T0211646

Lecture Notes in Computer Science   12104

More information about this series at http://www.springer.com/series/7407

Pedro A. Castillo · Juan Luis Jiménez Laredo ·
Francisco Fernández de Vega (Eds.)

Applications of Evolutionary Computation

23rd European Conference, EvoApplications 2020
Held as Part of EvoStar 2020
Seville, Spain, April 15–17, 2020
Proceedings

 Springer

Editors
Pedro A. Castillo ⓘ
University of Granada
Granada, Spain

Juan Luis Jiménez Laredo ⓘ
Université Le Havre Normandie
Le Havre, France

Francisco Fernández de Vega
Universidad de Extremadura
Mérida, Spain

ISSN 0302-9743   ISSN 1611-3349   (electronic)
Lecture Notes in Computer Science
ISBN 978-3-030-43721-3   ISBN 978-3-030-43722-0   (eBook)
https://doi.org/10.1007/978-3-030-43722-0

LNCS Sublibrary: SL1 – Theoretical Computer Science and General Issues

This Springer imprint is published by the registered company Springer Nature Switzerland AG
The registered company address is: Gewerbestrasse 11, 6330 Cham, Switzerland

Preface

This volume contains the proceedings of the International Conference on the Applications of Evolutionary Computation (EvoApplications 2020). The conference is part of EvoStar, the leading event on bio-inspired computation in Europe, and was held in Sevilla, Spain, during April 15–17, 2020.

EvoApplications, formerly known as EvoWorkshops, aims to bring together high-quality research with a focus on applied domains of bio-inspired computing. At the same time, under the EvoStar umbrella, EuroGP focused on the technique of genetic programming, EvoCOP targeted evolutionary computation in combinatorial optimization, and EvoMUSART was dedicated to evolved and bio-inspired music, sound, art, and design. The proceedings for all of these co-located events are available in the LNCS series.

EvoApplications received this year 62 high-quality submissions distributed among the main session Applications of Evolutionary Computation and six additional special sessions chaired by leading experts on the different areas: applications of bio-inspired techniques on social networks, evolutionary computation in digital healthcare and personalized medicine, soft-computing applied to games, applications of deep-bioinspired algorithms, parallel and distributed systems, and evolutionary machine learning. We selected 33 of these papers for full oral presentation, while a further 11 works were presented in short oral presentation and as posters. All contributions, regardless of the presentation format, appear as full papers in this volume (LNCS 12104).

Obviously, an event of this kind would not be possible without the contribution of a large number of people.

- We express our gratitude to the authors for submitting their works and to the members of the Program Committee for devoting a selfless effort in the review process.
- We would also like to thank the local organizing team led by Francisco Fernández de Vega (University of Extremadura, Spain) and Federico Divina (University Pablo de Olavide, Spain) for providing such an exciting venue and arranging a set of additional activities for delegates.
- José Francisco Chicano García (University of Málaga, Spain) for managing and maintaining the EvoStar website and João Correia (University of Coimbra, Portugal) for handling publicity: both did an impressive job.
- We credit the invited keynote speakers, José Antonio Lozano (University of the Basque Country, Spain) and Roberto Serra (University degli Studi di Modena e Reggio Emilia, Italy), for their fascinating and inspiring presentations.
- We would like to express our gratitude to the Steering Committee of EvoApplications for helping with the organization of the conference.

- We are grateful to the support provided by SPECIES, the Society for the Promotion of Evolutionary Computation in Europe and its Surroundings, and its individual members Marc Schoenauer (President), Anna I. Esparcia-Alcázar (Secretary and Vice-President), and Wolfgang Banzhaf (Treasurer), for the coordination and financial administration.

Finally, we express our continued appreciation to Anna I. Esparcia-Alcázar, from Universitat Politècnica de València, Spain, whose considerable efforts in managing and coordinating EvoStar helped towards building a unique, vibrant, and friendly atmosphere.

February 2020

Pedro A. Castillo
Juan Luis Jiménez Laredo
Francisco Fernández de Vega
Giovanni Iacca
Doina Bucur
Stephen Smith
Marta Vallejo
Antonio Mora
Pablo García Sánchez
Alberto P. Tonda
Juan Julián Merelo Guervós
Carlos Cotta
Paco Fernández
Penousal Machado
Wolfgang Banzhaf

Organization

Organizing Committee

EvoApplications Coordinator

Pedro A. Castillo   Universidad de Granada, Spain

EvoApplications Publication Chair

Juan Luis Jiménez Laredo   Université Le Havre Normandie, France

Local Chairs

Francisco Fernández   University of Extremadura, Spain
    de Vega
Federico Divina   University Pablo de Olavide, Spain

Publicity Chair

João Correia   University of Coimbra, Portugal

Applications of Bio-inspired Techniques on Social Networks

Giovanni Iacca   University of Trento, Italy
Doina Bucur   University of Twente, The Netherlands

Evolutionary Computation in Digital Healthcare and Personalized Medicine

Stephen Smith   University of York, UK
Marta Vallejo   Heriot-Watt University, UK

Soft Computing Applied to Games Chairs

Alberto P. Tonda   Université Paris-Saclay, INRA, France
Antonio M. Mora   Universidad de Granada, Spain
Pablo García-Sánchez   Universidad de Cádiz, Spain

Applications of Deep Bioinspired Algorithms Chairs

Carlos Cotta   Universidad de Málaga, Spain
Francisco Fernández   Universidad de Extremadura, Spain
    de Vega

Parallel and Distributed Systems Chairs

Juan Julián Merelo Guervós   Universidad de Granada, Spain
Juan Luis Jiménez Laredo   Université Le Havre Normandie, France

Evolutionary Machine Learning

Penousal Machado	University of Coimbra, Portugal
Wolfgang Banzhaf	Michigan State University, USA

EvoApps Steering Committee

Stefano Cagnoni	University of Parma, Italy
Anna I. Esparcia	Universidad Politécnica de Valencia, Spain
Mario Giacobinni	Universitá degli Studi di Torino, Italy
Antonio M. Mora	Universidad de Granada, Spain
Günther Raidl	Technische Universität Wien, Austria
Franz Rothlauf	Mainz University, Germany
Kevin Sim	Edinburgh Napier University, UK
Giovanni Squillero	Politecnico di Torino, Italy
Cecilia di Chio (Honorary Member)	University of Southampton, UK

Program Committee

Alberto Tonda	INRA, France
Aleksander Byrski	AGH University Science and Technology, Poland
Ales Zamuda	University of Maribor, Slovenia
Alison Motsinger-Reif	North Carolina State University, USA
Amir Dehsarvi	University of York, UK
Ana Soares	VITO, Belgium
Anabela Simões	Coimbra Institute of Engineering, Portugal
Anas Abou El Kalam	Cadi Ayyad University, Morocco
Anca Andreica	Babes-Bolyai University, Romania
Anders Christensen	University of Southern Denmark, Denmark
Andrea Tettamanzi	University Nice Sophia Antipolis, France
Andres Faina	IT University of Copenhagen, Denmark
Andries Engelbrecht	Stellenbosch University, South Africa
Anna Paszynska	Jagiellonian University, Poland
Anna I. Esparcia Alcazar	Universitat Politècnica de València, Spain
Annalisa Socievole	CNR-ICAR, Italy
Anthony Clark	Missouri State University, USA
Anthony Brabazon	University College Dublin, Ireland
Antonio Mora	University of Granada, Spain
Antonio Fernandez-Ares	University of Granada, Spain
Antonio Della Cioppa	University of Salerno, Italy
Antonio Cordoba	University of Seville, Spain
Antonio J. Fernández Leiva	University of Málaga, Spain
Antonio J. Nebro	University of Málaga, Spain
Antonios Liapis	University of Malta, Malta
Arindam K. Das	University of Eastern Washington, USA
Arkadiusz Poteralski	Silesian University of Technology, Poland

Ben Paechter	Napier University, UK
Carlos Cotta	University of Málaga, Spain
Changhe Li	China University of Geosciences Wuhan, China
Chien-Chung Shen	University of Delaware, USA
Clara Pizzuti	CNR-ICAR, Italy
David Megias	University Oberta de Catalunya, Spain
David Camacho	Universidad Politécnica de Madrid, Spain
David Pelta	University of Granada, Spain
Denis Robilliard	University Lille Nord de France, France
Dietmar Maringer	University of Basel, Switzerland
Doina Bucur	University of Twente, The Netherlands
Ed Keedwell	University of Exeter, UK
Edoardo Fadda	Politecnico di Torino, Italy
Elena Marchiori	Radboud University, The Netherlands
Ender Özcan	University of Nottingham, UK
Enrico Schumann	VIP Value Investment Professionals AG, Switzerland
Ernesto Costa	University of Coimbra, Portugal
Ernesto Tarantino	ICAR-CNR, Italy
Fabio D'Andreagiovanni	CNRS-Sorbonne University, France
Fabio Caraffini	De Montfort University, UK
Federico Divina	Pablo de Olavide University, Spain
Federico Liberatore	Universidad Carlos III, Spain
Fernando Lobo	University of Algarve, Portugal
Ferrante Neri	University of Nottingham, UK
Francesco Fontanella	Università di Cassino e del Lazio meridionale, Italy
Francisco Chicano	University of Málaga, Spain
Francisco Luna	University of Málaga, Spain
Frank Neumann	The University of Adelaide, Australia
Gabriel Luque	University of Málaga, Spain
Gareth Howells	University of Kent, UK
Geoff Nitschke	University of Cape Town, South Africa
Giovanni Iacca	University of Trento, Italy
Gordon Fraser	University of Passau, Germany
Gregoire Danoy	University of Luxembourg, Luxembourg
Hui Cheng	Liverpool John Moores University, UK
Igor Deplano	Liverpool John Moores University, UK
Iwona Karcz-Duleba	Wrocław University of Technology, Poland
J. Ignacio Hidalgo	University Complutense de Madrid, Spain
Jacopo Aleotti	University of Parma, Italy
James Foster	University of Idaho, USA
Janos Botzheim	Budapest University of Technology and Economics, Hungary
Jaroslaw Was	AGH University of Science and Technology, Poland
Jaume Bacardit	Newcastle University, UK
Jean-Marc Montanier	Norwegian University of Science and Technology, Norway

Sergio Damas	University of Granada, Spain
Sevil Sen	University of York, UK
Shayan Kavakeb	Liverpool John Moores University, UK
Simon Wells	Edinburgh Napier University, UK
Srini Ramaswamy	ABB Inc., USA
Stefano Cagnoni	University of Parma, Italy
Stefano Coniglio	University of Southampton, UK
Stenio Fernandes	Federal University of Pernambuco, Brazil
Stephane Doncieux	ISIR, UPMC, France
Thomas Farrenkopf	Technische Hochschule Mittelhessen, Germany
Ting Hu	Memorial University, Canada
Vicenc Torra	University of Skövde, Sweden
Vincenzo Moscato	University of Naples, Italy
Wolfgang Banzhaf	Michigan State University, USA
Ying-Ping Chen	National Chiao Tung University, Taiwan
Yoann Pigné	LITIS, University Le Havre Normandie, France

Contents

Applications of Bio-inspired Techniques on Social Networks

Evolutionary Machine Learning

Parallel and Distributed Systems

Applications of Evolutionary Computation

A Local Search for Numerical Optimisation Based on Covariance Matrix Diagonalisation

Ferrante Neri[1]($\boxtimes$)(iD) and Shahin Rostami[2](iD)

[1] Computational Optimisation and Learning (COL) Lab, School of Computer Science, University of Nottingham, Nottingham, UK
`ferrante.neri@nottingham.ac.uk`
[2] Department of Computing and Informatics, Bournemouth University, Bournemouth, UK
`srostami@bournemouth.ac.uk`

Abstract. Pattern Search is a family of optimisation algorithms that improve upon an initial solution by performing moves along the directions of a basis of vectors. In its original definition Pattern Search moves along the directions of each variable. Amongst its advantages, the algorithm does not require any knowledge of derivatives or analytical expression of the function to optimise. However, the performance of Pattern Search is heavily problem dependent since the search directions can be very effective on some problems and lead to poor performance on others. The present article proposes a novel enhancement of Pattern Search that explores the space by using problem-dependent search directions. Some points are sampled within the basin of attraction and the diagonalisation of the covariance matrix associated with the distribution of these points is performed. The proposed Covariance Pattern Search improves upon an initial point by varying it along the directions identified by the eigenvectors of the covariance matrix.

Keywords: Hooke-Jeeves · Pattern Search · Covariance matrix · Eigenvectors · Numerical optimisation

1 Introduction

In the context of optimisation, a basin of attraction of a search algorithm is the set of points of the decision space that would converge to the same local optimum, see [15]. For example, if we consider a multimodal problem in the continuous domain, a gradient based algorithm would process some randomly sampled solutions by converging to the nearest local optimum. If two points converge to the same optimum, they belong to the same basin of attraction with respect to the gradient based optimiser. Thus, for a given search algorithm (with its variation operator) a decision space can be seen as mapped into several (and possibly overlapping) subsets, with each of them being a basin of attraction.

© Springer Nature Switzerland AG 2020
P. A. Castillo et al. (Eds.): EvoApplications 2020, LNCS 12104, pp. 3–19, 2020.
https://doi.org/10.1007/978-3-030-43722-0_1

This concept is fundamental in optimisation, especially when complex, multivariate, and multimodal fitness landscapes are taken into consideration, see [1,19,28,31]. A popular strategy to address these issues is the use of multiple search operators within the same framework. This idea has been extensively applied over the past three decades in both continuous and combinatorial domains. Some of the keywords associated with this idea are Metaheuristics [9,25], Hyper-heuristics [2], Memetic Computing [19], Genetic Programming [11], Agent Systems [24], and Algorithm's Portfolio [22,33].

In these frameworks a distinction between global and local search operators has been traditionally presented as part of the nomenclature to describe algorithmic operations. Whilst the distinction between global and local optima is mathematically rigorous, the distinction between global and local search is more subtle, especially in the context of heuristic optimisation where there is no theoretical guarantee of the detection of an optimum. More specifically, global and local search algorithms differ in purpose: whilst global search algorithms search for a candidate solution with the lowest (or highest) function value within the entire decision space, local search algorithms search for a candidate solution with the lowest (or highest) function value within a subset of the entire space, often referred to as a neighbourhood, see [10].

In mathematical optimisation, and with reference to the continuous domain that is the focus of this paper, the concepts of basins of attraction and local search are well-defined. When considering a minimisation problem a basin of attraction is a set containing one or more infinite contiguous (saddle) points with null gradient (unless the optimum is on the bounds), surrounded by points with non-null gradient and higher function values. Local search algorithms that calculate the gradient, e.g. descent methods, Newtonian methods, Quasi-Newtonian methods, and conjugate gradient methods, would (approximately) detect the local optimum in a given time-frame from any starting point in the basin of attraction, see [21].

When the derivatives are not available and a heuristic method is applied, the concepts of basins of attraction and local search become unclear. For example, the Nelder-Mead algorithm [18], which is often considered a local search algorithm [17], can search for the optimum in an area with only one local optimum, a larger area, or potentially the entire decision space (depending on the initial simplex).

In the absence of derivatives, one of the simplest ideas to optimise a function is to vary one design variable at a time by steps of the same magnitude and calculate the function value at each step. Then, when no increase or decrease in any one design variable improves upon the performance of the current best solution, the algorithm halves the step size and repeats the process until the steps are sufficiently small. This simple algorithm was employed in the 1940s in Los Alamos laboratories by Fermi and Metropolis, see [8]. This idea has been refined and modified over the decades, and its most famous implementation is the **Pattern Search** (PS) algorithm by Hooke and Jeeves [14] which proved to be convergent in [34]. This idea has been conceptualised in [29] where Pattern

Search Algorithms are introduced as a family of optimisation algorithms, and the term Generalised Pattern Search was coined as a Pattern Search using any generic basis of a vector. The search logic of PS is used as part of many modern algorithms. One example is [30] where a greedy version of the Patter Search is used within a three algorithm portfolio for large scale problems. Furthermore, other recent examples of Pattern Search implementations have re-named the algorithm as "S" and put it into the context of Memetic Algorithms [5,7] and in a restarting scheme in [6].

The present article exploits this idea to propose a novel enhancement of Generalised Pattern Search. The proposed algorithm attempts to enhance the original scheme by using an alternative and more convenient reference system to move within the search space. This alternative system is provided by the eigenvectors of a covariance matrix of a set of points crowding a basin of attraction.

The remainder of this article is organised as follows. Section 2 introduces the notation, presents the naive Pattern Search and highlights its limitations. Section 3 presents the proposed algorithm including its theoretical justification, as well as its limitations. Section 4 provides the numerical results of this study. Finally, Sect. 5 gives the conclusions to this work.

2   Notation and Background

In order to clarify the notation used, we refer to the minimisation of an objective function $f(\mathbf{x})$, where the candidate solution $\mathbf{x}$ is a vector of n design variables in a decision space $D \subset \mathbb{R}^n$:

$$\mathbf{x} = (x_1, x_2, \ldots, x_n).$$

The Pattern Search (PS) processes a single solution and, whilst moving along the axes, improves upon its performance (objective function value). PS can be viewed as a simple deterministic local search algorithm which can be part of a more complex framework, see [3,5].

In this paper we will refer to the naive implementation of this idea proposed in one of the searchers in [30]. Starting from an elite solution $\mathbf{x}$, this local search generates a trial solution $\mathbf{x^t}$ by performing steps along each of the variables. For each design variable i,

$$\mathbf{x^t} = \mathbf{x} - \rho \cdot \mathbf{e^i}$$

is calculated, where ρ is the exploratory radius, $\cdot$ indicates the product of a scalar and a vector, and $\mathbf{e^i}$ is the ith versor that is a vector composed of zeros and one 1 in the ith position. Subsequently, if $\mathbf{x^t}$ outperforms $\mathbf{x}$, the trial solution $\mathbf{x^t}$ is updated (taking the value of $\mathbf{x}$), otherwise a half-step in the opposite direction is performed:

$$\mathbf{x^t} = \mathbf{x} + \frac{\rho}{2} \cdot \mathbf{e^i}.$$

This exploration is repeated for all the design variables and stopped when a prefixed budget is exceeded. For the purpose of this paper we will refer to the naive implementation used in [5,30]. The pseudo-code displaying the working principles of this PS implementation is given in Algorithm 1.

Algorithm 1. Pattern Search according to the implementation in [30]

```
INPUT x
while local budget condition do
    xᵗ = x
    for i = 1 : n do
        xᵗ = x − ρ · eⁱ
        if f (xᵗ) ≤ f (x) then
            x = xᵗ
        else
            xᵗ = x + ρ/2 · eⁱ
            if f (xᵗ) ≤ f (x) then
                x = xᵗ
            end if
        end if
    end for
    if x has not been updated then
        ρ = ρ/2
    end if
end while
RETURN x
```

2.1 Limitation of Pattern Search

The naive PS algorithm, albeit easy to implement, is characterised by heavy problem dependent performance due to its variation operators. Since the variables are perturbed/modified one by one, PS can lead to very good performance if the function is separable. In practice, PS can be successfully applied to various partly separable and non-separable problems (see [7]), but its performance would generally be poor. In order to illustrate this statement let us consider the ellipsoid function in two dimensions shown in Fig. 1. The PS algorithm would quickly solve the problem in Fig. 1a from any starting point, since one of the directions of the search (one of the axes) coincide with the direction of maximum gradient. However, the PS algorithm would not be efficient in optimising the problem in Fig. 1b, since the search directions are not along the maximum gradient. The algorithm would halve the radius in the early stages of the search and move slowly towards the optimum. In the case of optimisation in higher dimensions the difference in performance between the two scenarios would be significant.

3 The Proposed Covariance Pattern Search

If we could move along the direction of maximum gradient for every problem, PS would work efficiently regardless of the problem. Unfortunately, in real-world optimisation, problems are unknown and there is no prior knowledge of the most convenient reference system. This consideration is not novel and is common to several algorithms for numerical optimisation, such as the Rosenbrock Algorithm, see [27], where the gradient is estimated adaptively and by a new reference system determined by Gram-Schmidt orthogonalisation.

On the basis of this classical consideration, the present article proposes a novel local search implementation of Pattern Search. This section outlines and

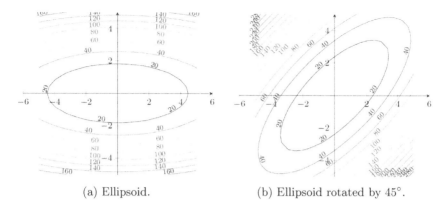

(a) Ellipsoid.   (b) Ellipsoid rotated by 45°.

Fig. 1. Non-rotated and 45° rotated ellipsoid in two dimensions: PS would be efficient at solving (a) and inefficient at solving (b).

discusses the proposal. Subsection 3.1 provides a theoretical justification for the method, Subsect. 3.2 describes the implementation details of the methods, and Subsect. 3.4 highlights the limitations of our proposal.

3.1   Theoretical Justification

Unlike the Rosenbrock Algorithm, the proposed method makes use of pre-processing of the problem under investigation to determine the most convenient search directions. In order to understand the theoretical foundation of the proposed method let us consider a population of m vectors/candidate solutions in an n-dimensional space

$$\mathbf{x^1} = \left(x_1^1, x_2^1, \ldots, x_n^1\right)$$
$$\mathbf{x^2} = \left(x_1^2, x_2^2, \ldots, x_n^2\right)$$
$$\ldots$$
$$\mathbf{x^m} = \left(x_1^m, x_2^m, \ldots, x_n^m\right).$$

These points can be interpreted as a statistical distribution characterised by a mean vector

$$\mu = (\mu_1, \mu_2, \ldots, \mu_n) = \frac{1}{m}\left(\sum_{i=1}^{m} x_1^i, \sum_{i=1}^{m} x_2^i, \ldots, \sum_{i=1}^{m} x_n^i\right)$$

and a covariance matrix

$$\mathbf{C} = \begin{pmatrix} c_{1,1} & c_{1,2} & \cdots & c_{1,n} \\ c_{2,1} & c_{2,2} & \cdots & c_{2,n} \\ \cdots & \cdots & \cdots & \cdots \\ c_{n,1} & c_{n,2} & \cdots & c_{n,n} \end{pmatrix}$$

where

$$c_{j,j} = \frac{1}{m} \sum_{i=1}^{m} \left(\left(x_j^i - \mu_j \right) \left(x_j^i - \mu_j \right) \right)$$

and

$$c_{j,k} = \frac{1}{m} \sum_{i=1}^{m} \left(\left(x_j^i - \mu_j \right) \left(x_k^i - \mu_k \right) \right).$$

Due to the commutative property of the product of numbers, it follows that $\forall j, k : c_{j,k} = c_{k,j}$, i.e. the covariance matrix is symmetric.

The vector μ represents the barycentre of the distribution. The covariance matrix $\mathbf{C}$ describes the geometry of the distribution with respect to the reference system. More specifically, the diagonal elements represent the deviation of the design variable from the barycentre whilst the extradiagonal elements represent a measurement of how two design variables vary together.

Let us consider an optimisation problem and let us imagine to sample m points, with m arbitrarily large, within the decision space D. With reference to Fig. 1a, let us imagine to crowd the elliptic inner contour with points and calculate the mean vector and covariance matrix. It can be verified that μ would be the optimum and the covariance matrix $\mathbf{C}$ would be diagonal. However, if we crowded with points the elliptic inner contour in Fig. 1b we would observe that the corresponding covariance matrix $\mathbf{C}$ would be full.

This observation could be extended to the general case: a basin of attraction that has the highest gradient along one of the axes is characterised by a diagonal covariance matrix of the points crowding it. Hence, we propose to use the reference system corresponding to a diagonal covariance matrix as move directions for PS in order to find the highest gradient direction. That is, we propose to run PS along the directions identified by the eigenvectors of $\mathbf{C}$, see [20]. These directions are the columns of a non-singular matrix $\mathbf{P}$ such that

$$\mathbf{D} = \mathbf{P}^{-1}\mathbf{C}\mathbf{P}$$

where $\mathbf{D}$ is a diagonal matrix.

Observation 1. *Since the covariance matrix $\mathbf{C}$ is symmetric, it follows that*

1. *$\mathbf{C}$ is always diagonalisable and hence there always exists a non-singular transformation matrix $\mathbf{P}$ that diagonalises $\mathbf{C}$.*
2. *each pair of the eigenvectors of $\mathbf{C}$ (column of matrix $\mathbf{P}$) is orthogonal, the proposed search directions compose an orthogonal system of coordinates.*

The matrix $\mathbf{P}$ is the linear transformation that changes the variables of the problem. For example, the directions of the eigenvectors associated with the covariance matrix or the rotated ellipsoid in Fig. 1b are shown in Fig. 2.

Equivalently to what is stated above, the proposed algorithm is based on the consideration that the nonseparability is not just a feature of the function to optimise. Nonseparability is a feature of the function within its reference system. Hence, a (local) change in the reference system can (locally) lead to a much easier optimisation problem.

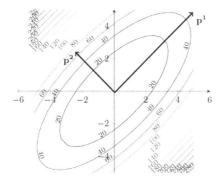

Fig. 2. Ellipsoid in two dimensions rotated by 45°: PS moving along the thick directions would be efficient.

3.2 Algorithmic Outline of the Proposed Method

Let us assume that we have a reliable matrix $\mathbf{C}$ available of the basin of attraction under investigation. The matrix $\mathbf{C}$ would be diagonalised and the eigenvectors would be the columns of a transformation matrix $\mathbf{P}$:

$$\mathbf{P} = \left(\mathbf{p}^1, \mathbf{p}^2, \ldots, \mathbf{p}^n\right).$$

In this article the diagonalisation is performed by the numerical method described and implemented in [20].

In order to better illustrate the relation between the change of coordinates and the diagonalisation of the covariance matrix, let us consider the ellipsoid function

$$f\left(x,y\right) = a\left(\cos\left(\alpha\right)x + \sin\left(\alpha\right)y\right)^2 + b\left(\sin\left(\alpha\right)x - \cos\left(\alpha\right)y\right)^2.$$

Figure 3 illustrates this function (with $a = 1$ and $b = 6$), for $\alpha = 0°$ and $\alpha = 30°$ respectively, a sample of points, the eigenvectors, and the directions identified by them. It can be observed that for $\alpha = 0°$ the directions of the eigenvectors coincide with those of the reference axes whilst for $\alpha = 30°$ the axes appear rotated.

The new version of PS operates on a starting point $\mathbf{x}$ and generates trial solutions for the ith design variable by computing

$$\mathbf{x^t} = \mathbf{x} - \rho \cdot \mathbf{Pe^i} = \mathbf{x} - \rho \cdot \mathbf{p^i}$$

and

$$\mathbf{x^t} = \mathbf{x} + \frac{\rho}{2} \cdot \mathbf{Pe^i} = \mathbf{x} + \frac{\rho}{2} \cdot \mathbf{p^i}$$

where the product of a matrix by a vector $\mathbf{Pe^i}$ is equal to $\mathbf{p^i}$.

The pseudocode of the proposed Covariance Pattern Search (CPS) Algorithm is shown in Algorithm 2.

Algorithm 2. The proposed Covariance Pattern Search

```
INPUT x
INPUT the covariance matrix C
Process the covariance matrix C and calculate the transformation matrix P = (p¹, p², ..., pⁿ)
whose columns are the eigenvectors of C
while local budget condition do
    xᵗ = x
    for i = 1 : n do
        xᵗ = x − ρ · pⁱ
        if f (xᵗ) ≤ f (x) then
            x = xᵗ
        else
            xᵗ = x + ρ/2 · pⁱ
            if f (xᵗ) ≤ f (x) then
                x = xᵗ
            end if
        end if
    end for
    if x has not been updated then
        ρ = ρ/2
    end if
end while
RETURN x
```

3.3   Working Example

In order to highlight the difference in functioning between Algorithms 1 and 2, and the benefits of the proposed CPS with respect to its standard counterpart, we have run both of the algorithms on the ellipsoid function above in this case with the arbitrary values $a = 1$ and $b = 76$. We arbitrarily chose an angle $\alpha = \frac{\pi}{3.5} \approx 51.43°$ and a starting point $(71.4, -49.1)$. The search directions of CPS are the columns of the following matrix $\mathbf{P}$:

$$\mathbf{P} = \begin{pmatrix} -0.7821 & 0.6231 \\ 0.6231 & 0.7821 \end{pmatrix}.$$

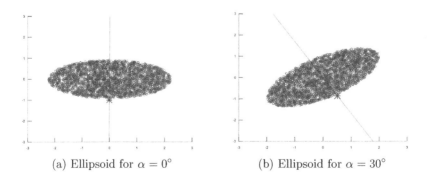

(a) Ellipsoid for $\alpha = 0°$ (b) Ellipsoid for $\alpha = 30°$

Fig. 3. Sampling of points (blue circles) within the basin of attraction of the ellipsoid, resulting eigenvectors (asterisks), and search directions of the proposed method (lines) (Color figure online)

We let both the algorithms run until $\rho < 10^{-75}$, which was considered to be when the problem to be solved. Whilst PS requires the calculation of 16169 objective function evaluations, CPS solves the problem after only 2040 evaluations. Figure 4 comparatively illustrates the functioning of the two algorithms. The proposed CPS moves along more convenient directions than the variable directions of PS, thus quickly reaching the optimum.

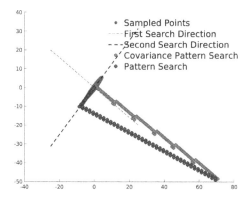

Fig. 4. Illustration of the functioning of the proposed Covariance Pattern Search and advantages with respect to the standard Pattern Search (the proposed algorithm solves the problem in 2040 whilst its standard counterpart requires 16169 steps)

3.4 Limitations of the Proposed Covariance Pattern Search

The most evident limitation of the proposed CPS is that a reliable matrix $\mathbf{C}$ of points of the basin of attraction must be estimated. In the present paper, when a basin of attraction is identified, a set of points populating this basin is found by treating the optimisation problem as a level set problem: random points are generated and those whose objective function values fall below a threshold are saved in a data structure, see Fig. 3. These points are then used to calculate the covariance matrix $\mathbf{C}$.

The major issue associated with this approach is that a suitable threshold is problem dependent and empirically determined in each case. Besides being inelegant, this procedure can also be computationally expensive in the high dimensional domain. Although, the initial computational effort may be paid off by a much faster solution to the optimisation problem, see Fig. 4.

The second limitation is that for multimodal optimisation problems promising basins of attraction must be identified before one basin is selected and CPS is executed. This limitation would make CPS unsuitable as a stand-alone algorithm and/or would require a preprocessing algorithm to estimate the locations of potential basins of attraction. However, CPS just like other local search algorithms can be embedded in a metaheuristic framework and can exploit the function calls performed by a global optimiser (or other local search algorithms) as part of the preprocessing, see [19].

Alternatively, CPS can be applied to a multimodal problem at the end of preprocessing for multimodal optimisation, see e.g. the method in [26] or the intelligent sampling proposed in [23]. In the latter, an initial population of m candidate solutions (n-dimensional vectors) is sampled within the decision space D. Each candidate solution undergoes the application, with a limited budget, of the two local searchers. The solutions returned by the two local search algorithms are then processed by the K-means clustering algorithm enhanced by a control on the Silhouette to decide the correct number of clusters, as explained in [23]. Each cluster represents a basin of attraction and its candidate solutions are the sampled points on which the covariance matrix $\mathbf{C}$ is computed.

4   Numerical Results

In order to experimentally demonstrate the effectiveness of CPS, and the idea inspiring it, we have tested CPS against PS in multiple scenarios. To simulate the local search conditions we have considered and adapted a sample of the functions from the CEC 2013 benchmark (focussing on unimodal problems), see [16]. We have used two versions of the ellipsoid since the use of two versions was relevant to demonstrate the performance of the local search. Each problem has been scaled to 10, 30, and 50 dimensions and has been studied in $[-100, 100]^n$. Table 1 displays the functions and depicts the shape of the corresponding basins of attraction. For each problem, a shift and a rotation has been applied: with reference to Table 1 the variable

$$\mathbf{z} = \mathbf{Q_k}\left(\mathbf{x} - \mathbf{o}\right)$$

where $\mathbf{o}$ is the shifting vector (the same used in [16]) and $\mathbf{Q_k}$ is a rotation matrix (a randomly generated orthogonal matrix) set for the kth problem, see [4].

The PS in Algorithm 1 has been executed with a budget of $10000 \times n$ function calls where n is the problem dimensionality. In order to guarantee a fair comparison, the budget of the proposed CPS in Algorithm 2 has been split into two parts: $5000 \times n$ function calls have been used to build the covariance matrix $\mathbf{C}$ whilst $5000 \times n$ function calls have been spent to execute the algorithm. Due to the nature of PS and CPS, i.e. deterministic local search, the bound handling has been performed by saturating the design variable to the bound. We preferred the saturation to the bound over the toroidal insertion or reflection [10] since the latter two mechanisms would be equivalent to the sampling of a point. This sampling would disrupt the gradient estimation logic of Pattern Search.

Although PS and CPS are deterministic algorithms, their performance can depend on the initial point and, for CPS, on the sampled points used to estimate the covariance matrix. Thus, for each scenario, we sampled 51 initial points within the entire domain and used them to execute PS and CPS. The average

Table 1. Basins of attraction functions

function name	function formula	basin of attraction in 2D
sphere	$f_1(\mathbf{x}) = \sum_{i=1}^{n} z_i^2$	
ellipsoid	$f_2(\mathbf{x}) = \sum_{i=1}^{n} 50 \left(i^2 z_i\right)^2$	
ill-conditioned ellipsoid	$f_3(\mathbf{x}) = \sum_{i=1}^{n} \left(10^6\right)^{\frac{i-1}{n-1}} z_i^2$	
bent cigar	$f_4(\mathbf{x}) = z_1^2 + 10^6 \sum_{i=2}^{n} z_i^2$	
discus	$f_5(\mathbf{x}) = 10^6 z_1^2 + \sum_{i=2}^{n} z_i^2$	
sum of powers	$f_6(\mathbf{x}) = \sqrt{\sum_{i=1}^{n} |z_i|^{\left(2 + 4\frac{i-1}{n-1}\right)}}$	

objective function values and standard deviations over the 51 runs have been calculated. The statistical significance of the results has been enhanced by the application of the Wilcoxon rank sum test, see [12,32]. In the Tables in this section, a "+" indicates that CPS significantly outperforms PS, a "−" indicates that PS significantly outperforms CPS, and a "=" indicates that there is no significant difference in performance. Regarding CPS, the threshold values used in this study are reported in Table 2.

Table 2. Thresholds thr in 10, 30, and 50 dimensions

n	f_1	f_2	f_3	f_4	f_5	f_6
10	10^4	10^9	5×10^8	10^9	10^9	10^4
30	5×10^4	5×10^{11}	2×10^9	2×10^9	10^8	10^5
50	10^5	5×10^{13}	5×10^9	2×10^9	5×10^7	3×10^5

Numerical results show that, besides f_1, the proposed CPS consistently outperforms the standard PS across the three dimensions under consideration. The problem f_1 is characterised by a central symmetry. This means that the rotation

Table 3. Average error avg $\pm$ standard deviation σ over 51 runs for the problems listed in Table 1

	Pattern Search		Covariance Pattern Search		
	Avg	σ	Avg	σ	W
10 dimensions					
f_1	**0.0000e+00**	0.0000e+00	2.7768e−29	1.4329e−29	−
f_2	1.8198e+03	1.9132e+03	**1.1062e−03**	3.4915e−03	+
f_3	7.0241e+04	9.5716e+04	**4.1064e+03**	6.6534e+03	+
f_4	5.3135e+03	3.7177e+03	**3.3017e−06**	9.9933e−06	+
f_5	9.3944e+03	1.2996e+04	**3.0984e−25**	5.3080e−25	+
f_6	5.5475e+01	9.4900e+01	**2.6276e−05**	1.3087e−05	+
30 dimensions					
f_1	**0.0000e+00**	0.0000e+00	1.3562e−28	5.1167e−29	−
f_2	1.1636e+08	2.3036e+08	**6.9435e+05**	6.4717e+05	+
f_3	2.9155e+05	2.4771e+05	**1.8116e+04**	1.1143e+04	+
f_4	5.2064e+03	5.3776e+03	**4.6182e−13**	3.2833e−12	+
f_5	8.4596e+03	3.4177e+04	**5.3340e−28**	3.2325e−27	+
f_6	1.2427e+02	1.7049e+02	**6.4462e−05**	1.7549e−05	+
50 dimensions					
f_1	**0.0000e+00**	0.0000e+00	4.1998e−28	9.9033e−29	−
f_2	4.3878e+08	8.6339e+08	**1.6151e+07**	1.3937e+07	+
f_3	3.7522e+05	2.7408e+05	**5.1237e+04**	3.4165e+04	+
f_4	5.6398e+03	7.4905e+03	**5.5627e−22**	1.4649e−21	+
f_5	2.8261e+01	1.3792e+02	**7.8822e−27**	1.2792e−26	+
f_6	1.8153e+02	2.0042e+02	**1.0584e−04**	2.3244e−05	+

is ineffective and any reference system would broadly perform in the same way. The use of the eigenvectors as search directions not only systematically improves upon PS but appears to solve some problems such as f_5 (discus).

In order to ensure that the results of proposed CPS are not biased by specific rotation matrices, the experiments have been repeated on the problems in Table 1 with a modified experimental condition. For each run a new rotation matrix has been generated and both PS and CPS have been run on the rotated problem. An additional 51 independent runs have been executed under this new condition. Table 4 displays the results for this set of experiments with random matrices.

Numerical results in Table 4 show that CPS maintains the same performance irrespective of the rotation matrix. These results allow us to conjecture that the proposed mechanism of optimising along the direction of the eigenvectors is effective and the generation of the covariance matrix is robust.

Table 4. Average error avg ± standard deviation σ over 51 runs for the problems listed in Table 1 subject to random rotation at each run

	Pattern Search		Covariance Pattern Search		
	Avg	σ	Avg	σ	W
10 dimensions					
f_1	**0.0000e+00**	0.0000e+00	3.6603e−29	2.0133e−29	−
f_2	1.2340e+03	1.2462e+03	**3.7683e−04**	1.1634e−03	+
f_3	1.3739e+05	2.3991e+05	**2.9764e+03**	2.7313e+03	+
f_4	3.5615e+03	6.8974e+03	**3.8205e+01**	1.0569e+02	+
f_5	7.8684e+03	1.1461e+04	**1.0087e−23**	3.1002e−23	+
f_6	1.3676e+02	4.3249e+02	**2.6698e−05**	1.0627e−05	+
30 dimensions					
f_1	**0.0000e+00**	0.0000e+00	1.3810e−28	5.9062e−29	−
f_2	9.8109e+07	2.6281e+08	**7.2563e+05**	9.0521e+05	+
f_3	1.7506e+05	1.8632e+05	**1.7248e+04**	1.0875e+04	+
f_4	5.8954e+03	1.0909e+04	**2.2632e−01**	1.6163e+00	+
f_5	1.1985e+03	5.2373e+03	**7.9322e−26**	4.2633e−25	+
f_6	1.3485e+02	1.8275e+02	**6.4239e−05**	1.8127e−05	+
50 dimensions					
f_1	**0.0000e+00**	0.0000e+00	4.2394e−28	9.7414e−29	−
f_2	8.2205e+08	1.7628e+09	**1.5302e+07**	1.2051e+07	+
f_3	3.1913e+05	2.8232e+05	**5.8034e+04**	3.0679e+04	+
f_4	9.3975e+03	1.0959e+04	**3.8535e−21**	1.4037e−20	+
f_5	1.2639e+02	4.5309e+02	**2.8811e−26**	1.2290e−25	+
f_6	1.8761e+02	1.8060e+02	**9.1000e−05**	1.8870e−05	+

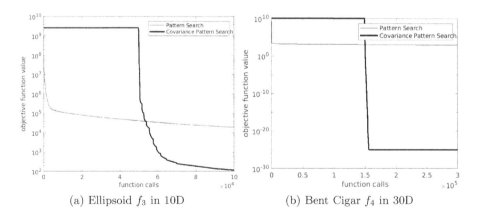

(a) Ellipsoid f_3 in 10D   (b) Bent Cigar f_4 in 30D

Fig. 5. Performance trend (logarithmic scale) of Pattern Search vs Covariance Pattern Search for two runs: for half of the budget CPS analyses the problem to generate the covariance matrix and then optimises the problem.

Table 5. Average error avg $\pm$ standard deviation σ over 51 runs for the problems listed in Table 1

	CMAES		Covariance Pattern Search		
	Avg	σ	Avg	σ	W
10 dimensions					
f_1	2.1589e−15	2.9083e−15	**2.7768e−29**	1.4329e−29	+
f_2	**1.4746e−15**	1.1443e−15	1.1062e−03	3.4915e−03	−
f_3	**1.0489e−15**	8.2847e−16	4.1064e+03	6.6534e+03	−
f_4	**1.8441e−14**	8.2847e−16	3.3017e−06	9.9933e−06	=
f_5	1.5539e−14	2.8869e−14	**3.0984e−25**	5.3080e−25	+
f_6	**9.8517e−13**	9.4715e−13	2.6276e−05	1.3087e−05	−
30 dimensions					
f_1	1.2862e−15	2.3923e−16	**1.3562e−28**	5.1167e−29	+
f_2	**1.2574e−15**	3.6076e−16	6.9435e+05	6.4717e+05	−
f_3	**1.1737e−15**	2.4995e−16	1.8116e+04	1.1143e+04	−
f_4	**1.2556e−14**	2.0370e−14	4.6182e−13	3.2833e−12	=
f_5	8.7935e−15	1.1728e−14	**5.3340e−28**	3.2325e−27	+
f_6	**1.1134e−11**	9.1361e−12	6.4462e−05	1.7549e−05	−
50 dimensions					
f_1	1.1017e−15	4.7700e−16	**4.1998e−28**	9.9033e−29	+
f_2	**9.1890e−15**	2.0913e−15	1.6151e+07	1.3937e+07	−
f_3	**1.2302e−15**	7.1779e−16	5.1237e+04	3.4165e+04	−
f_4	1.2606e+04	3.3045e+04	**5.5627e−22**	1.4649e−21	+
f_5	9.0248e−03	4.4211e−02	**7.8822e−27**	1.2792e−26	+
f_6	**4.8125e−11**	2.8066e−11	1.0584e−04	2.3244e−05	−

To further illustrate the functioning of CPS with respect to PS, Fig. 5 show the performance trend of two specific runs.

The results in Fig. 5 show that CPS achieves results orders of magnitude better than PS. It must be noted that we represented the performance of CPS as a constant for the first half of the trend. This is due to the objective function evaluation budget used to calculate the covariance matrix and the corresponding eigenvectors, with the optimisation only occurring in the second part of the budget. At half of the budget CPS starts the optimisation by exploiting the directions suggested by the preliminary phase. A dramatic decrease in the fitness value is evident in the illustration. When the proposed logic is considered within a local search/optimisation algorithm, this logic can be efficiently implemented by using the samples produced by a global searcher, whilst the local search can run with a short budget, just to exploit the abrupt improvement.

Finally, in order to highlight the potential and limitations of CPS, we have compared it against the Covariance Matrix Adaptation Evolution Strategy (CMAES), according to the implementation in [13] and the default parameters therein (initial σ set to one third of the domain). Table 5 displays the results of this comparison for the same problems in Table 3.

Table 5 shows that for about half of the problems CPS is competitive (f_1 and f_4) or outperforms CMAES (f_5), whilst for some other problems CMAES achieves results that are orders of magnitudes better in performance than CPS. This fact happens especially in cases of steep gradients, such as the ellipsoid functions f_2 and f_3. However, this paper proposes a principle about search directions rather than a full algorithm. For example, unlike CMAES, CPS employs a naive search operation based on the simple halving of a radius. Nonetheless, the proposed logic can be exported to other schemes and more sophisticated operators, e.g. an adaptive search radius, can enhance upon the current performance.

5   Conclusion

This article provides a proof of principle of a conjecture: the search directions identified by the eigenvectors of the covariance matrix of a population of points filling a basin of attraction are efficient to search for the local optimum. This idea has been tested on a naive implementation of pattern search, which has displayed a major systematic improvement over the standard version of pattern search for the problems considered in this study.

The main limitation of the proposed approach is that in order to build the covariance matrix a threshold value has to be set. This value is currently set manually. Our future work will include a protocol for setting this threshold to ensure that a sample of points representing the basin of attraction is detected.

Other future developments will include the extension of the proposed logic to more complex algorithms such as Hooke-Jeeves Pattern search and population based algorithms. Furthermore the proposed algorithm will also be tested within frameworks composed of multiple algorithms, such as Memetic Algorithms and Hyperheuristics.

References

1. Al-Dabbagh, R.D., Neri, F., Idris, N., Baba, M.S.: Algorithmic design issues in adaptive differential evolution schemes: review and taxonomy. Swarm Evol. Comput. **43**, 284–311 (2018)
2. Burke, E.K., Kendall, G., Soubeiga, E.: A tabu search hyperheuristic for timetabling and rostering. J. Heuristics **9**(6), 451–470 (2003). https://doi.org/10.1023/B:HEUR.0000012446.94732.b6
3. Caponio, A., Cascella, G.L., Neri, F., Salvatore, N., Sumner, M.: A fast adaptive memetic algorithm for on-line and off-line control design of PMSM drives. IEEE Trans. Syst. Man Cybern.-Part B **37**(1), 28–41 (2007)
4. Caraffini, F., Neri, F.: A study on rotation invariance in differential evolution. Swarm Evol. Comput. **50**, 100436 (2019)

5. Caraffini, F., Neri, F., Iacca, G., Mol, A.: Parallel memetic structures. Inf. Sci. **227**, 60–82 (2013)
6. Caraffini, F., Neri, F., Passow, B.N., Iacca, G.: Re-sampled inheritance search: high performance despite the simplicity. Soft. Comput. **17**(12), 2235–2256 (2013). https://doi.org/10.1007/s00500-013-1106-7
7. Caraffini, F., Neri, F., Picinali, L.: An analysis on separability for memetic computing automatic design. Inf. Sci. **265**, 1–22 (2014)
8. Davidon, W.C.: Variable metric method for minimization. SIAM J. Optim. **1**(1), 1–17 (1991)
9. Dumitrescu, I., Stützle, T.: Combinations of local search and exact algorithms. In: Cagnoni, S., et al. (eds.) EvoWorkshops 2003. LNCS, vol. 2611, pp. 211–223. Springer, Heidelberg (2003). https://doi.org/10.1007/3-540-36605-9_20
10. Eiben, A.E., Smith, J.E.: Introduction to Evolutionary Computation, 2nd edn. Springer, Berlin (2015). https://doi.org/10.1007/978-3-662-44874-8
11. Esparcia-Alcázar, A.I., Almenar, F., Vos, T.E.J., Rueda, U.: Using genetic programming to evolve action selection rules in traversal-based automated software testing: results obtained with the TESTAR tool. Memetic Comput. **10**(3), 257–265 (2018)
12. Garcia, S., Fernandez, A., Luengo, J., Herrera, F.: A study of statistical techniques and performance measures for genetics-based machine learning: accuracy and interpretability. Soft. Comput. **13**(10), 959–977 (2008)
13. Hansen, N.: The CMA Evolution Strategy (2012). http://www.lri.fr/hansen/cmaesintro.html
14. Hooke, R., Jeeves, T.A.: Direct search solution of numerical and statistical problems. J. ACM **8**, 212–229 (1961)
15. Krasnogor, N.: Toward Robust Memetic Algorithms. In: Hart, W.E., Krasnogor, N., Smith, J.E. (eds.) Recent Advances in Memetic Algorithms. STUDFUZZ, vol. 166, pp. 185–207. Springer, Heidelberg (2004). https://doi.org/10.1007/3-540-32363-5_9
16. Liang, J.J., Qu, B.Y., Suganthan, P.N., Hernndez-Daz, A.G.: Problem definitions and evaluation criteria for the CEC 2013 special session on real-parameter optimization. Technical report 201212, Zhengzhou University and Nanyang Technological University, Zhengzhou China and Singapore (2013)
17. Luersen, M.A., Riche, R.L.: Globalized neldermead method for engineering optimization. Comput. Struct. **82**(23), 2251–2260 (2004)
18. Nelder, A., Mead, R.: A simplex method for function optimization. Comput. J. **7**, 308–313 (1965)
19. Neri, F., Cotta, C.: Memetic algorithms and memetic computing optimization: a literature review. Swarm Evol. Comput. **2**, 1–14 (2012)
20. Neri, F.: Linear Algebra for Computational Sciences and Engineering, 2nd edn. Springer, Cham (2019). https://doi.org/10.1007/978-3-030-21321-3
21. Nocedal, J., Wright, S.: Numerical Optimization, 2nd edn. Springer, New York (2006). https://doi.org/10.1007/978-0-387-40065-5
22. Peng, F., Tang, K., Chen, G., Yao, X.: Population-based algorithm portfolios for numerical optimization. IEEE Trans. Evol. Comput. **14**(5), 782–800 (2010)
23. Poikolainen, I., Neri, F., Caraffini, F.: Cluster-based population initialization for differential evolution frameworks. Inf. Sci. **297**, 216–235 (2015)
24. Powers, S.T., Ekárt, A., Lewis, P.R.: Modelling enduring institutions: the complementarity of evolutionary and agent-based approaches. Cogn. Syst. Res. **52**, 67–81 (2018)

25. Puchinger, J., Raidl, G.R.: Combining metaheuristics and exact algorithms in combinatorial optimization: a survey and classification. In: Mira, J., Álvarez, J.R. (eds.) IWINAC 2005. LNCS, vol. 3562, pp. 41–53. Springer, Heidelberg (2005). https://doi.org/10.1007/11499305_5

26. Qu, B.Y., Suganthan, P.N., Liang, J.J.: Differential evolution with neighborhood mutation for multimodal optimization. IEEE Trans. Evol. Comput. **16**(5), 601–614 (2012)

27. Rosenbrock, H.H.: An automatic method for finding the greatest or least value of a function. Comput. J. **3**(3), 175–184 (1960)

28. Rostami, S., Neri, F.: A fast hypervolume driven selection mechanism for many-objective optimisation problems. Swarm Evol. Comput. **34**, 50–67 (2017)

29. Torczon, V.: On the convergence of pattern search algorithms. SIAM J. Optim. **7**(1), 1–25 (1997)

30. Tseng, L.Y., Chen, C.: Multiple trajectory search for large scale global optimization. In: Proceedings of the IEEE Congress on Evolutionary Computation, pp. 3052–3059 (2008)

31. Wang, Y., Li, H.X., Huang, T., Li, L.: Differential evolution based on covariance matrix learning and bimodal distribution parameter setting. Appl. Soft Comput. **18**, 232–247 (2014)

32. Wilcoxon, F.: Individual comparisons by ranking methods. Biom. Bull. **1**(6), 80–83 (1945)

33. Xu, L., Hutter, F., Hoos, H., Leyton-Brown, K.: SATzilla: portfolio-based algorithm selection for SAT. J. Artif. Intell. Res. **32**, 565–606 (2008)

34. Yu, W.C.: Positive basis and a class of direct search techniques. Sci. Sin. (in Chinese) **9**(S1), 53–67 (1979)

EvoCluster: An Open-Source Nature-Inspired Optimization Clustering Framework in Python

Raneem Qaddoura[1], Hossam Faris[2(✉)], Ibrahim Aljarah[2],
and Pedro A. Castillo[3]

[1] Information Technology, Philadelphia University, Amman, Jordan
`rqaddoura@philadelphia.edu.jo`
[2] King Abdullah II School for Information Technology, The University of Jordan,
Amman, Jordan
`{hossam.faris,i.aljarah}@ju.edu.jo`
[3] ETSIIT-CITIC, University of Granada, Granada, Spain
`pacv@ugr.es`
`http://www.evo-ml.com`

Abstract. EvoCluster is an open source and cross-platform framework implemented in Python which includes the most well-known and recent nature-inspired metaheuristic optimizers that are customized to perform partitional clustering tasks. The goal of this framework is to provide a user-friendly and customizable implementation of the metaheuristic based clustering algorithms which can be utilized by experienced and non-experienced users for different applications. The framework can also be used by researchers who can benefit from the implementation of the metaheuristic optimizers for their research studies. EvoCluster can be extended by designing other optimizers, including more objective functions, adding other evaluation measures, and using more data sets. The current implementation of the framework includes ten metaheristic optimizers, thirty datasets, five objective functions, and twelve evaluation measures. The source code of EvoCluster is publicly available at (http://evo-ml.com/2019/10/25/evocluster/).

Keywords: Clustering · Cluster analysis · Evolutionary computing · Framework · Python

1 Introduction

Clustering is an unsupervised learning task that are essential in many applications. The main goal of clustering is to find the similarities between every group of data to find common relationships between them. It is widely used in different domains such as customer segmentation [40], image processing [26], and pattern recognition [27].

© Springer Nature Switzerland AG 2020
P. A. Castillo et al. (Eds.): EvoApplications 2020, LNCS 12104, pp. 20–36, 2020.
https://doi.org/10.1007/978-3-030-43722-0_2

Swarm Intelligence (SI) and Evolutionary Algorithms (EA) as nature-inspired metaheuristic algorithms are commonly utilized for performing partitional clustering tasks. They are proven to be efficient for multiple scientific and engineering domains [36]. The main advantage of using these algorithms in clustering is the ability to explore and search for better grouping of data to achieve high quality clustering results [36]. In addition, they have reasonable running time [49], they can avoid falling in local optima [39], and they can work with noisy data.

Metaheuristic algorithms use predefined objective function to lead the solution toward the optimal one. The objective function directly affects the quality of the results [41]. Thus, considering the best objective function is very important, and is not an easy task.

Nature-inspired algorithms include well-regarded optimization algorithms like Genetic algorithm (GA) [20], Evolution Strategy (ES) [9], Particle Swarm Optimization (PSO) [23], and Ant Colony Optimization (ACO) [25]. While noticeable recent nature-inspired algorithms include Cuckoo Search (CS) [55], Grey Wolf Optimizer (GWO) [7,35], Multi-Verse Optimizer (MVO) [8,34,49], Moth-flame optimization (MFO) [31], Whale Optimization Algorithm (WOA) [33], Bat Algorithm (BAT) [57], Firefly Algorithm (FFA) [56], and many others [2,4–6].

In this paper, we introduce EvoCluster an open-source framework for partitional clustering based on using nature-inspired metaheuristic optimizers. Since Python is a rapid development language that is recognizably growing in the data science machine learning field, Python was selected for implementing this framework. The main contributions of the proposed framework are:

- Provide a set of nature-inspired optimizers for performing the partitional clustering task to facilitate using these algorithms by researchers and practitioners.
- Provide a wide set of objective functions that are customized for the partitional clustering task.
- Facilitate the evaluation process of clustering by including many well-known evaluation measures for clustering.
- Provide a set of well-known data sets which are widely used for performing experiments in clustering.

The remainder of this paper is organized as follows: Sect. 2 presents the latest evolutionary and clustering frameworks and libraries in the literature. Section 3 describes in detail the components and functionalities of the framework. Section 4 displays the design of population and the framework components. Section 5 shows some visual representation of some results and plots generated from the framework. Section 6 concludes the work and gives future possible extension to the framework.

2   Related Work

Many frameworks and libraries can be found in the literature that can be used for performing clustering tasks. Some popular examples are Weka [17], Elki [1], and scikit-learn [37]. Some other frameworks that are specific to clustering are clusterNOR [30] and ClustEval [54]. clusterNOR is a parallel framework which includes nine clustering algorithms, while ClustEval is a recent framework having around twenty well-known algorithms and fourteen evaluation measures. Other frameworks are specific to certain domains: TimeClust [28] is a clustering tool for gene expression time series having four clustering algorithms. A recent framework was developed in [43] named clusterExperiment for clustering single-cell RNA-Seq data. These clustering frameworks and libraries include the basic and traditional clustering algorithms and most of them do not include nature-inspired metaheuristic optimizers.

Since nature-inspired metaheuristic algorithms are commonly used in different applications, some general-purpose frameworks and libraries were developed to facilitate their use. EvoloPy [15] is one of the recent open-source python frameworks that includes well-known and recent optimizing algorithms. Evolopy-FS [24] is another version of Evolopy for feature selection. NiaPy [51] is a python microframework for building nature-inspired algorithms. Other popular frameworks include DEAP [16], ECJ [53], EO [22], HeuristicLab [52], jMetal [14], and ParadisEO [10]. Some frameworks are specific to certain domains: GEATbx [18] is a framework in MATLAB having many variants of the Genetic Algorithms and Genetic Programming. GAlib [29] is a C++ library of genetic algorithm tools and operators for parallel environments. These frameworks are used for optimizing general problems which do not include clustering.

Since the clustering task can be approached by optimizing the centroids for the clusters according to a predefined objective function, which needs special implementation, frameworks and libraries can be implemented for this purpose. To the best of our knowledge, we found only one framework for clustering with evolutionary algorithms which is LEAC [44]. LEAC is implemented using c++ which includes 23 Evolutionary Algorithms for partial clustering. However, most practitioners use other languages which have more libraries and packages than c++ language. In addition, the algorithms used in LEAC are only different variations of the evolutionary operators for fixed and variable k-clusters and do not include other algorithms. Thus, there is a need for a framework of the nature-inspired metaheuristic clustering optimizers which is not specific to the evolutionary algorithms.

EvoCluster is implemented as a flexible framework which includes several nature-inspired metaheuristic optimizers for performing the clustering task which allows user customization of the clustering algorithms, the objective functions, and the evaluation measures. EvoCluster is an extension to the aforementioned EvoloPy framework in which the algorithms are customized for the partitional clustering task. It also considers multiple objective functions to enhance the population at each iteration. Evaluation measures are also implemented for evaluating the clustering results. To the best of our knowledge,

EvoCluster framework is the first framework in python for clustering data using the selected metaheuristic optimizers. It is implemented efficiently considering the computation time and the quality of results.

3   Framework Overview

EvoCluster includes the most well-regarded nature-inspired metaheuristic optimizers that are adopted for performing the partitional clustering task with a very easy and useful interface. The framework is constructed with six main components which are described in the following sections:

3.1   The Optimizer

It serves as the main interface of the framework. Users can select the set of optimizers, data sets, and objective functions that they prefer for running their experiments. They can also specify the main parameters that are common for most optimizers which are the number of iterations and the population size. The number of runs can also be determined through this interface. In addition to selecting the evaluation measures the user prefer for evaluating the results generated from the framework.

3.2   Nature-Inspired Metaheuristics

The implementation of each optimizer are visible as a separate file in the framework. The optimizers that are available at the time of writing this paper are as follows:

- Genetic Algorithm (GA) [47]: It is inspired by biological evolution. The algorithm evolves toward better solutions based on four main operations: selection, crossover, mutation, and elitism.
- Particle Swarm Optimization (PSO) [23,48]: It is inspired by the flocking behavior of birds and the schooling behavior of fish. The algorithm evolves toward better solutions based on a mathematical formula considering the position and velocity of the particles. The movement of the particle is influenced by its local best and the global best positions.
- Salp Swarm Algorithm (SSA) [32]: It is inspired by the swarming behaviour of salps. The algorithm evolves toward better solutions based on two mathematical models to update the position of leading and follower salps.
- Firefly Algorithm (FFA) [56]: It is inspired by the flashing behavior of fireflies. The algorithm evolves toward better solutions by the attraction of fireflies based on the brightness of other fireflies calculated by the inverse square law.
- Gray Wolf Optimizer (GWO) [35]: It is inspired by grey wolves. The algorithm evolves toward better solutions based on hunting, searching for prey, encircling prey, and attacking prey.

- Whale Optimization Algorithm (WOA) [33]: It is inspired by social behavior of humpback whales. The algorithm evolves toward better solutions based on three operators to simulate the search for prey, encircling prey, and bubble-net foraging behavior of humpback whales.
- Multi-Verse Optimizer (MVO) [34]: It is inspired by the theory of multi-verse in physics. The algorithm evolves toward better solutions based on mathematical models of the white hole, black hole, and worm hole which reflect exploration, exploitation, and local search, respectively.
- Moth Flame Optimizer (MFO) [31]: It is inspired by the death behaviour of moths. The algorithm evolves toward better solutions based on logarithmic spiral update mechanism of moths.
- Bat Algorithm (BAT) [57]: It is inspired by the echolocation behaviour of bats. The algorithm evolves toward better solutions based on the pulse of loudness and pulse rate.
- Cuckoo Search Algorithm (CS) [55]: It is inspired by the brood parasitism of some cuckoo species. The algorithm evolves toward better solutions based on three idealized rules where the bird decide whether it should throw the eggs away or abandon its nest and create a new one.

3.3   Objective Functions

Consists of the implementation of the objective functions that are used to optimize the individuals at each iteration. The list of objective functions which are used with the data sets having k clusters of N points, which are available at the time of writing this paper are as follows:

- Sum of squared error (SSE) [11]:

$$\sum_{n=1}^{N} d_{nc}^2 \tag{1}$$

  where d_{nc} is the euclidean distance between the centroid and the point. By minimizing SSE, we obtain better results.
- Total Within Cluster Variance (TWCV) [38]:

$$TWCV = \sum_{n=1}^{N}\sum_{f=1}^{F} p_{nf}^2 - \sum_{k=1}^{K} \frac{1}{|p_k|} \sum_{f=1}^{F} (\sum p_{kf})^2 \tag{2}$$

  where F is the number of features, p_{nf} is feature f of the point n, p_{kf} is feature f of the point k, and $|p_k|$ is the number of points in cluster k. By minimizing TWCV, we obtain better results.
- Silhouette Coefficient (SC) [12,38]:

$$SC = \frac{\sum_{k=1}^{|K|}((b-a)/max(a,b)))}{N} \tag{3}$$

  where a is the average distance between a point and the other points in the same predicted cluster and b is the average distance between a point and the other points in the next nearest cluster. By maximizing SC, we obtain better results. We normalize the values of SC between 0 and 1 and then use the reversed value of the normalized SC $(1 - \text{norm}(SC))$ in the objective function.

– Davies–Bouldin (DB) index [13]:

$$DB = \frac{1}{|k|} \sum_{k=1}^{|K|} max_{k \neq j} \left(\frac{s_k + s_j}{d_{kj}} \right) \tag{4}$$

where s_k is the average distance between a point and the cluster center and d_{kj} is the distance between the centroid of cluster k and the centroid of cluster j. By minimizing DB, we obtain better results.

– Dunn Index (DI) [12, 19]:

$$DI = \frac{d_{min}}{d_{max}} \tag{5}$$

where d_{min} represents the ratio between the minimal distance between two points in different clusters and d_{max} represents the maximal distance between the farthest two points in a cluster. By maximizing DI, we obtain better results. Thus, we use the reversed value of DI $(1 - DI)$ in the objective function.

3.4 Evaluation Measures

The framework includes a set of evaluation measures to evaluate the results obtained from running the framework. Given T as the true classes of N points and P as the predicted clusters of these points. The evaluation measures that are available at the time of writing this paper are as follows:

– Purity (P) [6]:

$$Purity = \frac{1}{N} \sum_{j=1}^{k} max_i (|T_i \cap P_j|) \tag{6}$$

where P_j presents all points assigned to cluster j, k is the number of clusters, and T_i is the true assignments of points in cluster i.

– Entropy (E) [6]:

$$Entropy = \sum_{j=1}^{k} \frac{(|P_j|)}{n} E(P_j) \tag{7}$$

where $E(P_j)$ is the individual entropy of a cluster. Individual cluster entropy is calculated using Eq. 8:

$$E(P_j) = -\frac{1}{logk} \sum_{i=1}^{k} \frac{|P_j \cap T_i|}{P_j} log \left(\frac{|P_j \cap T_i|}{P_j} \right) \tag{8}$$

- Homogeneity Score (HS) [46]:

$$HS = 1 - \frac{H(T|P)}{H(T)} \tag{9}$$

where $H(T)$ is the classes Entropy and $H(T|P)$ is the classes conditional Entropy. $H(T)$ and $H(T|P)$ are calculated as follows [46]:

$$H(T) = -\sum_{t=1}^{|T|} \frac{n_t}{N} \cdot \log\left(\frac{n_t}{N}\right) \tag{10}$$

$$H(T|P) = -\sum_{p=1}^{|P|} \sum_{t=1}^{|T|} \frac{n_{pt}}{N} \cdot \log\left(\frac{n_{pt}}{n_p}\right) \tag{11}$$

where n_t and n_p are the number of points of the true class t and the predicted cluster p, respectively. n_{pt} is the number of points of the true class t which are clustered to the predicted cluster p.

- Completeness Score (CS) [46]:

$$CS = 1 - \frac{H(P|T)}{H(P)} \tag{12}$$

where $H(P)$ is the cluster Entropy and $H(P|T)$ is the clusters conditional Entropy. $H(P)$ and $H(P|T)$ are calculated as follows [46]:

$$H(P) = -\sum_{p=1}^{|P|} \frac{n_p}{N} \cdot \log\left(\frac{n_p}{N}\right) \tag{13}$$

$$H(P|T) = -\sum_{t=1}^{|T|} \sum_{p=1}^{|P|} \frac{n_{pt}}{N} \cdot \log\left(\frac{n_{pt}}{n_t}\right) \tag{14}$$

- V-measure (VM) [46]:

$$VM = 2 \cdot \frac{HS \cdot CS}{HS + CS} \tag{15}$$

- Adjusted Mutual Information (AMI) [50]:

$$AMI = \frac{MI - E[MI]}{\max(H(P), H(T)) - E[MI]} \tag{16}$$

where H(P) and and H(T) are the cluster Entropy (Eq. 13) and the class entropy (Eq. 10).
MI is the Mutual Index which is calculated by [50]:

$$MI = \sum_{p=1}^{|P|} \sum_{t=1}^{|T|} \frac{n_{pt}}{N} \log\left(\frac{\frac{n_{pt}}{N}}{\frac{n_p}{N} \cdot \frac{n_t}{N}}\right) \tag{17}$$

E[MI] is the Expected Mutual Index which is calculated by [45,50]:

$$E(MI) = \sum_{p=1}^{|P|} \sum_{t=1}^{|T|} \sum_{n_{pt}=max(0,n_p+n_t-N)}^{min(n_p,n_t)} \frac{n_{pt}}{N} log(\frac{N.n_{pt}}{n_p n_t}) \times$$
$$\left(\frac{n_p! n_t! (N-n_p)! (N-n_t)!}{N! n_{pt}! (n_p - n_{pt})! (n_t - n_{pt})! (N - n_p - n_t + n_{pt})!} \right) \tag{18}$$

– Adjusted Rand Index (ARI) [21]:

$$ARI = \frac{RI - E[RI]}{max(RI) - E[RI]} \tag{19}$$

where RI is the Rand Index, E[RI] is the Expected Rand Index, and max[RI] is the Maximum Rand Index. RI, E[RI], and max[RI] are calculated by [21,42]:

$$RI = \frac{a+b}{\binom{N}{2}} = \frac{\sum_{p,t} \binom{n_{pt}}{2}}{\binom{N}{2}} \tag{20}$$

$$E(RI) = E\left(\sum_{p,t} \binom{n_{pt}}{2}\right) = \frac{\sum_{p=1}^{|P|} \binom{n_p}{2} \sum_{t=1}^{|T|} \binom{n_t}{2}}{\binom{N}{2}} \tag{21}$$

$$max[RI] = \frac{1}{2}\left[\sum_{p=1}^{|P|} \binom{n_p}{2} + \sum_{t=1}^{|T|} \binom{n_t}{2}\right] \tag{22}$$

where a is the number of pair of points located in the same true class t and clustered at the same predicted cluster p. b is the number of pair of points located in a different true class t and clustered at a different predicted cluster p. $\binom{N}{2}$ is the number of pair of points.
– Sum of squared error (SSE) [11]
– Total Within Cluster Variance (TWCV) [38]
– Silhouette Coefficient (SC) [12,38]
– Davies–Bouldin (DB) index [13]
– Dunn Index (DI) [12,19]
The last five measures are discussed in the previous section and are used as evaluation measures.

3.5   Benchmark Data Sets

Most common and well-known data sets used for clustering can be found in the framework in which it can be extended to include other data sets. The list of data sets that are available at the time of writing this paper are summarized in Table 1. As shown from the table, the data sets have different number of points, features, and clusters. The data sets are either real or artificial data sets.

They are gathered from scikit learn[1], UCI machine learning repository[2], School of Computing at University of Eastern Finland[3], ELKI[4], KEEL[5], and Naftali Harris Blog[6].

3.6 Results Management

The results obtained by running the framework are gathered in three types of CSV files and two types of plots:

- Average results file: this file gives average results of the runs for performing each combination of optimizer, objective function, and data set. Each item in the CSV file includes the average execution time, the average value of each external measure, and the average value for each iteration.
- Detailed results file: this file gives detailed results for performing each run. Each item in the CSV file includes the execution time, the value of each external measure, and the value for each iteration.
- Best individual labels file: this file includes the values of the labels obtained from the best individual at the last iteration of each run.
- Convergence curve plot: after running the convergence curve script, a plot is generated for the convergence curves for each selected data sets, optimizers, and objective functions. The plot represents the convergence curves for multiple optimizers having the values of the objective function at each iteration.
- Box plot: a plot is generated to represent the evaluation measures for each data set for several runs of the framework. Each box represents one of the selected optimizers. The interquartile range, best value, and worst value are presented as the box, the upper whiskers, and the lower whiskers, respectively [3].

4 Design Issues

The nature-inspired metaheuristic optimizers, which are included in the framework, use population of individuals (s) at each iteration. Each individual represents one of the optimizer suggested clustering solution of centroids. Thus, consisting of the features (f) of each centroid for (k) clusters. Figure 1 shows how a population at a certain iteration is formed. For each individual in the group of s individuals in the population, there are k centroids having f features for each centroid.

In EvoCluster, populations are defined using the `Numpy` open-source python package which is based on the `N-dimensional array` data structure. The

---

[1] http://scikit-learn.org/stable/datasets/index.html.
[2] https://archive.ics.uci.edu/ml/.
[3] http://cs.uef.fi/sipu/datasets/.
[4] https://elki-project.github.io/datasets/.
[5] https://sci2s.ugr.es/keel/datasets.php.
[6] https://www.naftaliharris.com/blog/visualizing-K-means-clustering/.

Table 1. Data sets properties which show the name, number of clusters, number of points, number of features, data set type, and source

ID	Data set	k	#Points	#Features	Type	Source
1	Aggregation	7	788	2	Artificial	University of Eastern Finland (See footnote 3)
2	Aniso	3	1500	2	Artificial	Scikit learn (See footnote 1)
3	Appendicitis	2	106	7	Real	KEEL (See footnote 5)
4	Balance	3	625	4	Real	UCI (See footnote 2)
5	Backnote	2	1372	4	Real	UCI (See footnote 2)
6	Blobs	3	1500	2	Artificial	Scikit learn (See footnote 1)
7	Blood	2	748	4	Real	UCI (See footnote 2)
8	Circles	2	1500	2	Artificial	Scikit learn (See footnote 1)
9	Diagnosis II	2	120	6	Real	UCI (See footnote 2)
10	Ecoli	5	327	7	Real	UCI (See footnote 2)
11	Flame	2	240	2	Artificial	University of Eastern Finland (See footnote 3)
12	Glass	6	214	9	Real	UCI (See footnote 2)
13	Heart	2	270	13	Real	UCI (See footnote 2)
14	Iris	3	150	4	Real	UCI (See footnote 2)
15	Iris 2D	3	150	2	Real	UCI (See footnote 2)
16	Ionosphere	2	351	344	Real	UCI (See footnote 2)
17	Jain	2	373	2	Artificial	University of Eastern Finland (See footnote 3)
18	Liver	2	345	7	Real	UCI (See footnote 2)
19	Moons	2	1500	2	Artificial	Scikit learn (See footnote 1)
20	Mouse	3	490	2	Artificial	ELKI (See footnote 4)
21	Pathbased	3	300	2	Artificial	University of Eastern Finland (See footnote 3)
22	Seeds	3	210	7	Real	UCI (See footnote 2)
23	Smiley	4	500	2	Artificial	naftaliharris (See footnote 6)
24	Sonar	2	208	60	Real	UCI (See footnote 2)
25	Varied	3	1500	2	Artificial	Scikit learn (See footnote 1)
26	Vary Density	3	150	2	Artificial	ELKI (See footnote 4)
27	Vertebral2	2	310	6	Real	UCI (See footnote 2)
28	Vertebral3	3	310	6	Real	UCI (See footnote 2)
29	WDBC	2	569	30	Real	UCI (See footnote 2)
30	Wine	3	178	13	Real	UCI (See footnote 2)

`metrics` module of the `sklearn` package are used for the evaluation measures for HS, CS, VM, AMI, ARI, FM, SC, and DB. In addition, the `normalize` function of the `preprocessing` module in the `sklearn` package is used to convert the values of the features for a data set to the interval $[0, 1]$ to give similar weights to the features of the points. Each individual of a population in a certain iteration generates a corresponding vector of predicted labels which represent the cluster number for each point of the data set. This vector is evaluated using a selected objective function in the framework.

EvoCluster components and their relationships are illustrated as a class diagram in Fig. 2. EvoCluster contains fourteen classes which include ten classes for the metaheuristic algorithms and four other main classes. The main classes are `Optimizer`, `Solution`, `Objectives`, and `Measures`. The `Optimizer` class solves the partitional clustering task by using one of the metaheuristic algorithm which finds a `Solution` using an `Objective` function. This generates the global solution of the best clustering labels. The `Optimizer` then evaluates the labels using the `Measures` class.

5   Experiments and Visualizations

In this section, we show some examples of conducting some experiments using EvoCluster. The framework is run 10 times using a population size of 50 and iterations of 100.

Figure 3 shows the convergence curve for selected optimizers which are PSO, GA, GWO, FFA, and CS using the SSE objective function for different data sets which are Aggregation, Flame, Iris, and Seeds. The convergence curve represents the values of the objective/fitness function over the course of iterations. The convergence curve shows the progress of the optimizers toward the optimal solution by minimizing the value of the objective/fitness function. As can be seen in the figure, the optimizers show different behaviors. In addition, the same algorithm behaves differently for different data sets. Figure 4 shows the box plot for the selected optimizers which are PSO, GA, GWO, FFA, and CS using the SSE objective function for the Aggregation data set for different evaluation measure which are SSE, Purity, Entropy, and ARI. The box plot represents the range of values of different runs. It also shows the max, min, and mean value of the evaluation measure.

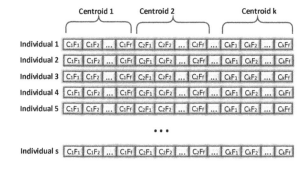

Fig. 1. Population of individuals at a specific iteration

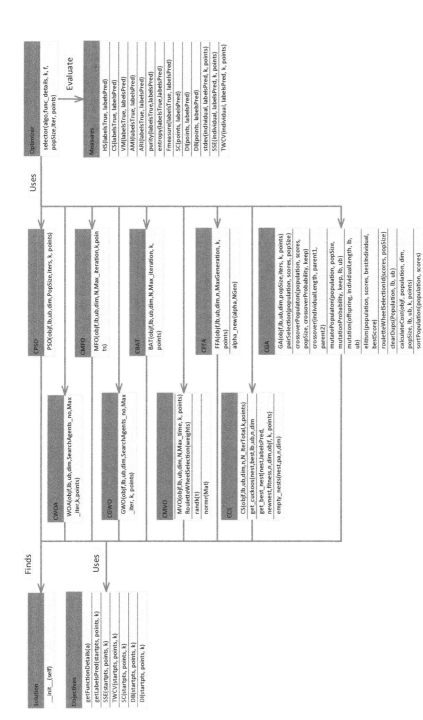

Fig. 2. Class diagram of EvoCluster

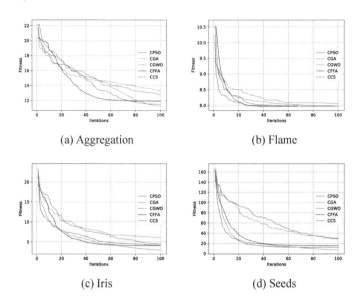

Fig. 3. Convergence curve for PSO, GA, GWO, FFA, and CS using SSE objective function for (a) Aggregation; (b) Fame; (c) Iris; and (d) Seeds

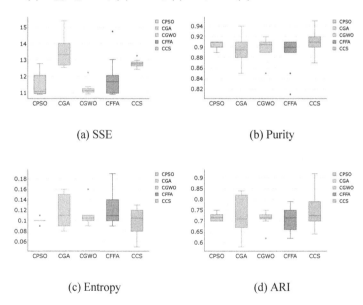

Fig. 4. Box plot of (a) SSE; (b) Purity; (c) Entropy; and (d) ARI for PSO, GA, GWO, FFA, and CS using SSE objective function for the Aggregation data set

6   Conclusion and Future Work

EvoCluster is an open-source framework implemented in python which provides so-far ten nature-inspired metaheuristic optimizers that are customized to solve partitional clustering tasks. EvoCluster provides the ability to select one of five well-known objective functions and twelve well-known evaluation measures. The framework is designed in a flexible way so that developers and researchers can customize it by implementing other optimizers, objective functions, and evaluation measures. In this paper, we showed some visualizations that are automatically generated based on the results of the conducted experiments using the EvoCluster in the form of the convergence curves and box plots. For future work, we plan to implement more existing nature-inspired metaheuristic algorithms and add any other new algorithms incrementally.

Acknowledgements. This work has been supported in part by: Ministerio español de Economía y Competitividad under project TIN2017-85727-C4-2-P (UGR-DeepBio).

References

1. Achtert, E., Kriegel, H.-P., Zimek, A.: ELKI: a software system for evaluation of subspace clustering algorithms. In: Ludäscher, B., Mamoulis, N. (eds.) SSDBM 2008. LNCS, vol. 5069, pp. 580–585. Springer, Heidelberg (2008). https://doi.org/10.1007/978-3-540-69497-7_41

2. Al-Madi, N., Aljarah, I., Ludwig, S.A.: Parallel glowworm swarm optimization clustering algorithm based on MapReduce. In: 2014 IEEE Symposium on Swarm Intelligence (SIS), pp. 1–8. IEEE (2014)

3. Aljarah, I., Ala'M, A.-Z., Faris, H., Hassonah, M.A., Mirjalili, S., Saadeh, H.: Simultaneous feature selection and support vector machine optimization using the grasshopper optimization algorithm. Cogn. Comput. **10**, 478–495 (2018). https://doi.org/10.1007/s12559-017-9542-9

4. Aljarah, I., Ludwig, S.A.: Parallel particle swarm optimization clustering algorithm based on MapReduce methodology. In: 2012 Fourth World Congress on Nature and Biologically Inspired Computing (NaBIC), pp. 104–111. IEEE (2012)

5. Aljarah, I., Ludwig, S.A.: MapReduce intrusion detection system based on a particle swarm optimization clustering algorithm. In: 2013 IEEE Congress on Evolutionary Computation (CEC), pp. 955–962. IEEE (2013)

6. Aljarah, I., Ludwig, S.A.: A new clustering approach based on Glowworm Swarm Optimization. In: 2013 IEEE Congress on Evolutionary Computation (CEC), pp. 2642–2649. IEEE (2013)

7. Aljarah, I., Mafarja, M., Heidari, A.A., Faris, H., Mirjalili, S.: Clustering analysis using a novel locality-informed grey wolf-inspired clustering approach. Knowl. Inf. Syst. **62**, 507–539 (2019). https://doi.org/10.1007/s10115-019-01358-x

8. Aljarah, I., Mafarja, M., Heidari, A.A., Faris, H., Mirjalili, S.: Multi-verse optimizer: theory, literature review, and application in data clustering. In: Mirjalili, S., Song Dong, J., Lewis, A. (eds.) Nature-Inspired Optimizers. SCI, vol. 811, pp. 123–141. Springer, Cham (2020). https://doi.org/10.1007/978-3-030-12127-3_8

9. Beyer, H.-G., Schwefel, H.-P.: Evolution strategies - a comprehensive introduction. Nat. Comput. **1**(1), 3–52 (2002). https://doi.org/10.1023/A:1015059928466

10. Cahon, S., Melab, N., Talbi, E.-G.: ParadisEO: a framework for the reusable design of parallel and distributed metaheuristics. J. Heuristics **10**(3), 357–380 (2004). https://doi.org/10.1023/B:HEUR.0000026900.92269.ec

11. Chang, D.-X., Zhang, X.-D., Zheng, C.-W.: A genetic algorithm with gene rearrangement for K-means clustering. Pattern Recogn. **42**(7), 1210–1222 (2009)

12. Chowdhury, K., Chaudhuri, D., Pal, A.K.: A novel objective function based clustering with optimal number of clusters. In: Mandal, J.K., Mukhopadhyay, S., Dutta, P., Dasgupta, K. (eds.) Methodologies and Application Issues of Contemporary Computing Framework, pp. 23–32. Springer, Singapore (2018). https://doi.org/10.1007/978-981-13-2345-4_3

13. Davies, D.L., Bouldin, D.W.: A cluster separation measure. IEEE Trans. Pattern Anal. Mach. Intell. **PAMI−1**(2), 224–227 (1979)

14. Durillo, J.J., Nebro, A.J.: jMetal: a Java framework for multi-objective optimization. Adv. Eng. Softw. **42**, 760–771 (2011)

15. Faris, H., Aljarah, I., Mirjalili, S., Castillo, P.A., Guervós, J.J.M.: EvoloPY: an open-source nature-inspired optimization framework in Python. In: IJCCI (ECTA), pp. 171–177 (2016)

16. Fortin, F.-A., De Rainville, F.-M., Gardner, M.-A., Parizeau, M., Gagné, C.: DEAP: evolutionary algorithms made easy. J. Mach. Learn. Res. **13**, 2171–2175 (2012)

17. Hall, M., Frank, E., Holmes, G., Pfahringer, B., Reutemann, P., Witten, I.H.: The WEKA data mining software: an update. ACM SIGKDD Explor. Newsl. **11**(1), 10–18 (2009)

18. Pohlheim, H.: GEATbx - the genetic and evolutionary algorithm toolbox for matlab (2006)

19. Hassani, M., Seidl, T.: Using internal evaluation measures to validate the quality of diverse stream clustering algorithms. Vietnam J. Comput. Sci. **4**(3), 171–183 (2017). https://doi.org/10.1007/s40595-016-0086-9

20. Holland, J.: Genetic algorithms. Sci. Am. **267**, 66–72 (1992)

21. Hubert, L., Arabie, P.: Comparing partitions. J. Classif. **2**(1), 193–218 (1985). https://doi.org/10.1007/BF01908075

22. Keijzer, M., Merelo, J.J., Romero, G., Schoenauer, M.: Evolving objects: a general purpose evolutionary computation library. In: Collet, P., Fonlupt, C., Hao, J.-K., Lutton, E., Schoenauer, M. (eds.) EA 2001. LNCS, vol. 2310, pp. 231–242. Springer, Heidelberg (2002). https://doi.org/10.1007/3-540-46033-0_19

23. Kennedy, J., Eberhart, R.: Particle swarm optimization. In: 1995 Proceedings of the IEEE International Conference on Neural Networks, vol. 4, pp. 1942–1948, November 1995

24. Khurma, R.A., Aljarah, I., Sharieh, A., Mirjalili, S.: EvoloPy-FS: an open-source nature-inspired optimization framework in Python for feature selection. In: Mirjalili, S., Faris, H., Aljarah, I. (eds.) Evolutionary Machine Learning Techniques. AIS, pp. 131–173. Springer, Singapore (2020). https://doi.org/10.1007/978-981-32-9990-0_8

25. Korošec, P., Šilc, J.: A distributed ant-based algorithm for numerical optimization. In: Proceedings of the 2009 Workshop on Bio-inspired Algorithms for Distributed Systems - BADS 2009. Association for Computing Machinery (ACM) (2009)

26. Kumar, S., Pant, M., Kumar, M., Dutt, A.: Colour image segmentation with histogram and homogeneity histogram difference using evolutionary algorithms. Int. J. Mach. Learn. Cybernet. **9**(1), 163–183 (2018). https://doi.org/10.1007/s13042-015-0360-7

27. Liu, A., Su, Y., Nie, W., Kankanhalli, M.S.: Hierarchical clustering multi-task learning for joint human action grouping and recognition. IEEE Trans. Pattern Anal. Mach. Intell. **39**(1), 102–114 (2017)
28. Magni, P., Ferrazzi, F., Sacchi, L., Bellazzi, R.: TimeClust: a clustering tool for gene expression time series. Bioinformatics **24**(3), 430–432 (2007)
29. Wall, M.: GAlib: a C++ library of genetic algorithm components (1996)
30. Mhembere, D., Zheng, D., Priebe, C.E., Vogelstein, J.T., Burns, R.: clusterNOR: a NUMA-optimized clustering framework. arXiv preprint arXiv:1902.09527 (2019)
31. Mirjalili, S.: Moth-flame optimization algorithm: a novel nature-inspired heuristic paradigm. Knowl.-Based Syst. **89**, 228–249 (2015)
32. Mirjalili, S., Gandomi, A.H., Mirjalili, S.Z., Saremi, S., Faris, H., Mirjalili, S.M.: Salp Swarm Algorithm: a bio-inspired optimizer for engineering design problems. Adv. Eng. Softw. **114**, 163–191 (2017)
33. Mirjalili, S., Lewis, A.: The whale optimization algorithm. Adv. Eng. Softw. **95**, 51–67 (2016)
34. Mirjalili, S., Mirjalili, S.M., Hatamlou, A.: Multi-Verse Optimizer: a nature-inspired algorithm for global optimization. Neural Comput. Appl. **27**(2), 495–513 (2015). https://doi.org/10.1007/s00521-015-1870-7
35. Mirjalili, S., Mirjalili, S.M., Lewis, A.: Grey wolf optimizer. Adv. Eng. Softw. **69**, 46–61 (2014)
36. Nanda, S.J., Panda, G.: A survey on nature inspired metaheuristic algorithms for partitional clustering. Swarm Evol. Comput. **16**, 1–18 (2014)
37. Pedregosa, F., et al.: Scikit-learn: machine learning in Python. J. Mach. Learn. Res. **12**(Oct), 2825–2830 (2011)
38. Peng, P., et al.: Reporting and analyzing alternative clustering solutions by employing multi-objective genetic algorithm and conducting experiments on cancer data. Knowl.-Based Syst. **56**, 108–122 (2014)
39. Prakash, J., Singh, P.K.: Particle swarm optimization with k-means for simultaneous feature selection and data clustering. In: 2015 Second International Conference on Soft Computing and Machine Intelligence (ISCMI), pp. 74–78. IEEE (2015)
40. Qaddoura, R., Faris, H., Aljarah, I.: An efficient clustering algorithm based on the k-nearest neighbors with an indexing ratio. Int. J. Mach. Learn. Cyber. **11**, 675–714 (2019). https://doi.org/10.1007/s13042-019-01027-z
41. Raitoharju, J., Samiee, K., Kiranyaz, S., Gabbouj, M.: Particle swarm clustering fitness evaluation with computational centroids. Swarm Evol. Comput. **34**, 103–118 (2017)
42. Rand, W.M.: Objective criteria for the evaluation of clustering methods. J. Am. Stat. Assoc. **66**(336), 846–850 (1971)
43. Risso, D., et al.: clusterExperiment and RSEC: a bioconductor package and framework for clustering of single-cell and other large gene expression datasets. PLoS Comput. Biol. **14**(9), e1006378 (2018)
44. Robles-Berumen, H., Zafra, A., Fardoun, H.M., Ventura, S.: LEAC: an efficient library for clustering with evolutionary algorithms. Knowl.-Based Syst. **179**, 117–119 (2019)
45. Romano, S., Vinh, N.X., Bailey, J., Verspoor, K.: Adjusting for chance clustering comparison measures. J. Mach. Learn. Res. **17**(1), 4635–4666 (2016)
46. Rosenberg, A., Hirschberg, J.: V-measure: a conditional entropy-based external cluster evaluation measure. In: EMNLP-CoNLL, vol. 7, pp. 410–420 (2007)
47. Sheikh, R.H., Raghuwanshi, M.M., Jaiswal. A.N.: Genetic algorithm based clustering: a survey. In: First International Conference on Emerging Trends in Engineering and Technology, pp. 314–319. IEEE (2008)

48. Shi, Y., Eberhart, R.: A modified particle swarm optimizer. In: 1998 IEEE International Conference on Evolutionary Computation Proceedings. IEEE World Congress on Computational Intelligence (Cat. No. 98TH8360), pp. 69–73. IEEE (1998)

49. Shukri, S., Faris, H., Aljarah, I., Mirjalili, S., Abraham, A.: Evolutionary static and dynamic clustering algorithms based on multi-verse optimizer. Eng. Appl. Artif. Intell. **72**, 54–66 (2018)

50. Vinh, N.X., Epps, J., Bailey, J.: Information theoretic measures for clusterings comparison: variants, properties, normalization and correction for chance. J. Mach. Learn. Res. **11**(Oct), 2837–2854 (2010)

51. Vrbančič, G., Brezočnik, L., Mlakar, U., Fister, D., Fister Jr., I.: NiaPY: python microframework for building nature-inspired algorithms. J. Open Source Softw. **3**, 613 (2018)

52. Wagner, S., Affenzeller, M.: The HeuristicLab optimization environment. Technical report, University of Applied Sciences Upper Austria (2004)

53. Wilson, G.C., Mc Intyre, A., Heywood, M.I.: Resource review: three open source systems for evolving programs-Lilgp, ECJ and grammatical evolution. Genet. Program Evolvable Mach. **5**(1), 103–105 (2004). https://doi.org/10.1023/B:GENP.0000017053.10351.dc

54. Wiwie, C., Baumbach, J., Röttger, R.: Comparing the performance of biomedical clustering methods. Nat. Methods **12**(11), 1033 (2015)

55. Yang, X.S., Deb, S.: Cuckoo search via Lévy flights. In: 2009 World Congress on Nature Biologically Inspired Computing, NaBIC 2009, pp. 210–214, December 2009

56. Yang, X.-S.: Firefly algorithm, stochastic test functions and design optimisation. Int. J. Bio-Inspired Comput. **2**(2), 78–84 (2010)

57. Yang, X.-S.: A new metaheuristic bat-inspired algorithm. In: González, J.R., Pelta, D.A., Cruz, C., Terrazas, G., Krasnogor, N. (eds.) NICSO 2010. SCI, vol. 284. Springer, Berlin (2010). https://doi.org/10.1007/978-3-642-12538-6_6

Optimizing the Hyperparameters of a Mixed Integer Linear Programming Solver to Speed up Electric Vehicle Charging Control

Takahiro Ishihara[1] and Steffen Limmer[2(✉)]

[1] Department of Systems and Control, Graduate School of Engineering,
Tokyo Institute of Technology, Tokyo 152-8552, Japan
`ishihara.t.af@m.titech.ac.jp`
[2] Honda Research Institute Europe GmbH, 63073 Offenbach am Main, Germany
`steffen.limmer@honda-ri.de`

Abstract. Optimization of charging profiles for controlled charging of electric vehicles is commonly done via mixed integer linear programming. The runtime of the optimization can represent an issue for the practical use. However, by tuning the parameter setting of the employed solver, it is possible to speed up the optimization process. The present work evaluates two popular hyperparameter tuning tools – irace (iterated racing) and SMAC (sequential model-based algorithm configuration) – for the optimization of parameters of the SCIP (Solving Constraint Integer Programs) solver with the objective to speed up the solving process for four common variants of the electric vehicle charging scheduling problem. Based on the results, the most important solver parameters are identified. It is shown that by tuning a very limited number of parameters, speed-ups of 60% and more can be achieved.

Keywords: Hyperparameter optimization · SMAC · irace · Mixed integer linear programming · SCIP · Electric vehicles

1 Introduction

Today, charging processes of electric vehicles (EVs) are typically uncontrolled, meaning that an EV is instantaneously charged with the maximum possible power after plugging in, until the EV is either plugged off or the EV's battery is fully charged. However, there is an increasing interest in smart charging, which controls and coordinates charging processes in an intelligent way. Smart charging can help distribution system operators to increase the stability of the power grid [1] and it can help charging providers and EV owners to charge more cost-efficiently [2,3]. Advanced approaches for controlled charging plan multiple time steps ahead, meaning that they construct a charging schedule, which consists of a charging power profile for each considered EV. The construction of a charging

© Springer Nature Switzerland AG 2020
P. A. Castillo et al. (Eds.): EvoApplications 2020, LNCS 12104, pp. 37–53, 2020.
https://doi.org/10.1007/978-3-030-43722-0_3

schedule with a certain objective, like minimizing the involved electricity costs, results in a potentially complex optimization problem. In the literature, different algorithms are proposed for EV charging schedule optimization, like evolutionary algorithms [4], dynamic programming [2] and non-linear programming [5]. However, if the underlying optimization problem can be formulated in linear form – what is often the case – mixed integer linear programming (MILP) is typically employed for its solution [6–9].

Although MILP is a very efficient optimization approach, the runtime can present a serious problem. For the practical application of EV charging scheduling, real-time requirements exist and the lower the runtime, the more EVs can be considered in the optimization. Furthermore, there exist dynamic pricing approaches for EV charging, which require the repeated optimization of charging schedules inside a bilevel optimization [10]. Thus, a runtime of a few seconds might be already too high. The choice of the MILP solver has a big influence on the runtime. There are different solvers available. Examples of commercial solvers are IBM ILOG CPLEX [11], Gurobi [12], and FICO Xpress [13]. Examples of non-commercial solvers are CBC [14], lp_solve [15], and SCIP [16]. Modern MILP solvers can be very complex and often contain advanced techniques and heuristics in order to speed up the optimization process. Besides the solver itself, the setting of its parameters can have a large effect on the runtime. For example, the SCIP solver has more than 1600 parameters. The default parameter settings of MILP solvers are usually in a way, that a good average performance is achieved on heterogeneous problem instances. Hence, it can be expected to be hard to find parameter settings, which outperform the default settings on arbitrarily chosen problems. However, it has been shown that restricted to a certain problem class, it can be worthwhile to tune the solver parameters in order to achieve a better performance on instances of that problem class. Thus, tuning the parameters of the used MILP solver is promising to speed up MILP-based EV charging scheduling.

Due to the large search space, a manual tuning of the parameters or a simple brute-force search are not efficient. There are different approaches for a more efficient tuning of parameters (in this context often referred to as hyperparameters) of an algorithm or a tool. Two popular representatives are irace (iterated racing) [17] and SMAC (sequential model-based algorithm configuration) [18]. A common application of such approaches is the tuning of hyperparameters of optimization algorithms [19,20], like for example, the crossover and mutation rate of evolutionary algorithms. Furthermore, they are often used in the field of machine learning (ML) in order to optimize the hyperparameters of ML models [21], like the learning rate and the number of layers of a neural network. The tool auto-sklearn [22] employs SMAC to not only tune the hyperparameters of given ML models, but to simultaneously decide, which models are used (known as *automated ML*).

In the present work, two questions are investigated: (1) To which degree can the automated tuning of the parameters of a MILP solver speed up the practically relevant problem of EV charging scheduling? (2) Which tool is better suited for this task – irace or SMAC? In order to answer these questions, SMAC and irace are evaluated for the tuning of parameters of the SCIP MILP solver on four common variants of the EV charging scheduling problem.

The rest of the paper is structured as follows: Sect. 2 briefly discusses related work on optimizing hyperparameters of MILP solvers. Section 3 provides an overview of hyperparameter optimization and the tools irace and SMAC. Section 4 outlines the SCIP MILP solver. Section 5, describes and discusses the experiments and their results. Finally, Sect. 6 provides a conclusion and an outlook.

2   Related Work

The tuning of MILP solver hyperparameters is studied in different works. Koripalli [23] describes the tuning of hyperparameters of CPLEX with help of design of experiments and statistical modelling. The proposed approach is evaluated on three problem classes, but only on a small number of problem instances, which are not split into training and test set.

Sorrell [24] uses an analogous approach for tuning parameters of CPLEX and evaluates it on three further problem classes, but also without splitting into training and test instances.

Smirnov [25] describes the tuning of SCIP hyperparameters in a public cloud environment with a simple approach: First a large number of parameter settings are evaluated, which differ only in one parameter from the default settings. Based on the results, the four parameters with the highest impact on the solving time are determined and these parameters are then tuned with a brute-force method. The approach is evaluated on traveling salesman problem instances on which a speed-up of around 1.4 was achieved.

Baz et al. [26] propose an approach called STOP and evaluate it for the tuning of parameters of the CBC, CPLEX and GLPK solvers. The evaluation is done on four problem classes and they conclude that the runtime was generally reduced from 31 to 81% compared to default solver settings.

In 2010, Hutter et al. [27] tuned hyperparameters of Gurobi, lp_solve and CPLEX with an approach called ParamILS. The hyperparameter tuning was done for 7 problem classes consisting of 50 training and 50 test instances, each. In most cases, they achieved to decrease the mean runtime on the test set, especially for CPLEX, for which speed-ups between 2 and 52 were achieved. In 2011, Hutter et al. [18] compared four approaches (ParamILS, ROAR, TB_SPO, and GCA) with a new approach called SMAC for tuning parameters of CPLEX. They come to the result that SMAC outperforms the other approaches in the conducted experiments.

López-Ibáñez and Stützle [28] describe the use of the tool irace to tune hyperparameters of SCIP with respect to *anytime behavior*. A good anytime behavior means that at each moment of the solving process the quality of the current solution is as high as possible. The tuning of SCIP hyperparameters is done for a set of 2000 combinatorial problems (1000 training instances and 1000 test instances). The results show that improving the anytime behavior does not necessarily reduce the time it takes to solve problems to optimality.

3 Hyperparameter Optimization

Tuning the hyperparameters of algorithms and tools is a recurrent problem in different application domains, like machine learning or mathematical optimization. Manual tuning is usually time consuming and involves the risk of being influenced by human bias. Grid and random search are widely used for the identification of good hyperparameter configurations. However, especially in the case of a large search space, a more structured search can be assumed to be more efficient. Thus, a promising alternative would be the use of a general black-box optimizer, like CMA-ES [29]. In addition, there are approaches and tools, which are designed specifically for hyperparameter optimization (HPO). Examples of such tools are STOP [26], ParamILS [30], GCA [31], irace [17], and SMAC [18]. Compared to a general optimizer, they are typically better suited for handling parameter spaces, which consist of discrete as well as continuous parameters.

Most HPO methods adopt an iterative algorithm, as outlined in Algorithm 1.

Algorithm 1. Outline of iterative HPO algorithm

Require: Target Algorithm A,
   Parameter configuration space Θ,
   Training instance set Π,
   Cost function C,
   Tuning budget B
1: $[\theta_{\text{inc}}, B_{\text{used}}] \leftarrow$ Initialize(Θ)
2: **while** $B_{\text{used}} \leq B$ **do**
3: $\theta_{\text{sample}} \leftarrow$ SampleConfiguration($\Theta, \theta_{\text{inc}}$)
4: **if** Evaluate($\theta_{\text{inc}}, C, \Pi, A$) $\leq$ Evaluate($\theta_{\text{sample}}, C, \Pi, A$) **then**
5:   $\theta_{\text{inc}} \leftarrow \theta_{\text{sample}}$
6: **end if**
7: $B_{\text{used}} \leftarrow$ UpdateBudget()
8: **end while**
9: **return** θ_{inc}

The inputs of the algorithm are a target Algorithm A whose parameters should be optimized, a search space Θ of parameter configurations, a set Π of problem instances of the target algorithm, a cost function $C : \Theta \times \Pi \rightarrow \mathbb{R}$, and a tuning budget B. The cost function $C(\theta, \pi)$ evaluates the performance (e.g., runtime or quality of the solution) of a given parameter configuration θ on a given problem instance π by running the target Algorithm A. The budget B is typically expressed in form of a time limit or a maximum number of cost function evaluations.

The algorithm starts with the creation of an initial parameter configuration, which is set as the current best known configuration (the *incumbent*) θ_{inc}. Then, a new parameter configuration θ_{sample} is created randomly and is compared to the incumbent, which is updated, if the new configuration is better. This is repeated until the budget is reached.

Modern HPO methods apply efficient ways for sampling new parameter configurations (line 3 in Algorithm 1) and for the evaluation of parameter configurations (line 4 in Algorithm 1). SMAC and irace are two popular representatives of such methods. They are applied in the experiments described later in the present work.

3.1 SMAC

SMAC applies Bayesian optimization [32] for the tuning of hyperparameters. In Bayesian optimization, a surrogate model is used to predict the fitness of points of the search space, which were not evaluated so far. In addition to the prediction, the surrogate model provides a measure for the uncertainty of the prediction. The optimization process is done iteratively, where in each iteration a new point is selected from the search space, is evaluated with the real cost function and the surrogate model is updated according to the new information. The new point to evaluate is selected according to a so called *infill criteria*. A common infill criteria, which is also used by SMAC is the *expected improvement*. The expected improvement is high for points with a high predicted fitness and a high uncertainty in this prediction.

While commonly a kriging model is used as surrogate in Bayesian optimization, SMAC employs a random forest, because it is better suited for discrete parameters. In order to be able to predict the performance of parameter configurations on multiple problem instances, SMAC requires features of the training instances, like for example the runtimes with default parameters, as additional inputs. SMAC applies a combination of neighboring and random search to identify parameter configurations with a high expected improvement in each iteration. In contrast to the basic Bayesian optimization, SMAC selects not only one parameter configuration in each iteration, but multiple configurations. These are compared with the current incumbent on the training instances with help of a so called *intensification* process. In this process, iteratively one of the new parameter configurations is picked and is evaluated (using a doubling scheme) on randomly selected training instances on which also the incumbent was evaluated before, until either the empirical performance of the new configuration is worse than that of the incumbent (and the new configuration is rejected) or the new configuration was evaluated on as many instances as the incument (and the new configuration becomes the incumbent).

3.2 irace

The irace software package implements a general iterated racing algorithm. Its optimization process starts with a set of uniformly distributed random parameter configurations. Then, from these configurations the best ones are selected via a so called *racing* process, which works as follows: First, all configurations are evaluated on a predefined number of randomly chosen problem instances. Then, a statistical test (per default a Friedman test) is applied in order to determine whether there are configurations, which performed significantly worse than the rest of configurations. If there are such configurations, then these configurations are discarded. The remaining configurations are evaluated on a number of further randomly chosen problem instances and then again a statistical test is applied and possibly more configurations are discarded. This is repeated until the number of surviving configurations falls under a certain minimum value and the racing stops. The surviving configurations are termed *elite configurations*.

After the racing, a set of new parameter configurations is generated via sampling around the elite configurations, where the sampling is done by sampling each parameter according to a truncated Gaussian distribution with a variance associated to the parameter. The sets of new and elite configurations are then combined to a set of candidate configurations, from which (possibly new) elite configurations are selected via racing. This procedure repeats until the budget is reached. In each iteration the variances of the Gaussian distributions, which are used to sample new configurations, are decreased. Thus, the search focuses more and more on promising regions of the search space.

4 SCIP

SCIP is one of the fastest non-commercial solvers for mixed integer linear programming (MILP) problems. A MILP problem is a problem of the following form:

$$
\begin{aligned}
\min \quad & \mathbf{c}^{\mathsf{T}}\mathbf{x} \\
\text{s.t.} \quad & \mathbf{A}\mathbf{x} \leq \mathbf{b}, \\
& \mathbf{l} \leq \mathbf{x} \leq \mathbf{u}, \\
& x_i \in \mathbb{Z} \qquad\qquad \forall i \in \mathcal{I},
\end{aligned}
$$

where $\mathbf{x} \in \mathbb{R}^N$ is a vector of N decision variables, $\mathbf{c} \in \mathbb{R}^N$ is a vector of coefficients of the (linear) objective function, $\mathbf{A} \in \mathbb{R}^{M \times N}$ and $\mathbf{b} \in \mathbb{R}^M$ are the coefficients and the right-hand side of M inequalities, $\mathbf{l}, \mathbf{u} \in \bar{\mathbb{R}}^N$ with $\bar{\mathbb{R}} := \mathbb{R} \cup \{-\infty, \infty\}$ are the lower and upper bounds of the decision variables, and the set $\mathcal{I} \subseteq \{1, 2, \cdots, N\}$ defines, which decision variables have to be integers.

If all decision variables have to be integers, the problem is called an integer linear programming (ILP) problem and if all decision variables are continuous, it is called a linear programming (LP) problem. LP problems can be solved in polynomial time. However, solving ILP and MILP problems is NP-complete.

SCIP employs a branch-and-cut approach to solve MILP problems exactly. Furthermore, it applies different heuristics in order to find and to improve feasible solutions at early stages of the solving process [33]. Since the exact solution of

MILP problems can be very time consuming, it is possible to specify a time limit. When the time limit is reached, SCIP outputs the best solution found so far (if at least one feasible solution was found) and an optimality gap, which is an upper bound for the relative gap between the solutions objective and the global optimum. In some cases, for example, when no feasible solution was found so far, an optimality gap of infinity is output.

SCIP has more than 1,600 discrete and continuous parameters, which affect the solving process. Besides the default parameter setting, SCIP provides three further settings called FAST, AGGRESSIVE, and OFF, which can be set in order to change the behavior of the employed heuristics.

5   Experiments

5.1   Use Cases

The problem of EV charging scheduling can be formulated with different objectives and constraints. In the experiments, we assume a basic version of the problem: We assume a charging station operator, who can purchase and sell energy for real-time electricity prices. The operator is interested in scheduling the charging and discharging of a number N of EVs so that all charging requirements are satisfied and the energy costs are minimized. Furthermore, it is assumed that there are lower and upper limits for the total charging power. This constraint might be required to avoid transformer overloads or to avoid high peak demand charges. An analogous problem definition is assumed in several works, like [34–37].

In the experiments, four variants of the described problem are considered, which are summarized in Table 1.

Table 1. Problem variants considered in the experiments.

Problem variant	CD-C	C-C	CD-D	C-D
Charging rates	$[-P^{max}, P^{max}]$	$[0, P^{max}]$	$\{-P^{max}, 0, P^{max}\}$	$\{0, P^{max}\}$

In the variants CD-C and CD-D, the EVs can be charged and discharged, while in variants C-C and C-D, only charging is allowed. In variants CD-C and C-C, the charging power can be modulated continuously and in variants CD-D and C-D only a discrete modulation is possible.

All four problem variants can be formulated as MILP problem. For example, the variant CD-D can be formulated as follows:

$$\min_{c_{t,n}, d_{t,n}} \sum_{t=1}^{T} \sum_{n=1}^{N} P_n^{max}(e_t^c c_{t,n} - e_t^d d_{t,n})\Delta t \qquad (1)$$

subject to

$$E_{t,n} = E_n^{init} + \sum_{k=1}^{t} P_n^{max}((1 - \delta_n)c_{k,n} - (1 + \delta_n)d_{k,n})\Delta t \qquad \forall n, \forall t, \quad (2)$$

$$E_{T,n} \geq E_n^{ref} \qquad \forall n, \quad (3)$$

$$E_n^{min} \leq E_{t,n} \leq E_n^{max} \qquad \forall n, \forall t, \quad (4)$$

$$c_{t,n} + d_{t,n} \leq 1 \qquad \forall n, \forall t, \quad (5)$$

$$P^{min} \leq \sum_{n=1}^{N} P_n^{max}(c_{t,n} - d_{t,n}) \leq P^{max} \qquad \forall t, \quad (6)$$

$$c_{t,n}, d_{t,n} \in \{0,1\} \qquad \forall n, \forall t, \quad (7)$$

where the objective function (1) represents the costs for charging N EVs over T time steps of length Δt, each. If the binary variable $c_{t,n}$ is one, EV n charges in time step t with its maximum power P_n^{max} and if the binary variable $d_{t,n}$ is one, it discharges with its maximum power. The parameters e_t^c and e_t^d are the prices for buying and selling, respectively, energy in time step t. Constraint (2) sets the charge levels of all EVs in all time steps, where E_n^{init} is the initial charge level of EV n and the factor δ_n encodes conversion losses. Constraints (3) and (4) ensure that at the end each EV n has its desired battery charge level E_n^{ref} and that the charge level is always within certain limits. The simultaneous charging and discharging of an EV in a time step is prevented by constraint (5) and constraint (6) sets the limits for the total charging power.

The other problem variants can be formulated analogously. It has to be noted that the variants CD-C and C-C have only continuous decision variables, what makes them easier to solve than variants CD-D and C-D. The hardest of the four problem variants is the variant CD-D.

5.2   Experimental Setup

We randomly generated for each problem variant 100 training instances and 60 test instances analogously to [35] based on the values shown in Tables 2 and 3. Values in brackets are sampled from a uniform distribution. Since the four

Table 2. Problem parameters used in the experiments.

Parameter	P_n^{max}	E_n^{min}	E_n^{max}	E_n^{init}	E_n^{ref}	δ_n
Unit	kW	kWh	kWh	kWh	kWh	–
Value	$[3,5]$	1	$[8,16]$	$[0.2,0.5] \cdot E_n^{max}$	$[0.55,0.8] \cdot E_n^{max}$	$[0.015,0.075]$
Parameter	Δt	T	P^{max}	P^{min}	e_t^c	e_t^d
Unit	min	–	kW	kW	cent/kWh	cent/kWh
Value	15	32	$3 \cdot N$	$-P^{max}$	$[1.9,3.5]$	$1.1 \cdot e_t^c$

Table 3. Ranges of number of EVs used in the experiments.

Problem variant	CD-C	C-C	CD-D	C-D
Number of EVs (N)	$[320, 800]$	$[320, 800]$	$[3, 10]$	$[80, 180]$

problem variants are differently hard to solve, the number of EVs is sampled from different ranges for the different problem variants.

In the experiments, the SCIP parameters are tuned with the objective to reduce the time it takes SCIP to solve the problem instances. However, some training instances are very difficult and it takes more than several days to solve them to optimality. Hence, we set a time limit t_{lim} of 40 s for the individual solving processes. If a problem instance cannot be solved in 40 s, the optimality gap, which is returned by SCIP is used as a penalty in the cost function. More precisely, the following cost function is used:

$$cost = \frac{t}{t_{lim}} + \frac{2 \tan^{-1}(g)}{\pi}, \tag{8}$$

where t is the runtime of SCIP in seconds, t_{lim} is the time limit in seconds and g is the relative optimality gap in percent. The inverse tangent function is used because g can have a value of infinity. If an optimal solution is found before the time limit is reached, the second term becomes 0 and the cost is between 0 and 1. If no optimal solution is found before the time limit is reached, the cost is between 1 and 2.

The parameters of SCIP are divided into different categories. For the CD-D and C-D problem variants, we tune the parameters of three categories: **presolving**, **heuristics** and **separating**. These are 420 parameters in total, from which 88 are continuous, 257 are discrete, 3 are categorical and 72 are binary. The parameters of the category **separating** have no effect for the problem variants CD-C and C-C, since these problem variants are purely continuous. Thus, for these two problem variants, we tune the 316 parameters of the categories **presolving**, **heuristics** and **lp**, from which 75 are continuous, 193 are discrete, 6 are categorical and 42 are binary.

In order to reduce the search space, continuous parameters are discretized and discrete parameters are sampled as follows: First, the default parameter value is 4 times iteratively halved, then it is 4 times iteratively doubled, and the set of possible values of the parameter is set to the resulting 8 values together with the default value.

In order to construct instance features for SMAC, SCIP is run with default parameters on all training instances and the following seven properties are used as instance features: runtime, relative optimality gap, average relative optimality gap, number of variables, number of variables after presolving, number of constraints and number of constraints after presolving.

For each problem variant, 40 trials are executed with irace and with SMAC. As a baseline, 40 additional trials are executed with random search. The random search is performed on 10 randomly chosen training instances. In each trial, the budget is set to 3,000 cost function evaluations (i.e., 3,000 calls of SCIP). All settings of irace and SMAC are left to the default with exception of the budget and the random seed. We use irace version 3.3, SMAC v3 version 0.11.0 and SCIP version 5.0.0. All experiments are executed on a dual 2.10 GHz Intel Xeon Silver 4110 computer with 93.1 GB RAM.

5.3   Experimental Results

The three considered approaches – irace, SMAC and random search – output the current incumbent parameter configuration after each iteration. In order to compare the performance of the three approaches, we evaluated the resulting incumbents on the 60 test instances and linearly interpolated the test performance over the number of evaluations and over time. The resulting optimization progresses on the four problem variants can be seen in Fig. 1.

Shown are the mean costs according Eq. (8) on the test instances averaged over the 40 trials. The initial costs (at evaluation and time 0, respectively) correspond to the costs with SCIP default parameter configuration. It can be seen that at the beginning of the optimization process, irace is outperformed by SMAC and even by random search. However, on the C-C, CD-D and C-D problem variants, irace converges to better results than SMAC and random search. On all problem variants, irace and SMAC yield better final results than random search. From the right-hand side of Fig. 1 it can be seen that random search takes more time than irace because it tends to evaluate poor parameter configurations, which result in high runtimes of SCIP. SMAC takes even longer for the parameter tuning process. This is probably caused by the internal updates of SMAC's surrogate model (random forest).

Table 4. Experimental result of parameter tuning approaches.

Problem		irace			SMAC			random search		
		Cost	Time	Gap	Cost	Time	Gap	Cost	Time	Gap
CD-C	Best	**0.172**	**6.86**	–	0.182	7.26	–	0.182	7.28	–
	Avg.	0.198	7.80	0.00530	**0.195**	**7.79**	–	0.209	8.28	0.00262
	STD	0.031	0.68	0.024	0.0082	0.33	–	0.022	0.56	0.0166
C-C	Best	**0.0642**	**2.57**	–	0.0661	2.65	–	0.0669	2.68	–
	Avg.	**0.0672**	**2.69**	–	0.0713	2.85	–	0.0778	3.11	–
	STD	0.0014	0.055	–	0.0033	0.13	–	0.0087	0.35	–
CD-D	Best	**1.14**	**25.4**	**0.789**	1.15	25.5	0.803	1.18	26.6	0.802
	Avg.	**1.21**	**26.8**	**0.845**	1.26	28.1	0.877	1.29	28.7	0.898
	STD	0.045	1.1	0.030	0.054	1.3	0.038	0.048	1.0	0.041
C-D	Best	**0.171**	**6.83**	**0.00959**	0.310	11.7	0.0282	0.290	11.2	0.0151
	Avg.	**0.350**	**12.5**	**0.0538**	0.455	16.6	0.0618	0.495	17.7	0.0824
	STD	0.10	2.8	0.061	0.099	3.2	0.040	0.12	3.7	0.058

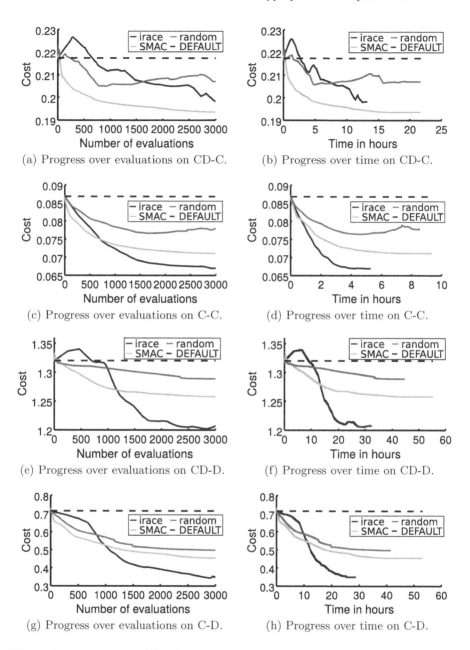

(a) Progress over evaluations on CD-C.

(b) Progress over time on CD-C.

(c) Progress over evaluations on C-C.

(d) Progress over time on C-C.

(e) Progress over evaluations on CD-D.

(f) Progress over time on CD-D.

(g) Progress over evaluations on C-D.

(h) Progress over time on C-D.

Fig. 1. Tuning progress of the three approaches over number of evaluations (left-hand side) and over time (right-hand side). Cost is the mean cost on the test set averaged over all trials. DEFAULT is the mean cost with default SCIP settings. random stands for random search.

The final results with the three approaches are shown in detail in Table 4. Shown are the mean cost over all test problems, the mean runtime of SCIP, and the mean inverse tangent function of the relative optimality gap. A gap of "–" means that all problem instances are solved to optimality within the time limit of 40 s. Avg. stands for average performance over all trials, STD for the standard deviation and Best for the best performance over all trials. Bold text denotes the best performance over the three methods. For comparison, Table 5 shows the corresponding performances with the four predefined parameter settings of SCIP. With exception of random search on the CD-D problem variant, all parameter

Table 5. Performance of the predefined parameter settings analogous to Table 4.

Problem	DEFAULT			FAST			AGGRESSIVE			OFF		
	Cost	Time	Gap	Cost	Time	Gap	Cost	Time	Gap	Cost	Time	Gap
CD-C	0.217	8.70	–	0.213	8.53	–	0.213	8.53	–	**0.213**	**8.52**	–
C-C	0.0868	3.47	–	0.0830	3.32	–	**0.0830**	**3.32**	–	0.0830	3.32	–
CD-D	1.32	**29.3**	0.925	1.27	30.1	0.817	**1.27**	29.9	0.818	1.27	30.1	**0.817**
C-D	0.715	24.5	0.162	**0.698**	**24.3**	0.140	0.699	24.4	0.140	0.699	24.4	**0.140**

tuning approaches yield better average costs than the predefined parameter settings. The achieved performance improvement varies over the problem variants. On C-D, the best result found by irace solves the test problems 72% faster than the best predefined setting FAST and on average, the results yielded by the three parameter tuning approaches reduce the time by 27% to 49% compared to FAST. By contrast, on the CD-D case, the tuning approaches are not able to achieve a speed-up higher than 15% compared to FAST and on average a speed-up of only 2% to 9% is achieved. Furthermore, the average optimality gap yielded by the tuning approaches is greater than with the OFF setting. On the CD-C and C-C problems, irace and SMAC yield an average time improvement from 9% to 20% compared to the corresponding best predefined setting.

In order to test whether the differences between the results of irace and SMAC are statistically significant, we applied a Mann-Whitney U test on the costs resulting from the individual trials. The corresponding p-values for the different problem variants are shown in Table 6. For the C-C, CD-D and C-D variants, the differences are statistically significant and since on these variants irace yields better average results than SMAC, irace is statistically better than SMAC in these cases.

Table 6. Results of Mann-Whitney U test on the different problem variants.

Problem variant	CD-C	C-C	CD-D	C-D
p-value	0.40	9.84×10^{-9}	3.19×10^{-5}	9.06×10^{-6}

To get a better insight into the optimization results, we identified the most important SCIP parameters based on the results of the parameter tuning processes. For each problem variant, we examined the distributions of the parameter values in the results of irace and SMAC. For less important parameters, the resulting values should follow a uniform distribution. Hence, we tested for each parameter with a chi-square test whether the distribution of its values in the optimization results is uniform. Then, we removed all parameters with a corresponding p-value higher than 5% and all parameters whose mode in the optimization results is identical to the default parameter setting. From the mode values of the remaining parameters and the default values of the removed parameters, we form a SCIP parameter configuration and evaluate it on the test set. Afterwards, we iteratively remove the parameters with the highest p-values from the remaining parameters until the performance on the test set gets significantly worse than before.

The remaining parameters and their mode values are shown in Table 7. It

Table 7. Important parameters and the performances of them on each problem variant.

Problem	Cost	Time	Gap	Configuration
CD-C	0.178	7.12	–	lp/initalgorithm=p
				lp/pricing=q
				heuristics/trivial/freq=-1
C-C	0.0659	2.63	–	lp/pricing=d
				presolving/maxrounds=4
				presolving/implfree/maxrounds=16
				heuristics/trivial/freq=-1
CD-D	1.21	26.5	0.857	separating/poolfreq=1
C-D	0.216	8.38	0.0111	separating/gomory/away=0.00125
				separating/poolfreq=1

can be seen that only 1 to 4 parameters remained for the different problem variants. The performances on the test set with the stated configurations (and all other parameters set to default) are also shown in Table 7. For each problem variant the performance is better than the average performances of the three parameter tuning approaches and the performances of the predefined settings. This means that in spite of the vast configuration space, the performance on the considered problem variants largely depends on only a few parameters and a notable performance increase can be achieved by adapting these parameters. However, which parameters these are and their optimal setting depends on the problem variant.

In a last experiment, we examined how well the results generalize to higher numbers of EVs. We generated two new sets of test instances with ranges for the number of EVs, which are five-fold and ten-fold, respectively, compared to Table 3. The results can be seen in Table 8. On all problem variants, new configurations still yield better performance than the default setting. However, as the number of EVs increases, the performance improvement tends to decrease with exception of the C-C problem variant.

Table 8. Performances for different numbers of EVs. DEF stands for DEFAULT, New for the configurations according Table 7, and Impv. is the performance improvement compared to DEFAULT.

Problem		Cost			Time			Gap		
		DEF	New	Impv.	DEF	New	Impv.	DEF	New	Impv.
CD-C	Normal	0.217	0.178	**18%**	8.70	7.12	**18%**	–	–	–
	Five-fold	0.522	0.484	**7.2%**	150	145	**3.4%**	0.230	0.191	**17%**
	Ten-fold	0.731	0.685	**6.4%**	332	319	**4.0%**	0.497	0.450	**9.5%**
C-C	normal	0.0868	0.0659	**24%**	3.47	2.63	**24%**	–	–	–
	Five-fold	0.108	0.0631	**42%**	43.3	25.2	**42%**	–	–	–
	Ten-fold	0.156	0.0837	**46%**	125	67	**46%**	–	–	–
CD-D	Normal	1.32	1.21	**8.5%**	29.3	26.5	**9.4%**	0.925	0.857	**7.4%**
	Five-fold	1.18	1.10	**6.6%**	249	230	**7.7%**	0.878	0.831	**5.4%**
	Ten-fold	1.29	1.13	**12%**	562	477	**15%**	0.916	0.832	**9.1%**
C-D	Normal	0.715	0.216	**70%**	24.5	8.38	**66%**	0.162	0.0111	**93%**
	Five-fold	0.997	0.435	**56%**	355	169	**52%**	0.171	0.0197	**88%**
	Ten-fold	1.12	0.477	**57%**	800	368	**54%**	0.182	0.0266	**85%**

6 Conclusion

The present work investigates the optimization of SCIP parameters with irace and SMAC on four variants of the practical important problem of electric vehicle charging scheduling. Experiments show that both, irace and SMAC, are able to speed up the solving process for all four problem variants and that they outperform a simple random search. Although SMAC is superior at the beginning of the parameter tuning process, irace converges to better final results. SMAC yields an average time improvement from 4% to 32% compared to predefined settings, while the average time improvement yielded by irace is between 8% and 49%.

A closer examination of the optimization results revealed that from the up to 420 parameters, which were tuned, only one to four are worth to tune. However, it depends on the problem variant, which parameters these are and what their optimal settings are. Furthermore, experimental results indicate that the performance tends to decrease with an increasing number of considered electric vehicles. Thus, the optimal parameter setting seems to depend on the number of considered electric vehicles. For a practical application, this issue might be solved by optimizing different parameter settings for different ranges of the number of electric vehicles.

In the experiments, default settings of SMAC and irace were used. Both tools have more than 10 parameters, which affect the search process. Thus, as future work, we plan to investigate whether the results can be improved by tuning the parameters of SMAC and irace. Furthermore, we plan to apply hyperparameter tuning for speeding up the optimization of energy system parameters based on simulations [38].

References

1. Waraich, R.A., Galus, M.D., Dobler, C., Balmer, M., Andersson, G., Axhausen, K.W.: Plug-in hybrid electric vehicles and smart grids: investigations based on a microsimulation. Transp. Res. Part C: Emerg. Technol. **28**, 74–86 (2013)
2. Rotering, N., Ilic, M.: Optimal charge control of plug-in hybrid electric vehicles in deregulated electricity markets. IEEE Trans. Power Syst. **26**(3), 1021–1029 (2011)
3. Goebel, C., Jacobsen, H.A.: Aggregator-controlled EV charging in pay-as-bid reserve markets with strict delivery constraints. IEEE Trans. Power Syst. **31**(6), 4447–4461 (2016)
4. Mehta, R., Srinivasan, D., Trivedi, A.: Optimal charging scheduling of plug-in electric vehicles for maximizing penetration within a workplace car park. In: IEEE Congress on Evolutionary Computation (CEC), pp. 3646–3653 (2016)
5. Sortomme, E., Hindi, M.M., MacPherson, S.D.J., Venkata, S.S.: Coordinated charging of plug-in hybrid electric vehicles to minimize distribution system losses. IEEE Trans. Smart Grid **2**(1), 198–205 (2011)
6. Jin, C., Tang, J., Ghosh, P.: Optimizing electric vehicle charging with energy storage in the electricity market. IEEE Trans. Smart Grid **4**(1), 311–320 (2013)
7. Igualada, L., Corchero, C., Cruz-Zambrano, M., Heredia, F.J.: Optimal energy management for a residential microgrid including a vehicle-to-grid system. IEEE Trans. Smart Grid **5**(4), 2163–2172 (2014)
8. Franco, J.F., Rider, M.J., Romero, R.: A mixed-integer linear programming model for the electric vehicle charging coordination problem in unbalanced electrical distribution systems. IEEE Trans. Smart Grid **6**(5), 2200–2210 (2015)
9. Naharudinsyah, I., Limmer, S.: Optimal charging of electric vehicles with trading on the intraday electricity market. Energies **11**(6), 1–11 (2018)
10. Limmer, S., Rodemann, T.: Peak load reduction through dynamic pricing for electric vehicle charging. Int. J. Electr. Power Energy Syst. **113**, 117–128 (2019)
11. IBM ILOG CPLEX. https://www.ibm.com/analytics/cplex-optimizer. Accessed Jan 2020
12. Gurobi. https://www.gurobi.com/. Accessed Jan 2020
13. Fico Xpress. https://www.fico.com/fico-xpress-optimization/docs/latest/overview.html. Accessed Jan 2020
14. CBC Solver. https://projects.coin-or.org/Cbc. Accessed Jan 2020
15. lp_solve. http://lpsolve.sourceforge.net/5.5/. Accessed Jan 2020
16. Gleixner, A., et al.: The SCIP optimization suite 5.0. Technical report 17-61, ZIB, Berlin (2017)

17. López-Ibáñez, M., Dubois-Lacoste, J., Cáceres, L.P., Birattari, M., Stützle, T.: The irace package: iterated racing for automatic algorithm configuration. Oper. Res. Perspect. **3**, 43–58 (2016)
18. Hutter, F., Hoos, H.H., Leyton-Brown, K.: Sequential model-based optimization for general algorithm configuration. In: Coello, C.A.C. (ed.) LION 2011. LNCS, vol. 6683, pp. 507–523. Springer, Heidelberg (2011). https://doi.org/10.1007/978-3-642-25566-3_40
19. Smit, S.K., Eiben, A.E.: Parameter tuning of evolutionary algorithms: generalist vs. specialist. In: Di Chio, C., et al. (eds.) EvoApplications 2010. LNCS, vol. 6024, pp. 542–551. Springer, Heidelberg (2010). https://doi.org/10.1007/978-3-642-12239-2_56
20. Roman, I., Ceberio, J., Mendiburu, A., Lozano, J.A.: Bayesian optimization for parameter tuning in evolutionary algorithms. In: 2016 IEEE Congress on Evolutionary Computation (CEC), pp. 4839–4845 (2016)
21. Feurer, M., Hutter, F.: Hyperparameter optimization. In: Hutter, F., Kotthoff, L., Vanschoren, J. (eds.) Automated Machine Learning. TSSCML, pp. 3–33. Springer, Cham (2019). https://doi.org/10.1007/978-3-030-05318-5_1
22. Feurer, M., Klein, A., Eggensperger, K., Springenberg, J.T., Blum, M., Hutter, F.: Efficient and robust automated machine learning. In: Proceedings of the 28th NIPS, pp. 2755–2763. MIT Press (2015)
23. Koripalli, R.S.: Parameter tuning for optimization software. Master's thesis, Virginia Commonwealth University, Richmond, Virginia (2012)
24. Sorrell, T.P.: Tuning optimization software parameters for mixed ineteger programming problems. Ph.D. thesis, Virginia Commonwealth University, Richmond, Virginia (2017)
25. Smirnov, S.: Tuning parameters of a mixed integer programming solver in the cloud. Int. Sci. J. "Sci. Bus. Soc." **1**(2), 3–5 (2016)
26. Baz, M., Brooks, J.P., Gosavi, A., Hunsaker, B.: Automated tuning of optimization software parameters. Technical report. University of Pittsburgh Department of Industrial Engineering, Pittsburgh, PA (2007)
27. Hutter, F., Hoos, H.H., Leyton-Brown, K.: Automated configuration of mixed integer programming solvers. In: Lodi, A., Milano, M., Toth, P. (eds.) CPAIOR 2010. LNCS, vol. 6140, pp. 186–202. Springer, Heidelberg (2010). https://doi.org/10.1007/978-3-642-13520-0_23
28. López-Ibáñez, M., Stützle, T.: Automatically improving the anytime behaviour of optimisation algorithms. Eur. J. Oper. Res. **235**(3), 569–582 (2014)
29. Hansen, N., Ostermeier, A.: Completely derandomized self-adaptation in evolution strategies. Evol. Comput. **9**, 159–195 (2001)
30. Hutter, F., Hoos, H.H., Leyton-Brown, K., Stützle, T.: ParamILS: an automatic algorithm configuration framework. J. Artif. Int. Res. **36**(1), 267–306 (2009)
31. Ansótegui, C., Sellmann, M., Tierney, K.: A gender-based genetic algorithm for the automatic configuration of algorithms. In: Gent, I.P. (ed.) CP 2009. LNCS, vol. 5732, pp. 142–157. Springer, Heidelberg (2009). https://doi.org/10.1007/978-3-642-04244-7_14
32. Jones, D.R., Schonlau, M., Welch, W.J.: Efficient global optimization of expensive black-box functions. J. Global Optim. **13**(4), 455–492 (1998)
33. Berthold, T.: Heuristics of the branch-cut-and-price-framework SCIP. In: Kalcsics, J., Nickel, S. (eds.) Operations Research Proceedings 2007. ORP, vol. 2007, pp. 31–36. Springer, Heidelberg (2008). https://doi.org/10.1007/978-3-540-77903-2_5

34. Ma, C., Rautiainen, J., Dahlhaus, D., Lakshman, A., Toebermann, J.C., Braun, M.: Online optimal charging strategy for electric vehicles. Energy Procedia **73**, 173–181 (2015). 9th International Renewable Energy Storage Conference, IRES 2015

35. Vujanic, R., Esfahani, P.M., Goulart, P.J., Mariéthoz, S., Morari, M.: A decomposition method for large scale MILPs, with performance guarantees and a power system application. Automatica **67**, 144–156 (2016)

36. Han, J., Park, J., Lee, K.: Optimal scheduling for electric vehicle charging under variable maximum charging power. Energies **10**(7), 933 (2017)

37. Mao, T., Zhang, X., Zhou, B.: Intelligent energy management algorithms for EV-charging scheduling with consideration of multiple EV charging modes. Energies **12**(2), 265 (2019)

38. Rodemann, T.: A comparison of different many-objective optimization algorithms for energy system optimization. In: Kaufmann, P., Castillo, P.A. (eds.) EvoApplications 2019. LNCS, vol. 11454, pp. 3–18. Springer, Cham (2019). https://doi.org/10.1007/978-3-030-16692-2_1

Automatic Rule Extraction from Access Rules Using Genetic Programming

Paloma de las Cuevas[1], Pablo García-Sánchez[2]([⊠]),
Zaineb Chelly Dagdia[3,4], María-Isabel García-Arenas[1],
and Juan Julián Merelo Guervós[1]

[1] Department of Computer Architecture and Computer Technology,
ETSIIT and CITIC, University of Granada, Granada, Spain
{palomacd,mgarenas,jmerelo}@ugr.es
[2] Department of Computer Engineering, ESI, University of Cádiz, Cádiz, Spain
pablo.garciasanchez@uca.es
[3] Université de Lorraine, CNRS, Inria, LORIA, 54000 Nancy, France
[4] LARODEC, Institut Supérieur de Gestion de Tunis, Bouchoucha, Tunisia
chelly.zaineb@gmail.com

Abstract. The security policy rules in companies are generally proposed by the Chief Security Officer (CSO), who must, for instance, select by hand which access events are allowed and which ones should be forbidden. In this work we propose a way to automatically obtain rules that generalise these single-event based rules using Genetic Programming (GP), which, besides, should be able to present them in an understandable way. Our GP-based system obtains good dataset coverage and small ratios of false positives and negatives in the simulation results over real data, after testing different fitness functions and configurations in the way of coding the individuals.

Keywords: Security · Corporate Security Policy · Genetic Programming · Rule extraction · Bring your own device

1 Introduction and Related Work

In general, companies establish a series of rules to allow or reject access to assets from company-owned or bring-your-own devices (BYOD). These rules often depend on the context these devices are in and their specific characteristics. Although in general, asset access needs to be regulated, and the existence of devices not owned or controlled by the company adds a layer of complexity that makes the job of establishing an access policy more difficult. To this end, the Corporate Security Policies (CSPs) [12], approved by the company's Chief Security Officer (CSO), are the core at the identification of threats and the construction of a set of security rules. CSOs build the set of CSPs based on their expertise, and as such, in many cases access events are allowed or not depending on white- or blacklists or the simple presence or absence of a feature such as the fact that the asset is being accessed from a public, non-encrypted, WiFi.

© Springer Nature Switzerland AG 2020
P. A. Castillo et al. (Eds.): EvoApplications 2020, LNCS 12104, pp. 54–69, 2020.
https://doi.org/10.1007/978-3-030-43722-0_4

The aim of this paper is to propose a novel technique for extracting inference rules from past behaviour instances that might help the CSO in the definition and refinement of security policies that, eventually, would classify an upcoming event or user action as permitted or not permitted. The objective, thus, is to obtain a way to classify correctly as many incoming events as possible, avoiding false positives [13], that is, avoiding the possibility of unsafe events being classified as safe.

Rules generated by GP could be used in two different scenarios. In the first one a CSO has hand-coded a set of security policies and wants to simplify or generalise them. The second scenario would simply dispense with rules and have the CSO manually decide which particular events are to be granted or denied access, and have a system such as the one described here generate a set of security policies by creating a set of rules from particular events. The main objective in both scenarios is to create a reliable rule set which is able to cover every new situation that might be a threat, allowing the system to go beyond the limited set of known pre-defined rules. Additionally, this feature can be used as "reverse engineering", so that the rules initially made by the current or former CSO are found in the solution along with additional ones. In order to have a space of conceivable policy rules as wide as possible, it is necessary a technique that explores the rule space efficiently and with the least assumptions about rule structure.

This is why we have decided to use Genetic Programming (GP) for dealing with the problem of discovering novel, interesting knowledge and rules from large amounts of data [8], given that the up-to-date approaches are based in general on pre-defined or manually defined rules [1]. One of the advantages of GP is that by making the solutions to a problem available as trees, they themselves can be seen as decision tree classifiers [15] and can be expressed as a set of rules. Moreover, GP can outperform other methods such as SVM or naive-Bayes [4].

To the best of our knowledge, there is not a tool that helps CSOs in developing new security rules via GP, even as this method has been indeed applied to classification, as described by Espejo et al. in [6]. In fact, their survey theoretically supports our decision of applying GP to obtain security rules in a BYOD environment.

In our case, the assigned classes, or leaves of the tree, would be either "allow" or "deny", acting over a certain incoming event; whilst the nodes are the conditions that have to be met to apply the action. Taking this into account, GP can be used to generate these classification trees, optimising an objective function called *fitness*. In this case the fitness can be defined as the accuracy of a rule or set of rules, being this the most used metric in classification [17], along with the classification error. But since there are other metrics that influence in "how good" a rule or a set of rules is, such as the depth of the created tree, the number of nodes it has, or the obtained false positives [3], it would be convenient to use them in the definition of the fitness.

The main issue we face is how to create a set of rules from a series of instances that those rules are bound to follow; initially we have a set of URIs and hand-coded tags that deny access to them, or allow it by default. Espejo et al. review in [6] three papers which use GP for classification with communications data, but mainly for intrusion detection and e-mail spamming. Thus, the works they review have applications in all fields but not exactly the one we focus on here. In [16] the authors also extract rules with IF ... THEN structure through GP, although for medical purposes. Furthermore, Freitas deeply studied the application of GP to Data Mining (DM) in [8], providing the necessary knowledge and guidelines to design a GP framework for DM applications. Also, in [7], a system which discovers rules for the PROBEN1 databases [14], a collection of real-world datasets, via GP is described and a new fitness function is introduced. As happened in the survey of Espejo et al., out of six of the databases inside PROBEN1 and analysed by these authors, none is related to security. However, the authors' proposed fitness function is indeed of interest for this research, and as such we compare the performance or our algorithm using two different fitness ones: the more classical approach that measures only the correctly classified instances (accuracy); and De Falco's et al. [7] suggestion, also taking into account the complexity of the solution.

We thus demonstrate the utility of our framework by using it on a real-world dataset, and comparing two ways of coding the individuals – as a set of rules, or as a single rule – so that we are able to choose the best approach for our system. We make this comparison because while obtaining a set of rules as a solution is computationally expensive due to the need of longer evaluations, to present and evaluate a single rule not taking into account how it interacts with what the others cover [8] can lead to massive overlapping. Hence, we must study their accuracy despite of their advantages and disadvantages. In addition, we choose the most appropriate (fastest to converge and with best value) fitness after comparing the use of a most simpler one that only measures the accuracy, and a complex one which takes into account the complexity of the individuals. Finally, we propose the approach with the best performance in terms of best coverage over a validation set.

As previously highlighted, the main idea behind corporate security policies, which are defined by the CSO, is to build a basic, fixed, and well defined set of rules, which take the form of IF ... THEN clauses. By applying them, the company system decides if certain conditions are met in order to allow or deny access to an asset, being company owned or not, and wherever it is accessed from. Therefore, these rules can be visualised as the actions, taking place in a precise environment, being classified as allowed or denied. In this sense and while facing a security breach from a BYOD system, the set of rules will be tested looking for matches between the access characteristics and the rules premises – the conditions expressed in the IF part, also known as the description of the rule [7]. If it matches then the decision can be made, by checking the conclusion part of the rule, which comes after the THEN and indicates the class [7], either by allowing or denying employees' access to non-confidential or non-certified data, for example. However, it is important to mention that the companies' set of security rules defined by the CSO is based on known and previously recognised accesses and thus it cannot cover the whole, safe and unsafe, search spaces.

Therefore, there is an urgent need to develop a system capable of discovering a more reliable rule set which should be able to cover every new situation that may be a threat. Hence, allowing the company security system to go beyond the limited set of known, pre-defined rules.

The rest of the paper is organised as follows. Next (Sect. 2) describes the proposed methodology, depicting the problem this work tries to solve and describing the available dataset and the proposed GP framework. The experimental setup, as well as the different set of experiments that have been carried out are also described in that section. Section 3 shows and discusses the obtained results from the application of GP to security rules extraction and, finally, the conclusions of this work along with some suggestions about how to continue our research are given in Sect. 4.

2   Methodology

Our proposed solution is based on a novel GP framework dedicated for the BYOD context and capable of performing an automatic and wider discovery of classification rules. More precisely, our GP based framework will, first, extract all the possible values of every attribute in the data at hand and then make the GP algorithm evolving. Specifically, in this context, we have decided to follow the more conventional approach in Genetic Programming, the Pittsburgh approach [8], meaning that each individual is seen as a set of rules. However, in this work we have also implemented the Michigan approach, where every individual is a single rule. The aim of having these two different implementations is to choose the most efficient, in terms of time to find the solution, best fitness, accuracy in the validation phase, and readability.

The last step would be to present the rules – solution – to the CSO of the company and tune up the algorithm according to the decision of finally including or not the set of rules in the main security policy. The description of the used data and further explicit details about our proposed solution are given next.

The set of used data has been gathered from the evaluations that were performed during the development of an FP7 European Project, called Anon. In these evaluations, a group of users tested a smartphone and PC *app* meant for securing a BYOD environment. The app generates warnings when the users act in a dangerous way. Technically, these warnings are triggered by a set of initial and pre-defined rules. When certain conditions are met in an "event" (action performed by a user), the corresponding action could be allowed - nothing happened - or denied with a warning explaining the rule that the user did not comply with. Then, the app displays the steps to perform the action in a more secure way or environment.

The dataset contains a collection of these "events" from which a number of attributes (variables) have been extracted or were given by the application itself. User data has been also extracted but anonymised, in the sense that from all the attributes extracted from the user actions, those that could lead to identifying the user are not included as variables to build rules with. The attributes can be classified in different ways; one of them is based on whether they are directly read from the application or inferred after processing the data. Therefore, we distinguish between:

- Attributes given by the tested application: these attributes are related to the type of the event (action), its timestamp, or the application which originated the event, among others.
- Attributes inferred from the information in the database: the information given by the aforementioned attributes, along with the rest of information already existing in the database, helps inferring other attributes. These are, for instance: all extra information related to the origin, like the user position in the company or the device Operating System; the configuration of the device, such as WiFi or Bluetooth being enabled; and even lexical properties of the user password, in order to avoid storing the password itself or using it for classification or rule generation.

The tests had a duration of five weeks, and a total of 153270 events were registered in the database. We discarded those events that did not imply access to assets, meaning that they were not useful for knowledge extraction purposes, such as events of *log in*, *log out*, or *restarting the server*. The remaining was a 35% (53296 instances) of the total, and were considered as *important* because they contain information about meaningful user actions such as opening files or sending emails in a certain connection environment, changing security properties, or installing apps. Altogether, there are 38 attributes, plus the class, which can take two possible values: GRANTED or STRONGDENY.

As previously highlighted, in this work we propose a system which is able to process a set of user actions that have been allowed or denied based on initial, simple rules, and discover new rules through GP by exploring the whole space of possible combinations among the attribute values. The coding of the individual might take two approaches, named *Pittsburgh* and *Michigan* [8].

The Pittsburgh approach uses GP to create an individual tree that models a set of different rules, given that the problem can be seen as a classification one and therefore the model can be a decision tree [15]. Then, the generated tree is a binary tree of expressions formed by two different types of nodes:

- *Variable*: it is a logical expression formed by a prefix, a name, an operator and a value. It is the equivalent to a "primitive" in the field of GP [3]. The operators depend on the type of variable, being $\{=>\}$ (an arrow, as in "takes the value of") in the case of categorical attributes, $\{=\}$ for binary attributes, and $\{<, <=, =, =>, >\}$ for numeric ones. At the same time, the prefix can be $\{AND, OR\}$, and NOT can appear before these.

Examples: $\left\{ \begin{array}{l} \texttt{password\_length<5} \\ or \\ \texttt{event\_level=>COMPLEX\_EVENT} \end{array} \right.$

- *Action*: it is a leaf of the tree and therefore, a "terminal" state. Each decision is the result of applying the rule, so it is limited to two terms which are GRANTED or STRONGDENY. Only one leaf must hung from a parent (variable) node.

Rules are constructed starting from each leaf of the tree and iterating to the upper parents, or variables, reading their data as string. Therefore, the number of rules of the set produced by the tree is equal to the number of its leafs. It is worth mentioning that some rules might have contradictory conditions inside them during the evolution. This is not a problem because those rules will not cover any instance and thus they will not contribute to the fitness value.

The second approach tested, called Michigan approach, assigns a single rule to every individual. In this paper we have expressed the rule as a list of conditions, with a fixed class, obtaining just one rule per execution. That means we are not using GP in this case, because the generated individual is not a tree, but a vector, so we are applying a regular Genetic Algorithm (GA) instead. Therefore, in order to cover all classes, the algorithm has to be executed once for each class; in our case, GRANTED, allowed actions, and STRONGDENY, for the denied actions.

Indeed, each approach has its advantages and disadvantages. The Pittsburgh approach allows to directly obtain a set of rules able to classify instances of every existing class, meanwhile Michigan approach solution is coded as a single rule, so that we obtain as many rules as classes are defined. The possibility of having many rules for every class instead of just one, more general, per class might seem to better help the CSO in detecting specific dangerous situations. At the same time, obtaining a set of rules as a solution is more computationally expensive due to the need of longer evaluations. Lastly, to evaluate a single rule not taking into account how it interacts with what the others cover [8] can lead to massive overlapping with the consequent loss of efficiency.

With respect to the variables, both approaches use three different types, described as follows [17]:

- *Binary Variable*: those with a boolean value, for instance, variables that are related to the device services switched on or off and important features such as the device having or not an antivirus installed.
- *Categorical Variable*: the ones with nominal values, where a list is defined with the possible values it may have, in order to randomly pick up one in the creation of the rules.
- *Numerical Variable*: those with a numerical value, for which both maximum and minimum values are specified.

We distinguish the variables used by the GP expressions in order to create the rules in those that are specific to the BYOD context and those that will show up in any environment:

BYOD-specific: DeviceHasAccessibility, DeviceHasAntivirus, DeviceHasPassword, DeviceIsRooted, DeviceOS, DeviceOwnedBy, WifiEncryption, DeviceScreenTimeout, PasswordLength

General: BluetoothConnected, MailHasAttachment, WifiConnected, WifiEnabled, AssetConfidentialLevel, DeviceType, EventLevel, EventType, UserRole

There is no difference, however, in how do we deal with the two types of variables; this only shows the exhaustiveness of the set of terminals that we will be using in this work. At the end of the process, either as part of a set of rules or just being a single rule, they can be presented as follows:

```
device_has_antivirus=false AND
password_length<5 AND
user_role=>Administration OR
device_is_rooted=true THEN=STRONGDENY
```

Rules presented in this way offer good readability which is key to understand the relationship between attributes and how the described situation might, or might not, be dangerous. In the example, the system would have inferred that an action from a device without antivirus, a short password, and rooted or belonging to an administration employee, should be denied.

In the application of GP to classification the most used metric to evaluate the individuals, i.e. the fitness function, is the accuracy [6]. The accuracy is normally obtained as the ratio of the correctly classified instances among the total of instances. Witten et al. use in [17] the concepts of true positive/negative and false positive/negative. The first refers to the correctly classified instances, and the latter are those instances that are classified as the contrary, and consequently they are called false positives or false negatives. Using this nomenclature – true negative (TN) and true positive (TP) –, a fitness function defined for accuracy would be expressed as follows:

$$f_{Acc} = (TP + TN)/T_{tr} \qquad (1)$$

This kind of fitness has to be maximised, given that the ideal value of f_{Acc} is the whole training dataset, T_{tr}. Equation 1 has the advantage of not being computationally expensive, but it does not penalise the badly predicted instances (false positives and negatives), which in security environments such as this one can be very harmful. Furthermore, a false negative would mean that the system denies an event that should be allowed, but the worst-case scenario is having a false positive, when a dangerous event is classified as allowed. To this end, in [17] the authors define the coverage as:

$$C_{ind} = TP + TN - (FP + FN) \qquad (2)$$

Additionally, to take into account the complexity of the individuals, whether they are a rule or a set of rules, in [17] they introduce a measure of the generated trees or list size by this expression:

$$S_{ind} = N_{nodes} + depth \qquad (3)$$

Where N_{nodes} is the number of nodes of the tree (or elements in a list), and $depth$ is the tree depth. So that combining C_{ind}, S_{ind} and introducing an α variable inside $[0, 1]$ to tune up the degree of allowed complexity, the problem becomes now a matter of minimising this formula:

$$f_{CS} = (T_{tr} - C_{ind}) + \alpha S_{ind} \tag{4}$$

Therefore, in our experimental section we are going to compare both f_{Acc} and f_{CS}, with different alpha values, to check two statements:

- How do they influence in the number of evaluations taken to find the best solution.
- Which fitness function is able to minimise false positives and negatives.

And finally decide which fitness function offers, taking into account these measures, the best performance.

Once the methods to compare have been explained, the rest of the experimental setup is now described.

The configurations that will be compared involve two different encoding of individuals (Pittsburgh tree individuals vs. Michigan list individuals), two types of fitness (f_{CS} and f_{Acc}), and three different values for α in the case of f_{Acc}.

With respect to the GP parameters, different decisions for experimental design have been taken into account. First, sub-tree crossover and 1-node mutation evolutionary operators have been used, as indicated by, for instance, [9]. In this case, during the mutation operation, there is a 50% of probability to change the complete variable (prefix, name, operator, and value) or only the value. A population of 32 individuals and a 2-tournament selector for a pool of 16 parents have been used. These parameters have been also previously used in, for instance, [9]. Table 1 summarises all the parameters used.

Table 1. Parameters used in the experiments.

Parameter name	Value
Population size	32
Crossover type	Sub-tree crossover
Crossover rate	0.5
Mutation	1-node mutation
Selection	2-tournament
Replacement	Generational with elitism
Stopping criterion	150 generations
Maximum tree depth	10
Runs per configuration	10
Compared configurations	
Individual representation	Pittsburgh vs. Michigan
Fitness	f_{CS} VS f_{Acc}
α for f_{CS}	0, 0.5, and 1

During the fitness evaluation, the generated individual is transformed into a string, which can become a single rule or set of rules depending on the approach, as previously described. Then, the chosen fitness is evaluated for a particular rule – the single rule or each one inside the set – and over the 90% of the data. For further reliability of the results, it is advised to perform 10-fold cross-validation, and as such the WEKA Java Library [10] has been used to generate the 10 folds or distributions of data into 90% training (fitness evaluation) and 10% validation. This way, each experiment has been executed 10 times, each one with a different distribution of data.

The algorithms have been executed in a cluster node with 16 Intel(R) Xeon(R) CPU E5520 @2.27 GHz processors, 16 GB RAM, CentOS 6.8 and Java Version 1.8.0_80. The specific source code of the proposed method is available under a LGPL V3 License at github.com/anon, as a module for the framework Anonymous n.

3   Results from Genetic Programming Application

As our purpose in this paper is to obtain a system which proposes to a CSO useful security rules that improve the existing ones, and present them in an understandable way, in this section we compare the results from using two fitness functions described in Eqs. 1 and 4, as well as the two approaches taken – Pittsburgh and Michigan –. In addition, an example of the individuals obtained will be presented in order to understand how the different approaches affect them, along with their advantages and disadvantages. Lastly, we will choose the best approach, justifying this choice.

The aim of this comparison is to conclude which fitness function should be used, discussing the results from the point of view of convergence, and that means finding which one reaches the best value faster. To study this we have displayed the obtained fitness through the iterations for the Pittsburgh approach in Fig. 1 and for the Michigan approach in Figs. 2 and 3. Figures for GRANTED and STRONGDENY classes are separated because the solution is a single rule instead of a set of rules, and therefore the algorithm has to be executed once per class. With regard to the best fitness obtained for each fitness function, they are similar in the same scope, which means that the different values of α in f_{CS} did not present significant differences in the two approaches separately.

For the sake of clarity, f_{CS} has been divided by the maximum value – the number of instances for training – it might take. By looking at the Pittsburgh approach values in Fig. 1, we show that mostly all configurations tend to converge around iteration 40, but it seems that f_{CS} with $\alpha = 0.5$ is the configuration that reaches the best solution faster, around the 30th iteration.

With respect to the Michigan approach, a higher variability is noticeable in Figs. 2 and 3, but in average we see that for f_{CS} with $\alpha = 0$ or 1, the fitness do not converge until generation 120. The best ones are for f_{Acc} and f_{CS} with $\alpha = 0.5$, being the latter the one that converges faster, around the 50th iteration.

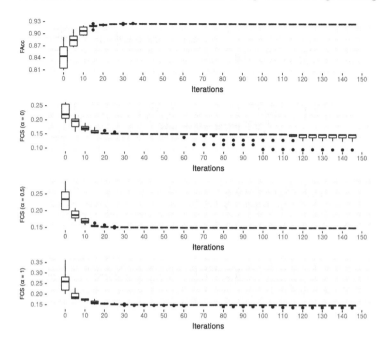

Fig. 1. Convergence of fitness for each one of the tested fitness functions, following the Pittsburgh approach. Note that f_{Acc} has to be maximised, whereas f_{CS} has to be minimised.

We can advance that the best results might be obtained for f_{CS} with $\alpha = 0.5$. However, there is a considerable difference between the performance, in terms of best obtained fitness, of the two used approaches. In this way, we have to thoroughly compare them. In the next section we do so by choosing the validation coverage and the ratio of false positives and negatives as independent measurements.

Once the variability of the obtained fitness has been studied, and always taking into account that those values come from their evaluation in a training subset of the data, now we *validate* the proposed approaches with a validation set, similar to the validation set used in classification problems [17]. The way to evaluate this is similar to Eq. 1, but using the validation subset of the data:

$$v_{Acc} = (TP + TN)/T_{val} \tag{5}$$

This measure will be the same independently of the approach or fitness function has used to evaluate the individuals. Table 2 shows the average, best, median, and worst results from the evaluations with f_{Acc} and also f_{CS}.

In Sect. 3 we have shown that the performance in the fitness of the Michigan approach was worse than that of Pittsburgh, and now it is more clear, given that the accuracy over the validation set is not even 50%. In fact, the dataset we are using is highly imbalanced; there are 1 instance in the training set of

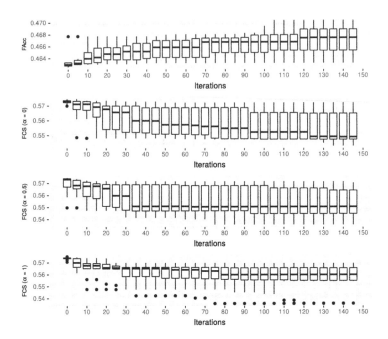

Fig. 2. Evolution of fitness for the Michigan approach and the GRANTED class.

Table 2. Validation (accuracy in classification of a new dataset) scores for the Pittsburgh and Michigan approaches. ∗ marks statistically significant best values.

| | | Fitness function | Validation measurement | | | | | |
			Average	Best	Median	Worst	FP	FN
Pittsburgh: Individual eq. set of rules		f_{Acc}	0.925 ± 0.379e-2	0.929	0.926	0.917	0.075 ± 0.045e-1	0
		f_{CS} $\alpha = 0$	0.926 ± 0.744e-2	0.945	0.926	0.917	0.072 ± 1.272e-2	0.002 ± 0.564e-2
		$\alpha = 0.5$	0.924 ± 0.371e-2	0.929	0.924	0.917	0.074 ± 0.451e-2	0
		$\alpha = 1$	0.925 ± 0.384e-2	0.929	0.926	0.917	0.075 ± 0.378e-2	0
Michigan: Individual eq. one rule	Class: GRANTED	f_{Acc}	0.467 ± 0.143e-2	0.472	0.468	0.459	0.023 ± 0.095e-1	0
		f_{CS} $\alpha = 0$	0.466 ± 0.441e-2	0.472	0.467	0.459	0.021 ± 0.094e-1	0
		$\alpha = 0.5$	0.467 ± 0.305e-2	0.472	0.467	0.462	0.019 ± 0.088e-1	0
		$\alpha = 1$	0.465 ± 0.43e-2	0.472	0.467	0.458	0.023 ± 0.099e-1	0
	Class: STRONGDENY	f_{Acc}	0.046∗ ± 0.74e-2	0.065	0.045	0.037	0	0.307 ± 0.745e-1
		f_{CS} $\alpha = 0$	0.025 ± 1.527e-2	0.045	0.023	0.003	0	0.004 ± 0.039e-1
		$\alpha = 0.5$	0.02 ± 1.603e-2	0.061	0.015	0.002	0	0.007 ± 0.063e-1
		$\alpha = 1$	0.025 ± 1.948e-2	0.047	0.036	0	0	0.004 ± 0.049e-1

data labelled as STRONGDENY for every 13 labelled as GRANTED. Thus, the results we have obtained are biased towards the majority class [11].

At the same time, and because of the distributions for the Michigan approach follow the normal, an ANOVA test has been performed in every class [5], obtaining a p-value of 0.5538 for the GRANTED class, meaning that there are not statistically significant differences in the results. However, in the case of the STRONGDENY class, using f_{CS} significantly (p-value of 0.001736) decreases the accuracy over the validation set. With regard to how many FP and FN are obtained in every approach, we see in Table 2 that for the Pittsburgh approach we generally obtain low rates or 0 – ideal – false negatives, and around 7% rate

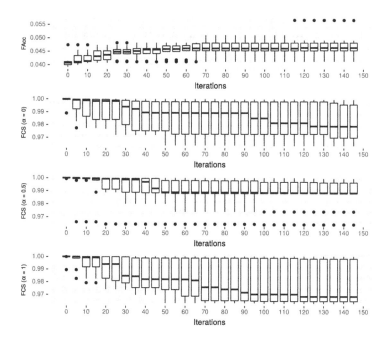

Fig. 3. Evolution of fitness for the Michigan approach and the STRONGDENY class.

of false positives – almost 400 in average for our validation set –. On the other hand, best rates are found for the Michigan approach, where the rate of FP is, at most, 2.8% – around 113 instances in average –. And even if there were FN found, the average for the used validation set is 29 instances out of 5330, which is a very low number and as we explained before, in this BYOD scenario it is less worse to have FN than FP. Also, this imbalance in the FP and FN values is also caused by the imbalance in the dataset.

To evaluate computation costs of the two approaches, and taking into consideration the infrastructure available for the experiments (see Sect. 2), we present the execution times in Table 3, detailed by their average value and standard deviation, along with the best, worst, and median values. Time is expressed in hours, for the sake of clarification. In addition, the values for the Michigan approach are not separated by class this time, because in order to have the two rules - one for each class – the CSO would have to wait for both executions.

In this table we see that best times are obtained when f_{CS} is used. More precisely, in the Pittsburgh approach, the distributions follow the normal and after performing the ANOVA test, we can say that the shorter execution time (the best) is found for $\alpha = 0.5$ with statistical significance (p-value of 0.008623). In the case of the Michigan approach, we again find statistical differences (p-value of 5.537e−405) between the results, and thus we can say that the best execution time is obtained when we use f_{CS} with an α value of 0. It seems that the time does decrease when α is different from 0, meaning that the depth of the tree has influence on the evaluation of the fitness.

Table 3. Execution time, Pittsburgh and Michigan approaches; this one adds times for GRANTED and STRONGDENY. * marks statistically significant best values.

	Fitness function		Time measurement (h)			
			Average	Best	Median	Worst
Pittsburgh: individual eq. set of rules	f_{Acc}		18.371 ± 7.178	8.545	17.366	31.366
	f_{CS}	$\alpha = 0$	14.424 ± 2.938	7.016	14.352	17.43
		$\alpha = 0.5*$	11.934 ± 2.22	8.267	11.609	16.166
		$\alpha = 1$	13.176 ± 1.923	9.283	13.424	16.517
Michigan: individual eq. one rule	f_{Acc}		10.627 ± 0.187	10.307	10.64	10.956
	f_{CS}	$\alpha = 0*$	9.342 ± 0.3	8.993	9.261	9.854
		$\alpha = 0.5$	9.435 ± 0.348	9.039	9.401	10.281
		$\alpha = 1$	9.612 ± 0.508	8.946	9.509	10.38

To study this effect, we have to look at the sizes of the best individuals obtained for each configuration, which are displayed in Table 4.

Table 4. Tree size of the best individuals for the Pittsburgh approach. An * indicates the statistically significant best value for α.

	Fitness function		Best individual size			
			Average	Best	Median	Worst
Pittsburgh: individual eq. set of rules	f_{Acc}		60.2 ± 10.922	47	60	79
	f_{CS}	$\alpha = 0$	60 ± 11.086	43	60	83
		$\alpha = 0.5$	40 ± 4.447	35	40	47
		$\alpha = 1*$	36.2 ± 3.011	31	37	39

In this table we only show the results for the Pittsburgh approach, given that the sizes of the trees do change in GP, but the size of a list – number of conditions in the rule – does not, and in this case is always 10. Certainly, the size of the trees decreases when the value of α grows. Since the distributions do not follow the normal, a non-parametric test (Kruskal-Wallis) has been used to asset the statistical significance [5], obtaining a p-value of $1.679e-10$. Then, the smaller individual is found for f_{CS}, and $\alpha = 1$. In the context of this problem, a smaller number of rules increases their explainability, which is why this particular value and fitness function will have to be considered if that is a priority.

What we also have to determine is which kind of presented solution is better: showing the CSO a set of rules or a single rule for each class. Figure 4 shows an example of best individual obtained using f_{CS} and $\alpha = 0$. The tree in this figure represents a set of 16 rules, two of them classifying to the STRONGDENY class, whilst the rest classify towards the GRANTED class. The ones that classify to STRONGDENY have been highlighted and presented in string form in the figure.

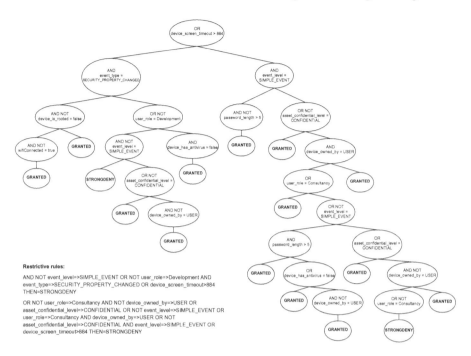

Fig. 4. Example with f_{CS} and $\alpha = 0$.

The STRONGDENY rules in Fig. 4 imply that the developers are more probably to get a GRANTED in their actions, and this conclusion makes sense because they are supposed to be more familiar with systems security. Also, from the second rule we can infer that the complex events – not simple – and the BYOD devices imply a certain degree of unsafety. The root, and thus most important, condition, is related to the time that the the device takes to enter into sleep mode (screen turns off).

4   Conclusions and Future Work

In this work, we wanted to help companies adopting the BYOD philosophy by developing a tool that is able to discover rules using a GP approach, extracting knowledge from the users behaviours when interacting with their devices, at the time it minimises the false positives, so that a dangerous action is never taken as permitted. To this end, in Sect. 2 we have presented different ways to implement a methodology based on GP, by two approaches: Pittsburgh, in which the individuals are coded as set or rules; and Michigan, where the individuals are a single rule, and thus a rule for every class has to be generated. In addition, two different fitness functions have been used to study their effect over the validation accuracy rate and the number of false positives and negatives.

The results in Sect. 3 make a fine proof of concept of a tool that helps the CSO of a company discovering dangerous situations through the presentation of GP generated rules. We obtained promising rates for the number of false positives (around 7%), and good coverage over the validation data set, as is shown in Sect. 3. However, since the ideal value for both false positives and negatives is 0, there is room for improvement. In addition, Fig. 4 shows that the individuals are presented in a readable form, but the ratio between rules classifying to one or another class is too biased towards the GRANTED class.

With regard to the execution time, the solution we propose takes between 16 and 17 h, in the worst case and taking into account the used infrastructure, to obtain the best individual. Although these times could be acceptable, in the sense that the CSO would have new rules every day, they can still be reduced. A possible way to achieve better values for FP and FN is to set up the problem as a multiobjective one, so that we try to minimise f_{CS}, but also FP and FN. Additionally, we will try to reduce the execution time by adapting the algorithm parameters, for instance, the number of generations, as has been shown in Sect. 3 that in some cases 50 generations is enough. Other enhancements could be to study every tree individual and not to directly evaluate the fitness for the contradictory rules of each one.

On the other hand, the imbalance of the dataset should be taken into account, given that it affects the results in terms of obtained accuracy in the validation process and the ratio among classes in the obtained individuals [2], so different solutions to deal with this issue will be applied.

For our future work we will implement these solutions to continue improving our system. Furthermore, we will extend the approach to other problems where data is available. For example, particularisations of the BYOD problem as it could be Internet navigation during work hours. We will explore network traffic from public data repositories, such as http://www.secrepo.com/#3p_network, and try to apply our approach.

Acknowledgements. This work has been partially funded by projects RTI2018-102002-A-I00 (Ministerio de Ciencia, Innovación y Universidades), TIN2017-85727-C4-2-P (Ministerio español de Economía y Competitividad), and TEC2015-68752 (also funded by FEDER), as well as project B-TIC-402-UGR18 (FEDER y Junta de Andalucía).

References

1. Ali, S., Qureshi, M.N., Abbasi, A.G.: Analysis of BYOD security frameworks. In: 2015 Conference on Information Assurance and Cyber Security (CIACS), pp. 56–61. IEEE (2015)
2. de Arruda Pereira, M., Carrano, E.G., Davis Junior, C.A., de Vasconcelos, J.A.: A comparative study of optimization models in genetic programming-based rule extraction problems. Soft Comput. **23**(4), 1179–1197 (2019). https://doi.org/10.1007/s00500-017-2836-8

3. Back, T.: Evolutionary Algorithms in Theory and Practice: Evolution Strategies, Evolutionary Programming, Genetic Algorithms. Oxford University Press, Oxford (1996)
4. Castellanos-Garzón, J.A., Ramos, J., Martín, Y.M., de Paz, J.F., Costa, E.: A genetic programming approach applied to feature selection from medical data. In: Fdez-Riverola, F., Mohamad, M.S., Rocha, M., De Paz, J.F., González, P. (eds.) PACBB2018 2018. AISC, vol. 803, pp. 200–207. Springer, Cham (2019). https://doi.org/10.1007/978-3-319-98702-6_24
5. Derrac, J., García, S., Molina, D., Herrera, F.: A practical tutorial on the use of nonparametric statistical tests as a methodology for comparing evolutionary and swarm intelligence algorithms. Swarm and Evolutionary Computation $1(1)$, 3–18 (2011). https://doi.org/10.1016/j.swevo.2011.02.002
6. Espejo, P.G., Ventura, S., Herrera, F.: A survey on the application of genetic programming to classification. IEEE Trans. Syst. Man Cybern. Part C $40(2)$, 121–144 (2010)
7. Falco, I.D., Cioppa, A.D., Tarantino, E.: Discovering interesting classification rules with genetic programming. Appl. Soft Comput. $1(4)$, 257–269 (2002). https://doi.org/10.1016/S1568-4946(01)00024-2. http://www.sciencedirect.com/science/article/pii/S1568494601000242
8. Freitas, A.A.: Data Mining and Knowledge Discovery with Evolutionary Algorithms. Springer, Heidelberg (2002). https://doi.org/10.1007/978-3-662-04923-5
9. García-Sánchez, P., Fernández-Ares, A., Mora, A.M., Castillo, P.A., González, J., Guervós, J.J.M.: Tree depth influence in genetic programming for generation of competitive agents for RTS games. In: Esparcia-Alcázar, A.I., Mora, A.M. (eds.) EvoApplications 2014. LNCS, vol. 8602, pp. 411–421. Springer, Heidelberg (2014). https://doi.org/10.1007/978-3-662-45523-4_34
10. Hall, M., Frank, E., Holmes, G., Pfahringer, B., Reutemann, P., Witten, I.H.: The WEKA data mining software: an update. SIGKDD Explor. $11(1)$, 10–18 (2009)
11. Japkowicz, N., Stephen, S.: The class imbalance problem: a systematic study. Intell. Data Anal. $6(5)$, 429–449 (2002)
12. Kaeo, M.: Designing Network Security, 2nd edn. Cisco Press, Indianapolis (2003)
13. Pietraszek, T., Tanner, A.: Data mining and machine learning - towards reducing false positives in intrusion detection. Inf. Secur. Techn. Rep. $10(3)$, 169–183 (2005)
14. Prechelt, L.: PROBEN 1-a set of benchmarks and benchmarking rules for neural network training algorithms (1994)
15. Safavian, S.R., Landgrebe, D.: A survey of decision tree classifier methodology. IEEE Trans. Syst. Man Cybern. $21(3)$, 660–674 (1991). https://doi.org/10.1109/21.97458
16. Tsakonas, A., Dounias, G., Jantzen, J., Axer, H., Bjerregaard, B., von Keyserlingk, D.G.: Evolving rule-based systems in two medical domains using genetic programming. Artif. Intell. Med. $32(3)$, 195–216 (2004). https://doi.org/10.1016/j.artmed.2004.02.007. http://www.sciencedirect.com/science/article/pii/S0933365704001058. Adaptive Systems and Hybrid Computational Intelligence in Medicine
17. Witten, I.H., Frank, E.: Data Mining: Practical Machine Learning Tools and Techniques. Morgan Kaufmann, Burlington (2005)

Search Trajectory Networks
of Population-Based Algorithms
in Continuous Spaces

Gabriela Ochoa[1]([envelope]) [ID], Katherine M. Malan[2] [ID], and Christian Blum[3] [ID]

[1] University of Stirling, Scotland, UK
gabriela.ochoa@stir.ac.uk
[2] Department of Decision Sciences, University of South Africa, Pretoria, South Africa
malankm@unisa.ac.za
[3] Artificial Intelligence Research Institute (IIIA-CSIC), Campus of the UAB,
Bellaterra, Spain
christian.blum@iiia.csic.es

Abstract. We introduce *search trajectory networks* (STNs) as a tool
to analyse and visualise the behaviour of population-based algorithms
in continuous spaces. Inspired by local optima networks (LONs) that
model the global structure of search spaces, STNs model the search trajectories of algorithms. Unlike LONs, the nodes of the network are not
restricted to local optima but instead represent a given state of the search
process. Edges represent search progression between consecutive states.
This extends the power and applicability of network-based models to
understand heuristic search algorithms. We extract and analyse STNs
for two well-known population-based algorithms: particle swarm optimisation and differential evolution when applied to benchmark continuous
optimisation problems. We also offer a comparative visual analysis of the
search dynamics in terms of merged search trajectory networks.

Keywords: Continuous optimisation · Local optima networks ·
Metaheuristics behaviour · Search trajectory networks

1 Introduction

There is a lack of tools for understanding the dynamics of heuristic search algorithms and the global structure of fitness landscapes. It is also difficult to visualise high-dimensional search spaces. Local optima networks (LONs) [15,24] help
to fill this gap by providing a compressed model of landscapes, where nodes are
local optima and edges possible transitions among them. LONs model the distribution and connectivity pattern of local optima, and thus help to characterise
the underlying landscape global structure. Once a network model has been constructed, it can be visualised and analysed with the plethora of powerful analytical and visualisation tools provided by the science of complex networks [14].
However, there are limitations to LONs, as they have been applied mainly to

© Springer Nature Switzerland AG 2020
P. A. Castillo et al. (Eds.): EvoApplications 2020, LNCS 12104, pp. 70–85, 2020.
https://doi.org/10.1007/978-3-030-43722-0_5

fully enumerated networks [10,15,24], combinatorial optimisation in the context of single-point metaheuristics [16,22] or population-based approaches where there there is a local search component [4,23]. The major limitation of LONs is that the nodes have been restricted to local optima of standard neighbourhood operators, and only recently have been extended to large-neighbourhoods within hybrid metaheuristics [1]. The contributions of this article are as follows:

- To propose search trajectory networks (STNs) as a tool to analyse and visualise the behaviour of population-based algorithms.
- To show how the concept of STNs could be implemented in the context of continuous search spaces.
- To conduct STN analyses of two well-known evolutionary algorithms in continuous optimisation.
- To conduct a visual comparative analysis of the studied algorithms using merged STNs.

2 Population-Based Algorithm Behaviour

In the last few decades there has been a huge increase in the number of metaheuristics inspired by different natural and social phenomena. One of the problems with all of these new algorithms is that it is not clear whether they are in fact "new". When the metaphor is stripped away, is the search process any different from the search process of existing established algorithms [20]?

Combined with this increase in the choice of algorithms is the lack of expert knowledge required to use the algorithms effectively. It has taken many decades of empirical and theoretical research for well-established metaheuristics to be understood even to a very limited extent. Every new approach comes with a blank record of established knowledge around behaviour with respect to algorithm setup, parameter choices and suitable or unsuitable problem classes. A need clearly exists for approaches to analysing search algorithm behaviour.

It is often stated that the success of any metaheuristic boils down to finding the right balance between exploration and exploitation (or the broader concept of intensification/diversification [2]). However, there is no generally accepted understanding of the concept in the evolutionary computing research community [8]. Part of the problem is that controlling this aspect of algorithmic behaviour is not trivial. In the case of evolutionary algorithms, there are three levels at which exploration/exploitation can be controlled [8]: at individual level (when solutions share information with each other), at sub-individual level (when solutions are combined) and at gene level (when components of individual solutions are modified).

In population-based algorithms, exploration/exploitation is related to the notion of diversity. The more diverse or spread-out the solutions in the population are, the more the algorithm is exploring. Conversely, if the solutions are clustered closely together in the search space, then the algorithm is exploiting a specific part of the search space. The way in which diversity changes over time is therefore one approach to characterising the behaviour of a population-based algorithm. Bosman and Engelbrecht [3] proposed a single numerical measure called diversity rate of change (DRoC) for characterising the exploration-exploitation trade-off in particle swarms. Their premise was that the profile of the reduction in diversity (measured using the average Euclidean distance around the centre of the swarm [17]) could be captured by the slopes of a two-piecewise linear approximation of the diversity over time. Although diversity provides one important view of algorithm behaviour, it ignores where in the search space the population is moving and hence whether convergence is premature or not.

The STN model proposed in this paper provides a complementary view of the behaviour of population-based algorithms. Instead of studying the diversity of the population over time, we study the trajectory of a representative solution (the current best solution) over time. The visualisations and metrics of STNs provide an additional tool for analysing algorithm behaviour that may provide insights that are not captured by commonly used convergence plots or the DRoC measure.

3   Search Trajectory Networks (STNs)

Our proposal to provide new insights into the search dynamics of different algorithms is to model their search trajectories by means of a network model. Specifically, we modify the local optima networks (LON) model [15] to analyse the trajectories of population-based algorithms. We also use the recently proposed idea [1] of merging the network models induced by two different algorithms in order to compare their trajectories with a graphical support.

In order to define a network model, we need to specify the nodes and edges. The relevant definitions are given below, as well as a description of the sampling process to construct the network models.

Trajectory. A sequence of solutions corresponding to the best solution in the population over time. The frequency of recording the best solution is controlled by a parameter.

Location. A partition of the search space containing a subset of solutions within a predefined neighbourhood.

Nodes. The nodes correspond to the locations of the corresponding best solutions in a trajectory. The set of nodes is denoted by N.

Edges. Edges are directed and connect two consecutive locations of best solutions in the search trajectory. Edges are weighted with the number of times a transition between two given nodes occurred during the process of sampling and constructing the STN. The set of edges is denoted by E.

Search Trajectory Network (STN). Is the directed graph $G^{\mathrm{STN}} = (N, E)$, with node set N, and edge set E as defined above.

Sampling and STN Model Construction. The STNs were generated for a selection of well-studied benchmark instances. For each of these instances an STN was constructed by aggregating all the unique nodes and edges encountered across 10 independent runs (search trajectories) of each algorithm. The details of the sampling and STN setup are given in Sect. 4.4.

4   Experimental Setting

This section describes the algorithms and problems used in the experiments as well as the setup required for the STN model.

4.1   Candidate Algorithms

Two candidate population-based algorithms were chosen for testing the proposed STN model – one evolutionary, namely differential evolution (DE), and one swarm-based, namely particle swarm optimisation (PSO). The particular version of DE used in the study was DE/rand/1 [21], with uniform crossover, a population size of 50, a scale factor of 0.5, and a crossover rate of 0.5. The version of PSO used in the study was traditional global best PSO [6,12] with an inertia weight term [19], 50 particles, 1.496 for both the cognitive and social acceleration constants, and 0.7298 for the inertia weight (although the optimal choice of parameters is problem dependent, this is a common choice that works reasonably well for many problems [7]).

Note that no parameter tuning was performed on the two algorithms. The purpose of this paper is to introduce a mechanism for understanding and contrasting population-based algorithm behaviour in continuous spaces. No judgements are made on the performance of DE in relation to PSO. We are rather showing that if one search process is more successful than another on a particular problem, the STN model can shed some light on why this is the case.

The behaviour of the two candidate algorithms can be understood on a high level as follows:

- DE/rand/1: At each iteration, new perturbed solutions are formed for each individual of the population by adding a scaled weighted difference between two other random solutions in the population to another random solution. A trial solution is then formed through crossover of the current solution with the perturbed solution. If the trial solution is better, then it will replace the current solution. On a high level DE/rand/1 can be understood as each solution being attracted towards a combination of three other random solutions of the population, but only moving if the new combination is better.
- Global best PSO: At each iteration, the position of each solution is influenced by three terms: the solution's previous velocity, the position of the best solution in the individual trajectory and the position of the best solution of the population. All solutions therefore have two attractors: the current best solution in the population and the previous best solution in the individual's trajectory. The solution will move regardless of whether it is better or not.

A significant difference between the two algorithms is in the size of the neighbourhood for sharing information. In the case of DE/rand/1, the neighbourhood is three other individuals, whereas for global best PSO, the neighbourhood is the entire population, since all solutions are attracted towards one global best solution.

4.2 Benchmark Functions

A sample of five minimisation benchmark functions (defined in Table 1) with different characteristics were chosen for testing the proposed STN model. Function instances were chosen that demonstrated performance differences between the two candidate algorithms in our preliminary experiments. The purpose was to investigate whether the STN visualisations and metrics could be used to explain relative algorithm success and failure for problems in different dimensions. Two-dimensional plots of the functions are provided in Fig. 1 to provide insight into the global structure of the problems.

Quadric (also known as Schwefel 1.2) [25] is the only unimodal function. Michalewicz [13] is multimodal, but also has large plateaus at high fitness values. Schwefel 2.26 [25] is multimodal and also multi-funnelled. Both Salomon [18] and Rana [18] are extremely rugged, but Salomon has a single-funnel global structure (evident in Fig. 1d), whereas Rana has a multi-funnel structure. Figure 1e shows the Salomon function zoomed in to the domain around the origin (the global optimum), showing that the function "resembles a pond with ripples" [18] on a micro scale.

Table 1. Benchmark functions

Function	Definition	Domain
Michalewicz	$f(\mathbf{x}) = -\sum_{i=1}^{D} \sin(x_i) \left(\sin(ix_i^2/\pi)\right)^{2p}$	$x_i \in [0, \pi]$
Quadric	$f(\mathbf{x}) = \sum_{i=1}^{D} \left(\sum_{j=1}^{i} x_j\right)^2$	$x_i \in [-100, 100]$
Rana	$f(\mathbf{x}) = \sum_{i=1}^{D} x_i \sin(\alpha) \cos(\beta)$ $+ \left(x_{(i+1)\bmod D} + 1\right) \cos(\alpha) \sin(\beta), \quad D \geq 2,$ $\alpha = \sqrt{|x_{i+1} + 1 - x_i|}, \quad \beta = \sqrt{|x_i + x_{i+1} + 1|}$	$x_i \in [-512, 512]$
Salomon	$f(\mathbf{x}) = -\cos\left(2\pi \sqrt{\sum_{i=1}^{D} x_i^2}\right) + 0.1\sqrt{\sum_{i=1}^{D} x_i^2} + 1$	$x_i \in [-100, 100]$
Schwefel 2.26	$f(\mathbf{x}) = -\sum_{i=1}^{D} \left(x_i \sin(\sqrt{|x_i|})\right)$	$x_i \in [-500, 500]$

4.3 Experimental Runs

Ten runs of each of the two candidate algorithms (using the parameters specified in Sect. 4.1) were executed on the five benchmark problem instances: Michalewicz

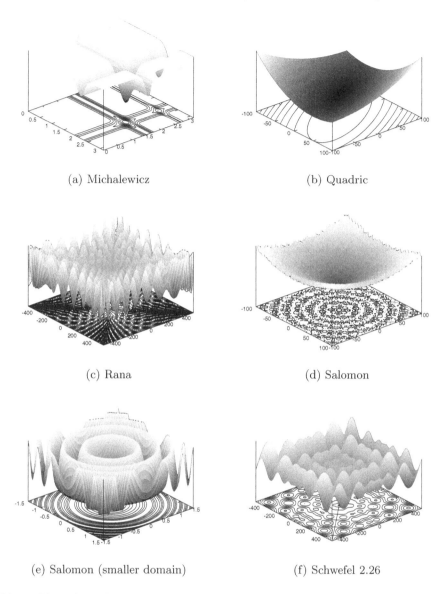

(a) Michalewicz   (b) Quadric

(c) Rana   (d) Salomon

(e) Salomon (smaller domain)   (f) Schwefel 2.26

Fig. 1. Plots of two-dimensional versions of the benchmark functions used in the experiments

in 5D, Quadric in 10D, Rana in 3D, Salomon in 3D and Schwefel 2.26 in 5D. Each run had a budget of $5000 \times D$ function evaluations ($100 \times D$ iterations for a population size of 50). The positions and fitness values of the best solutions in the current population were saved to represent the trajectories.

To ensure that the visualisations were not too cluttered, the best solutions of every D^{th} iteration were stored. Problems of different dimensions therefore had representative trajectories of equal length (100 in this case). The fitness of solutions was stored rounded off to a precision of 10^{-8}.

4.4 STN Setup

In a discrete domain, nodes of the STN could be modelled as unique solutions. In the continuous domain, however, considering unique solutions is not feasible, so each node instead represents a number of solutions that are within a specified non-overlapping sub-space of the solution space, which we call a *location*. A location can therefore be thought of as a small portion of the search space through which trajectories might pass. Each solution in the trajectory is represented by one node in the STN, but the same node may represent multiple solutions (meaning that the trajectories passed through the location multiple times).

In this study, a solution precision parameter (SP) was used to portion the continuous search space into equal-sized discrete portions equal to a hypercube with length 10^{-SP}. For example, if $SP = 2$, then the solution space is divided into hypercubes of size 10^{-2} and each node in the STN is equivalent to one of these hypercubes or locations. Solutions are mapped to locations by rounding off all components of the position to the nearest 10^{-SP} to determine the identity of the enclosing hypercube.

To extract meaningful insights from the STN model, the value of the parameter SP should decrease as the search space increases. In this study, (assuming that the domain of values is the same for each dimension of the problem) the value for SP was expressed as a function of the range of the domain ($x_{max}-x_{min}$) and dimension (D) of the problem as follows: SP is set to $2 - n$, where n is the largest integer for which the following is true:

$$(x_{max} - x_{min}) \times D \geq 10^{n}. \tag{1}$$

For example, given a problem in 3 dimensions with domain $[-1, 1]$ in all dimensions, SP would be set to 2, since $2 \times 3 \geq 10^{0}$, so $n = 2-0 = 2$. For this problem, a location/node in the STN would be equivalent to a unique $10^{-2} \times 10^{-2} \times 10^{-2}$ cube in the search space.

Since each location comprises multiple solutions, there are many different fitness values for each location. For visualisation purposes, each location in the trajectory was assigned a representative fitness value equal to the minimum fitness value of all visited solutions within that location.

5 Results

5.1 Visualisation

Visualisation is a powerful tool for network data analysis, allowing us to appreciate structural features difficult to infer from the raw data and statistical analysis. The network visualisations in Figs. 2 and 3 model the search trajectories traversed by 10 independent runs of both candidate algorithms on the benchmark instances. Plots were produced with the R statistics package, using graph layout methods implemented in the igraph library [5]. Specifically, we considered *force-directed* layout algorithms, such as Fruchterman-Reignold [9] and Kamada-Kawai [11]. Force-directed layout algorithms are based on physical analogies and do not rely on any assumptions about the structure of the networks. These algorithms strive to satisfy the following generally accepted criteria [9]:

- Vertices are distributed roughly evenly on the plane (a circle in the igraph implementation).
- The number of crossing edges is minimised.
- The lengths of edges are approximately uniform.
- The inherent symmetries in the networks are respected, i.e., sub-networks with similar inherent structure are usually laid out in a similar manner.

The left plots in Figs. 2, 3 and 4, show the STNs 2D force-directed layouts, while the right plots give a 3D visualisation of the same layouts where the z coordinate indicates the fitness values. In the 3D plots, locations appearing lower in the plot have better fitness as we are dealing with minimisation problems. The features of the nodes and edges in all the STN visualisations (Figs. 2, 3 and 4) reflect properties of the search dynamics. The size of the nodes is proportional to their incoming degree (number of incoming edges), which indicates how often a node was visited and thus 'attracts' the search process. The nodes and edges visited by only one of the two algorithms are distinguished in different colours; light orange for PSO, and blue for DE. The initial locations for all runs are visualised as yellow nodes. Both algorithms started from the same 10 randomly generated initial solutions, so each yellow node has one blue (DE) and one orange (PSO) outgoing edge. Red nodes illustrate the location of the global optimum. Nodes in green indicate locations that were visited (shared) by both algorithms in their combined search trajectories, while dark grey nodes represent the end point of search trajectories, i.e. where the final location was not the location containing the global optimum. A visualisation legend summarising the colours used in Figs. 2, 3 and 4 is given in Fig. 2(a).

The STN visualisation of the Salomon function (Fig. 3(b)) appears crowded towards its centre. In order to have a clearer perspective, Fig. 4 shows a zoomed view near the global optimum. Specifically, the plots in Fig. 4 visualise the subgraph containing the nodes which are within the first quantile in fitness value; that is, the best 25% of the set of nodes.

5.2 Structural and Performance Metrics

Table 2 reports the following STN metrics for each algorithm:

- nodes: The total number of nodes, which corresponds to the number of unique locations visited.
- edges: The total number of edges, which corresponds to the number of unique search transitions between locations.

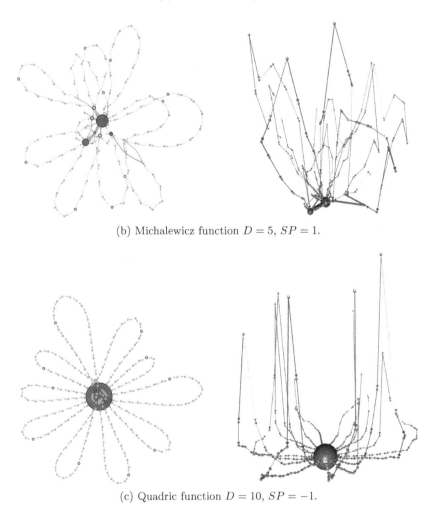

Locations visited by PSO
Search transitions by PSO
Locations visited by DE
Search transitions by DE
Locations visited by both algorithms
Locations at the start of runs
Locations at the end of runs
Location of the global optimum

(a) Visualisation legend.

(b) Michalewicz function $D = 5$, $SP = 1$.

(c) Quadric function $D = 10$, $SP = -1$.

Fig. 2. Merged STN visualisations for functions 1 and 2. The visualisation legend is shown at the top. The dimension D, and solution precision SP are indicated in the captions. The left plots use a force-directed layout, while the right plots use the same layout and adds a 3rd dimension indicating fitness. (Color figure online)

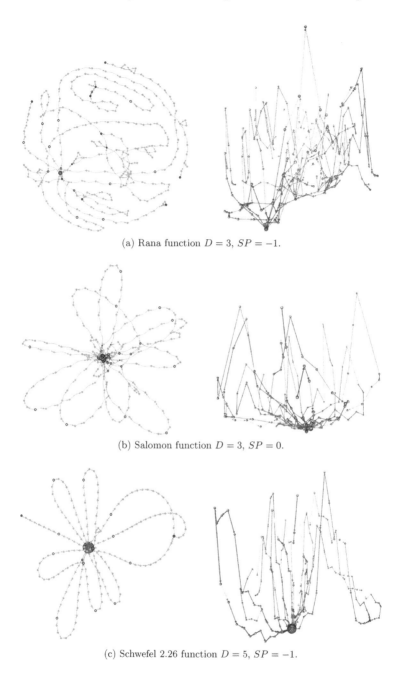

(a) Rana function $D = 3$, $SP = -1$.

(b) Salomon function $D = 3$, $SP = 0$.

(c) Schwefel 2.26 function $D = 5$, $SP = -1$.

Fig. 3. Merged STN visualisations for functions 3, 4 and 5. The dimension D, and solution precision SP used for each function are indicated in the captions. For each function, the left plot uses a force-directed layout, while the right plot considers the same layout and adds a 3rd dimension indicating fitness. (Color figure online)

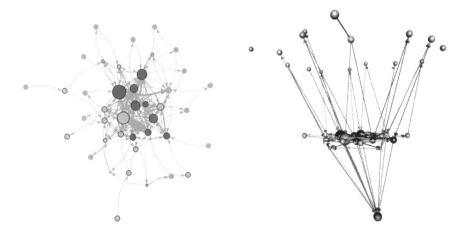

Fig. 4. Zoomed merged STN visualisation for the Salomon function. The plots show only those nodes within the first quantile of fitness values (i.e. the best 25% solutions). The left plot uses a force-directed layout, while the right plot considers the same layout and adds a 3rd dimension indicating fitness. (Color figure online)

- ends: The number of (unique) nodes corresponding to the end of runs. These include both the global optimum and other locations to which the runs converged.
- avg. path length: Average (with standard deviation) path length from start to end nodes. The length of a path is the number of edges it contains.

The table also reports the success rate of the algorithms as a percentage of the 10 runs that ended in the global optimum location. For example, in the case of DE on the Michalewicz problem instance, 8 out of the 10 runs reached the node that contains the global minimum.

The values in Table 2 indicate that the PSO trajectories are generally longer than those of DE, with the exception of the Quadric function. This means that the best solution in the PSO population traversed through more nodes than the best solution in the DE population. This could be as a result of the absence of elitism in the PSO implementation, resulting in more exploration than DE (that did use elitism), except in the unimodal function (Quadric) where the single global best attractor resulted in faster convergence to the global optimum.

Table 3 reports network metrics for the merged STNs that include the trajectories of both DE and PSO. The columns report, from left to right, the total number of nodes, the total number of edges, the number of end nodes, and the number of *shared* nodes, that is, locations visited by both algorithms. Remember that both algorithms start from the same 10 initial solutions, so the 10 start nodes are always shared. The global optimum is also a shared visited node in most functions, except Rana where PSO was not able to converge to it. Table 3 indicates that other search points are shared between the algorithms in all functions, with Salomon having the largest number of shared nodes.

Table 2. STN structural metrics and success rate of each algorithm.

	Nodes		Edges		Ends		Avg. path length		Success (%)	
	DE	PSO	DE	PSO	DE	PSO	DE	PSO	DE	PSO
Michalewicz	61	76	71	81	2	3	$7.0_{1.88}$	$7.5_{2.63}$	80	40
Quadric	154	93	160	92	1	1	$15.1_{3.51}$	$9.2_{1.55}$	100	100
Rana	49	211	54	249	2	10	$4.7_{0.95}$	$13.5_{7.22}$	90	0
Salomon	85	131	129	221	3	7	$8.3_{1.21}$	$10.4_{2.08}$	80	30
Schwefel 2.26	81	138	80	143	1	4	$8.0_{2.11}$	$12.6_{3.23}$	100	50

Table 3. Merged STN structural metrics.

	Nodes	Edges	Ends	Shared
Michalewicz	120	151	2	17
Quadric	233	252	1	14
Rana	245	303	10	15
Salomon	178	338	3	38
Schwefel 2.26	205	220	4	14

Metrics on merged STNs, such as those given in Table 3, can be used to provide insight into the nature of problems in relation to each other. For example, in the case of the Michalewicz function there are far fewer nodes than for the other algorithms (recall that all recorded trajectories were of equal length). This could be due to the neutrality present in the function (see Fig. 1a), resulting in less movement of the best solution, due to lack of information in the landscape.

5.3 Performance Comparison

In the following we analyse the behaviour of the two candidate algorithms on the basis of the graphics from Figs. 2, 3 and 4 and the metrics from Tables 2, 3 and 4. Remember that both the graphics and the metrics were generated on the basis of 10 runs per algorithm and per function.

Michalewicz Function. The STN concerning the Michalewicz function (see Fig. 2(a)) shows two important attractors: the global minimum (red dot) and the large grey dot. In addition, smaller attractors such as the smaller grey dot can be identified. The success rate of DE for this problem is 80%, while the one for PSO is 40%. The graphics clearly show that, although both algorithms are attracted by the portion of the search space representing the large grey dot, DE is much better than PSO at escaping from this basin of attraction (see the thick blue edge to the global optimum node). Moreover, note that a number of PSO runs are attracted by the smaller grey dot, but that none of these runs is able to escape from there. The opposite is the case for DE: although two runs are attracted by the smaller grey dot, the algorithm is able to leave from there and to proceed with the search. Finally, note that the search trajectories of PSO can be seen to be generally longer than those of DE (also reflected in the average path length in Table 2).

Quadric Function. The STN obtained for the Quadric function shows that all runs—for both DE and PSO—are attracted by the global minimum. This is reasonable, because this function does not have any local minima. Moreover, with respect to the considered precision, all runs of PSO and DE finally reach the location containing the global minimum (success rate of 100% – see Table 2). However, consulting Table 4 we can see that the DE runs finish, on average, further from the global minimum than the PSO runs. This indicates that DE suffers from premature convergence in the case of function Quadric. Interestingly, the search trajectories of DE (in terms of the number of steps) are clearly longer than those of PSO (visually and seen in Table 2) indicating that PSO took a more direct route in the direction of the global optimum.

Rana Function. Already a first visual inspection of the STN for the Rana function (see Fig. 3(a)) indicates that this function is very different from the Michalewicz and Quadric functions. This is also evident in the merged metrics of Table 3, showing more unique nodes than for all other functions. In fact, PSO does not seem to be attracted by any particular part of the search space and can be seen to have 10 different end points (Table 2), compared to only 2 for DE. The normalised average distance from the end of the PSO trajectories to the global minimum is ≈0.5 (Table 4), which is about half the distance between the two most distant points in the search space. This divergent behaviour is also reflected in the low success rate – no PSO runs end in the location of the global minimum, while DE has a success rate of 90%, that is, nine out of 10 runs end in the global minimum node. Moreover, the trajectories of DE are rather short and seem to move towards the global minimum without suffering from too many detours (also reflected in the low average path length in Table 2). On the opposite, PSO comes often back to the same solutions (portions of the search space), which is indicated by directed cycles in the STN.

Salomon Function. The Salomon function is another example of a function that is characterised by a big valley structure (like Quadric, for example). However, instead of being smooth, there are many ripples (see Fig. 1(d) and Fig. 1(e)). In each of these ripples we find numerous local minima of the same quality. The STN for this function (see Fig. 3(b)) nicely shows that both algorithms move rather quickly towards the global minimum. Then, however, they get often stuck in the last or in the second-last ripple. In fact, note that DE has a success rate of 80%, while PSO has a success rate of 30% (Table 2). The fact that both algorithms have difficulties in overcoming the last ripple before reaching the global minimum is shown in a zoomed visualisation of the merged STN shown in Fig. 4. Note that some of the green and grey dots located on that ripple are actually larger in size

Table 4. Normalised average distances of the end of the search trajectories from the global minimum of each considered function. The value of the algorithm that, on average, finishes closer to the global minimum is indicated in bold font.

Algorithm	Benchmark function				
	Michalewicz	Quadric	Rana	Salomon	Schwefel 2.26
DE	**2.305e−02**	5.702e−06	**8.080e−02**	**6.645e−04**	**4.637e−08**
PSO	6.426e−02	**7.947e−14**	5.058e−01	2.020e−03	1.752e−01

than the red dot representing the global minimum. This means that these nodes have more incoming edges than the global minimum node.

Schwefel 2.26 Function. From the 2D graphics of the considered functions in Fig. 1 it can be seen that Schwefel 2.26 is somewhat related to Rana, in the sense that there are rather high-quality basins of attraction scattered all over the search space. This observation goes in line with the fact that the end of the PSO trajectories are, on average, again much further away from the global minimum than the ones of DE (see Table 4). Moreover, studying the STN graphics from Fig. 3(c) it can be observed that there are four of the 10 PSO runs that converge to basins of attraction rather far away from the global minimum. Interestingly, three of these four runs are attracted by the same basin of attraction. Moreover, as in the case of Rana, the PSO trajectories are—in terms of the number of steps—longer than those of DE.

As a general conclusion we might say that for those functions with rugged landscapes and high-quality solutions scattered all over the search space, an algorithm with elitism and multiple attractors (as with DE/rand/1) seems to be more successful than an algorithm without elitism and a shared global attractor (as with global best PSO).

6   Conclusion

We proposed a network-based model to characterise and visualise the search behaviour of population-based metaheuristics: search trajectory networks (STNs). We tested the model by studying the search process of two well-known algorithms (DE and PSO) when optimising a set of continuous benchmark functions with different characteristics and dimensions. Our analysis illustrates that the qualitative (visualisations) and quantitative (network metrics) analysis of STNs give insight into the convergence behaviour of algorithms and their performance differences. STNs allow us to observe and quantify which portions of the search space attract the process and thus act as traps in the way of locating the global optimum. We can also identify frequently traversed areas of the search space by a given algorithm or pair of algorithms. We argue that this information gives new insights in understanding the dynamics of metaheuristics, and thus can be used to improve their design and to inform the selection of the most suitable algorithm for a given problem.

Future work will generalise the model to combinatorial optimisation and other metaheuristics, and will analyse real-world optimisation problems. We will also explore further case scenarios where intriguing performance differences among algorithms are observed, which can potentially be clarified with our proposed analysis.

References

1. Blum, C., Ochoa, G.: A comparative analysis of large neighborhood search and construct, merge, solve & adapt by means of merged local optima networks (submitted)
2. Blum, C., Roli, A.: Metaheuristics in combinatorial optimization. ACM Comput. Surv. **35**(3), 268–308 (2003)
3. Bosman, P., Engelbrecht, A.P.: Diversity rate of change measurement for particle swarm optimisers. In: Dorigo, M., et al. (eds.) ANTS 2014. LNCS, vol. 8667, pp. 86–97. Springer, Cham (2014). https://doi.org/10.1007/978-3-319-09952-1_8
4. Chicano, F., Whitley, D., Ochoa, G., Tinós, R.: Optimizing one million variable NK landscapes by hybridizing deterministic recombination and local search. In: Genetic and Evolutionary Computation Conference, GECCO 2017, pp. 753–760. ACM (2017)
5. Csardi, G., Nepusz, T.: The igraph software package for complex network research. Int. J. Complex Syst. **1695**, 1–9 (2006)
6. Eberhart, R., Kennedy, J.: A new optimizer using particle swarm theory. In: Proceedings of the Sixth International Symposium on Micromachine and Human Science, pp. 39–43 (1995)
7. Eberhart, R., Shi, Y.: Comparing inertia weights and constriction factors in particle swarm optimization. In: Proceedings of the IEEE Congress on Evolutionary Computation, vol. 1, pp. 84–88 (2000)
8. Eiben, A.E., Schippers, C.A.: On evolutionary exploration and exploitation. Fundam. Inform. **35**(1–4), 35–50 (1998)
9. Fruchterman, T.M.J., Reingold, E.M.: Graph drawing by force-directed placement. Softw. Pract. Exper. **21**(11), 1129–1164 (1991)
10. Herrmann, S., Ochoa, G., Rothlauf, F.: Pagerank centrality for performance prediction: the impact of the local optima network model. J. Heuristics **24**(3), 243–264 (2018)
11. Kamada, T., Kawai, S.: An algorithm for drawing general undirected graphs. Inf. Process. Lett. **31**(1), 7–15 (1989)
12. Kennedy, J., Eberhart, R.: Particle swarm optimization. In: Proceedings of the IEEE International Joint Conference on Neural Networks, pp. 1942–1948 (1995)
13. Mishra, S.K.: Performance of repulsive particle swarm method in global optimization of some important test functions: a Fortran program. Technical report, Social Science Research Network (SSRN), August 2006
14. Newman, M.E.J.: Networks: An Introduction. Oxford University Press, Oxford (2010)
15. Ochoa, G., Tomassini, M., Verel, S., Darabos, C.: A study of NK landscapes' basins and local optima networks. In: Genetic and Evolutionary Computation Conference, GECCO, pp. 555–562. ACM (2008)

16. Ochoa, G., Veerapen, N.: Deconstructing the big valley search space hypothesis. In: Chicano, F., Hu, B., García-Sánchez, P. (eds.) EvoCOP 2016. LNCS, vol. 9595, pp. 58–73. Springer, Cham (2016). https://doi.org/10.1007/978-3-319-30698-8_5

17. Olorunda, O., Engelbrecht, A.P.: Measuring exploration/exploitation in particle swarms using swarm diversity. In: 2008 IEEE Congress on Evolutionary Computation (IEEE World Congress on Computational Intelligence). IEEE, June 2008

18. Price, K.V., Storn, R.M., Lampinen, J.A.: Appendix A.1: Unconstrained uni-modal test functions. In: Price, K.V., Storn, R.M., Lampinen, J.A. (eds.) Differential Evolution: A Practical Approach to Global Optimization. Natural Computing Series, pp. 514–533. Springer, Berlin (2005). https://doi.org/10.1007/3-540-31306-0

19. Shi, Y., Eberhart, R.: A modified particle swarm optimizer. In: Proceedings of the 1998 IEEE World Congress on Computational Intelligence, pp. 69–73 (1998)

20. Sörensen, K.: Metaheuristics-the metaphor exposed. Int. Trans. Oper. Res. **22**(1), 3–18 (2013)

21. Storn, R., Price, K.: Minimizing the real functions of the ICEC'96 contest by differential evolution. In: Proceedings of the International Conference on Evolutionary Computation, pp. 842–844 (1996)

22. Thomson, S.L., Ochoa, G., Verel, S.: Clarifying the difference in local optima network sampling algorithms. In: Liefooghe, A., Paquete, L. (eds.) EvoCOP 2019. LNCS, vol. 11452, pp. 163–178. Springer, Cham (2019). https://doi.org/10.1007/978-3-030-16711-0_11

23. Veerapen, N., Ochoa, G., Tinós, R., Whitley, D.: Tunnelling crossover networks for the asymmetric TSP. In: Handl, J., Hart, E., Lewis, P.R., López-Ibáñez, M., Ochoa, G., Paechter, B. (eds.) PPSN 2016. LNCS, vol. 9921, pp. 994–1003. Springer, Cham (2016). https://doi.org/10.1007/978-3-319-45823-6_93

24. Verel, S., Ochoa, G., Tomassini, M.: Local optima networks of NK landscapes with neutrality. IEEE Trans. Evol. Comput. **15**(6), 783–797 (2011)

25. Yao, X., Liu, Y., Lin, G.: Evolutionary programming made faster. IEEE Trans. Evol. Comput. **3**(2), 82–102 (1999)

Evolving-Controllers Versus Learning-Controllers for Morphologically Evolvable Robots

Karine Miras[✉], Matteo De Carlo, Sayfeddine Akhatou, and A. E. Eiben

Vrije Universiteit Amsterdam, Amsterdam, Netherlands
k.s.m.a.dasilvamirasdearaujo@vu.nl

Abstract. We investigate an evolutionary robot system where (simulated) modular robots can reproduce and create robot children that inherit the parents' morphologies by crossover and mutation. Within this system we compare two approaches to creating good controllers, i.e., evolution only and evolution plus learning. In the first one the controller of a robot child is inherited, so that it is produced by applying crossover and mutation to the controllers of its parents. In the second one the controller of the child is also inherited, but additionally, it is enhanced by a learning method. The experiments show that the learning approach does not only lead to different fitness levels, but also to different (bigger) robots. This constitutes a quantitative demonstration that changes in brains, i.e., controllers, can induce changes in the bodies, i.e., morphologies.

Keywords: Morphological evolution · Life-time learning · Evolutionary Robotics · Modular robots

1 Introduction

In the field of Evolutionary Robotics, evolving the controllers of robots has been much more explored than evolving their morphologies [4,5]. This is not surprising, considering that the challenge of evolving both morphology and controller is much greater than evolving the controller alone. In case of the joint evolution of morphologies and controllers there are two search spaces and the search space for the controllers changes with every new robot morphology produced. This challenge was firstly explored in Sims' seminal work [15], and more recently in multiple studies [6,10,11,16].

In the present study we consider morphologically evolving robot populations. Our main goal is to investigate the effects of life-time learning in these populations. To this end, we set up a system where (simulated) modular robots can reproduce and create offspring that inherits the parents' morphologies by crossover and mutation. Regarding the controllers, we implement and compare two methods. Method 1 works by evolving the robot controllers. In this method, controllers are inheritable, where the controller of the offspring is produced by

© Springer Nature Switzerland AG 2020
P. A. Castillo et al. (Eds.): EvoApplications 2020, LNCS 12104, pp. 86–99, 2020.
https://doi.org/10.1007/978-3-030-43722-0_6

applying crossover and mutation to the controllers of the parents. In Method 2, controllers are not only inheritable (hence, evolvable), but also learnable. In this method, the controller of the offspring is produced by a learning method that starts with the inherited brain.

The specific research questions we are to answer here are as follows:

– How does life-time learning affect evolvability?
– How does life-time learning affect the morphological properties of the population?
– How does life-time learning drive the course of evolution?

2   Methodology

The datasets and code of this study are stored at ssh.data.vu.nl in the karinemiras-evostar2020 directory, and can be accessed given administrative request.

2.1   Morphology

We are using simulated robots based on RoboGen [2] whose morphologies ("morphologies") are composed of modules shown in Fig. 1. Any module can be attached to any other module through its attachable slots, except for the sensors, which can not be attached to joints. Our morphologies consist of a single layer, i.e., the modules do not allow attachment on the top or bottom slots, only on the lateral ones, but the joints can bend, so the robots can 'stand' in a 3D-shape. Each module type is represented by a distinct symbol in the genotype.

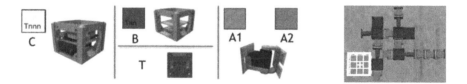

Fig. 1. At the left, the robot modules: Core-component with controller board (C); Structural brick (B); Active hinges with servo motor joints in the vertical (A1) and horizontal (A2) axes; Touch sensor (T). C and B have attachment slots on their four lateral faces, and A1 and A2 have slots on their two opposite lateral faces; T has a single slot which can be attached to any slot of C or B. The sequence of letters (T or n) in C and B indicate if there is a sensor on the laterals left, front, right and back (for C only), in this order. At the right, an example of robot in simulation.

2.2   Controller

The controller ("controller") is a hybrid artificial neural network, which we call Recurrent CPG Perceptron (Fig. 2, right).

For every joint in the morphology, there exists a corresponding oscillator neuron in the network, whose activation function is calculated through a Sine wave with three parameters: Phase offset, Amplitude, and Period. The oscillators are not interconnected, and every oscillator may or may not possess a direct recurrent connection. Additionally, every sensor is reflected as an input for the network, which might connect to one or more oscillators, having the weights of its connections ranging from -1 to 1. The CPG [9] generates a constant pattern of movement, even if the robot is not sensing anything, so that the sensors are used either to suppress or to reinforce movements.

Representation and Operators. We use an evo-devo style generative encoding to represent the robots. Specifically, our genomes –that encode both morphology and controller– are based on a Lindenmayer-System (L-system) inspired by [8]. The grammar of an L-System is defined as a tuple $G = (V, w, P)$, where

- V, the alphabet, is a set of symbols containing replaceable and non-replaceable symbols.
- w, the axiom, is a symbol from which the system starts.
- P is a set of production-rules for the replaceable symbols.

The following didactic example illustrates the process of iterative-rewriting of an L-System. For a given number of iterations, each replaceable symbol is simultaneously replaced by the symbols of its production-rule. Given $w = X$, $V = \{X, Y, Z\}$ and $P = \{X : \{X, Y\}, Y : \{Z\}, Z : \{X, Z\}\}$, the rewriting goes as follows.

$$\text{Iteration 0: } X$$

$$\text{Iteration 1: } XY$$

$$\text{Iteration 2: } XYZ$$

$$\text{Iteration 3: } XYZXZ$$

In our system each genotype is a distinct grammar in the syntax specified by the types of modules we have. The alphabet is formed by symbols denoting the morphological modules and commands to attach them together, as well as commands for defining the structure of the controller. The construction of a phenotype (robot) from a genotype (grammar) is done in two stages. In the first stage (early development), the axiom of the grammar is rewritten into a more complex string of symbols (intermediate phenotype), according to the production-rules of the grammar. (Here we set the number of iterations to 3). In the second stage (late development), this string is decoded into a phenotype. The second stage of this process is illustrated in Fig. 2. The first stage was omitted because it is somewhat extensive, but it follows work flow shown in the example above. During the second stage of constructing a phenotype two positional references are always maintained in it, one for the morphology (pointing to the current module) and one for the controller (pointing to the current sensor and the current oscillator). The application of the commands happens in the current module in the case of the morphology, while for the controller it happens in (or between) the current sensor and the current oscillator. More details about the representation can be found in [12,13].

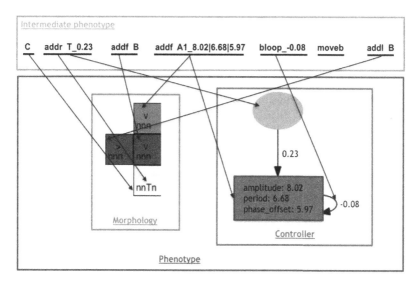

Fig. 2. Process of late development: decoding an intermediate phenotype into a (final) phenotype with morphology and controller.

The initialization of a genotype adds, to each production rule, one random (uniformly) symbol of each the following categories, in this order: Controller-moving commands, and Controller-Changing commands, Morphology-mounting commands, Modules, Morphology-moving commands. This can be repeated for r times, being r sampled from a uniform random distribution ranging from 1 to e. This means that each rule can end up with 1 or maximally e sequential groups of five symbols (here e is set to 3). The symbol C is reserved to be used exclusively at the beginning of the production rule C.

The crossovers are performed by taking complete production-rules randomly (uniform) from the parents. Finally, individuals undergo mutation by adding, deleting, or swapping one random (uniform) symbol from a random production-rule/position. All symbols have the same chance of being removed or swapped. As for the addition of symbols, all categories have equal chance of being chosen to provide a symbol, and every symbol of the category also has equal chance of being chosen. An exception is always made to C to ensure that a robot has one and only one core-component. This way, the symbol C is added as the first symbol of the C production rule, and can not be added to any other production rules, neither removed or moved from the production rule of C.

Once it is possible that only the rules of one single parent end up being expressed in the final phenotype, and also as it is not rare that one mutation happens for non-expressed genes, both crossover and mutation probabilities were set high, to 80%, aiming to minimize this effect.[1]

For practical reasons (simulator speed and physical constructability) we limit the number of modules allowed in a robot to a maximum of 100.

2.3 Morphological Descriptors

For quantitatively assessing morphological properties of the robots, we utilized the following set of descriptors:

1. **Size:** Total number of modules in the morphology.
2. **Relative Number of Limbs:** The number of extremities of a morphology relative to a practical limit. It is defined with Eq. (1)

$$L = \begin{cases} \frac{l}{l_{max}}, & \text{if } l_{max} > 0 \\ 0 & \text{otherwise} \end{cases}$$

$$l_{max} = \begin{cases} 2 * \lfloor \frac{(m-6)}{3} \rfloor + (m-6) \pmod 3 + 4, & \text{if } m \geq 6 \\ m-1 & \text{otherwise} \end{cases}$$

(1)

where m is the total number of modules in the morphology, l the number of modules which have only one face attached to another module (except for the core-component) and l_{max} is the maximum amount of modules with one face attached that a morphology with m modules could have, if containing the same amount of modules arranged in a different way (Fig. 3).

(a) Limbs: 0.5   (b) Limbs: 1

Fig. 3. Morphology (a) has four modules that could be extremities (considering the limit determined by the size of the morphology), but only the two indicated by green arrows are; (b) has the maximum number of extremities it could have. (Color figure online)

3. **Relative Length of Limbs:** The length of limbs relative to a practical limit. It is defined with Eq. (2):

$$E = \begin{cases} \frac{e}{e_{max}}, & \text{if } m \geq 3 \\ 0 & \text{otherwise} \end{cases}$$

(2)

---

[1] This means that around 80% of the offspring will be result of crossovers, and also that around 80% of the offspring will suffer the above explained mutation.

where m is the total number of modules of the morphology, e is the number of modules which have two of its faces attached to other modules (except for the core-component), and $e_{max} = m - 2$ – the maximum amount of modules that a morphology with m modules could have with two of its faces attached to other modules, if containing the same amount of modules arranged in a different way[2] (Fig. 4).

(a) Length of limbs: 0.67   (b) Length of limbs: 1

Fig. 4. While in morphology (b) the maximum possible quantity of modules was used as the extension of a limb, in (a), the module indicated by an orange arrow was used as an extra limb. (Color figure online)

4. **Proportion:** The length-width ratio of the rectangular envelope around the morphology. It is defined with Eq. (3):

$$P = \frac{p_s}{p_l} \tag{3}$$

where p_s is the shortest side of the morphology, and p_l is the longest side, after measuring both dimensions of length and width of the morphology (Fig. 5).

(a) Proportion: 0.2   (b) Proportion: 1

Fig. 5. Morphology (a) is disproportional and (b) is proportional.

A complete search space analysis of the utilized robot framework and its descriptors is available in [12,13], demonstrating the capacity of these descriptors to capture relevant robot properties, and proving that this search space allows high levels of diversity.

2.4   Evolution

We are using overlapping generations with population size $\mu = 100$. In each generation $\lambda = 50$ offspring are produced by selecting 50 pairs of parents through binary tournaments (with replacement) and creating one child per pair by crossover and mutation. From the resulting set of μ parents plus λ offspring, 100 individuals are selected for the next generation, also using binary tournaments. The evolutionary process is stopped after 30 generations, thus all together

---

[2] The types of modules would not have to be necessarily the same, as long as the morphology had the same amount of modules.

we perform 1.550 fitness evaluations per run. For each environmental scenario the experiment was repeated 10 times independently.

The task used was undirected locomotion, and the fitness utilized was the speed (cm/s) of the robot's displacement in any direction, as defined by Eq. 4.

$$s_x = \frac{e_x - b_x}{t} \qquad (4)$$

where b_x is x coordinate of the robot's center of mass in the beginning of the simulation, e_x is x coordinate of the robot's center of mass at the end of the simulation, and t is the duration of the simulation.

2.5 Learning

The life-time learning of the robots was carried out by optimizing the parameters of the oscillators of their controllers (Fig. 2, right) using the algorithm CMA-ES [7]. The μ (population size) and λ (offspring size) values are defined according to the dimension N of the controller (number of oscillators in the controller and its parameters), and is defined as with Eqs. 5 and 6, respectively.

$$\lambda = 4 + \lfloor 3 \times log(N) \rfloor \qquad (5)$$

$$\mu = \lfloor \lambda/2 \rfloor \qquad (6)$$

These parameters were chosen based on [7], and the maximum number of evaluations was set to be at least 100. Because not always λ is a divisor of 100, some runs can have a few more evaluations than that.

Given that we decided to experiment with evolution-only versus learning-only, the initial mean and standard deviation of the multivariate normal distributions were defined randomly, instead of derived from the parameters that the L-System defines.

2.6 Experimental Setup

All experiments were carried out on a plane flat floor with no obstacles. While the morphologies were evolving in all of the experiments, we tested two different methods for optimizing controllers: Method 1 works by evolving the robot controllers. In this system, controllers are inheritable, whereas the controller of the offspring is produced by applying crossover and mutation to the controllers of the parents. We refer to this method as Evolvable throughout the paper. In Method 2, controllers are not only inheritable (hence, evolvable), but also learnable. In this method, the controller of the offspring is produced by a learning method that starts with the inherited brain. We refer to this method as Learnable throughout the paper.

3   Results and Discussion

3.1   Evolvability and the Production Costs

As expected, adding a life-time learning capacity to the system increased the speed of the population, as depicted by Figs. 6 and 7. This was expected for two reasons: (a) the number of evaluations performed by Learnable is around 100 times higher than by Evolvable; (b) in Learnable, robots have time to fine-tune their controllers to the morphologies they were born with.

On the other hand, while the average speed of Learnable seems to be going to flatten soon, the average speed of Evolvable keeps growing. Nevertheless, this is not the aspect we are interested in discussing. Instead, we are interested in observing which method presents a faster growth of the average speed. In Fig. 6, the black line shows that around generation 9, Learnable had already obtained an average speed that took the whole evolutionary period, i.e., 30 generations, for Evolvable to achieve. Of course, we should not neglect that, as previously mentioned, Learnable at generation 9 had already spent around 55.000 evaluations, while at the final generation Evolvable spent only 1.550. However, we should consider that Learnable at generation 9 created only 550 robots while Evolvable created 1.550, i.e., around 3 times more. If we consider real physical robots, and assuming that the production cost of each robot is substantially higher than the evaluation cost, we can clearly see the advantage of introducing learning. For instance, the evaluation cost could be around 30 s and creation cost around 4 h. In this case, Evolvable would take 327.775 min versus 159.500 min for Learnable, representing a difference of 116 days.

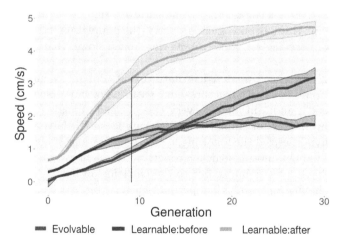

Fig. 6. Speed: progression of the mean of the population (quartiles over all runs). Black lines mark generation (9), when the Learnable method (after learning) achieved the levels of speed that the Evolvable method managed to achieve only in the end of the evolutionary period

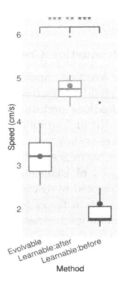

Fig. 7. Comparison of speed in the final generations. The method Learnable:before is equivalent to a random controller. Significance levels for the Wilcoxon tests in the boxplots are $* < 0.05$, $** < 0.01$, $* * * < 0.001$, while NS means non-significant.

3.2   Morphological Properties

In [12], a study utilizing this same robot framework observed a strong selection pressure for robots with few limbs, most often one single long limb, i.e., a snake-like morphology. Furthermore, they demonstrated that by explicitly adding a penalty to having this morphological property, the population did indeed develop multiple limbs, nevertheless, these robots were much slower than the single-limb ones.

Interestingly, we have observed in nature that "for many animals, natural selection may tend to favor structures and patterns of movement that increase maximum speed", and, "in almost every case, legged animals can move faster over land than animals of similar size that lack legs" [1]. Given such notions, in [12] it was hypothesized the following, concerning few long limbs having shown to be a predominant morphological property: "it might be due, not to some advantage of having fewer limbs, but to the challenge of having multiple limbs. For example, having one limb that permits locomotion is a challenge in itself, while having multiple limbs not only multiplies this challenge but also carries an additional challenge of synchronization, to avoid limbs pulling in different directions and impairing displacement. Perhaps adding a life-time learning ability to the robots would allow them to learn how to use their limbs better and obtain higher speed."

Though such a hypothesis seems plausible, our experiments have proven it wrong. Figures 8 and 9 show the comparison between the methods for the emergent morphological properties in the population. We see that the average Num-

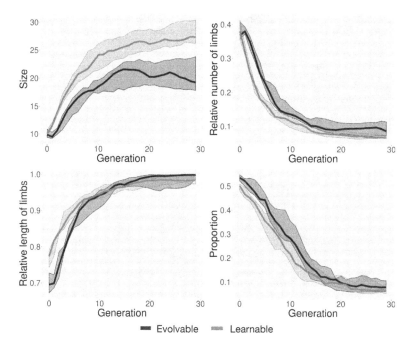

Fig. 8. Morphological properties: progression of the mean of the population (quartiles over all runs).

bers of Limbs, Length of Limbs, and Proportion in Learnable converge to non significantly different values than in Evolvable. In summary, with both methods, the population converged to big, disproportional robots that have few, long limbs (Fig. 10).

Despite all these similarities, there was one morphological property that showed to be different, i.e., Size, so that robots in Learnable are significantly bigger than in Evolvable. A video showing examples of robots from both types of experiments can be found in https://www.youtube.com/watch?v=szwZvJnEfYw.

3.3   Morphological Exploitation Through Learning

In Fig. 11 we see that the average learning Δ of the method Learnable, i.e., average speed after the parameters were learned minus average speed before the parameters were learned, grows across the generations. This growth is rather quick up to generation 15, from when becomes more moderate. Not coincidentally, it is also from generation 15 that the curves of the average morphological properties started to flatten out. These observations suggest that the life-time learning led the evolutionary search to more quickly exploit the high performing morphological properties. In other words, it was faster for the population to turn into morphologies that are big, disproportional, with few, long limbs.

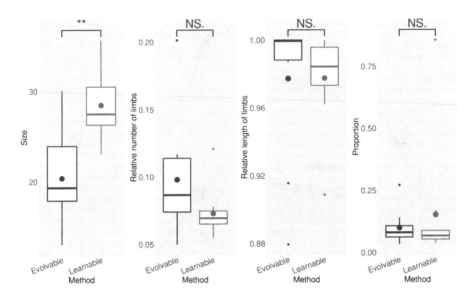

Fig. 9. Comparison between the morphological properties in the final generations. Significance levels for the Wilcoxon tests in the boxplots are $* < 0.05$, $** < 0.01$, $*** < 0.001$, while NS means non-significant.

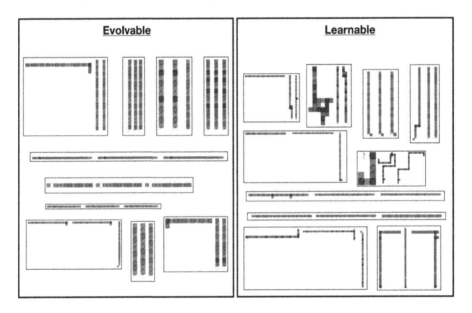

Fig. 10. The three best robots of each run for both control methods. Figures were scaled to fit the frame.

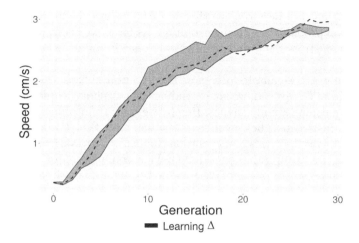

Fig. 11. Learning Δ, i.e., average speed after the parameters were learned minus average speed before the parameters were learned. Progression of the mean of the population (quartiles over all runs).

4   Conclusions and Future Work

The main goal of this paper was to investigate the effects of life-time learning in populations of morphologically evolving robots. To this end, we have set up a system where (simulated) modular robots can reproduce and create offspring that inherits the parents' morphologies by crossover and mutation. In this system we implemented two options to produce controllers (for the task of locomotion). In the evolutionary method controllers are inheritable, where the controller of the offspring is produced by applying crossover and mutation to the controllers of the parents. In the learning method controllers of the offspring are also inheritable, but additionally, they are fine-tuned by a learning algorithm (specifically, we employed the CMA-ES as a learner). Conducting experiments with both methods we obtained answers to our research questions.

Firstly, if we measure time by the number of generations, learning boosts evolvability in terms of efficiency as well as efficacy, i.e., solution quality at termination, once its growth curve was steeper and ended higher than that of the evolutionary method. Of course, this is not a surprise, since the learning version performs much more search steps. However, a learning trial (testing another controller) is much cheaper than an evolutionary trial (making another robot), so we can firmly conclude the advantage of adding lifetime-learning to an evolutionary robot system.

Secondly, we have witnessed a change in the evolved morphologies when lifetime learning was applied. In particular, the sizes at the end of evolution were clearly different (while the shapes were not). We find this the most interesting outcome because it is the opposite of the well-known effect of how the body shapes the brain [14]. Our results show how the brains can shape the bodies through affecting task performance that in turn changes the fitness values that define selection probabilities during evolution. As far as we know, previously this has been demonstrated and documented only once in an artificial evolutionary context [3].

For future work, we aim to look more deeply into the "how the brain shapes the body" effect. To this end, we are extending the morphological search space by allowing more complex body shapes. Hereby we hope to introduce more regions of attraction in the morphological search space, such that the snakes are not the most dominant life forms and evolution can converge to various shapes. Last but not least, we are working on a Lamarckian combination of evolution and life-time learning, where (some of) the learned traits are inheritable.

References

1. Alexander, R.M.: Principles of Animal Locomotion. Princeton University Press, Princeton (2003)
2. Auerbach, J., et al.: RoboGen: robot generation through artificial evolution. In: Artificial Life 14: Proceedings of the Fourteenth International Conference on the Synthesis and Simulation of Living Systems, pp. 136–137. The MIT Press (2014)
3. Buresch, T., Eiben, A.E., Nitschke, G., Schut, M.: Effects of evolutionary and lifetime learning on minds and bodies in an artificial society. In: Proceedings of the IEEE Conference on Evolutionary Computation (CEC 2005), pp. 1448–1454. IEEE Press (2005). http://www.cs.vu.nl/~schut/pubs/Buresch/2005.pdf
4. Doncieux, S., Bredeche, N., Mouret, J.B., Eiben, A.: Evolutionary robotics: what, why, and where to. Frontiers Robot. AI **2**, 4 (2015)
5. Floreano, D., Husbands, P., Nolfi, S.: Evolutionary robotics. In: Siciliano, B., Khatib, O. (eds.) Springer Handbook of Robotics, Part G. 61, pp. 1423–1451. Springer, Heidelberg (2008). https://doi.org/10.1007/978-3-540-30301-5_62
6. Hamann, H., Stradner, J., Schmickl, T., Crailsheim, K.: A hormone-based controller for evolutionary multi-modular robotics: from single modules to gait learning. In: 2010 IEEE World Congress on Computational Intelligence, WCCI 2010 - 2010 IEEE Congress on Evolutionary Computation, CEC 2010 (2010)
7. Hansen, N., Akimoto, Y., Brockhoff, D., Chan, M.: CMA-ES/pycma: r2.7.0, April 2019. https://doi.org/10.5281/zenodo.2651072
8. Hornby, G.S., Pollack, J.B.: Body-brain co-evolution using L-systems as a generative encoding. In: Proceedings of the 3rd Annual Conference on Genetic and Evolutionary Computation, pp. 868–875. Morgan Kaufmann Publishers (2001)
9. Ijspeert, A.J.: Central pattern generators for locomotion control in animals and robots: a review. Neural Netw. **21**(4), 642–653 (2008)
10. Jelisavcic, M., Kiesel, R., Glette, K., Haasdijk, E., Eiben, A.: Analysis of Lamarckian evolution in morphologically evolving robots. In: Artificial Life Conference Proceedings, vol. 14. pp. 214–221. MIT Press (2017)
11. Marbach, D., Ijspeert, A.J.: Co-evolution of configuration and control for homogenous modular robots. In: Proceedings of the Eighth Conference on Intelligent Autonomous Systems (IAS8), pp. 712–719 (2004)
12. Miras, K., Haasdijk, E., Glette, K., Eiben, A.E.: Effects of selection preferences on evolved robot morphologies and behaviors. In: Proceedings of the Artificial Life Conference, Tokyo (ALIFE 2018). MIT Press (2018)

13. Miras, K., Haasdijk, E., Glette, K., Eiben, A.E.: Search space analysis of evolvable robot morphologies. In: Sim, K., Kaufmann, P. (eds.) EvoApplications 2018. LNCS, vol. 10784, pp. 703–718. Springer, Cham (2018). https://doi.org/10.1007/978-3-319-77538-8_47
14. Pfeifer, R., Bongard, J.: How the Body Shapes the Way We Think: A New View of Intelligence. MIT Press, Cambridge (2006)
15. Sims, K.: Evolving 3D morphology and behavior by competition. Artif. Life $\mathbf{1}(4)$, 353–372 (1994)
16. Sproewitz, A., Moeckel, R., Maye, J., Ijspeert, A.J.: Learning to move in modular robots using central pattern generators and online optimization. Int. J. Robot. Res. $\mathbf{27}(3\text{--}4)$, 423–443 (2008)

Simulation-Driven Multi-objective Evolution for Traffic Light Optimization

Alessandro Cacco[ID] and Giovanni Iacca[(✉)][ID]

Department of Information Engineering and Computer Science,
University of Trento, 38123 Povo, Italy
alessandro.cacco@studenti.unitn.it, giovanni.iacca@unitn.it

Abstract. The constant growth of vehicles circulating in urban environments poses a number of challenges in terms of city planning and traffic regulation. A key aspect that affects the safety and efficiency of urban traffic is the configuration of traffic lights and junctions. Here, we propose a general framework, based on a realistic urban traffic simulator, SUMO, to aid city planners to optimize traffic lights, based on a customized version of NSGA-II. We show how different metrics -such as number of accidents, average speed of vehicles, and number of traffic jams- can be taken into account in a multi-objective fashion to obtain a number of Pareto-optimal light configurations. Our experiments, conducted on two city scenarios in Italy and different combinations of fitness functions, demonstrate the validity of this approach and show how evolutionary optimization is an effective tool for traffic light optimization.

Keywords: Traffic light optimization · Simulation of urban mobility · Multi-objective evolutionary algorithm

1 Introduction

Almost every day, we experience long waits at traffic lights or, even worse, we get stuck in traffic jams. In fact, the ever growing number of cars has made road congestion a phenomenon that is almost impossible to control, especially in larger cities where, even in the presence of efficient public transport, cars are still the preferred choice for private mobility. A recent study from the European Union reported that congestion in the EU costs nearly *100 billion* EUR, or 1% of the EU's GDP, annually[1]. It has been estimated that in 2017 in Europe, where over 60% of the population lives in urban areas of over 10,000 inhabitants and urban mobility accounts for 40% of all CO2 emissions of road transport, an average driver spent in congestion, over a period of 220 working days, a number of hours ranging between 45.73 (UK) and 18.13 (Finland)[2].

---

[1] Source: https://ec.europa.eu/transport/themes/urban/urban_mobility_en.

[2] Data collected by TomTom: https://ec.europa.eu/transport/facts-fundings/scoreboa rd/compare/energy-union-innovation/road-congestion_en.

© Springer Nature Switzerland AG 2020
P. A. Castillo et al. (Eds.): EvoApplications 2020, LNCS 12104, pp. 100–116, 2020.
https://doi.org/10.1007/978-3-030-43722-0_7

These numbers speak for themselves: road congestion is a substantial problem in terms of economy, safety and drivers' comfort, which makes the question of how to enhance urban mobility, while at the same time reducing congestion, accidents and pollution, one of the greatest challenges of our time.

To handle this problem, the traditional approach is to use decentralized (self-regulated) traffic lights, or queue-based models based on traffic statistics. In this sense, the traffic light timing settings are usually tested *live*, and then adjusted *a posteriori* based on the traffic statistics. However, not only this way of managing the problem is expensive and time consuming, but also it can also create confusion in drivers, who would find that the road configurations change over time. Thus, this solution might cause even more congestion and accidents, exacerbating the problem or jeopardizing the safety on the streets.

Here, we tackle this problem by performing computer simulations coupled with numerical optimization. In particular, we focus on how to define the optimal traffic light configuration for controlling the crossroads (in the following, we will refer to them interchangeably also as junctions, or intersections) in a certain area of interest, taking into account different traffic densities (to model time-variant traffic conditions) and different contrasting goals. We model this problem in terms of multi-objective optimization, that we solve *in silico* by means of a realistic mobility simulator, SUMO [1,2], coupled with the well-known multi-objective evolutionary algorithm NSGA-II [3]. The latter is configured with custom mutation/crossover operators capable to handle our solution representation, which encompasses various parameters of traffic junctions and traffic lights timings.

Our approach continues a research path initially opened in [4], a seminal paper where a (single-objective) evolutionary algorithm (EA) was tested for the first time -although in a limited experimental setup- in connection with the microscopic traffic simulator FLEXSYT-II [5], to optimize traffic light timings.

Later research has further investigated the use of Evolutionary Algorithms for traffic optimization, with most of the existing studies being limited to single-junction optimization, and differing mainly for the kind of traffic simulation adopted. For instance, a microscopic simulation approach base on Cellular Automata was proposed in [6–8], coupled with a standard Genetic Algorithm (GA). A custom Matlab simulator was implemented instead in [9], where a GA was used to optimally control in "real-time" (i.e., during the traffic light operations) the light timings. A simplified, custom simulator was also used with a GA in [10], while a more realistic traffic simulator called Traffic Simulator Framework (TSF) was used in [11].

More recently, two works by Nguyen et al. [12] and Bravo et al. [13] used for the first time SUMO in connection with EAs to perform traffic light optimization. In fact, these two papers inspired our work. In particular, in [12] SUMO was coupled with a memetic version of NSGA-II (including a local search algorithm) to improve the anytime behavior of the evolutionary algorithm. The main difference w.r.t. our work is that in [12] only one objective (the no. of vehicles entering and leaving the simulation scenario) was related to a specific domain goal, being the other simply the simulation time: in other words, there was no actual domain multi-objective optimization. Furthermore, in [12] the experimental setup consisted of a single urban map, where the traffic lights in only one junction were tuned by the EA. Here, we instead tune the traffic lights of *all* the junctions in a certain area of interest (potentially, an entire city), which makes the problem space much larger and more difficult to explore. This kind of holistic approach is indeed more similar to the one -named HITUL- proposed by Bravo et al. [13], who for the first time called for a shift from traditional junction-local control to global control approaches based on advanced computational resources and techniques. This concept was implemented in [13] by connecting SUMO with a single and multi-objective EA, and tested it on a large-scale scenario in Málaga.

Our work here follows a similar approach: despite the increased computational complexity, as shown in [13] optimizing simultaneously all the junctions in a certain area of interest -thus leveraging synergistic effects between multiple junctions' traffic lights- makes it possible to provide high-quality solutions even in the most complex traffic scenarios that characterize modern urban mobility. However, while our work shares a several similarities with the paper by Bravo et al. [13], we further improve upon their work in at least two main aspects:

- We consider multiple traffic densities *at the same time*, i.e. we look for solutions that are robust against multiple traffic conditions (while in [13] one traffic profile at a time is considered: this feature represents a major novelty of our framework w.r.t. previous works).
- We implement a fully customizable mechanism to combine multiple objectives in a robust optimization fashion: with our framework, the user can for instance decide to optimize w.r.t. the worst or average traffic conditions, reducing the variance of the objectives across various conditions, etc. This feature -that we deem as crucial in practical contexts- is not present in [13].

Finally, we conduct an extensive experimental analysis on two areas of Trento and Milan, Italy, having very different topologies and sizes, thus showing the flexibility of our framework to different city scenarios.

The rest of the paper is organized as follows. Section 2 describes the proposed framework. Section 3 presents the experimental setup and the numerical results. Finally, Sect. 4 concludes this work.

2   Proposed Framework

The impact of traffic lights on road performance is strongly related to the specific road network configuration. For instance, different speed limits, lane directions, potential reservations etc. may heavily influence the traffic flow. Furthermore, performance indicators can also be specific, depending on the scenario road types (i.e., arterial, urban, suburban roads) and on particular needs (e.g. reduce incidents or emissions in a certain area).

The fundamental idea of our framework is to account for these aspects by using a microscopic traffic simulator, namely SUMO [1,2], and connect it to a

multi-objective evolutionary algorithm, NSGA-II [3], in order to optimize the
traffic junction and light configurations in a certain area of interest w.r.t. user-
defined fitness functions (and combinations thereof). In the next sections, we
describe the details of the proposed framework.

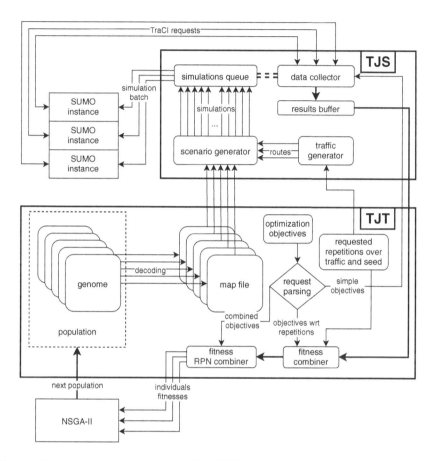

Fig. 1. The framework architecture. The TJS module manages the batch-execution
of multiple SUMO simulation instances and provides the data needed for the fitness
evaluations. The TJT module acts as an interface between NSGA-II and the simulator.

2.1 Framework Architecture

An overview of the architecture is shown in Fig. 1, where the main components
are represented:

– *Traffic Junction Tuner (TJT)*: builds the initial generation, translates each
  candidate solution generated by the NSGA-II module to make it available

in SUMO, collects the fitness values to allow user-defined combinations, and provides the combined fitness functions to the NSGA-II module.
- *Traffic Junction Tuner - SUMO tools (TJS)*: provides a batch-execution interface for the SUMO simulator, abstracting the TraCI [14] APIs to launch and advance simulations, and gathering all the performance information needed for the fitness evaluation of a scenario. Moreover, it exposes the *NETCONVERT* and *randomTrips* SUMO tools, needed to prepare the scenario and generate synthetic traffic, respectively.
- *SUMO* [1,2]: the microscopic traffic scenario simulator.
- *NSGA-II* [3]: the algorithm module, based on the *inspyred* Python library [15].

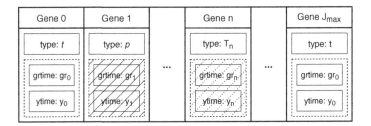

Fig. 2. Graphical representation of the genome. The type T_n of a gene can either be p or t. Genes with type p maintain the traffic light timings values inactive. The length of the genome corresponds to the total number of junctions in the scenario.

2.2   Solution Representation

The individuals composing the population that NSGA-II optimizes are particular instances of the input map. Specifically, each traffic junction corresponds to a specific gene in the genome of an individual, which can either be of type p or t: in the former case, the corresponding junction is based on standard priority[3], in the latter case the gene corresponds to a traffic light. This solution representation is based on some fundamental simplifications, which considerably reduce the overall complexity of the optimization process:

- A traffic junction can only be of type t or p. Roundabouts, zip merges and other junction types are not considered, being converted to an allowed type during the initialization.
- Traffic light phases apply to an entire edge incoming to a junction, meaning that dedicated light phases for specific lanes are not possible (e.g. no right-turn preferential lanes).

---

[3] Vehicles on a low-priority edge have to wait until vehicles on a high-priority edge have passed the junction.

– Each edge incoming to a junction has a dedicated traffic light phase. Each edge has its own phase and no combinations are allowed (e.g. the classic four-way 2-phases traffic light cannot be modeled).

Additionally, a t gene carries additional parameters, namely *grtime* and *ytime*, corresponding to the traffic light timings for green and yellow lights. A graphical representation of the genome is shown in Fig. 2.

2.3   Mutation and Crossover Operators

At the first generation, individuals are randomly generated with randomized junction types and random timings within the allowed boundaries. Subsequent generations are manipulated via *ad-hoc* mutation and crossover operators. When an individual is randomly selected for mutation, each of its genes is subject to mutation with a certain probability mr, to generate an offspring I_i as follows:

– The junction type may switch from t to p (or vice versa) if:

$$\sigma_{I_i} \times \rho_{I_i} > 1, \quad \rho_{I_i} \sim \mathcal{N}(0,1) \tag{1}$$

where σ_{I_i} (initialized to 1) is a hyper-parameter that adaptively decreases over the generations until it reaches a threshold $\epsilon = 0.01$ (see [16]).
– The traffic light timings can change by a random amount (even in the case of a junction type p, where they will be ignored) as follows:

$$grtime'_{I_i} = grtime_{I_i} + 10 \times \tau^g_{I_i}, \quad \tau^g_{I_i} \sim \mathcal{N}(0,1) \tag{2}$$
$$ytime'_{I_i} = ytime_{I_i} + 10 \times \tau^y_{I_i}, \quad \tau^y_{I_i} \sim \mathcal{N}(0,1) \tag{3}$$

As for crossover, it is applied with probability cr on two randomly selected individuals (I_i and I_j), to generate two offspring I_k obtained as follows:

– For each junction, the type is randomly inherited from one of the parents, with an equal probability;

Table 1. Main parameters of the evolutionary algorithm.

Parameter	Description
mr	Probability of a mutation happening on a selected individual (0.5)
cr	Probability of crossover happening on two selected individuals (0.5)
$[gr_{min}, gr_{max}]$	Time boundaries for the green light, enforced in initialization, mutations and crossover ($[1, 40]$ s)
$[y_{min}, y_{max}]$	Time boundaries for the yellow light, enforced in initialization, mutations and crossover ($[1, 40]$ s)
N_{pop}	Population size (50)
N_{gen}	Number of generations (50)

– The traffic light timings are computed as a randomized weighted average of the parents' values:

$$grtime_{I_k} = w^g_{I_k} \times grtime_{I_i} + (1 - w^g_{I_k}) \times grtime_{I_j}, \quad w^g_{I_k} \sim U(0,1) \quad (4)$$
$$ytime_{I_k} = w^y_{I_k} \times ytime_{I_i} + (1 - w^y_{I_k}) \times ytime_{I_j}, \quad w^y_{I_k} \sim U(0,1) \quad (5)$$

A summary of the algorithm parameters is reported in Table 1.

2.4   Simulations and Data Collection

In order to evaluate each individual in SUMO, its genome is decoded into a pair of *.nod* and *.tll* files, containing respectively the junctions types and the traffic light logics (i.e., phases definitions). These files are then loaded by the TJS module in order to generate a *.net* scenario file, along with the necessary amount of *.rou* files, containing synthetic traffic routes with a given *period*[4]. Further information about SUMO files can be found in the SUMO documentation [17]. In our framework, every individual is then simulated in SUMO with various traffic densities, and for each density multiple times with different seeds (every time with randomly generated vehicle routes). For what concerns the vehicle model, only a standard automobile model has been considered, as per the SUMO default vehicle controller *carFollowing-Krauss*, a modification of the original Krauß controller [18], please refer to the SUMO documentation for further details.

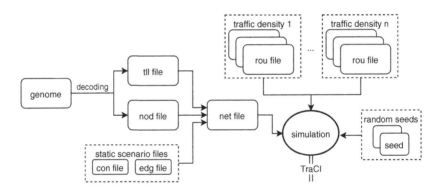

Fig. 3. Simulation flow of a single individual. The genome is decoded into a *.tll* and a *.nod* file, which are then combined with a *.con* connection file and a *.edg* file, representing how the road segments are connected to junctions. The simulations are therefore performed on an individual final scenario file *.net*.

---

[4] By default, this generates vehicles with a constant period and arrival rate of 1/period per second. By using values below 1, multiple arrivals per second can be achieved. Routes are generates such that a new vehicle with a random path and destination is inserted at a certain starting position every *period* seconds, determining a certain average traffic density.

Table 2. Main parameters of the simulation process.

Parameter	Description
traffic-rates	List of traffic *periods* for the synthetic traffic generation. These values are representative of the expected traffic on the scenario (e.g. at different times of the day) (1.5 s, 2 s, 2.5 s)
random-routes	No. of random vehicle routes sets (i.e. *.rou* files) to generate and simulate on the scenario, for each value of *traffic-rates* (5)
single-route-repetition	No. of simulation repetitions to perform for each value of *traffic-rates*, with different random seeds (3)
end	Simulation duration, used also for routes generation (1 h)
step-size	Simulation time-step (1 s)

The simulation flow is represented in Fig. 3, while Table 2 describes the main parameters of the simulation process.

2.5   Optimization Objectives

The fitness evaluation is based on information gathered via the TraCI API available in SUMO: information about simulation events are retrieved at every simulation step by TJS, to be later combined into the final individual fitness vector considering all traffic densities, routes sets and seed repetitions. Specifically, *simple objectives* (*SO*) can be defined as:

$$
\begin{aligned}
fit_k^{id} &\in \{arrived, accidents, teleported, avg\_speed, var\_speed\} \\
T_k^{RR} &\in \{H, L, M, V\} \\
T_k^{TR} &\in \{H, L, M, V\} \\
SO_k &= T_k^{TR} \, T_k^{RR} \, fit_k^{id}
\end{aligned}
\tag{6}
$$

with fit^{id} being the original value collected via TraCI (see Table 3), and T^{RR} and T^{TR} specifying how to combine the information from the different repetitions (Highest, Lowest, Mean, Variance), respectively for routes sets and traffic densities. Additionally, some of the TraCI-collected values can be normalized prior to be combined, according to the rules in Table 3. It should be noted that the framework can be easily extended to collect further TraCI data, for instance about fuel consumption or emissions.

Simple objectives are then combined into an *objective definition* O_j, which consists of an identifier ϕ_j and a valid reverse polish notation (RPN) expression of *SO*, operators in RPN_{ops}, and real numbers:

Table 3. Fitness request identifiers available in TJS.

Identifier (fit_{id})	Description	Normalization
arrived	Number of vehicles which were able to complete their entire route and arrive at their final destination	Arrived over departed vehicles ratio
accidents	Number of vehicles which were involved in an accident. Note that crashed vehicles are removed from the simulation according to SUMO standard logic	Crashed over departed vehicles ratio
teleported	As specified in the SUMO documentation [17], the default behavior for a vehicle in a traffic jam is to "teleport" to the next edge of its route (as such, it can be used as a proxy to measure congestion). The *teleported* identifier keeps track of the number of teleports that happened during the execution. Note that a vehicle may teleport multiple times in the same simulation	Number of teleports over 10 times the departed vehicles
avg_speed	Average speed of all the vehicles in the scenario throughout all the simulation duration	Average speed over 2 times the maximum speed limit of the scenario
var_speed	Speed variance of all the vehicles in the scenario throughout all the simulation duration	N.A

$$RPN_{ops} = \{+, -, \times, /, min, Max\}$$
$$tk_j^i \in \{SO_0\ SO_1\ \dots\ SO_s\} \cup RPN_{ops} \cup \mathbb{R}$$
$$\phi_j \in \{+, -, *\} \tag{7}$$
$$O_j = \phi_j[tk_j^0\ tk_j^1\ \dots\ tk_j^n]$$

An objective (as handled by NSGA-II) is then given by the evaluation of the corresponding RPN expression on the SO values of the individuals. The ϕ symbol specifies whether the objective has to be maximized, minimized, or just saved without using it as fitness, respectively with $+$, $-$ and $*$. An example of valid notation of (semicolon separated) objectives is as follows:

$+[MMarrived\ 2\ *]$; $-[HMteleported\ MMaccidents\ *\ 10\ /]$; $-[HHaccidents]$.

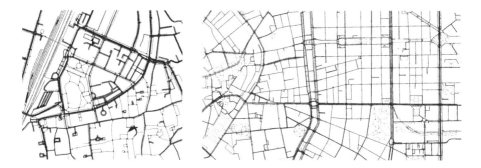

Fig. 4. Urban maps used in the experiments: Trento (left), Milan (right).

Table 4. Objective configurations used in the experiments.

id	Scenario	Objectives	Normalization
TN0	Trento	−[MMteleported]; −[HHaccidents]; +[MMarrived]	Yes
TN1	Trento	−[MMteleported]; −[HHaccidents]; +[MMarrived]; *[VMarrived]; *[VMteleported]	No
TN2	Trento	−[MMteleported 2 *]; −[HHaccidents]; +[MMarrived]; −[VMarrived]; −[VMteleported]	Yes
MI0	Milan	−[MMteleported]; −[HHaccidents]; +[MMarrived]; *[VMarrived]; *[VMteleported]	Yes
MI1	Milan	−[MMteleported]; −[HHaccidents 20 *]; +[MMarrived]; *[VMarrived]; *[VMteleported]	Yes

3   Numerical Results

We have extensively tested the proposed framework on two different maps, respectively of Trento and Milan city center (see Fig. 4). These map files have been obtained from OpenStreetMap [19] and automatically converted to the SUMO compatible XML files via the NETCONVERT tool. The objective configurations are shown in Table 4. The main difference between the two scenarios are the number of traffic junction to optimize, and the map complexity: Trento has 998 junctions in a smaller space, with many curves and links, while Milan has 3776 junctions that are farther apart, along mostly straight perpendicular roads. Trento is more challenging from in terms of synergy across junctions, whereas on Milan the algorithm must explore a much larger search space.

All the experiments have been executed on an Intel® i9-7940X@3.10 GHz 14 cores-28 threads CPU with 64 GB RAM, running Ubuntu 18.10. The SUMO simulations has been performed in parallel, to take advantage of the processor multi-threading capabilities. All code and numerical results are available as Supplementary Information online[5].

---

[5] https://github.com/alecacco/Traffic-Junction-Tuner.

For both the scenarios, first we ran 50 test simulations on the original junction configuration, in order to compare the results of the individuals fitness with this *reference scenario*. It should be noted that the simplifications made in Sect. 2.2 for the genome encoding does not apply to these original maps, so in this case the traffic is able to exploit preferential lanes and dedicated light phases, making the comparison biased against the evolving individuals. In the next two sections we will see the details results of the evolutionary algorithm on the two scenarios.

3.1   Trento Optimization Runs

The TN0 boxplots (Fig. 5), matrix plots (Fig. 6) and parallel coordinates plot (Fig. 7) clearly show how the fitness improves over the generations, eventually reaching a performance similar to the *reference scenario* (shown in gray in the matrix and parallel coordinate plots). Similar results (not shown here for brevity) have been achieved with TN1 and TN2, with even better results in the former. Interestingly, an improvement over the non-fitness data (i.e., metrics that are not explicitly optimized by the evolutionary algorithm), *[VMarrived];*[VMteleported], has also been observed in TN1: this highlights how the optimization collaterally reduced the performance difference across different traffic densities. On the other hand, while TN2 objectives included explicitly the optimization of these parameters, the best individuals didn't perform as well as the best ones of TN1 (this might be due to a more difficult identification of Pareto-optimal solutions with an increased number of objectives). Additionally, TN2 progress was slower, also probably due to the higher number of objectives.

Overall, the TN experiments can be considered successful, especially considering the complexity of the Trento scenario, our simplifications in the model, and their direct impact on traffic junction synergies.

3.2   Milan Optimization Runs

Due to the characteristics of the Milan scenario, individuals are expected to evolve slower than the ones in the case of Trento. In fact, this behavior has been observed in the MI0 and MI1 runs, still achieving interesting results: the boxplots in Fig. 8 show how the fitness values improve over the generations, while the matrix plot in Fig. 9 gives more insights on the progress w.r.t. the reference scenario (shown in gray). As it can be observed in the latter the reference is almost outperformed by the best evolved individuals. The parallel coordinates plot (Fig. 10) also show how the evolution progressed towards the reference fitness, reaching it and outdoing at the last generation.

The difference between MI0 and MI1 runs is the second objective (as stated in Table 4), which in the former case caused the decrease of accidents to be less significant, while in the latter the *20* * factor better guided the optimization, reaching the reference *HHaccidents* fitness.

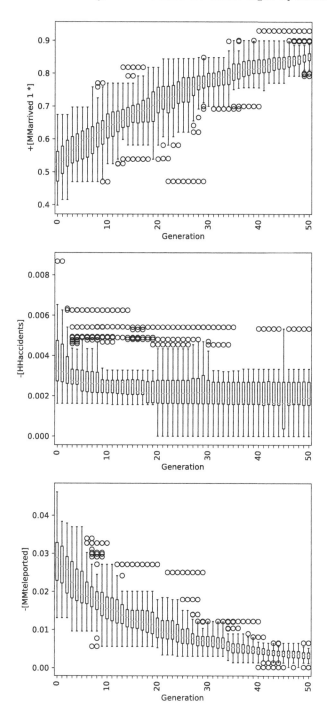

Fig. 5. TN0 scenario: generational plot. Each boxplot represents the distribution of the objective function value within a generation.

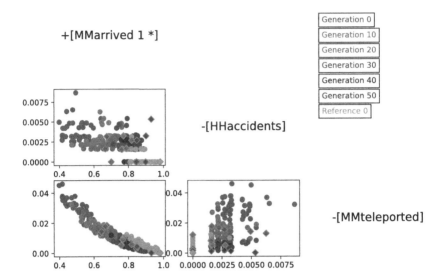

Fig. 6. TN0 scenario: matrix plot. The labels on the diagonal indicate the x axis of the plots in the same column and the y axis of the plots in the same row. The diamond markers indicate the final Pareto-optimal solutions.

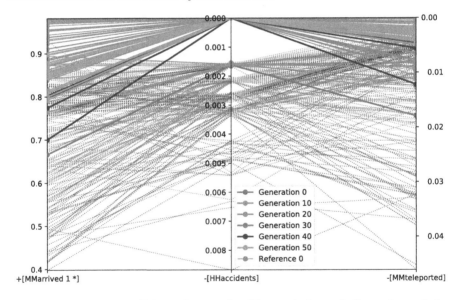

Fig. 7. TN0 scenario: parallel coordinates plot. The vertical axes indicate the optimization objectives, while the connected lines represent the fitness of each individual. The Pareto-optimal solution (at each generation) and the reference solutions are highlighted with thicker lines.

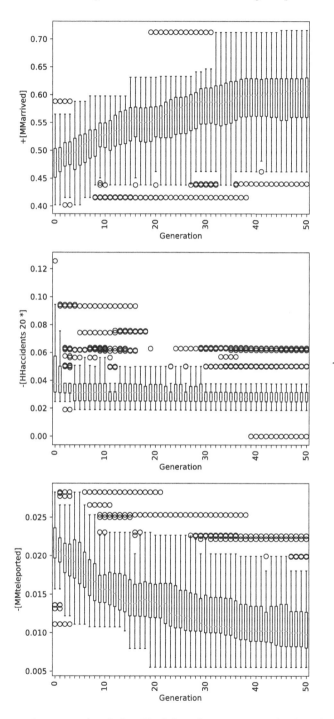

Fig. 8. MI1 scenario: generational plot. Each boxplot represents the distribution of the objective function value within a generation.

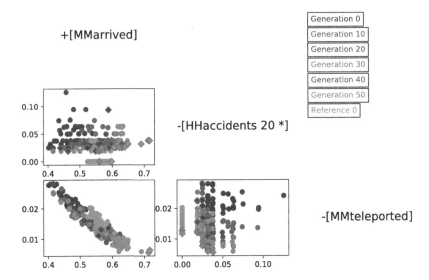

Fig. 9. MI1 scenario: matrix plot. The labels on the diagonal indicate the x axis of the plots in the same column and the y axis of the plots in the same row. The diamond markers indicate the final Pareto-optimal solutions.

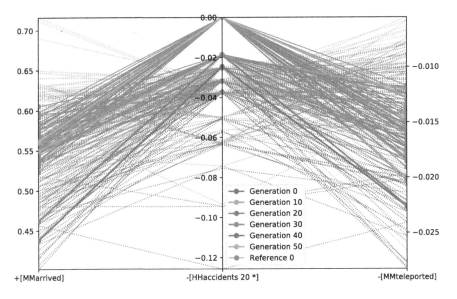

Fig. 10. MI1 scenario: parallel coordinates plot. The vertical axes indicate the optimization objectives, while the connected lines represent the fitness of each individual. The Pareto-optimal solution (at each generation) and the reference solutions are highlighted with thicker lines.

Overall, the MI runs achieved satisfying results, in particular considering the scale of the scenario and, again, the simplification that has been made on the genome encoding.

4   Conclusions

In this paper we presented a general framework for traffic light optimization. The framework couples a realistic simulator for urban mobility, SUMO, with a multi-objective Evolutionary Algorithm based on NSGA-II. We tested the framework on two city maps with various combinations of optimization goals, taking into account the robustness of each solution (i.e., a traffic light configuration generated by NSGA-II) w.r.t. different levels of traffic density. This latter aspect shows how the tool can be applied in practical urban scenarios with time-variant traffic density, giving the user the possibility to optimize e.g. w.r.t. the worst or the average density scenarios.

Our results provided a number of interesting insights on the possible trade-off solutions that can be obtained on the two maps, taking into account conflicting goals. Furthermore, they showed the flexibility of the proposed framework, that has been designed such that it can be easily extended to additional goals and arbitrary combinations thereof.

In future works, we will include into our framework the possibility to take into account different types of vehicles (such as buses, trams, bicycles, etc.), each with its own traffic behavior and density. In addition to that, we will focus our attention on more detailed intersection models, and test the framework on larger and more complex city maps. As for what concerns the algorithmic details, we will try to investigate alternative mutation/crossover operators, in order to characterize their behavior, and compare single vs multi-objective evolutionary algorithms as well as incremental local search methods.

Finally, we will consider the possibility to provide our framework as a Software-as-a-Service, available to the general public and the local administrators in order to make better informed city plan choices.

Acknowledgments. We thank Andrea Ferigo for his contribution to a preliminary implementation of the framework proposed in the paper.

References

1. Krajzewicz, D., Erdmann, J., Behrisch, M., Bieker, L.: Recent development and applications of SUMO - Simulation of Urban MObility. Int. J. Adv. Syst. Meas. **5**(3&4), 128–138 (2012)
2. Lopez, P.A., et al.: Microscopic traffic simulation using SUMO. In: International Conference on Intelligent Transportation Systems, pp. 2575–2582 (2018)
3. Deb, K., Pratap, A., Agarwal, S., Meyarivan, T.: A fast and elitist multiobjective genetic algorithm: NSGA-II. IEEE Trans. Evol. Comput. **6**(2), 182–197 (2002)

4. Taale, H., Bäck, T., Preuss, M., Eiben, A., De Graaf, J., Schippers, C.: Optimizing traffic light controllers by means of evolutionary algorithms. In: European Congress on Intelligent Techniques and Soft Computing, vol. 3, pp. 1730–1734 (1998)
5. Taale, H., Middelham, F.: FLEXSYT-II-A validated microscopic simulation tool. IFAC Proc. Vol. **30**(8), 883–888 (1997)
6. Sanchez, J.J., Galan, M., Rubio, E.: Genetic algorithms and cellular automata: a new architecture for traffic light cycles optimization. In: Congress on Evolutionary Computation, vol. 2, pp. 1668–1674. IEEE (2004)
7. Turky, A.M., Ahmad, M.S., Yusoff, M.Z.M.: The use of genetic algorithm for traffic light and pedestrian crossing control. Int. J. Comput. Sci. Netw. Secur. **9**(2), 88–96 (2009)
8. Turky, A.M., Ahmad, M.S., Yusoff, M.Z.M., Hammad, B.T.: Using genetic algorithm for traffic light control system with a pedestrian crossing. In: Wen, P., Li, Y., Polkowski, L., Yao, Y., Tsumoto, S., Wang, G. (eds.) RSKT 2009. LNCS (LNAI), vol. 5589, pp. 512–519. Springer, Heidelberg (2009). https://doi.org/10.1007/978-3-642-02962-2_65
9. Singh, L., Tripathi, S., Arora, H.: Time optimization for traffic signal control using genetic algorithm. Int. J. Recent Trends Eng. **2**(2), 4–6 (2009)
10. Teo, K.T.K., Kow, W.Y., Chin, Y.: Optimization of traffic flow within an urban traffic light intersection with genetic algorithm. In: International Conference on Computational Intelligence, Modelling and Simulation, pp. 172–177. IEEE (2010)
11. Gora, P.: A genetic algorithm approach to optimization of vehicular traffic in cities by means of configuring traffic lights. In: Ryżko, D., Ryńbiski, H., Gawrysiak, P., Kryszkiewicz, M. (eds.) Emerging Intelligent Technologies in Industry. SCI, vol. 369, pp. 1–10. Springer, Heidelberg (2011). https://doi.org/10.1007/978-3-642-22732-5_1
12. Nguyen, P.T.M., Passow, B.N., Yang, Y.: Improving anytime behavior for traffic signal control optimization based on NSGA-II and local search. In: International Joint Conference on Neural Networks, pp. 4611–4618. IEEE (2016)
13. Bravo, Y., Ferrer, J., Luque, G., Alba, E.: Smart mobility by optimizing the traffic lights: a new tool for traffic control centers. In: Alba, E., Chicano, F., Luque, G. (eds.) Smart-CT 2016. LNCS, vol. 9704, pp. 147–156. Springer, Cham (2016). https://doi.org/10.1007/978-3-319-39595-1_15
14. API TraCI. https://sumo.dlr.de/docs/TraCI.html
15. inspyred. https://pypi.python.org/pypi/inspyred
16. Garrett, A.: inspyred: bio-inspired algorithms in Python (2015)
17. SUMO. https://sumo.dlr.de/docs
18. Krauß, S.: Microscopic modeling of traffic flow: investigation of collision free vehicle dynamics. Ph.D. thesis, Dt. Zentrum für Luft-und Raumfahrt eV, Abt. Unternehmensorganisation und-information (1998)
19. OpenStreetMap. https://www.openstreetmap.org

Automatic Generation of Adversarial Metamorphic Malware Using MAP-Elites

Kehinde O. Babaagba[(✉)] [ID], Zhiyuan Tan[ID], and Emma Hart[ID]

School of Computing, Edinburgh Napier University, Edinburgh EH10 5DT, UK
{K.Babaagba,Z.Tan,E.Hart}@napier.ac.uk

Abstract. In the field of metamorphic malware detection, training a detection model with malware samples that reflect potential mutants of the malware is crucial in developing a model resistant to future attacks. In this paper, we use a Multi-dimensional Archive of Phenotypic Elites (MAP-Elites) algorithm to generate a large set of novel, malicious mutants that are diverse with respect to their behavioural and structural similarity to the original mutant. Using two classes of malware as a test-bed, we show that the MAP-Elites algorithm produces a large and diverse set of mutants, that evade between 64% to 72% of the 63 detection engines tested. When compared to results obtained using repeated runs of an Evolutionary Algorithm that converges to a single solution result, the MAP-Elites approach is shown to produce a significantly more diverse range of solutions, while providing equal or improved results in terms of evasiveness, depending on the dataset in question. In addition, the archive produced by MAP-Elites sheds insight into the properties of a sample that lead to them being undetectable by a suite of existing detection engines.

Keywords: Metamorphic malware · MAP-Elites · Machine-learning

1 Introduction

The proliferation of malicious attacks on networked devices and internet infrastructures at large has become a source of concern for companies and cybersecurity researchers. These attacks often emanate from a vast range of malicious groups. One of such dangerous groups is metamorphic malware. These malware transform their code between generations using various obfuscation techniques thereby making detection difficult. These techniques include the insertion of junk code into the original program code i.e. garbage code insertion, renaming variables in the original program code a process calling variable renaming among others. [3] provides a comprehensive list of such techniques used by metamorphic malware.

One recent approach to improving detection of metamorphic malware is through the use of *adversarial learning* [11]: these approaches generate new malicious input data (attacks) that reveals vulnerabilities in the detection models,

© Springer Nature Switzerland AG 2020
P. A. Castillo et al. (Eds.): EvoApplications 2020, LNCS 12104, pp. 117–132, 2020.
https://doi.org/10.1007/978-3-030-43722-0_8

then improve detection models as a result. Adversarial learning has received significant attention from cybersecurity experts recently for malware analysis and detection as it gives insights to researchers on the processes malware writers use in generating malware [7,12,17].

However, the search for adversarial samples which comprise of several variants of malware can be a difficult task as it involves the traversal of a large search space of potential malicious variants. In addition, in order to drive improvements in detection models, it is desirable to create as many new samples as possible for a model to learn from, and furthermore, that the samples are as *diverse* as possible to improve model generality. A number of evolutionary algorithms (EA) have been proposed in the past to generate adversarial samples, for example in the domains of pdf-malware [19] and in android malware [1,2]. However, these algorithms generate only a single new sample with each run of the algorithm: given that most machine-learning approaches require large amounts of training data, not only is it time-consuming to generate multiple samples in this way, but in addition, there is no guarantee that the samples will be diverse. Furthermore, existing methods do not provide much insight into the properties of the generated samples.

To address this, we propose a solution that generates a *set* of variants that are *diverse* with respect to two features, the Structural Similarity (SS(x)) and Behavioral Similarity (BS(x)) of the variants with respect to the original malware. Specifically, we apply a quality-diversity algorithm—MAP-Elites [13]—to generate a set of diverse variants that are optimised with respect to their ability to evade a large set of well-known detection engines. MAP-Elites algorithm traverses a high-dimensional search space in search of the best solution at every point of a feature space with low dimension defined by the user and is one of a new raft of quality-diversity optimisation algorithms [14] that aim to return an archive of diverse, high-quality behaviors in a single run. The algorithm has multiple documented successes in evolutionary robotics [13], but also in design applications, car wing-mirror design [8].

We address two questions in this paper:

1. How does diversity of samples produced by running MAP-Elites algorithm compare to repeated executions of the standard Evolutionary algorithm described in [2] and in Sect. 2?
2. How does the evasiveness of samples produced by MAP-Elites algorithm compare to repeated executions of a standard Evolutionary algorithm?

The contributions of the paper is three-fold. To the best of our knowledge, this is the first use of an illumination algorithm to generate a diverse set of adversarial samples of mutant malware. The approach is rigorously evaluated in terms of the number of samples generated, their evasiveness, and their diversity with respect to two features that measure the behavioural and structural similarity to the original malware. Secondly, we provide a comparison to results obtained by running a single evolutionary algorithm multiple times in order to generate a set of variants [2], comparing the same metrics as above. Results show that MAP-Elites generates larger, more diverse sets of variants than the EA, while retaining approximately the same levels of performance (in terms of the evasiveness of the samples generated). Finally, we provide novel insights into the factors that contribute to evasiveness, based on the results obtained from the illumination algorithm.

The rest of the paper is structured as follows. Section two presents a background of the work and reviews related works presenting distinguishing points between this work and the related works. In section three, we present our methodology. Our experimental design is explained in section four. We discuss and analyse our results in section five. Section six concludes the paper and provides areas of future research work.

2   Background

Previous research has been geared towards creating evasive malware that goes undetected by antivirus engines and other detectors. One of the pioneering systems used to assess the ability of antivirus engines in detecting evasive malware is ADAM [20]. This system automatically transforms an original malware sample to different variants via repackaging and obfuscation techniques in order to evaluate the robustness of different detection systems against malware mutation. Similar to the work of [20] is DroidChameleon [16] which extends [20] by considering more advanced forms of attacks including metamorphic and polymorphic attacks.

Recently, the use of evolutionary computing as a technique in the generation of evasive malware has been explored by a number of authors. Genetic Programming (GP) was used by [19] to create pdf malware that evades detection by pdf detectors while retaining their malicious functionality. [1] used GP to create a single malware variant that maximised an evasiveness score when presented to 8 detection engines, however the characteristics of the evolved malware were not considered. In addition, it is likely that many distinct variants could map to the same fitness value, given that the fitness function takes one of only 9 distinct values.

Inspired by this work, we recently proposed a mutation only EA [2] for generating adversarial samples. Our work advanced that of [1] in (1) evaluating a set of new fitness functions that optimised for behavioral and structurally diverse variants as well as for evasiveness and (2) extended the evaluation to a much larger set of 63 detection engines. However in both this work and prior work of [1], it was necessary to run the evolutionary engine multiple times to generate a set of samples. While the work presented in [2] was shown in fact to lead to some diversity across multiple runs, this cannot be guaranteed.

On contrast, the MAP-Elites algorithm was explicitly designed with the goal of providing multiple high-performing solutions that are diverse with respect to a user-defined feature-space [13]. The seminal paper showed that the technique can illuminate the close links between performance and interesting features in the search space as well as creating diverse and high quality solutions. Following the initial work in the robotics domain, the algorithm has found application in other domains such as video games, with the introduction of MAP-Elites with Sliding Boundaries (MESB)[5] showing MAP-Elites ability to discover varying and diverse styles of playing the game, and in the combinatorial optimisation domain in evolving delivery schedules in a feature-space that includes carbon-emissions and staff-costs [18].

Here, we use MAP-Elites algorithm in the malware analysis domain to generate new malicious variants that evade current detectors and are structurally and behaviourally dissimilar to their parent malware. As far as we are aware, this is the first time that this algorithm has been used in the exploration of the search space of malware.

3   Methodology

In this section, we describe the malware mutant generator that uses MAP-Elites algorithm to generate an archive of highly evasive but diverse mutants that can be used as future training data by a machine-learning model.

3.1   MAP-Elites Algorithm

The algorithm is given in Algorithm 1. First, an empty archive is created as a two-dimensional grid defined by two features: the behavioural similarity and the structural similarity of a solution to the original malware. The grid is divided in 20×20 equally sized cells: these are created by equally "binning" the range of each feature (which take values between 0 and 1), thereby creating a potential archive of 400 solutions. The algorithm is then initialised with a random population of mutants, each created by applying a single mutation to the original malware. After calculating the feature descriptor for the mutant (see Sect. 3.2), the mutant is mapped to the corresponding cell in the archive.

Mutants are generated by applying a single mutation to an existing malware by selecting a mutation operator at random from the following list:

- Garbage Code Insertion (GCI) - This inserts a piece of junk code, e.g. a line number into the original program code.
- Instructional Reordering (IR) - This adds a goto statement in the original program code that jumps to a label that does nothing.
- Variable Renaming (VR) - This renames a variable with another valid variable name in the original program code.

As the original malware is in the form of an executable *apk file*, to create mutants we first reverse engineer the apk by converting it to a *smali* format using apktool[1]. Thereafter, we execute the following steps:

1. Apply a mutation operator to the smali code.
2. Recompile the smali to apk in order to test that the variant created is executable.

---

[1] APKTOOL - http://ibotpeaches.github.io/Apktool.

3. Sign the recompiled apk using apksigner[2] and align using zipalign[3].
4. Calculate the feature descriptor of the mutant.
5. Calculate the fitness of the mutant (detection-rate).

Subsequent solutions are created by random selection from the elites in the map. Upon selecting each random elite, they are also mutated by applying a randomly selected mutation operator from the list given above. New mutants are placed in the archive if the corresponding cell is empty *or* replace an existing solution in a cell if their fitness is better than the existing solution.

Algorithm 1. MAP-Elites algorithm for mutant generation, modified from [13]

 1: **procedure** MAP-ELITES(I, G)
 2:     $(\mathcal{E} \leftarrow \phi, \mathcal{X} \leftarrow \phi)$ ▷ N-dimensional map of elites: mutants $\mathcal{X}$ and their evasiveness $\mathcal{E}$
 3:     **for** iter $= 1 \rightarrow \mathcal{I}$ **do**   ▷ Repeat for I iterations
 4:         **if** iter $> \mathcal{G}$ **then** ▷ Initialize by generating G random solutions created by mutating original malware
 5:             $x' \leftarrow random\_solution()$
 6:         **else**   ▷ Subsequent solutions are generated from elites in the map
 7:             $x \leftarrow random\_selection(\mathcal{X})$▷ Randomly select an elite x from the map $\mathcal{X}$
 8:             $x' \leftarrow random\_mutation(x)$ ▷ Create a mutant of x
 9:         **end if**
10:         **if** $executable(x')$ **then**   ▷ Confirm that mutated solution compiles and executes
11:             $b' \leftarrow feature\_descriptor(x')$ ▷ Calculate and record the behavioral and structural similarity between x' and the original malware
12:             $e' \leftarrow evasiveness(x')$ ▷ Record the evasiveness e' of x'
13:             **if** $\mathcal{E}(b') = \phi$ or $\mathcal{E}(b') > e'$ **then** ▷ If the appropriate cell is empty or its occupants's evasiveness is $>=$ e', then
14:                 $\mathcal{E}(b') \leftarrow e'$ ▷ store the value for evasiveness of x' in the map of elites according to its feature descriptor b'
15:                 $\mathcal{X}(b') \leftarrow x'$ ▷ store the solution x' in the map of elites according to its feature descriptor b'
16:             **end if**
17:         **else**
18:             delete x'
19:         **end if**
20:     **end for**
21:     **return** feature-evasiveness map ($\mathcal{E}$ and $\mathcal{X}$)
22: **end procedure**

---
[2] APKSIGNER - https://developer.android.com/studio/command-line/apksigner.
[3] ZIPALIGN - https://developer.android.com/studio/command-line/zipalign.

3.2   Feature Descriptor

The feature descriptor of the mutants is defined by the behavioural and structural similarity between the original malware and a mutant. A *behavioural signature* of the mutant is derived from monitoring its system calls using Strace[4] using Monkeyrunner[5] to simulate user interaction. This creates a behavioural signature represented as a vector of 251 elements, each corresponding to the frequency of 251 possible system calls made by the mutant. The behavioural similarity between the original malware and the mutant is calculated as the cosine similarity between the two system call vectors, returning a value between 0 and 1, where the former indicates that the original malware and the mutant share no behavioral similarity while 1 means the original malware and the mutant have equivalent behaviour.

The *structural similarity* between the mutants and the original malware is measured using both text based and code level similarity metrics. The text based similarity measures the cosine similarity, fuzzy string match [4] and Levenshtein distance [10] between the original malware and the mutant. The code level similarity on the other hand, uses the jplag and sherlock plagiarism detectors [9] and normalised compression distance [15] in computing the similarity between the original malware and the mutant. The similarity metrics are then *averaged*, returning a value from 0 to 1 where 0 means the original malware and the mutant are completely dissimilar and 1 means they are the same. These metrics are chosen following previous work by [15].

3.3   Fitness Evaluation

The fitness of a mutant is measured in terms of its ability to evade a set of well known detection engines. Mutants are evaluated using Virustotal[6] which comprises of 63 up-to-date antivirus engines and reports how many of its engines flags a sample as malicious. The fitness measures the *detection-rate*, i.e. the percentage of the antivirus engines that *fail* to detect a mutant. A detection-rate of 0 denotes that no engine detected the variant while a value of 1 denotes all the engines detected the mutant. The problem is thus treated as a *minimisation* problem.

4   Experimental Design

The dataset utilised in this work is the Contagio Minidump[7] which comprises of mobile malware archived as APKs collected between the period of December

---

[4] Strace - https://linux.die.net/man/1/strace.

[5] Monkeyrunner - https://developer.android.com/studio/test/monkey.

[6] Virustotal - https://developers.virustotal.com/reference#getting-started.

[7] Contagio Minidump - http://contagiominidump.blogspot.com/2015/01/android-hideicon-malware-samples.html.

2011 and March 2013. We randomly select two samples belonging to two families from this dump to serve as the parent malware. The parent malware chosen belong to Dougalek[8] and Droidkungfu[9] family. Dougalek family is known for stealing personal information from mobile phone users such as the user's account details or contacts. The Droidkungfu family on the other hand is known for privilege escalation and unauthorised remote control of mobile phones. Experiments are conducted separately on each family.

To assess the quality of the MAP-Elites based mutant generator, we compare its performance against that of an EA proposed in [2] for the same task. The EA in [2] is a classical EA which uses a single objective performance-based fitness function to drive evolution with no regard to features of the resulting solutions. The EA is referred to from here on as *MAL_EA*. MAL_EA is a steady-state EA that uses same mutation operators as the MAP-Elites based mutant generator and no crossover. It uses tournament selection and replaces the worst solution in the population with the best solution produced in the tournament provided that it is better than the worst solution. The reader is referred to [2] for a detailed description of this algorithm and parameter settings. The parameters used are given in Table 1. The parameters used in MAL_EA were derived following empirical analysis. For MAP-Elites on the other hand, two of its parameters namely, selection and mutation rate are standard settings from previous literature. However, as a result of the computational cost involved in running the experiments, we limit the number of iterations to 120. The number of bootstrap iterations is then set proportionally.

Table 1. Evolutionary based parameter settings

MAL_EA		MAP-Elites	
Parameter	Setting	Parameter	Setting
Selection	Tournament	Selection	Random selection
Population size	20	Bootstrap	20
Iterations	120	Iterations	120
Mutation rate	1	Mutation rate	1

To compare between the MAL_EA method proposed in [2] and the new MAP-Elites approach proposed here, we use four standard metrics for measuring algorithm performance which include global performance, coverage, reliability and precision, taken from [13].

Global performance (Eq. 1) computes for each run, the fitness of the single best performing solution s divided by the fitness of the best solution S possible. Following the approach described in previous literature, as the theoretical

---

[8] Dougalek - https://www.trendmicro.com/vinfo/us/threat-encyclopedia/malware/androidosdougalek.a.

[9] Droidkungfu - https://www.f-secure.com/v-descs/trojan_android_droidkungfu_c.shtml.

optimum is unknown, we take the value for the best solution possible to be the single best solution obtained from any run of either algorithm. This is given as:

$$Global\ Performance = \frac{s}{S} \tag{1}$$

Coverage (Eq. 2) measures how many cells of the feature space a run of an algorithm is able to fill of the total number that are possible to fill. For a single map, it is defined as number of filled cells $n(f_c)$ in the map divided by the total number of cells that theoretically could be filled. As this number is generally unknown, it is approximated by counting the total number of unique cells that have been filled considering all runs of all algorithms $n(F_c)$. Coverage is therefore an indicator of diversity.

$$Coverage = \frac{n(f_c)}{n(F_c)} \tag{2}$$

The *reliability* metric measures for each run, the closeness of the best solution found for each cell to the best possible performance for that cell, averaged over the whole map. As above, as the best possible performance is unknown, the value is approximated as the best solution obtained for the cell from any run of any algorithm. Supposing that $M_{x,y}$ represents the highest performing solution found from all runs of the algorithm for both MAP-Elites and MAL_EA at coordinate x, y. Assuming that $M = m_1...m_k$ is a vector which contains the final performance map derived from every run of the algorithm for both MAP-Elites and MAL_EA. Then

$$M_{x,y} = \max_{\{i \in [1,...,k]\}} m_i(x,y) \tag{3}$$

The reliability of a performance map m is given as:

$$Reliability = \frac{1}{n(M)} \sum_{x,y} \frac{m_{x,y}}{M_{x,y}} \tag{4}$$

where $x,y \in \{[x_{min},...,x_{max}; y_{min},...,y_{max}]\}$, and $n(M)$ is count of unique cells filled by any run of the algorithm for both MAP-Elites and MAL_EA.

Precision is similar to reliability but for a single run, averages only the performance of only cells that were filled for that run and provides an indication of how high-performing a solution is relative to what is possible for that cell.

The precision of a performance map m is given as:

$$Precision = \frac{1}{n(M)} \sum_{x,y} \frac{m_{x,y}}{M_{x,y}} \tag{5}$$

for $x,y \in \{[x_{min},...,x_{max}; y_{min},...,y_{max}]\}|filled_m(x,y) = 1$, where $filled_m(x,y) = 1$ is a matrix that takes on either value 1 in an (x,y) cell if the algorithm generated a solution in that cell or 0 otherwise and where $n(M)$ is count of unique cells filled by any run of the algorithm for both MAP-Elites and MAL_EA.

Note that the standard definition of these metrics assumes a maximisation problem, therefore in order to calculate these values, we define performance as (1-*detection_rate*), using the definition of *detection_rate* given in Sect. 3.3, i.e. a solution that was not detected by any of the antivirus engines has a performance of 1.

To ensure a fair comparison, we run each algorithm for exactly same number of fitness evaluations, i.e. 120. In the case of MAP-Elites, this includes boot-strapping with $\mathcal{G} = 20$ iterations (step 4 of the Algorithm 1) and then running for 100 more iterations (step 6 on-wards). 10 repeated runs are performed, each returning an archive of solutions.

For the EA comparison experiments, as in [2], a population size of 20 is used. The EA was run 10 times with each of the three fitness functions defined in [2], the first optimising directly for evasiveness, the second optimising for behavioral similarity and the third for structural similarity. Each run results in a single solution, giving 30 variants in total which are then combined into a single archive. The feature descriptor b is calculated for each of these 30 variants as described above so that the results can be directly compared with MAP-Elites.

5   Results and Analysis

Here, we first provide a qualitative comparison between the MAP-Elites based mutant generator and the EA from [2]. Then, using the metrics described in Sect. 4, we carry out a quantitative comparison. We then provide additional analysis to gain insights into which of the anti-virus engines prove weakest in failing to detect the evolved variants.

5.1   Qualitative Comparison of MAP-Elites and MAL_EA

Figures 1 and 2 show the maps obtained from merging the repeated runs of (a) the EA and (b) MAP-Elites for both Dougalek and Droidkungfu families. The x and y axes are defined by the selected feature descriptors, i.e. the behavioral (BS(x)) and structural similarity (SS(x)) between the original malware and the mutants respectively. A value of 0 for each axis indicates 0% similarity and 1 represents a 100% similarity between the original malware and the mutants. The color bar represents the detection rates (DR(x)) of the mutants with a value of 0 meaning 0% of detectors detected the variants and 1 meaning 100% of detectors detected the variants. For both the x and y axes as well as the detection rates, the lower the values, the better. Hence, the lighter the shade of the filled cells in the map, the better.

It is obvious from Fig. 1 that MAP-Elites generates a larger archive of solutions than MAL_EA for the Dougalek family. Although the solutions from both algorithms cover approximately the same *range* for each feature, the MAL_EA map is sparsely occupied with the 30 solutions obtained from the multiple runs filling only 12 cells: this indicates a lack of diversity with respect to the two features obtained from multiple runs of the EA. In contrast, MAP-Elites finds

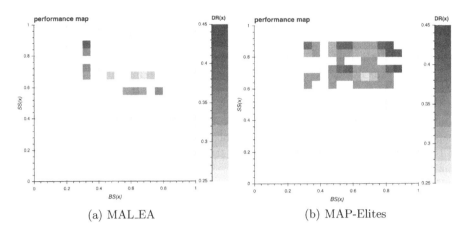

(a) MAL_EA   (b) MAP-Elites

Fig. 1. Performance map of MAL_EA and MAP-Elites for Dougalek family

50 solutions that are evenly distributed along the range of each feature. Similar observations apply to the Droidkungfu archives shown in Fig. 2. Although the range of the structural similarity feature extends more widely in the MAL_EA archive than that observed in the MAP-Elites archive, MAP-Elites finds solutions that are distributed more consistently across the range, as opposed to the more sparse distribution found by MAL_EA. For this malware, the 30 solutions obtained by MAL_EA occupy only 14 cells, again in stark contrast to that of MAP-Elites which finds a diverse set of solutions occupying 44 cells.

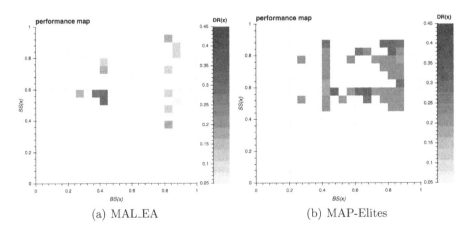

(a) MAL_EA   (b) MAP-Elites

Fig. 2. Performance map of MAL_EA and MAP-Elites for Droidkungfu family

Table 2. The table shows the median results obtained for the 4 metrics on each dataset. Values in bold indicate the best performing algorithm where the difference between the medians is statistically significant (at a level of 0.05).

		Performance	Coverage	Reliability	Precision
Dougalek	MAP-Elites	**0.94**	**0.5**	**0.48**	0.96
	MAL_EA	0.92	0.06	0.06	0.97
Droidkungfu	MAP-Elites	0.85	**0.49**	**0.46**	0.94
	MAL_EA	0.86	0.07	0.07	**0.97**

5.2 Quantitative Comparison of MAP-Elites and MAL_EA

In Figs. 3 and 4, we show the performance of both MAP-Elites and MAL_EA in terms of the global performance, coverage, reliability and precision metrics for both Dougalek and Droidkungfu families. Mann-Whitney U tests with a 95% confidence interval are used to determine statistical significance. Table 2 provides a summary of the median results derived for the 4 metrics on each dataset. Values are given in bold where the p-value indicates significance at a confidence level of 0.05. Where neither values is shown in bold, the significance test failed to reject the null hypothesis that the distributions are different.

We see from Table 2 that for Dougalek, MAP-Elites does significantly better than MAL_EA in terms of global performance, reliability and coverage. For *precision* however, the significance tests fails to reject the null hypothesis that the distributions are different.

For Droidkungfu, MAP-Elites performs significantly better than MAL_EA for coverage and reliability. In terms of global performance, the significance test failed to reject the null hypothesis that the distributions are different. In terms of the precision metric, MAL_EA outperforms MAP-Elites with the statistical test showing this difference is significant, i.e. when MAL_EA is able to fill a cell, it reliably finds a high-performing solution for the cell.

Table 3. Fitness of the best, median and worst variants produced by MAP-Elites and MAL_EA, where fitness is defined by the detection-rate, i.e. the percentage of detectors that recognise the variant as malicious. Hence, 0 represents a failure of all 63 detectors.

Parameter	Dougalek		Droidkungfu	
	MAP-Elites	MAL_EA	MAP-Elites	MAL_EA
Best	0.28	0.28	0.18	0.06
Median	0.32	0.34	0.2	0.19
Worst	0.33	0.46	0.21	0.33
Original malware	0.6		0.35	

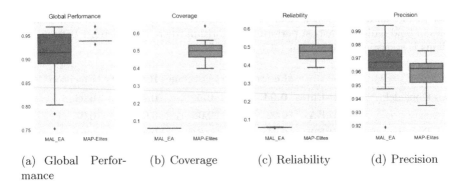

(a) Global Perfor-   (b) Coverage   (c) Reliability   (d) Precision
mance

Fig. 3. Boxplots of Global Performance, Coverage, Reliability and Precision for MAL_EA and MAP-Elites for Dougalek family

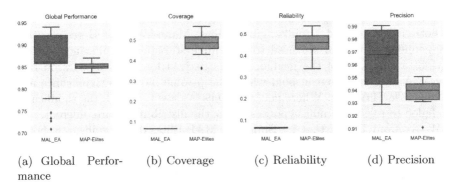

(a) Global Perfor-   (b) Coverage   (c) Reliability   (d) Precision
mance

Fig. 4. Boxplots of Global Performance, Coverage, Reliability and Precision for MAL_EA and MAP-Elites for Droidkungfu family

From Table 3, we see that both MAL_EA and MAP-Elites produce variants that are more evasive than the original malware for both Dougalek and Droidkungfu, i.e their detection rates are lower. For Dougalek, both methods produce a variant that is only detected by 28% of the detectors (compared to the original malware that was detected by 60%). For Droidkungfu, MAL_EA produces a single variant that is only detected by 6% of the detection engines, outperforming MAP-Elites in which the single best variant is detected by 18%. Although the median values are similar, the worst variant produced by MAP-Elites is more evasive than the worst variant from MAL_EA for both Dougalek and Droidkungfu.

In summary, MAP-Elites consistently outperforms the EA in terms of the *coverage* and *reliability* metrics, while finding solutions that are better or comparable in terms of the *performance* metric. Although for the Droidkungfu family, the *single* most evasive variant is found by MAL_EA, recall that the goal of the study is to produce a *set* of diverse, hard to detect variants to provide an improved training set for a machine-learning algorithm: in this respect a diverse set of evasive variants is significantly preferable to a small set of highly evasive variants.

5.3 Analysis of the Antivirus Engines

In order to gain more insight into which engines are most susceptible to potential mutated versions of the original malware, we determine the percentage of new variants evolved using MAP-Elites that a detector fails to recognise. We only consider the engines which recognised the original parent malware in this analysis in order to understand which engines are vulnerable to potential mutants and which remain capable of detecting the malware. The results are shown for each malware family in Fig. 5(a) and (b).

It can be seen from Fig. 5(a), that 9 of the 37 engines that detected the original Dougalek parent malware also recognise all of the mutants evolved by MAP-Elites. Examples include Avast Mobile, Avira and Tencent. At the other extreme, 12 engines failed to detect 100% of the newly generated mutants. Examples include GData, Symantec, BitDefender and McAfeeGW. For the Droid-kungfu malware, 4 of the 21 engines that detected the original malware also detect all of the evolved mutants. Examples again include the Avast Mobile and Avira engines that also proved robust to the Dougalek mutants. Three of the 21 engines failed to recognise *all* of the evolved mutants—AegisLab, DrWeb and McAfeeGW. We note that the McAfeeGW engine appears very vulnerable to both families of metamorphic malware.

6 Conclusion

The ability of metamorphic malware to change its code over time poses significant challenges for detection models that are trained on static sets of data. One approach to this is to train models with datasets that include potential variants of the malware. It is therefore desirable to create new datasets that (a) contain large numbers of new malicious samples and (b) that those samples are as diverse as possible in order to maximise the performance of the model. In order to challenge the model and drive improvements, it is also desirable to create new samples that are highly evasive with respect to current detection methods.

Quality-Diversity (QD) algorithms that produce diverse archives of high-performing solutions offer an obvious solution to this problem. Although they have proved effective in a range of domains in recent years, we believe this to be their first use in generating a diverse set of adversarial malware samples within the metamorphic malware detection domain. We have shown that MAP-Elites—an example of a QD algorithm—is capable of generating high-performing and diverse samples for two malware families. When compared to an EA (MAL_EA [2]), it produces larger sets of data with more diversity (with 50% (Dougalek) and 49% (Droidkungfu) coverage for MAP-Elites, as opposed to MAL_EA's coverage of 0.06% (Dougalek) and 0.07% (Droidkungfu)), while still producing comparable performance in terms of minimising detection rates. There remains significant

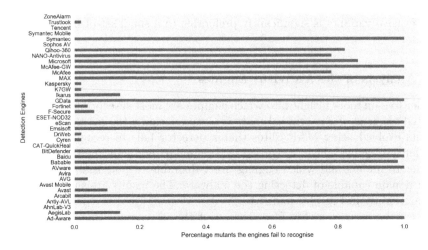

(a) Dougalek

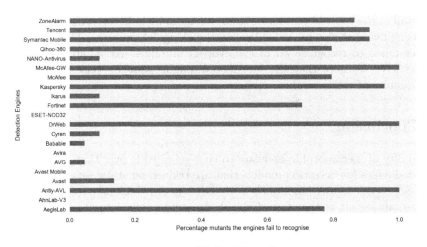

(b) Droidkungfu

Fig. 5. Percentage of the mutants evolved from MAP-Elites that a specific detection engine failed to recognise for (a) Dougalek and (b) Droidkungfu

scope to optimise the model suggested, particularly in terms of investigating an appropriate size for the archive and running the algorithm over longer periods to increase coverage.

We believe that quality-diversity algorithms are a ripe avenue for exploration in this field, particularly if they can be combined in a setting typical in generative adversarial networks (GAN [6]) in which improvements in the generated samples drive improvements in the detection method and vice versa. This will form the basis of future work.

References

1. Aydogan, E., Sen, S.: Automatic generation of mobile malwares using genetic programming. In: Mora, A.M., Squillero, G. (eds.) EvoApplications 2015. LNCS, vol. 9028, pp. 745–756. Springer, Cham (2015). https://doi.org/10.1007/978-3-319-16549-3_60

2. Babaagba, K.O., Tan, Z., Hart, E.: Nowhere metamorphic malware can hide - a biological evolution inspired detection scheme. In: Wang, G., Bhuiyan, M.Z.A., De Capitani di Vimercati, S., Ren, Y. (eds.) DependSys 2019. CCIS, vol. 1123, pp. 369–382. Springer, Singapore (2019). https://doi.org/10.1007/978-981-15-1304-6_29

3. Bruschi, D., Martignoni, L., Monga, M.: Code normalization for self-mutating malware. IEEE Secur. Priv. **5**(2), 46–54 (2007)

4. Dhakal, A., Poudel, A., Pandey, S., Gaire, S., Baral, H.P.: Exploring deep learning in semantic question matching. In: 2018 IEEE 3rd International Conference on Computing, Communication and Security, ICCCS 2018, pp. 86–91 (2018)

5. Fontaine, M.C., Lee, S., Soros, L.B., De Mesentier Silva, F., Togelius, J., Hoover, A.K.: Mapping hearthstone deck spaces through map-elites with sliding boundaries. In: Proceedings of the Genetic and Evolutionary Computation Conference, GECCO 2019, pp. 161–169. ACM, New York (2019)

6. Goodfellow, I., et al.: Generative adversarial nets. In: Advances in Neural Information Processing Systems, pp. 2672–2680 (2014)

7. Grosse, K., Papernot, N., Manoharan, P., Backes, M., McDaniel, P.: Adversarial examples for malware detection. In: Foley, S.N., Gollmann, D., Snekkenes, E. (eds.) ESORICS 2017. LNCS, vol. 10493, pp. 62–79. Springer, Cham (2017). https://doi.org/10.1007/978-3-319-66399-9_4

8. Hagg, A., Asteroth, A., Bäck, T.: Modeling user selection in quality diversity. In: Proceedings of the Genetic and Evolutionary Computation Conference, GECCO 2019, pp. 116–124. ACM, New York (2019)

9. Heres, D.: Source Code Plagiarism Detection using Machine Learning. Ph.D. thesis, Utrecht University (2017)

10. Gomaa, W.H., Fahmy, A.A.: A survey of text similarity approaches. Int. J. Comput. Appl. **68**(13), 13–18 (2013)

11. Lowd, D., Meek, C.: Adversarial learning. In: Proceedings of the Eleventh ACM SIGKDD International Conference on Knowledge Discovery in Data Mining, KDD 2005, pp. 641–647. ACM, New York (2005)

12. Maiorca, D., Biggio, B., Giacinto, G.: Towards adversarial malware detection: lessons learned from pdf-based attacks. ACM Comput. Surv. **52**(4), 78:1–78:36 (2019)

13. Mouret, J.B., Clune, J.: Illuminating search spaces by mapping elites (2015)

14. Pugh, J.K., Soros, L.B., Stanley, K.O.: Quality diversity: a new frontier for evolutionary computation. Front. Rob. AI **3**, 40 (2016)

15. Ragkhitwetsagul, C., Krinke, J., Clark, D.: A comparison of code similarity analysers. Empirical Softw. Eng. **23**(4), 2464–2519 (2018)

16. Rastogi, V., Chen, Y., Jiang, X.: Droidchameleon: evaluating android anti-malware against transformation attacks. In: Proceedings of the 8th ACM SIGSAC Symposium on Information, Computer and Communications Security, ASIA CCS 2013, pp. 329–334. ACM, New York (2013)

17. Suciu, O., Coull, S.E., Johns, J.: Exploring adversarial examples in malware detection. In: 2019 IEEE Security and Privacy Workshops, SPW 2019, pp. 8–14. IEEE (2019)

18. Urquhart, N., Hart, E.: Optimisation and illumination of a real-world workforce scheduling and routing application (WSRP) via Map-Elites. In: Auger, A., Fonseca, C.M., Lourenço, N., Machado, P., Paquete, L., Whitley, D. (eds.) PPSN 2018. LNCS, vol. 11101, pp. 488–499. Springer, Cham (2018). https://doi.org/10.1007/978-3-319-99253-2_39

19. Xu, W., Qi, Y., Evans, D.: Automatically evading classifiers: a case study on PDF malware classifier. In: 23rd Annual Network and Distributed System Security Symposium, NDSS 2016, San Diego, California, USA. The Internet Society (2016)

20. Zheng, M., Lee, P.P.C., Lui, J.C.S.: ADAM: an automatic and extensible platform to stress test android anti-virus systems. In: Flegel, U., Markatos, E., Robertson, W. (eds.) DIMVA 2012. LNCS, vol. 7591, pp. 82–101. Springer, Heidelberg (2013). https://doi.org/10.1007/978-3-642-37300-8_5

EvoDynamic: A Framework for the Evolution of Generally Represented Dynamical Systems and Its Application to Criticality

Sidney Pontes-Filho[1,2]([✉]) [iD], Pedro Lind[1], Anis Yazidi[1], Jianhua Zhang[1],
Hugo Hammer[1], Gustavo B. M. Mello[1], Ioanna Sandvig[3], Gunnar Tufte[2],
and Stefano Nichele[1,4]

[1] Department of Computer Science, Oslo Metropolitan University, Oslo, Norway
`sidneyp@oslomet.no`
[2] Department of Computer Science,
Norwegian University of Science and Technology, Trondheim, Norway
[3] Department of Neuromedicine and Movement Science,
Norwegian University of Science and Technology, Trondheim, Norway
[4] Holistic Systems, SimulaMet, Oslo, Norway

Abstract. Dynamical systems possess a computational capacity that may be exploited in a reservoir computing paradigm. This paper presents a general representation of dynamical systems which is based on matrix multiplication. That is similar to how an artificial neural network (ANN) is represented in a deep learning library and its computation can be faster because of the optimized matrix operations that such type of libraries have. Initially, we implement the simplest dynamical system, a cellular automaton. The mathematical fundamentals behind an ANN are maintained, but the weights of the connections and the activation function are adjusted to work as an update rule in the context of cellular automata. The advantages of such implementation are its usage on specialized and optimized deep learning libraries, the capabilities to generalize it to other types of networks and the possibility to evolve cellular automata and other dynamical systems in terms of connectivity, update and learning rules. Our implementation of cellular automata constitutes an initial step towards a more general framework for dynamical systems. Our objective is to evolve such systems to optimize their usage in reservoir computing and to model physical computing substrates. Furthermore, we present promising preliminary results toward the evolution of complex behavior and criticality using genetic algorithm in stochastic elementary cellular automata.

Keywords: Cellular automata · Dynamical systems ·
Implementation · Reservoir computing · Evolution · Criticality

ⓒ Springer Nature Switzerland AG 2020
P. A. Castillo et al. (Eds.): EvoApplications 2020, LNCS 12104, pp. 133–148, 2020.
https://doi.org/10.1007/978-3-030-43722-0_9

1   Introduction

A cellular automaton (CA) is the simplest computing system where the emergence of complex dynamics from local interactions might take place. It consists of a grid of cells with a finite number of states that change according to simple rules depending on the neighborhood and own state in discrete time-steps. Some notable examples are the elementary CA [30], which is unidimensional with three neighbors and eight update cases, and Conway's Game of Life [24], which is two-dimensional with nine neighbors and three update cases.

Table 1 presents some computing systems that are capable of giving rise to the emergence of complex dynamics. Those systems can be exploited by reservoir computing, which is a paradigm that resorts to dynamical systems to simplify complex data. Such simplification means that reservoir computing utilizes the non-linear dynamical system to perform a non-linear transformation from non-linear data to higher dimensional linear data. Such linearized data can be applied in linear machine learning methods which are faster for training and computing because has less trainable variables and operations. Hence, reservoir computing is more energy efficient than deep learning methods and it can even yield competitive results, especially for temporal data [25,27]. Basically, reservoir computing exploits a dynamical system that possesses the echo state property and fading memory, where the internals of the reservoir are untrained and the only training happens at the linear readout stage [16].

Reservoir computers are most useful when the substrate's dynamics are at the "edge of chaos" [17], meaning a range of dynamical behaviors that is between order and disorder. Cellular automata with such dynamical behavior are capable of being exploited as reservoirs [21,22]. Other systems can also exhibit similar dynamics. The coupled map lattice [15] is very similar to CA, the only exception is that the coupled map lattice has continuous states which are updated by a recurrence equation involving the neighborhood. Random Boolean network [10] is a generalization of CA where random connectivity exists. Echo state network [13] is an artificial neural network (ANN) with random topology while liquid state machine [18] is similar to echo state network with the difference that it is a spiking neural network that communicates through discrete-events (spikes) over continuous time.

Table 1. Examples of dynamical systems.

Dynamical system	State	Time	Connectivity
Cellular automata	Discrete	Discrete	Regular
Coupled map lattice	Continuous	Discrete	Regular
Random Boolean network	Discrete	Discrete	Random
Echo state network	Continuous	Discrete	Random
Liquid state machine	Discrete	Continuous	Random

One important aspect of the computation performed in a dynamical system is the trajectory of system states traversed during the computation [19]. Such trajectory may be guided by system parameters [23]. Another characteristic of a dynamical system, which is crucial for computation, is to be in a critical state, as indicated by Langton [17]. If the attractors of the system are in the critical state, this characteristic is called self-organized criticality [7].

Besides, computation in dynamical systems may be carried out in physical substrates [27], such as networks of biological neurons [3] or in nanoscale materials [8]. Finding the correct abstraction for the computation in a dynamical system, e.g. CA, is an open problem [20].

All the systems described in Table 1 are sparsely connected and can be represented by a weighted adjacency matrix, such as a graph. The connectivity from a layer to another in a fully connected feedforward ANN is represented with a weighted adjacency matrix that contains the weights of each connection. Our CA implementation is similar to this, but the connectivity goes from the "layer" of cells to itself.

The goal of representing CA with a weighted adjacency matrix is to implement a framework which facilitates the development of all types of CAs, from unidimensional to multidimensional, with all kinds of lattices and without any boundary conditions during execution; and also allowing the inclusion of other major dynamical systems, independent of the type of the state, time and connectivity. Such initial implementation is the first component of a Python framework under development, based on TensorFlow deep neural network library [4]. Therefore, it benefits from powerful and parallel computing systems with multi-CPU and multi-GPU. One of the framework's goals is to have a balance between performance and generalization of computing dynamical systems, since general methods are slower than specialized ones. Nevertheless, this framework, called EvoDynamic[1], aims at evolving (i.e., using evolutionary algorithms) the connectivity, update and learning rules of sparsely connected networks to improve their usage for reservoir computing guided by the echo state property, fading memory, state trajectory, and other quality measurements. Such improvement of reservoirs is applied similarly in [26], where the internal connectivity of a reservoir is trained to increase its performance to several tasks. Moreover, evolution will model the dynamics and behavior of physical reservoirs, such as *in-vitro* biological neural networks interfaced with microelectrode arrays, and nanomagnetic ensembles. Those two substrates have real applicability as reservoirs. For example, the former substrate is applied to control a robot, in fact making it into a cyborg, a closed-loop biological-artificial neuro-system [3], and the latter possesses computation capability as shown by a square lattice of nanomagnets [14]. Those substrates are the main interest of the SOCRATES project [1] which aims to explore a dynamic, robust and energy efficient hardware for data analysis.

There exist some implementations of CA similar to the one of EvoDynamic framework. They typically implement Conway's Game of Life by applying 2D

---

[1] EvoDynamic open-source repository is available at https://github.com/Socrates NFR/EvoDynamic.

convolution with a kernel that is used to count the "alive" neighbors, then the resulting matrix consists of the number of "alive" neighboring cells and is used to update the CA. One such implementation, also based on TensorFlow, is available open-source in [2]. We do not use this type of method because it works only with a regular grid topology and not with a random or custom one. Therefore, that cannot be a general method for simulating the different types of dynamical systems.

This paper is organized as follows. Section 2 describes our method according to which we use weighted adjacency matrix to compute CA. Section 3 presents the results obtained from the method. Section 4 discusses the initial advances and future plan of EvoDynamic framework and Sect. 5 concludes this paper.

2   Method

In our proposed method, the equation to calculate the next states of the cells in a cellular automaton is

$$\mathbf{c}_{t+1} = f(\mathbf{A} \cdot \mathbf{c}_t). \tag{1}$$

It is similar to the equation of the forward pass of an artificial neural network, but without the bias. The layer is connected to itself, and the activation function f defines the update rules of the CA. The next states of the CA $\mathbf{c}_{t+1}$ is calculated from the result of the activation function f which receives as argument the dot product between the weighted adjacency matrix $\mathbf{A}$ and the current states of the CA $\mathbf{c}_t$. $\mathbf{c}$ is always a column vector of size $len(\mathbf{c}) \times 1$, that does not depend on how many dimensions the CA has, and $\mathbf{A}$ is a matrix of size $len(\mathbf{c}) \times len(\mathbf{c})$. Hence the result of $\mathbf{A} \cdot \mathbf{c}$ is also a column vector of size $len(\mathbf{c}) \times 1$ as $\mathbf{c}$.

The implementation of cellular automata as an artificial neural network requires the procedural generation of the weighted adjacency matrix of the grid. In this way, any lattice type or multidimensional CAs can be implemented using the same approach. The adjacency matrix of a sparsely connected network contains many zeros because of the small number of connections. Since we implement it on TensorFlow, the data type of the adjacency matrix is preferably a `SparseTensor`. A dot product with this data type can be up to 9 times faster than the dense counterpart. However, it depends on the configuration of the tensors (or, in our case, the adjacency matrices) [28]. The update rule of the CA alters the weights of the connections in the adjacency matrix. In a CA whose cells have two states meaning "dead" (zero) or "alive" (one), the weights in the adjacency matrix are one for connection and zero for no connection, such as an ordinary adjacency matrix. Such matrix facilitates the description of the update rule for counting the number of "alive" neighbors because the result of the dot product between the adjacency matrix and the cell state vector is the vector that contains the number of "alive" neighbors for each cell. If the pattern of the neighborhood matters in the update rule, each cell has its neighbors encoded as a n-ary string where n means the number of states that a cell can have. In this case, the weights of the connections with the neighbors are n-base identifiers and

Algorithm 1. Generation of weighted adjacency matrix for 1D cellular automaton

---

1: **procedure** GENERATECA1D
2:     $numberOfCells \leftarrow widthCA$
3:     $\mathbf{A} \leftarrow \mathbf{0}^{numberOfCells \times numberOfCells}$ ▷ Adjacency matrix initialization
4:     **for** $i \leftarrow \{0..(numberOfCells - 1)\}$ **do**
5:         **for** $j \leftarrow \{-indexNeighborCenter..(len(neighborhood) - indexNeighborCenter - 1)\}$ **do**
6:             $currentNeighbor \leftarrow neighborhood_{j+indexNeighborCenter}$
7:             **if** $currentNeighbor \neq 0 \wedge (isWrappedGrid \vee (\neg isWrappedGrid \wedge (0 \leq (i + j) < widthCA))$ **then**
8:                 $\mathbf{A}_{i,((i+j) \bmod widthCA)} \leftarrow currentNeighbor$
9:         **return** $\mathbf{A}$

---

are calculated by

$$neighbor_i = n^i, \forall i \in \{0..len(\mathbf{neighbors}) - 1\} \qquad (2)$$

where **neighbors** is a vector of the cell's neighbors. In the adjacency matrix, each neighbor receives a weight according to (2). The result of the dot product with such weighted adjacency matrix is a vector that consists of unique integers per neighborhood pattern. Thus, the activation function is a lookup table from integer (i.e., pattern) to next state.

Algorithm 1 generates the weighted adjacency matrix for one-dimensional CA, such as the elementary CA, where $widthCA$ is the width or number of cells of a unidimensional CA and **neighborhood** is a vector which describes the region around the center cell. The connection weights depend on the type of update rule as previously explained. For example, in case of an elementary CA **neighborhood** $= [4 \ 2 \ 1]$. $indexNeighborCenter$ is the index of the center cell in the **neighborhood** whose starting index is zero. $isWrappedGrid$ is a Boolean value that works as a flag for adding a wrapped grid or not. A wrapped grid for one-dimensional CA means that the initial and final cells are neighbors. With all these parameters, Algorithm 1 creates an adjacency matrix by looping over the indices of the cells (from zero to $numberOfCells - 1$) with an inner loop for the indices of the neighbors. If the selected $currentNeighbor$ is a non-zero value and its indices do not affect the boundary condition, then the value of $currentNeighbor$ is assigned to the adjacency matrix $\mathbf{A}$ in the indices that correspond to the connection between the current cell in the outer loop and the actual index of $currentNeighbor$. Finally, this procedure returns the adjacency matrix $\mathbf{A}$.

To procedurally generate an adjacency matrix for 2D CA instead of 1D CA, the algorithm needs to have small adjustments. Algorithm 2 shows that for two-dimensional CA, such as Conway's Game of Life. In this case, the height of the CA is an argument passed as $heightCA$. **Neighborhood** is a 2D matrix and **indexNeighborCenter** is a vector of two components meaning the indices of the center of **Neighborhood**. This procedure is similar to the one in Algorithm 1, but it contains one more loop for the additional dimension.

Algorithm 2. Generation of adjacency matrix of 2D cellular automaton

---

1: **procedure** GENERATECA2D
2:     $numberOfCells \leftarrow widthCA * heightCA$
3:     $\mathbf{A} \leftarrow \mathbf{0}^{numberOfCells \times numberOfCells}$ ▷ Adjacency matrix initialization
4:     $widthNB, heightNB \leftarrow shape(\mathbf{Neighborhood})$
5:     **for** $i \leftarrow \{0..(numberOfCells - 1)\}$ **do**
6:         **for** $j \leftarrow \{-\mathbf{indexNeighborCenter}_0..(widthNB - \mathbf{indexNeighborCenter}_0 - 1)\}$ **do**
7:             **for** $k \leftarrow \{-\mathbf{indexNeighborCenter}_1..(heightNB - \mathbf{indexNeighborCenter}_1 - 1)\}$ **do**
8:                 $currentNeighbor \leftarrow Neighborhood_{j+indexNeighborCenter}$
9:                 **if** $currentNeighbor \neq 0 \wedge (isWrappedGrid \vee (\neg isWrappedGrid \wedge (0 \leq ((i \bmod heightCA)+j) < widthCA) \wedge (0 \leq (\lfloor i/widthCA \rfloor +k) < heightCA))$ **then**
10:                     $\mathbf{A}_{i,(((i+k) \bmod widthCA)+((\lfloor i/widthCA \rfloor +j) \bmod heightCA)*widthCA)} \leftarrow currentNeighbor$
11:     **return A**

The activation function for CA is different from the ones used for ANN. For CA, it contains the update rules that verify the vector returned by the dot product between the weighted adjacency matrix and the vector of states. Normally, the update rules of the CA are implemented as a lookup table from neighborhood to next state. In our implementation, the lookup table maps the resulting vector of the dot product to the next state of the central cell.

3   Results

This section presents the results of the proposed method and it also stands for the preliminary results of the EvoDynamic framework.

Figure 1 illustrates a wrapped elementary CA described in the procedure of Algorithm 1 and its generated weighted adjacency matrix. Figure 1a shows the appearance of the desired elementary CA with 16 cells (i.e., $widthCA = 16$). Figure 1b describes its pattern 3-neighborhood and the indices of the cells. Figure 1c shows the result of the Algorithm 1 with the neighborhood calculated by (2) for pattern matching in the activation function. In Fig. 1c, we can verify that the left neighbor has weight equal to 4 (or 2^2 for the most significant bit), central cell weight is 2 (or 2^1) and right neighbor weight is 1 (or 2^0 for the least significant bit) as defined by (2). Since the CA is wrapped, we can notice in row index 0 of the adjacency matrix in Fig. 1c that the left neighbor of cell 0 is the cell 15, and in row index 15 that the right neighbor of cell 15 is the cell 0.

Figure 2 describes a wrapped 2D CA (similar to Game of Life but with less number of neighbors) for Algorithm 2 and shows the resulting adjacency

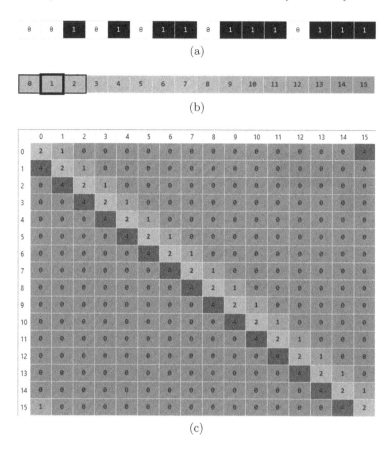

Fig. 1. Elementary cellular automaton with 16 cells and wrapped grid. (a) Example of the grid of cells with states. (b) Indices of the cells and standard pattern neighborhood of elementary CA where thick border means the central cell and thin border means the neighbors. (c) Generated weighted adjacency matrix for the described elementary CA.

matrix. Figure 2a illustrates the desired two-dimensional CA with 16 cells (i.e., $widthCA = 4$ and $heightCA = 4$). Figure 2b presents the von Neumann neighborhood [29] which is used for counting the number of "alive" neighbors (the connection weights are only zero and one, and **Neighborhood** argument of Algorithm 2 defines it). It also shows the index distribution of the CA whose order is preserved after flatting it to a column vector. Figure 2c contains the generated adjacency matrix of Algorithm 2 for the described 2D CA. Figure 2b shows an example of a central cell with its neighbors, the index of this central cell is 5 and the row index 5 in the adjacency matrix of Fig. 2c presents the same neighbor indices, i.e., 1, 4, 6 and 9. Since this is a symmetric matrix, the columns have the same connectivity of the rows. That means the neighborhood of a cell considers this cell as a neighbor too. Therefore, the connections are bidirectional and the adjacency matrix represents an undirected graph. The wrapping effect is also observable. For example, the neighbors of the cell index 0 are 1, 3, 4 and 12. So the neighbors 3 and 12 are the ones that the wrapped grid allowed to exist for cell index 0.

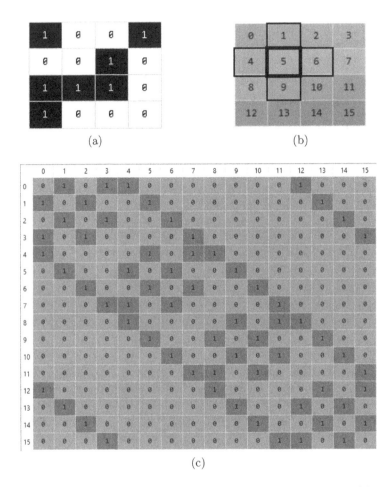

Fig. 2. 2D cellular automaton with 16 cells (4 × 4) and wrapped grid. (a) Example of the grid of cells with states. (b) Indices of the cells and von Neumann counting neighborhood of 2D CA where thick border means the current cell and thin border means the neighbors. (c) Generated adjacency matrix for the described 2D CA.

4   On-Going and Future Applications with EvoDynamic

The method of implementing a CA as an artificial neural network is beneficial for the further development of EvoDynamic framework. Since the implementation of all sparsely connected networks in Table 1 is already planned in forthcoming releases of the Python framework, EvoDynamic shall have a general representation to all of them. Therefore, CAs are treated as ANNs and then can be extended to random Boolean network by shuffling the connections, and to the models that are already ANNs, such as echo state networks and liquid state machines. Moreover, EvoDynamic framework will evolve the connectivity, update and learning rules of the dynamical systems for reservoir computing improvement and physical substrate modeling. This common representation facilitates the evolution of such systems and models which will be guided by several methods that measure the quality of a reservoir or the similarity to a dataset. The following subsections explain two on-going applications with CA that use the EvoDynamic framework.

4.1 State Trajectory

An example of methods to guide the evolution of dynamical system is the state trajectory. This method can be used to cluster similar states for model abstraction and to measure the quality of the reservoir. Therefore, a graph can be formed and analysis can be made by searching for attractors and cycles. For visualization of the state trajectory, we use principal component analysis (PCA) to reduce the dimensionality of the states and present them as a state transition diagram as shown in Fig. 3. The depicted dynamical system is Conway's Game of Life with 7×7 cells and wrapped boundaries. A glider is its initial state (Fig. 3a) and this system cycles over 28 unique states as illustrated in the state transition diagram of Fig. 3l.

4.2 Towards the Evolution for Criticality

Evolution of dynamical systems is a feature currently under development of EvoDynamic framework. The first on-going evolution task of our framework is to find systems with criticality [7] using genetic algorithm, in order to allow for better computational capacity [17]. The first dynamical system for this task is a modified version of stochastic elementary cellular automata (SECA) introduced by Baetens et al. [6]. Our stochastic elementary cellular automaton works as a 1D three neighbors elementary CA, but the next state in time $t+1$ of the central cell c_i is defined by a probability p to be 1 and a probability $1-p$ to be 0 for each of the eight different neighborhood patterns this CA has. Formally, probability p is represented by

$$p = P(c_{i,t+1} = 1 | N(c_{i,t})) \tag{3}$$

where the neighborhood pattern $N(c_{i,t})$ is denoted as

$$N(c_{i,t}) = (c_{i-1,t}, c_{i,t}, c_{i+1,t}). \tag{4}$$

The genetic algorithm for criticality is guided by a fitness function which mainly verifies if the probability distributions of avalanche size (i.e., cluster size[2]

---

[2] Cluster size stands for the number of repetitions of a state that happened consecutively without any interruption of another state.

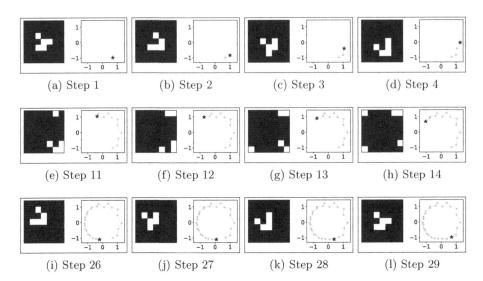

| (a) Step 1 | (b) Step 2 | (c) Step 3 | (d) Step 4 |

| (e) Step 11 | (f) Step 12 | (g) Step 13 | (h) Step 14 |

| (i) Step 26 | (j) Step 27 | (k) Step 28 | (l) Step 29 |

Fig. 3. States of Conway's Game of Life in a 7×7 wrapped lattice alongside their PCA-transformed state transition diagrams of the two first principal components. (a) Initial state is a glider. (a)–(d) Four first steps in this CA. (e)–(h) Four intermediate steps in this CA while reaching the wrapped border. (i)–(l) Four last steps in this CA before repeating the initial state and closing a cycle.

in space) and duration (i.e., cluster size in time) follow a power-law distribution. Such verification can be done by checking how linear is the probability distribution in a log-log plot, by performing goodness-of-fit tests based on the Kolmogorov-Smirnov (KS) statistic and by comparing the power-law model with the exponential model using log-likelihood ratio [9]. For our fitness function, we estimate the candidate distributions with the linear fitting of the first 10 points of the log-log plot using least squares regression, which was verified to be not biased and gives a fast and acceptable estimation of the slope of the power-law distribution [12]. After the linear 10-points fitting, the model is tested using KS statistic. One benefit of using such estimation method is that when the model is not a power-law, the KS statistic reports a large error, i.e., an error greater than one. Another objective in the fitness function is the coefficient of determination [31], but for a complete linear fit of the log-log plot. The fitness function also considers the number of unique states of the stochastic elementary CA, the number of bins in the raw histogram and the value of the estimated power-law exponent. All these fitness function objectives are calculated using a randomly initialized CA of 1,000 cells with wrapped boundaries during 1,000 time-steps. The avalanche size and duration are computed for the cell values 0 and 1, thus producing four different distributions (see Fig. 4) for extracting vectors of their normalized number of histogram bins[3] bin; coefficient of determination R^2 of complete linear fitting; KS statistic D and estimated power-law exponent $\hat{\alpha}$ from the 10-points linear estimation. The fitness score s for each objective is then calculated by the following equations:

$$bin_s = \tanh(5 * (0.9 * \max(bin) + 0.1 * \mathrm{mean}(bin))), \tag{5}$$

$$R_s^2 = \mathrm{mean}(R^2), \tag{6}$$

$$D_s = \exp(-(0.9 * \min(D) + 0.1 * \mathrm{mean}(D))), \tag{7}$$

$$\hat{\alpha}_s = \mathrm{mean}(\hat{\alpha}), \tag{8}$$

$$unique_s = \frac{\#uniqueStates}{\#timesteps}. \tag{9}$$

The (5)–(9) are all objective values for calculating the fitness score s. Those values are real numbers between zero and one, except the score for the estimated power-law exponent $\hat{\alpha}_s$, and they have weights attributed to them regarding their level of importance and for compensating small and large values. The following equation denotes how the fitness score s is calculated:

$$s = 10 * bin_s + 10 * R_s^2 + 10 * D_s + 0.1 * \hat{\alpha}_s + 10 * unique_s. \tag{10}$$

The genetic algorithm has 40 individuals that evolve through 100 generations. The optimization performed by GA is to maximize the fitness score. The genome of the individuals has eight real number genes with a value range between zero and one. Each gene represents the probability of the next state becoming one

Table 2. Best individual

Neighborhood $N(c_{i,t})$	Probability p
(0,0,0)	0.103009
(0,0,1)	0.536786
(0,1,0)	0.216794
(0,1,1)	0.393468
(1,0,0)	0.679836
(1,0,1)	0.175458
(1,1,0)	0.724778
(1,1,1)	1.000000

---

[3] The actual number of histogram bins is normalized or divided by the possible total number of bins.

Table 3. Fitness score of the best individual

Objective	Score
$10 * bin_s$	9.780749590096136
$10 * R_s^2$	8.832520186440096
$10 * D_s$	9.655719560019996
$0.1 * \hat{\alpha}_s$	0.18022617747972156
$10 * unique_s$	10.0
s	**38.44921551403595**

(i.e., p in (3)) for its respective neighborhood pattern. The selection of two parents is done by deterministic tournament selection [11]. After that, the crossover between the genomes of the parents can happen with probability 0.8, then each gene can be exchanged with probability 0.5. Afterward, a mutation occurs to a gene with probability 0.1. This mutation adds a random value from a normal distribution with mean and standard deviation equals to, respectively, 0 and

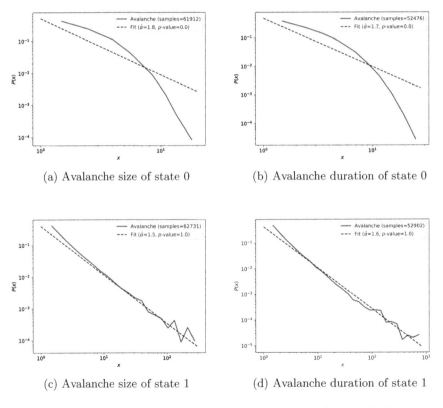

(a) Avalanche size of state 0   (b) Avalanche duration of state 0

(c) Avalanche size of state 1   (d) Avalanche duration of state 1

Fig. 4. Avalanche size and duration of the two states 0 and 1 of the evolved stochastic elementary CA.

0.2. The mating process of the two parents produces an offspring of two new individuals who replace the parents in the next generation.

An example of an evolved genome for the best resulting individual is presented in Table 2. The fitness score s and all objective scores with their respective weights for calculating s are in Table 3.

With the genome or probabilities of the eight different neighborhood patterns of the best evolved individual, we can produce the log-log plots of the probability distribution of avalanche size and duration for the states zero and one. Such plots are depicted in Fig. 4. The p-value of goodness-of-fit test is calculated using 1,000 randomly generated data with 10,000 samples applying the power-law exponent $\hat{\alpha}$ estimated by maximum likelihood estimation method with minimum x of the distribution fixed to 1. The Figs. 4a and b show the avalanche size and

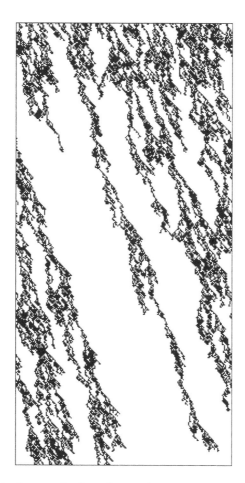

Fig. 5. Sample of the best evolved stochastic elementary CA of 200 cells (horizontal axis) randomly initialized with wrapped boundaries through 400 time-steps (vertical axis).

duration for the state 0 or black. They present distributions that are not a power-law because they do not fit the power-law estimation (the black dashed line). Moreover, the p-value is equal to 0.0 which proves that those two distributions are not a power-law. The Figs. 4c and d present the avalanche size and duration for the state 1 or white. Those distributions follow a power-law because, visually, the estimated power-law distribution fits the empirical probability distribution and, quantitatively, the p-value is equal to 1.0 which means that 100% of the KS statistic of the generated data is greater than the KS statistic of the empirical distribution of avalanche size and duration of state 1. The number of samples in those distributions (62,731 for avalanche size and 52,902 for avalanche duration) confirms that the p-value is trustworthy. Such power-law analysis is performed by utilizing the powerlaw Python library [5]. It is important to warn that high fitness scores do not mean p-values closer to 1.0 and the goodness-of-fit test is not part of the fitness score because it is a slow process.

A sample of the resulting stochastic elementary cellular automaton of the best individual is illustrated in Fig. 5. This CA, as seen, has no static nor periodic states, and no random evolution of its states. Therefore, this dynamical system is between a strongly and weakly coupled substrate. Therefore, the CA presents patterns or structures that mean the cells are interdependent in this system.

5   Conclusion

In this paper, we present an alternative method to implement a cellular automaton. This allows any CA to be computed as an artificial neural network. That means, any lookup table can be an activation function, and any neighborhood and dimensionality can be represented as a weight matrix. Therefore, this will help to extend the CA implementation to more complex dynamical systems, such as random Boolean networks, echo state networks and liquid state machines. Furthermore, the EvoDynamic framework is built on a deep learning library, TensorFlow, which permits the acceleration and parallelization of matrix operations when applied on computational platforms with fast CPUs and GPUs. The planned future implementations of EvoDynamic are presented and discussed. The state trajectory is an important feature for the targeted future tasks. The evolution with genetic algorithm towards criticality of stochastic CA is showing promising results and our next goal can be for self-organized criticality. The future work for the CA implementation is to develop algorithms to procedurally generate weighted adjacency matrices for 3D and multidimensional cellular automata with different types of cells, such as the cells with hexagonal shape in a 2D CA.

Acknowledgments. We thank Kristine Heiney for thoughtful discussions about self-organized criticality.

References

1. SOCRATES – Self-Organizing Computational substRATES. https://www.ntnu.edu/socrates
2. Conway's game of life implemented using tensorflow 2d convolution function (2016). https://github.com/conceptacid/conv2d_life
3. Aaser, P., et al.: Towards making a cyborg: a closed-loop reservoir-neuro system. In: The 2018 Conference on Artificial Life: A Hybrid of the European Conference on Artificial Life (ECAL) and the International Conference on the Synthesis and Simulation of Living Systems (ALIFE), no. 29, pp. 430–437 (2017). https://doi.org/10.1162/isal_a_072
4. Abadi, M., et al.: Tensorflow: a system for large-scale machine learning. In: 12th USENIX Symposium on Operating Systems Design and Implementation (OSDI 16), pp. 265–283. USENIX Association, Savannah, GA (2016)
5. Alstott, J., Bullmore, E., Plenz, D.: Powerlaw: a python package for analysis of heavy-tailed distributions. PLOS ONE 9(1), 1–11 (2014). https://doi.org/10.1371/journal.pone.0085777
6. Baetens, J.M., Van der Meeren, W., De Baets, B.: On the dynamics of stochastic elementary cellular automata. J. Cell. Automata 12, 63–80 (2016)
7. Bak, P., Tang, C., Wiesenfeld, K.: Self-organized criticality: an explanation of the 1/f noise. Phys. Rev. Lett. 59, 381–384 (1987). https://doi.org/10.1103/PhysRevLett.59.381
8. Broersma, H., Miller, J.F., Nichele, S.: Computational Matter: Evolving Computational Functions in Nanoscale Materials. In: Adamatzky, A. (ed.) Advances in Unconventional Computing. ECC, vol. 23, pp. 397–428. Springer, Cham (2017). https://doi.org/10.1007/978-3-319-33921-4_16
9. Clauset, A., Shalizi, C.R., Newman, M.E.: Power-law distributions in empirical data. SIAM Rev. 51(4), 661–703 (2009)
10. Gershenson, C.: Introduction to random boolean networks (2004). arXiv preprint nlin/0408006
11. Goldberg, D.E., Deb, K.: A comparative analysis of selection schemes used in genetic algorithms. In: Foundations of Genetic Algorithms, vol. 1, pp. 69–93. Elsevier (1991)
12. Goldstein, M.L., Morris, S.A., Yen, G.G.: Problems with fitting to the power-law distribution. Eur. Phys. J. B-Condens. Matter Complex Syst. 41(2), 255–258 (2004)
13. Jaeger, H., Haas, H.: Harnessing nonlinearity: predicting chaotic systems and saving energy in wireless communication. Science 304(5667), 78–80 (2004). https://doi.org/10.1126/science.1091277
14. Jensen, J.H., Folven, E., Tufte, G.: Computation in artificial spin ice. In: The 2018 Conference on Artificial Life: A Hybrid of the European Conference on Artificial Life (ECAL) and the International Conference on the Synthesis and Simulation of Living Systems (ALIFE), no. 30, pp. 15–22 (2018). https://doi.org/10.1162/isal_a_00011
15. Kaneko, K.: Overview of coupled map lattices. Chaos: Interdisc. J. Nonlinear Sci. 2(3), 279–282 (1992)
16. Konkoli, Z., Nichele, S., Dale, M., Stepney, S.: Reservoir Computing with Computational Matter. Comput. Matter. NCS, pp. 269–293. Springer, Cham (2018). https://doi.org/10.1007/978-3-319-65826-1_14

17. Langton, C.G.: Computation at the edge of chaos: phase transitions and emergent computation. Phys. D: Nonlinear Phenom. **42**(1), 12–37 (1990). https://doi.org/10.1016/0167-2789(90)90064-V
18. Maass, W., Markram, H.: On the computational power of circuits of spiking neurons. J. Comput. Syst. Sci. **69**(4), 593–616 (2004). https://doi.org/10.1016/j.jcss.2004.04.001
19. Nichele, S., Tufte, G.: Trajectories and attractors as specification for the evolution of behaviour in cellular automata. In: IEEE Congress on Evolutionary Computation, pp. 1–8, July 2010. https://doi.org/10.1109/CEC.2010.5586115
20. Nichele, S., Farstad, S.S., Tufte, G.: Universality of evolved cellular automata in-materio. Int. J. Unconv. Comput. **13**(1) (2017)
21. Nichele, S., Gundersen, M.S.: Reservoir computing using nonuniform binary cellular automata. Complex Syst. **26**(3), 225–245 (2017). https://doi.org/10.25088/complexsystems.26.3.225
22. Nichele, S., Molund, A.: Deep learning with cellular automaton-based reservoir computing. Complex Syst. **26**(4), 319–339 (2017). https://doi.org/10.25088/complexsystems.26.4.319
23. Nichele, S., Tufte, G.: Genome parameters as information to forecast emergent developmental behaviors. In: Durand-Lose, J., Jonoska, N. (eds.) UCNC 2012. LNCS, vol. 7445, pp. 186–197. Springer, Heidelberg (2012). https://doi.org/10.1007/978-3-642-32894-7_18
24. Rendell, P.: Turing Universality of the Game of Life, pp. 513–539. Springer, London (2002). https://doi.org/10.1007/978-1-4471-0129-1_18
25. Schrauwen, B., Verstraeten, D., Van Campenhout, J.: An overview of reservoir computing: theory, applications and implementations. In: Proceedings of the 15th European Symposium on Artificial Neural Networks 2007, pp. 471–482 (2007)
26. Subramoney, A., Scherr, F., Maass, W.: Reservoirs learn to learn (2019). arXiv preprint arXiv:1909.07486
27. Tanaka, G., et al.: Recent advances in physical reservoir computing: a review. Neural Netw. **115**, 100–123 (2019). https://doi.org/10.1016/j.neunet.2019.03.005
28. TensorFlow: tf.sparse.sparse_dense_matmul — tensorflow core r1.14 — tensorflow. https://www.tensorflow.org/api_docs/python/tf/sparse/sparse_dense_matmul
29. Toffoli, T., Margolus, N.: Cellular Automata Machines: A New Environment for Modeling. MIT press, Cambridge (1987)
30. Wolfram, S.: A New Kind of Science, vol. 5. Wolfram Media, Champaign (2002)
31. Wright, S.: Correlation and causation. J. Agric. Res. **20**, 557–580 (1921)

A Decomposition-Based Evolutionary Algorithm with Adaptive Weight Vectors for Multi- and Many-objective Optimization

Guang Peng$^{(\boxtimes)}$ and Katinka Wolter

Department of Mathematics and Computer Science,
Free University of Berlin, Berlin, Germany
{guang.peng,katinka.wolter}@fu-berlin.de

Abstract. The multi-objective evolutionary algorithms based on decomposition (MOEA/D) have achieved great success in the area of evolutionary multi-objective optimization. Numerous MOEA/D variants are focused on solving the normalized multi- and many-objective problems without paying attention to problems having objectives with different scales. For this purpose, this paper proposes a decomposition-based evolutionary algorithm with adaptive weight vectors (DBEA-AWV) for both the normalized and scaled multi- and many-objective problems. In the light of this direction, we compare existing popular decomposition approaches and choose the best suitable one incorporated into DBEA-AWV. Moreover, one novel replacement strategy is adopted to attain the balance between convergence and diversity for multi- and many-objective optimization problems. Our experimental results demonstrate that the proposed algorithm is efficient and reliable for dealing with different normalized and scaled problems, outperforming several other state-of-the-art multi- and many-objective evolutionary algorithms.

Keywords: Multi-objective · Many-objective · Evolutionary computation · Adaptive weight vectors · Decomposition approach

1 Introduction

Multi-objective optimization problems (MOPs), which involve more than one conflicting objective to be optimized, can be described as follows:

$$\min \ F(x) = (f_1(x), f_2(x), \cdots, f_m(x))^T \qquad (1)$$
$$\text{subject to } x \in \Omega \subseteq R^n$$

where Ω is the decision space and $\boldsymbol{x} = (x_1, x_2, \cdots, x_n)$ is an n-dimensional decision vector; $F : \Omega \to \Theta \subseteq R^m$ denotes an m-dimensional objective vector and Θ is the objective space. Specially, MOPs with more than three objectives are

© Springer Nature Switzerland AG 2020
P. A. Castillo et al. (Eds.): EvoApplications 2020, LNCS 12104, pp. 149–164, 2020.
https://doi.org/10.1007/978-3-030-43722-0_10

known as many-objective optimization problems (MaOPs). Due to the conflicts between objectives, a number of optimal solutions can be achieved to set a trade-off between different conflicting objectives, termed Pareto optimal solutions. The set of Pareto optimal solutions are the Pareto optimal set in the decision space. The Pareto optimal set in the objective space is called Pareto front (PF). A variety of multi-objective evolutionary algorithms (MOEAs) has been developed for solving MOPs and MaOPs during the last two decades, which can be classified into three categories [24].

The first category are the Pareto dominance-based MOEAs, where the Pareto dominance criterion is the main feature to push the candidate solutions to approximate the PF. NSGA-II [6] is a typical Pareto dominance-based MOEA for MOPs, all non-dominated solutions are first identified by fast non-dominated sorting and then the crowding distance strategy is used to preserve population diversity. Due to the loss of selection pressure with the increasing number of objectives, the traditional Pareto dominance-based MOEAs face the dominance resistance phenomenon with regard to MaOPs [14]. To address this issue, some modified Pareto dominance relationships have been put forward to solve MaOPs, such as grid dominance-based MOEA (GrEA) [21] and θ dominance-based MOEA (θ-DEA) [22].

The second category are the decomposition-based MOEAs, where an MOP can be decomposed into a series of scalar optimization subproblems. MOEA/D [25] is a typical MOEA of this category, the decomposition approaches can decompose an MOP into different subproblems and optimize them simultaneously based on a set of uniformly-distributed weight vectors. Owing to the efficient framework, MOEA/D with differential evolution (DE) has been applied for solving complicated Pareto sets [11]. Some other novel decomposition-based MOEAs try to decompose an MOP into different subspace, such as NSGA-III [5] and RVEA [3]. It is worth noting that NSGA-III combines Pareto dominance and decomposition ideas to maintain the convergence and diversity.

The third category are the indicator-based MOEAs, where the performance indicators are adopted as criteria to select candidate solutions. IBEA [27] and SMS-EMOA [2] are two representative indicator-based MOEAs, where the indicators are designed as predefined binary indicator and hypervolume (HV) indicator. HV is a popular indicator for it's strictly monotonic to the Pareto optimality, but its main issue is that the computational complexity grows exponentially with the increasing number of objectives in MaOPs. HypE [1] adopted the Monte Carlo simulation to estimate the HV value for accelerating the computing speed. Other performance indicators with lower computational complexity have also been proposed for MaOPs, such as IGD [16] and IGD-NS [17].

Although many MOEAs using decomposition approaches in the MOEA/D framework have been verified on different normalized MOPs and MaOPs, the literature [5] and [10] have demonstrated the unstable performance of MOEA/D variants when dealing with scaled problems. In other words, even adopting different normalization approaches into MOEA/D framework, MOEA/D versions can't always get good results with regard to scaled problems. To address the issue, we propose a decomposition-based evolutionary algorithm with adaptive reference vectors (DBEA-AWV) for both the normalized and scaled MOPs and MaOPs. The main contributions of this work are summarized as follows: (1) An adaptive weight vectors adjusting method is proposed for the problems with disparately scaled objectives instead of using normalization approaches. (2) Based on the adaptive weight vectors, we analyze the characteristics of existing six popular decomposition approaches and find the best one. Further, one novel replacement strategy is adopted to keep the balance between convergence and diversity for solving MOPs and MaOPs. (3) The proposed DBEA-AWV is competitive compared with several state-of-the-art multi- and many-objective evolutionary algorithms on a variety of normalized and scaled MOPs and MaOPS.

The rest of this paper is organized as follows. In Sect. 2, existing popular decomposition approaches and normalization approaches are briefly reviewed. The details of proposed DBEA-AWV are presented in Sect. 3. Section 4 shows the experimental results of DBEA-AWV compared with other state-of-the-art algorithms. Finally, conclusions and future work are drawn in Sect. 5.

2   Background

In this section, five popular decomposition approaches used in MOEA/D framework are firstly given. Then, two common normalization approaches incorporated into MOEAs for scaled problems are introduced.

2.1   Decomposition Approaches

In the original MOEA/D, three decomposition approaches are reported: the weighted sum, Tchebycheff and penalty-based boundary intersection (PBI). The weighted sum approach has some shortcomings to deal with concave Pareto fronts [25].

In the Tchebycheff approach, a scalar optimization problem can be defined as follows:

$$\min_{x \in \Omega} g^{te}\left(x \,|\, \lambda, z^*\right) = \min_{x \in \Omega} \max_{1 \le i \le m} \left\{\lambda_i \,|\, f_i\left(x\right) - z_i^*\,|\right\} \tag{2}$$

where $\lambda = (\lambda_1, \lambda_2, \cdots, \lambda_m)^T$ is a weight vector and $\sum_{i=1}^{m} \lambda_i = 1, \lambda_i \ge 0, i = 1, 2, \cdots, m$. $z^* = (z_1^*, z_2^*, \cdots, z_m^*)^T$ is the reference point, for each objective, $z_i^* = \min\left\{f_i\left(x\right) \,|\, x \in \Omega\right\}, i = 1, 2, \cdots, m$.

In the PBI approach, a scalar optimization problem can be stated as follows:

$$\min_{x \in \Omega} g^{pbi}\left(x \,|\, \lambda, z^*\right) = \min_{x \in \Omega} \left(d_1 + \theta d_2\right) \tag{3}$$

where

$$\begin{cases} d_1 = \frac{\left\|(f(x) - z^*)^T \lambda\right\|}{\|\lambda\|} \\ d_2 = \left\|f(x) - \left(z^* + d_1 \frac{\lambda}{\|\lambda\|}\right)\right\| \end{cases} \tag{4}$$

Here θ is a user-predefined penalty parameter. PBI approach has gained particular research interest because of the ability to control the convergence and diversity. To improve the performance of original PBI with a constant penalty value, Yang et al. [20] proposed two new penalty schemes, i.e., adaptive penalty scheme (APS) and subproblem-based penalty scheme (SPS). APS is defined as follows:

$$\theta = \theta_{\min} + (\theta_{\max} - \theta_{\min}) \frac{t}{t_{\max}} \tag{5}$$

where t is the iteration number, $t_{\max}$ is maximum number of iterations. $\theta_{\max}$ and $\theta_{\min}$ are the upper and lower bounds of θ, respectively. $\theta_{\min} = 1$ and $\theta_{\max} = 10$ are recommended in the original paper.

SPS is described as follows:

$$\theta_j = e^{\alpha \beta_j} \tag{6}$$

$$\beta_j = \max_{1 \le i \le m} \lambda_i^j - \min_{1 \le i \le m} \lambda_i^j \tag{7}$$

where θ_j represents the penalty value for a weight vector λ^j. β_j is the difference between the maximum and minimum value of λ^j. α is a control parameter, and $\alpha = 4$ is suggested.

Moreover, an adaptive PBI selection is developed in literature [9], an angle-based dynamic penalty factor adaptation strategy is determined as follows:

$$\theta_k = K \cdot m \cdot \left(\alpha_k^{ind} + \alpha_k^{neighbor} \right) \tag{8}$$

where α_k^{ind} is the angle between the current solution x_k and λ^k, $\alpha_k^{neighbor}$ is the angle between the weight vector λ^k and the closest neighboring one. m is the number of objectives. K is pre-defined scaling parameter, and $K = 0.06$ is suggested.

2.2   Normalization Approaches

For decomposition base MOEAs, one important issue is to tackle the MOPs with objectives having different scales. Nowadays, there are two typical normalization approaches dealing with scaled problems.

In MOEA/D, a simple normalization method is suggested:

$$\bar{f}_j(x_i) = \frac{f_j(x_i) - z_j^*}{z_j^{\max} - z_j^*} \tag{9}$$

where $f_j(x_i)$ is the j-th objective value of solution x_i, and $z_j^{\max}$ is the maximum value of objective f_j in the current population. $\bar{f}_j(x_i)$ is the normalized objective value.

In NSGA-III, one adaptive normalization method is proposed and the main idea is to adopt some extreme points to construct a hyperplane. The intercept a_j of j-th objective axis on the hyperplane substitutes $z_j^{\max}$, then the transformed objective can be computed as the method in MOEA/D. The extreme points are determined by minimizing the achievement scalarizing function (ASF):

$$ASF(x, w) = \max_{i=1}^{m} \frac{f_i(x) - z_i^*}{w_i}, \quad for \ x \in S_t \tag{10}$$

where S_t represents the current population. w is the axis direction, $w_i = 10^{-6}$ when it is zero.

The above two normalization approaches are the popular methods incorporated into MOEA/D framework to solve scaled problems. However, the literature [5] and [10] demonstrate MOEA/D variants where these normalization methods cannot obtain good results even for some common scaled problems. For better dealing with disparately scaled objectives, this paper selects a weight vector adaptation method instead of normalization approaches.

3 The Proposed DBEA-AWV

This section presents the details of the proposed algorithm.

3.1 General Framework

The general framework of the proposed DBEA-AWV is described as Algorithm 1. First, Das and Dennis's systematic approach [4] is used to generate a set of uniform weight vectors. The population $P \leftarrow \{x_1, x_2, \cdots, x_N\}$ is randomly generated, then the reference point is initialized. The neighborhood set of each weight vector can be derived based on the Euclidean distance. The widely used simulated binary crossover (SBX) and polynomial mutation [25] are applied to produce the offspring. The other two main components, i.e., weight vector adaptation and replacement strategy of updating population will be introduced in details in the following sections.

3.2 Adaptive Weight Vectors

Given a set of uniform weight vectors in a hyperplane, the MOEA/D variants can often produce the uniformly distributed solutions with regard to normalized problems. For scaled problems, it is a challenge to use fixed weight vectors or some normalization approaches [5,10]. This paper adopts a weight vector adaptation method to solve both the normalized and scaled problems. The adaptive weight vectors are adjusted by the ranges of objective values as follows:

$$\lambda_{t+1,k}^{i} = \frac{\lambda_{0,k}^{i} \times \left(f_{t+1,k}^{\max} - f_{t+1,k}^{\min}\right)}{\sum_{j=1}^{m} \times \left(\lambda_{0,j}^{i} \times \left(f_{t+1,j}^{\max} - f_{t+1,j}^{\min}\right)\right)} \tag{11}$$

where $i = 1, 2, \cdots, N$ and $k = 1, 2, \cdots, m$, $\lambda_{t+1,k}^{i}$ denotes k-th value of i-th adaptive weight vector for the next generation $t+1$. $\lambda_{0,k}^{i}$ denotes the k-th value of i-th

---

Algorithm 1. Framework of DBEA-AWV

Input: A set of uniform weight vectors $\Lambda_0 \leftarrow \{\lambda_0^1, \lambda_0^2, \cdots, \lambda_0^N\}$, the maximum number of generations $t_{\max}$

Output: The final population

1 Initialize the population $P \leftarrow \{x_1, x_2, \cdots, x_N\}$;

2 Initialize the reference point $z^* \leftarrow (z_1^*, z_2^*, \cdots, z_m^*)^T$;

3 Set $\Lambda = \Lambda_0$;

4 **for** $i = 1 : N$ **do**

5    $\quad B(i) \leftarrow \{i_1, i_2, \cdots, i_T\}$, where $\lambda^{i_1}, \lambda^{i_2}, \cdots, \lambda^{i_T}$ are T closest weight vectors to λ^i;

6 **end**

7 **while** $t < t_{\max}$ **do**

8    $\quad$ **for** $i = 1 : N$ **do**

9    $\quad\quad y = \text{offspring\_creation}\left(P_t, \lambda^i, B(i)\right)$;

10   $\quad\quad z^* = \text{Update\_Ideal\_Point}(y, z^*)$;

11   $\quad\quad P_{t+1} = \text{Update\_Population}(y, z^*, \Lambda_t, P_t)$;

12   $\quad$ **end**

13   $\quad \Lambda_{t+1} = \text{Weight\_Vector\_Adaption}(t, P_{t+1}, \Lambda_t, \Lambda_0)$;

14   $\quad t = t + 1$;

15 **end**

---

weight vector in Λ_0. $f_{t+1,k}^{\max}$ and $f_{t+1,k}^{\min}$ represent the maximum and minimum values of the population in the generation $t+1$. The denominator in Eq. (11) makes sure that $\sum_{k=1}^m \lambda_{t+1,k}^i = 1$ is suitable for different decomposition approaches in MOEA/D framework, which is different from the strategy in RVEA [3]. Based on the weight vector adaption strategy, the proposed DBEA-AWV is able to deal with disparately scaled problems.

The literature [8] suggested that weight vector adaptation should be periodically executed to ensure convergence in the search process. The parameter f_r is used to control the frequency, the smaller f_r is, the higher of frequency of weight vector adaptation will be employed. The weight vector adaptation method is described as Algorithm 2.

3.3   Modified Tchebycheff Approach

The modified Tchebycheff approach is defined as follows:

$$\min_{x \in \Omega} g^{mte}(x \,|\, \lambda, z^*) = \min_{x \in \Omega} \; \max_{1 \leq i \leq m} \left\{ \frac{1}{\lambda_i} |f_i(x) - z_i^*| \right\} \tag{12}$$

It has been proved that the modified Tchebycheff approach can produce more uniformly distributed solutions against the original one [15]. Furthermore, we compare six different decomposition approaches (introduced in Sect. 2.1) based on the adaptive weight vectors to solve the SDTLZ1 problem having objectives with different scales [5], and the results are shown in Fig. 1.

Algorithm 2. Weight vector adaptation

Input: Weight vector set Λ_0 and Λ_t, generation index t, population P_{t+1}
Output: Weight vector set Λ_{t+1} and neighborhood set B

1 **if** $\left(\frac{t}{t_{\max}} \bmod f_r\right) == 0$ **then**
2   Calculate the maximum and minimum objective values of $f_{t+1,k}^{\max}$ and $f_{t+1,k}^{\min}$ of P_{t+1}, respectively;
3   **for** $i \leftarrow 1\ to\ N$ **do**
4   **for** $k \leftarrow 1\ to\ m$ **do**
5             $\lambda_{t+1,k}^i = \dfrac{\lambda_{0,k}^i \times \left(f_{t+1,k}^{\max} - f_{t+1,k}^{\min}\right)}{\sum_{j=1}^{m} \times \left(\lambda_{0,j}^i \times \left(f_{t+1,j}^{\max} - f_{t+1,j}^{\min}\right)\right)};$
6   **end**
7   **end**
8   **for** $i \leftarrow 1\ to\ N$ **do**
9   Calculate the neighborhood set $B(i) \leftarrow \{i_1, i_2, \cdots, i_T\}$;
10   **end**
11 **else**
12    $\Lambda_{t+1} = \Lambda_t$;
13 **end**

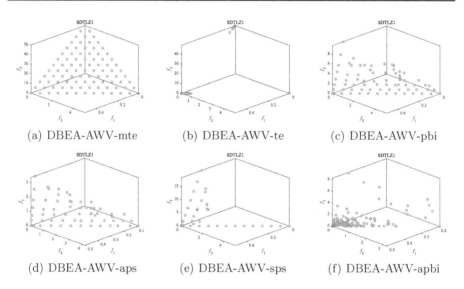

(a) DBEA-AWV-mte   (b) DBEA-AWV-te   (c) DBEA-AWV-pbi

(d) DBEA-AWV-aps   (e) DBEA-AWV-sps   (f) DBEA-AWV-apbi

Fig. 1. The obtained fronts of six decomposition approaches on SDTLZ1.

From Fig. 1, we can see that except for the modified Tchebycheff approach, the proposed algorithm with other decomposition methods cannot find the true Pareto fronts. Therefore we select the modified Tchebycheff approach combined with adaptive weight vectors as our algorithm, denoted as DBEA-AWV to replace DBEA-AWV-mte for convenience.

3.4 Replacement Strategy

Compared with MOPs, in MaOPs it should be paid more attention to balancing the diversity and convergence based on a set of uniform weight vectors. Instead of updating the whole neighboring solutions, we choose one novel replacement strategy for MOPs and MaOPs.

With respect to MOPs and MaOPs, we calculate the acute angles between the offspring and all the solutions in the current population when a offspring is produced. A cluster of front K solutions are marked based on the sort of increasing acute angles. Then the offspring is compared with these K solutions one by one using the modified Tchebycheff value, and the process is terminated until one of K solutions is replaced with the offspring. In this way, the balance factor K is vital for the controlling the convergence and diversity and the influence of K will be discussed in Sect. 4.

3.5 Computational Complexity

In the proposed DBEA-AWV, the major computational costs are the iteration process in Algorithm 1. Step 9 randomly chooses two solutions from the neighborhood set for genetic operators. Step 10 requires $O(m)$ comparisons to update the reference point. Step 11 performs $O(mN)$ operations to update the population for MOPs and MaOPs at the worst case. For the weight vector adaptation strategy in Step 13, it needs $O(mN)$ and $O(N^2)$ operations to update the weight vectors and the neighborhood set. Since it has N passes from Step 8 to Step 12, the overall computational complexity becomes $O(mN^2)$ for one generation of DBEA-AWV.

4 Experimental Studies

In this section empirical experiments are conducted on different MOPs and MaOPs to compare DBEA-AWV with other state-of-the-art algorithms. We then analyze the influence of parameters in DBEA-AWV.

4.1 Experimental Design

The experimental design includes four parts.

(1) Test problems. The test problems are chosen form the widely used benchmark test suites ZDT [26] (included scaled ZDT, i.e. SZDT), DTLZ [7] (included scaled DTLZ, i.e. SDTLZ). SZDT and SDTLZ test suites are modified by ZDT and DTLZ. To illustrate, if the scaling factor is a, the objective value f_i of SZDT and SDTLZ is multiplied by a^{i-1}, that is:

$$f_i = a^{i-1}f_i, \quad i = 1, 2, \cdots, m \tag{13}$$

DTLZ and SDTLZ test problems can be scaled to any number of objectives. The scaling factors used in SZDT and SDTLZ with different number of objectives are listed as Table 1.

Table 1. The scaling factor.

No. of objectives (m)	Scaling factor (a)
2	10
3	10
5	10
8	3
10	2

(2) Performance metrics. The inverted generational distance (IGD) [28] and hypervolume (HV) [28] are adopted to evaluate the performance of the tested algorithms. For scaled problems, the objectives values are normalized by the ideal and nadir points of exact PF. The smaller IGD and larger HV means better.

(3) Comparing algorithms. To assess the performance of the proposed DBEA-AWV, overall ten different state-of-the-art algorithms are chosen to evaluate. Five MOEAs are considered for MOPs. NSGA-II and IBEA are the representative Pareto dominance and indicator-based MOEAs, respectively. Other three MOEA/D (using Tchebycheff), MOEA/D-AWA [15] and MOEA/D-STM [13] are the popular MOEA/D variants. Five many-objective optimization algorithms are selected for MaOPs. NSGA-III and RVEA are two widely used algorithms with good performance. Other three MOEA/DD [12], MOEA/D-DU [23] and MOEA/D-PaS [19] are the typical decomposition-based algorithms for many-objective optimization. All the algorithms are implemented in the PlatEMO framework [18].

(4) Parameter settings. The population size of decomposition-based algorithms is controlled by a parameter H ($N = C_{H+m-1}^{m-1}$). To obtain the uniform weight vectors, a two-layered weight vectors method [5] is used. Table 2 lists the population size used for different number of objectives of proposed DBEA-AWV. For comparison, other tested algorithms adopt same population size.

Table 2. The population size.

No. of objectives (m)	Parameter (H_1, H_2)	Population size (N)
2	99, 0	100
3	13, 0	105
5	5, 0	210
8	3, 2	156
10	3, 2	275

The neighborhood size of decomposition-based algorithms is set to $0.1N$. The crossover probability and distribution index of SBX are set to $p_c = 1$ and $\eta_c = 20$, respectively. For polynomial mutation, the mutation probability and distribution index are set to $p_m = 1/n$ and $\eta_m = 20$, where n is the number of decision variables. For other parameters for specific algorithms, we use the same settings as the original references.

In DBEA-AWV, the frequency control parameter is set to $f_r = 0.2$, and the factor in replacement strategy is set to $K = 5$. More details of parameter analysis will be discussed in Sect. 4.4.

The termination of each run is the maximal number of generations, which is set to 1000 for all test problems. Each algorithm is run 30 times independently on each test instance, and the average and standard deviation of metric values are recorded. The Wilcoxon rank sum test at a 5% significance level is used to compare the experimental results, where the symbol '+', '−' and '≈' denotes that the result of another algorithm is significantly better, significantly worse and similar to that obtained by DBEA-AWV, respectively.

4.2   Comparative Results on MOPs

Table 3 presents the IGD metric values obtained by NSGA-II, IBEA, MOEA/D, MOEA/D-AWA, MOEA/D-STM, and DBEA-AWV on MOPs, including ZDT1-ZDT6, SZDT1-SZDT6, DTLZ1-4 and SDTLZ1-SDTLZ4. The proposed DBEA-AWV could achieve the best performance on 15 of 18 instances of all the test problems, while compared algorithms could get one or two best results at most. According to the Wilcoxon rank sum test, the proposed DBEA-AWV has great advantages. It is still noted that NSGA-II and MOEA/D-AWA show some features suitable for the non-uniform distributed solutions especially for disconnected Pareto fronts.

Figures 2 and 3 show the obtained fronts with medium value of IGD metric of all six algorithms for 2-objective ZDT4 and 3-objective SDTLZ3. We can find that some algorithms can deal well with the normalized ZDT4, whereas only DBEA-AWV can get the true Pareto front of the scaled SDTLZ3 with better convergence and diversity. It is obvious that the proposed DBEA-AWV is competitive for all the normalized and scaled MOPs.

4.3   Comparative Results on MaOPs

Table 4 presents the HV metric values obtained by NSGA-III, RVEA, MOEA/DD, MOEA/D-DU, MOEA/D-PaS, and DBEA-AWV on MaOPs, including many-objective DTLZ1-4 and SDTLZ1-SDTLZ4. The proposed DBEA-AWV could achieve the best performance on 15 of 24 instances, while the number of best results obtained by NSGA-III, RVEA, MOEA/DD, MOEA/D-DU and MOEA/D-PaS are 1, 0, 2, 6, and 0, respectively. Although NSGA-III can get only one best result, it has the stable performance for most of the MaOPs. MOEA/D-DU and MOEA/DD can acquire some best results for normalized many-objective DTLZ problems, while they seem to encounter difficulties when

Table 3. The IGD values obtained by tested algorithms.

Problem	m	NSGA-II	IBEA	MOEA/D	MOEA/D-AWA	MOEAD-STM	DBEA-AWV
ZDT1	2	4.6126e-3 (1.69e-4) −	4.5333e-3 (1.44e-4) −	3.8878e-3 (6.84e-8) ≈	3.9579e-3 (3.64e-5) −	3.9352e-3 (2.16e-5) −	**3.8876e-3 (6.06e-7)**
ZDT2	2	4.7196e-3 (1.31e-4) −	9.5288e-3 (1.11e-3) −	**3.8070e-3 (8.79e-9) +**	3.8303e-3 (1.70e-5) −	3.8367e-3 (1.18e-5) −	3.8070e-3 (1.23e-8)
ZDT3	2	1.1804e-2 (1.33e-2) −	4.9370e-2 (3.98e-2) −	1.1079e-2 (6.36e-6) −	**5.0208e-3 (1.34e-4) +**	1.1012e-2 (2.61e-5) −	7.0573e-3 (1.55e-2)
ZDT4	2	4.4721e-3 (1.48e-4) −	1.9465e-2 (2.60e-3) −	3.8975e-3 (1.27e-5) ≈	3.9465e-3 (5.25e-5) −	3.9749e-3 (1.21e-4) −	**3.8907e-3 (1.37e-5)**
ZDT6	2	3.8764e-3 (1.00e-4) −	5.3567e-3 (1.43e-4) −	3.2597e-3 (3.78e-7) −	3.2617e-3 (1.44e-5) −	3.2594e-3 (8.86e-8) −	**3.1575e-3 (2.27e-7)**
SZDT1	2	4.5832e-3 (1.49e-4) −	4.4852e-3 (1.81e-4) −	1.2390e-2 (2.16e-6) −	4.3416e-3 (1.21e-4) −	1.2406e-2 (2.13e-5) −	**3.8875e-3 (7.56e-7)**
SZDT2	2	4.7551e-3 (2.19e-4) −	9.1512e-3 (9.84e-4) −	1.5905e-2 (2.39e-7) −	6.7764e-3 (9.80e-4) −	1.6000e-2 (5.40e-5) −	**3.8070e-3 (1.27e-8)**
SZDT3	2	8.5945e-3 (9.99e-3) +	5.0946e-2 (3.93e-2) −	5.4132e-2 (7.66e-5) −	**7.1083e-3 (1.38e-3) ≈**	5.3839e-2 (1.83e-4) −	1.0178e-2 (9.86e-3)
SZDT4	2	4.6028e-3 (1.51e-4) −	1.8516e-2 (2.32e-3) −	1.2400e-2 (2.38e-5) −	4.3634e-3 (1.21e-4) −	1.2422e-2 (2.22e-5) −	**3.9264e-3 (3.12e-5)**
SZDT6	2	4.0015e-3 (2.01e-4) −	5.3703e-3 (9.87e-5) −	1.5110e-2 (1.92e-6) −	3.6376e-3 (8.29e-5) −	1.5109e-2 (2.13e-6) −	**3.1672e-3 (2.22e-5)**
+/−/≈		1/9/0	0/10/0	1/7/2	1/8/1	0/10/0	
DTLZ1	3	5.3162e-2 (2.73e-3) −	3.1082e-1 (5.65e-2) −	5.6991e-2 (2.11e-5) −	4.0135e-2 (5.80e-4) −	3.8079e-2 (5.46e-5) −	**3.7967e-2 (2.47e-5)**
DTLZ2	3	6.7512e-2 (2.40e-3) −	7.9687e-2 (2.17e-3) −	6.9623e-2 (5.18e-5) −	5.0666e-2 (2.13e-4) −	5.1043e-2 (2.03e-4) −	**5.0318e-2 (1.09e-5)**
DTLZ3	3	6.7180e-2 (2.59e-3) −	4.7455e-1 (7.88e-3) −	6.9437e-2 (2.02e-4) −	5.1034e-2 (3.45e-4) −	5.3434e-2 (1.04e-3) −	**5.0627e-2 (1.67e-4)**
DTLZ4	3	6.6333e-2 (2.01e-3) −	7.7829e-2 (2.01e-3) −	3.4147e-1 (3.43e-1) −	1.1616e-1 (1.69e-1) −	7.6677e-2 (6.17e-2) −	**5.0327e-2 (2.01e-5)**
SDTLZ1	3	5.2909e-2 (2.25e-3) −	3.0006e-1 (3.67e-2) −	2.9216e-1 (2.80e-4) −	1.4347e-1 (5.21e-2) −	3.3976e-1 (8.95e-2) −	**3.7971e-2 (2.02e-5)**
SDTLZ2	3	6.7847e-2 (2.88e-3) −	7.8525e-2 (2.31e-3) −	3.4039e-1 (1.06e-4) −	1.2649e-1 (1.20e-2) −	2.7225e-1 (2.09e-4) −	**5.0368e-2 (9.58e-5)**
SDTLZ3	3	6.8050e-2 (3.08e-3) −	4.7493e-1 (9.90e-3) −	3.4169e-1 (1.12e-3) −	1.3736e-1 (1.21e-2) −	1.3067e+0 (2.36e+0) −	**5.1217e-2 (7.75e-4)**
SDTLZ4	3	9.5373e-2 (1.61e-1) −	1.0637e-1 (1.59e-1) −	6.0224e-1 (2.58e-1) −	2.7603e-1 (2.45e-1) −	2.9495e-1 (3.71e-2) −	**5.0329e-2 (1.06e-5)**
+/−/≈		0/8/0	0/8/0	0/8/0	0/8/0	0/8/0	

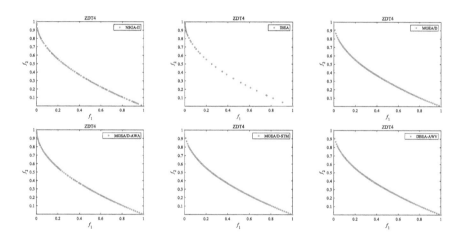

Fig. 2. The obtained fronts of tested algorithms on 2-objective ZDT4.

facing the scaled test instances. The proposed DBEA-AWV perform much better than other compared algorithms on MaOPs with disparately scaled objectives. As shown in Table 4, DBEA-AWV is always reliable and effective to achieve the good performance for both normalized and scaled MaOPs.

Figures 4 and 5 show the obtained fronts with medium value of HV metric of all six algorithms for 10-objective DTLZ1 and SDTLZ3. It can be observed that NSGA-III, RVEA, MOEA/DD, MOEA/D-DU and DBEA-AWV have obtained good approximations to true Pareto front of 10-objective DTLZ1. For 10-objective SDTLZ3, only NSGA-III, MOEA/D-DU and DBEA-AWV get the right fronts. Furthermore, DBEA-AWV can acquire a better performance with

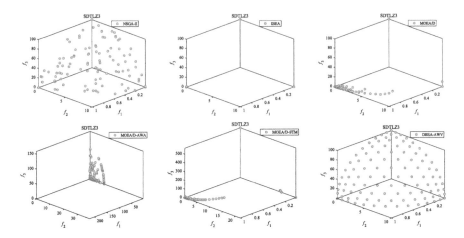

Fig. 3. The obtained fronts of tested algorithms on 3-objective SDTLZ3.

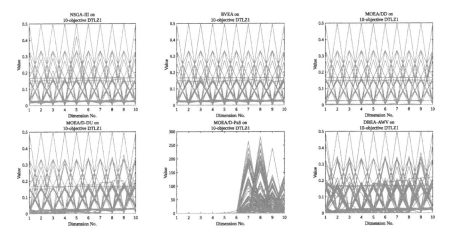

Fig. 4. The obtained fronts of tested algorithms on 10-objective DTLZ1.

regard to convergence and diversity compared with NSGA-III, MOEA/D-DU. In general the proposed DBEA-AWV has a promising versatility of solving normalized and scaled MaOPs.

4.4 Parameter Sensitivity Analysis

There are two major parameters to be specified in the proposed DBEA-AWV, i.e., K controlling the balance between convergence and diversity and f_r controlling frequency of employing the weight vector adaptation. To investigate the sensitivity about these two parameters, different settings of K and f_r are used in DBEA-AWV on DTLZ2 and SDTLZ3, which represent normalized and scaled problems, respectively.

Table 4. The HV values obtained by tested algorithms.

Problem	m	NSGA-III	RVEA	MOEA/DD	MOEA/D-DU	MOEA/D-PaS	DBEA-AWV
DTLZ1	5	9.7985e-1 (1.62e-4) ≈	9.7982e-1 (1.18e-4) ≈	9.7989e-1 (1.53e-4) ≈	9.7990e-1 (1.60e-4) ≈	5.5473e-1 (4.53e-1) −	9.7985e-1 (1.56e-4)
	8	9.9714e-1 (1.12e-3) ≈	9.9761e-1 (4.64e-5) +	9.9756e-1 (6.69e-5) +	9.9765e-1 (6.60e-5) ≈	6.1110e-2 (1.67e-1) −	9.9732e-1 (1.42e-3)
	10	9.9680e-1 (1.32e-2) −	9.9969e-1 (1.87e-5) −	9.9967e-1 (1.46e-5) −	9.9969e-1 (1.80e-5) −	2.7064e-2 (1.48e-4) −	9.9970e-1 (1.58e-5)
DTLZ2	5	8.1254e-1 (4.40e-4) ≈	8.1261e-1 (4.47e-4) ≈	8.1263e-1 (4.13e-4) ≈	8.1263e-1 (3.38e-4) ≈	7.6761e-1 (2.02e-2) −	8.1250e-1 (3.68e-4)
	8	9.1111e-1 (3.34e-2) −	9.2411e-1 (2.45e-4) −	9.2411e-1 (2.73e-4) −	9.2436e-1 (8.79e-4) −	4.6198e-1 (2.37e-1) −	9.2475e-1 (3.91e-4)
	10	9.5953e-1 (2.12e-2) −	9.6976e-1 (1.58e-4) −	9.6979e-1 (1.82e-4) −	9.7019e-1 (3.45e-4) −	1.5943e-1 (1.90e-1) −	9.7043e-1 (2.01e-4)
DTLZ3	5	8.1105e-1 (1.11e-3) ≈	8.1131e-1 (1.04e-3) ≈	8.1190e-1 (7.01e-4) +	8.1191e-1 (6.71e-4) +	4.6863e-1 (3.02e-1) −	8.1141e-1 (8.05e-4)
	8	8.7304e-1 (1.73e-1) −	9.2233e-1 (1.39e-3) ≈	9.2182e-1 (1.62e-3) ≈	9.2242e-1 (1.60e-3) ≈	4.7565e-1 (5.00e-2) −	9.1732e-1 (1.54e-2)
	10	9.2389e-1 (1.56e-1) −	9.6936e-1 (4.14e-4) +	9.6950e-1 (2.36e-4) +	9.6880e-1 (5.82e-4) ≈	4.8485e-2 (4.61e-2) −	9.6021e-1 (1.22e-2)
DTLZ4	5	8.0895e-1 (1.98e-2) ≈	8.1264e-1 (2.81e-4) ≈	8.1270e-1 (4.78e-4) ≈	8.1260e-1 (3.98e-4) ≈	7.5010e-1 (3.86e-2) −	8.1276e-1 (4.83e-4)
	8	9.1312e-1 (3.64e-2) −	9.2400e-1 (2.16e-4) −	9.2406e-1 (1.87e-4) −	9.2665e-1 (5.08e-4) +	8.9996e-1 (6.68e-3) −	9.2617e-1 (3.53e-4)
	10	9.6840e-1 (6.21e-3) −	9.6975e-1 (1.81e-4) −	9.6979e-1 (1.79e-4) −	9.7123e-1 (1.92e-4) +	9.5729e-1 (7.90e-3) −	9.7106e-1 (2.36e-4)
SDTLZ1	5	9.7833e-1 (2.96e-3) −	7.0877e-1 (1.68e-1) −	4.4899e-1 (6.13e-3) −	9.7655e-1 (4.68e-4) −	6.1446e-1 (4.65e-1) −	9.7978e-1 (3.18e-4)
	8	9.9638e-1 (3.12e-3) −	8.5694e-1 (6.72e-2) −	6.6415e-1 (1.21e-2) −	9.9470e-1 (4.49e-4) −	3.0818e-2 (8.90e-2) −	9.9729e-1 (5.77e-4)
	10	9.9467e-1 (1.39e-2) −	9.7052e-1 (9.45e-3) −	8.2216e-1 (8.84e-3) −	9.9927e-1 (4.96e-5) −	5.8189e-2 (1.60e-1) −	9.9961e-1 (9.88e-5)
SDTLZ2	5	8.1255e-1 (4.18e-4) +	7.7032e-1 (4.27e-3) −	2.4895e-1 (1.89e-2) −	6.7704e-1 (1.05e-3) −	7.5242e-1 (5.37e-2) −	8.1221e-1 (5.38e-4)
	8	9.2012e-1 (1.10e-2) −	7.7615e-1 (3.49e-2) −	3.2121e-1 (1.59e-2) −	8.9447e-1 (2.91e-3) −	4.8659e-1 (2.49e-1) −	9.2255e-1 (7.29e-4)
	10	9.6749e-1 (6.36e-3) −	9.1550e-1 (9.00e-3) −	5.0061e-1 (2.32e-2) −	9.5674e-1 (1.24e-3) −	1.2844e-1 (1.41e-1) −	9.6933e-1 (4.21e-4)
SDTLZ3	5	8.0842e-1 (6.29e-3) −	2.9667e-1 (1.66e-1) −	2.6951e-1 (1.55e-2) −	6.7218e-1 (5.08e-3) −	5.1518e-1 (3.01e-1) −	8.0941e-1 (9.55e-4)
	8	8.4412e-1 (2.08e-1) −	4.7586e-1 (1.24e-1) −	3.2048e-1 (1.84e-2) −	8.7872e-1 (7.63e-3) −	8.2632e-2 (1.13e-1) −	9.0631e-1 (1.74e-2)
	10	9.1410e-1 (1.21e-1) −	7.8909e-1 (7.86e-2) −	4.9249e-1 (1.57e-2) −	9.5030e-1 (2.14e-3) −	6.9697e-2 (3.91e-2) −	9.6090e-1 (5.65e-3)
SDTLZ4	5	8.1213e-1 (4.80e-4) −	7.8040e-1 (2.00e-3) −	2.8442e-1 (1.94e-2) −	6.7723e-1 (4.42e-4) −	7.5781e-1 (3.21e-2) −	8.1232e-1 (4.05e-4)
	8	9.1587e-1 (2.38e-2) −	8.4798e-1 (5.48e-3) −	3.6363e-1 (3.29e-2) −	8.9998e-1 (2.86e-4) −	8.9667e-1 (1.96e-2) −	9.2619e-1 (3.18e-4)
	10	9.6701e-1 (9.66e-3) −	9.4574e-1 (2.87e-3) −	5.4249e-1 (1.74e-2) −	9.6072e-1 (2.02e-4) −	9.5751e-1 (6.86e-3) −	9.7110e-1 (1.49e-4)
$+/-/\approx$		1/12/11	2/17/5	3/17/4	3/14/7	0/24/0	

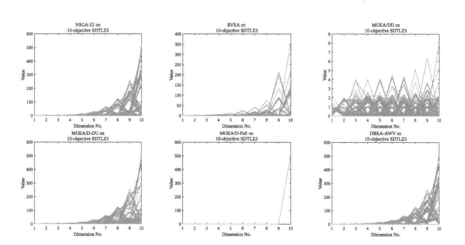

Fig. 5. The obtained fronts of tested algorithms on 10-objective SDTLZ3.

We first analyze the sensitivity of parameter K, where K varies from 1 to 20 and f_r is fixed to 0.2. The average HV values obtained by DBEA-AWV with different K over 30 independent runs are shown in Fig. 6. Two observations from the results can be noted. The first observation is that DTLZ2 having a simple search landscape is not sensitive to the parameter K. Second, SDTLZ3 is a representative disparately scaled problem with multimodality, where as the number of objectives increases the performance starts to be better with increasing values

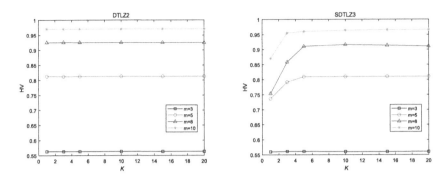

Fig. 6. The average HV values obtained by DBEA-AWV with different K.

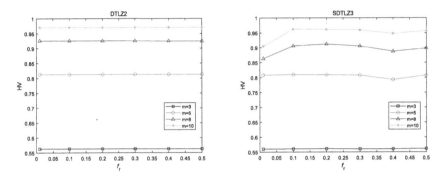

Fig. 7. The average HV values obtained by DBEA-AWV with different f_r.

of K. However, the optimization results cannot always be better with increasing of K when K becomes larger than 15. It implies that a suitable setting of K can achieve better balance between convergence and diversity especially for many-objective optimization. Based on the analysis, K is recommended to be selected between $[5, 15]$.

The sensitivity analysis of parameter f_r is carried out, where f_r varies from 0.01 to 0.5 and K is fixed to 5. The average HV values obtained by DBEA-AWV with different f_r over 30 independent runs are shown in Fig. 7. It can be observed that the normalized problem DTLZ2 having the same range of objectives is insensitive to the parameter f_r. For SDTLZ3 with high dimensional objectives, a too small f_r, employing weight vector adaptation frequently, will lead to deterioration of performance of DBEA-AWV. On the other hand, a too large f_r is also not beneficial for the performance. Therefore, f_r is recommended to be selected between $[0.1, 0.3]$.

5   Conclusions and Future Work

In this paper, we have proposed the DBEA-AWV algorithm for solving MOPs and MaOPs. In order to improve the performance of DBEA-AWV on disparately scaled problems, a strategy for adapting weight vectors is adopted to tune weight vectors according to the range of each objective with respect to candidate solutions. Based on the adaptive weight vectors, we compare several existing popular approaches and find out that the modified Tchebycheff approach shows high efficiency in dealing with both normalized and scaled problems. What's more, a novel replacement strategy is developed to achieve better balance between convergence and diversity especially for MaOPs.

To investigate the performance of DBEA-AWV, we compare DBEA-AWV with ten state-of-the-art MOEAs. The experimental results demonstrate that DBEA-AWV is competitive and efficient compared with other algorithms.

In the future, further investigation on how to extend the algorithm to solve other problems is still desirable, such as MOPs with irregular PFs and constrained problems. The use of DBEA-AWV in practice is also to be investigated.

References

1. Bader, J., Zitzler, E.: HypE: an algorithm for fast hypervolume-based many-objective optimization. Evol. Comput. **19**(1), 45–76 (2011)
2. Beume, N., Naujoks, B., Emmerich, M.: SMS-EMOA: multiobjective selection based on dominated hypervolume. Eur. J. Oper. Res. **181**(3), 1653–1669 (2007)
3. Cheng, R., Jin, Y., Olhofer, M., Sendhoff, B.: A reference vector guided evolutionary algorithm for many-objective optimization. IEEE Trans. Evol. Comput. **20**(5), 773–791 (2016)
4. Das, I., Dennis, J.E.: Normal-boundary intersection: a new method for generating the Pareto surface in nonlinear multicriteria optimization problems. SIAM J. Optim. **8**(3), 631–657 (1998)
5. Deb, K., Jain, H.: An evolutionary many-objective optimization algorithm using reference-point-based nondominated sorting approach, part I: solving problems with box constraints. IEEE Trans. Evol. Comput. **18**(4), 577–601 (2013)
6. Deb, K., Pratap, A., Agarwal, S., Meyarivan, T.: A fast and elitist multiobjective genetic algorithm: NSGA-II. IEEE Trans. Evol. Comput. **6**(2), 182–197 (2002)
7. Deb, K., Thiele, L., Laumanns, M., Zitzler, E.: Scalable test problems for evolutionary multiobjective optimization. In: Abraham, A., Jain, L., Goldberg, R. (eds.) Evolutionary Multiobjective Optimization, pp. 105–145. Springer, London (2005). https://doi.org/10.1007/1-84628-137-7_6
8. Giagkiozis, I., Purshouse, R.C., Fleming, P.J.: Towards understanding the cost of adaptation in decomposition-based optimization algorithms. In: 2013 IEEE International Conference on Systems, Man, and Cybernetics, pp. 615–620. IEEE (2013)
9. Han, D., Du, W., Du, W., Jin, Y., Wu, C.: An adaptive decomposition-based evolutionary algorithm for many-objective optimization. Inf. Sci. **491**, 204–222 (2019)
10. Li, H., Sun, J., Zhang, Q., Shui, Y.: Adjustment of weight vectors of penalty-based boundary intersection method in MOEA/D. In: Deb, K., et al. (eds.) EMO 2019. LNCS, vol. 11411, pp. 91–100. Springer, Cham (2019). https://doi.org/10.1007/978-3-030-12598-1_8

11. Li, H., Zhang, Q.: Multiobjective optimization problems with complicated Pareto sets, MOEA/D and NSGA-II. IEEE Trans. Evol. Comput. **13**(2), 284 (2009)
12. Li, K., Deb, K., Zhang, Q., Kwong, S.: An evolutionary many-objective optimization algorithm based on dominance and decomposition. IEEE Trans. Evol. Comput. **19**(5), 694–716 (2014)
13. Li, K., Zhang, Q., Kwong, S., Li, M., Wang, R.: Stable matching-based selection in evolutionary multiobjective optimization. IEEE Trans. Evol. Comput. **18**(6), 909–923 (2013)
14. Purshouse, R.C., Fleming, P.J.: On the evolutionary optimization of many conflicting objectives. IEEE Trans. Evol. Comput. **11**(6), 770–784 (2007)
15. Qi, Y., Ma, X., Liu, F., Jiao, L., Sun, J., Wu, J.: MOEA/D with adaptive weight adjustment. Evol. Comput. **22**(2), 231–264 (2014)
16. Sun, Y., Yen, G.G., Yi, Z.: IGD indicator-based evolutionary algorithm for many-objective optimization problems. IEEE Trans. Evol. Comput. **23**(2), 173–187 (2018)
17. Tian, Y., Cheng, R., Zhang, X., Cheng, F., Jin, Y.: An indicator-based multiobjective evolutionary algorithm with reference point adaptation for better versatility. IEEE Trans. Evol. Comput. **22**(4), 609–622 (2017)
18. Tian, Y., Cheng, R., Zhang, X., Jin, Y.: PlatEMO: a MATLAB platform for evolutionary multi-objective optimization [educational forum]. IEEE Comput. Intell. Mag. **12**(4), 73–87 (2017)
19. Wang, R., Zhang, Q., Zhang, T.: Decomposition-based algorithms using Pareto adaptive scalarizing methods. IEEE Trans. Evol. Comput. **20**(6), 821–837 (2016)
20. Yang, S., Jiang, S., Jiang, Y.: Improving the multiobjective evolutionary algorithm based on decomposition with new penalty schemes. Soft. Comput. **21**(16), 4677–4691 (2017)
21. Yang, S., Li, M., Liu, X., Zheng, J.: A grid-based evolutionary algorithm for many-objective optimization. IEEE Trans. Evol. Comput. **17**(5), 721–736 (2013)
22. Yuan, Y., Xu, H., Wang, B., Yao, X.: A new dominance relation-based evolutionary algorithm for many-objective optimization. IEEE Trans. Evol. Comput. **20**(1), 16–37 (2015)
23. Yuan, Y., Xu, H., Wang, B., Zhang, B., Yao, X.: Balancing convergence and diversity in decomposition-based many-objective optimizers. IEEE Trans. Evol. Comput. **20**(2), 180–198 (2015)
24. Zhang, J., Xing, L.: A survey of multiobjective evolutionary algorithms. In: 2017 IEEE International Conference on Computational Science and Engineering (CSE) and IEEE International Conference on Embedded and Ubiquitous Computing (EUC), vol. 1, pp. 93–100, July 2017
25. Zhang, Q., Li, H.: MOEA/D: a multiobjective evolutionary algorithm based on decomposition. IEEE Trans. Evol. Comput. **11**(6), 712–731 (2007)
26. Zitzler, E., Deb, K., Thiele, L.: Comparison of multiobjective evolutionary algorithms: empirical results. Evol. Comput. **8**(2), 173–195 (2000)
27. Zitzler, E., Künzli, S.: Indicator-based selection in multiobjective search. In: Yao, X., et al. (eds.) PPSN 2004. LNCS, vol. 3242, pp. 832–842. Springer, Heidelberg (2004). https://doi.org/10.1007/978-3-540-30217-9_84
28. Zitzler, E., Thiele, L., Laumanns, M., Fonseca, C.M., Da Fonseca Grunert, V.: Performance assessment of multiobjective optimizers: an analysis and review. TIK-Report 139 (2002)

Differential Evolution Multi-Objective for Tertiary Protein Structure Prediction

Pedro Henrique Narloch[ID] and Márcio Dorn[(✉)][ID]

Institute of Informatics, Federal University of Rio Grande do Sul,
Porto Alegre, Brazil
mdorn@inf.ufrgs.br

Abstract. The determination of proteins' structure is very expensive
and time-consuming, making computer-aided methods attractive. However, in computational terms, the protein structure prediction is a NP-
Hard problem [17], meaning that there is no efficient algorithm that can
find a solution in a viable computational time. Nonetheless, the energy
terms that compose different force fields seem to be conflicting among
themselves, leading to a multi-objective problem. In this sense, different works in the literature have proposed multi-objective formulations
of search mechanisms. Hence, we use the Differential Evolution Multi-
Objective (DEMO) algorithm with the Rosetta score3 energy function as
a force field. In our work, we split the energy terms into two objectives,
one with only the *van der Waals* values, while the second one contains
the remaining bonded and non-bonded, including the secondary structure reinforcement. Moreover, we enhance the DEMO algorithm with
structural knowledge provided by the Angle Probability List (APL).
From this perspective, our work provides different contributions to the
research area, since the DEMO algorithm was never used in this problem,
neither the APL with this algorithm. Also, the multi-objective formulation using Rosetta score3 was not yet explored by related works, even
though its relevance for the problem. Results obtained show that the
DEMO found better structures than the single-objective differential evolution that uses the same mutation mechanism, energy function, and
APL. Also, DEMO reached competitive results when comparing with
state-of-art bi-objective approaches.

Keywords: Protein structure prediction · Differential evolution ·
Multi-objective optimization

1 Introduction

Proteins are macromolecules responsible for vital biological functions in every
living organism. The protein function is directly related to the three-dimensional
arrangement of its structures – also known as tertiary structure or protein native
state [32]. Due to its relevance, the determination of 3D shapes of proteins plays
an essential role in the understanding of how life works, since the misfolding

© Springer Nature Switzerland AG 2020
P. A. Castillo et al. (Eds.): EvoApplications 2020, LNCS 12104, pp. 165–180, 2020.
https://doi.org/10.1007/978-3-030-43722-0_11

of a protein can lead to several different types of illness. Although there are different experimental methods to determine the tertiary protein structure, such as X-ray crystallography and Nuclear Magnetic Resonance (NMR), they are either expensive and time-consuming. In this sense, computational approaches could be helpful to the structural determination, leading to a cheaper and faster identification of structures, and for the understanding of protein's biological function. For these reasons, the Protein Structure Problem (PSP) became a well-known problem in Structural Bioinformatics, which still an open-problem [14].

In order to develop a computational approach to predict the tertiary structure of proteins, there are three main definitions needed: (i) a well-defined protein representation; (ii) a way to measure the three dimensional shape of the protein, and (iii) a search method to explore the conformational search space for finding the best structure overall [14]. There are different ways to represent proteins in a computational model, from the simpler versions of 2D *in lattice* shapes until the all-atom 3D representation (*off lattice*). It is fundamental to state that the tertiary structure prediction in *off lattice* is considered an NP-Hard problem by computational theory, meaning that there is not an exact algorithm that could solve the problem in polynomial time. This complexity is directly related to the number of possible conformations a protein can assume. In light of the computational limitation related to exact search algorithms, bio-inspired algorithms became an exciting class of search methods for the PSP problem in a viable computational time, although they do not guarantee the optimum solution.

Over the years, many studies provided substantial evidence regarding the Differential Evolution algorithm (one well-known evolutionary algorithm) capabilities, leading it to one of the most competitive algorithms in different benchmarks [12] and real-life problems – such as PSP. For this reason, in this work, we use it as the search algorithm. For the tertiary PSP problem, the DE algorithm has been employed in different studies [23,24,29], with different energy functions, and with the multi-objective formulation of the problem as well [31].

Although there is much contribution from previous works, the PSP problem still an open real-world problem, with some gaps that should be covered, contributing to the problem understanding. Nonetheless, it can also provide an understanding of different behaviors and capabilities that the DE algorithm can have in complex real-world problems. In this sense, the purpose of this work is to apply the differential evolution in a multi-objective formulation of PSP problem with structural knowledge provided by the Angle Probability List [4], something not yet explored in the literature body of research. For energy measurement, the score3 energy function is used, setting the first objective as *van der Waals* energy and the second one as bonded energy terms and secondary structure reinforcement. For the simulations, we have selected a set of eight structures, from 29 to 73 amino acids long. Comparisons were made with the single-objective version of DE [23] and four different multi-objective approaches [11,22,31]. The results obtained in this work show that our approach can find better solutions than the single-objective formulation of the problem as well as competitive results in comparison with related works for all test cases.

In a way to present the contributions of the current work, this paper begins by a description (Sect. 2) about the tertiary PSP problem, outlining the characteristics of the problem and different components that build a predictor, as well as related works in the area. It will then go on to the methodology (Sect. 3) used and its contributions. The Sect. 4 presents the results obtained by our experiments, with some numerical comparison and visual representation of predicted proteins. Finally, the work is concluded in Sect. 5, reviewing the fundamentals and contributions obtained by this work, as well as further research projections.

2   Preliminaries

2.1   Protein Structure Prediction

The linear sequence of amino acids represents the composition of a protein, also known as the primary structure. As stated by Anfinsen [2], the functional structure of a protein is related to its unique primary structure and the environment conditions, leading to a unique conformation with the minimum possible free energy of the system. During the biological folding process, amino acids rearrange themselves, creating local geometrical structures (secondary structures) accordingly to energy forces employed among the interaction of atoms. There are different structures, but the most common ones are α-helices and β-sheets [32]. Finally, the global adjustment of all these structures in a 3D space creates the functional protein, known as tertiary structure or native state. These three structures can be visualized in Fig. 1. There is the fourth structure, called a quaternary structure, composed by the interaction of different proteins in order to exert a specific function.

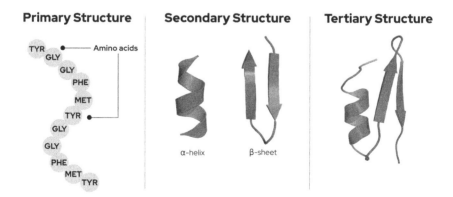

Fig. 1. The three structures that composes a single protein.

Over the years, different approaches were proposed to represent proteins computationally. Among all of them, the most forthright version is the all-atom representation, which depicts the protein in atomic positions in a three-dimensional space. Although this is the most realistic approach, it becomes computationally expensive regarding the number of atoms present in the protein. In this way, many computational approaches describe a protein as a set of torsional angles, keeping the high-quality representation and reducing the computational cost of its representation. For each amino acid, three angles compose the backbone (ϕ, ψ, and ω) and χ_n angles the side-chain of each amino acid. All these angles can assume free rotations in the space, ranging from -180.0 to $+180.0$ degrees, which thereafter are expressed as Cartesian's coordinates for the energy evaluation step. It is important to state that each amino acid has a unique side chain, while the composition of their backbones are equals [32]. Figure 2 presents the computation representation of a small peptide (1PLW) in the torsion angles model. Even though the torsion angles representation reduces the amount of information to describe each atom position, the PSP problem continues to be considered as an NP-Hard problem [17].

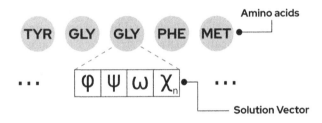

Fig. 2. Protein representation for the torsion angle model

In order to evaluate the energy of a protein structure, different force fields were introduced by different researchers. The most well-known are CHARMM [7], AMBER [18], GROMOS [28] and Rosetta [1]. Although they have their ways to measure the energy of a molecule, all of them consider atomic forces related to bonded and non-bonded interactions. The energy function used in the current work is provided by the PyRosetta[1], a python interface for the Rosetta package containing the energy function used by high-resolution predictors.

2.2 Angle Probability List

Even though different approaches were proposed to solve the PSP problem, none of them genuinely solved it. Since the problem has a high level of complexity associated, it is reasonable to aggregate structural information from proteins that have been described from high-resolution techniques, such as X-ray crystallography. In this context, the Angle Probability List (APL) was created by

---

[1] www.pyrosetta.org.

Borguesan et al. [4], taking into consideration the conformational preference of amino acids accordingly with their expected secondary structure [21]. All the structural information used was obtained in the Protein Data Bank (PDB) [3] using resolutions ≤2.5 Å, creating a set of more than 11,130 structures.

The APL forms a histogram matrix ($H_{aa,ss}$) of $[-180, 180] \times [-180, 180]$ for each amino acid residue (aa) and secondary structure (ss). With this information, it is possible to create different combinations of amino acids considering their dihedral angles preferences. The usage of this information has been very promising, showing that the APL is beneficial for energy reduction and better structure formation. Authors provided a web interface for APL generation called NIAS[2]– Neighbors Influence of Amino acids and Secondary structures [5].

2.3   Multi-Objective Optimization

Although single-objective problems and their optimization tasks are relevant for problem-solving, most real problems do not have only a single-objective function that should be considered. With this purpose, multi-objective formulation of problems became an exciting field of research, since they take into consideration more than one objective in its optimization process [15], becoming more truthful with reality. A multi-objective problem can be formalized as:

$$minimize\ \{f_1(x), f_2(x), f_3(x), ..., f_k(x)\}$$
$$subject\ to\ x \in X \tag{1}$$

where each k is a different cost function of the problem to be solved. It is interesting to state that these functions could be in conflict, where a good value of $f_k(x)$ can have a bad value of $f_{k-1}(x)$. In this sense, for multi-objective problems, we have two types of spaces: the objective space (as shown by Eq. 1), and the decision space (noted as X). Each possible solution $x \in X$ encapsulates properties for a feasible solution, being measured by a vector containing the values of the objective space. With these characteristics, the definition of the best solution (with better fitness) in a set of solutions becomes a non-trivial task since there are conflicts among the objectives of other solutions. In light of this fact, the usage of the Pareto Dominance concept is essential to identify dominant solutions for further analysis.

2.4   Differential Evolution

The Differential Evolution algorithm was firstly proposed by Storn and Price in 1997 [30], being classified as a population-based evolutionary algorithm (EA). Since its very first participation in optimization competitions, the DE achieved better results in comparison with different well-known algorithms [12]. Four components comprise a DE algorithm, the initialization, selection, mutation, and crossover. Algorithm 1 exposes how all these components are linked together.

---

[2] http://sbcb.inf.ufrgs.br/nias.

Also, the DE algorithm has three parameters that must be set before the optimization process: the population size (NP) – how many solutions will be generated, the mutation factor (F), and the crossover rate (CR). Unlike the GAs, that the crossover operation does significant changes in the individual, the mutation mechanism is the main component for the generation of new individuals in the DE algorithm. The first proposed, and yet one of the most used configuration, is the rand/1/bin mutation mechanism, which uses three randomly selected individuals from the population to create the new one. Further, different mechanisms were proposed and evaluated in different applications, taking into consideration more individuals in its composition and elitism.

Algorithm 1. Classical Differential Evolution

Data: NP, F and CR
Result: The best individual in population
Generate initial population with NP individuals
while $g \leq$ *number of generations* **do**
    for *each i individual in population* **do**
        select three random individuals (x_{r1}, x_{r2}, x_{r3})
        $d_{rand} \leftarrow$ select a random dimension to mutate
        for *each d dimension* **do**
            if $d = d_{rand}$ **or** *random* $\leq CR$ **then**
             | $\boldsymbol{u}_{i,d} \leftarrow \boldsymbol{x}^g_{r1,d} + F \cdot (\boldsymbol{x}^g_{r2,d} - \boldsymbol{x}^g_{r3,d})$
            else
             | $\boldsymbol{u}_{i,d} \leftarrow \boldsymbol{x}_{i,d}$
            end
        end
        if $\boldsymbol{u}_{i,fitness} \leq \boldsymbol{x}_{i,fitness}$ **then**
        | add $\boldsymbol{u}_i$ in the offspring
        else
        | add $\boldsymbol{x}_i$ in the offspring
        end
    end
    population $\leftarrow$ offspring
    $g \leftarrow g + 1$
end

In light of the capacity that DE had to handle continuous complex problems as a single-objective algorithm, some multi-objective formulations of the algorithm were performed. Some of them are the Generalized Differential Evolution (GDE – currently on the third version) [20], Differential Evolution Multi-Objective (DEMO) [25] and, the Adaptive Differential Evolution Multi-Objective based on Decomposition (ADEMO/D) [31]. Despite their differences, they all have the influence of one of the most well-known multi-objective algorithm, the second versionf of the Nondominated Sorting Genetic Algorithm (NSGA-II) [13].

2.5   Related Works

Different approaches were proposed to the PSP problem, with different protein representations, energy functions, and search algorithms − most of them as a single-objective optimization problem. In this sense, one of the first researches that explored the multi-objectiveness of the PSP problem was made by Cutello, Narzisi, and Nicosia [11], where the CHARMM [7] force field was divided in two objectives, one considering the bonded forces and other the non-bonded ones. Authors used a Pareto Evolutionary Strategy with immune inspired mechanisms (IPAES) [10, 11]. Following this line of research, Venske et al. [31] used the same bi-objective problem formulation with the ADEMO/D, an adaptive differential evolution algorithm based on decomposition. Both works showed that the multi-objective formulation of the problem could be beneficial for problem-solving since their predicted structures were quite similar to the experimental ones.

Besides the bi-objective formulation of works provided by Cutello, Narzisi, and Nicosia [11], by Venske et al. [31], and their contribution to the problem, other formulations also appeared. The work of Calvo, Ortega, and Anguita [8] evaluated the parallel version of the well-known NSGA-II algorithm with a three-objective formalization, taking into consideration the bonded energies as the first objective, the *van der Waals* interactions as a second objective, and the other non-bonded energies as the third one. For evaluations, the authors used five proteins, comparing the NSGA-II with the PAES algorithm in a 250 thousand of energy evaluations. As expected, the NSGA-II algorithm reached better results in terms of structural similarity. Another work that used the three-objectives is called as PITAGORAS-PSP proposed in [9]. In this case, the authors use the bonded, non-bonded, and structural differences among the initial solution and the current one to define the objective space. The algorithm used in this case is an enhanced version of PAES, with a specific initialization process using random, template-based, or rotamer library information. As far as our concern, this was the first work that tried to add some structural information in the multi-objective formulation of the problem.

Other works have tried different combinations of possible energy terms as in [16], where the solvent effect was taken into consideration, creating a three-objective version of the problem (bonded, non-bonded, and solvent effect). In the analysis made by authors, the solvent effects are beneficial for structural improvements. The search mechanism used was the evolutionary strategy algorithm. Further, a fourth-objective formulation was provided in [6], considering the *van der Waals*, electrostatic, hydrogen bond, and solvation contributions as four energetic objectives to be optimized. As most of the multi-objective algorithms have some limitations to the number of objectives, the authors proposed an algorithm called "multi-objective evolutionary algorithms with many tables" to handle the four objectives. Final remarks state that the algorithm can achieve good structural results without any prior knowledge.

Finally, there is some effort in adding different structural information in multi-objective formulations. In [26], authors used predicted contact maps to evaluate whether predicted proteins respect the predicted contact map or do not, accordingly to a fitness function based on this information. In this sense, a bi-objective formulation can be done, taking into consideration the energy function and the contact map information. Results show that using contact-maps information as an objective could enhance algorithms' capabilities for finding better structures. Following this research, author of [22] used the contact-maps strategy as a second objective and the APL as structural information to enhance the probability of generating more accurate initial structures.

Even though the mentioned works have profoundly contributed to the advancement of multi-objective optimization in the PSP problem, only two of them used some structural information to enhance the algorithm. Also, only the work of Venske et al. [31] used the DE as a search mechanism, even though its outstanding performance on single-objective problems, including the single-objective PSP problem. This gap indicates a need to understand the behavior of a multi-objective DE algorithm using structural information, something not yet explored neither discussed, indicating the importance in this work.

3   Methods

Energy Function: In order to evaluate the molecules, we use the centroid version (score3) [27] of Rosetta energy function provided by a Python interface known as PyRosetta. The *score3* uses a centroid-based representation of amino acids side chains, reducing the problem dimensionality and speeding up the time used to compute the energy of a single protein. In this way, the problem representation became a $2N$ vector, where N is the number of amino acids in the primary structure. As ten terms compose the energy function, depicted in Eq. 2, it is possible to split the terms for a multi-objective formulation based on previous works, which were non-bonded terms (mainly *van der Waals*) compose one of the objectives.

$$E_{total} = \frac{E_{cenpack} + E_{pair} + E_{env} + E_{cbeta} + E_{rg}+}{E_{hs\_pair} + E_{ss\_pair} + E_{rsigma} + E_{sheet} + E_{vdW}} \qquad (2)$$

In this context, our multi-objective formulation will follow related works, where the first objective is composed of *van der Waals* energy, and the second objective is composed of other terms, including the bonded ones. In addition to the second objective, we use a secondary structure scoring term, giving a better score for solutions that match the identified structure from the DSSP [19] method provided by PyRosetta.

Search Strategy: In order to optimize the multi-objective formulation of the problem, the differential evolution multi-objective (DEMO) [25] is used. This algorithm reached good results when applied to benchmark problems in comparison with other multi-objective algorithms. Furthermore, this is the first work that tested DEMO in a Structural Bioinformatics problem. In Fig. 3 it is possible to see the workflow of the DEMO algorithm, a very similar workflow in the canonical DE algorithm shown in Sect. 2.

In our approach, the initialization of the population uses structural data obtained by APL, creating high-value individuals as already other works shown [4,23]. After the initial evaluation of all individuals using the multi-objective formulation of score3, the main loop begins, and it only stops when a stopping criterion is achieved, in our case, the maximum number of fitness evaluations. As in the canonical versions of DE, the algorithm creates a new individual, through a mutation process, for each one of the current population. The differences of DEMO from the canonical DE are in the replacement and truncation operators. In the replacement operator, newly generated individuals are evaluated according to its dominance of their parent (the current individual in the population). Three conditions are checked during this process: **(i)** if the new individual dominates the parent, it replaces the parent in the population for the next generation; **(ii)** if the parent dominates the candidate, then the new individual is discarded. Finally, **(iii)** if there is no dominance between the new individual and its parent, the new solution is attached in the population, increasing the population size by 1. In this sense, if the new solution is a valuable candidate, it can be used for the next mutation processes, emphasizing the elitism during the creation of new solutions.

With the population growing, reaching two times its initial size in the worst case $(2NP)$, it is needed to truncate it to the original size before the next step. For this specific case, the truncation operator is used. The truncation consists of sorting the individuals with the non-dominant sorting algorithm and evaluating the front solutions with the crowding distance metric. This truncation process is derived from the NSGA-II algorithm. Finally, after the optimization process, the post-processing step is done by Pareto front analysis and structural evaluation.

In order to verify the structural information reached by the DEMO_{APL} algorithm, two metrics are used, the root mean square deviation (RMSD) and the global distance metric (GDT). The $\text{RMSD}_{C\alpha}$ is used to measure the distance among C_α atoms present in the protein's backbone, as shown in Eq. 3.

$$\text{RMSD}(a, b) = \sqrt{\frac{\sum\limits_{i=1}^{n} \mid r_{ai} - r_{bi} \mid^2}{n}} \tag{3}$$

where r_{ai} and r_{bi} are the ith atoms in a set of n atoms from structures a and b. The closer RMSD is from 0 Å more similar are the structures. Since there is no unique structure state in the protein conformation, we also consider a second metric, called as GDT, in order to give more information about the protein folding. The GDT considers the mean ratio of the maximum number of atoms that can be aligned using a cutoff. This metric is widely used as an assessment criterion in the Critical Assessment of Structure Prediction (CASP) giving the possibility to compare different computational methods and energies.

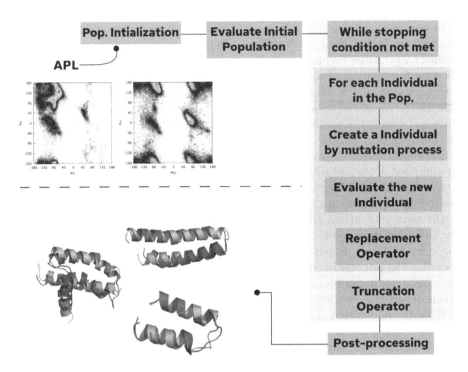

Fig. 3. Workflow used in the current work. The highlighted areas show the DEMO operations and optimization loops. The two main differences between the DEMO and the single objective DE are the replacement operator and the truncation operators.

4   Results and Analysis

In order to evaluate the $DEMO_{APL}$ performance in the PSP problem, we have selected eight structures used in different works present in the literature. These proteins have different secondary structures and sizes, ranging from 29 to 73 amino acids. Table 1 summarizes the proteins, their size in terms of amino acids, and secondary structures in each one of them. The $DEMO_{APL}$ parameters setting is present in Table 2. All these parameters are based on other PSP works in the literature [23,31]. For all proteins listed in Table 1 we performed 30 independent simulations for statistical relevance. Our comparison takes into consideration the works that used the DE as a search algorithm since it is the objective of the current work.

In order to evaluate the quality of the structures found by the $DEMO_{APL}$, we compare the multi-objective approach with the single-objective version of DE used in [23]. Although energy values are not comparable, we can use the RMSD as a metric. Also, in this work, we provide the GDT score, unavailable information in the single-objective work [23]. Results are shown in Table 3. The first column identifies the structure PDB ID, while the second column brings the algorithms. In the third column, the maximum GDT information is provided as well as the

Table 1. Target protein sequences.

PDB ID	Size	Secondary structure
1ACW	29	$\alpha + \beta$
1ZDD	34	α
2MR9	44	α
2P81	44	α
1CRN	46	$\alpha + \beta$
1ENH	54	α
1ROP	63	α
1AIL	73	α

Table 2. DE parameters.

Parameter	Value	Description
NP	100	Population size
CR	0.9	Crossover factor
F	0.5	Mutation factor
Fitness Eval.	10^6	Stop criterion

mean and standard deviation. Finally, on column number 4, the RMSD values are disposed with the minimum value with minimum and standard deviation in parenthesis.

The present results, concerning the data provided by Table 3, are significant in different aspects. The first one is the difference of RMSD values when comparing the $DEMO_{APL}$ with the single-objective $DE_{rand/1/bin}$. In all reported RMSD values, DEMO achieved lower RMSD, showing that the bi-objective formulation of the problem proposed in the current work reaches better structural results rather than the single-objective version of it. The second aspect is the comparison with other state-of-art bi-objective formulations that do not take into consideration the structural knowledge provided by contact maps, nor using solvent surface energy term. In this case, our approach got competitive results with ADEMO/D [31] for protein 1CRN and better RMSDs for proteins 1ROP and 1ZDD. In comparison with IPAES [11], DEMO got slightly bad results for protein 1CRN, but better values for 1ROP and 1ZDD. With this in mind, we can conclude that our approach is competitive with other similar multi-objective approaches, one using DE [31] and the second one using a modified ES [11].

One last comparison can be made with a work that provides a multi-objective formulation of the problem using contact maps and solvent energy terms in its simulation [22]. For the three comparable proteins (1ACW, 1AIL, and 2MR9), all algorithms achieved very similar results regarding the minimum RMSD value, although the results provided in [22] have better mean values and lower standard deviation. When taking into consideration the GDT values, our algorithm did not achieve competitive solutions. The difference can be related to the two additional terms used in [22], where both contact maps and solvent interactions are beneficial for the protein packing. In this sense, it would be interesting to add these terms in future versions of the algorithm.

Additionally, to the numerical analysis, it is interesting to make a visual comparison among the predicted structures and the experimentally determined ones. In this sense, Fig. 4 bring a visual comparison among the best GDT structure (red), the minimum RMSD structure (blue), and the experimental ones (green) for each protein. For those that do not have the visible blue color, means that the same structure represents the best GDT and RMSD value.

Table 3. Results obtained by the approach we used in this work compared with some literature works, with single-objective formulation, different energy functions, and bi-objective formulation. **Highlighted cells** display the best-achieved result in terms of GDT and RMSD.

PDB ID	Algorithm	GDT	RMSD
1ACW	$DEMO_{APL}$	62.75(48.89 ± 6.07)	3.82(7.17 ± 1.81) Å
	$DE_{rand/1/bin}$[23]	–	4.87 Å
	MO-ABC-1 [22]	**77.59(67.03 ± 5.97)**	**1.54(2.8 ± 0.74) Å**
	MO-ABC-2 [22]	74.14(67.24 ± 4.8)	2.05(2.89 ± 0.82) Å
1AIL	$DEMO_{APL}$	**61.71(48.80 ± 6.97)**	**3.14(7.40 ± 2.55) Å**
	MO-ABC-1 [22]	56.79(52.46 ± 5.95)	3.8(5.24 ± 1.57) Å
	MO-ABC-2 [22]	61.43(53.44 ± 6.09)	3.82(5.30 ± 1.33) Å
1CRN	$DEMO_{APL}$	**50.00(38.81 ± 4.71)**	6.32(9.31 ± 2.79) Å
	$DE_{rand/1/bin}$[23]	–	7.40 Å
	ADEMO/D [31]	–	6.06 Å
	IPAES [11]	–	**4.43 Å**
	MOEA [16]	–	5.34 Å
1ENH	$DEMO_{APL}$	**72.96(49.07 ± 7.82)**	**4.29(7.47 ± 1.67) Å**
	$DE_{rand/1/bin}$[23]	–	6.24 Å
1ROP	$DEMO_{APL}$	**66.42(46.01 ± 6.96)**	3.04(6.80 ± 1.61) Å
	$DE_{rand/1/bin}$[23]	–	8.54 Å
	ADEMO/D [31]	–	4.48 Å
	IPAES [11]	–	3.70 Å
	MOEA [16]	–	**3.07 Å**
1ZDD	$DEMO_{APL}$	**93.52(62.72 ± 12.92)**	**1.19(4.01 ± 1.98) Å**
	$DE_{rand/1/bin}$[23]	–	2.78 Å
	ADEMO/D [31]	–	2.14 Å
	IPAES [11]	–	2.27 Å
	MOEA [16]	–	2.16 Å
2MR9	$DEMO_{APL}$	70.45(48.57 ± 8.82)	2.62(7.21 ± 1.87) Å
	$DE_{rand/1/bin}$[23]	–	5.90 Å
	MO-ABC-1 [22]	75.57(71.09 ± 3.13)	2.0(2.27 ± 0.28) Å
	MO-ABC-2 [22]	**76.70(71.45 ± 2.87)**	**1.84(2.44 ± 0.35) Å**
2P81	$DEMO_{APL}$	**69.09(49.81 ± 6.61)**	**5.06(7.72 ± 1.44) Å**
	$DE_{rand/1/bin}$[23]	–	8.11 Å

An important observation is that our approach did not find the β-sheets in 1ACW and 1CRN. This inconsistency can be observed in different literature works, since the β-sheets need an almost perfect alignment between coils, a very flexible structure. Despite the problem with the β-sheet structures, the

DEMO$_{APL}$ achieved very similar structures in comparison with the structures found by experimental methods.

Taken together, this analysis suggests that the bi-objective formulation of the problem is a promising approach, and it can provide more accurate predictions when comparing it with the single-objective formulation. Besides, it is possible to observe that the DEMO algorithm is suitable for the PSP problem, achieving competitive results with state-of-art approaches. In this sense, our work contributes with a different approach to the problem, considering a barely explored multi-objective formulation with Rosetta energy function, and providing data to further comparisons.

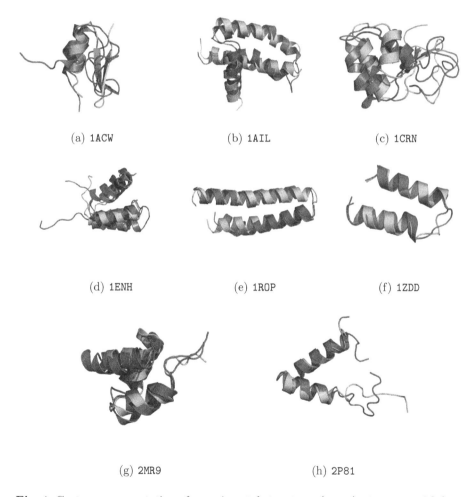

(a) 1ACW   (b) 1AIL   (c) 1CRN

(d) 1ENH   (e) 1ROP   (f) 1ZDD

(g) 2MR9   (h) 2P81

Fig. 4. Cartoon representation of experimental structures (green), structure with best GDT (red), and lowest RMSD structure (blue) found by DEMO. (Color figure online)

5 Conclusions

Although researchers made many contributions to the prediction of tertiary protein structures, the problem still unsolved and challenging. Moreover, there are conflicts regarding the energy terms, indicating that single-objective search mechanisms might struggle with the energy landscape. In light of these facts, in this investigation, our objective was to evaluate the Differential Evolution algorithm in the Multi-Objective version of the PSP problem, using the energy function provided by Rosetta modeling software, and information from the Angle Probability List (DEMO$_{APL}$).

In our approach, we have grouped the energy terms into two objectives, one containing only the *van der Waals* interactions, while the second objective is composed of different *score3* terms and the secondary structure reinforcement score. The proposed approached was not yet explored in literature works, contributing in different ways to the development of the research area. In order to evaluate the efficiency of our approach, we used two structural measurements (GDT and RMSD), and compare them with literature works in a set of 8 proteins. Additionally, a visual analysis was made.

Results obtained by DEMO$_{APL}$ showed that the multi-objective formulation of the PSP problem could find better structural conformations in comparison with the single mutation version of it in terms of RMSD. Also, it was possible to verify that DEMO$_{APL}$ is very competitive with different multi-objective approaches from the literature works, taking into consideration the RMSD and the GDT metrics. In our visual comparison, it was possible to verify that DEMO$_{APL}$ found well defined secondary structures. A limitation of this study was observed when the visual comparison was made, in which our approach was unable to find β-sheet structures for proteins 1ACW and 1CRN, something also observed in other works in the literature. Besides this issue, our study indicates that the DEMO algorithm can contribute to the PSP problem and the research field.

Besides the contributions achieved by our work, there are different possible ways to improve our algorithm. In this sense, future works involve the study of the surface solvent area since it evaluates the compaction of the protein. Another interesting topic would be the self-adaptive version of the algorithm as well as exploring different mutation mechanisms in the mutation process, analyzing their impact in terms of Pareto optimality and structural quality. Finally, the usage of different domain data of the problem with the APL information could be impactful for the research field, enhancing, even more, the capability of different algorithms to explore the search space.

Acknowledgements. This work was supported by grants from MCT/CNPq [*311611/2018-4*], CAPES PROBRAL [*88881.198766/2018-01*] - Brazil, Alexander von Humboldt-Stiftung (*AvH*) [*BRA 1190826 HFST* CAPES-P] - Germany, and FAPERGS [19/2551-0001906-8, APE]. This study was financed in part by the Coordenação de Aperfeiçoamento de Pessoal de Nível Superior - Brasil (CAPES) - Finance Code 001.

References

1. Alford, R.F., et al.: The Rosetta all-atom energy function for macromolecular modeling and design. J. Chem. Theory Comput. **13**(6), 3031–3048 (2017)
2. Anfinsen, C.B.: Principles that govern the folding of protein chains. Science **181**, 223–230 (1973)
3. Berma, H.M., et al.: The protein data bank. Nucleic Acids Res. **28**, 235–242 (2000)
4. Borguesan, B., E Silva, M.B., Grisci, B., Inostroza-Ponta, M., Dorn, M.: APL: an angle probability list to improve knowledge-based metaheuristics for the three-dimensional protein structure prediction. Comput. Biol. Chem. **59**, 142–157 (2015)
5. Borguesan, B., Inostroza-Ponta, M., Dorn, M.: NIAS-server: neighbors influence of amino acids and secondary structures in proteins. J. Comput. Biol. **24**, 255–265 (2017)
6. Brasil, C.R.S., Delbem, A.C.B., Da Silva, F.L.B.: Multiobjective evolutionary algorithm with many tables for purely *ab initio* protein structure prediction. J. Comput. Chem. **34**(20), 1719–1734 (2013)
7. Brooks, B.R., et al.: CHARMM: the biomolecular simulation program. J. Comput. Chem. **30**(10), 1545–1614 (2009)
8. Calvo, J.C., Ortega, J., Anguita, M.: Comparison of parallel multi-objective approaches to protein structure prediction. J. Supercomput. **58**(2), 253–260 (2011)
9. Calvo, J.C., Ortega, J., Anguita, M.: PITAGORAS-PSP: including domain knowledge in a multi-objective approach for protein structure prediction. Neurocomputing **74**(16), 2675–2682 (2011)
10. Cutello, V., Narzisi, G., Nicosia, G.: A class of Pareto archived evolution strategy algorithms using immune inspired operators for ab-initio protein structure prediction. In: Rothlauf, F., et al. (eds.) EvoWorkshops 2005. LNCS, vol. 3449, pp. 54–63. Springer, Heidelberg (2005). https://doi.org/10.1007/978-3-540-32003-6_6
11. Cutello, V., Narzisi, G., Nicosia, G.: Computational studies of peptide and protein structure prediction problems via multiobjective evolutionary algorithms. In: Knowles, J., Corne, D., Deb, K., Chair, D.R. (eds.) Multiobjective Problem Solving from Nature. Natural Computing Series, pp. 93–114. Springer, Heidelberg (2008). https://doi.org/10.1007/978-3-540-72964-8_5
12. Das, S., Mullick, S.S., Suganthan, P.N.: Recent advances in differential evolution–an updated survey. Swarm Evol. Comput. **27**, 1–30 (2016)
13. Deb, K., Pratap, A., Agarwal, S., Meyarivan, T.: A fast and elitist multiobjective genetic algorithm: NSGA-II. IEEE Trans. Evol. Comput. **6**(2), 182–197 (2002)
14. Dorn, M., E Silva, M.B., Buriol, L.S., Lamb, L.C.: Three-dimensional protein structure prediction: methods and computational strategies. Comput. Biol. Chem. **53**, 251–276 (2014)
15. Emmerich, M.T., Deutz, A.H.: A tutorial on multiobjective optimization: fundamentals and evolutionary methods. Nat. Comput. **17**(3), 585–609 (2018)
16. Gao, S., Song, S., Cheng, J., Todo, Y., Zhou, M.C.: Incorporation of solvent effect into multi-objective evolutionary algorithm for improved protein structure prediction. IEEE/ACM Trans. Comput. Biol. Bioinf. **15**(4), 1365–1378 (2018)
17. Guyeux, C., Côté, N.M.L., Bahi, J.M., Bienie, W.: Is protein folding problem really a NP-complete one? First investigations. J. Bioinf. Comput. Biol. **12**, 1350017 (2014)
18. Hornak, V., Abel, R., Okur, A., Strockbine, B., Roitberg, A., Simmerling, C.: Comparison of multiple Amber force fields and development of improved protein backbone parameters. Proteins: Struct. Funct. Bioinf. **65**(3), 712–725 (2006)

19. Kabsch, W., Sander, C.: Dictionary of protein secondary structure: pattern recognition of hydrogen-bonded and geometrical features. Biopolymers **22**, 2577–2637 (1983)
20. Kukkonen, S., Lampinen, J.: GDE3: the third evolution step of generalized differential evolution. IEEE Congr. Evol. Comput. **1**, 443–450 (2005)
21. Ligabue-Braun, R., Borguesan, B., Verli, H., Krause, M.J., Dorn, M.: Everyone is a protagonist: residue conformational preferences in high-resolution protein structures. J. Comput. Biol. **25**, 451–465 (2017)
22. de Lima Corrêa, L., Dorn, M.: A multi-objective swarm-based algorithm for the prediction of protein structures. In: Rodrigues, J.M.F., et al. (eds.) ICCS 2019. LNCS, vol. 11538, pp. 101–115. Springer, Cham (2019). https://doi.org/10.1007/978-3-030-22744-9_8
23. Narloch, P.H., Dorn, M.: A knowledge based differential evolution algorithm for protein structure prediction. In: Kaufmann, P., Castillo, P.A. (eds.) EvoApplications 2019. LNCS, vol. 11454, pp. 343–359. Springer, Cham (2019). https://doi.org/10.1007/978-3-030-16692-2_23
24. Narloch, P.H., Dorn, M.: A Knowledge based self-adaptive differential evolution algorithm for protein structure prediction. In: Rodrigues, J.M.F., et al. (eds.) ICCS 2019. LNCS, vol. 11538, pp. 87–100. Springer, Cham (2019). https://doi.org/10.1007/978-3-030-22744-9_7
25. Robič, T., Filipič, B.: DEMO: differential evolution for multiobjective optimization. In: Coello Coello, C.A., Hernández Aguirre, A., Zitzler, E. (eds.) EMO 2005. LNCS, vol. 3410, pp. 520–533. Springer, Heidelberg (2005). https://doi.org/10.1007/978-3-540-31880-4_36
26. Rocha, G.K., dos Santos, K.B., Angelo, J.S., Custódio, F.L., Barbosa, H.J.C., Dardenne, L.E.: Inserting co-evolution information from contact maps into a multiobjective genetic algorithm for protein structure prediction. In: IEEE Congress on Evolutionary Computation (CEC), pp. 1–8 (2018)
27. Rohl, C.A., Strauss, C.E., Misura, K.M., Baker, D.: Protein structure prediction using Rosetta, pp. 66–93 (2004)
28. Scott, W.R., et al.: The GROMOS biomolecular simulation program package. J. Phys. Chem. A **103**(19), 3596–3607 (1999)
29. Silva, R.S., Stubs Parpinelli, R.: A self-adaptive differential evolution with fragment insertion for the protein structure prediction problem. In: Blesa Aguilera, M.J., Blum, C., Gambini Santos, H., Pinacho-Davidson, P., Godoy del Campo, J. (eds.) HM 2019. LNCS, vol. 11299, pp. 136–149. Springer, Cham (2019). https://doi.org/10.1007/978-3-030-05983-5_10
30. Storn, R., Price, K.: Differential evolution - a simple and efficient heuristic for global optimization over continuous spaces. J. Global Optim. **11**, 341–359 (1997)
31. Venske, S.M., Gonçalves, R.A., Benelli, E.M., Delgado, M.R.: ADEMO/D: an adaptive differential evolution for protein structure prediction problem. Expert Syst. Appl. **56**, 209–226 (2016)
32. Walsh, G.: Proteins: Biochemistry and Biotechnology. Wiley, Hoboken (2014)

Particle Swarm Optimization: A Wrapper-Based Feature Selection Method for Ransomware Detection and Classification

Muhammad Shabbir Abbasi[1,2(✉)], Harith Al-Sahaf[1], and Ian Welch[1]

[1] School of Engineering and Computer Science, Victoria University of Wellington,
P.O. Box 600, Wellington 6140, New Zealand
{shabbir.abbasi,harith.al-sahaf,ian.welch}@ecs.vuw.ac.nz
[2] Department of Computer Science, University of Agriculture Faisalabad,
Faisalabad, Punjab, Pakistan
shabbir.abbasi@uaf.edu.pk

Abstract. Ransomware has emerged as a grave cyber threat. Many of the existing ransomware detection and classification models use datasets created through dynamic or behaviour analysis of ransomware, hence known as behaviour-based detection models. A big challenge in automated behaviour-based ransomware detection and classification is high dimensional data with numerous features distributed into various groups. Feature selection algorithms usually help to deal with high dimensionality for improving classification performance. In connection with ransomware detection and classification, the majority of the feature selection methods used in existing literature ignore the varying importance of various feature groups within ransomware behaviour analysis data set. For ransomware detection and classification, we propose a two-stage feature selection method that considers the varying importance of each of the feature groups in the dataset. The proposed method utilizes particle swarm optimization, a wrapper-based feature selection algorithm, for selection of the optimal number of features from each feature group to produce better classification performance. Although the proposed method shows comparable performance for binary classification, it performs significantly better for multi-class classification than existing feature selection method used for this purpose.

Keywords: Evolutionary computation · Ransomware detection · Feature selection

1 Introduction

The use of the Internet and modern devices for personal and organizational needs, especially for business and banking, has become the norm in today's modern world. Automation adds convenience to the lives of common people, however,

© Springer Nature Switzerland AG 2020
P. A. Castillo et al. (Eds.): EvoApplications 2020, LNCS 12104, pp. 181–196, 2020.
https://doi.org/10.1007/978-3-030-43722-0_12

it provides opportunities for cyber criminals to make money illicitly. The utter reliance of public and private sectors on technology and modern devices for day-to-day tasks makes these sectors vulnerable to contemporary cyber threats like advanced persistent threats (APT), malvertising, and cryptojacking. One of such modern threats is ransomware, which is a type of malware, that hijacks victim's access to data or machine by employing encryption or locking the machine down. The attackers hold the access to victim's data or machine hostage until a ransom is paid to these cyber extortionists [25]. The prevalent method of ransom collection today is crypto-currency, often in the form of bitcoins [15].

Although the first ever attack of ransomware known as *PC-Cyborg* was observed in year 1989 [24], it came to prominence as a grave cyber threat in 2013 with the introduction of new families like RansomCrypt, and Cryptolocker [25]. From 2013 to 2015 various new families and multiple variants of ransomware of the existing families were introduced. To increasing the financial returns, a few of the sophisticated attackers started offering *ransomware-as-a-service* (RAAS) which gave birth to notorious ransomware like Cryptolocker, CryptoWall, Locky and TeslaCrypt. The damage done by Cryptowall alone was more than $320 million [13]. Yet other notorious ransomware like Petya and WannaCry started hitting government and private networks widely in years 2016 and 2017 respectively [13]. The majority of the targets of ransomware attacks were individuals by the end of year 2016 [35]. However, most of the ransomware attacks in recent times are observed as targeted attacks on big organizations, perhaps for their potential to pay big amount of money as ransom [3]. The major game players in these targeted ransomware attacks are LockerGoga, MegaCortex, SamSam, Ryuk, and RobinHood [26].

Malware analysis is conducted for characterization of various attributes and the behaviour of the malware to develop effective anti-malware systems [32]. Generally, there are two approaches to malware analysis: static and dynamic [4]. In static analysis, the sample of malware is analysed without executing it to learn its various static characteristics, such as string signatures, byte sequences, and operation codes (OPCodes). In dynamic or behaviour analysis, the malware binary is executed in controlled environment to learn its behaviour in terms of operations it performs with the operating system and machine's other resources. Anti-malware evasion techniques such as code obfuscation and polymorphism utilized by ransomware developers make signature-based ransomware detection ineffective [19,21]. To complement the static detection process behaviour-based detection (dynamic analysis based) approaches are used. Most of the existing ransomware detection models utilize the behaviour-based detection approach, for instance [7,17,18,20]. Existing analysis work on ransomware detection has identified some key behavioural features for ransomware detection, e.g., API calls patterns to tracking file system activity and changes made to user data by ransomware [19]. An automated way to characterize the signature behaviour of ransomware by means of behaviour analysis of ransomware samples can be achieved by utilizing machine learning methods, but dynamic analysis of ransomware generates a huge amount of high-dimensional data which makes it hard to develop an effective automated model for ransomware detection.

Processing and analysing high dimensional data has become a challenge for researchers working in various disciplines, especially machine learning and data mining [6]. Fortunately, data mining approaches serve the purpose of dimensionality reduction by exploiting machine learning techniques of feature selection and construction [33]. Feature selection is a process of selecting a subset of features from the given set of features on the basis of feature ranking or feature evaluation criteria [6]. Feature selection has been proven effective in improving training and prediction time, and performance of classification algorithms [14,16] in many domains including intrusion detection [2], and malware detection and classification [12,30]. Feature selection methods can largely be divided into filter, wrapper and embedded or hybrid methods [16]. The major difference between filter and wrapper methods is evaluation of features which is independent of any classification algorithm in filter methods, whereas wrappers use a classification algorithm for feature evaluation [34]. Embedded methods integrate feature selection and classifier learning [34].

Particle swarm optimization (PSO) [10] is an evolutionary computation method that iteratively improves a candidate solution with respect to a given measure. It has been widely used for optimization and as a wrapper-based feature selection method in problems of classification [34]. PSO has been effective for feature selection in many application areas, such as image recognition [23], and spam detection [36].

The overall aim of this research is to improve the performance of ransomware detection and classification using behaviour analysis data of ransomware and goodware (benign software) by means of employing effective feature selection methods. We propose a feature selection model that utilizes PSO for selection of an optimal number of features from various feature groups structuring the ransomware detection model.

2 Literature Survey

In this section, some of the directly related research work to this study is discussed which is followed by a discussion on the baseline studies (in Sect. 2.2) that we used in our experiments for the purpose of comparison of the results of the proposed method.

2.1 Related Work

Kharraz et al. [19] first proposed that ransomware of many families could be detected by means of effective monitoring of file system activity. The authors conducted a large scale dynamic analysis of 1359 ransomware coming from 15 different families, found between year 2006 and 2014. Subsequently, Kharraz et al. [17] proposed ransomware analysis and detection solution named as UNVEIL that utilized patterns of input output (I/O) traces left by user-level processes as signature behaviour for ransomware detection. These I/O traces contained multifaceted information, in particular I/O operations performed and entropy of read/write data buffer. Unfortunately, UNVEIL was able to detect ransomware only after a few files at victim machine had already been encrypted, hence, the solution left the victims partially unprotected. Moreover, the authors themselves mentioned that UNVEIL could be thwarted by any ransomware executing with kernel-level privilege.

ShieldFS [7] was a step forward and addressing the limitation of file loss in case of UNVEIL. The solution incorporated a self-healing module that automatically restored the encrypted files on detection of ransomware. However, the implementation of ShieldFS suffered from operational overheads on all I/O operations with file system which made it inapplicable.

PayBreak [20] could extract and store the symmetric session keys used by ransomware for encryption of victim's data. These keys could be retrieved and used for decryption of victim's data. However, PayBreak was only able to detect ransomware that used Windows default cryptographic libraries for encryption of victims' files. Moreover, it was unable to detect ransomware variants using incremental unpacking and advanced obfuscation techniques.

Redemption [18] is a ransomware detection model that employed a similar approach for ransomware detection to that of ShieldFS, and PayBreak [7,20,29]. It also incorporates a recovery module for recovering any encrypted files before ransomware detection. The solution suffers from operational overheads on I/O with the disk and it is also unable to detect ransomware executing with elevated privileges.

Cusack et al. [9] proposed a ransomware detection model based on machine learning methods using network traffic data. The researchers monitored the network communication between victim's machine and C&C to detect and prevent the delivery of encryption key required for encryption of victim's files without which the encryption process did not start. The authors used dimensionality reduction techniques to find the eight most contributing features for ransomware detection from network traffic. The proposed solution achieved false negative rate of 0.0% and false positive rate of 12.5%. However, the solution suffers for two reasons: firstly, the solution is unable to detect a new unseen variant of ransomware, and secondly, a false positive rate of 12.5% is going to raise many false alarms.

2.2 Background

Sgandurra et al. [30] proposed an anti-ransomware solution, named *Elderan*. The authors conducted dynamic analysis of ransomware and goodware samples. The samples were executed for 30 s in an analysis environment to record their behaviour in terms of program operations (represented as features). In total 30,967 features categorized into seven groups were recorded. To address the challenge of high dimensional behaviour analysis data, the researchers used a filter-based feature selection method using mutual information (MI) [8] to select 400 top-ranked features. A regularized logistic regression classification algorithm

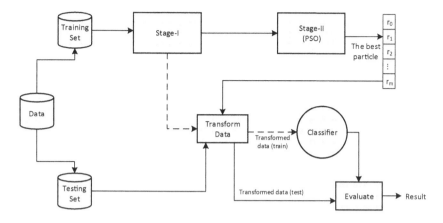

Fig. 1. The overall algorithm of the proposed feature selection method.

was used for classification of ransomware and goodware. The selection of 400 features was rationalised by scaling of the classification results with 100 to 1500 features selected using MI, where classification results with 400 features were found producing the best results. The results of Elderan were compared with 5 different models including virusTotal[1]. Although the authors proposed a complete anti-ransomware solution that analyzed the applications and then used machine learning for the purpose of ransomware detection, the model suffers a relatively high false positive rate than VirusTotal and a high false negative rate. The feature selection algorithm used in Elderan completely ignored the presence of various groups of features and the difference in number of features among various groups in the data set. The feature selection method used in [30] (the baseline) is run in our experimental environment to select 400 top-ranked featured for binary and multi-class tasks.

3   Proposed Features Selection Method

We hypothesize that in high dimensional behaviour analysis data (of ransomware) consisting of multiple feature groups, the selection of only top-ranked features (using MI feature ranking approach) from the whole feature space (without considering the feature groups) may be a limitation. Such a method can select all the features from a single group based on the MI score, the features belonging to other groups may have fewer chances of selection despite of having comparable MI scores. To create effective behaviour profiles covering most of the feature groups in data set, the feature groups may be considered while performing feature selection. In this way, providing features belonging to various groups a better chance of selection in the final model might improve the classification performance.

---

[1] https://www.virustotal.com/gui/home/upload.

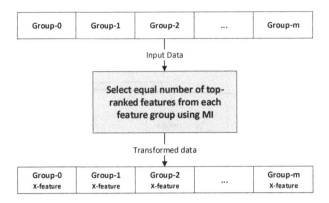

Fig. 2. Stage-I of the proposed feature selection method.

In connection with automated behaviour-based ransomware detection and classification, different feature groups may have varying impacts on accuracy. Hence, we propose a two-stage PSO-based feature selection method (Fig. 1) which considers all the feature groups by performing group-wise feature selection. It first selects an adequate and equal number of top-ranked features from each group to eliminate the difference among groups with respect to the number of features and then selects an optimal number of features from each of the groups for better classification performance. The functionality and objective of the stages of the proposed model are described in this section.

3.1   Stage-I

This stage uses MI feature ranking method to select equal number of top-ranked features from each of the feature groups in the data set as shown in Fig. 2. This stage aims to balance the number of features in all feature groups in order to eliminate the difference in number of features among various groups. In this way, features with low probability of selection previously may get a better chance of selection for the final feature set at the upcoming stage of the proposed method.

3.2   Stage-II

The aim of this stage is to select an optimal number of features from each of the feature groups to achieve the best classification performance since the transformed data obtained from Stage-I may still have redundant and irrelevant features. This stage utilizes PSO for feature selection where a wrapper classifier is used to find the optimal ratios for the feature groups for the final selected feature set as shown in the Fig. 3.

A particle in our implementation is a vector consisting of m values as shown in Fig. 4, where m is equal to number of features groups in the data set. These values are named as r_i, where $i \in \{0, 1, \ldots, m\}$ mapped to a feature group in the data set as shown in Fig. 4. r_i is a continuous number between 0 and 1.

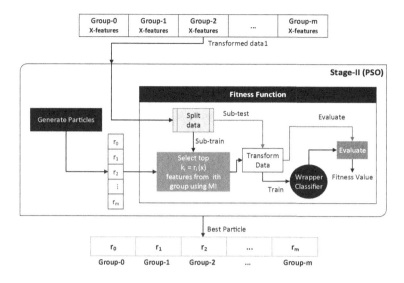

Fig. 3. Stage-II of the proposed feature selection method.

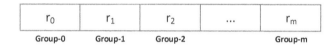

Fig. 4. Particle in PSO.

In this study, the fitness function of PSO aims at minimizing the classification error calculated using balanced accuracy by only selecting optimal number of features from each group. The fitness function is defined as:

$$Fitness = 1 - Accuracy \tag{1}$$

$$Accuracy = \frac{1}{n} \sum_{i=1}^{n} \frac{correct_i}{total_i} \tag{2}$$

where n is the number of classes, $correct_i$ is the number of instances of the ith class identified correctly, and $total_i$ is the total number of instances of the ith class.

For evaluation of a candidate solution, the input data (transformed training data received from Stage-I) is further split into sub-training and sub-testing sets within fitness function. The wrapper method performs group-wise feature selection using MI to select k number of top-ranked features from each feature group. The number k for each feature group is calculated as:

$$k_i = r_i \times t_i \tag{3}$$

where k_i is an integer value depicting the number of features to be selected from the ith feature group, r_i is the ratio value in the particle for the ith feature group, and t_i is the total number of features in the ith feature group.

In this way the fitness function translates continuous values to integer values to select k number of features for each group. To evaluate the fitness of selected features a wrapper classifier (Regularized Logistic Regression classification algorithm in our case) is used. The wrappers classifier is trained using sub-training data and the model is evaluated using sub-testing data.

4   Experimental Design

In this section, details of the data set used for experiments is provided in Sect. 4.1 which is followed by Sect. 4.2 which discusses the implementation details of the experiments. Afterwards, the setting of the evolutionary parameters are discussed. The section is concluded with the discussion about the performance evaluation metrics and the way of reporting of results.

4.1   Data Set

Finding an existing data set for automated behaviour-based ransomware detection and classification is hard despite the many existing work on ransomware analysis. One reason for the unavailability of data is that analysis of ransomware can be performed with a variety of perspectives, e.g., to learn the network traffic patterns [1,5], and API call patterns [17,20]. It has been observed that most of the researchers working in domain of ransomware detection start with analysis work for the following reasons. Firstly, the rate of growth of ransomware in terms of families and variants has been too high for the past few years [11] which makes existing analysis work outdated soon. Secondly, any existing analysis work may not match the analysis perspective (mentioned above) of these researchers.

For experimentation purpose, we utilized an existing behaviour data set containing both ransomware and goodware provided by Sgandurra et al. [30]. The data set was created through dynamic analysis of samples of ransomware from 11 different families and variety of benign software (also known as goodware). The details on number of samples of ransomware and goodware in this data set can be found in Table 1. The samples of ransomware (obtained from VirusShare[2]) and goodware were executed in Cuckoo Sandbox[3] to record their interaction (in terms of operations performed) with operating system and machine's other resources. A feature in data set represents an operation performed by a sample. Every feature has a value 0 or 1 representing absence or presence of the corresponding operation. In total, 30,967 different features were recorded. These features were categorised into seven groups, the details can be found in Table 2.

---

[2] https://virusshare.com/ is an online malware repository that produces active malware samples to security researchers.

[3] https://cuckoosandbox.org/.

Table 1. A summary of the data set instances [30].

Family	# Instances	Family	# Instances	Family	# Instances
Citroni	50	Kovter	64	Reveton	90
CryptoLocker	107	Locker	97	TeslaCrypt	6
CryptoWall	46	Matsnu	59	Trojan-Ransom	34
Kollah	25	Pgpcoder	4	Goodware	942

Table 2. Groups of features in the data set [30].

Group ID	Description	# Features
API	API invocations	232
DROP	Extensions of the dropped files	346
REG	Registry key operations	6622
FILE	File operations	4141
FILES_EXT	Extension of the files involved in file operations	935
DIR	File directory operations	2424
STR	Embedded strings	16267

4.2   Implementation

The wrapper classification algorithm in our experiments is regularized logistic regression (RLR), however, we used other classification algorithms, namely, random forest (RF), decision tree (DT), and support vector machines (SVMs) with linear kernel (SVM) to generalize the performance of our model. These classifiers were selected in order to investigate the impact of the selected features by the proposed method on a diverse set of classification algorithms. All four classification algorithms were used with their default settings, i.e., no parameter tuning was performed. We implemented the classifiers using Scikit-learn libraries version 0.21.3 [27] for Python version 3.7 [28]. We used Pyswarms library [22] for implementation of PSO algorithm. We compared the proposed method in this study with the baseline method proposed by Sgandurra et al. [30]. The baseline method utilizes regularized logistic regression where the parameters have been tuned. Hence, the same parameter settings suggested by the authors have been used for the Baseline.

Four-fold cross validation is used to split the data into four folds. A data split into 4-folds is chosen, because of the fact *PgpCoder* family of ransomware contains the least number of ransomware samples, i.e., 4. Therefore, a four fold split ensures the presence of one ransomware sample from this family in each fold.

4.3   The Evolutionary Parameters

Thirty runs of PSO with 100 epochs for each run and the following parameters settings. The value of cognitive and social parameters are both set to 1.149618, the value of inertia is set to 0.729844, and number of particles in swarm is set to 30. Note that We set the values of all the PSO parameters to their recommended values [31]. The Scikit-learn library [27] is utilized for implementation of filter feature selection approach. For calculation of MI, info-gain library for python 3.7 is brought to service.

Within the objective function of PSO, we split the data into three folds because of the reason that training data fed to PSO contained only three samples of ransomware from PgpCoder family. Therefore, a three fold split on one hand ensured the presence a sample per fold, on the other hand it prevented any overfitting while evaluation of the fitness of the selected features. The value of the fitness function was treated as an average value for all the three folds for the purpose of evaluation of selected features.

4.4   Performance Evaluation Metrics

For evaluation of classification results, we used balanced accuracy with Eq. (2) instead of accuracy due to unbalanced number of samples of goodware and ransomware in EldeRan data set.

The results of the baseline method are reported as an average of single run for all four folds after running the baseline method in our experimental settings. Whereas, the results of the proposed feature selection method are reported as an average of 30 runs of PSO per fold for all of the four folds of the data.

One sample two tailed t-test is performed to calculate the significance of difference of the classification results using features selected with the baseline and the proposed method, where a 95% confidence interval is used. The "+", "−", and "=" signs in the results table indicate a significantly better, poor, and equal (no difference) performance, respectively, using the features selected by the proposed method as compared to the features selected by the baseline method.

In order to avoid feature selection bias, we split the data into training and testing data at the earliest stage prior to performing feature selection. Only training data is utilized for feature selection at stages I and II of the proposed method, and finally for training the classifiers, whereas test data is only utilized for the purpose of evaluation of the proposed method.

5   Results and Discussions

Table 3 shows the results for binary and multi-class classification with both the baseline and the proposed feature selection methods. The average accuracy with the baseline feature selection method is given under the column of the Baseline method. Whereas, the performance of the proposed feature selection method is recorded after each of the two stages given in the column of Stage-I and Stage-II, respectively.

Table 3. Average (%) accuracy ($\bar{x} \pm s$) for binary and multi-class classification with features selected using the baseline and the proposed feature selection (FS) methods.

Type	Classifiers	Baseline FS method	Two-stage PSO-based FS method	
			Stage-I	Stage-II
Binary	RLR	97.29	97.61 ± 0.0044	$97.29 \pm 0.0011^=$
	RF	97.48	97.43 ± 0.0058	$97.06 \pm 0.0021^-$
	DT	95.08	96.49 ± 0.0156	$95.06 \pm 0.0024^=$
	SVC	96.62	96.81 ± 0.0094	$96.33 \pm 0.0019^-$
	Baseline	97.20	97.66 ± 0.0037	$97.34 \pm 0.0011^+$
Multi-class	RLR	52.00	54.16 ± 0.2667	$54.61 \pm 0.0044^+$
	RF	55.81	53.91 ± 0.2564	$54.68 \pm 0.0090^-$
	DT	52.80	55.92 ± 0.2409	$52.94 \pm 0.0131^=$
	SVC	52.85	55.04 ± 0.2556	$54.57 \pm 0.0047^+$
	Baseline	50.87	54.24 ± 0.2675	$53.86 \pm 0.0043^+$

It can be observed from the results of binary classification with the baseline method that RF (with average accuracy as 97.48%) and DT (with average accuracy as 95.08%) are the best and the worst performing classifiers, respectively. The difference in the classification performance with different classification algorithms may be due to the individual characteristics of the classification algorithms. A slight difference in performance for binary classification with the Baseline method can be observed as compared to RLR, i.e., RLR dominates the Baseline, which is evidently due to the difference in settings of classifier parameters since both of the classifiers are same. For multi-class classification with the baseline feature selection method, RLR (with average accuracy as 52.00%) dominated the Baseline method (with average accuracy as 50.87%) which was also the case for binary classification with the features selected by Baseline. We can conclude that the default settings of regularized logistic regression as in case of RLR shows better performance than that of used in Baseline.

It is to be noted here that we used RLR as wrapper classification algorithm in PSO for evaluation of the fitness value with selected features at stage-II of the proposed method. The results with other classifiers are provided for the sake of generality of the goodness of the selected features. For comparison of classification results using the baseline and the proposed methods, a drop in performance of RF, DT, SVC was observed, whereas a rise in performance of the Baseline was observed. The classification performance of RLR is of our greatest interest as the proposed method uses RLR as wrapper classifier. The performance of RLR remained consistent using the features selected with both of the baseline and the proposed feature selection methods. This shows that for binary classification, the proposed feature selection method enhanced the performance at Stage-I and then dropped it slightly at Stage-II.

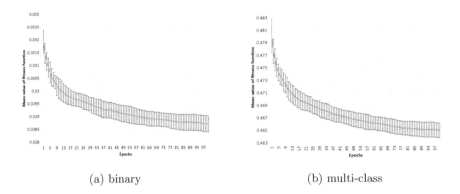

(a) binary   (b) multi-class

Fig. 5. PSO convergence graphs for binary and multi-class classification.

Although, the proposed feature selection method produces better classification results for multi-class classification, it shows comparable performance for binary class classification as compared to the baseline feature selection method. A significant improvement in performance of RLR shows that the proposed feature selection method selected good features that increased the classification performance as compared to the features selected using the baseline method.

6 Analysis

To have a deeper insight into the proposed features selection method, we analyzed the convergence of the algorithms, and the number of features selected from each of the various group of features in the data set.

6.1 Convergence

Figure 5(a) and (b) show the convergence graphs of PSO for binary and multi-class classification, respectively. The convergence graphs are generated using average results of the 30 independent runs of PSO for the best particle at each epoch. Both of the convergence graphs show that PSO explores the search space rapidly in the first 20 epochs, whereas it performs exploitation for the rest of the epochs. The whiskers in the graphs show that the proposed algorithm is stable among different runs.

6.2 Features Analysis

Although the proposed method selects a variable number of features, i.e., 822 ± 59 for binary and 803 ± 49 for multi-class tasks on the average which is more than that of selected by the baseline method, it enhances the classification performance significantly, especially for multi-class task. Our particular interest in

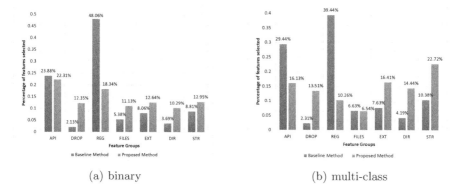

(a) binary   (b) multi-class

Fig. 6. The percentage of average number of features selected from each group by the baseline and the proposed methods for binary and multi-class classification.

this research is how the proposed algorithm mixes features belonging to various groups by selecting an optimal number of features from each of the feature groups in the data.

Figure 6(a) and (b) show the percentage of the features selected from each of the seven feature groups using the baseline and the proposed feature selection method for binary and multi-class tasks, respectively. For the baseline method, the pattern of selection of features is consistent for binary and multi-class tasks with REG being the group at top (i.e., 48.06% for binary and 39.44% for multi-class task), API being the second (i.e., 23.88% for binary and 29.44% for multi-class task) and STR being the third largest group (i.e., 08.81% for binary and 10.38% for multi-class task) with respect to number of features. Out of the rest of the feature groups, EXT has been the top contributor followed by DIR, FILES, and DROP features categories, respectively.

The proposed feature selection method shows a variation in the pattern of selected features due to the number of features selected from different groups for binary and multi-class classification being different. For binary classification, the proposed method selected most of the features from API group, i.e., 22.31%, whereas for multi-class classification, the top group with the most number of features is STR, i.e., 22.72%. The pattern of the number of selected features from each group for binary and multi-class tasks using both of the features selection methods, i.e., the baseline and the proposed method, can be observed in Fig. 6. The pattern suggests the goodness of the proposed method as PSO is selecting an optimal number of features from each of the seven groups to achieve the best classification performance.

It can be further observed that for binary classification, the proposed method selected most of the features from API group which is in line with existing literature since many authors have used the API calls in connection with ransomware detection, e.g, [19,21,30]. Similarly, for multi-class classification, the proposed method selected the most number of features from STR group. The STR group contains information about imported libraries and functions calls. This makes it

Table 4. Family-wise Average (%) accuracy ($\bar{x} \pm s$) for multi-class task with RLR classifier using proposed feature selection model.

Family	Accuracy	Family	Accuracy
Citroni	70.10 ± 0.0038	Matsnu	42.52 ± 0.0216
CryptoLocker	70.76 ± 0.0147	Pgpcoder	00.00 ± 0.0000
CryptoWall	45.95 ± 0.0041	Reveton	73.57 ± 0.0084
Kollah	44.19 ± 0.0076	TeslaCrypt	37.50 ± 0.0000
Kovter	78.93 ± 0.0266	Trojan-Ransom	34.17 ± 0.0219
Locker	58.74 ± 0.0130	Goodware	99.43 ± 0.0007

an important group for ransomware detection because many ransomware import standard cryptographic libraries for encryption [20].

6.3   Family-Wise Classification Performance

Table 4 presents class-wise average (%) classification accuracy for all four folds with RLR classifier for multi-class classification. It can be seen that classification accuracy of *PgpCoder* family remains consistently zero for all four folds in multi-class classification due to insufficient number of samples for training the classifier. Similarly, TeslaCrypt family has only six samples in the data set and so average classification accuracy for this family is poor, although for one fold the classifier was able to produce 100% accuracy.

7   Conclusion

In this paper, we proposed a feature selection method for ransomware detection and classification using high dimensional behaviour analysis data of ransomware and goodware. The proposed feature selection method considers the importance of different feature groups present in the analysis data set. At first stage, the proposed method selects an equal number of top-ranking features using MI from each of the feature group and then at second stage, it selects an optimal number of top ranking features from each of the group using PSO. The proposed feature selection method produces comparable results for binary classification but better results for multi-class classification as compared to the baseline method. The results of the experiment proves that classification performance of the model is dependent on the number of features selected from each of the feature groups in the data set.

In future, we consider conducting the analysis of ransomware and goodware to create behaviour analysis data set with time stamps to consider the sequence of different operations performed by a sample in analysis environment. The incorporation of time stamps of various operation while creating data set may proves good for extracting distinguishing behavioural patterns which can eventually improves the classification performance.

References

1. Alhawi, O.M.K., Baldwin, J., Dehghantanha, A.: Leveraging machine learning techniques for windows ransomware network traffic detection. In: Dehghantanha, A., Conti, M., Dargahi, T. (eds.) Cyber Threat Intelligence. AIS, vol. 70, pp. 93–106. Springer, Cham (2018). https://doi.org/10.1007/978-3-319-73951-9_5
2. Ambusaidi, M.A., He, X., Nanda, P., Tan, Z.: Building an intrusion detection system using a filter-based feature selection algorithm. IEEE Trans. Comput. **65**(10), 2986–2998 (2016)
3. Brewer, R.: Ransomware attacks: detection, prevention and cure. Netw. Secur. **2016**(9), 5–9 (2016)
4. Burnap, P., French, R., Turner, F., Jones, K.: Malware classification using self organising feature maps and machine activity data. Comput. Secur. **73**, 399–410 (2018)
5. Cabaj, K., Gawkowski, P., Grochowski, K., Osojca, D.: Network activity analysis of cryptowall ransomware. Przeglad Elektrotechniczny **91**(11), 201–204 (2015)
6. Cai, J., Luo, J., Wang, S., Yang, S.: Feature selection in machine learning: a new perspective. Neurocomputing **300**, 70–79 (2018)
7. Continella, A., et al.: ShieldFS: a self-healing, ransomware-aware filesystem. In: Proceedings of the 32nd Annual Conference on Computer Security Applications, pp. 336–347. ACM (2016)
8. Cover, T.M., Thomas, J.A.: Elements of Information Theory. Wiley, Hoboken (2012)
9. Cusack, G., Michel, O., Keller, E.: Machine learning-based detection of ransomware using SDN. In: Proceedings of the 2018 ACM International Workshop on Security in Software Defined Networks & Network Function Virtualization, pp. 1–6. ACM (2018)
10. Eberhart, R., Kennedy, J.: A new optimizer using particle swarm theory. In: Proceedings of the 6th International Symposium on Micro Machine and Human Science, pp. 39–43. IEEE (1995)
11. Fagioli, A.: Zero-day recovery: the key to mitigating the ransomware threat. Comput. Fraud Secur. **2019**(1), 6–9 (2019)
12. Feizollah, A., Anuar, N.B., Salleh, R., Wahab, A.W.A.: A review on feature selection in mobile malware detection. Digit. Invest. **13**, 22–37 (2015)
13. Groot, J.D.: A history of ransomware attacks: the biggest and worst ransomware attacks of all time, January 2019. https://digitalguardian.com/blog/history-ransomware-attacks-biggest-and-worst-ransomware-attacks-all-time#4. Accessed 03 Jan 2019
14. Guyon, I., Elisseeff, A.: An introduction to variable and features selection. J. Mach. Learn. Res. **3**, 1157–1182 (2003)
15. Huang, D.Y., et al.: Tracking ransomware end-to-end. In: Proceedings of 2018 IEEE Symposium on Security and Privacy, vol. 2018-May, pp. 618–631. IEEE (2018)
16. Khalid, S., Khalil, T., Nasreen, S.: A survey of feature selection and feature extraction techniques in machine learning. In: Proceedings of 2014 Science and Information Conference, pp. 372–378. IEEE (2014)
17. Kharaz, A., Arshad, S., Mulliner, C., Robertson, W., Kirda, E.: UNVEIL: a large-scale, automated approach to detecting ransomware. In: Proceedings of 25th USENIX Security Symposium, pp. 757–772. USENIX Association (2016)
18. Kharraz, A., Kirda, E.: Redemption: real-time protection against ransomware at end-hosts. In: Dacier, M., Bailey, M., Polychronakis, M., Antonakakis, M. (eds.) RAID 2017. LNCS, vol. 10453, pp. 98–119. Springer, Cham (2017). https://doi.org/10.1007/978-3-319-66332-6_5

19. Kharraz, A., Robertson, W., Balzarotti, D., Bilge, L., Kirda, E.: Cutting the gordian knot: a look under the hood of ransomware attacks. In: Almgren, M., Gulisano, V., Maggi, F. (eds.) DIMVA 2015. LNCS, vol. 9148, pp. 3–24. Springer, Cham (2015). https://doi.org/10.1007/978-3-319-20550-2_1

20. Kolodenker, E., Koch, W., Stringhini, G., Egele, M.: PayBreak. In: Proceedings of the 2017 ACM on Asia Conference on Computer and Communications Security, pp. 599–611. ACM (2017)

21. Maiorca, D., Mercaldo, F., Giacinto, G., Visaggio, C.A., Martinelli, F.: R-packdroid: API package-based characterization and detection of mobile ransomware. In: Proceedings of the Symposium on Applied Computing, pp. 1718–1723. ACM (2017)

22. Miranda, L.J.V., et al.: PySwarms: a research toolkit for particle swarm optimization in Python. J. Open Source Softw. 3(21), 433 (2018)

23. Mistry, K., Zhang, L., Neoh, S.C., Lim, C.P., Fielding, B.: A micro-GA embedded PSO feature selection approach to intelligent facial emotion recognition. IEEE Trans. Cybern. 47(6), 1496–1509 (2016)

24. Mohurle, S., Patil, M.: A brief study of wannacry threat: ransomware attack 2017. Int. J. Adv. Res. Comput. Sci. 8(5), (2017)

25. Monika, Zavarsky, P., Lindskog, D.: Experimental analysis of ransomware on windows and android platforms: evolution and characterization. Procedia Comput. Sci. 94, 465–472 (2016)

26. O'Brien, D., DiMaggio, J., Nguyen, H.G.: Targeted Ransomware: An ISTR Special Report. Whitepaper, Symantec Corporation (2019)

27. Pedregosa, F., et al.: Scikit-learn: machine learning in Python. J. Mach. Learn. Res. 12(Oct), 2825–2830 (2011)

28. Rossum, G.: Python library reference. Technical report (1995)

29. Scaife, N., Carter, H., Traynor, P., Butler, K.R.B.: Cryptolock (and drop it): stopping ransomware attacks on user data. In: Proceedings of the 36th International Conference on Distributed Computing Systems, pp. 303–312. IEEE (2016)

30. Sgandurra, D., Muñoz-González, L., Mohsen, R., Lupu, E.C.: Automated dynamic analysis of ransomware: benefits, limitations and use for detection. Computing Research Repository abs/1609.03020 (2016)

31. Shi, Y., Eberhart, R.C.: Parameter selection in particle swarm optimization. In: Porto, V.W., Saravanan, N., Waagen, D., Eiben, A.E. (eds.) EP 1998. LNCS, vol. 1447, pp. 591–600. Springer, Heidelberg (1998). https://doi.org/10.1007/BFb0040810

32. Souri, A., Hosseini, R.: A state-of-the-art survey of malware detection approaches using data mining techniques. Hum.-Centric Comput. Inf. Sci. 8(1) (2018). https://doi.org/10.1186/s13673-018-0125-x

33. Sun, Z.L., Huang, D.S., Cheung, Y.M., Liu, J., Huang, G.B.: Using FCMC, FVS, and PCA techniques for feature extraction of multispectral images. IEEE Geosci. Remote Sens. Lett. 2(2), 108–112 (2005)

34. Xue, B., Zhang, M., Browne, W.N., Yao, X.: A survey on evolutionary computation approaches to feature selection. IEEE Trans. Evol. Comput. 20(4), 606–626 (2016)

35. Young, A.L., Yung, M.: Cryptovirology. Commun. ACM 60(7), 24–26 (2017)

36. Zhang, Y., Wang, S., Phillips, P., Ji, G.: Binary PSO with mutation operator for feature selection using decision tree applied to spam detection. Knowl.-Based Syst. 64, 22–31 (2014)

A Method for Estimating the Computational Complexity of Multimodal Functions

Juan Luis Jiménez Laredo[1]([⊠]) [iD], Juan Julián Merelo Guervós[3] [iD],
Carlos M. Fernandes[2] [iD], and Eric Sanlaville[1] [iD]

[1] RI2C-LITIS, University of Le Havre Normandy, Le Havre, France
{juanlu.jimenez,eric.sanlaville}@univ-lehavre.fr
[2] LARSyS, University of Lisbon, Lisbon, Portugal
cfernandes@laseeb.org
[3] Department of Computer Architecture, University of Granada, Granada, Spain
jmerelo@ugr.es

Abstract. This paper addresses the issue of estimating the computational complexity of optimizing real-coded multimodal functions where the aim is to find all global optima. The proposed complexity method provides a partial answer to this question in the form of the estimated sample size needed to sample all basins of attraction of all global optima at least once. The rationale behind the approach is that, in optimization, in order to locate all possible optima of a multimodal function, we should first locate all its basins of attraction and then exploit them using, e.g., gradient information. Therefore, estimating the cost of locating all basins of attraction provides a lower bound on the computational budget necessary to optimize a multimodal function. This lower bound can serve as a measure of the computational complexity of the problem. From the conducted experimentation, we show that the proposed model can be very useful in determining the computational complexity of specialized benchmarks and can also be used as a heuristic in case of having some partial knowledge of the features of the targeted function.

Keywords: Multimodal optimization · Sampling · Basins of attraction · Benchmarking · Computational complexity

1 Introduction and State of the Art

Population-based metaheuristics, such as Evolutionary Algorithms, were initially conceived as methods for locating a single global solution to a problem – or function optimum – provided as input [6]. The general canonical procedure establishes that a randomly initialized population of candidate solutions, with high likelihood, iteratively converges towards a promising region in the solution space. If the algorithm performs well, a global solution to the problem will be found within this region. Nonetheless, real problems may not only have a single but

© Springer Nature Switzerland AG 2020
P. A. Castillo et al. (Eds.): EvoApplications 2020, LNCS 12104, pp. 197–211, 2020.
https://doi.org/10.1007/978-3-030-43722-0_13

multiple solutions: all feasible and equally good. These kinds of problems are referred to as multimodal problems [21].

Multimodality poses a series of new challenges to the design of an efficient metaheuristic when the aim is to locate all possible solutions. Particularly, the exploration/exploitation tradeoff [12] in population-based algorithms needs to be rethought from the ground up in order to induce a more exploratory behavior to the algorithm and to be able to locate and exploit all the different promising regions of the problem; on the one hand, "natural" exploitation will lead us to hone in on a single, or maybe a few, optimums; however, in order to solve these problems we also need exploration *in depth*, so that local optima insufficiently explored are not abandoned in pursuit of a deceptively unique global optimum.

In order to cope with the issue, metaheuristics are typically intertwined with the so-called niching techniques. Among others, these techniques include fitness sharing [10], crowding [5], spatial distribution of the population using fine-grained parallelization [15] or coarse-grained parallelization [4] as well as some other additional forms of diversity maintenance techniques [2,16,17]. The difficulty of establishing the relative performance of these approaches to one another has been, however, an obstacle to their adoption by the community at large.

This is why, in 2013, a framework of reference for comparing the performance of different multimodal algorithms was introduced in the form of a benchmark during the CEC Competition on Niching Methods for Multimodal Optimization [18]. The proposed benchmark is composed of 20 problems of different difficulties obtained by tuning the dimensionality and the modality of 12 functions. Each of these problems has, additionally, an associated maximum computational budget (provided as a maximum number of fitness evaluations) which depends on the estimated difficulty of each problem. In particular, the budget of 1D and some 2D functions is 50K evaluations, the rest of 2D functions 200K evaluations, and 3D and higher dimension functions 400k evaluations. The difficulty of a given problem is therefore established mostly based on its dimensionality. However, some state-of-the-art approaches[1], such as HillVallEA [19] or NMMSO [7], suggest that the prescribed budget is much larger than required for some functions while, for others, the budget is insufficient to locate all solutions. This hints at the fact that, possibly, establishing a maximum budget based on the dimensionality and not on the modality of a given function is not the best strategy to follow in relation to multimodal optimization.

This paper aims to explore a new method for establishing more accurate estimates on the computational complexity of a given function based on its modality (and implicitly also on its dimensionality). The objective is to relate the complexity of a function with the number and the distribution of solutions in the solution space. To that end, we propose a probabilistic model inspired

---

[1] HillVallEA is the winner of GECCO'19 Competition on Niching Methods for Multimodal Optimization https://cs.adelaide.edu.au/~markus/temp/gecco2019_certificates2019-ALL.pdf and NMMSO winner of the competition at IEEE CEC 2015 https://titan.csit.rmit.edu.au/~e46507/cec15-niching/competition/NichingCEC2015.pdf. Accessed on November 2019.

by the coupon collector problem: a classical problem in probability that studies the number of trials *"needed to collect a given number of distinct coupons that are drawn from a set of coupons with an arbitrary probability distribution"* [1]. In our case, obtaining a coupon translates into hitting a basin of attraction enclosing a global optimum by uniformly sampling at random the solution space. In simple terms, the method is equivalent to finding the minimum population size that guarantees that all basins of attraction of a function are sampled at least once with a given probability. The working hypothesis is therefore that hard multimodal problems will require larger population sizes than simpler problems and, that way, the obtained population size will serve as a lower bound on the number of fitness evaluations. In turn, this can provide an estimate on the experimental complexity of the problem. In fact, relating the complexity of a problem to the population size is not a novel approach.

Population sizing theory, based on Goldberg's facetwise decomposition for designing competent GAs [8, 11], focuses on determining the population size according to the problem difficulty. The underlying idea is that a small instance of an easy problem will require a smaller population size than a larger instance of a more difficult problem. In further studies, population sizing has also been studied from the perspective of random walks [14] and also counts with empirical estimation methods, such as Sastry bisection method [20] used to estimate the minimum size of the initial population required to supply enough building blocks (BBs) so that a fixed-size selectorecombinative GA (without mutation) can converge to the problem optimum. However, the first study that relates population sizing to multimodal optimization is the work of Goldberg, Den and Horn [9]. The authors propose a massively multimodal and deceptive problem based on unitation and are able to locate all of the 32 global optima of the problem by using an appropriate population size and fitness sharing. The foundations of population sizing theory are based on these previous works. However, they are all based on the schemata theorem and have been devoted to unitation-based combinatorial optimization. The novelty of our approach relies on that, to the extent of our knowledge, this is the first time that a population sizing model is employed to investigate the complexity of multimodal continuous optimization problems. Once the complexity of the problem has been determined, methodologies such as the one established by Harik et al. in [13] (which extends [14], that confusingly has the same title), can be used to size the population. However, this goes a step beyond what we focus in this paper, which is a foundational methodology for establishing the computational complexity of a real-coded multimodal function.

The remainder of the paper is organized as follows: Sect. 2 describes the problem of estimating the number of trials required for sampling all basins of attraction in a multimodal function and provides a probabilistic model as a solution. In order to validate our claims, different experiments are conducted in Sect. 3. First, in Sect. 3.1, two functions of the CEC2013 benchmark are analyzed from the perspective of the proposed model. Then, in Sect. 3.2, we propose a synthetic benchmark to assess the impact of different problem landscapes on the sampling size. Finally, some conclusions are drawn in Sect. 4 and some future lines of works presented.

2   Estimating the Sample Size Needed to Hit All Basins Enclosing Global Optima

This section provides a definition and a resolution to the problem of estimating the number of trials required for sampling all basins of attraction in a multimodal function – the trials are drawn from the uniform random variable. Additionally, upper and lower bounds are also derived. To that end, we will consider that a basin of attraction of a function f is a region with a well-defined boundary that encloses a local or global optimum and where, for every point within the region, there exists at least a monotonically decreasing path – or increasing if considering maximization – from the point to the enclosed optimum (see e.g. [3] for a more detailed mathematical notions on the definition).

2.1   Problem Definition

Let $f : \mathbb{R}^D \to \mathbb{R}, x \mapsto y = f(x)$ be a D-dimensional multimodal function having different basins of attraction that can enclose either a global or a suboptimal solution. Provided that m of these basins of attraction enclose a global optimum, estimate the number of independent trials n drawn from the uniform random variable necessary to sample all m basins of attraction with a probability P.

2.2   Problem Resolution

For the sake of simplicity but without any loss of generality, we will use a 2-dimensional nomenclature[2] where:

- A, is the total area of the function f determined by the ranges of the variables.
- m, is the total number of basins of attraction enclosing a global optimum. Henceforth, we will generically refer to *basins of attraction* to only those basins enclosing a global optimum, i.e., the proposed model does not take into account the basins enclosing local optima.
- b_i, is the area of the $i - th$ basin of attraction where $i \in [1, \ldots, m]$.
- n, is a number of independent samples in A generated uniformly at random,
- s_j, is the $j - th$ sample in A, $j \in [1, \ldots, n], s_j \in A$
- Finally, $P(B)$ is the probability that for every basin of attraction there exists at least one sample s_j within the area of the basin, $\forall b_i, i \in [1, \ldots, m] : \exists s_j \in b_i$

Let $P(b_{i,1})$ be the probability of the $i - th$ basin being sampled by a single random trial:

---

[2] Note here that for other number of dimensions we can equivalently talk about length (1 dimension), volume (3 dimensions) or hypervolume (> 3 dimensions).

$$P(b_{i,1}) = \frac{b_i}{A} = 1 - \left(1 - \frac{b_i}{A}\right)$$

from the hypothesis of independence it is straightforward to see that, after n trials drawn from the uniform random variable, this probability becomes:

$$P(b_{i,n}) = 1 - \left(1 - \frac{b_i}{A}\right)^n$$

so that the probability that every basin is sampled after n samples can be approached by:

$$P(B) \approx \prod_{i=1}^{m} P(b_{i,n}) = \prod_{i=1}^{m} 1 - \left(1 - \frac{b_i}{A}\right)^n \tag{1}$$

For the sake of simplicity, in this last equation, we consider the $(b_{i,n})$ events to be independent which is not true. But the error is negligible for n sufficiently large, as our experiments confirm. Please refer to [1] for a full characterization of the problem based on Markov chains analysis of the generalized coupon collector problem.

2.3   Deriving an Upper Bound

It can be fairly argued that, in order to provide an effective estimate, Eq. 1 requires perfect information about the number and the shape of all basins of attraction of the problem at hand. This issue will be discussed later on in Sect. 3 along the line that this estimate can still be useful for determining, for example, a fair termination criterion in specialized benchmarks such as the one of CEC2013 on niching methods [18]. However, if the aim is at tackling a problem as a black box, an estimate of this kind is of little use.

In order to provide estimates for an unknown function f, we aim at deriving an upper bound on the sampling size with only minimal information on the problem. Namely, the input parameters will be a given probability $P(B)$ (a probability of e.g. $P(B) = 0.98$ means that all basins of attraction will be sampled in 98 out of 100 runs), a number m of sought global optima, and the area b_{min} of the smallest basin of attraction to be considered.

From Eq. 1 and assuming that each of the m basins of attraction has an equal area b, i.e. $\forall b_i \forall b_j, i \neq j : b_i = b_j$, it can be stated that:

$$P(B) = \left(1 - \left(1 - \frac{b}{A}\right)^n\right)^m$$

so that n can be expressed as:

$$n = \frac{ln\left(1 - P(B)^{\frac{1}{m}}\right)}{ln\left(1 - \frac{b}{A}\right)}.$$

In order to determine an **upper bound** for a function f with basins of attraction of different areas, it is required to consider the smallest one:

$$b_{min} : \min(b_i \in [b_1, \ldots, b_m])$$

$$n_{upper} = \frac{ln\left(1 - P(B)^{\frac{1}{m}}\right)}{ln\left(1 - \frac{b_{min}}{A}\right)} \qquad (2)$$

We will show throughout a set of conducted experiments that Eq. 2 is a robust approach to determine an upper bound on the number of trials n necessary to sample all m basins of attraction in f with a given probability $P(B)$.

Alternatively, and following the same logic, we could also derive a **lower bound** by considering the basin with the largest area, i.e. $b_{max} : \max(b_i \in [b_1, \ldots, b_m])$. However, a lower bound is of less interest when the aim is at sampling all basins of attraction as it will only work for a best case scenario in which all basins of attraction are of the same area.

3   Experimental Setup and Results

Let us define a sample S of size n as a set of coordinates generated uniformly at random $S = (s_1, s_2, \ldots, s_n) : S \subset A$. We will say that S is a successful sample if for every basin of attraction b_i there is at least one coordinate $s_j \in S$ within its bounds:

$$\forall b_i \exists s_j : s_j \in b_i.$$

Over a number of different runs, we can compute the **success rate (SR)** (or alternatively the probability of success of a sample S of size n) as the ratio between the number of successful runs over the number of total runs:

$$SR = \frac{no. \; of \; successful \; runs}{no. \; of \; total \; runs}$$

3.1   First Insights Using Two Functions from the CEC2013 Benchmark

In order to gain insights in the quality of Eqs. 1 and 2 as estimators of the sampling size, experiments were conducted[3] using two functions of the CEC2013 benchmark [18]: F_7 2D Vincent and F_8 2D modified Rastrigin. Both functions were selected because of their distinct features in terms of either relative areas of the basins of attraction or number of global optima. Figure 1 shows the contours of the functions.

---

[3] Code for the experiments is available at https://www-apps.univ-lehavre.fr/forge/jimenezj/multistartnomad published under GNU Public License v3.0.

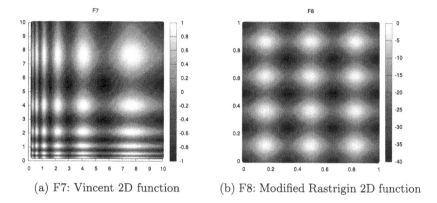

(a) F7: Vincent 2D function   (b) F8: Modified Rastrigin 2D function

Fig. 1. Contours of the two functions selected from the CEC2013 benchmark. Both problems are formulated as maximization problems.

F_7 *Vincent D = 2.* This function has 36 global optima, there are no local optima and therefore all basins of attraction lead to a global solution. The challenge of this function is that the basins of attraction have very different areas. The range of the variables is $x_i \in [0.25, 10]^D$.

$$F_7(x) = \frac{1}{D} \sum_{i=1}^{D} sin(10log(x_i))$$

F_8 *Modified Rastrigin D = 2.* This function has 12 global optima and 0 local optima. Unlike the previous function, all basins of attraction have the same area. The range of the variables is $x_i \in [0, 1]^D$.

$$F_8(x) = - \sum_{i=1}^{D} (10 + 9cos(2\pi k_i x_i))$$

where $k_1 = 3$ and $k_2 = 4$.

The aim of these experiments is to compare the results estimated by Eq. 1 (model of the sampling size) and Eq. 2 (upper bound) to the actual values computed when sampling the two functions uniformly at random. As for the setup of experiments, increasing values of the sampling size n were used as to obtain a sampling size vs. success rate curve. Note that success rate is equivalent in this context to the probability $P(B)$.

Figure 2 shows the results obtained for the functions F_7 and F_8. At a first sight, these results suggest that Eq. 1 provides a good estimate on the experimental data obtained when sampling a multimodal function uniformly at random. Additionally, the following conclusions can also be drawn from this set of experiments:

- In the case of functions where all the basins of attraction have an equal area (e.g. F_8), Eqs. 1 and 2 are equivalent. In other words, the upper bound is identical to the estimation. In fact, this conclusion can be straightforwardly extracted from Sect. 2.3 as the condition to derive Eq. 2 from Eq. 1 is $\forall b_i \forall b_j, i \neq j : b_i = b_j$.

- In the case of functions such as F_7 where $\forall b_i \exists b_j, i \neq j : b_i \neq b_j$, Eq. 2 provides, indeed, an upper bound on the sampling size. However, these results are not sufficient to establish further conclusions about the quality of such an equation and its ability to generalize in other search landscapes. In Sect. 3.2, we will try to explore this question with a new set of experiments.
- Finally, in a more qualitative interpretation of the results, the large number of trials needed to sample all basins of attraction (in the order of 10^4 for F_7 or 10^2 for F_8) emphasizes the difficulty of multimodal optimization when compared, for instance, with unimodal optimization; in the latter case a single trial necessarily guarantees the sampling of the unique basin of attraction.

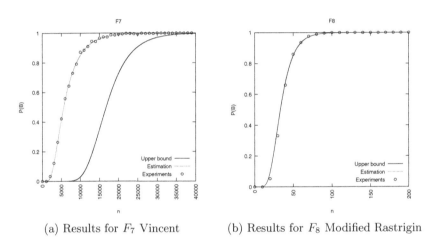

(a) Results for F_7 Vincent   (b) Results for F_8 Modified Rastrigin

Fig. 2. Results for the estimation produced by Eq. 1 (dotted red line), upper bound by Eq. 2 (black line) and actual values calculated as the average of 1000 independent runs on both functions ($\circ$). In F_8 the estimation and the upper bound are superposed as the areas of all basins of attraction are equal. For F_7, the area A is 95.0625 and the b_i values are {9.92, 5.90, 5.90, 3.51, 2.835, 2.835, 1.68, 1.68, 1.41, 1.41, 0.84, 0.84, 0.81, 0.70, 0.70, 0.47, 0.47, 0.42, 0.42, 0.40, 0.40, 0.28, 0.28, 0.20, 0.20, 0.20, 0.13, 0.13, 0.10, 0.10, 0.06, 0.06, 0.05, 0.03, 0.03, 0.02}. For F_8 the area A is 1 and $\forall b_i = 0.0825$. (Color figure online)

3.2 Assessing the Impact of the Problem Landscape on the Sampling Size with a Synthetic Benchmark

In this second round of experiments, the aim is at assessing the impact of different problem landscapes on the sampling size. To that end, Eqs. 1 and 2 are used as estimators of the sampling size and confronted with different types of landscapes. In order to provide a systematic experimentation, a synthetic benchmark with the following features is proposed:

- m, stands for the number of basins of attraction.
- A_b, stands for the total area covered by the different basins of attraction, i.e. $A_b = \sum_{i=1}^{m} b_i$
- For simplicity, we will treat henceforth the area of the basin b_i with respect to A as a probability $p_i = \frac{b_i}{A}$ so that Eqs. 1 and 2 can be respectively rewritten as Eqs. 3 and 4, where $p_{min} : \min(p_i \in [p_1, \ldots, p_m])$.
- We also define the ratio of the area covered by all the basins A_b with respect to the total area A as $Ratio = \frac{A_b}{A}$.

$$P(B) \approx \prod_{i=1}^{m} 1 - (1 - p_i)^n \tag{3}$$

$$n_{upper} = \frac{ln\left(1 - P(B)^{\frac{1}{m}}\right)}{ln\left(1 - p_{min}\right)} \tag{4}$$

In order to generate different problem landscapes a triangular distribution is proposed. The triangular distribution provides a powerful -yet simple- way to tune the skewness of a distribution. This is important because by controlling the skewness we can synthetically generate problems landscapes with different features. For example, by positively skewed distribution we mean that the function contains more small basins of attraction than large ones. On the other hand, in a negatively skewed distribution, the function contains more large basins of attraction than small ones. Without any loss of generality, we assume the lower and upper limits of the distribution respectively be at 0 and 1 with the mode c as the only tunable parameter of the distribution, i.e. $c : 0 \leq c \leq 1$.

Under these settings the Probability Density Function (PDF) of the triangular distribution is:

$$pdf(x) = \begin{cases} \frac{2x}{c} & \text{if } 0 \leq x < c \\ \frac{2-2x}{1-c} & \text{if } c \leq x \leq 1 \end{cases}$$

In particular three instances of the distribution are considered. By setting the respective values of the mode to $c = 0.1$, $c = 0.5$ and $c = 0.9$ we respectively obtain distributions with positive skewness, no skewness and negative skewness. Additionally, in order to calculate the different probabilities p_i, the Inverse Cumulative Distribution Function (ICDF) is employed.

$$F_x^{-1}(\alpha) = \begin{cases} \sqrt{\alpha c} & \text{if } 0 \leq \alpha < c \\ 1 - \sqrt{(1-\alpha)(1-c)} & \text{if } c \leq \alpha \leq 1 \end{cases}$$

PDF and ICDF distributions for the experiments are depicted in Fig. 3 and the full parameterization of experiments is shown in Table 1.

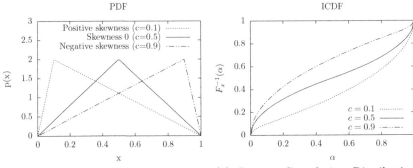

(a) Probability Distribution Function   (b) Inverse Cumulative Distribution Function

Fig. 3. PDF and ICDF curves for $c = 0.1$, $c = 0.5$ and $c = 0.9$ which respectively stand for positive, zero and negative skewness of the distribution.

Table 1. Parameterization of the experiments.

Parameter	Values
m	$1, 2, \ldots, 100$
ratio	0.2, 0.5, 0.8
c	0.1, 0.5, 0.9

We consider m regular intervals on the ICDF as shown in Fig. 4. In order to obtain the respective values of these m intervals, the following sequence has to be applied: $F_x^{-1}(\frac{1}{m+1}), \ldots, F_x^{-1}(\frac{m}{m+1})$.

With the intervals above and given that the *ratio* for the experiments is provided as a parameter in Table 1, we establish:

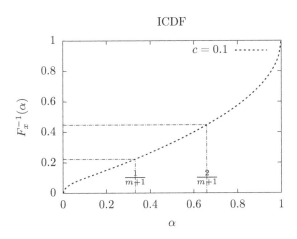

Fig. 4. Example depicting how to obtain the intervals in $F_x^{-1}(\alpha)$ for $m = 2$ and $c = 0.1$.

$$ratio = \frac{\sum_{i=1}^{m} F_x^{-1}(\frac{i}{m+1})}{A}$$

where the only unknown is A so that:

$$A = \frac{\sum_{i=1}^{m} F_x^{-1}(\frac{i}{m+1})}{ratio}$$

that way, for the given $ratio$ and the obtained value for A the respective probabilities p_i can be obtained for every basin of attraction as:

$$p_i = \frac{F_x^{-1}(\frac{i}{m+1})}{A}, i \in [1, \ldots, m]$$

Figure 5 shows the results obtained for the different parameterization proposed in Table 1 from where we can drawn the following conclusions.

- The parameter m (number of basins of attraction) has a non-linear impact in the sampling size n. Independently of the scenario, it holds that the larger m is the larger the sampling size n must be in order to guarantee a certain success rate.
- Surprisingly, there is almost no difference between the curves when $c = 0.5$ or $c = 0.9$. That points out that negative skewness has a negligible impact on the sampling size n. However, when the distribution of the basins' areas is positively skewed such as for $c = 0.1$ (see also F_7 in Sect. 3.1), the sampling problem becomes harder. In the light of these results, we can state that skewness has a non-linear effect on the difficulty of the problem.
- Independently of the scenario, the upper bound (Eq. 4) is steadily twice as large as the value of n (Eq. 3). As a rule of thumb – at least for the case of the triangular distribution –, it can be stated that Eq. 4 provides an estimate which roughly doubles that of Eq. 3.
- The ratio, which indicates the proportion of the whole area occupied by the basins of attraction, has also a major impact in the results. In general, the smaller the ratio the larger the sampling size n.

These results provide some hints about how to design challenging multimodal problems. In addition, for given problems such as those in the CEC2013 benchmark, the provided models may also help establishing some quantifiable measure to assess their degree of difficulty.

To check the accuracy of the bounds, we will make several runs of the algorithms that are considered state of the art for multimodal optimization, and got the best results in the GECCO'19 competition: HillVallEA [19] or NMMSO [7]. Table 2 shows[4] these results. The number of evaluations for F_7 is roughly double the estimated sample size for both algorithms. However, in the case of F_8, the

---

[4] Results for HillVallEA, which is available from https://github.com/scmaree/HillVallEA, were obtained by making 50 independent runs of the algorithm.

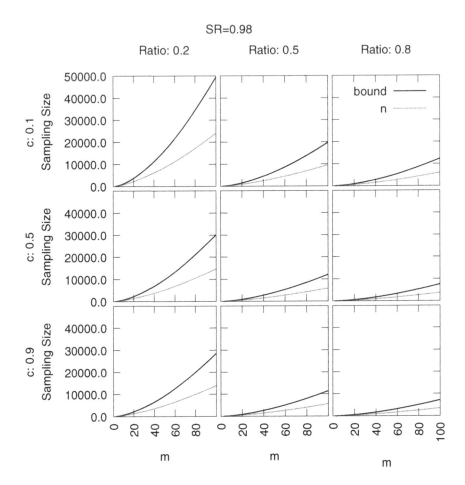

Fig. 5. Results of the experiments for different parameterizations of c and *ratio*. The x-axis corresponds to the number of basins of attraction m and the y-axis the respective sampling size n. The upper bound is established by Eq. 4 (solid black line) and n by Eq. 3 (dotted red line). In all the experiments the success rate is fixed to 0.98 (or equivalently $P(B) = 0.98$). (Color figure online)

Table 2. Convergence rates for NMMSO and HillVallEA.

Algorithm	Function ($\epsilon = 10^{-1}$)	F_7	F_8
NMMSO [7]	Mean ± St. D	27349 ± 14198	1422 ± 444
HillVallEA [19]	Mean ± St. D	28901 ± 7628	4428 ± 335
MaxFEs [18]		200000	200000
Sampling size $P(B) \geq 0.98$		18000	80

estimated sample size is quite small (80), with NMSSO needing approximately 17 times this size, and HillVallEA needing more than 55 times this sample size.

These results, first, support the claim that the evaluation budget set for these problems is too large (i.e. 200k evaluations), because any of the algorithms needs just a fraction of the budget to find the solution. In addition, they also support the claim that a budget based only on dimensionality is not accurate enough: despite both functions having 2 dimensions, F_7 is largely more complex than F_8. Dimensionality, however, has an impact on the complexity of a function that our model encapsulates implicitly since the ratio *area of the basin/total area of the function* will be different in 1, 2 or D dimensions.

Our estimated sampling size also establishes the difficulty of the problems, but as a lower bound on their complexities. The estimates give a hint on the performance of the algorithms on these problems, pointing out that F_7 is harder than F_8.

4   Conclusions and Future Works

In this paper we have presented a probabilistic model that estimates the number of independent trials required to sample all basins of attraction in a multimodal function. The aim of the model is to establish an estimate on the computational complexity of a given function based on its modality, i.e. the number and the distribution of the solutions in the problem space. Additionally, we also present a simplified model in order to provide an upper bound on the sampling size in the case that little or no information on the problem is available.

Two series of experiments have been conducted for analyzing and validating the proposed model. In a first set of experiments, the accuracy of the model is analyzed over two test functions of the CEC2013 benchmark. In the second set of experiments, we propose a synthetic benchmark to systematically analyze the complexity of different problem distributions. From both sets of experiments the following conclusions can be drawn:

1. With respect to the accuracy of the model:
   (a) The conducted experimentation shows that the proposed model provides a good estimate when compared to the experimental values obtained by sampling a multimodal function uniformly at random.
   (b) The model and the upper bound produce the same results in functions where all the basins of attraction have an equal area size.
   (c) If the basins of attraction have different area sizes, the probabilistic model obtains an accurate estimate on the sampling size while the upper bound, as a rule of thumb for the tested distributions, provides a value twice as large.
2. With respect to the complexity of multimodal problems:
   (a) The number of basins of attraction has a non-linear impact on the sampling size and therefore on the complexity of the problem. It holds that a larger number of basins of attraction implies a much larger sampling size.

(b) The distribution of the areas of the basins of attraction has a major impact on the complexity of the problem:
   i. Negative to zero skewed distributions do not seem to significantly increase the complexity of the problem.
   ii. Positive skewed distributions, however, seem to have a non-linear effect on the complexity of the problem as they demand larger sampling sizes.
(c) The ratio (i.e. area occupied by the basins of attraction vs. total area of the problem space) has also a major impact on the complexity of the problem. As the ratio diminishes, the sampling size becomes increasingly larger.
(d) Overall, it can be concluded that *the most challenging multimodal problems are those with a large number of basins of attraction, where the distribution of the areas of the basins of attraction is positively skewed and where a large part of the solution space is **not** occupied by basins of attraction.*

In future works, we aim to establish the sampling size for all CEC2013 functions and then propose an individualized maximum evaluation budget for each of them. To that end, the plan is to conduct Montecarlo simulations in order to estimate the areas (i.e. lengths, areas, volumes or hypervolumes) of all functions in the benchmark.

Acknowledgments. This paper has been supported in part by projects DeepBio (TIN2017-85727-C4-2-P) funded by the Spanish Ministry of Economy, Industry and Competitiveness and FCT project (UID/EEA/50009/2013). We would also like to thank Petr Pošík for his valuable comments on this paper.

References

1. Anceaume, E., Busnel, Y., Sericola, B.: New results on a generalized coupon collector problem using markov chains. J. Appl. Probab. **52**(2), 405–418 (2015). https://doi.org/10.1239/jap/1437658606
2. Bessaou, M., Pétrowski, A., Siarry, P.: Island model cooperating with speciation for multimodal optimization. In: Schoenauer, M., Deb, K., Rudolph, G., Yao, X., Lutton, E., Merelo, J.J., Schwefel, H.-P. (eds.) PPSN 2000. LNCS, vol. 1917, pp. 437–446. Springer, Heidelberg (2000). https://doi.org/10.1007/3-540-45356-3_43
3. Bilgin, A., Kulenović, M.R.S., Pilav, E.: Basins of attraction of period-two solutions of monotone difference equations. Adv. Differ. Eqn. **2016**(1), 1–25 (2016). https://doi.org/10.1186/s13662-016-0801-y
4. Cohoon, J., Hegde, S., Martin, W., Richards, D.: Punctuated equilibria: a parallel genetic algorithm. In: Genetic Algorithms and Their Applications: Proceedings of the Second International Conference on Genetic Algorithms, pp. 148–154. L. Erlhaum Associates, Hillsdale, July 1987
5. De Jong, K.A.: An analysis of the behavior of a class of genetic adaptive systems. Ph.D. thesis, Ann Arbor, MI, USA (1975). aAI7609381
6. Eiben, A.E., Smith, J.E.: Introduction to Evolutionary Computing. Springer, Heidelberg (2003). https://doi.org/10.1007/978-3-662-05094-1

7. Fieldsend, J.E.: Running up those hills: multi-modal search with the niching migratory multi-swarm optimiser. In: 2014 IEEE Congress on Evolutionary Computation (CEC), pp. 2593–2600, July 2014. https://doi.org/10.1109/CEC.2014.6900309
8. Goldberg, D.E., Deb, K., Clark, J.H.: Genetic algorithms, noise, and the sizing of populations. Complex Syst. **6**, 333–362 (1992)
9. Goldberg, D.E., Deb, K., Horn, J.: Massive multimodality, deception, and genetic algorithms. In: Parallel Problem Solving from Nature, vol. 2. Elsevier Science Publishers, B. V., Amsterdam (1992). http://citeseer.ist.psu.edu/133799.html
10. Goldberg, D.E., Richardson, J.: Genetic algorithms with sharing for multimodal function optimization. In: Proceedings of the Second International Conference on Genetic Algorithms on Genetic Algorithms and Their Application, pp. 41–49. L. Erlbaum Associates Inc., Hillsdale (1987). http://dl.acm.org/citation.cfm?id=42512.42519
11. Goldberg, D.: The Design of Innovation - Lessons from and for Competent Genetic Algorithms. Kluwer Academic Publishers, Norwell (2002)
12. Hansheng, L., Lishan, K.: Balance between exploration and exploitation in genetic search. Wuhan Univ. J. Natl. Sci. **4**(1), 28–32 (1999)
13. Harik, G., Cant-Paz, E., Goldberg, D.E., Miller, B.L.: The Gambler's ruin problem, genetic algorithms, and the sizing of populations. Evol. Comput. **7**(3), 231–253 (1999). https://doi.org/10.1162/evco.1999.7.3.231
14. Harik, G., Goldberg, D.E., Cantú-paz, E., Miller, B.L.: The gambler's ruin problem, genetic algorithms, and the sizing of populations. In: IEEE Conference on Evolutionary Computation (IEEE-CEC 1997), pp. 7–12 (1997)
15. Laredo, J.L.J., Castillo, P.A., Mora, A.M., Merelo, J.J.: Evolvable agents, a fine grained approach for distributed evolutionary computing: walking towards the peer-to-peer computing frontiers. Soft Comput. **12**(12), 1145–1156 (2008). https://doi.org/10.1007/s00500-008-0297-9
16. Jiménez Laredo, J.L., Nielsen, S.S., Danoy, G., Bouvry, P., Fernandes, C.M.: Cooperative selection: improving tournament selection via altruism. In: Blum, C., Ochoa, G. (eds.) EvoCOP 2014. LNCS, vol. 8600, pp. 85–96. Springer, Heidelberg (2014). https://doi.org/10.1007/978-3-662-44320-0_8
17. Li, J.P., Balazs, M.E., Parks, G.T., Clarkson, P.J.: A species conserving genetic algorithm for multimodal function optimization. Evol. Comput. **10**(3), 207–234 (2002). https://doi.org/10.1162/106365602760234081
18. Li, X., Engelbrecht, A., Epitropakis, M.: Benchmark functions for CEC'2013 special session and competition on niching methods for multimodal function optimization. Technical report, Evolutionary Computation and Machine Learning Group, RMIT University, Australia (2013). https://titan.csit.rmit.edu.au/e46507/cec13-niching/competition/cec2013-niching-benchmark-tech-report.pdf
19. Maree, S., Alderliesten, T., Bosman, P.: Benchmarking HillVallEA for the GECCO 2019 competition on multimodal optimization. arXiv:1907.10988 (2019). https://arxiv.org/abs/1907.10988
20. Sastry, K.: Evaluation-relaxation schemes for genetic and evolutionary algorithms. Technical report 2002004, University of Illinois at Urbana-Champaign, Urbana, IL (2001)
21. Žilinskasi, A.: On statistical models for multimodal optimization. Stat. A J. Theor. Appl. Stat. **9**(2), 255–266 (1978)

Locating Odour Sources with Geometric Syntactic Genetic Programming

João Macedo[1,2(✉)], Lino Marques[1], and Ernesto Costa[2]

[1] ISR, Department of Electrical and Computer Engineering, University of Coimbra,
3030 290 Coimbra, Portugal
{jmacedo,lino}@isr.uc.pt
[2] CISUC, Department of Informatics Engineering, University of Coimbra,
3030 290 Coimbra, Portugal
ernesto@dei.uc.pt

Abstract. Using robots to locate odour sources is an interesting problem with important applications. Many researchers have drawn inspiration from nature to produce robotic methods, whilst others have attempted to automatically create search strategies with Artificial Intelligence techniques. This paper extends Geometric Syntactic Genetic Programming and applies it to automatically produce robotic controllers in the form of behaviour trees. The modification proposed enables Geometric Syntactic Genetic Programming to evolve trees containing multiple symbols per node. The behaviour trees produced by this algorithm are compared to those evolved by a standard Genetic Programming algorithm and to two bio-inspired strategies from the literature, both in simulation and in the real world. The statistically validated results show that the Geometric Syntactic Genetic Programming algorithm is able to produce behaviour trees that outperform the bio-inspired strategies, while being significantly smaller than those evolved by the standard Genetic Programming algorithm. Moreover, that reduction in size does not imply statistically significant differences in the performance of the strategies.

Keywords: Evolutionary Robotics · Odour source localisation · Genetic Programming · Geometric operators

1 Introduction

Olfaction enables the detection and localisation of distant targets, even if they are silent and invisible. While in nature animals use this sense to locate food, detect danger and mates, humans may use it for locating victims in disaster scenarios, detecting illegal substances or tracking sources of pollution. But, locating odour sources in realistic environments is not easy as the odour particles released flow with the wind, spreading through molecular diffusion and turbulent dispersion. The resulting chemical plumes are intermittent, containing local voids and peaks of concentration which hinder the ability to estimate local gradients. The process of locating an odour source has three well-defined stages [1],

© Springer Nature Switzerland AG 2020
P. A. Castillo et al. (Eds.): EvoApplications 2020, LNCS 12104, pp. 212–227, 2020.
https://doi.org/10.1007/978-3-030-43722-0_14

each requiring a distinct behaviour: (1) plume searching, where the agent must explore the environment, searching for initial odour cues; (2) plume tracking, where the agent is sensing the odour plume and must follow it to the vicinity of its source; and (3) source localisation, where the agent is close to the odour source and must pinpoint its location. Most of the existing works, including the present one, focus only on the plume finding and tracking stages, assuming that other sensory perceptions (e.g., vision) are used to identify the odour source once it is close enough.

Due to the great ability of animals to locate odour sources, many of the published works draw inspiration from their behaviours to devise search strategies [2,3]. The present paper proposes to go one step further, creating new strategies by means of a new kind of Evolutionary Algorithm. Evolutionary Algorithms (EA) are stochastic search heuristics inspired by Darwin's principles of evolution and by Mendel's genetics, which have produced good solutions to difficult problems from many application domains. They have been successfully applied to design robots and their controllers, yielding the field of Evolutionary Robotics (ER) [4]. In this work, a sub-family of EAs entitled Genetic Programming (GP) [5] is used to improve the search strategies encoded as behaviour trees. One of the purposes of evolving robotic controllers in the form of behaviour trees is to enable their interpretation by humans. However, GP suffers from bloat, a phenomenon which translates into an uncontrolled growth of the behaviour trees without a correspondent increase in performance. This growth not only renders the trees hard to be interpreted by humans, but also hampers their interpretation by computers, consequently slowing down the evolutionary process. While there are methods available in the literature to cope with bloat [6] these methods typically restrict the search ability of the evolutionary algorithm.

This work investigates the ability of Geometric Syntactic Genetic Programming (GSynGP) [7] to evolve the robotic controllers for locating odour sources. In its original version, this method has been shown to produce controlled variations of the individuals, resulting in an implicit control of their growth. The present paper extends GSynGP to enable it to evolve expression trees with multiple symbols per node. The best controllers produced by GSynGP are compared to those evolved by the standard Genetic Programming algorithm (SGP) and to two bio-inspired strategies from the literature, both in simulation and in the real world. The statistically validated experimental results show that GSynGP is able to produce behaviour trees that outperform the bio-inspired strategies, while being significantly smaller than those evolved by SGP. Moreover, there are no statistically significant differences between the fitness of the strategies evolved by the two GP algorithms.

2 Background and Related Work

Consider a mobile robot r moving in R^2. The robot is equipped with the necessary sensors to measure the wind direction, the concentration of a target odour and the distance to nearby obstacles. The robot is placed in a bounded arena A where there is a single odour source S emitting at a constant rate. The location of the odour source is unknown. The goal of the robot is to fulfil the first two stages of the odour source localisation process (i.e., to detect the plume and follow it to the vicinity of its source) before a time limit T. This section briefly presents some of the background and related works on odour source localisation.

2.1   Odour Source Localisation Strategies

Over the past decades, researchers have proposed various bio-inspired strategies for locating odour sources. Similarly to the natural organisms that provide inspiration, those strategies are meant to work under particular environmental conditions. The wind speed is amongst the most relevant environmental variables. In the presence of very weak winds, odour disperses mainly through diffusion, whereas in environments with strong wind the odour spreads mainly through turbulent advection. The resulting dispersion patterns are quite distinct, requiring fundamentally different search strategies.

In environments lacking strong wind, chemotactic strategies are typically employed, which use only chemical information to guide their search process. An example of such strategies is the method inspired by the *E. coli* bacteria [8], which consists of a biased random walk composed only by rotations and linear motions. On each iteration, the search agent compares the local chemical concentration to its previous measurement. If the concentration has increased, the agent makes a small rotation followed by a large straight motion, continuing searching roughly in the same direction. Otherwise, it makes a large rotation followed by a short straight motion, directing the search to another direction.

In environments where there is a strong air-flow, animals typically employ strategies that use the direction of the wind for guiding the search, i.e., they perform anemotaxis. A popular anemotactic strategy is inspired by the behaviour of the Male Silkworm Moth (SM) while tracking a trail of pheromone released by a female moth [9]. This algorithm is based on three behaviours: straight line upwind surges when detecting odour, and upwind-centred zigzag or spiral motions for re-encountering the chemical plume. Another popular anemotactic strategy is inspired by the Dung Beetle (DB) tracking a cow's pat [9]. In this approach, the robot starts with a plume finding behaviour, moving crosswind in search for odour cues. Upon sensing odour, it performs an odour-centred zigzag behaviour for tracking the plume to its source. In this behaviour, the robot moves diagonally upwind, changing direction every time it stops sensing odour.

2.2   Evolutionary Algorithms

Evolutionary Algorithms (EA) are a family of stochastic search heuristics loosely inspired by the principles of evolution through natural selection and Mendel's genetics. The application of these heuristics to the automatic design of robots and their controllers yielded a novel research area known as Evolutionary Robotics (ER) [4]. While there are many ways to represent robotic controllers, a popular choice are Behaviour Trees (BT), which are human-readable directional graphs. The trees are composed by inner nodes, encoding decision or sequence functions, and leaf nodes that encode the actions of the robot. In this work, a Genetic Programming (GP) algorithm is used for evolving robotic controllers in the form of Behaviour Trees. GPs [5] are a family of EAs which evolve computer programs that produce the solutions to a given problem, rather than evolving that solution directly. The evolved programs are typically represented by expression trees, composed by inner and leaf nodes. Thus, GPs may be seamlessly used to evolve behaviour trees. Genetic Programming has already been applied to the evolution of robotic controllers for odour source localisation [10]. That work differs from the present one as it focused solely on the evolution of chemotactic strategies, which where tested in an indoor environment without air flow. Moreover, the standard Genetic Programming algorithm used is known to suffer from bloat, producing large expression trees that hinder their interpretation by humans. The present paper investigates the applicability of a recently proposed geometric GP algorithm [7] which has been shown to implicitly control bloat. An extension to that algorithm is made to enable it to evolve expression trees with multiple symbols per node. This is useful to be able to evolve strategies with complex behaviours (e.g., zigzag), rather than elementary actions (e.g., move, rotate) as used in [10]. This algorithm is presented in Sect. 3.

3   Geometric Syntactic Genetic Programming

Geometric variation operators are representation-independent operators based on a distance defined in the search space interpreted as a metric space [11]. A geometric crossover operator produces offspring that are on a shortest path (i.e., line segment) linking its parents. In turn, a geometric mutation operator produces an individual in the neighbourhood of the original individual, i.e., within a ball centred on the original individual whose radius defines the magnitude of the mutation. Geometric Syntactic Genetic Programming (GSynGP) [7] differs from the other GP algorithms by performing geometric crossover between two individuals in the syntactic space. The genotype of each individual is a string that encodes an expression tree in prefix notation. The crossover operation uses the Longest Common Subsequence to align the genomes of the two parent individuals and to create two modification masks, which are used to alter a copy of one individual so that it becomes more similar to the other. Each iteration of this crossover consists of performing one of four modifications: (1) removing one terminal symbol and inserting another of the same type; (2) removing a non-terminal symbol and inserting another of the same type; (3) removing a terminal and a non-terminal symbol; and (4) inserting a terminal and a non-terminal symbol.

As an example, consider the Santa Fe Ant trail benchmark problem [5], for which the terminal set is {*left*, *right*, *move*} and the function set is {*IfFoodAhead*, *Progn*}. Two possible strategies are:

A:	IfFoodAhead	move	Progn	left	move

B:	Progn	Progn	move	move	right

The Longest Common Subsequence between the two individuals is [*Progn, move*], and the modification masks created by GSynGP are:

Due to space limitations, the algorithm for creating the modification masks is not reproduced in this work and we direct the interested reader to [7]. The modification masks contain three types of symbols: (1) the aligned symbols that constitute the longest common subsequence (i.e. the aligned common symbols, whose nodes are presented with a grey background); (2) blank spaces where insertions or deletions must be made; and (3) the non-common symbols, marked with a T_- or F_- depending on whether they belong to the terminal or function set, and that should either be deleted or inserted. The crossover operator uses these masks to make a copy of parent A more similar to parent B. This process can be repeated for various iterations, generating individuals at different points in the paths linking the original parents. Two possible offspring for the first iteration of this crossover operator are:

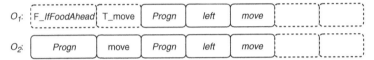

where O_1 results from deleting *IfFoodAhead* and *move*, whereas O_2 is created by deleting *IfFoodAhead* and inserting *Progn* in its place. In this work, only a single iteration of the crossover operator is used.

3.1   Extended GSynGP

The original version of Geometric Syntactic Genetic Programming considered expression trees where each node contains a single symbol. However, in many cases the nodes of the expression trees may contain more than one symbol. This work is one of such cases, where the symbols in the function and terminal sets, called main symbols, take a list of parameters. The proposed variant of the crossover operator works in the same manner as before when two nodes (one of each type) are to be removed or inserted. The novelty is when a node is to be deleted and another of the same type is to be inserted. For the sake of clarity, the node to be deleted shall be referred to as N_d, whereas the node to be inserted shall be called N_i. The new crossover operator works as follows:

1. A new node N_n is created with the main symbol of N_i;
2. The parameters that are present only in N_d are ignored, whereas those that only exist in N_i are added to the new node.
3. The parameters that are common to N_d and N_i are merged as follows: if a parameter takes a numerical value, it takes the mean value from the parents; otherwise, k randomly chosen parameters take the value from N_i, while the remaining take the value from N_d. In this work k was set to 1.

As an example consider the following two nodes:

- N_d: $ZZ(dir = U, dist = 0.5, iters = 1, off = \pi/4, term = PL(5))$
- N_i: $SP(s\_dir = r, dist = 1, dist\_inc = 0.1, intvs = 7, term = SO())$

which are contained in the terminal set described in Sect. 4.3. Further consider that during a crossover operation, N_d is to be deleted and N_i is to be inserted. The creation process of the new node N_n is depicted in Fig. 1. As before, N_n is created with the symbol SP. The parameters dir, $iters$ and off from N_d are not present in N_i and thus are ignored. The parameters s_dir, $dist\_inc$ and $intvs$ are only present in N_i and thus are added to N_n with their original values. The parameter $term$ is present in both nodes but takes a non-numerical value and thus it is added to N_n with the value from N_i. The only remaining parameter is dis, which is added to N_n with the mean of the values from N_d and N_i. N_n is then inserted in the appropriate place using the same method as in the original version of the crossover operator. The proposed extension to GSynGP enables it to perform smaller, geometric modifications to the individuals, rather than simply replacing the different nodes as a whole.

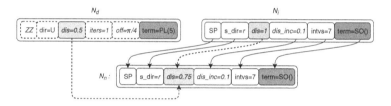

Fig. 1. Creation of a new node, merging the parameters of its parent nodes.

4 Experimental Setup

This section presents the robot, simulator and validation environments used for conducting the experiments, as well as provides details regarding the Genetic Programming algorithms used.

4.1 Odour-Seeking Robot

The robot used for validating the strategies is an in-house built two-wheeled differential unit based on DFRobot's MiniQ 2WD v2.1, that has been extensively modified. The robot is equipped with a E2V MICS 5524 sensor for measuring the gas concentration, two SHARP 2YOA21F57 proximity sensors for detecting nearby obstacles and an in-house built wind vane, which is able to sense the wind direction in 45° intervals. Figure 2 depicts a photograph of this robot, as well a schematic pointing out its various components. The robot uses a nodeMCU

ESP8266 to communicate through WiFi with a remote server running the Robot
Operating System Framework [12]. The server receives the sensory information
from the robot, executes the active controller and returns to the robot a motion
command, in the form of a rotation or a linear motion. The STM32 board in
the robot interprets the command and performs the low-level motion-control.
The ESP8266 is also responsible for interfacing with the sensors, through the
ADS1115 analog-to-digital converter.

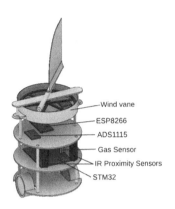

Fig. 2. (Left) developed robot; (right) schematic of the robot.

4.2   Testing Environments

The robotic simulator presented in [9] is used to evaluate the search strategies
during evolution. The simulated arena is a scaled up version of the real world
arena, measuring 40 by 30 m and containing no obstacles. A single odour source,
modelled according to [13], is placed randomly within a bounded region. Its
behaviour is characterised by two parameters: (1) the chemical release rate,
which is set at $8.3 \cdot 10^9$ molecules/s; and (2) the filament release rate, which is
set accordingly to the intended type of environment. The wind is simulated in a
grid that covers the entire arena. The cells of this grid have a square shape, being
the width of each cell equal to 7% of the arena's width. At each simulation step
(which is set to 0.5 s), a wind vector is computed for each vertex of this grid. A
Gaussian noise is then added to each vector, emulating the random phenomena
of turbulence. Modifying the standard deviation of this Gaussian distribution, it
is possible to achieve different levels of wind stability. The standard deviation,
along with the filament emission rate and the initial wind velocity are used to
create diverse environmental conditions, as described in the Sect. 4.3. The real
world test arena (Fig. 3) is a 4 by 3 m enclosed rectangular environment with
50 cm of height. The walls along its length are made of plywood, whereas the

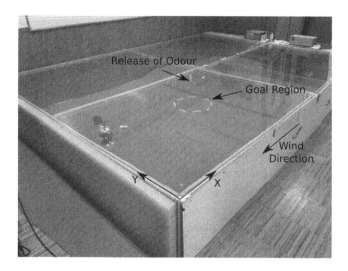

Fig. 3. Validation arena.

others are made of a honeycomb mesh to reduce turbulence. Behind the mesh, on one of the walls, a set of fans are mounted to create air flow with a mean speed of 1.6 m/s. A single odour source is created using an air pump and a bubbler with a 96% solution of ethanol. The bubbler is connected to a hose that emits the odour at the centre of the arena, i.e., at location (2, 1.5) m. A 25 cm circle centred on the end of this hose is marked on the floor, representing the goal region for the robot. The coordinate system of the arena has its origin in the corner closest to the camera, with the x-axis coinciding with the wall along its length and the y-axis coinciding with the wall along its width.

4.3   Genetic Programming Algorithms

The Genetic Programming algorithms used in this work evolve the robotic search strategies in the form of behaviour trees. Each tree is composed by inner and leaf nodes, both of which contain a main symbol (i.e. the function or action to execute) and a list of parameters required by that symbol. The algorithms work as follows: at each generation, a number $n\_offspring$ of individuals are created. Each offspring may result from crossover (sub-tree or geometric) from two parents, or be a copy of an existing individual. In either case, the individuals are chosen from the population by tournament selection. The offspring may then be mutated, at which case either its main symbol or a parameter is altered with equal probability. At the end of each generation, a new population is created containing the $elite\_size$ best individuals from the old population, as well as the best $pop\_size\text{-}elite\_size$ new individuals to ensure that the population size remains constant. During preliminary experiments, the algorithms exhibited signs of premature convergence, which was fought by injecting a set of random and elitist immigrants (in equal number) into the population at each generation. The parameters used by the algorithms are presented on Table 1. The two Genetic Programming algorithms use the same parameters, differing solely in the type of crossover. SGP uses sub-tree crossover, whereas GSynGP uses geometric crossover with one iteration.

Table 1. Parameters of the Genetic Programming algorithms

Parameter	Value	Description
gens	75	Number of generations used
pop_size	50	Size of the population used by the algorithm
n_immigrants	20	Number of immigrants injected per generation
n_offspring	30	Number of offspring created per generation
max_depth	5	Maximum depth of the trees in the initial population
p_cross	0.7	Crossover rate
p_mut	0.3	Mutation rate
tourn_size	2	Size of the tournaments for selecting the parent individuals

The function set used by the GPs contains a set of binary functions devised to make it easier to use the sensors' signals, both from the present and past moments: $F_{set} = \{SO, HDO, PL(t), WS(s), Progn\}$. *Progn* is a sequence function, which executes its two sub-trees in order; *SO* and *HDO* respectively inform whether the robot is currently sensing odour and if it has already sensed odour in this trial; $PL(t)$ informs whether the robot has not sensed odour for a period longer than t seconds, $t \in [1, plume\_lost\_time * 0.75]$, where $plume\_lost\_time$ is a predefined threshold, set at 60 s, above which it is considered that the robot has definitively lost the plume; $WS(s)$ returns true if the sensed wind speed is higher than s m/s, $s \in \{0.5, 1.0\}$.

The terminal set used by the GPs contains the elementary behaviours that constitute the strategies of the Silkworm Moth and Dung Beetle, which are adapted from [1]: $T\_set = \{Break, ZZ(dir, dis, iters, off, term), PCZZ(dir, dis, off, term), SP(s\_dir, dis, dis\_inc, intvs, iters, term)\}$. *Break* stops the robot for a control step and the interpretation of the behaviour tree is resumed from its root; *ZZ* encodes a simple zigzag motion, which is carried out with an offset *off* to a specified direction *dir*, with each linear motion having a given length *dis*. This behaviour is made for a number of iterations *iters* until a termination criteria *term* is met; *PCZZ* encodes an odour-centred zigzag motion similar to that of the dung beetle, where the robot attempts to regain contact with the plume once its lost. It consists of performing straight motions, each with a predefined length *dis* and an offset *off* to a specified direction *dir*. This behaviour is performed until a termination criteria *term* is met; *SP* encodes a rectilinear spiral motion, composed by *intvs* line segments until a termination criteria *term* is met. Each iteration of this motion is composed by three steps: (1) rotating $2 \cdot \pi/intvs$

radians, (2) moving linearly for a given distance *dis* and increment *dis* with an amount *dis_inc*. *s_dir* controls whether the spiral is made to the left (*l*) or to the right (*r*). The values of the aforementioned parameters, found through preliminary experimentation, are:

- *term* $\in \{C, PL(t = 5), PL(t = 40)\}$, where C halts the behaviour when all iterations are completed.
- *dir* $\in \{U, D, X\}$, where U, D, X respectively stand for upwind, downwind and crosswind;
- *off* $\in \{0, \pi/3, \pi/4, \pi/6\}$;
- *dis* $\in \{motion\_length/2, motion\_length, motion\_length * 2\}$;
- *iters* $\in \{1, 2, 3\}$;
- *s_dir* $\in \{l, r\}$;
- *dis_inc* $\in \{motion\_length * x\}$, where $x \in [0, 1]$;
- *intvs* $\in \{4, 5, 6, 7, 8, 9, 10\}$;

where *motion_length* is set to 0.5 m.

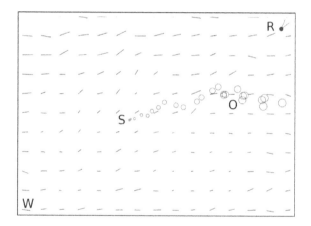

Fig. 4. Screenshot of the second evaluation environment. The wind vectors W are presented as black line segments, the odour source S is the filled green circle, the odour filaments O are empty green circles and the robot R is the filled blue circle with two red lines representing the ranges of its proximity sensors. (Color figure online)

Evaluation Mechanism. Evaluating odour source localisation strategies is not straightforward, as chance may enable a bad strategy to find the source. Moreover, accurately matching the odour and air flow conditions created in simulation and in the real world is not an easy task. For those reasons, an evaluation mechanism was devised to provide a good assessment of a strategy's quality while increasing its robustness to the reality gap. This evaluation mechanism consists of evaluating each strategy in 3 environments, each having different air flow and odour dispersion patterns. Using distinct sets of environmental conditions should encourage the GPs to find strategies that perform well across various scenarios. The environments are made different by varying the initial wind speed WS, the stability of the wind and the rate at which the odour filaments are emitted. The stability of the wind is varied by using different values for the standard deviation (WAV) of the Gaussian noise added to the computed wind vectors (see Sect. 3.1.1 of [9]). As described in Sect. 4.2, the modelled chemical source emits odour in filaments. Two variables regulate odour emission: the chemical emission rate $(\bar{Q})$, which is set at $8.3 \cdot 10^9$ molecules/s and the filament emission rate (FER), which is set differently for each environment. A screenshot of the second evaluation environment is presented in Fig. 4.

Table 2. Environmental parameters

Parameter	Env. 1	Env. 2	Env. 3
WS	0.1 m/s	1.5 m/s	1.5 m/s
Wind direction	0 rad	0 rad	0 rad
WAV	0.3 rad	0.2 rad	0.3 rad
FER	0.05 Hz	0.7 Hz	2.0 Hz
Kx	6	6	6
Arena size	40 m × 30 m	40 m × 30 m	40 m × 30 m
Cell size	2.8 m	2.8 m	2.8 m
Start region	(38 m, 28 m)	(38 m, 2 m)	(30 m, 28 m)
Simulation step	0.5 s	0.5 s	0.5 s
Simulation time	600 s	600 s	600 s

In each of the three evaluation environments the robot departs from a different start region, reducing the possibility of chance enabling bad solutions to find the chemical source. The start position of the robot in each environment is chosen at the beginning of each run and used for all evaluations. The coordinates of those positions are drawn randomly from Gaussian distributions centred on the corresponding coordinates of each start region and with a standard deviation of 0.5. The position of the odour source is also drawn randomly for each trial. Its x-coordinate is drawn from a uniform distribution, ranging between 40% and 45% of the arena's length, while its y-coordinate is between 48% and 53% of the arena's width. The values of the parameters used to create the three environments are presented on Table 2. As previously described, the process of locating odour sources has different stages, each requiring a distinct behaviour. On each evaluation, the search strategy must lead the robot to find and track the odour plume as efficiently as possible. A trial ends successfully when the robot reaches a location within 25 cm from the odour source. Conversely, it ends unsuccessfully if the time limit runs out or if the plume is lost for longer than *plume_lost_time*. The fitness of an individual S is given by the mean performance values attained in the three environments, being the performance $F_i(S)$ in environment i computed by Eq. 1.

$$F_i(S) = \begin{cases} \alpha \frac{t_{si}}{T} + (1 - \alpha)(\frac{t_{ti}}{T} + \frac{d_i}{D_i}) & \text{if the plume has been found} \\ c & \text{if the plume has not been found} \end{cases} \quad (1)$$

where t_{si} is the time taken to find the plume, t_{ti} is the time spent tracking the plume, T is the evaluation time, d_i is the final distance to the source and D_i is the maximum possible distance to the source in environment i. α and c are constant values which, after preliminary experimentation, were set respectively to 0.5 and 2. This is a minimisation problem.

5   Experimental Results

The first step of this work consisted on devising modular implementations of two well-known strategies from the literature (SM and DB), where each module is a elementary behaviour that can later be used by the evolutionary process, as described in [1]. The two strategies were then optimised using a $(1 + 1)$ version of the standard Genetic Programming algorithm that relied solely on parameter mutation. Each optimisation trial was given the same amount of evaluations as the population-based approaches (i.e., each trial ran for *pop_size · gens* iterations). All of the other parameters are equal to those used by the population-based approaches, which were presented in Sect. 4.3. Thirty independent optimisation trials were made for these approaches, being the performance of the strategies measured with Eq. 1. The population-based versions of SGP and GSynGP also ran for 30 independent trials using the parameters described in Sect. 4.3. The mean performance values and sizes of the best strategies found by each algorithm are presented on Table 3. As can be seen, the bio-inspired strategies attain worse mean performance values than those produced by evolution. The worst performing strategies are produced by SM, with a mean fitness of 0.299, whereas the best strategies are produced by GSynGP, with a mean performance of 0.258. The strategies produced by GSynGP are also the most consistent, having the lowest std. dev. of 0.03. Regarding the sizes of the evolved strategies, those evolved by SGP are on average 17 nodes larger than those produced by

Table 3. Results of the search strategies.

		SM	DB	SGP	GSynGP
Fitness	Mean	0.299	0.285	0.273	0.258
	Std. Dev.	0.044	0.0468	0.044	0.030
Size	Mean	15	5	26.133	9.133
	Std. Dev.	-	-	17.600	8.131

GSynGP. Moreover, the strategies produced by GSynGP can be considered to be of an appropriate size, being only 4 nodes larger than DB and 6 nodes smaller than SM.

Table 4. Results of the Wilcoxon test applied to the fitness values.

	SM-DB	SGP-SM	SGP-DB	SGP-GSynGP	GSynGP-SM	GSynGP-DB
Z	−1.18	−2.29	−1.14	−1.51	−3.30	−2.7
p	0.237	0.022	0.254	0.131	0.001	0.007

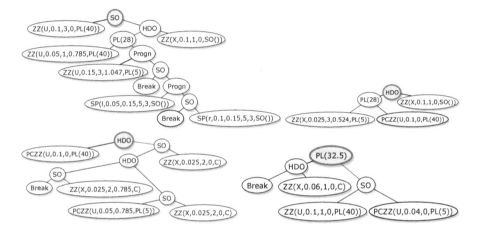

Fig. 5. Overall best strategy for the Silkworm Moth (top-left), Dung Beetle (top-right), SGP (bottom-left) and GSynGP (bottom-right) algorithms. The root nodes are shaded and are drawn with thicker strokes. The parameters of each node follow the same order as presented in Sect. 4.3.

In order to be able to draw more robust conclusions, the results obtained are statistically validated using a confidence interval of 95%. The Kolmogorov-Smirnov test is used to assess the normality of the distributions. Its results show that, at the chosen confidence interval, the fitness values of the DB cannot be considered to follow a normal distribution and, consequently, this analysis must resort to non-parametric tests. The Friedman's Anova is applied to assess whether there are significant differences between the performance of all strategies. It outputs a p-value of 0.009, indicating the presence of statistically significant differences. The next step consists of using the Wilcoxon test to perform pairwise comparisons between the strategies. The Bonferroni correction is used to adjust the significance value to 0.0083. The results of the Wilcoxon test are presented on Table 4, showing that the two bio-inspired strategies are not significantly different. At the chosen confidence level, the strategies produced by SGP do not outperform those produced by any other algorithm. On the other hand, the strategies produced by GSynGP are found to perform significantly better than those of the two bio-inspired approaches. Analysing the sizes of the trees produced, the Kolmogorov-Smirnov test indicates that the data produced by GSynGP cannot be considered to follow a normal distribution. For that reason, the Wilcoxon test is used to compare the sizes of the strategies. Its results show that the trees evolved by GSynGP are significantly smaller than those produced by SGP ($Z = -4.48$, $p = 0.0$).

5.1   Real World Validation

This section presents the real world validation of the best strategy produced by each algorithm. In the previous simulation experiments, each algorithm produced 30 strategies, one for each run. As the environments used in the evaluation process have stochastic components, it is not possible to directly compare fitness values obtained from different trials. For that reason, the best strategies produced by each algorithm were evaluated in the conditions of the 30 independent trials and the one with the lowest mean fitness value was chosen as the overall best for that algorithm. The overall best strategies are depicted in Fig. 5. The real world validation consists of using the overall best strategy found by each algorithm to control a mobile robot tasked with locating an odour source in the indoor environment described in Sect. 4.2. Due to the real world arena being significantly smaller than the simulated one, the distance parameters of the strategies presented in Fig. 5 are a tenth of the values found in simulation. Similarly to the simulation experiments, each strategy has a maximum evaluation time of 600s and the evaluation is halted if the robot reaches a 25 cm distance from the odour source (goal region) or if it looses contact with the plume for a period longer than 60 s. The robot departs from location $(0.5, 0.5)$ m with its heading set at 0 rad. Odour is emitted at location $(2, 1.5)$ m. Due to the time required for the validation, only 5 trials were made for each strategy. In most experiments, the strategies were able to consistently lead the robot to the vicinity of the odour source within the available time. The two unsuccessful trials occurred when the robot was being controlled by DB and by the best strat-

Table 5. Validation results

Strategy	Time search		Time track		Success rate
	Mean	Std. Dev.	Mean	Std. Dev.	
SM	42.710 s	3.899	44.072s	1.993	5/5
DB	67.757 s	4.672	61.896s	8.979	4/5
SGP	125.801 s	4.358	71.141s	5.411	4/5
GSynGP	60.288 s	3.487	46.876s	3.487	5/5

egy of SGP. Despite not reaching the goal region, the strategies made the robot halt its motion at approximately 35 cm from goal region, remaining still until the end of the trial. From an observers' perspective, all strategies exhibited a plume searching behaviour, moving crosswind while attempting to sense odour. All strategies also exhibited similar plume tracking behaviours, moving upwind after sensing odour. The main difference between the behaviours exhibited was the speed, as the strategies produced by SGP and DB were considerably slower than the others due to making shorter motions. These short motions also meant that the robot did not go as deep into the plume before starting the tracking stage. As a result, the robot is more likely to loose contact with the odour plume when controlled by the SGP and DB strategies than when using the GSynGP and SM strategies. While this may not have been an issue in simulation, the anemometer used in the real world experiments has a resolution of only 45°, making it possible for the robot to unintentionally move diagonally to upwind and thus increasing the chance of losing the plume. The time periods taken by the strategies to find and track the odour plume are presented in Table 5. As can be seen, the SM is the fastest strategy, requiring an average of 42.71 s to find the odour plume and 44.072 s to reach the vicinity of its source. The strategy produced by GSynGP is the second fastest, requiring 60.288 s to find the plume and 46.876 s to reach the goal region. The DB and SGP strategies are the slowest, being their average times affected by the trials where the goal was not reached and the robot remained still until the end of the trial. The larger standard deviations are also indications of this.

6   Conclusions and Future Work

This paper presented an extension to Geometric Syntactic Genetic Programming that enables it to evolve expression trees with multiple symbols per node. This method is applied to evolve search strategies for a mobile robot tasked with locating an odour source. The search strategies produced are compared to those evolved by a standard Genetic Programming algorithm and to two bio-inspired search strategies from the literature. The statistically validated results show that the extended GSynGP is able to evolve solutions that are significantly smaller than those produced by SGP without loss of performance. Moreover, the results show that GSynGP is able to outperform the two strategies from the literature, while the SGP can only match their performance. The best strategy of each algorithm was validated by controlling a real robot attempting to locate an odour source in an indoor environment. In this experiment, GSynGP and SM managed to successfully locate the odour source in all trials, whereas DB and SGP failed 1 of the 5 trials conducted. Furthermore, the SM was the fastest to find and track the plume, followed by GSynGP, whereas SGP required the most time.

In the future, efforts should be made to encourage behavioural diversity as a means to counteract premature convergence and, possibly, achieve better quality solutions. The strategies should also be encouraged to re-encounter the odour plume rather than simply halting the motion after loosing contact with the odour. Finally, efforts should be made to quantify and reduce the reality gap, so that strategies perform more similarly both in simulation and in the real world.

Acknowledgement. J. Macedo acknowledges the Portuguese Foundation for Science and Technology (FCT) for Ph.D. studentship SFRH/BD/129673/2017. This work was supported by national funds of FCT/MCTES under projects UID/EEA/00048/2019 and UID/CEC/00326/2019, and it is based upon work from COST Action CA15140: Improving Applicability of Nature-Inspired Optimisation by Joining Theory and Practice (ImAppNIO).

References

1. Macedo, J., Marques, L., Costa, E.: A performance comparison of bio-inspired behaviours for odour source localisation. In: 2019 IEEE International Conference on Autonomous Robot Systems and Competitions (ICARSC), pp. 1–6. IEEE (2019)
2. Russell, R.A., Bab-Hadiashar, A., Shepherd, R.L., Wallace, G.G.: A comparison of reactive robot chemotaxis algorithms. Robot. Auton. Syst. **45**(2), 83–97 (2003)
3. Harvey, D.J., Lu, T.F., Keller, M.A.: Comparing insect-inspired chemical plume tracking algorithms using a mobile robot. IEEE Trans. Robot. **24**(2), 307–317 (2008)
4. Nolfi, S., Floreano, D., Floreano, D.D.: Evolutionary Robotics: The Biology, Intelligence, and Technology of Self-organizing Machines. MIT Press, Cambridge (2000)
5. Koza, J.: Genetic Programming: On the Programming of Computers by Means of Natural Selection, vol. 1. MIT Press, Cambridge (1992)
6. Silva, S., Costa, E.: Dynamic limits for bloat control in genetic programming and a review of past and current bloat theories. Genet. Program Evolvable Mach. **10**(2), 141–179 (2009)
7. Macedo, J., Fonseca, C.M., Costa, E.: Geometric crossover in syntactic space. In: Castelli, M., Sekanina, L., Zhang, M., Cagnoni, S., García-Sánchez, P. (eds.) EuroGP 2018. LNCS, vol. 10781, pp. 237–252. Springer, Cham (2018). https://doi.org/10.1007/978-3-319-77553-1_15
8. Marques, L., Nunes, U., de Almeida, A.T.: Particle swarm-based olfactory guided search. Auton. Robots **20**(3), 277–287 (2006)
9. Macedo, J., Marques, L., Costa, E.: A comparative study of bio-inspired odour source localisation strategies from the state-action perspective. Sensors **19**(10), 2231 (2019)
10. Villarreal, B.L., Olague, G., Gordillo, J.L.: Synthesis of odor tracking algorithms with genetic programming. Neurocomputing **175**, 1019–1032 (2016)
11. Moraglio, A.: Towards a geometric unification of evolutionary algorithms (2007)
12. Quigley, M., et al.: ROS: an open-source Robot Operating System. In: Proceedings of the IEEE International Conference on Robotics and Automation (ICRA) Workshop on Open Source Robotics, Kobe, Japan, May 2009
13. Farrell, J.A., Murlis, J., Long, X., Li, W., Cardé, R.T.: Filament-based atmospheric dispersion model to achieve short time-scale structure of odor plumes. Environ. Fluid Mech. **2**(1), 143–169 (2002)

Designing Cable-Stayed Bridges
with Genetic Algorithms

João Correia[1(✉)] and Fernando Ferreira[2,3]

[1] CISUC, Department of Informatics Engineering, University of Coimbra,
Coimbra, Portugal
jncor@dei.uc.pt
[2] Department of Civil Engineering, University of Coimbra, UC, Coimbra, Portugal
fferreira@uc.pt
[3] MATEREO, Coimbra, Portugal

Abstract. Cable-stayed bridges construction involves the determination of a high number of design variables, both static and dynamic. Moreover, the properties of such variables make them statically indeterminate, meaning that a change in one design variable affects the response of the entire structure. This property makes the design of cable-stayed bridges a complex optimization problem. In this work, we use a Genetic Algorithm to evolve solutions for this problem. A set of experiments are executed, where conventional variation operators are used for exploring the solution space. The first experiments suggest that this is a problem with a deceptive landscape. However, we show that we can design solutions that optimize structural objectives. Moreover, we want also to minimize costs while presenting different optimized solutions. In the second set of experiments, we included a baseline solution in the population to evaluate if we could find better solutions using this approach. The results on the second set showed that it was possible, thus we moved to the third set of experiments with more parameter tuning. The experimental results suggest that we are able to find new and suitable solutions for the problem comparable to the existing baseline approach.

Keywords: Genetic Algorithm · Bridge design · Optimal design ·
Deceptive landscape · Structural dynamics

1 Introduction

Structural Engineering is a fertile ground for new ideas, structural systems, concepts, in particular when designing complex structures [1]. Usually, the work of structural engineers is performed as a series of 'trial and error' iterations, where changes are made to a computer model of the structure until the structure is stable and satisfies standard requirements presented in the Eurocodes – the structural design codes for the European Union, in this case, EN 1991 to EN 1998 and Setra Footbridge guidelines. This process is strongly dependent on each designer capability, creativity and experience.

© Springer Nature Switzerland AG 2020
P. A. Castillo et al. (Eds.): EvoApplications 2020, LNCS 12104, pp. 228–243, 2020.
https://doi.org/10.1007/978-3-030-43722-0_15

Structures can be roughly divided into two groups: statically determinate and indeterminate structures [2]. Statically determinate structures are easier to solve and, for a fixed geometry, the stresses in all internal elements are known. Statically indeterminate structures become more complex because a change in a particular structural element changes the stress distribution in the entire structure, even without changing the geometry. A complex statically determinate structure can be calculated by hand in a reasonable amount of time, while an indeterminate structure with moderate complexity cannot. In recent years, the advance in computers using the finite element method allows engineers to analyse even complex, indeterminate structures in a reasonable amount of time [3].

Artificial Intelligence (AI) has long been identified with high potential to improve the work of structural engineers [4]. Moreover, Evolutionary computation has been used for solving structural design problems [5,6]. Other AI methods have been proposed to tackle specific problems such as pattern recognition and machine learning for damage detection and structural health monitoring [7].

Research works on the optimum design of Cable Stayed Bridges (CSBs) have increased over the past three decades. Most of this can be attributed to the increase in computational performance for the analysis of the structure as well as CSB construction technology [8,9]. These two key factors contributed, for example, to the increase of the CSB record span from 490 m in 1991 (Ikuchi Bridge in Japan) to 1104 m in 2012 (Russky Bridge in Russia). The same trend does not happen to other types of structures. For example, suspension bridges where the record span of 1991 m dates back to 1998 (Akashi Kaikyo Bridge in Japan), or arch bridges where the current record span of 552 m in 2009 (Chaotianmen Bridge in China) is not much longer than older structures such as the Bayonne Bridge opened in 1931 in the USA with 510 m or the famous Sydney Harbour Bridge opened in 1931 with 503m. The reason for this is that it was not possible to calculate recent CSB without the advances in computer science since they are highly nonlinear and static indeterminate structures. Even in 1999, structural engineers did not have the necessary computational capabilities to solve all load cases in the most complex cable-stayed bridges [8]. Evolutionary computation was not possible back then as a single analysis of the structure was very time-consuming.

The optimum design of CSB can be viewed as a relevant benchmark for artificial intelligence algorithms as it requires to consider both the geometry, cross-section, cable tensioning and control devices to address the real-world problems. Other types of structures such as arch bridges require mostly to compute the section sizing [10].

In terms of contributions we enumerate the following: (i) an out-of-the-shelf evolutionary approach to optimise and explore different solutions for a controlled cable-stayed bridge problem; (ii) different fitness functions designs based on various criteria and objectives of the problem; (iii) comparison between a set of optimisation approaches proposed on this work and; (iv) the obtained results suggest that the system dynamic properties create a deceptive landscape that must be adequately addressed in order for the algorithm to find efficient solutions.

Fig. 1. An example of a CSB bridge.

The remainder of the document is organised as follows. In Sect. 2, we overview the related work regarding optimising the design of bridges. Next, Sect. 3, we explain the approach of this work for modelling this problem and system dynamics with a traditional Genetic Algorithm (GA). In Sect. 4, we present the set of experiments performed around this case study. Afterwards we present the results in Sect. 5 and we draw our final conclusions in Sect. 6.

2   Related Work

The previous research works on the optimum design of CSB started by addressing the cable tensioning problem with fixed geometry and structural sections [11–13]. This problem has also been addressed more recently using genetic algorithms (GA) [14,15].

The simultaneous optimization of the geometry, sizing and cable tensioning has also been studied using gradient-based optimization techniques [16,17] and more recently with genetic algorithms [18] with simpler modelling constraints, conditions and with a smaller number of variables than the work presented in this document. Overall, based on the literature, the performance of gradient-based optimization using multi-start procedure is faster than using GA. However, the main drawback is that it requires a very high amount of time to program the details and sensitivities of the problem, unlike GA that it is a more hands-off approach, i.e. that can be used with much lower implementation effort.

Another drawback is that if one changes the structural analysis software, the sensitivity-based code will no longer be available, while the GA can be more easily adapted to another software.

The inclusion of the dynamic loads creates additional constraints for the design problem. Previous researches have focused on earthquakes [19,20], wind aerodynamics [21–23] and pedestrian induced action in cable stayed footbridges [24–26].

Both wind aerodynamics and pedestrian induced action cause resonance in the structure, which magnitudes are strongly dependent on the structural damping (ξ) by a factor of $(1/2\xi)$. Usually, steel footbridges are vibration prone since they exhibit very low damping (0.4%) and thus the dynamic criteria are a governing factor for the design. There are mainly three options to mitigate the vibrations of footbridges: (i) increase the mass of the structure. This is not efficient or desirable since footbridges are required to be slender and aesthetically appealing to become part of the landmark; (ii) Changing the bridge dynamic properties such that the vibration frequency of each mode does not fall within the critical range for the pedestrian induced actions; (iii) Inclusion of control devices such as viscous dampers or tuned mass dampers (TMDs) which was the option to retrofit the London Millennium Footbridge, for example, [27,28].

To the author's knowledge, no previous work addressed the optimum design problem of controlled pedestrian CSB using evolutionary computation algorithms. The problem is based on previous works by [25,26] was a sensitivity based algorithm is used to find the optimum results for both geometry, section sizing, cable tensioning and control device properties. This has the advantage of having already a feasible and improved solution (not necessarily a global optimum) to compare the results with. Also, the sensitivity based algorithm requires the researchers to employ the sensitivities analysis, the derivation of the equilibrium equations, which constitute a high time expenditure in the implementation of the optimization algorithm. We are aware that the nature of the problem can call for different approaches, including multi-objective optimization, nevertheless we intend to explore and harness the complexity of the problem using a standard GA.

3   The Approach

We use a standard Genetic Algorithm [29] to search for solutions in the search space. The individuals are a set of Design Variable (DV)s that parameterize the design of the bridge. To that effect the following fixed DVs have been considered:

- Bridge Length: LTotal = 220 m;
- Bridge Width: 4 m;
- Tower Height below deck: 10 m;
- Number of cables (Ncables) = 4

The number of cables is considered for each side of each tower. The structure is parameterized with four towers leading to a total of 8 cables for the entire structure. An example of such a structure is depicted in Fig. 1.

The DVs have been considered similar to works available in the literature, nonetheless, they were normalized. The objective of this normalization is for

Table 1. Design variables description.

	Description
Geometry	
DV1	Central span (tower to tower distance) of the structure
DV2	Distance between the first and second cables anchorage in the lateral span of the deck
DV3	Distance between the tower and the first cable in the central span
DV4	Distance between the last cable anchorage and the bridge symmetry axis
DV5	Height of the towers
DV6	Distance where the cables are distributed in the top of the towers
DV7	Distance between the top of each tower
DV8	Distance between each tower at the base
Control	
DV9	Transversal stiffness of the tower-deck connection
DV10	Vertical stiffness of the tower-deck connection
DV11	Transversal damping of the tower-deck connection
DV12	Vertical damping of the tower-deck connection
Sectional and tensioning	
DV13	Added mass of the concrete slab
DV14	Deck section
DV15	Deck section (triangular section)
DV16-19	Tower sections (rectangular hollow section) above and below the deck
DV20	Cables pre-stress
DV21	Cables cross section

future works to obtain a database of solutions that could be more easily correlated even for different bridges. A more detailed explanation about the DVs can be found in Ferreira et al. work [25]. Each specific DV affect a specific geometric, sectional or control property of the bridge as shown in Table 1.

The implementation is a standard GA, where a fixed-sized population of solutions is evaluated, selected and submitted to variation operators in a loop with a certain termination criterion (i.e., a predetermined number of generations). The representation of an individual of the population consists of an array of floats representing the values of the DVs. An aspect of the representation of the individuals is that each DV has its domain of range values, which are presented in Table 2. The selection implemented is the tournament selection where the best N individuals are selected to apply variation operators. The conventional

Table 2. Individual's domain values.

	Domain
Geometry	
DV1	$[0.9, 1.2]$
DV2	$[0.7, 1.3]$
DV3	$[0.7, 1.3]$
DV4	$[0.7, 1.3]$
DV5	$[0.1, 2.0]$
DV6	$[0.1, 4.0]$
DV7	$[0.1, 1.3]$
DV8	$[0.1, 1.13]$
Control	
DV9	$[0.001, 1000]$
DV10	$[0.001, 1000]$
DV11	$[0.001, 1000]$
DV12	$[0.001, 1000]$
Sectional and tensioning	
DV13	$[0.1, 7.0]$
DV14	$[0.1, 80.0]$
DV15	$[0.5, 1.3]$
DV16	$[0.4, 1.5]$
DV17	$[0.1, 20.0]$
DV18	$[0.3, 20.0]$
DV19	$[0.3, 9.0]$
DV20	$[0.7, 3.0]$
DV21	$[0.5, 9.0]$

variation operators, crossover and mutation are applied. The crossover of this approach is the uniform crossover, where each DV has a chance to swap between the parents. The mutation is the replacement of a DV value for another drawn from a uniform distribution in the domain of the corresponding DV.

We are designing variables for the CSB, a task normally done by structural engineers. The objectives in a real-world scenario are to minimize the costs of constructions while maintaining the structural and safety constraints. Thus, we consider the following objectives for our approach: minimize the bridge costs and minimizing the structural constraints. These two objectives are affected by the chosen DVs. In order to complete the modelling of the GA, we need to design a proper fitness assignment that guides towards the solution of the problem. In Eq. 1 is depicted as the fitness function used for the set of experiments of this work.

Table 3. GA's Parameters for *exp1* and *exp2*.

Parameter	Setting
Number of generations	5000
Population size	50
Elite size	1
Tournament size	2
Crossover operator	Uniform crossover
Crossover rate	0.8
Mutation operator	Gene replacement
Mutation rate per gene	0.1
a fitness constant	50
b fitness constant	0.9

$$f(x) = \begin{cases} 1/S(x), & \text{if } S(x) > 1.04 \\ a + b/C(x), & \text{if } S(x) \leq 1.04 \end{cases} \tag{1}$$

Where x is an individual, $C(x)$ is a function that computes the cost of an individual, $S(x)$ is a function that evaluates the structural constraints of and individual, "a" is a bonus value constant for the "$S(x) > 1.00$" constraint and "b" is a constant for the target cost. The $C(x)$ is used to calculate the cost of the bridge according to some pre-determined pricing of the materials. The $S(x)$ calculates all security and structural constraints and returns the maximum value of each variable considered. From a practical perspective, we have only to ensure that the maximum value of $S(x)$ is bellowed 1.04, preferably, around 1.00. These two functions represent the two objectives that we must optimize, as minimization problems. Note that both, from a structural engineering perspective, are correlated. By increasing some of the values of the DVs we are strengthening the structure of the bridge which results in a low S(x) value but could translate to a costly solution, i.e., a high value of C(x).

4   Experimental Setup

We developed three experiments for this case study. The first experiment referred to as *exp1*, are the first set of experiments where we aim to optimize the problem further than a baseline conventional approach from [25]. Based on the results of *exp1*, later explained in Sect. 5, we performed experiments in which we insert in the starting population an individual of the best baseline approach. After drawing some conclusions from *exp3* we moved to some adaptations on the hyper-parameters and performed the experiments of *exp3*.

Note that, as said in Sect. 3, for this problem we had some fixed constraints and objectives. However, the approach can be adapted and some of these constraints can be included in the set of DVs. We fixed some of these constraints

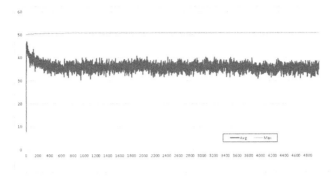

Fig. 2. The average and maximum fitness across generations for *exp1*. The results are averages of 15 evolutionary runs.

such as, the size of the bridge to 220 meters and the number of cables to 4, to compare with a baseline conventional solution which has the following optimized solution:

– Bridge cost: 91.354 k€
– Max Structural Constraints value: 0.9962

The evolutionary engine settings are presented in Table 3. For *exp3* we changed the "Tournament size" to 3, the "Mutation rate per gene" to 0.2 and the "Crossover rate" to 0.85. Due to the stochastic nature of the approach, we performed 15 evolutionary runs for each experiment.

5   Experimental Results

For *exp1* we evaluate the approach in terms of fitness optimization, cost values and structural constraints. In Fig. 2 we can observe that we can optimize the fitness function. However, while looking at the average population, we see instability on the curve behaviour. After the first few 200 we have a lot of ups and downs from one generation to the other, around the same average value. This fast growth and the average population values oscillation suggest that the fitness landscape is deceptive. Fully investigating this, is out of the scope of the paper but it is an avenue of research that is already being pursued. Regarding the best solutions per generation, we can observe that rapidly grows and stabilizes. To further see the variations, we analyse the cost and structural constraints for the best individuals.

In terms of structural constraints, part of the first objective of the fitness function, we can observe on Fig. 3 that is achievable and maintained. It starts with lower values, which is normal but there is a small correlation between having this value low and the cost of the solution high, showing that we must find a solution that balances the two objectives.

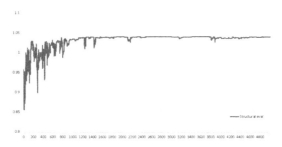

Fig. 3. The structural constraint value of the best individual across generations for *exp1*. The results are averages of 15 evolutionary runs.

Fig. 4. The cost of the best individual across generations for *exp1*. The results are averages of 15 evolutionary runs.

In Fig. 4 we can observe the cost of the best individual across the generations. As expected, inversely like the fitness, the values rapidly decrease although in the first 100 iterations it is quite high. To see the results with more detailed we also provide a "close-up" plot, which shows the values of the cost after 400 iterations as shown in Fig. 5. We can observe that there are some alterations along the iterations, but, for the number of evaluations defined in the setup, the best solution on average only reaches the $110k$€ which is higher than the baseline approach. Since we have done several seeds and arrived at this result, at the time we questioned if it was possible to get or improve on the baseline approach using this approach.

Thus, we then move to *exp2* where we use the GA but we include a copy of the baseline solution in the starting population, promoting local exploration of solutions. We can observe the fitness behaviour in Fig. 6. The results suggest that the behaviour as not changed. In terms of structural constraints we obverse little to none differences across generations in Fig. 7. The main point of conclusions here is the Fig. 8. It shows that we can further improve from the baseline solution, showing that there are other solutions for the problem. Furthermore, suggests that the parameters need to be adjusted for the problem at hand, something that motivated the final set of experiments of this work, the *exp3*.

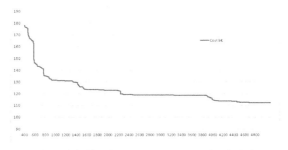

Fig. 5. The cost of the best individual across generations, starting from generation 400, for *exp1*. The results are averages of 15 evolutionary runs.

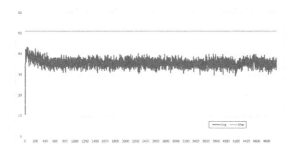

Fig. 6. The average and maximum fitness across generations for *exp2*. The results are averages of 15 evolutionary runs.

After *exp1* and *exp2* we performed *exp3* knowing that it was possible to evolve solutions for the problem and it was possible to improve beyond the baseline solution. We performed some tests and determined the changes of parameters empirically. The rationale beyond the defined values is the following: we wanted to promote more changes from one iteration to the other, hence changing the increase on the mutation rate. We also increase the crossover rate and the size of the tournament to increase selective pressure.

A close up of the results after 400 iterations, in terms of cost, is presented in Fig. 9. We tend to have the same behaviour of *exp1* but now it surpasses the baseline approach under the same number of evaluations. We get values of cost around almost 90.00k€. In terms of structural, we have the values around 1.0 as shown in Fig. 10. The solutions evolved in this set of experiments are able of achieving the desired objective, while maintaining low costs.

We can observe in Table 4 that the algorithm arrives at different solutions. Note that the results that are shown are from the best solutions found in each experiment and are just representative of the universe of solutions that the GA encounters. We can observe that some of the DVs are unchanged when compared to the baseline solution, which could be indicating that the best optimize solution only changes a few variables once we arrived at the baseline one. The best result

Fig. 7. The structural constraint value of the best individual across generations for *exp2*. The results are averages of 15 evolutionary runs.

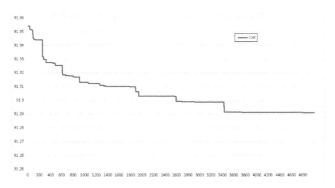

Fig. 8. The cost of the best individual across generations, starting from generation 400, for *exp2*. The results are averages of 15 evolutionary runs.

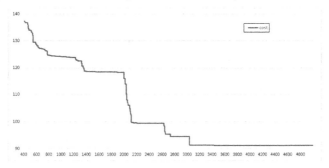

Fig. 9. The cost across generations, starting from generation 400, for *exp3*. The results are averages of 15 evolutionary runs.

observed during the set of three experiments is the a solution with the cost of: 90.893*k€* and structural constraints of 1.016. Overall the results show that we can find different and better solutions than the baseline solution obtained via gradient optimization.

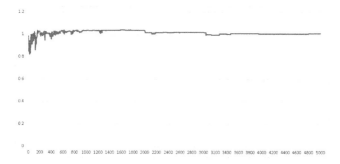

Fig. 10. The structural constraint value of the best individual across generations for *exp3*. The results are averages of 15 evolutionary runs.

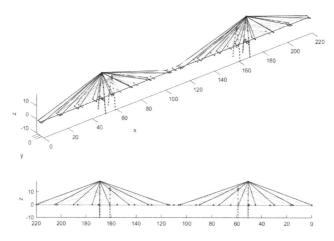

Fig. 11. Baseline (blue) vs Best Exp1 (red) structural model geometry of the bridge. (Color figure online)

Figures 11 and 12 present the structural model geometry where each line represents a structural element. The Best *exp1* solution is awkward from a structural Engineering perspective at the first impression. The central span is lower than half of the bridge length (DV1 < 1) which is not an usual CSB geometry. Also, the tower height to central span ratio (affected by DV5) is markedly low. The reason for this is that, in *exp1*, the GA could not balance the bridge, probably due to the lower mutation rate in this experiment. It then converged to a extra-dosed bridge where the cable stay system becomes secondary and the bridge deck works as a continuous beam. This can also be seen in DV10 which has a very high value in Best *exp1*. In the other solutions the bridge floats over the tower intersection as only a very slender connection is required. the opposite happens in Best *exp1* where the tower-deck connection needs to be very rigid to support the bridge deck. This solution is not governed by the dynamic constraints, but rather by the static response, in particular, the deck stresses. As it

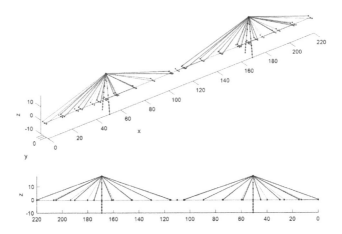

Fig. 12. Baseline vs Best Exp2 = Best Exp3 structural model of the bridge.

Table 4. Best solutions of all the three experiments and the difference between cost, structural constraints and DVs values against the baseline approach.

	Baseline (B)	dif (B, exp1)	Best exp1	dif (B, exp2)	Best exp2	dif (B, exp3)	Best exp3
C(x)	91.354	−13.006	104.360	0.461	90.893	0.481	90.873
S(x)	0.996	−0.043	1.039	−0.022	1.018	−0.021	1.017
DV1	1.075	0.147	0.927	0.000	1.075	0.000	1.075
DV2	0.700	−0.224	0.924	−0.598	1.298	−0.599	1.299
DV3	0.892	0.118	0.774	−0.136	1.028	−0.136	1.028
DV4	1.300	0.001	1.299	0.000	1.300	−0.009	1.309
DV5	0.498	0.146	0.352	0.000	0.498	0.000	0.498
DV6	0.100	−0.717	0.817	0.000	0.100	−0.002	0.102
DV7	0.100	−0.003	0.103	0.000	0.100	−0.001	0.101
DV8	1.300	0.058	1.242	0.020	1.280	0.020	1.280
DV9	3.690	−10.422	14.112	0.000	3.690	0.001	3.689
DV10	0.986	−316.751	317.738	−16.039	17.025	−15.039	16.025
DV11	2.775	1.785	0.990	0.000	2.775	−0.009	2.784
DV12	33.113	−301.763	334.876	7.160	25.953	8.160	24.953
DV13	0.792	0.452	0.340	0.000	0.792	0.001	0.791
DV14	3.989	−0.975	4.964	0.016	3.973	0.017	3.972
DV15	0.500	−0.066	0.566	0.000	0.500	0.000	0.500
DV16	0.497	−0.251	0.748	−0.017	0.514	−0.017	0.514
DV17	0.840	0.095	0.744	0.000	0.840	0.001	0.839
DV18	0.667	−0.411	1.078	0.000	0.667	0.000	0.667
DV19	0.667	−0.222	0.889	0.000	0.667	−0.002	0.669
DV20	1.913	−0.130	2.043	0.029	1.884	0.029	1.883
DV21	6.552	−1.585	8.137	0.000	6.552	0.002	6.550

can be seen in Fig. 13, the response is well below the established limits. This is because the bridge is much stiffer than the baseline solution which also makes it more expensive.

The best solutions for *exp2* and exp *exp3* are very similar to the baseline. In terms of geometry the relevant difference is in the cable anchorage position that

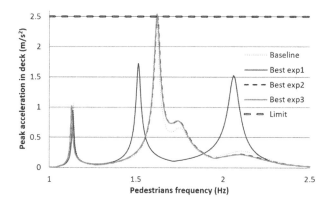

Fig. 13. Comparison between the dynamic responses of each of the bridge solutions. This represents the peek of acceleration of the deck peak accelerations in the vertical direction with the increase of pedestrians frequency in the bridge.

change in Best *exp2* and *exp3* (see Fig. 12). Another main difference seems to be in DV10, which is the stiffness of the tower-deck connection in the vertical direction. Even if the numerical value is quite different the solutions have similar properties since the baseline stiffness is relatively low (this is why DV9 to DV12 have an exponential type domain as presented in Table 4). DV12 (damping in the vertical tower-deck connection) also presents a difference in the results. The constraints have a sensitivity to this parameter. Figure 13 presents the deck peak accelerations in the vertical direction for three different solutions. The 1.018 S(x) value for the Best *exp2* solution can be viewed in this figure as the vertical acceleration slightly exceeds the limits.

6   Conclusions

We perform different experiments using a GA and compare them with a domain knowledge baseline solution. First, we show that a conventional Evolutionary approach is able to optimize the fitness function and find solutions that are: (i) suitable in terms of requirements; (ii) and that minimize the cost. Furthermore, the approach is able to find solutions that are suitable and comparable to the baseline solution.

The preliminary results using a conventional Genetic Algorithm to evolve towards the maximization of the structural objectives indicate that we are able to optimize the fitness function. However, while optimizing the structural objectives, the solutions found do not minimize the cost of solutions. When combining both objectives, the experiments reveal that the fitness landscape is deceptive. Small local changes either make no impact on the objectives of the fitness function or high impact one of the objectives making the solution not viable. However, the results from the last experiment allowed us to surpass the baseline approach by tweaking the starting parameters.

As future work, we plan to develop other variation operators and fitness functions to optimize the solutions towards both objectives. We intend to further study the fitness landscape and analyse how we can minimize the deceptive nature of the search space. We plan on exploring both optimal and diverse solutions via novelty search for this problem with different constraints, starting objectives and more DVs. Another topic of interest to go is the re-utilization of solutions, i.e., some variables from one bridge configuration could be re-utilized to solve other bridges. Furthermore, we feel that this a problem that could be used for benchmark and we are moving efforts to provide this problem to the community.

Acknowledgments. This work is partially supported by national funds through the Foundation for Science and Technology (FCT), Portugal, within the scope of the project UID/CEC/00326/2019 and it is based upon work from COST Action CA15140: Improving Applicability of Nature-Inspired Optimisation by Joining Theory and Practice (ImAppNIO).

References

1. Alan, H.: The art of Structural Engineering: The Work of Jorg Schlaich and His Team. Edition Axel Menges Stuttgart, London (1997)
2. Hibbeler, R.C., Kiang, T.: Structural Analysis. Pearson Prentice Hall, Upper Saddle River (2015)
3. Zienkiewicz, O., Taylor, R., Fox, D.: The Finite Element Method for Solid and Structural Mechanics. Elsevier, Amsterdam (2014)
4. Adeli, H.: Artificial intelligence in structural engineering. Eng. Anal. **3**(3), 154–160 (1986)
5. Arciszewski, T., De Jong, K.A.: Evolutionary computation in civil engineering: research frontiers. In: Civil and Structural Engineering Computing: 2001, pp. 161–184. Saxe-Coburg Publications (2001)
6. Kicinger, R., Arciszewski, T., Jong, K.D.: Evolutionary computation and structural design: a survey of the state-of-the-art. Comput. Struct. **83**(23–24), 1943–1978 (2005)
7. Salehi, H., Burgueño, R.: Emerging artificial intelligence methods in structural engineering. Eng. Struct. **171**, 170–189 (2018)
8. Virlogeux, M.: Recent evolution of cable-stayed bridges. Eng. Struct. **21**(8), 737–755 (1999)
9. Chen, W.F., Duan, L. (eds.): Bridge Engineering Handbook. CRC Press, Boca Raton (2014)
10. Latif, M., Saka, M.: Optimum design of tied-arch bridges under code requirements using enhanced artificial bee colony algorithm. Adv. Eng. Softw. **135**, 102685 (2019)
11. Qin, C.: Optimization of cable-stretching planning in the construction of cable-stayed bridges. Eng. Optim. **19**(1), 1–20 (1992)
12. Sung, Y.C., Chang, D.W., Teo, E.H.: Optimum post-tensioning cable forces of Mau-Lo Hsi cable-stayed bridge. Eng. Struct. **28**(10), 1407–1417 (2006)
13. Baldomir, A., Hernandez, S., Nieto, F., Jurado, J.: Cable optimization of a long span cable stayed bridge in La Coruña (Spain). Adv. Eng. Softw. **41**(7–8), 931–938 (2010)

14. Hassan, M.M.: Optimum design of cable-stayed bridges. Ph.D. Western Ontario University (2010)
15. Hassan, M.: Optimization of stay cables in cable-stayed bridges using finite element, genetic algorithm, and B-spline combined technique. Eng. Struct. **49**, 643–654 (2013)
16. Negrão, J., Simões, L.: Optimization of cable-stayed bridges with three-dimensional modelling. Comput. Struct. **64**(1–4), 741–758 (1997)
17. Simões, L., Negrão, J.: Optimization of cable-stayed bridges with box-girder decks. Adv. Eng. Softw. **31**(6), 417–423 (2000)
18. Hassan, M.M., El Damatty, A.A., Nassef, A.O.: Database for the optimum design of semi-fan composite cable-stayed bridges based on genetic algorithms. Struct. Infrastr. Eng. **11**(8), 1054–1068 (2015)
19. Simões, L.M.C., Negrão, J.H.J.O.: Optimization of cable-stayed bridges subjected to earthquakes with non-linear behaviour. Eng. Optim. **31**(4), 457–478 (1999)
20. Ferreira, F., Simoes, L.: Optimum design of a controlled cable stayed bridge subject to earthquakes. Struct. Multidisc. Optim. **44**(4), 517–528 (2011)
21. Baldomir, A., Kusano, I., Hernandez, S., Jurado, J.: A reliability study for the Messina bridge with respect to flutter phenomena considering uncertainties in experimental and numerical data. Comput. Struct. **128**, 91–100 (2013)
22. Jurado, J.Á., Nieto, F., Hernández, S., Mosquera, A.: Efficient cable arrangement in cable stayed bridges based on sensitivity analysis of aeroelastic behaviour. Adv. Eng. Softw. **39**(9), 757–763 (2008)
23. Nieto, F., Hernández, S., Jurado, J.Á., Mosquera, A.: Analytical approach to sensitivity analysis of flutter speed in bridges considering variable deck mass. Adv. Eng. Softw. **42**(4), 117–129 (2011)
24. Ferreira, F., Simões, L.: Optimum cost design of controlled cable stayed footbridges. Comput. Struct. **106–107**, 135–143 (2012)
25. Ferreira, F., Simões, L.: Least cost design of curved cable-stayed footbridges with control devices. Structures **19**, 68–83 (2019)
26. Ferreira, F., Simões, L.: Optimum design of a controlled cable-stayed footbridge subject to a running event using semiactive and passive mass dampers. J. Perform. Constr. Fac. **33**(3), 04019025 (2019)
27. Dallard, P., et al.: London millennium bridge: pedestrian-induced lateral vibration. J. Bridge Eng. **6**(6), 412–417 (2001)
28. Dallard, P.: The London millennium footbridge. Struct. Eng. **79**(22), 17–21 (2001)
29. Mitchell, M.: An Introduction to Genetic Algorithms. MIT Press, London (1996)

A Fast, Scalable Meta-Heuristic for Network Slicing Under Traffic Uncertainty

Thomas Bauschert[✉] and Varun S. Reddy

Chair of Communication Networks, Technische Universität Chemnitz,
09126 Chemnitz, Germany
{thomas.bauschert,srva}@etit.tu-chemnitz.de

Abstract. Perceived to be one of the cornerstones of the emerging next generation (5G) networks, *Network slicing* enables the accommodation of multiple logical networks with diverse performance requirements on a common substrate platform. Of particular interest among different facets of network slicing is the problem of designing an individual network slice tailored specifically to match the requirements of the big-bandwidth next generation network services. In this work, we present an exact formulation for the network slice design problem under traffic uncertainty. As the considered mathematical formulation is known to pose a high degree of computational difficulty to state-of-the-art commercial mixed integer programming solvers owing to the inclusion of robust constraints, we propose a meta-heuristic based on ant colony optimisation algorithms for the robust network slice design problem. Experimental evaluation conducted on realistic network topologies from SNDlib reveals that the proposed meta-heuristic can indeed be an efficient alternative to the commercial mixed integer programming solvers.

Keywords: Ant colony optimisation · Meta-heuristics · Robust optimisation · Data uncertainty · Network slicing

1 Introduction

Powered by cloud computing and virtualisation techniques, Network softwarisation has paved the way for a holistic transformation of the underlying monolithic ICT infrastructure into a software-defined infrastructure where the legacy hardware-based networking components are replaced by software-based functions executed on general-purpose hardware [1,17]. While this increases the flexibility in deployment, operation and management of immersive next generation services, it is also expected to significantly improve the revenue of the network operators [22]. To leverage the benefits of network softwarisation, NGMN proposes the concept of *Network slicing* as a basis for enabling co-existence of a myriad of logical, self-sufficient, autonomous networks with distinct attributes on a shared substrate platform further opening up newer business prospects in the form of

© Springer Nature Switzerland AG 2020
P. A. Castillo et al. (Eds.): EvoApplications 2020, LNCS 12104, pp. 244–259, 2020.
https://doi.org/10.1007/978-3-030-43722-0_16

Over-The-Top (OTT) content/service providers such as Amazon, Hulu, Netflix [23,24]. Each of these logical networks, henceforth termed as network slices, represents an abstraction of a fraction of the shared physical substrate network resources tailored to meet customer/vertical-specific performance requirements.

Network slicing has gained traction in the recent years for its ability to provide "on-demand", end-to-end slices composed of an assortment of compute, storage, network, radio resources for a wide array of verticals/use-cases thereby empowering network operators to achieve the stringent yet diverse requirements of the emerging next generation (5G) services [19,24,26]. For example, deploying a network slice along a dynamic railway corridor will require very specific characteristics like high mobility, low latency and low throughput whereas a slice dedicated for collaborative automation within an industrial environment demands high reliability, guaranteed throughput with a relaxed mobility policy. Notwithstanding the imminent benefits, realising network slicing in practise entails several algorithmic challenges ranging from efficient resource provisioning mechanisms to online admission control policies [29].

Earlier proposals handled network slicing exclusively as a resource partitioning problem as in the virtual network embedding (VNE) problem addressed in [10,16,18]. Recent works have attempted to broaden the problem statement from merely assigning substrate network resources to pre-defined network slice requests to encompassing the design of the individual network slices (i.e., the network slice topology, the number of required virtual functions, their dimensioning, and the interconnections) as well as considering the impact of the stochastic traffic demands in the problem formulation [3,4]. In this work, we consider the problem of designing a large-scale logical network slice capable of handling the uncertain nature of traffic demands proposed in [4]. We first present an exact formulation for the network slice design problem (NSDP) under uncertainty where the uncertain traffic demands in the network slice request are characterised using the multi-band uncertainty model proposed by Büsing and D'Andreagiovanni [9]. The multi-band uncertainty model extends the Γ-robustness model [5] by partitioning the deviation interval into multiple sub-intervals thereby returning solutions with reduced conservatism without compromising on their robustness guarantees against traffic uncertainty.

The robust counterpart of the network slice design problem is known to pose computational challenges to state-of-the-art commercial mixed integer programming (MIP) solvers due to the inclusion of robust constraints. This observation is in line with prior works that tackle the presence of uncertainty in the problem formulation as in [10,11]. Inspired by the performance of the ant colony optimisation (ACO) algorithms on several real-world problems such as the travelling salesman problem (TSP), vehicle routing problem (VRP) and so on [8], we propose a meta-heuristic approach to solve the robust network slice design problem. Our approach employs the $\mathcal{MAX} - \mathcal{MIN}$ ant system [27] variant of the ACO algorithms within a hyper-cube framework [7] to guide the variable fixing procedure for the considered problem. Experiments conducted on a range of realistic network topologies from SNDlib [25] reveal that the proposed ACO-

based meta-heuristic returns solutions of improved quality in comparison to the
commercial MIP solvers.

The paper is structured as follows: We present a mathematical model for the
robust NSDP by employing a multi-band uncertainty model in Sect. 2 followed
by our ant colony optimisation approach to solve the robust NSDP in Sect. 3.
Experimental results are presented in Sect. 4 with a conclusion in Sect. 5.

2   Robust Network Slice Design

In this section, we present the mathematical model for the robust network slice
design problem. The physical substrate network infrastructure is modelled as an
undirected graph G composed of a network of nodes V connected by edges E. The
residual (i.e. unused) capacities of the nodes and edges are denoted by $c_v^0 \in \mathbb{R}_{\geq 0}$
and $c_e^0 \in \mathbb{R}_{\geq 0}$, respectively. The costs per allocated unit of the substrate network
resources to the network slice is given by $\gamma_v^0 \in \mathbb{R}_+$ and $\gamma_e^0 \in \mathbb{R}_+$, respectively.
Additionally, we allow the expansion of substrate network capacity in discrete
steps of size $c_v \in \mathbb{Z}_+$ and $c_e \in \mathbb{Z}_+$ incurring a one-time installation costs denoted
by $\gamma_v \in \mathbb{R}_+$ and $\gamma_e \in \mathbb{R}_+$, respectively.

We assume the network slice to be composed of a set of demands K, where
each demand k is associated with an uncertain traffic volume $d^k \in \mathbb{R}$ that must
be routed from source s^k to destination t^k through a sequence of network functions $F^k = \langle f_i \mid i \in \mathbb{N} \rangle$ usually derived from the corresponding service graph
[2]. To comply with the restrictions arising due to technological, economic or
geographical limitations, or security issues, we assume that only a subset of the
substrate nodes $V(f_i) \subseteq V$ are capable of offering the functionality f_i in virtual
modules of size $c_f \in \mathbb{Z}_+$.

In this work, we cast the NSDP under uncertainty within a layered graph
framework [20]. This is achieved through the following steps: The given undirected graph G is converted into a directed graph $G' = (V, A)$, where for every
edge $\{u, v\} \in E$ we add two arcs (u, v), (v, u) to A. The digraph G' is then transformed into a layered graph $G_L^k = (V_L^k, A_L^k)$, where the newly-constructed vertex
set $V_L^k = \{v_i \mid v \in V, 1 \leq i \leq |F^k| + 1\}$ is obtained by creating $|F^k| + 1$ copies of
the nodes in V. We retain the connection of the vertices according to the original
digraph G' to obtain $A_L^{k,E} = \{(u_i, v_i) \mid (u, v) \in A, 1 \leq i \leq |F^k| + 1\}$. We then
encode the potential routing of the demand k through the network functions F^k
by creating a set of inter-layer arcs $A_L^{k,V} = \{(v_i, v_{i+1}) \mid v \in V(f_i), 1 \leq i \leq |F^k|\}$.
Finally, we let $A_L^k = A_L^{k,V} \cup A_L^{k,E}$ to complete the transformation.

A formal problem statement for the robust network slice design problem can
now be stated as:

Definition 1. The robust network slice design problem. *Let $G = (V, E)$ denote
the physical substrate network infrastructure with residual node and edge capac-
ities $c^0 \colon V \to \mathbb{R}_{\geq 0}$ and $c^0 \colon E \to \mathbb{R}_{\geq 0}$ expressed in bits per second, whose costs
per occupied unit bandwidth is given as $\gamma^0 \colon V \to \mathbb{R}_{\geq 0}$ and $\gamma^0 \colon E \to \mathbb{R}_{\geq 0}$. Let
the node and edge capacities be expanded, optionally, in discrete steps of size*

$c \colon V \to \mathbb{Z}_+$ and $c \colon V \to \mathbb{Z}_+$ costing $\gamma \colon V \to \mathbb{Z}_{\geq 0}$ and $\gamma \colon E \to \mathbb{Z}_{\geq 0}$ per unit module of installed capacity. Given a set of demands K, where each demand k is associated with an uncertain traffic flow of volume $d \colon K \to \mathbb{R}$ from s^k to t^k through a sequence of network functions F^k, the robust network slice design problem on a transformed layered graph instance $G_L^k = (V_L^k, A_L^k)$ concerns routing the uncertain traffic volume of each demand over the layered graph instance such that the cumulative costs of substrate resource utilisation and potential capacity expansions to host the network slice are minimised.

To this end, we employ the following family of decision variables to model the robust NSDP. Variables $x_a^k \in \{0, 1\}$ indicate if demand k is routed over arc a of the layered graph. Variables $y_{vf} \in \mathbb{Z}_{\geq 0}$ specify the number of virtual modules allocated to the network function f hosted on node v. Variables $y_v \in \mathbb{Z}_{\geq 0}$ and $y_e \in \mathbb{Z}_{\geq 0}$ specify the number of capacity modules installed on the nodes and edges of the substrate network, respectively. The robust network slice design problem takes the form:

$$\min_{} \max_{d \in \mathcal{D}} \quad \sum_{v \in V} \gamma_v y_v + \sum_{f \in F} \sum_{v \in V(f)} \gamma_v^0 c_f y_{vf}$$

$$+ \sum_{e \in E} \gamma_e y_e + \sum_{e \in E} \sum_{k \in K} \sum_{a \in A_L^{k,E}(e)} \gamma_e^0 d^k x_a^k \tag{1a}$$

$$\text{s.t.} \quad \sum_{a \in \delta_v^+} x_a^k - \sum_{a \in \delta_v^-} x_a^k = b^k \qquad \forall v \in V_L^k, k \in K \tag{1b}$$

$$\sum_{k \in K : f \in F^k} \sum_{a \in A_L^{k,V}(f,v)} d^k x_a^k \leq c_f y_{vf} \qquad \forall d \in \mathcal{D}, f \in F, v \in V(f) \tag{1c}$$

$$\sum_{f \in F : v \in V(f)} c_f y_{vf} \leq c_v^0 + c_v y_v \qquad \forall v \in V \tag{1d}$$

$$\sum_{k \in K} \sum_{a \in A_L^{k,E}(e)} d^k x_a^k \leq c_e^0 + c_e y_e \qquad \forall d \in \mathcal{D}, e \in E \tag{1e}$$

$$x_a^k \in \{0, 1\} \tag{1f}$$

$$y_{vf}, y_v, y_e \in \mathbb{Z}_{\geq 0} \tag{1g}$$

Objective function (1a) minimises, for the worst-case realisation of the uncertain demands, the sum of capacity consumption and capacity installation costs for accommodating the network slice request on the substrate network infrastructure. Constraints (1b) are standard flow conservation constraints, where $b^k = 1$ if $v = s^k$, $b^k = -1$ if $v = t^k$, else 0. Constraints (1c) denote the capacity requirements of the network functions on the substrate nodes. Constraints (1d) and (1e) ensure that the consumption of the substrate network resources doesn't exceed the available capacity (residual and installed together) at the substrate nodes and edges, respectively. Note that constraints (1c) and (1e) must hold good for every realisation of the uncertain traffic flow d contained in the uncertainty set $\mathcal{D}$.

2.1   Multi-band Uncertainty Model

We consider the multi-band uncertainty model proposed in [9] to design the uncertainty set $\mathcal{D}$ for the robust NSDP. Under this model, we assume the uncertain coefficient $d^k, \forall k \in K$ to be an independent and bounded random variable represented by the nominal (or forecast) traffic volume $\bar{d}^k > 0$ and a deviation from the forecast traffic volume $\hat{d}^k$ belonging to the deviation range $[\hat{d}^k_{R^-}, \hat{d}^k_{R^+}]$, where $\hat{d}^k_{R^-} < 0$ and $\hat{d}^k_{R^+} > 0$ represent the maximum negative and positive deviation from the forecast traffic volume $\bar{d}^k$. The deviation range of each uncertain coefficient is partitioned into $R = R^- + 1 + R^+$ disjoint ranges on the basis of R deviation values:

$$-\infty < \hat{d}^k_{R^-} < \cdots < \hat{d}^k_{-1} < \hat{d}^k_0 = 0 < \hat{d}^k_1 < \cdots < \hat{d}^k_{R^+} < \infty$$

A band $r \in \{R^- + 1, \cdots, R^+\}$ now corresponds to the range $(\hat{d}^k_{r-1}, \hat{d}^k_r]$, and band $r = R^-$ corresponds to the single value $\hat{d}^k_{R^-}$. We impose a lower bound θ_r and an upper bound Θ_r on the number of realisations of the uncertain traffic coefficients in band r, where $0 \le \theta_r \le \Theta_r \le |K|$ with $\Theta_0 = |K|$. To guarantee a feasible realisation of the uncertain traffic coefficients, we ensure $\sum_{r \in \{R^-, \cdots, R^+\}} \theta_r \le |K|$.

The multi-band uncertainty set for the robust NSDP can now be defined as:

$$\mathcal{D} = \{d^k \in \mathbb{R} \mid d^k = \bar{d}^k + \sum_{r=R^-}^{r=R^+} \hat{d}^k_r z^k_r, \forall k \in K, z \in \mathcal{Z}\}$$

where

$$\mathcal{Z} = \{\theta_r \le \sum_{k \in K} z^k_r \le \Theta_r \qquad \forall r \in \{R^-, \cdots, R^+\}$$

$$\sum_{r=R^-}^{r=R^+} \hat{d}^k_r z^k_r = 1 \qquad \forall k \in K$$

$$z^k_r \in \{0, 1\}\}$$

2.2   The Multi-band Robust NSDP

Since the goal of the decision maker is to be protected against the worst-case realisation of the uncertain traffic coefficients in multi-band uncertainty set $\mathcal{D}$, we introduce additional terms $\mathrm{DEV}^\Gamma_{vf}(x, \mathcal{D})$ and $\mathrm{DEV}^\Gamma_e(x, \mathcal{D})$ in every equation affected by the uncertain coefficients d^k in the robust NSDP indicating additional capacities required at the network functions and the substrate edges in order to cope with traffic uncertainty. These terms, however, render the robust NSDP formulation non-linear and can be linearised by transforming the inner maximisation problem into its dual equivalent as follows:

$$\text{DEV}_{vf}^{\Gamma}(x,\mathcal{D}) = \max \sum_{k\in K:f\in F^k}\sum_{a\in A_L^{k,V}(f,v)}\sum_{r\in R}\hat{d}_r^k x_a^k z_{rvf}^k \tag{2a}$$

$$\text{s.t.} \sum_{k\in K:f\in F^k} z_{rvf}^k \leq \Gamma_r \qquad \forall r\in R \tag{2b}$$

$$\sum_{r\in R} z_{rvf}^k \leq 1 \qquad \forall k\in K:f\in F^k \tag{2c}$$

$$z_{rvf}^k \in \{0,1\} \tag{2d}$$

where binary variables $z_{rvf}^k, \forall k\in K:f\in F^k, r\in R$ take the value 1 if the coefficient $\hat{d}^k$ falls in the r-th band. Objective function (2a) maximises the worst-case deviation for each constraint (1c). Constraints (2b) ensure that not more than Γ_r coefficients deviate in each band whereas constraints (2c) impose that each coefficient deviates in at most one band. As the constraint matrix of the problem is totally unimodular [9], variables z_{rvf}^k can be relaxed. By virtue of strong LP duality, the resulting LP can be replaced by its dual equivalent:

$$\text{DEV}_{vf}^{\Gamma}(x,\mathcal{D}) = \min \sum_{r\in R}\Gamma_r\pi_{vf}^r + \sum_{k\in K:f\in F^k}\rho_{vf}^k \tag{3a}$$

$$\text{s.t.} \ \pi_{vf}^r + \rho_{vf}^k \geq \sum_{a\in A_L^{k,V}(f,v)}\hat{d}_r^k x_a^k$$

$$\forall r\in R, k\in K:f\in F^k \tag{3b}$$

$$\pi_{vf}^r, \rho_{vf}^k \in \mathbb{R}_{\geq 0} \tag{3c}$$

where $\pi_{vf}^r, \forall r\in R$ and $\rho_{vf}^k, \forall k\in K:f\in F^k$ are dual variables. The dual equivalent of $\text{DEV}_e^{\Gamma}(x,\mathcal{D})$ can be obtained in a similar fashion. Substituting the inner maximisation problems with their dual equivalents, we can obtain the compact reformulation of the robust NSDP for the multi-band uncertainty set.

3   An ACO-Based Meta-Heuristic for the Robust NSDP

In the previous section, we presented a compact reformulation of the robust NSDP for the multi-band uncertainty set. Through the inclusion of (hard) robust constraints in the formulation, we restrict the solution space to contain only those solutions that are robust against traffic uncertainty. Such inclusion is known to pose computational challenges to state-of-the-art commercial MIP solvers such as CPLEX as observed in [4,11,12]. To circumvent this computational difficulty, we present a resolution method that employs the $\mathcal{MAX} - \mathcal{MIN}$ ant system [27] variant of the ACO algorithms within a hyper-cube framework [7] to solve the robust NSDP.

Ant colony optimisation is a stochastic meta-heuristic that draws influence from the foraging behaviour of real ants [13]. A standard ACO meta-heuristic involves a family of computing agents iteratively constructing candidate solutions for the considered problem by means of probabilistic sampling from a set of solution components. Each solution component is typically associated with two values of attractiveness - an *a-priori* pheromone trail value and an *a-posteriori* desirability value - that influence the transition probability of the solution components. During the construction phase, a computing agent makes a probabilistic move from the current state (with a partial solution) to the next state by augmenting the incumbent solution with a new solution component until a complete solution is found. The probability of selecting the next move from a set of plausible moves is usually governed by a state transition rule. Upon the completion of the solution construction phase, the pheromone trail values of the solution components are reinforced essentially creating a positive feedback mechanism to aid the construction of improved solutions. The process is repeated until a termination condition is satisfied. For an exhaustive introduction to the theory and applications of ACO algorithms, we refer the reader to the works of [8,14].

3.1   A Meta-Heuristic for the Multi-band Robust NSDP

In this section, we sketch our meta-heuristic that employs the $\mathcal{MAX} - \mathcal{MIN}$ ant system within a hyper-cube framework to guide the decision making strategy for our robust NSDP. A crucial decision within the problem formulation is to determine the routing paths for the network slice demands K in given substrate network infrastructure. Once the routing template for the network slice demands is identified, we can easily compute the capacities required to support the identified routing template to complete the robust network slice design solution. We accomplish the vital task of identifying the routing template through the ant-based solution construction module. Algorithm 1 presents a high-level description of the proposed ACO-based meta-heuristic. In the following, we explain, in further detail, the different phases involved in the meta-heuristic.

Initialisation. In the first step, we set the global-best (x^{gb}, y^{gb}) and restart-best (x^{rb}, y^{rb}) ant solutions to a null value, the convergence factor cf to 0, and the boolean variable gb_update to FALSE. Similar to [7], the pheromone trail values T are initialised to 0.5.

Ant-Based Solution Construction. The algorithm starts with a family of $\Psi > 0$ computing agents that set out to build feasible solutions to the multi-band robust NSDP at each iteration. Within the inner construction loop, agent $\psi \in \Psi$ incrementally constructs the solution to the problem as outlined in the CONSTRUCTNSDP(T) module. For every $k \in K$, agent ψ probabilistically selects a path p from the set of candidate paths P_k over which the traffic of the demand k can be possibly routed. The probabilities of the candidate paths to feature in the solution are determined by the following state transition rule proposed in [21]:

$$\mathfrak{pr}_{pk}^{\psi} = \frac{\alpha \cdot \tau_{pk} + (1 - \alpha) \cdot \eta_{pk}}{\sum_{p \in P_k} \alpha \cdot \tau_{pk} + (1 - \alpha) \cdot \eta_{pk}} \tag{4}$$

Algorithm 1. A meta-heuristic for the multi-band robust NSDP

Input: Problem instance, parameter file
1: $\left(x^{gb}, y^{gb}\right) := \emptyset; \left(x^{rb}, y^{rb}\right) := \emptyset; cf = 0; gb\_update := \text{FALSE}$
2: **for all** $\tau_{pk} \in \mathrm{T}$ **do**
3:      $\tau_{pk} = 0.5$
4: **end for**
5: **while** an arrest condition is not met **do**
6:      $\mathcal{S} := \emptyset$
7:      **for** $\psi = 1 : \Psi$ **do**
8:          $(\bar{x}, \bar{y})_\psi := \text{ConstructNSDP}\,(\mathrm{T})$
9:          $\mathcal{S} := \mathcal{S} \cup \{(\bar{x}, \bar{y})_\psi\}$
10:     **end for**
11:     **if** (iter % 50) = 0 **then**
12:         **for** $\psi = \Psi + 1 : \Psi + 3$ **do**
13:             $(\bar{x}, \bar{y})_\psi := \text{ConstructElitistNSDP}\,(\mathrm{T})$
14:             $\mathcal{S} := \mathcal{S} \cup \{(\bar{x}, \bar{y})_\psi\}$
15:         **end for**
16:     **end if**
17:     $\left(x^{ib}, y^{ib}\right) := \arg\min\{f(\bar{x}, \bar{y}) \mid (\bar{x}, \bar{y}) \in \mathcal{S}\}$
18:     **if** $f\left(x^{ib}, y^{ib}\right) < f\left(x^{rb}, y^{rb}\right)$ **then**
19:         $\left(x^{rb}, y^{rb}\right) := \left(x^{ib}, y^{ib}\right)$
20:     **end if**
21:     **if** $f\left(x^{ib}, y^{ib}\right) < f\left(x^{gb}, y^{gb}\right)$ **then**
22:         $\left(x^{gb}, y^{gb}\right) := \left(x^{ib}, y^{ib}\right)$
23:     **end if**
24:     $\text{ReinforcePheromone}\left(cf, gb\_update, \mathrm{T}, \left(x^{ib}, y^{ib}\right), \left(x^{rb}, y^{rb}\right), \left(x^{gb}, y^{gb}\right)\right)$
25:     $cf := \text{ComputeConvergenceFactor}\,(\mathrm{T})$
26:     **if** $cf > 0.999$ **then**
27:         **if** $gb\_update = \text{TRUE}$ **then**
28:             **for all** $\tau_{pk} \in \mathrm{T}$ **do**
29:                 $\tau_{pk} = 0.5$
30:             **end for**
31:             $\left(x^{rb}, y^{rb}\right) := \emptyset$
32:             $gb\_update := \text{FALSE}$
33:         **else**
34:             $gb\_update := \text{TRUE}$
35:         **end if**
36:     **end if**
37: **end while**
38: **return** $\left(x^{gb}, y^{gb}\right)$

---

where $\alpha \in [0, 1]$ controls the level of influence of the pheromone trail value τ and the desirability value η. We remark that this rule has the advantage of using simpler computational operations and lesser parameters over the classical transition rule. Upon termination of the inner construction cycle by agent ψ, we execute the variable fixing strategy for the robust NSDP as follows: For every demand k, we activate the arcs comprising the chosen routing path while deactivating the remaining arcs, consequently arriving at the fixing of the binary routing variables x_a^k. Having established a complete routing template for the network slice request, we determine the number capacity modules y_{vf} to be allocated network functions $f \in F$ using (1c). We then check if the substrate network has enough resources to fulfill the routing template under traffic uncertainty thereby deriving the fixings for variables y_v, and y_e, respectively. If no constraint of the problem is violated, we declare that the computing agent ψ has found a complete feasible solution to the multi-band robust NSDP, the costs for which can be assessed by using the equation (1a). A formal representation of the solution construction is depicted in Algorithm 2. At the end of the solution construction phase, we update variable (x^{ib}, y^{ib}) to contain the best solution found by the ants in the current iteration.

Algorithm 2. Ant-based solution construction (CONSTRUCTNSDP)

Input: Problem instance, T
1: $\mathfrak{Pr} := \emptyset; \mathcal{P} = \emptyset$
2: **for all** $k \in K$ **do**
3:     **for all** $p \in P_k$ **do**
4:         $\mathfrak{pr}_{pk} := \text{STATETRANSITIONRULE}(T)$
5:     **end for**
6:     $p := \text{PROBABILISTICSAMPLING}(\mathfrak{Pr}, P_k)$
7:     $\mathcal{P} := \mathcal{P} \cup \{p\}$
8: **end for**
9: $(\bar{x}, \bar{y}) := \text{VARIABLEFIXING}(\mathcal{P})$
10: **return** $(\bar{x}, \bar{y})$

Pheromone Reinforcement. Traditional pheromone reinforcement models consider only the iteration-best solution to update the pheromone trails. We employ a rather sophisticated model to update the pheromone trail values of the candidate paths wherein the pheromone deposit each candidate path receives is influenced by three different solutions: the iteration-best (x^{ib}, y^{ib}), the restart-best (x^{rb}, y^{rb}) and the global-best (x^{gb}, y^{gb}) solutions. The level of influence of each of these solutions on the pheromone reinforcement depends on the state of convergence of the algorithm indicated by convergence factor cf. An update to the pheromone trail values is now performed by the following rule:

$$\tau_{pk} := \min\{\max\{\tau^-, \tau_{pk} + \varrho \cdot (\omega_{pk} - \tau_{pk})\}, \tau^+\} \tag{5}$$

where $\varrho \in (0, 1]$ is the pheromone evaporation rate, and τ^+, τ^- are the upper and lower bounds of the pheromone trail values. The update ensures that pheromone trail values of the solution components remain in the range $[\tau^-, \tau^+]$. Finally, parameter $\omega_{pk} \in [0, 1]$ is expressed as:

$$\omega_{pk} := \kappa_{ib} \cdot \delta\big((x^{ib}, y^{ib}), (p, k) \big) + \kappa_{rb} \cdot \delta\big((x^{rb}, y^{rb}), (p, k) \big) \tag{6}$$
$$+ \kappa_{gb} \cdot \delta\big((x^{gb}, y^{gb}), (p, k) \big)$$

where κ_{ib}, κ_{rb}, and κ_{gb} are the weights of the solutions (x^{ib}, y^{ib}), (x^{rb}, y^{ib}), and (x^{gb}, y^{ib}), respectively such that the total sum of the weights doesn't exceed 1. These weights are chosen according to the schedule specified in Table 1. The term $\delta\big((x, y), (p, k)\big) \in \{0, 1\}$ takes the value 1 if the solution component (p, k) features in the solution (x, y), else 0.

Table 1. The schedule for weights κ_{ib}, κ_{rb}, and κ_{gb} depending on the convergence factor cf and the Boolean update variable gb_update.

	$gb_update = $ FALSE				$gb_update = $ TRUE
	$cf < 0.4$	$cf \in [0.4, 0.6)$	$cf \in [0.6, 0.8)$	$cf \geq 0.8$	
κ_{ib}	1	2/3	1/3	0	0
κ_{rb}	0	1/3	2/3	1	0
κ_{gb}	0	0	0	0	1

Convergence Factor. In the final phase of the solution construction, we compute the convergence factor cf which estimates the state of convergence of the algorithm using the formula (7). A convergence factor of $cf \geq 0.999$ indicates that the algorithm has converged and the probability of finding better solutions in the future iterations is extremely low. To overcome this, the boolean variable gb_update is set to TRUE and the pheromone trail values are reset to 0.5.

$$cf := 2 \times \left(\left(\frac{\sum_{\tau_{pk} \in T} \max(\tau^+ - \tau_{pk}, \tau_{pk} + \tau^-)}{|T| \times (\tau^+ - \tau^-)} \right) - 0.5 \right) \tag{7}$$

This concludes one complete iteration of the ACO-based meta-heuristic for the robust NSDP. To accelerate the search towards solutions of improved quality, at every 50th iteration of the algorithm, we introduce a small number of elitist agents that conduct the probabilistic search on a smaller pool of the shortest candidate paths $P_k^e \subset P_k$ for each demand k. As a result of working on a smaller solution space, these elitist ants may not only find solutions of (possibly) improved quality but also influence the search towards such solutions in the subsequent iterations.

4   Performance Evaluation

In this section, we validate the performance of the proposed solution methodologies using realistic problem instances. We consider ten different network topologies from SNDlib [25] to model the underlying substrate network infrastructure. For each network topology, the residual capacities of the nodes are drawn at random from the tuple (2.0,3.0,4.0) Tbps weighted by (0.3,0.4,0.3), and the cost per occupied unit of the node resources is set to EUR 12.5/Gbps. Auxiliary capacity modules of size 40 Gbps can be installed on the nodes at a cost of EUR 50,000 per module. The residual capacities of the edges are sampled at random from (0.2,0.3,0.4) Tbps with probability (0.3,0.4.0.3). The cost per occupied unit of the edge resources is set to EUR 5/Gbps. The capacity of the edges can be optionally expanded in steps of size 10 Gbps with each module costing EUR 20,000.[1]

We consider the design of a network slice for the use-case of next generation emergency services for which the set of network functions comprising the service is assumed to be $F = \langle \text{VF1}, \text{VF2}, \text{VF3}, \text{VF4}, \text{VF5} \rangle$. These network functions can be instantiated on substrate nodes in virtual modules of size 1 Gbps. For every network function $f \in F$, we draw samples of size $\lceil |V|/2 \rceil$ uniformly at random from the physical substrate node set V to construct the candidate physical substrate nodes that support the functionality. Historical traffic traces for the demands of the network slice are generated using the following three-step procedure: First, for every demand k, we randomly draw a value from the tuple (10.0,20.0,50.0) Gbps with probability (0.3,0.4,0.3). Second, to enforce that the traffic coefficients d^k are normal distributed, for each demand k, we draw 1440 samples at random from a normal distribution of mean 0 and standard deviation of 50% of the respective value chosen in the first step. In the final step, the value determined in the first step is added to each of these 1440 samples to obtain the historical traffic traces. Each of the constructed problem instances is now solved using the proposed solution methodologies for bands $|R| \in \{2, 4, 6\}$, encompassing the 68-95-99.7 areas of the normal distribution of the uncertain traffic demands.

We employ a single-threaded Linux machine with Intel® Core™ i3-3120M CPU @ 2.5GHz and 8 GB RAM to conduct the performance evaluation. The compact reformulation (1) is implemented in JuMP v0.18 [15] —a modelling language for mathematical optimisation embedded in Julia v0.6 [6] and is solved using IBM® ILOG® CPLEX® Optimization Studio v12.7.1 [28] with a time limit of 3600 s. The ACO-based meta-heuristic is coded in Julia v0.6 and a truncated time limit of 2400 s is imposed on each problem instance. The parameters of the ACO-based meta-heuristic are hand-tuned to the following values: Candidate paths considered for the construction of the network slice design solution are computed using the $k-$shortest path algorithm [30], where k is set to 10. Six computing agents are considered for the ant-based solution construction. Additionally, three computing agents periodically conduct an elitist search to find improved solutions in quick intervals. The lower and upper bounds for the pheromone trail values are fixed at $\tau^- = 0.001$ and $\tau^+ = 0.999$, respectively and the pheromone evaporation rate ϱ is set to 0.1.

---

[1] As large coefficients are known to pose some problems at various stages of the solution process in CPLEX, the capacities and demands were scaled down by a factor of 1 Gbps, and the costs by EUR 1000.

We evaluate the performance of the proposed solution methods by comparing the absolute gap of the slice design solutions obtained from the respective methods. The absolute gap of a solution is defined as the difference between its best integer objective value and the best lower bound to the problem (returned by CPLEX). Table 2 reports the absolute gaps of the robust network slice design solutions obtained from the considered solutions methodologies, where $|R|$ indicates the number of bands employed in the multi-band uncertainty set to capture the uncertain traffic coefficients, "LB" indicates the lower bound to the considered problem instance which, in this case, is produced by CPLEX, and the values under columns labelled "Exact" and "ACO" indicate the absolute gaps of the robust network slice design solutions obtained from the commercial MIP solver CPLEX and the ACO-based meta-heuristic.

Firstly, the absolute gaps of the robust network slice design solutions from CPLEX are observed to be exceedingly high as compared to their ACO-based counterparts consequently rendering these solutions cost-ineffective to implement in practise. In addition, for 27% of the problem instances, CPLEX couldn't find a non-trivial solution. Despite solving these failed instances using a computationally powerful IBM Decision Optimisation on Cloud service, we observed a negligible improvement in the absolute gaps of the solutions (in the range of 0–3%). We remark that this behaviour is in line with many of the previous works where the robust counterparts were often hard to solve for the commercial MIP solvers thereby justifying the need for scalable heuristic methods [4,11]. The ACO-based meta-heuristic, on the other hand, performs significantly better by yielding solutions of reduced absolute gap for 97% of the considered instances. In most cases, we observe that these solutions are at least an order of magnitude better when compared to the state-of-the-art commercial MIP solvers. The improved performance of the ACO-based meta-heuristic is particularly evident for larger problem instances (i.e., GERMANY50, JANOS-US, PIORO40) thereby establishing the effectiveness of the proposed ACO-based meta-heuristic.

In order to further assess the performance of the meta-heuristic, we develop a simple greedy algorithm to solve the robust NSDP and compare the resulting solution costs with that of the proposed ACO-based meta-heuristic. The algorithm employs a greedy strategy of routing each demand k of the network slice request over the shortest path in the substrate network infrastructure. In the next step, the binary routing variables x_a^k are fixed to reflect the shortest path routings for each demand. After setting up the routing template for the network slice, the remaining variables and the costs of the constructed solution are derived similar to the procedure outlined in Algorithm 2. While the solutions returned by the simple greedy algorithm outperform those of CPLEX for 29 of the considered problem instances, these solutions are still found to be of inferior quality when compared to those of our ACO-based meta-heuristic.

Table 2. Numerical results for the robust network slice design problem.

ID	Network	$|R|$	LB	Absolute gap		
				Exact	Greedy	ACO
1	FRANCE	2	5.21E+4	-	1.48E+4	6.40E+3
		4	6.40E+4	7.89E+6	1.43E+4	7.59E+3
		6	6.76E+4	9.48E+6	1.41E+4	9.05E+3
2	GEANT	2	1.35E+5	-	1.66E+4	1.18E+4
		4	1.51E+5	9.26E+6	1.80E+4	1.27E+4
		6	1.55E+5	1.12E+7	1.87E+4	1.49E+4
3	GERMANY50	2	1.80E+5	-	3.30E+4	2.54E+4
		4	0.00E+0	3.32E+7	2.48E+5	2.43E+5
		6	0.00E+0	4.02E+7	2.60E+5	2.57E+5
4	INDIA35	2	1.26E+5	5.24E+4	3.26E+4	2.17E+4
		4	0.00E+0	2.80E+7	1.88E+5	1.80E+5
		6	0.00E+0	3.36E+7	1.96E+5	1.90E+5
5	JANOS-US	2	2.21E+5	1.14E+5	2.67E+4	1.67E+4
		4	2.49E+5	1.51E+7	2.57E+4	1.94E+4
		6	0.00E+0	1.86E+7	2.82E+5	2.78E+5
6	NEWYORK	2	3.10E+4	-	1.59E+4	8.79E+3
		4	3.82E+4	6.85E+6	1.49E+4	8.76E+3
		6	3.98E+4	8.17E+6	1.50E+4	9.51E+3
7	NOBEL-EU	2	9.36E+4	-	1.92E+4	9.14E+3
		4	1.09E+5	-	1.96E+4	1.11E+4
		6	0.00E+0	1.01E+7	1.34E+5	1.27E+5
8	NOBEL-US	2	1.54E+4	-	4.12E+3	5.28E+2
		4	1.77E+4	4.97E+5	3.95E+3	9.35E+2
		6	1.84E+4	3.75E+2	3.88E+3	7.53E+2
9	NORWAY	2	2.26E+5	2.03E+5	1.74E+4	1.09E+4
		4	0.00E+0	2.03E+7	2.76E+5	2.71E+5
		6	0.00E+0	2.45E+7	2.84E+5	2.82E+5
10	PIORO40	2	2.02E+5	-	4.63E+4	3.08E+3
		4	0.00E+0	3.93E+7	2.85E+5	2.77E+5
		6	0.00E+0	4.71E+7	2.95E+5	2.90E+5

We now focus on the performance of the ACO-based meta-heuristic over the course of its execution. Figure 1 traces the evolution of the costs of the robust network slice design solutions during the ACO-based meta-heuristic execution for two exemplary networks: JANOS-US and PIORO40. We observe from Fig. 1 that the final best solutions yielded by the ACO-based meta-heuristic show, on

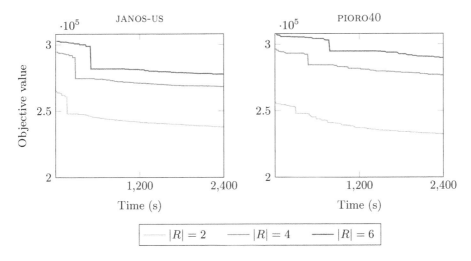

Fig. 1. Evolution of the objective value of the robust network slice design solutions yielded by the ACO-based meta-heuristic for bands $|R| \in \{2, 4, 6\}$.

average, a cost improvement of 8.27% against the initial best solutions over the course of 2400 s. This improvement is noticeably higher (9.91%) for instances with $|R| = 2$, and reduces (to 7.85% and 7.05%) with the increase in the number of bands. This can be explained as follows: The computational difficulty of the considered instances increases with the number of bands employed to capture the uncertain traffic coefficients. As a result, each computing agent ψ consumes more time at every iteration to construct a feasible solution to the robust NSDP, limiting the number of ant-based solution construction iterations. We remark that the computational burden of repetitive evaluation of the objective function after every iteration of the ant-based solution construction can be lessened by means of fitness approximation techniques. Re-defining the cost function (1a) using an approximate cost function may not only reduce the time consumed to execute the CONSTRUCTNSDP module in Algorithm 1 but can also accelerate the search process of the meta-heuristic through quick identification of good solutions in the modified solution landscape.

5   Conclusion

In this work, we propose a meta-heuristic based on the ACO algorithms to solve the robust network slice design problem. Experimentations conducted using realistic problem instances reveal that the proposed heuristic is capable of yielding solutions with improved absolute gaps in comparison to the commercial MIP solver CPLEX. As a further step, the ACO-based meta-heuristic can be integrated with a perturbative method relying on an exact solver to further improve the quality of the obtained network slice design solutions. We plan to evaluate the performance of the integrated ACO-based meta-heuristic with the existing solution methods [4] for the robust network slice design problem.

References

1. Afolabi, I., Taleb, T., Samdanis, K., Ksentini, A., Flinck, H.: Network slicing and softwarization: a survey on principles, enabling technologies, and solutions. IEEE Commun. Surv. Tutor. **20**(3), 2429–2453 (2018). Thirdquarter
2. Barcelo, M., Llorca, J., Tulino, A.M., Raman, N.: The cloud service distribution problem in distributed cloud networks. In: 2015 IEEE International Conference on Communications (ICC), pp. 344–350, June 2015
3. Baumgartner, A., Bauschert, T., D'Andreagiovanni, F., Reddy, V.S.: Towards robust network slice design under correlated demand uncertainties. In: ICC 2018–2018 IEEE International Conference on Communications, pp. 1–7, May 2018
4. Bauschert, T., Reddy, V.S.: Genetic algorithms for the network slice design problem under uncertainty. In: Proceedings of the Genetic and Evolutionary Computation Conference Companion, GECCO 2019, pp. 360–361. ACM, New York (2019)
5. Bertsimas, D., Sim, M.: The price of robustness. Oper. Res. **52**(1), 35–53 (2004)
6. Bezanson, J., Edelman, A., Karpinski, S., Shah, V.B.: Julia: a fresh approach to numerical computing. SIAM Rev. **59**(1), 65–98 (2017)
7. Blum, C., Dorigo, M.: The hyper-cube framework for ant colony optimization. IEEE Trans. Syst. Man Cybern. Part B (Cybern.) **34**(2), 1161–1172 (2004)
8. Blum, C.: Ant colony optimization: introduction and recent trends. Phys. Life Rev. **2**(4), 353–373 (2005)
9. Bsing, C., D'Andreagiovanni, F.: New results about multi-band uncertainty in robust optimization. In: Klasing, R. (ed.) SEA 2012. LNCS, vol. 7276, pp. 63–74. Springer, Heidelberg (2012). https://doi.org/10.1007/978-3-642-30850-5_7
10. Coniglio, S., Koster, A., Tieves, M.: Data uncertainty in virtual network embedding: robust optimization and protection levels. J. Netw. Syst. Manage. **24**(3), 681–710 (2016). https://doi.org/10.1007/s10922-016-9376-x
11. D'Andreagiovanni, F., Krolikowski, J., Pulaj, J.: A fast hybrid primal heuristic for multiband robust capacitated network design with multiple time periods. Appl. Soft Comput. **26**, 497–507 (2015)
12. D'Andreagiovanni, F., Mett, F., Nardin, A., Pulaj, J.: Integrating LP-guided variable fixing with MIP heuristics in the robust design of hybrid wired-wireless FTTx access networks. Appl. Soft Comput. **61**, 1074–1087 (2017)
13. Dorigo, M., Maniezzo, V., Colorni, A.: Ant system: optimization by a colony of cooperating agents. IEEE Trans. Syst. Man Cybern. Part B (Cybern.) **26**(1), 29–41 (1996)
14. Dorigo, M., Blum, C.: Ant colony optimization theory: a survey. Theoret. Comput. Sci. **344**(2), 243–278 (2005)
15. Dunning, I., Huchette, J., Lubin, M.: JuMP: a modeling language for mathematical optimization. SIAM Rev. **59**(2), 295–320 (2017)
16. Esposito, F., Matta, I., Ishakian, V.: Slice embedding solutions for distributed service architectures. ACM Comput. Surv. **46**(1), 6:1–6:29 (2013)
17. ETSI White Paper: Network functions virtualisation: an introduction, benefits, enablers, challenges and call for action. Technical report, October 2012
18. Fischer, A., Botero, J.F., Beck, M.T., de Meer, H., Hesselbach, X.: Virtual network embedding: a survey. IEEE Commun. Surv. Tutor. **15**(4), 1888–1906 (2013, Fourth)

19. Foukas, X., Patounas, G., Elmokashfi, A., Marina, M.K.: Network slicing in 5G: survey and challenges. IEEE Commun. Mag. **55**(5), 94–100 (2017)
20. Gouveia, L., Leitner, M., Ruthmair, M.: Layered graph approaches for combinatorial optimization problems. Comput. Oper. Res. **102**, 22–38 (2019)
21. Maniezzo, V.: Exact and approximate nondeterministic tree-search procedures for the quadratic assignment problem. INFORMS J. Comput. **11**(4), 358–369 (1999)
22. Mijumbi, R., Serrat, J., Gorricho, J., Bouten, N., De Turck, F., Boutaba, R.: Network function virtualization: state-of-the-art and research challenges. IEEE Commun. Surv. Tutor. **18**(1), 236–262 (2016). Firstquarter
23. NGMN Alliance: 5G White Paper. Technical report, February 2015
24. Ordonez-Lucena, J., Ameigeiras, P., Lopez, D., Ramos-Munoz, J.J., Lorca, J., Folgueira, J.: Network slicing for 5G with SDN/NFV: concepts, architectures, and challenges. IEEE Commun. Mag. **55**(5), 80–87 (2017)
25. Orlowski, S., Wessäly, R., Pióro, M., Tomaszewski, A.: SNDlib 1.0—survivable network design library. Networks **55**(3), 276–286 (2010)
26. Soenen, T., Banerjee, R., Tavernier, W., Colle, D., Pickavet, M.: Demystifying network slicing: from theory to practice. In: 2017 IFIP/IEEE Symposium on Integrated Network and Service Management (IM), pp. 1115–1120, May 2017
27. Stützle, T., Hoos, H.H.: $\mathcal{MAX} - \mathcal{MIN}$ ant system. Fut. Gener. Comput. Syst. **16**(8), 889–914 (2000)
28. CPLEX User's Manual: IBM ILOG CPLEX Optimization Studio (2017)
29. Vassilaras, S., et al.: The algorithmic aspects of network slicing. IEEE Commun. Mag. **55**(8), 112–119 (2017)
30. Yen, J.Y.: An algorithm for finding shortest routes from all source nodes to a given destination in general networks. Q. Appl. Math. **27**(4), 526–530 (1970)

What Is Your MOVE: Modeling Adversarial Network Environments

Karlo Knezevic[1]($\boxtimes$), Stjepan Picek[2]($\boxtimes$), Domagoj Jakobovic[1]($\boxtimes$), and Julio Hernandez-Castro[3]($\boxtimes$)

[1] Faculty of Electrical Engineering and Computing,
University of Zagreb, Zagreb, Croatia
{karlo.knezevic,domagoj.jakobovic}@fer.hr
[2] Delft University of Technology, Delft, The Netherlands
stjepan@computer.org
[3] University of Kent, Canterbury, UK
J.C.Hernandez-Castro@kent.ac.uk

Abstract. Finding optimal adversarial dynamics between defenders and attackers in large network systems is a complex problem one can approach from several perspectives. The results obtained are often not satisfactory since they either concentrate on only one party or run very simplified scenarios that are hard to correlate with realistic settings. To truly find which are the most robust defensive strategies, the adaptive attacker ecosystem must be given as many degrees of freedom as possible, to model real attacking scenarios accurately. We propose a coevolutionary-based simulator called MOVE that can evolve both attack and defense strategies. To test it, we investigate several different but realistic scenarios, taking into account features such as network topology and possible applications in the network. The results show that the evolved strategies far surpass randomly generated strategies. Finally, the evolved strategies can help us to reach some more general conclusions for both attacker and defender sides.

Keywords: Coevolutionary algorithms · Network security · Attack/defense strategies

1 Introduction

Cyber attacks are becoming more powerful, dangerous, and prevalent due to constant improvements in attackers' strategies. There are powerful attacks like Advanced Persistent Threats (APTs) that can hide their presence, conduct reconnaissance, and run exploits [15]. Defender mechanisms, at the same time, try to detect possible threats as early as possible and run defensive actions to thwart the attacker's moves. At the same time, the defender's actions are constrained by not being disruptive to the normal operation of the network. In most modern systems, there is a significant asymmetry between attackers and defenders. That notion of asymmetry is a well-known phenomenon with many

© Springer Nature Switzerland AG 2020
P. A. Castillo et al. (Eds.): EvoApplications 2020, LNCS 12104, pp. 260–275, 2020.
https://doi.org/10.1007/978-3-030-43722-0_17

attempts to make such a relationship more balanced [2,16]. Unfortunately, while the defender needs to protect the whole system at all times, for an attacker, it is enough to find a single weakness at a certain moment in time.

As an example, consider a defender strategy where one is randomly changing the network topology to deceive an attacker (for instance, implementing a Moving Target Defense (MTD) [4]). Such a strategy will thwart many attackers, but will not be capable of adapting to any specific scenario. Ideally, we want to develop strategies that are: (1) powerful enough to fulfill their goals (e.g., mounting a successful exploit or defending against it), (2) general enough to encompass many scenarios, and (3) adaptive, to react to new not previously observed scenarios. Developing such strategies can present multiple benefits, from simply testing the limits of a system (for example, we develop a system and we want to test how resilient it is against an adaptable attacker) to finding new strategies not previously used or even considered.

In this paper, we propose a new simulator (MOVE) based on coevolutionary algorithms, which can model adversarial network cybersecurity scenarios. To do so, we abstract networks with graphs and we define several capabilities for each side.

When considering adaptive scenarios, we start with seminal work by Miller, where he investigated the coevolution of strategies in the repeated prisoner's dilemma [10]. To find new strategies, Miller used genetic algorithms and modeled strategies in the form of finite automata (Moore machine) with individuals encoded as strings of bits. Winterrose et al. evolved attackers' strategies against moving target defenses [17]. There, the attackers' goal is to find the optimal scheduling strategy for introducing exploits to a system by using genetic algorithms. At the same time, the defenders switch between several platforms, i.e., they use migration-based techniques, to reduce the attackers' chances of mounting a successful exploit. Due to the limited number of considered resources and the limitation to only two defender's strategies, genetic algorithms were able to find highly successful strategies in all cases. Rush et al. presented CANDLES, a system designed to coevolve attacker and defender agent strategies and evaluate potential solutions with an abstract computer network defense simulation [12]. As far as we are aware, this is the first system considering coevolutionary algorithms for security scenarios. Garcia et al. considered modeling real-world attackers and defenders in a peer-to-peer network [6]. They develop a system able to generate defense strategies where the defenders can choose one of three different network routing protocols: shortest path, flooding, and a peer-to-peer ring overlay to try to maintain their performance.

Duan et al. presented a random route mutation technique, which by randomly changing the route of the multiple flows in a network, simultaneously defends against attackers while preserving network usability [4]. Zaffarano et al. investigated the influence of moving target defenses for network environments and discussed different metrics designed to evaluate the success of MTD [18]. Achleitner et al. developed a network reconnaissance system based on SDNs to achieve deception by simulating virtual network topologies [2]. There, the authors discussed several deceptive methods to slow down the scanning attempts by an attacker who needs to scan the whole network. Prado Sánchez explored several variants of coevolutionary algorithms to model adversarial behavior in cybersecurity domains [13]. Kelly et al. developed a system based on a coevolutionary genetic algorithm, which produces a virtual network topology that delays the attacker and detects the attacker's scan as quickly as possible [8]. Hemberg et al. used coevolutionary algorithms to examine a defensive measure called network segmentation, which divides a network into enclaves serve as threat isolation units [7].

The main contributions of this work are:

1. Design of a coevolutionary scheme able to model a wide range of realistic adversarial dynamics in complex networks. The developed simulator MOVE enables running simulations to find the best strategies for both attackers and defenders. MOVE is an open-source and publicly available project under development [1].
2. Besides modeling attackers and defenders, we also take into account the normal network traffic, which puts important constraints on defense strategies. Consequently, a defender's strategy will not only try to incapacitate attackers but simultaneously opt not to disrupt normal network operation.
3. We propose a new metric called *Network Spatial Topology* to measure changes in the network from the defender's perspective.
4. To better describe the adversarial dynamics, we add a temporal component to our strategies. As a consequence, the opponents play against each other in a series of games, where each game takes place after both players have performed their actions. The defender can maximize the impact of his actions by considering the network state at various moments in time.

Our simulator significantly differs from previous works (e.g., CANDLES [12] and RIVALS [6]), notably in contributions (2), (3), and (4) which, to the best of our knowledge, were never considered before. Naturally, the actions we define for the attacker and defender are also different from those considered in previous works.

2 Problem Definition

2.1 Network Model

Let NM be a network model consisting of a finite number of elements (e.g., switches, hosts, firewalls, honeypots, etc.). Accordingly, the network consists of a number of elements that are used in actual traffic but also some elements that are used to deceive an attacker. From the operational perspective, we distinguish between two types of elements: firewalls and everything else. The difference is that the attacker cannot conduct actions on nodes behind a firewall until he has the firewall under his control (i.e., he successfully performed an exploit on that node). Without loss of generality, we continue by calling all nodes hosts.

The host elements are connected to form a network and each host has certain resources related to it. For instance, one resource can be an operating system running on a station. Each host must have at least one resource allocated to it. Finally, each node has a set of ports to serve as endpoints for communication.

We represent our network NM as an n-tuple: $<H, R, C, P>$. Here, H represents the set of hosts, R represents the set of resources, C represents the connections between hosts (i.e., their adjacencies), and P denotes the set of ports. Next, we represent every host H as an n-tuple: $<RH, PH, Firewall, Honeypot>$, where RH represents the resources allocated on the host, PH represents the ports available on a specific host, $Firewall$ denotes whether a node is a firewall (1) or not (0), and finally, $Honeypot$ denotes whether a node is a honeypot (1) or not (0).

In our model, hosts are connected with edges that can be undirected or directed (e.g., a firewall that allows traffic in one direction but not in the other). To model the connections among hosts, we use an adjacency matrix. There is a finite number of possible resources in a network, and there is a degree of similarity between some of those resources. The resource similarity is defined with the resource similarity matrix. As an example, consider resources R_1, R_2, and R_3. The resources R_1 and R_2 have a similarity equal to 0.7, while resources R_1 and R_3 have a similarity equal to 0.5. This means that if there is a successful attack on resource R_1, then there is a greater probability that the same attack will work for resource R_2 than for resource R_3. Since not all resources are equally likely to be observed in a network, we model this phenomenon through the resource popularity table that defines the probability of a resource to occur in a network. Finally, each node has a number of ports where a certain port number is reserved to identify specific services.

2.2   Attacker Model

We assume that the attacker has already infiltrated the network and is controlling one internal host (location is not known, and at the beginning of each run, it is assigned uniformly at random). The attacker does not know the network topology, the resources allocated to each host, or which ports are used. From inside the network, he can use various scan techniques to discover details about the network topology and to run remote exploits to move laterally within the network. Note that by combining these actions, we encompass the main functionalities of the Discovery phase of a cyber attack [14]. This set of actions enable the attacker to obtain (partial) information about the network, i.e., n-tuple $<H, R, C, P>$ and a number of nodes, i.e., n-tuples $<RH, PH, Firewall, Honeypot>$. Then, he attempts to exploit specific resources (e.g., operating system, services, protocols) associated with hosts/ports. The attacking approach is to find a strategy that will maximize the amount of information about hosts gathered, and consequently, the success of the exploits deployed. To allow the attacker to (theoretically) assume control of any part of a network, we assume that each resource can be exploited (with a certain probability). The set of actions that are available to the attacker are:

Scan a Node of the Network. This is the basic move for the attacker and the only reliable way to explore the whole network – identifying hosts, used ports, and resources as well as the information on the connectivity between the hosts. Results from the literature show that the network scanning is often the predecessor of an attack, and consequently represents an integral part of our model [11]. We start each simulation with the assumption that the attacker does not know anything about the network, except for the node he is located at. Only once a node is scanned (e.g., using Nmap [9]), the attacker knows the potential weaknesses (resources) present there. To scan the network, the attacker can use either a horizontal scan or a vertical scan. A *horizontal scan* is a scan performed against a group of nodes for a single given port. A *vertical scan* is a scan where a single node is scanned for multiple ports. Note, we assume that the attacker can rescan nodes to keep an updated database to perform more successful attacks. It is not possible to scan the nodes behind a firewall before mounting a successful exploit on the firewall. There is a cost of scanning a node/port. To model it, we define those costs as a cost of accessing a node and the cost of scanning a port. The cost amounts can be set arbitrarily to match the actual network properties.

Attempt of an Exploit. A successfully mounted exploit is the end goal of the attacker. The exploit can be attempted on both previously scanned hosts and hosts that were not scanned before. In the former case, the attacker attempts to run the exploit corresponding to the most observed resource in the scanned network. Naturally, he will attempt the exploit only on the nodes that have that resource. Additionally, the attacker will also try to mount exploits on resources that are similar to the most observed resource. In the latter case, we distinguish two strategies. The first strategy is *Maximize*, where the attacker attempts to use the exploit that is the most "popular". The motivation for this type of exploit is that the attacker can use his previous experience or available information on the network to attempt the exploit he deems most likely to be successful. If the host does not have that specific resource, the attack is not successful. The second strategy is called *Diversify* and it differs from the previous one by using random exploits. Similarly, the host must have at least one of the corresponding resources for the exploit to be successful.

We assume there is a cost of running exploits where we assign these costs uniformly at random for each resource (but this can easily be configured differently). Note, the notion of exploit cost can be interpreted as a set of actions necessary for the attacker to run an exploit (the concept used in [17]). Regardless of the interpretation, we can work without loss of generality with a notion of a *budget* that the attacker must spend to perform a scan or to launch a successful exploit.

2.3   Defender Model

The defender's goal is to minimize the success of an attacker by either preventing him from mounting exploits or at least slowing him down. To do so, the defender has at his disposal several actions that will enable him to deceive the attacker with incorrect information. Since each of the hosts can be infected, we assume that our defense strategy can deploy different defense mechanisms for each host. By utilizing these actions, the defender changes the n-tuple corresponding to the actual network (i.e., "True View Network") $TV_N = <H, R, C, P>$ into n-tuples belonging to the Virtual View Network $VV_N = <H', R', C', P'>$ and n-tuple corresponding to host $TV_H = <RH, PH, Firewall, Honeypot>$ into $VV_H = <RH', PH', Firewall, Honeypot>$. With these actions, the defense deceives the attacker since he has access only to the virtual views. Consequently, when the attacker runs the attack, he will obtain knowledge only of a small part of a true network, which will reduce the chances of his successful exploits. Actions available to the defender are:

Add/Remove a Honeypot. A honeypot is isolated and monitored by the defense system, and users accessing it can be immediately labeled as attackers, since legitimate users do not enter honeypots. Each honeypot has resources/ports of the same type as real hosts and there is a limit on the maximal number of honeypots in the network.

Add/Remove a Connection. This action corresponds to re-routing traffic between hosts.

Add/Remove a Resource. This action corresponds to migration-based techniques.

Move Ports. This action corresponds to replacing a resource from the present port to another randomly chosen unused one.

Note that, by default, all actions affect a randomly selected part of the network. The defender has an additional goal connected with the network usability: he must maintain the normal operation of the network, which we encode as not being possible to remove nodes (or their corresponding connections) that participate in the normal (true) traffic. The set of nodes that must not be affected by defender actions is given at the beginning of the simulation.

3   Experimental Setup

Both the defender and the attacker have at their disposal a certain *budget* for their actions. With this, we try to avoid that the evolution finds solutions that are trivial or not particularly insightful (e.g., scanning the whole network at once or adding thousands of honeypots to a physical network of only ten hosts). Different actions have different costs which limit their use. The actual values can be defined in the simulator by the user to reflect the current network model.

We differentiate three scenarios concerning the capabilities of adversaries: (1) static defender, adaptive attacker, (2) adaptive defender, static attacker, and (3) adaptive defender, adaptive attacker. In all scenarios, both defender and attacker populations are initialized at random and at the beginning each member of both populations is evaluated in simulation against every member of the opposing population. This way, we obtain an initial estimate of the quality of randomly generated attack and defense strategies.

In the first scenario where the defense is static, we then select only the best strategy from the defender population and run the evolution on the attacker population only. In every iteration of the GA, each attacker is evaluated by simulating its actions against the preselected defender. The attacker population is then subject to evolution, trying to find the best strategy against the static defender. In the second scenario, the same principle is applied inversely; the best attacker from the initial population is used in the evolution of improved defense strategies.

Finally, in the most general case, both attacker and defender populations undergo evolution; in every iteration of the GA, we simulate the actions of each attacker against each defender and vice versa separately, and their fitness value is accumulated over all simulations. In this case, the aim is to evolve a strategy that would perform well against a wide range of opponents.

In all the scenarios, a single simulation is performed in one or more *games*: a single game includes both the attacker and the defender performing their actions up to exhausting the allotted budget. After a game is completed, their budgets are restored to the initial amount and the next game is commenced. In our experiments, a default number of 5 games is used in all experiments.

In MOVE, we use a simple genetic algorithm (GA) with a 3-tournament selection [5]. With the 3-tournament selection, three solutions are selected randomly and the worst one is discarded. From the remaining two solutions, one offspring is created by the crossover operator. We note that this algorithm has the property of elitism, which means that the best solution will always remain intact in the next population [5].

The initial population is created uniformly at random. As a stopping criterion, we use the number of generations. Each simulation is run for R runs where each run is independent and consists of G generations. The size of the attacker population is P_A and that of the defender population P_D. The simulation is run in a setting where time advances in discrete steps.

We use parameters defined for the coevolutionary algorithms as given in Table 1. Note, the mutation rate is per individual, which means there is a p_m chance an individual will be mutated, but the mutation happens only on a single, randomly selected gene.

Table 1. Coevolutionary algorithm parameters.

Parameter name	Parameter value
Number of runs R	30
Number of generations G	150
Number of games	5
Attacker (defender) population size A (B)	30
Tournament size k	3
Mutation rate per individual p_m	0.3

3.1   Encoding of Solutions

To encode strategies efficiently, we use integer representation, where each gene represents one part of the strategy. Each solution (i.e., an individual) is represented as an array of integer values – integer-based encoding. The encodings of solutions for attackers and defenders differ, but we define one that ensures a minimal number of non-coding genes, as explained in the next section. For both sides, the values for each gene are in the range $[0, 100]$. Each value represents a *relative probability* (as a percentage) of choosing a specific action. The relative percentages are always scaled during genotype decoding so that the total sum of probabilities of all considered actions equals 100%. After an action is chosen based on those probabilities, it is performed either in full (depending on the action type) or until the budget is exhausted. If there is a remaining budget after the current action is completed, the next action is chosen and performed in the same way until the budget is depleted. Note that although it may seem possible to run an exhaustive search over the set of all possible strategies, besides the number of strategies, one also needs to take into account the network layout and all possible choices in running the strategies, making exhaustive search infeasible.

To encode the attacker, we require seven genes. The first gene determines the amount of the budget spent on the *scan* action. The *scan* action can occur only on accessible nodes (i.e., those that are not behind a firewall). After a scan action is chosen, it can be performed either via a horizontal or vertical scan, and the relative probabilities of these variants are encoded in gene two and gene three, respectively.

The fourth gene decides the probability of mounting exploits on previously scanned nodes, while the fifth gene determines the choice of exploits attempted without a prior scan. After an exploit without a prior scan is chosen, gene six determines the probability of attempting to mount the most popular exploit on a node accessible by the attacker. Conversely, gene seven determines the relative probability of mounting a random exploit on the accessible nodes of the attacker.

All actions, i.e., scan and exploit are mounted on randomly selected accessible nodes. We randomly select a known resource and a known related port to be attacked on a previously scanned node. In the case when no scan action has been performed on a node, we take a resource from a list of the most popular resources and a random ordering of ports for the exploit attempt.

To clarify the encoding, we give a small example next. For easing the interpretation, we normalize the values. Let us see what coding $|15||35||65||75||10||72||28|$ represents: The first gene corresponds to the scan action, which is chosen with 15% probability, 75% on exploits after scanning and 10% on exploits without scan. From the scan budget, we choose a horizontal scan with 35% and a vertical scan with 65%. Finally, from the budget allocated to exploit without scan, we choose to diversify with 72% and maximize with 28%. Note that not all genes need to contribute to the fitness (e.g., if the exploit without scan is 0, then the values for gene five and six would not contribute to the strategy).

The defender encoding consists of nine genes. The first gene (at position 0) decides the probability of add actions. Genes two to four decide the relative probability for adding paths, hosts, and resources, respectively. Gene five decides the probability for remove actions. Analogously, genes six to eight decide the amount of remove budget to be spent on removing paths, hosts, and resources, respectively. Finally, gene nine decides the probability for moving ports (more precisely, replacing a resource from the present one to another randomly chosen port that is not used).

In both attacker and defender encodings, we use well-known genetic operators; namely, a simple mutation that alters a randomly chosen gene with uniform probability over the gene values, and one-point crossover between two parents.

3.2 Fitness Functions

The goal of the attacker is to mount as many as possible successful exploits and at the same time minimize the chances of being discovered by the defense system. Accordingly, he aims to maximize the following fitness function:

$$fitness_A = \#Successful\_Exploits. \tag{1}$$

If the attacker is simulated against multiple defenders (scenario 3), then the total fitness is simply the sum of all fitness values from separate simulations. The goal of avoiding being discovered is encoded implicitly in this fitness function since the attacker will not gain a reward for exploits mounted on honeypots.

The goal of the defender is to thwart the attacker by making the changes in the network where those changes cannot interfere with the normal operation of the network. To measure the changes in the network, we propose a metric called Network Spatial Topology – $NST(NM)$ that encompasses changes on hosts, paths, and resources. This metric is defined in three separate components:

$$NST(NM) = \left(\frac{n}{max\_network\_size}, \frac{number\_of\_paths}{n^2}, RSN \right). \tag{2}$$

RSN considers the number of resources on each host and their similarities:

$$RSN = \sum_{i=1}^{n} \left(\sum_{j=1}^{m} RH_{j,i} + \sum_{k=j+1}^{m} S\left(R_j, R_k\right) \right), \tag{3}$$

where n is the number of hosts, m is the maximal number of resources per host, $RH_{j,i}$ is the resource j on host i, and $S(R_j, R_k)$ is the similarity between resources R_j and R_k. To capture the effect of changes, we include a time component into the metric and compare the values of $NST(NM)$ at discrete moments t and $t + 1$ occurring after each game (each move) in the simulation.

All three components of NST are normalized into the $[0, 1]$ range to avoid one component having a much larger influence than the other components. Besides *maximizing* the changes in the network configuration, the defender has as a goal to *minimize* the number of successful exploits of an attacker. Note, this could be a less realistic goal since the defense will in practice rarely know immediately that a node is compromised. Still, we add this to our fitness function to be able to evolve strategies that can fight more actively against attackers. The number of successful exploits is normalized by dividing with the maximum number of nodes in the network (*max_network_size*). In our fitness function, we maximize *NST* and minimize the number of successful exploits (we subtract that value since the overall goal is fitness maximization):

$$fitness_D = |NST(NM, t) - NST(NM, t + 1)| - \#Successful\_Exploits. \quad (4)$$

Note that we do not add information about honeypot nodes that the attacker visited into the defender fitness. This is because such discovery is a consequence of fitness (i.e., because the fitness is enabling the development of good strategies, the attacker often visits honeypots) and not a behavior encoded in the fitness function.

3.3   Simulation Parameters and MOVE Simulator

In Table 2, we give parameters defining specific scenarios we investigate. *Max network size* represents the largest network size we allow in a simulation. We work with three sizes that represent a small, medium, and large network, respectively. Naturally, we are aware that our large network is small when considering many realistic scenarios (for instance, a university could easily have 20 000 or more hosts). Still, the network sizes we use are either comparable to or larger than those explored in similar literature [2,3]. *Init network size* represents the network size at the beginning of a simulation. *Number of real nodes* represents the part of the *Init network size* that is composed of real nodes, i.e., not honeypots. For instance, if the *Max network size* is 100, then there are 60 hosts at the beginning of the simulation, and of those 60, 54 are real hosts, meaning six hosts are honeypots. Finally, *Number of firewalls* is set to 10% of real hosts, which means there are five firewalls in the configuration. We set the costs of any defender action, as well as when the attacker is conducting the scan action (accessing a host, scanning a port) to the value of 1. For both the attacker and defender side, we allocate a budget equal to 10% of the *Init network size*.

We start each run by randomly generating a network with connections/paths between those hosts and resources belonging to each host. The exploit cost for each resource is selected uniformly in the range [1,5]. We report the average values and standard deviation of the fitness for both attacker and defender populations over 30 runs.

4   Results

For each scenario we consider, we give an average and standard deviation values calculated over several experimental runs. Those values are good indicators of the

Table 2. Network and adversary parameters.

Parameter name	Parameter value
Max network size	$[100, 500, 1\,000]$
Initial network size	60% of max network size
Number of real nodes	90% of initial network size
Number of firewalls	20% of real nodes
Budget for attacker	15% of initial network size
Budget for defender	15% of initial network size
Cost of any defender action	1
Cost of accessing a node (attacker)	1
Cost of scanning a port (attacker)	1
Max number of resources	$[10, 20, 30]$
Max number of ports on a node	20
Max number of resources per host	$[3, 5, 7]$

more general behavior and are less affected by a certain choice of experimental parameters. We do not give Min and Max values since they represent the extreme cases that are less interesting from the perspective of having good strategies.

It is to be expected that there will be some defense strategies behaving extremely poor for certain attack strategies and good for some other strategies. Naturally, such behavior is highly dependent on the current network and adversary, so it should not be considered as a good strategy in general. One goal of evolutionary optimization is to attain a set of possible solutions that behave well over a large number of problem instances. Consequently, a smaller deviation of the best fitness values over multiple runs would imply the optimization algorithm is consistently able to perform well.

Note that attacker and defender strategies could have significantly different fitness values; this is a natural consequence of different fitness functions. In Table 3, we present results for all three scenarios we experiment with, and in the next paragraphs, we discuss the obtained results as well as give examples of evolved strategies.

4.1 S1 – Static Defender, Adaptive Attacker

Since the defense is static, we simply create uniformly at random 30 defense strategies (since the population size equals 30) and we investigate how those strategies behave against attackers that can adapt to them. First, we observe that the fitness value of the attacker increases with the network size, while the defender fitness does not show a significant increase with the increase in the network size. At the same time, we see that the standard deviation for the defense is large (the larger the network size, the larger is the standard deviation), which indicates that there are many attack strategies for which a static defense is not that successful. Consequently, for a large number of attack strategies, static defense cannot provide adequate protection. Finally, we observe how attack strategies have a steady increase in their average values, which is expected since, with the increased size of the network, the attacker also has more freedom to select where and what to attack.

Differing from that, the defense strategies do not display consistent behavior with the increase of the network size. More precisely, the best fitness is obtained for the largest network size, which is not surprising since there the defense has the most freedom to change the topology of the network significantly. More surprisingly, the worst average fitness for defense is for the medium sized network. These results simply suggest that with random changes, it is impossible to predict the behavior of the defender.

Table 3. Results for all scenarios. NS denotes the network size and SD is the standard deviation.

NS	Strategy	S1 - SDAA		S2 - ADSA		S3 - ADAA	
		Avg	SD	Avg	SD	Avg	SD
100	Attack	3.23	1.17	0.39	6.09	12.70	3.69
	Defense	0.77	17.51	3.63	0.80	71.30	3.71
500	Attack	4.23	1.10	0.79	12.68	38.73	9.98
	Defense	0.66	24.82	4.00	0.82	80.09	4.38
1000	Attack	6.10	1.58	0.94	17.45	53.50	11.40
	Defense	1.19	26.41	3.87	0.93	82.05	3.91

When considering adaptive attack strategies, we give a typical high performing example for a large network: $|7||55||1||95||5||93||66|$. Here, we see that a large part of the budget is spent on mounting exploits after scanning, where strategy almost always prefers a horizontal scan rather than a vertical scan. Attempts to mount exploits without scan actions are deemed not to be very lucrative, fitness-wise. Still, when running the exploit without scan action, maximize strategy is preferred over the diversify strategy. Another fact to observe is the budget spent on scanning: better strategies spend lower budget in scanning, which means that the attacker scans a small part of the network and then conducts several exploits.

4.2 S2 – Adaptive Defender, Static Attacker

Analogously to the first scenario, now we randomly create a population of attack strategies and try to evolve defense strategies that are effective against such random attacker strategies. Here, we can see that having the ability to adapt reduces significantly the standard deviation of defense strategies, which means that we can evolve strategies successful against different attacks. At the same time, large standard deviation values for the attacker strategies indicate that random attacker strategies are not successful against a variety of defense strategies.

Small average values for the attacker further indicate that the random strategies are not a good choice to use since such strategies will not give a good performance even for particular cases. We observe how the increase in the network size brings improvement to the fitness of the attacker. Still, while the network size increases five times, the fitness increases only two times when comparing the small and medium networks. Similarly, when going from medium to large network (double the network size), the fitness increases for only around 20%.

Interestingly, we can see that both the average and standard deviation values for defense strategies remain similar even for significantly different network sizes. Finally, relatively small changes in the average value for the defender strategies indicate that the allocated budget is sufficient even for the largest network and that it could be smaller for the medium and small networks.

From the best evolved defense strategy for a small network |86||50||16||32||49|| 10||94||91||61|, we observe that add action is more lucrative than the remove action, and adding paths is the best option. When considering the remove action, we see there are many removed hosts and resources. This indicates that the strategy is aiming to produce a much better connected network while reducing the complexity of the elements in the network (by either removing the elements of a network or a number of resources). The move port action is also used relatively often, the success of which will depend on the actual number of port allocated to each host.

4.3   S3 – Adaptive Defender, Adaptive Attacker

Finally, in this setting, we run experiments where both attackers and defenders evolve and adapt over the course of the evolution process. We observe that the average values for both attack and defense strategies are higher than in the first two scenarios. With the network sizes increase, we see that the attacker's average results increase as well. When considering the standard deviation values for the attacker, we see that the values increase with the increase in the network size, which indicates that there is still a number of cases where the attack strategies show significantly various behavior, regardless good or bad. At the same time, there is a very stable behavior in the defense average values and standard deviations. This indicates that defense strategies can cope with attackers (to a certain extent) but also that it is difficult to increase the fitness of the defense by simply using a larger network. Still, the stability of the standard deviation indicates that the evolved defense strategies are indeed able to handle a variety of attacks.

The best obtained defense strategy for a small network |50||99||21||17||34|| 8||66||80||42| indicates that the adding action is preferred over remove action. Adding paths seem to be the best option, while from the removing side, resources represent the preferred choices. Along with moving resources to different ports, the defender balances between all three types of actions, which seems to be the most beneficial option. Despite having somewhat smaller values than in the second scenario, it is interesting to note that again remove host and remove resource are preferred actions over remove paths.

Finally, one of the best attack strategies for large networks is $|1||84||99||84||0||25||31|$ and indicates that to maximize fitness the attacker should invest a large part of the budget into attempting exploits after scanning. We see that there seems to be no incentive for running exploits without previous scans. Similarly (but even more pronounced) to the first scenario, we see that the budget to be spent on scan action is very small. There, some more budget is to be spent on a vertical scan, but we can consider both scanning techniques to be similarly represented. This is a reasonable step since now the network size is large when compared to the number of ports, so using any of those options will give comparable results in terms of exploration.

4.4 Discussion

We emphasize that although we consider specific scenarios where results depend on selected parameters, there are some general conclusions we can make. First, we observe that a random strategy (regardless of whether it is defense or attack strategy) cannot compete with an evolved one. This is clear from observing standard deviation for all cases where smaller values mean that the strategy is adapted for a large number of adversaries. Additionally, larger average values indicate that the tested strategies were able to make more impact on the network. As such, we see that random strategies do not provide good adaptation against a variety of different competing strategies.

When considering the defense, we see as a general trend that add action is favored over the remove action. Additionally, we see that the best option seems to be adding paths as much as possible and removing hosts/resources. For attackers, we observe that the scan action is almost not used since the mounting of exploits could be regarded as easy. Naturally, this depends on the perspective one takes since we see that the average values indicate a number of successful exploits. These numbers are still relatively small considering the size of the tested networks but represent a serious security breach. Finally, it is better to first scan (remember, the scan is not favored, so the number of scanned nodes is not large) and then conduct exploit on scanned nodes. Since the chances of the successful exploit are then much better than mounting exploit without prior scan, a vast majority of highly successful attack strategies involve only a smaller budget in the exploit without prior scan action.

In all scenarios, we used the budget equal to 15% of the network size. The results we obtained suggest that the defender requires a larger budget to be able to cope with the attacker. Naturally, these observations only confirm the intuition that the adversarial dynamic is more difficult for the defender since he needs to protect the whole network while the attacker only needs to find some weak hosts to exploit. In Fig. 1a and b, we depict the network topology after running both attack and defense strategies evolved for 20 generations. The real nodes are depicted in green color, the firewall in grey color, and honeypots in blue color. The nodes that are exploited by the end of the process (i.e., in the final network state) are depicted in red color. The paths that are accessed by the attacker are given in red color while those not traversed by the attacker are in black color. As can be seen, the attacker was able to successfully mount four exploits by the end of the simulation, 3 in real nodes, and 1 in the firewall. Note that the network is rather small and should serve only as an illustrative example.

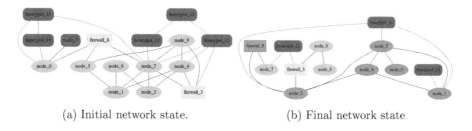

(a) Initial network state.   (b) Final network state

Fig. 1. Initial and evolved networks for scenario 3. (Color figure online)

5   Conclusions and Future Work

In this paper, we present the MOVE simulator as a tool to model adversarial behavior in networks. With it, we can construct attacker and defender strategies that offer high competitiveness in networks of various sizes. Our simulator can be used either as a tool to help decide the network layout, early in the design phase or as a driving force for on-the-fly network changes in reconfigurable environments such as software-defined networks. To be able to construct defensive strategies that are more resilient over different attack strategies, we propose a new metric called the Network Spatial Topology. Besides considering the attacker and defender side, our network model also includes normal behavior, which adds additional but realistic constraints on the defender.

Our scenarios consider only cases where all attacker strategies have the same agenda. It would be interesting to add several attackers (i.e., to have more than two populations) in adversarial dynamics where those attackers can be completely independent, but can also either collaborate or compete.

References

1. Move simulator (2019). https://github.com/MOVESimulator/
2. Achleitner, S., La Porta, T., McDaniel, P., Sugrim, S., Krishnamurthy, S.V., Chadha, R.: Cyber deception: virtual networks to defend insider reconnaissance. In: Proceedings of the 8th ACM CCS International Workshop on Managing Insider Security Threats, MIST 2016, pp. 57–68. ACM, New York (2016)
3. Achleitner, S., La Porta, T., McDaniel, P., Sugrim, S., Krishnamurthy, S.V., Chadha, R.: Reconnaissance deception system prototype implementation (2016). https://github.com/deceptionsystem/master

4. Duan, Q., Al-Shaer, E., Haadi Jafarian, J.: Efficient random route mutation considering flow and network constraints. In: IEEE Conference on Communications and Network Security, CNS 2013, National Harbor, MD, USA, 14–16 October 2013, pp. 260–268. IEEE (2013)
5. Eiben, A.E., Smith, J.E.: Introduction to Evolutionary Computing. Springer, Berlin (2003)
6. Garcia, D., Lugo, A.E., Hemberg, E., O'Reilly, U.-M.: Investigating coevolutionary archive based genetic algorithms on cyber defense networks. In: Proceedings of the Genetic and Evolutionary Computation Conference Companion, GECCO 2017, pp. 1455–1462. ACM, New York (2017)
7. Hemberg, E., Zipkin, J.R., Skowyra, R.W., Wagner, N., O'Reilly, U.-M.: Adversarial co-evolution of attack and defense in a segmented computer network environment. In: Proceedings of the Genetic and Evolutionary Computation Conference Companion, GECCO 2018, pp. 1648–1655. ACM, New York (2018)
8. Kelly, J., DeLaus, M., Hemberg, E., O'Reilly, U.: Adversarially adapting deceptive views and reconnaissance scans on a software defined network. In: 2019 IFIP/IEEE Symposium on Integrated Network and Service Management (IM), pp. 49–54, April 2019
9. Lyon, G.F.: Nmap Network Scanning: The Official Nmap Project Guide to Network Discovery and Security Scanning. Insecure, Los Angeles (2009)
10. Miller, J.H.: The coevolution of automata in the repeated prisoner's dilemma. J. Econ. Behav. Organ. **29**(1), 87–112 (1996)
11. Panjwani, S., Tan, S., Jarrin, K.M., Cukier, M.: An experimental evaluation to determine if port scans are precursors to an attack. In: 2005 International Conference on Dependable Systems and Networks (DSN 2005), pp. 602–611, June 2005
12. Rush, G., Tauritz, D.R., Kent, A.D.: Coevolutionary agent-based network defense lightweight event system (CANDLES). In: Proceedings of the Companion Publication of the 2015 Annual Conference on Genetic and Evolutionary Computation, GECCO Companion 2015, pp. 859–866. ACM, New York (2015)
13. Prado Sánchez, D.: Visualizing adversaries: transparent pooling approaches for decision support in cybersecurity. M. Eng, thesis, Massachusetts Institute of Technology (2018)
14. Symantec: Preparing for a cyber attack, January 2017
15. Tankard, C.: Advanced persistent threats and how to monitor and deter them. Netw. Secur. **2011**(8), 16–19 (2011)
16. Winterrose, M.L., Carter, K.M.: Strategic evolution of adversaries against temporal platform diversity active cyber defenses. In: Proceedings of the 2014 Symposium on Agent Directed Simulation, ADS 2014, pp. 9:1–9:9. Society for Computer Simulation International, San Diego (2014)
17. Winterrose, M.L., Carter, K.M., Wagner, N., Streilein, W.W.: Adaptive attacker strategy development against moving target cyber defenses. CoRR, abs/1407.8540 (2014)
18. Zaffarano, K., Taylor, J., Hamilton, S.: A quantitative framework for moving target defense effectiveness evaluation. In: Proceedings of the Second ACM Workshop on Moving Target Defense, MTD 2015, pp. 3–10. ACM, New York (2015)

Using Evolution to Design Modular Robots: An Empirical Approach to Select Module Designs

Rodrigo Moreno[1]([⊠])[ID] and Andres Faina[2][ID]

[1] Universidad Nacional de Colombia, Bogota, Colombia
rmorenoga@unal.edu.co
[2] IT University of Copenhagen, Copenhagen, Denmark
https://unal.edu.co
https://www.itu.dk

Abstract. In modular robots, the shape of the building blocks (robotic modules) greatly influences the end result. By changing the physical properties of the module, different robotic structures with better performance for a given task can be found. In this paper, we modify the modules of a modular robot platform, the EMERGE modular robot, in two different ways: changing the length of the module and changing the shape of the starting module (base). We use artificial evolution to optimize robots for a locomotion task using each different module length and base, and also evolve robots with combinations of modules of different length. Results show that, as the length of the module increases, the best robots obtained use fewer modules and fewer connections per module. However, the increase in length results also in a decrease in locomotion performance for large length increases. Interestingly, very few of the best robots found show symmetric structures, which can be attributed to their tendency to roll over as their main means of locomotion. Modular robot designers can use the information about the effectiveness of modules with different lengths, and the use of different starting bases, to reach trade-offs between the desired number of modules in a robot and their effectiveness for a given task.

Keywords: Modular robots · Evolutionary algorithms · Design optimization

1 Introduction

In physical structures, the shape of the building blocks greatly influences the end result. Therefore, the design of the building blocks should be carefully optimized. However, there are many areas where these building blocks are difficult to analyse in isolation, that is, when they are not part of an structure. This is the case of modular robots.

Robots are usually designed and built for a specific task, normally without reusing components developed for other kind of robots. In contrast with this

© Springer Nature Switzerland AG 2020
P. A. Castillo et al. (Eds.): EvoApplications 2020, LNCS 12104, pp. 276–290, 2020.
https://doi.org/10.1007/978-3-030-43722-0_18

approach, modular robots are built by connecting reusable robotic units, called modules, together. Modules are autonomous and encapsulate functionality (sensors, actuation, computational resources and energy).

Over the last decades, multiple modular robot designs have been proposed [8,22,26]. Modular robot systems have been demonstrated for locomotion and manipulation tasks and studied for their use in space exploration, among other tasks. In most modular robot works, an engineer decides the configuration of the robot for a task, given a module design, and then focus on how to control and coordinate individual modules, usually by using gait tables [27], hormone-inspired methods [19] or central pattern generators [11].

Some works have addressed the problem of enumerating all the different configurations that can be generated by using a module design [21]. However, knowing how many configurations are possible does not shed light on their performance for a specific task. Artificial evolution has been proposed as a method to find suitable combinations of morphologies and controllers for different tasks [22].

The simultaneous evolution of morphology and control was first proposed by Karl Sims [20]. In his work he evolves morphologies and controllers for virtual creatures which, however, are very difficult to be built physically. Similar techniques have been applied to modular robots [6,7,9,13,23], with the advantage being that designed robots can be easily built by joining modules together.

In this paper, we address how can we optimize robotic modules to maximize the performance of modular robots for a given task and how the different types of modules give way to different robotic structures that have advantages and disadvantages when solving the task at hand. We will focus on changing modules in two different ways: (1) changing the length of the module and (2) changing the shape of the starting (base) module. Two bases will be tested: a cuboid base, similar in size to a normal length module, and a bigger and heavier flat base. A test with robots that combine modules with different lengths is also performed. Changing the length of the module allows the module to perform wider movements while reducing the strength of that movement. Therefore, selecting the length of the module imposes a trade-off that is worth studying.

Similar questions have been studied before. In [14], Miras et al. studied how codification of the morphology of a modular robot (direct encoding or generative encoding) influences the morphological features of evolved robots. Their results indicate that there are no differences in the diversity of morphological features of the resulting robots when using either encoding. Additionally, Liu et al. [12] researched how the number of faces in the module influences the resulting evolved morphology for a given task. The results showed that a lower number of connection faces could help the evolutionary algorithm to get better results as long as the faces removed are chosen carefully.

This paper is organized as follows: Sect. 2 describes the methodology, including brief descriptions of the modular robot prototype and the evolutionary framework used. Section 3 describes the experimental setup and Sect. 4 details the tests results. The paper follows with a discussion of the results and a conclusion.

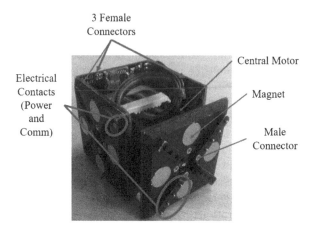

Fig. 1. EMERGE Module: The magnetic connections in their faces allows a quick assembly of the modules to build a robot, which is useful to test evolved morphologies and controllers.

2 Methodology

The methodology employed makes use of the EDHMOR system which is an evolutionary framework specifically designed to evolve morphologies and controllers for modular robots. In this paper, we evolve robots from modified versions of the EMERGE modular robot prototype. This section describes both of these tools.

2.1 EMERGE Modules

The EMERGE (Easy Modular Embodied Robot Generator) modular robot is a robotic platform designed to be easy to build, maintain and modify [16]. This enables us to quickly assemble morphologies, be it using homogeneous modules [15] or heterogeneous modules [12].

Each module has only one hinge, comprised of a servo motor attached to a pair of brackets, and resembles a small cube. Attached to the brackets are PCBs (Printed Circuit Boards) and 3D printed mating magnetic connector faces. A male connector has protrusions that match holes in three female connectors. The connector assembly maintains mechanical and electrical connections between any two modules (Fig. 1). Magnetic connectors provide a quick and practical way of assembling evolved robot morphologies and controllers. The simple design of the module also allows for an uncomplicated simulation model (See Table 1), which can be easily modified for the purposes of this work.

2.2 EDHMOR

The Evolutionary Designer of Heterogeneous Modular Robots (EDHMOR) [7] has been selected as the evolutionary framework to evolve the robotic structures in this work. It is based on the Java Evolutionary Algorithm Framework (JEAF) [4], but specifically designed to evolve modular robots.

EDHMOR generates a direct encoding that represents the modular robot and its controller. Specifically designed mutation operators are applied to individual robot solutions. After an initial population of robots has been generated, EDHMOR performs the following phases in a loop, until the stop criteria is met:

1. Growing phase: Add a module in a random position.
2. Morphological adaptation phase: Change some of the connections of the robot (the place a module is attached to or its orientation).
3. Control adaptation phase: Change some of the control parameters.
4. Pruning phase: Remove all the modules that do not contribute to the fitness
5. Replacement phase: Remove the worst N individuals and replace them with N/2 random individuals and N/2 variations of the best individuals of the population after applying a symmetry mutation.

In all these phases, the resulting individual only replaces its parent if it can beat the parent fitness, except in the growing phase. This means that the growing phase always adds modules, even if the fitness gets worse. This is done to protect innovations and give them some time to be tested and adapt (morphological and control adaptation phase) before the pruning phase. For a more detailed explanation of EDHMOR, see [7]. The EDHMOR system can be adapted to different kind of modules and it has already been used in conjunction with EMERGE modules before [12].

3   Experimental Setup

Using the EDHMOR framework, robots are evolved for a locomotion task. The algorithm is configured to use 2 growing phases, 2 morphological adaptation phases, 1 control adaptation phase and 2 pruning phases. Each growing and morphological adaptation phases test 3 different individual variations, while the control adaptation phase tests 10 individual variations for each mutation. A population of 40 individuals is used and 10 robots are replaced in the replacement phase.

Robot morphologies, the number and way in which modules are connected to each other, are encoded using a tree style encoding genotype. The genotype also includes information about the movements of the individual modules: each module joint position (*pos*) is controlled using a sinusoidal generator as in Eq. 1.

$$pos = \alpha \cdot A_{max} \cdot sin(\omega \cdot V_{max} \cdot t + \varphi) \tag{1}$$

Where α, the amplitude ($[0, 1]$), ω, the angular velocity ($[0, 1]$) and φ, the phase shift ($[0, 2\pi)$), are control parameters encoded in the individual's chromosome. The quantities A_{max} and V_{max} are fixed and based on the module properties, and t is the simulation time. Individual robot solutions are tested by placing them in the center of a simulated flat surface environment and allowing

Table 1. Different properties of all the modules employed in these work: EMERGE modules, starting with their original size $(1 \times L)$ and up to 8 times longer $(8 \times L)$, and two different types of bases, a cuboid base and a flat base, are shown. All EMERGE modules have the same motor and both bases are passive. The cuboid has connectors in all faces except for the upper face $(+Z)$ and the flat base has four connectors pointing in all outward directions at each corner.

	1xL	1.25xL	1.5xL	1.75xL	2xL	4xL	8xL	cuboid base	flat base
Length (mm)	77	86.6	96.2	105.9	115.5	192.5	346.5	5.5(x3)	27/5.5
Weight (g)	165	174	183	192	201	275	420	100	250
Connection faces				4				5	16
Torque (Nm)				1.5				-	-

them to move for about 20 s. Simulation is carried out in the V-REP simulator [17]. Modules are connected to each other in simulation by using a special element in V-REP called force sensors, these allow modules to break if affected by a force or torque that exceeds a certain value. Using force sensors, individual robots can break, however, they are not penalized for this. Instead, the fitness associated to each evaluation is calculated as the final position of the robot (center of mass) measured in a straight line, in the (x,y) plane, from the position of the robot at $t = 2.5$ s (Eq. 2). This starting time guarantees that the transitory effects at the beginning of the movement are not taken into account as all the robots are placed with at least one module in contact with the floor, but can fall if they are not stable.

$$F = d((x_{final}, y_{final}), (x_{t=2.5}, y_{t=2.5})) \tag{2}$$

3.1   Modifying Module Length

For the different tests performed, the distance between the motor axle and the male face of the EMERGE module is varied by adding a extension to the base of the motor (Table 1). Each different module type portrays a different distance, or length, from the motor to the male face: Starting with their original length $(1 \times L)$, modules are extended to have 1.25, 1.5, 1.75, 2, 4 and 8 times $(8 \times L)$ the original module length. In this way, the effect of the added length can be measured for small changes $(1.25 \times L, 1.5 \times L, 1.75 \times L, 2 \times L)$ and for extreme values $(4 \times L$ and $8 \times L)$. In the real world, the extension can also be added to the module by means of a part attached between the male face and the base of the motor.

The increase in length also implies an increase in the overall weight of the module and changes the weight distribution, which in turn makes bigger forces and torques appear in the module connectors, possibly increasing the number of disconnections. The central motor is also required to use bigger torque values when lifting a chain of modules, reducing the overall strength of the robot.

3.2 Different Starting Base Modules

Tests are also performed using two different types of base modules as the first building block for each robot: A cuboid base and a flat base (Table 1). The main difference between both bases is their size: the cuboid base is similar in dimensions and weight to a normal EMERGE module while the flat base is bigger and heavier, the number of connectors each base has is also different: the cuboid base has 5 connectors and the flat base has 16 connectors.

Using these two bases, robots are evolved using only one type of module at the same time and results are compared to determine whether there is a difference through various measures: fitness obtained by the best individuals, which provides an estimate of locomotion performance, number of modules and average number of connections per module, which provide a look into the shape of the robot, and number of broken connections (See Sect. 4). A final evolutionary run is performed for each base, combining modules of all different types. Evolutionary runs are repeated 20 times and configured to perform a total of 25000 fitness evaluations.

4 Results

As mentioned in the last section, the increase in module dimensions strains the module motor and connections. Bigger forces and torques lead to a decrease in the fitness of the best individuals obtained as length is increased, which can be seen on Fig. 2. This effect can also be seen in Fig. 3, in which the best individual fitnesses at the end of each evolutionary run are grouped in box-plots.

The fitness of the best individuals for modules of length $1 \times L$, $1.25 \times L$, $1.5 \times L$, $1.75 \times L$, $2 \times L$ and combined module robots ($1\text{-}8 \times L$) are very similar to each other, whereas fitness of individuals using modules of length $4 \times L$ an $8 \times L$ are statistically significantly different from other lengths and present a sharp decrease of fitness ($p = 2.33e^{-12}$ in the case of Fig. 3a and $p = 9.87e^{-12}$ in the case of Fig. 3b). In the cuboid base case, modules of length $2 \times L$ and $1.75 \times L$ also present a statistically significant difference ($p = 2.22e^{-2}$). Statistically significant differences for these and subsequent comparisons, are tested using a Kruskal-Wallis non parametric test for multiple samples, and pairwise statistically significant differences are verified using a post-hoc Mann-Whitney-Wilcoxon test.

The number of modules also shows a sharp decrease as the length of the module goes over 2 times the length ($2 \times L$) of the original (See Fig. 4) for the best individuals of each evolutionary run. In this case, robots using combinations of modules of different length ($1\text{-}8 \times L$) also have a lower measure than robots built with modules of length below $2 \times L$. The number of modules present a statistically significant difference between robots built using modules of length

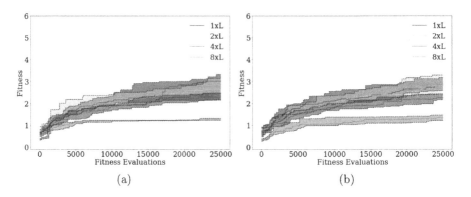

Fig. 2. Evolution of the best individuals fitness for (a) a cuboid base, (b) a flat base. For the sake of clarity, only evolution plots corresponding to robots with modules of lengths $1 \times L$, $2 \times L$, $4 \times L$ and $8 \times L$ are shown in each graph, the plots corresponding to robots with modules of lengths $1.25 \times L$, $1.5 \times L$ and $1.75 \times L$ overlap with $1 \times L$.

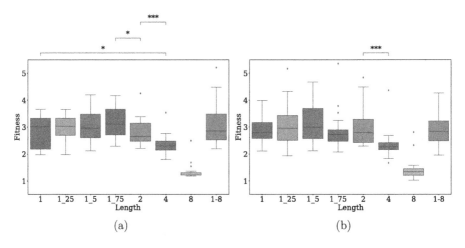

Fig. 3. Fitness obtained by the best individuals at the end of each evolutionary run, when using (a) a cuboid base, (b) a flat base. Fitness values for robots with combined modules (1-8) are similar to those of robots built with modules of lengths below $2 \times L \times L$. Stars indicate the level of statistical significance: $*p < 0.05, **p < 0.01, ***p < 0.001, ****p < 0.0001$.

$1 \times L$ and $2 \times L$, between modules of length $4 \times L$, $8 \times L$ and all other lengths, and between combined module robots (1-8 $\times$ L) and robots with modules below $1.75 \times L$ ($p = 9.05e^{-15}$) for the cuboid base. For the flat base, statistically significant differences also arise between robots built using modules of lengths $4 \times L$ and $8 \times L$ and robots built with modules of length below $2 \times L$, and between combined module robots (1-8 $\times$ L) and robots built with modules of length below $2 \times L$ ($p = 6.43e^{-16}$).

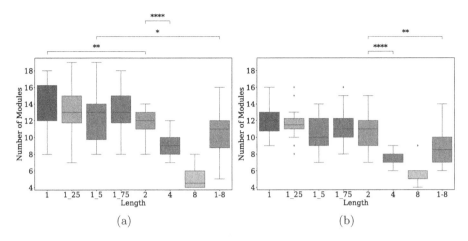

(a)   (b)

Fig. 4. Number of modules of the best individuals at the end of each evolutionary run, when using (a) a cuboid base, (b) a flat base. The number of modules decreases sharply for extreme length values ($4 \times L$ and $8 \times L$) as well as for robots with combined modules ($1\text{-}8 \times L$). Stars indicate the level of statistical significance: $*p < 0.05, **p < 0.01, ***p < 0.001, ****p < 0.0001$.

A similar phenomenon appears for the average number of connections per module (See Fig. 5): Robots built with modules of length $1 \times L$, $1.25 \times L$, $1.5 \times L$ and $1.75 \times L$ show similar average number of connections per module and there is a decrease in this measure for robots built using modules of length $2 \times L$, $4 \times L$, $8 \times L$ and $1\text{-}8 \times L$, in the case of the cuboid base. In the case of the flat base, robots built using modules of length $1 \times L$, $1.25 \times L$, $1.5 \times L$, $1.75 \times L$ and $2 \times L$ present a similar behavior, while robots built using modules of length $4 \times L$, $8 \times L$ and $1\text{-}8 \times L$ show a decrease. Statistically significant differences reappear between robots built using modules of length $1 \times L$ and $2 \times L$ and between robots built using modules of length $4 \times L$, $8 \times L$, $1\text{-}8 \times L$ and robots built using modules of length below $1.75 \times L (p = 8.88e^{-13})$ for the cuboid base, and between modules of length $4 \times L$, $8 \times L$, $1\text{-}8 \times L$ and robots built modules of length below $2 \times L$ $(p = 6.43e^{-16})$ for the flat base.

These two measures indicate that robots tend to maintain a small form factor by using less modules and less connections per modules as module length increases. This leads to robots that resemble long chains more and more and can be seen in Figs. 7 and 8. Robots built using a combination of modules of different length also show this behavior, although less pronounced, as can also be seen on Figs. 4 and 5. The increase in connector strain also leads to more broken connections as module length increases. When using the cuboid base and lengths $1 \times L$ to $2 \times L$, most of the best individuals obtained in each evolutionary run did not break connections, by contrast, the majority of the best individuals of lengths $4 \times L$ and $8 \times L$ broke at least 1 connection. In the case of using the flat base, most of the best individuals using lengths $1 \times L$ to $1.75 \times L$ did not break connections, while the majority of the best individuals of lengths $2 \times L$ to $8 \times L$

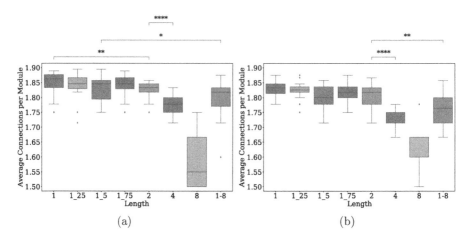

Fig. 5. Average connections per module of the best individuals at the end of each evolutionary run, when using (a) a cuboid base, (b) a flat base. The average number of connections per module decreases sharply for extreme length values ($4 \times L$ and $8 \times L$) as well as for robots with combined modules ($1\text{-}8 \times L$). Stars indicate the level of statistical significance: $*p < 0.05, **p < 0.01, ***p < 0.001, ****p < 0.0001$.

broke at least one connection, with some $8 \times L$ individuals breaking up to three connections. When mixing modules of different lengths, most of the best individuals tested did not break connections when using the cuboid base, and most of the individuals using the flat base broke at least 1 connection. The number of broken connections presents a statistically significant difference between groups in the case of both starting bases ($p = 6.75e^{-20}$ cuboid base and $p = 7.58e^{-20}$ flat base).

The type of base also influences the final number of modules and number of connections that the evolutionary algorithm finds. A direct comparison of these measures between base types can be seen on Fig. 6. A statistically significant difference is found between the number of modules that robots evolved with the cuboid base end up with and the number of modules that robots evolved with the flat base have at the end of the run ($p = 3.1e^{-4}$), a statistically significant difference can also be found in the case of the average number of connections per module ($p = 3.1e^{-4}$). In both measures, the flat base presents the lower values, something that can be attributed to robots trying to maintain a small shape given the bigger dimensions of the flat base. In these figures is also noticeable the sharp drop in the number of modules, and connections per module when module length exceeds 2 times the original value.

In all of the best robot obtained, mainly two types of movement arise: a rolling movement in which the whole robot structure rolls over, taking advantage of the small shape in the case of robots made of modules of lengths below $2 \times L$ or the thin shape in the case of robots with modules of lengths $4 \times L$ and $8 \times L$, and an oscillatory movement in which part of the structure oscillates or tumbles to generate traction, this last movement type can be seen specially in robots built

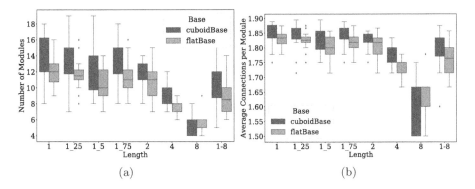

Fig. 6. Comparison of (a) the number of modules and (b) the average connections per module of the best individuals at the end of each evolutionary run, when using a cuboid base and a flat base. The smaller number of modules and average connections per module in the flat base case can be attributed to robots trying to maintain a small shape given the bigger dimensions of the base.

using the flat base as a starting point. Examples of this movements can be seen on Figs. 7 and 8. A third type of movement is also observed, in which some parts of the structure move almost independently, in a fashion similar to wheels, while the rest remains somewhat stable.

5   Discussion

Evolving modular robots with different module lengths sheds lights on the influence of module dimensions on the final performance of the robots obtained. This is beneficial from the point of view of modular robot designers since they can explore the limitations and advantages that each type of module offers. Furthermore, using easy to build modules of predefined lengths provides an easier and quicker alternative to approaches in which modular robots have to be fabricated from scratch [2]. In this case, results clearly show a drop in the performance of the best robots as length goes past 2 × L with both bases (Figs. 3 and 6), but also a decrease in the number of modules used. This means the designer can choose for module designs that produce robots with fewer modules at the cost of losing some performance in the locomotion task. Interestingly, the module lengths at which evolved robots show the best performance (115.5 mm and below) roughly match with human designed module dimensions, which usually reach between 100 and 150 mm of length [3], with a tendency to use smaller dimensions in the latest prototypes [5]. However, a direct comparison with human designed lengths must take into account the maximum torque of the chosen actuator and the strength of the module connectors. Furthermore, results show that evolution is also able to find robots with good locomotion performance, and fewer modules than if they used only one length, in the case of evolving robots that mix different lengths. This is similar to the results in [1], in which robots evolved

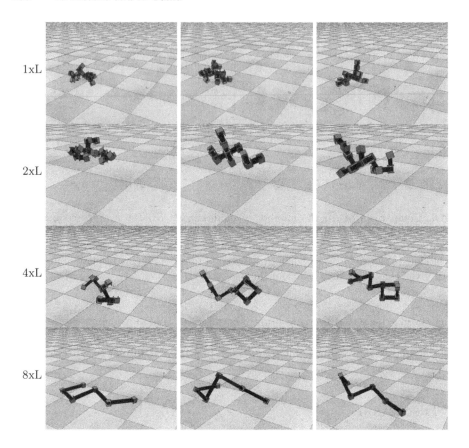

Fig. 7. Examples of the movement of some of the best robots obtained for each module length with the cuboid base. Each row shows a different robot. Robots with longer modules tend to have fewer modules and module connections, which make them resemble a long chain.

using modules of mixed sizes are also able to perform a locomotion task. Thus making evolution a good automatic aid when selecting among module designs.

The decrease in the number of modules and module connections can be attributed to the increase in weight: As the forces exerted on the module connectors increase and the maximum torque of the motor remains constant for bigger module lengths, moving the weight of more modules becomes less advantageous for the locomotion task defined. This loss in strength due to an increase in the number of modules is characteristic of modular robots [1,18]. And this helps maintain a small form factor (fewer modules with fewer connections per module as the length of the module increases, see Fig. 6) of the best robots found throughout all module lengths. It also leads to more broken connections in robot evaluations. The decrease in the number of modules and the average connections per module is even more visible for robots using the flat base. As

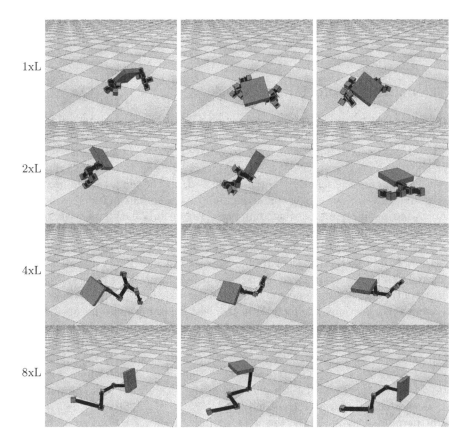

Fig. 8. Examples of the movement of some of the best robots obtained for each module length with the flat base. Each row shows a different robot. Robots with longer modules tend to have fewer modules and module connections, which make them resemble a long chain.

this base is heavier, robots tend to have fewer modules to be able to move with the extra weight. This is also seen on morphologies found in [10], in which a set of predefined parts containing a big core component is used to build robots.

Velde et al. [24], also in a locomotion experiment, found a correlation between the maximum fitness and the average symmetry of a population of modular robots. Surprisingly, very few of the best robots found have symmetric properties in our results, despite the evolutionary algorithm using symmetry operators as in the original EDMHOR work [7]. Nevertheless, symmetric structures were only found in [7] when robots were tested in environments with rough terrains or while they were made to carry loads. A rolling non-symmetric structure is probably a more efficient way of locomotion in flat terrains. Similar experiments in rough terrains are needed to determine whether symmetry would appear in the robots used in here. Finally, this work concentrates only on modules with fixed shape, but there are also modules that can change shape, for example soft modular robots [25]. Checking the validity of the results presented here with this kind of modules is still pending.

6   Conclusions and Future Work

In this work, we present a way of optimizing robotic modules to maximize the performance of modular robots for a locomotion task. Different types of modules give way to different robotic structures that have advantages and disadvantages when solving the task at hand. We focused on changing modules in two different ways: (1) changing the length of the module and (2) changing the shape of the base module. Two bases are available: a cuboid base, similar in size to a normal module, and a bigger and heavier flat base. An evolutionary run with robots that combine modules of different lengths is also performed.

Changing the length of the module, in this case enlarging it, implies an increase not only in the range of its movements but also in its overall weight, which reduces the effective force of the module actuator. This reduction in the strength of the module movements results in a decrease in the number of modules and average connections per module in the best robots found, and an increase in the number of broken connections, as the length of the module increases (Fig. 6). Consequently, resulting robots tend to have similar sizes across module lengths and robots become thinner (resembling long chains) as module length increases (Figs. 7 and 8). The strength reduction even makes robots with big module lengths ($4 \times L$, $8 \times L$) less effective in the locomotion task compared to their shorter counterparts (Figs. 2 and 3).

Furthermore, the shape of the base module, used as a starting point for the robot, also influences the morphological configuration of the best robots obtained. As the flat base is heavier and bigger than the cuboid base, robots using the former are inclined to use fewer modules than robots using the latter one (Fig. 6). Additionally, although robots combining modules of different lengths also present the same reduction in strength, they are able to achieve fitness values on par with robots built using modules between $1 \times L$ and $2 \times L$ (Fig. 3). Future work includes further testing of evolution as an automatic aid for the modular robot designer to select among module designs with different advantages and disadvantages for a given task.

Interestingly, very few of the best robots found show symmetric structures. This can be attributed to the tendency of resulting robots to produce rolling movements, which may be more efficient in flat terrains. Experiments in different kinds of terrains must be performed in future works to study when symmetry could be an advantage.

As a final conclusion, modular robot designers can use the information about the effectiveness of modules with different length, and the use of different starting bases, presented in this work to strike trade-offs between the desired number of modules in a robot and their effectiveness for a given task. Future work will focus on other module properties, like motor strength or movement speed, for different tasks.

References

1. Akrour, D., et al.: Joint evolution of morphologies and controllers for realistic modular robots. In: 22nd Symposium on Artificial Life And Robotics (AROB 2017), pp. 57–62, hal-01782566 (2017). https://hal.archives-ouvertes.fr/hal-01782566
2. Alattas, R.J., Patel, S., Sobh, T.M.: Evolutionary modular robotics: survey and analysis. J. Intell. Robot. Syst.: Theory Appl. **95**(3), 1–14 (2018). https://doi.org/10.1007/s10846-018-0902-9
3. Brunete, A., Ranganath, A., Segovia, S., de Frutos, J.P., Hernando, M., Gambao, E.: Current trends in reconfigurable modular robots design. Int. J. Adv. Rob. Syst. **14**(3), 1–21 (2017). https://doi.org/10.1177/1729881417710457
4. Caamaño, P., Tedín, R., Paz-Lopez, A., Becerra, J.A.: JEAF: a Java evolutionary algorithm framework. In: IEEE Congress on Evolutionary Computation, pp. 1–8. IEEE (2010)
5. Chennareddy, S.S.R., Agrawal, A., Karuppiah, A.: Modular self-reconfigurable robotic systems: a survey on hardware architectures. J. Robot. **2017** (2017). https://doi.org/10.1155/2017/5013532
6. Chocron, O.: Evolving modular robots for rough terrain exploration. In: Nedjah, N., Coelho, L.S., Mourelle, L.M. (eds.) Mobile Robots: The Evolutionary Approach, vol. 50, pp. 23–46. Springer, Heidelberg (2007). https://doi.org/10.1007/978-3-540-49720-2_2
7. Faíña, A., Bellas, F., López-Peña, F., Duro, R.J.: EDHMoR: evolutionary designer of heterogeneous modular robots. Eng. Appl. Artif. Intell. **26**(10), 2408–2423 (2013)
8. Faina, A., Bellas, F., Orjales, F., Souto, D., Duro, R.J.: An evolution friendly modular architecture to produce feasible robots. Robot. Auton. Syst. **63**, 195–205 (2015)
9. Haasdijk, E., Rusu, A.A., Eiben, A.E.: HyperNEAT for locomotion control in modular robots. In: Tempesti, G., Tyrrell, A.M., Miller, J.F. (eds.) ICES 2010. LNCS, vol. 6274, pp. 169–180. Springer, Heidelberg (2010). https://doi.org/10.1007/978-3-642-15323-5_15
10. Jelisavcic, M., et al.: Real-world evolution of robot morphologies: a proof of concept. Artif. Life **23**(2), 206–235 (2017). https://doi.org/10.1162/ARTL_a_00231
11. Kamimura, A., Kurokawa, H., Yoshida, E., Murata, S., Tomita, K., Kokaji, S.: Automatic locomotion design and experiments for a modular robotic system. IEEE/ASME Trans. Mechatron. **10**(3), 314–325 (2005)
12. Liu, C., Liu, J., Moreno, R., Veenstra, F., Faina, A.: The impact of module morphologies on modular robots. In: 2017 18th International Conference on Advanced Robotics (ICAR), pp. 237–243, July 2017. https://doi.org/10.1109/ICAR.2017.8023524
13. Marbach, D., Ijspeert, A.J.: Online optimization of modular robot locomotion. In: IEEE International Conference Mechatronics and Automation, vol. 1, pp. 248–253. IEEE (2005)
14. Miras, K., Haasdijk, E., Glette, K., Eiben, A.E.: Search space analysis of evolvable robot morphologies. In: Sim, K., Kaufmann, P. (eds.) EvoApplications 2018. LNCS, vol. 10784, pp. 703–718. Springer, Cham (2018). https://doi.org/10.1007/978-3-319-77538-8_47
15. Moreno, R., et al.: Automated reconfiguration of modular robots using robot manipulators. In: 2018 IEEE Symposium Series on Computational Intelligence (SSCI), pp. 884–891, November 2018. https://doi.org/10.1109/SSCI.2018.8628628

16. Moreno, R., Liu, C., Faina, A., Hernandez, H., Gomez, J.: The emerge modular robot, an open platform for quick testing of evolved robot morphologies. In: Proceedings of the Genetic and Evolutionary Computation Conference Companion, pp. 71–72. ACM (2017)
17. Rohmer, E., Singh, S.P.N., Freese, M.: V-REP: a versatile and scalable robot simulation framework. In: IROS 2013, pp. 1321–1326. IEEE, Tokyo, November 2013. https://doi.org/10.1109/IROS.2013.6696520, http://ieeexplore.ieee.org/lpdocs/epic03/wrapper.htm?arnumber=6696520
18. Seo, J., Paik, J., Yim, M.: Modular reconfigurable robotics. Annu. Rev. Control Robot. Auton. Syst. **2**(1), 63–88 (2019). https://doi.org/10.1146/annurev-control-053018-023834
19. Shen, W.M., Salemi, B., Will, P.: Hormone-inspired adaptive communication and distributed control for conro self-reconfigurable robots. IEEE Trans. Robot. Autom. **18**(5), 700–712 (2002)
20. Sims, K.: Evolving 3D morphology and behavior by competition. Artif. Life **1**(4), 353–372 (1994)
21. Stoy, K., Brandt, D.: Efficient enumeration of modular robot configurations and shapes. In: 2013 IEEE/RSJ International Conference on Intelligent Robots and Systems, pp. 4296–4301. IEEE (2013)
22. Stoy, K., Brandt, D., Christensen, D.J.: Self-Reconfigurable Robots: An Introduction. MIT Press (2010)
23. Veenstra, F., Faina, A., Risi, S., Stoy, K.: Evolution and morphogenesis of simulated modular robots: a comparison between a direct and generative encoding. In: Squillero, G., Sim, K. (eds.) EvoApplications 2017. LNCS, vol. 10199, pp. 870–885. Springer, Cham (2017). https://doi.org/10.1007/978-3-319-55849-3_56
24. van de Velde, T., Rossi, C., Eiben, A.E.: Body symmetry in morphologically evolving modular robots. In: Kaufmann, P., Castillo, P.A. (eds.) EvoApplications 2019. LNCS, vol. 11454, pp. 583–598. Springer, Cham (2019). https://doi.org/10.1007/978-3-030-16692-2_39
25. Vergara, A., Lau, Y.S., Mendoza-Garcia, R.F., Zagal, J.C.: Soft modular robotic cubes: toward replicating morphogenetic movements of the Embryo. PLoS ONE **12**(1), 1–17 (2017). https://doi.org/10.1371/journal.pone.0169179
26. Yim, M., et al.: Modular self-reconfigurable robot systems (grand challenges of robotics). IEEE Robot. Autom. Mag. **14**(1), 43–52 (2007)
27. Yim, M., Zhang, Y., Duff, D.: Modular robots. IEEE Spectr. **39**(2), 30–34 (2002)

Iterated Granular Neighborhood Algorithm for the Taxi Sharing Problem

Houssem E. Ben-Smida[1], Francisco Chicano[1(✉)] [iD], and Saoussen Krichen[2]

[1] Departamento de Lenguajes y Ciencias de la Computación,
Universidad de Malaga, Malaga, Spain
`he.bensmida@uma.es`, `chicano@lcc.uma.es`
[2] Laboratoire de Recherche Opérationnelle de Décision et de Contrôle de processus,
Université de Tunis, Tunis, Tunisia
`krichen-s@yahoo.fr`

Abstract. One of the most popular issues that we can find in cities is transportation problems: traffic jams, pollution and the transportation cost fees. The concept of taxi sharing is considered as a promising idea to reduce some of the transportation problems. A group of people travels from the same origin to different destinations. Our goal is to assign them to several taxis while reducing the cost of all trips. The taxi sharing problem is NP-hard, since it is a variant of the car pooling problem. We adapt Capacitated Vehicle Routing Problem (CVRP) to solve the taxi sharing problem, in which goods are changed by passengers and trucks by taxis. We describe a new algorithm, called Iterated Granular Neighborhood Algorithm (IGNA), based on the use of the restricted swap neighborhoods in the local search phase, eliminating moves that involve long arcs that may not be part of the best solution. We empirically analyze our algorithm solving different real-like instances of the problem with 9 to 57 passengers. The results show that the proposed IGNA is quite competitive with the parallel micro evolutionary algorithm (pμEA).

Keywords: Taxi sharing problem · Swap neighborhood · Smart mobility

1 Introduction

With the advent of the "sharing economy" based on information and communication technologies, services may not be purchased but can be shared, leading to the replacement of existing businesses. Peer-to-peer banking may substitute traditional banks, house sharing may trump the hotel business and carpooling

This research is partially funded by the Spanish Ministry of Economy and Competitiveness and FEDER under contract TIN2017-88213-R (6city); and Universidad de Málaga, Andalucía Tech, Consejería de Economía y Conocimiento de la Junta de Andaluía, and European Regional Development Fund under grant number UMA18-FEDERJA-003 (PRECOG).

P. A. Castillo et al. (Eds.): EvoApplications 2020, LNCS 12104, pp. 291–304, 2020.
https://doi.org/10.1007/978-3-030-43722-0_19

may replace taxicab service, etc. The carpooling gained massive public attention and taxi drivers lost a large part of their clients. For this reason, taxi drivers gathered in all the world to protest the launch of the ride sharing service [4]. The concept of taxi sharing is seen as the best solution, it can strike a balance between maximizing the benefits of the citizens and protecting the livelihood of the taxi drivers. All people agree that carpooling saves money, protects the environment, reduces stress and saves parking space. In order to maximize the benefits of the taxi-sharing system usage, we need to optimize taxi routes. The taxi sharing problem presented by Massobrio et al. [3] shows that evolutionary algorithms are able to reach significant improvements in the total cost of all trips. In previous work, Capacitated Vehicle Routing Problem (CVRP) was adapted to solve the taxi sharing problem, and this served as a motivation to adapt existing algorithms for the Vehicle Routing Problem. We are interested in this paper in finding good solutions in a reasonable time for the taxi sharing problem for medium, large and very large instances. We develop a new algorithm called Iterated Granular Neighborhood Algorithm (IGNA) to solve the taxi sharing problem. We compare it with the Parallel Micro Evolutionary Algorithm pμEA [10]. The rest of the paper is organized as follows: Sect. 2 describes the problem and Sect. 3 presents a literature review, Sects. 4 and 5 present the solution methodology and the computational experiments, respectively. Finally, Sect. 6 gives the conclusions of the research.

2   Taxi Sharing Problem

Taxi sharing problem is defined on a complete graph $G = (V, A)$. Let us imagine that a group of people in the same place, node 0 of our graph, decides to travel to different destinations using taxis. The destinations are numbered with 1, 2, etc. The taxi sharing problem consists in determining the appropriate number of taxis, the assignment of people to taxis and the order in which the taxis must drop the people off, in order to minimize the total monetary cost of the group of people. Despite there are some differences between CVRP and Taxi Sharing, we adapt the MILP formulation of CVRP to Taxi Sharing. We assume c_{0i} is the cost from the origin to the location plus the minimum fare that the customers have to pay to the taxi. Because taxis do not have to go back to the depot (as in CVRP), we do the cost of return equals zero and therefore the values c_{i0} will be 0. The problem can be formulated as Mixed Integer Linear Programming formulation (MILP) as follows:

$$\min \sum_{i=0}^{n} \sum_{j=0}^{n} c_{ij} x_{ij}, \tag{1}$$

subject to:

$$\sum_{i=0}^{n} x_{ij} = 1 \quad \text{for } 1 \leq j \leq n \tag{2}$$

$$\sum_{j=0}^{n} x_{ij} = 1 \quad \text{for } 1 \leq i \leq n \tag{3}$$

$$y_i - y_j + n x_{ij} \leq n - 1 \quad \text{for } 1 \leq i \neq j \leq n \tag{4}$$

$$u_i - u_j + k x_{ij} \leq k - 1 \quad \text{for } 1 \leq i \neq j \leq n \tag{5}$$

where x_{ij} are binary variables and $x_{ij} = 1$ if and only if a taxi visits node j after node i. Constraints (2) and (3) ensures that each node except the origin (node 0) are visited exactly once. Variables u_i and y_i are real-valued, Eq. (4) avoids subtour generation and Eq. (5) ensures that the capacity of any taxi is not exceeded. The previous MILP can be solved using CPLEX for small and some medium-sized instances. However, for large and very large instances, it is not possible to obtain the optimal solution in a reasonable time. In order to maximize the benefits of the taxi-sharing system, we need to optimize taxi routes and minimize passengers' fare. This optimization is known in the literature as a dial a ride problem (DARP), which is a problem of transportation requests from specific pickup locations to specific drop off locations while imposing certain requirements, such as earliest pickup time and latest drop off time of passengers and the capacity of vehicles [2]. Taxi Sharing variants could be static or dynamic. Dynamic Taxi sharing problem allows a new passenger to enter the system (taxi routes) that have been made, thus Hosni et al. proposed a formulation of taxi sharing problem and its solution by using heuristics method in 2014 [5]. The static version of the problem does not accept new passengers during the trip and the pick up of all the passengers should be from the same origin. Massobrio et al. had solved taxi sharing problem using a parallel micro evolutionary algorithm [10]. The pμEA was tested over a benchmark of 24 realistic problem instances generated in the city of Beijing. We will compare our proposed algorithm against the pμEA.

3   Iterated Granular Neighborhood Algorithm (IGNA)

The proposed algorithm is based on the Iterated Local Search metaheuristic (ILS) [8] with a Granular Neighborhood (GN) [1,11] in the local search phase. This is the first Iterated Granular Local Search (IGNA) approach for the Taxi Sharing Problem. The pseudo-code is in Algorithm 1:

The basic idea of the IGNA is extended from the ILS [7] to perform randomized walks in solution space. This algorithm escape from being trapped in a local minimum by perturbing the local optima. The search in the IGNA starts from an initial solution, commonly generated by a fast heuristic. In the first step, we apply the swap neighborhood to the current solution until the search is stuck in a local optimum. The swap neighborhood is generated by swapping

---

Algorithm 1. Iterated Granular neighborhood

1: **Initialization:** $S =$ Generate randomly an initial solution.
2: **Granularity:** $\vartheta \geq$ short arcs.
3: $S^* = SwapLS\,(S, \vartheta)$.
4: **while** stopping condition not reached **do**
5:     $S' = Perturbation\,(S^*)$;
6:     $S'^* = SwapLS(S', \vartheta)$;
7:     $S^* = Acceptance(S^*, S'^*)$;
8: **end while**

---

only the pair of nodes which can minimize the total cost. In the second step, an acceptance criteria can determine whether the new solution must replace the current solution or not. Whenever a new overall best solution is found in the local search step and has not been accepted before, it replaces the current solution. The third step is to escape from the current local optimum by perturbing the solution. Then, it repeatedly utilizes these three steps to improve this solution. The perturbation should be strong enough to get away from the current local optimum, but low enough to exploit knowledge from previous iterations [6]. To explore more solutions in the search space, we employed the first heuristic (the one applied to generate the initial solution) to perturb the local optima. A solution to the problem is a set of m sequences of locations $(s_1, s_1, ..., s_m)$, such that each sequence starts by 0 and finishes by 0. The number 0 plays two roles in the solution, it is considered as an origin in the first place and in the second place as a separator between the sequences. Then, we remove the separators from the solution S^* to get a path starting and finishing in the depot that contains all the destinations, we change the position of vertices randomly and we apply the initialization procedure explained in Sect. 3.1. The stopping condition of this algorithm is to reach a given runtime. In our experiments we set this runtime to the same required by $p\mu EA$ in [3].

3.1 Initial Solution

The goal of this contribution is to reach high-quality solutions as quickly as possible, this is why it is very important to start from a good initial solution. At the beginning, all the passengers must be assigned to taxis. A constructive heuristic is used to provide an initial solution for the Taxi Sharing Problem. We propose a new effective method to find an acceptable initial solution. Let us imagine that we have n destinations, while 0 is the origin for all passengers. We generate a random path, starting and returning to the same origin while visiting each vertex exactly once. The purpose of this path is to arrange travelers randomly and then divide them into groups. Each group must not exceed the capacity of one taxi. The main idea of our heuristic is how to divide the random path in many groups. The partitioning method is sequential and starts by the first passenger of the random path. Before taxis leave the origin, we fix the group of passengers. That's why we have to imagine a good scenario that can minimize the costs of all trips. We will exploit the new model that we have adapted from CVRP to the taxi sharing problem. We fix the first passenger of each group without any constraint. The first traveler of each group is the first one in the random path or who follows the last passenger assigned in a previous group. After defining the first passenger, next passenger is assigned according to the following constraints:

– The taxi capacity must not be exceeded.
– As long as the cost of returning to the depot is zero, the distance from the first vertex and the next one must be less than the distance from the depot to the next vertex, otherwise the actual taxi has to return to the origin and the next passenger will be the first passenger assigned in new taxi.

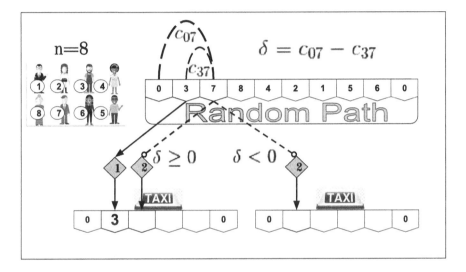

Fig. 1. Example of solution representation for the taxi sharing problem.

We will apply the same principle for all other vertices until we divide all the path. We want to remind that each taxi has to return to the origin from which he had started, so the separators should be 0, to distinguish groups of passengers assigned to different taxis. Figure 1 shows an example of n passengers and explains the criteria that applied to separate between taxis.

1. The first traveler (number 3) in the tuple will be assigned to the first taxi.
2. We calculate δ; the difference between the cost c_{07} and the cost c_{37}.
   – If $\delta \geq 0$, we assign the second traveler (number 7) to the same taxi.
   – Otherwise, we assign the second traveler to another taxi.
   – Before assigning each traveler, we check the capacity of the taxi, if there is still a place for a new traveler we calculate δ. Otherwise the traveler will be automatically assigned to another taxi without doing the distance calculation.

3. We repeat this method with all passengers until we get a first solution.

It is obvious that the result will be better if we start from a good solution. So we will study later the impact of the first solution in our algorithm.

3.2 Granular Neighborhood Algorithm (GNA)

The Granular Neighborhood is a reduced neighborhood with a particular focus on adjustment of the search space size. GNA doesn't include moves which are unlikely to belong to good solutions. Toth and Vigo [11] proposed the Granular tabu search algorithm (**GTS**) for solving the standard vehicle routing problem. They eliminated up to 80% of the edges, while for the taxi sharing problem, the experiments showed that the best solution always appears after the elimination of 5% of edges. Usually long arcs have a small probability of being part of high-quality solutions in a complete graph. Toth and Vigo [11] created an efficient filtering rule to eliminate long arcs. An arc is short if its cost is not greater than the granularity threshold value ϑ, defined by $\vartheta = \beta \cdot \frac{z'}{n+m}$.

Where, z' is the value of the initial solution given by the heuristic of this paper, n is the number of passengers and m is the number of taxis. As a result, $\frac{z'}{n+m}$ is the average cost of an arc of the solution. β is a parameter that adjusts the size of the granular neighborhood. In the case of $\beta = 1$, only arcs whose cost is less than or equal to the average belong to the granular neighborhood. The granular neighborhood is associated with a sparse graph $G = (V, A')$ that contains short arcs, whose cost c_{ij} is not greater than the granularity threshold ϑ, and a set I of important arcs such as those incident to the depot or belonging to high quality solutions. The arc set is:

$$A' = \{(i,j) \in A : c_{i,j} \leq \vartheta\} \cup I$$

The arcs in A' are used to determine the other arcs involved in each type of move, such as the swap neighborhood exchange. In our contribution, we identify important arcs I from the initial solution and we eliminate long arcs to build a set of the most important arcs. GNA is a K-exchange neighborhood with $K = 2$ that permute any two elements, irrespective of whether they are adjacent. Given an initial solution s_1 with m taxis and n passengers, the swap neighborhood generates solutions by interchanging the positions of nodes i and j for $1 \leqslant i < j \leqslant N$. Before making a swap, we must do these following tests shown in Figs. 2 and 3:

- Constraint 1: ensures that the capacity of each taxi is not exceeded after any swap.
- Constraint 2: check the cost of new edges which could be appear after the swap, and compare it with the granularity value (we do this swap only if each edge is less than the granularity value).
- Constraint 3: δ is the difference between the edges that disappear and the edges that appear after the swap. δ has to be negative to accept this swap.

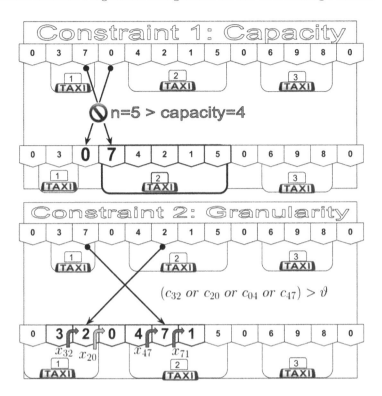

Fig. 2. Example of solution representation for constraint 1 and 2.

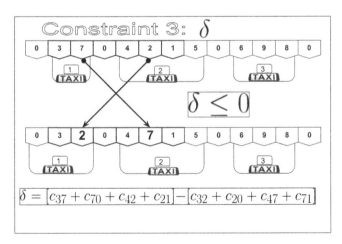

Fig. 3. Example of solution representation for constraint 3.

Subsequently, it is a first improvement neighborhood exploration, in which the current solution is replaced with the first better solution found in the neighborhood. The main handicap of the swap neighborhood is its short and limited movement: it looks only one single move ahead, and any move can lead to local optimum that may be substantially worse than a global optimum. On the positive side, the swap neighborhood is generally much faster and easier to implement. That's why we applied an effective approach such as IGNA which can allow dependent runs by generating the new starting solution from one of the previous local optima by a suitable perturbation method. This method leads to a high quality solution at relatively low computational time, without resorting to more complicated local search algorithms.

3.3 Running Example

We present in this section an example how IGNA works using the second small size instance with 12 travelers. We show how IGNA is able to provide a cheaper route for passengers by drawing a graph for each step.

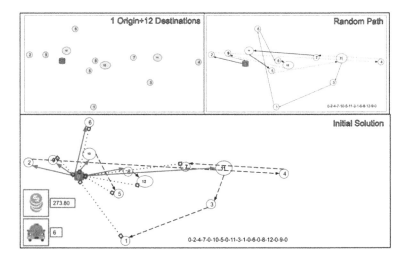

Fig. 4. Example of the second small instance representing the approach of the initial solution. (Color figure online)

In Fig. 4, we present 12 passengers willing to travel from the same origin which is represented in red color. Then, we create randomly a path that visits all the vertices, and starts and returns to the origin. The last step of the heuristic, applies the idea of dividing the path in many routes, and each route represents a taxi. The cost is 273.80 using a fleet of 6 taxis. This is the first solution and helps us to calculate the granularity ϑ, defined by $\vartheta = \beta \cdot \frac{z'}{n+m}$.

Figure 5 shows long arcs removed from the graph. In this instance $\vartheta = 72.06$. We removed all edges with $Distance \geq 72.06$. We fixed β to 5, and the number of edges removed is 8.

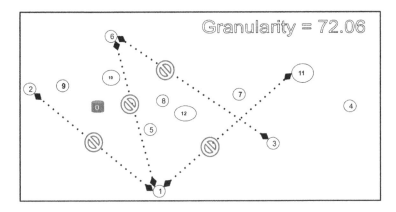

Fig. 5. Example of the second small instance representing long arcs removed from the graph.

Figure 6 describes the last four solutions in the first granular neighborhood iteration. We applied 13 swaps to optimise the cost to 212.31. The number of taxis is always the same: 6.

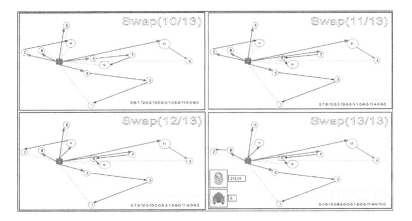

Fig. 6. Example of the second small instance representing the last four solutions in the swap neighborhood.

In Fig. 7 we show the result after the second iteration of the local search. The cost is 168.76 and the number of taxis is 3. Thanks to the exploitation of the ILS model in this algorithm, we could obtain the best solution in all the small instances and it scales well for larger instances.

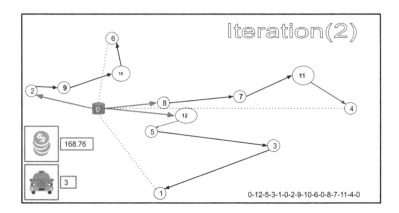

Fig. 7. Example of the second small instance representing the last solution obtained from the IGNA.

4   Experiments and Results

In order to evaluate the proposed IGNA and compare it with the pµEA, we use the same set of real-like instances used by Ma et al. [9]. These instances were generated with the help of Taxi Query Generator (TQG). TQG produces a list of origins and destinations for individual trips. To adapt those data to this problem, Massobrio et al. grouped the destinations having the same origin. They built instances with different sizes: small, with 9 to 25 passengers, medium, with 25 to 40 passengers, large with 40 to 55 passengers, and very large, with 55 to 70 passengers. This way, they created a benchmark of 24 realistic instances of the Taxi Sharing Problem. We use IBM Ilog CPLEX to solve the Taxi Sharing Problem using the MILP formulation described in Sect. 2. In Tables 1, 2, 3 and 4 we show the results of IGNA and pµEA for the small, medium large and very large instances. In the case of the small instances we also show the results obtained by CPLEX. In larger instances the runtime of CPLEX is too high to be useful in practice.

The results shows that we are able to find the optimal solution for small instances in a reasonable time. However, for medium, large and very large instances the time required to find the optimal solutions is not reasonable (several hours). For 21 passengers, the execution time is 1.18 s, which is reasonable. However, when the number of passengers is 24, CPLEX is no longer giving solutions in a reasonable time. The parallel micro evolutionary algorithm previously proposed for this problem in the literature, is able to find approximate solutions to the problem in a few seconds regardless the size of the instance, but it obtains low quality solutions. We run IGNA for the same time as the pµEA for medium, large and very large instances. The experimental results show that the difference in the cost is in all the cases significant in favor of the IGNA algorithm.

The experimental evaluation was performed in a machine with Quad core Xeon E5430 processor at 2.66 GHz and 8 GB of RAM. We carry out the code

Table 1. Comparison between the IGNA, pμEA and CPLEX with 24 sub populations and greedy initialization strategy for the small instances of the Taxi Sharing Problem. For pμEA, the best cost of 20 independent runs. For IGNA the best cost of 30 independent runs.

Instance small	IGNA		pμEA		CPLEX	
	Best	Runtime(s)	Best	Runtime(s)	Cost	Runtime(s)
#1 (10)	125.5	0.0	125.5	0.0	125.5	0.1
#2 (13)	168.7	0.0	168.7	0.0	168.7	0.8
#3 (18)	191.0	0.2	191.0	0.5	191.0	1.4
#4 (22)	215.5	0.4	215.5	0.1	215.5	1.18
#5 (25)	297.5	1.7	297.5	0.3	N/A	>64000
#6 (25)	244.0	2.4	246.1	2.4	N/A	>64000

by a virtual machine having the same characteristics as the machine used to execute the pμEA algorithm. Regarding the execution time of the IGNA solver and pμEA, we have to be careful with the conclusions, since the IGNA algorithm is sequential and the pμEA executes several instructions simultaneously on different processing devices. We run the code in the same time for medium, large and very large instances. We used the runtime of pμEA as stopping condition just because we couldn't run the pμEA again.

Table 2. Comparison between the IGNA and pμEA with 24 sub populations and greedy initialization strategy for the medium instances of the Taxi Sharing Problem. For pμEA, the best cost and the average of 20 independent runs. For IGNA the best cost and the average of 30 independent runs.

Instance medium	IGNA		pμEA		Runtime(s)
	Avg	Best	Avg	Best	
#1	336.4	336.4	344.5	336.5	5.6
#2	319.2	319.0	323.1	320.2	3.4
#3	793.6	793.6	801.2	795.5	4.2
#4	349.7	347.0	357.4	351.2	3.4
#5	435.0	433.8	443.7	436.8	3.8
#6	364.5	360.4	367.0	359.3	5.0

The first three instances show the potential of this approach, the best solutions are obtained in few seconds. The time required to find the optimal solutions by CPLEX is several hours and more than three days for the third instance. We knew that the cost should be lower than pμEA, since IGNA finds the optimal solution and the Table 1 shows that.

Table 3. Comparison between the IGNA and pμEA with 24 sub populations and greedy initialization strategy for the large instances of the Taxi Sharing Problem. For pμEA, the best cost and the average of 20 independent runs. For IGNA the best cost and the average of 30 independent runs.

Instance large	IGNA		pμEA		Runtime(s)
	Avg	Best	Avg	Best	
#1	413.1	410.4	429.9	412.6	7.1
#2	307.4	302.5	319.8	306.4	7.5
#3	419.3	410.0	425.0	417.2	4.3
#4	366.0	360.9	367.7	361.6	3.2
#5	438.1	427.2	446.3	437.6	2.6
#6	552.3	542.3	562.1	554.2	4.3

Table 4. Comparison between the IGNA and pμEA with 24 sub populations and greedy initialization strategy for the very large instances of the Taxi Sharing Problem. For pμEA, the best cost and the average of 20 independent runs. For IGNA the best cost and the average of 30 independent runs.

Instance very large	IGNA		pμEA		Runtime(s)
	Avg	Best	Avg	Best	
#1	632.9	619.9	637.7	626.3	3.6
#2	508.7	502.2	524.8	517.2	4.5
#3	489.8	482.2	498.4	490.0	3.5
#4	729.8	720.0	744.9	736.8	6.1
#5	550.5	542.6	560.6	548.7	4.7
#6	1416.8	1408.1	1424.6	1412.6	6.1

Tables 2 and 3 show the solution quality (cost) and the runtime required by our approach and pμEA to solve the 12 real-like instances of the Taxi Sharing Problem. We compare the average and the best solution obtined during the same runtime.

Table 5. Wilcoxon rank sum test between the IGNA and pμEA with 24 sub populations and greedy initialization strategy for medium, large and very large instances of the Taxi Sharing Problem.

Instance		#1	#2	#3	#4	#5	#6
p-value	Medium	1.26e-09	2.12e-09	3.38e-09	1.75e-08	2.99e-09	1.62e-07
	Large	1.70e-13	2.56e-06	1.38e-03	6.09e-02	1.81e-08	1.83e-09
	Very large	1.17e-04	4.24e-14	4.98e-09	1.27e-12	2.76e-07	2.11e-06

We applied the non-parametric Wilcoxon Sum-rank test (see Table 5) to compare the two algorithms and check if the differences between the algorithms are statistically significant. The results of the Wilcoxon Sum-rank test show that all the differences are statistically significant except the 4th large instance because the p-value > 0.05. For the remaining instances, the p-value <0.05, this confirms that IGNA is better than pμEA for taxi sharing problem.

5   Conclusions and Future Work

In this paper we propose Iterated Granular Swap Neighborhood Algorithm to solve the taxi sharing problem. We compared the proposed algorithm with a parallel micro evolutionary algorithm, and we can observe in all the cases that the average obtained by the IGNA is lower than the average obtained by pμEA. In our future work we will try to reduce the time complexity by dynamic and parallel techniques. We will try to extend the optimization problem by creating a new formulation, adding the delay as a second objective, impose the distance as new constraint and give the possibility to passengers to start the trip from different origins to make the problem more realistic.

References

1. Ahuja, R.K., Ergun, Ö., Orlin, J.B., Punnen, A.P.: A survey of very large-scale neighborhood search techniques. Discrete Appl. Math. **123**(1–3), 75–102 (2002)
2. Cordeau, J.-F., Laporte, G.: The dial-a-ride problem: models and algorithms. Ann. Oper. Res. **153**(1), 29–46 (2007)
3. Fagundez, G., Massobrio, R., Nesmachnow, S.: Online taxi sharing optimization using evolutionary algorithms. In: 2014 XL Latin American Computing Conference (CLEI), pp. 1–12. IEEE (2014)
4. Yann, H.: Les taxis confirment une manifestation européenne anti Uber le 11 juin (2014). https://www.01net.com/actualites/vtc-les-taxis-confirment-une-manifestation-europeenne-anti-uber-le-11-juin-621416.html/. Accessed 09 June 2014
5. Hosni, H., Naoum-Sawaya, J., Artail, H.: The shared-taxi problem: formulation and solution methods. Transp. Res. Part B: Methodol. **70**, 303–318 (2014)
6. Kramer, O.: Iterated local search with Powell's method: a memetic algorithm for continuous global optimization. Memetic Comput. **2**(1), 69–83 (2010). https://doi.org/10.1007/s12293-010-0032-9
7. Li, J., Pardalos, P.M., Sun, H., Pei, J., Zhang, Y.: Iterated local search embedded adaptive neighborhood selection approach for the multi-depot vehicle routing problem with simultaneous deliveries and pickups. Expert Syst. Appl. **42**(7), 3551–3561 (2015)
8. Lourenço, H.R., Martin, O.C., Stützle, T.: Iterated local search. In: Glover, F., Kochenberger, G.A. (eds.) Handbook of Metaheuristics, vol. 57, pp. 320–353. Springer, Boston (2003). https://doi.org/10.1007/0-306-48056-5_11
9. Ma, S., Zheng, Y., Wolfson, O.: T-share: a large-scale dynamic taxi ridesharing service. In: 2013 IEEE 29th International Conference on Data Engineering (ICDE), pp. 410–421. IEEE (2013)

10. Massobrio, R., Fagúndez, G., Nesmachnow, S.: A parallel micro evolutionary algorithm for taxi sharing optimization. In: VII ALIO/EURO workshop on applied combinatorial optimization, montevideo, uruguay (2014)
11. Toth, P., Vigo, D.: The granular Tabu search and its application to the vehicle-routing problem. Informs J. Comput. **15**(4), 333–346 (2003)

Applications of Bio-inspired Techniques on Social Networks

Multiobjective Optimization of a Targeted Vaccination Scheme in the Presence of Non-diagnosed Cases

Krzysztof Michalak[(✉)][iD]

Department of Information Technologies, Faculty of Management,
Wrocław University of Economics, Wrocław, Poland
krzysztof.michalak@ue.wroc.pl

Abstract. One of the problems in disease prevention and epidemics control is the large level of uncertainty present in the solved problems. If an optimization of targeted vaccination scheme is attempted, the evaluation of solutions usually involves simulating the non-deterministic spreading of the disease. However, the non-determinism of the epidemic dynamics is just one of the sources of uncertainty in this problem. This paper studies another source of uncertainty in optimization of targeted vaccination schemes, which is the existence of non-diagnosed cases of the disease.

In the paper the multiobjective optimization of a targeted vaccination scheme is carried out under an assumption that only a fraction of really existing cases of the disease are known. Solutions found by the optimization algorithm in this limited-knowledge scenario are then evaluated in a simulation in which all existing cases of the disease are taken into account. Optimized solutions are compared with the mass vaccination scheme which is not based on the knowledge of existing cases of the disease. An uncertainty-handling technique is proposed that randomly adds infected individuals to the simulations in order to compensate for the unknown ones.

Keywords: Disease prevention · Epidemics control · DPEC · Combinatorial optimization · Graph-based problems

1 Introduction

One of the problems studied in the area of Disease Prevention and Epidemics Control (DPEC) is elaboration of effective vaccination schemes intended to limit the extent of epidemic outbreaks. There are different approaches to this problem ranging from the mass vaccination scheme, which aims at reaching as many members of the population as possible, thereby providing herd immunity, to more complex schemes that target selected individuals. Especially in case of bioterrorism, targeted vaccination schemes are preferred to the mass vaccination, because of the unpredictable nature of intentionally initiated outbreaks [2].

© Springer Nature Switzerland AG 2020
P. A. Castillo et al. (Eds.): EvoApplications 2020, LNCS 12104, pp. 307–322, 2020.
https://doi.org/10.1007/978-3-030-43722-0_20

Also, targeted vaccination is a better choice when the vaccine is in short supply or when the complications of vaccination can be severe. In the case of some animal diseases, such as the Foot-and-Mouth Disease (FMD), preemptive mass vaccinations are prohibited in certain countries. For example, in the European Union only reactive FMD vaccinations are allowed.

Contrary to mass vaccinations, targeted schemes require a better understanding of the sources of the outbreak and the resulting spreading of the disease in the population. Modelling the dynamics of an epidemic involves various uncertainties. One of them is the fact that it cannot be exactly predicted which contacts will cause the disease to be transmitted and which will not. Therefore, a common approach is to use compartmental models [3], which, instead of modelling each individual, assume that the population is divided into compartments and that every individual in the same compartment has the same characteristics. These models reflect the uncertain nature of the spreading of the disease by calculating fractions of the population that belong to each compartment at a given time without referring to the state of each individual. However, even the global parameters of such models cannot be determined with certainty [4]. Other sources of uncertainty include difficult to predict outcomes of various preventive actions [6] and diverse scenarios of initial outbreaks that are possible [2].

This paper focuses on an optimization-based approach to targeted vaccination. It is assumed that an initial outbreak has already taken place and the optimization algorithm is used for finding a good vaccination scheme intended to minimize the number of infected individuals, but also to minimize the number of vaccinations. Therefore, the proposed scenario is related to the one discussed in [2] in which vaccination schemes are discussed for containment of a smallpox outbreak resulting from bioterrorist attacks. The nature of such events, which are highly unpredictable and usually limited to a small area makes mass vaccinations problematic. Also, the fact that smallpox vaccines may cause complications, means that mass vaccinations are not without risks and in the case of localized outbreaks may cause more harm than good.

In the scenario considered in this paper it is assumed that not all the cases of the disease have been diagnosed at the time when vaccinations are planned. The optimization algorithm works using only known cases of the disease for simulating its spreading and for assessing the effectiveness of vaccination schemes found during the optimization run. Solutions found by the optimization algorithm are compared with the mass vaccination scheme which is not based on the knowledge of existing cases of the disease.

The paper is structured as follows. Section 2 defines the optimization problem, Sect. 3 presents how the experiments were conducted in this paper, Sect. 4 discusses the results and Sect. 5 concludes the paper.

2   Problem Definition

This paper concerns a problem of optimizing a vaccination scheme with the goal of reducing the number of infected individuals in a scenario where an outbreak of a disease occurs. The spreading of the disease is modelled in discrete time steps on an undirected graph $G = \langle V, E \rangle$ with N_v vertices according to the SIRV (Susceptible, Infected, Recovered, Vaccinated) model [7]. Therefore, the state of the vertices of G at time t is represented as a vector $S_t \in \{$ 'S', 'I', 'R', 'V' $\}^{N_v}$. State transitions occur with the transmission probability β ('S' → 'I') and the recovery probability γ ('I' → 'R') per a time step. Vaccinated individuals change their state permanently to 'V' and, similarly, recovered individuals remain in the 'R' state indefinitely. In the initial state S_0 (at $t = 0$) a fraction α_{inf} of the vertices is in the state 'I' (Infected) and the remaining vertices are in the state 'S' (Susceptible). Next, a vaccine is administered and some vertices change their state from 'S' to 'V'. In this paper the vaccination scheme is represented as a binary vector $v \in \{0, 1\}^{N_v}$ in which elements equal 1 represent the vertices to vaccinate. Note, that only for non-infected individuals the vaccine works, so if $S_0[i] = $ 'I' and $v[i] = 1$ for some $i \in \{1, \ldots, N_v\}$ such vertex remains infected. In subsequent time steps each infected vertex transmits the disease to each of its susceptible neighbours with the transmission probability β. Infected vertices recover with the recovery probability γ and, following the SIRV model, they become immune to the disease, so the epidemic is guaranteed to stop (for $\gamma > 0$).

The optimization problem solved in this paper is the problem of determining which vertices to vaccinate in order to minimize the number of vertices that become infected. The search space in this problem is $\Omega = \{0, 1\}^{N_v}$, that is, solutions are binary vectors of length N_v, where N_v is the number of vertices in graph G. A solution $v \in \Omega$ is evaluated in the following manner. The graph state is set to the initial state with some vertices infected. Non-infected vertices for which the corresponding element in v equals 1 are vaccinated (change their state to 'V'). The spreading of the disease is simulated according to the SIRV model with the transmission probability β and the recovery probability γ. After the simulation stops (when all infected vertices recover, which is guaranteed to happen for $\gamma > 0$), values of two objective functions are calculated for v. The first objective is the number of vaccinated vertices which is the number of elements equal 1 in v, so: $f_1 = |\{i : v[i] = 1\}|$. The second objective is the number of vertices that became infected during the simulation, which is equal to the number of vertices in the 'R' state at the end of the simulation: $f_2 = |\{i : S_{t_{stop}}[i] = 'R'\}|$. Both objectives are to be minimized. In this multiobjective approach the costs of vaccinations and infections are not explicitly taken into account. Instead, the decision maker is presented with a set of non-dominated solutions to choose from. Each of these solutions represents the best known trade-off minimizing the number of infections for a given number of vaccinations. Because in this paper the vaccine is considered to be 100% effective the vaccinated vertices can be considered as removed from the graph. Thus, finding the smallest f_2 for a given f_1 is equivalent to solving the optimal node removal problem, which is known to be NP-complete [10].

Note, that in this paper it is assumed, that not all the cases of the disease have been diagnosed when the vaccination scheme is optimized. Instead, it is possible to add some artificially generated disease cases to the initial state from which the simulation starts. Therefore, simulations used for evaluating solutions during optimization do not start from the actual initial state S_0, but from a different state S_0'. Two parameters are used for generating the initial state S_0' for the simulations: α_{known} - the fraction of disease cases which are known, and R_a - the multiplier controlling the addition of artificial disease cases to S_0'. The construction of S_0' is performed as follows. First, $N_{known} = \alpha_{known} \cdot \alpha_{inf} \cdot N_v$ infected vertices from S_0 are selected, which represent these cases of the disease which we consider as the known ones. These vertices are also set to the state 'I' in S_0' and all the remaining vertices in S_0' are set to 'S'. Next, some artificially generated disease cases are added to S_0' by randomly selecting $R_a \cdot N_{known}$ vertices which are in the 'S' state in S_0 and setting them to the state 'I' in S_0'. Thus, apart from the N_{known} known cases of the disease the simulation starts with an additional number of artificial cases proportional to the number of already known ones and the multiplication factor R_a (for $R_a = 0$ there are no artificial cases, for $R_a = 1$ there are as many artificial as the known ones, etc.). Only after the optimization algorithm produces a set of solutions, these solutions are evaluated by simulating the spreading of the disease from the actual initial state S_0. This way, the optimization algorithm works with limited knowledge, but the solutions it produces are evaluated as if applied to the actual initial state S_0.

3   Experiments

In the experiments a multiobjective evolutionary algorithm was used to solve the targeted vaccinations optimization problem described in Sect. 2. Solutions processed by the optimization algorithm were evaluated according to the number of vaccinated individuals (f_1, minimized) and the number of individuals infected by the disease during simulations (f_2, minimized). As discussed in Sect. 2 the simulations during optimization were performed using the initial state S_0' different from the actual one S_0, thereby representing limited knowledge about the disease outbreak.

After the optimization concluded, the solutions found by the optimization algorithm were compared to the mass vaccination scheme which was not based on the knowledge of existing cases of the disease. For each solution $v \in \{0,1\}^{N_v}$ found by the algorithm the real value of objective $f_2^{(targ)}(v)$ was determined using a simulation in which all initially infected vertices were known. The effectiveness of the mass vaccination scheme was assessed by randomly vaccinating the same number of vertices as in the solution v, that is $f_1(v)$. Then, the number of vertices that became infected $f_2^{(mass)}(v)$ was determined using a simulation in which, again, all initially infected vertices were known. Thus, an optimized, targeted vaccination scheme was compared to the non-targeted mass vaccination scheme with the same number of vaccinated vertices. The ratio:

$$\Delta(v) = f_2^{(mass)}(v)/f_2^{(targeted)}(v) \tag{1}$$

can be used to determine which scheme resulted in fewer infections with $\Delta(v) > 1$ indicating that the targeted vaccinated scheme v produced by the optimization algorithm was better than the mass vaccination scheme with the same number of vaccinations $f_1(v)$.

In the experiments the following matters were considered:

- Finding a good parameterization of the optimization algorithm.
- Determining if the local search procedure proposed in this paper improves the optimization results.
- Verifying if the optimization of the targeted vaccination scheme yields better results than a mass vaccination scheme.
- Assessing the influence of the non-diagnosed cases on the optimization effectiveness.
- Testing an uncertainty handling technique which adds random infected individuals to the initial state of the simulations.

3.1   Problem Instances

Instances of the targeted vaccinations optimization problem tackled in this paper consist of:

- an undirected graph $G = \langle V, E \rangle$ with N_v vertices,
- the initial state S_0 in which a fraction α_{inf} vertices are in the 'I' state,
- the state S_0' in which only a fraction α_{known} of infected vertices from the state S_0 is in the state 'I', an additional number $R_a \cdot \alpha_{known} \cdot \alpha_{inf} \cdot N_v$ of vertices are set to 'I', and the remaining ones are in the state 'S'.

In this paper 30 optimization problem instances were generated for each number of vertices N_v. To generate the graph G the REDS model was used [1], which produces graphs with a distribution of edges resembling that of a social network. This model was chosen in order to simulate the epidemic on a graph as similar as possible to a real-life network of contacts, while still being able to generate graphs with different number of vertices. Apart from the number of vertices N_v, REDS graphs are parameterized by: R - the maximum radius within which a vertex can connect to other vertices, E - an energy budget that each vertex has for generating new connections and S - a parameter that controls the strength of the synergy effect. Vertices of an REDS graph are randomly placed with the uniform probability on a unit square $[0, 1] \times [0, 1]$. Subsequently, pairs of vertices located at a distance of at most R from each other are drawn with the uniform probability. The cost of adding an edge between vertices v_i and v_j is proportional to the distance $D_{ij} = d(v_i, v_j)$. This cost is discounted by the factor $\frac{1}{1+Sk_{ij}}$, where k_{ij} is the number of neighbours the vertices v_i and v_j have in common. The addition of a new edge between the vertices v_i and v_j may result in the costs of other edges adjacent to these vertices being discounted also. This may happen if v_i becomes a new common neighbour for v_j and one of its adjacent vertices, or if v_j becomes a new common neighbour for v_i and one of its adjacent vertices. Therefore, the total costs of edges adjacent to the vertices v_i and v_j have to be recalculated when the addition of the edge between the vertices v_i

and v_j is attempted. If the total (discounted) cost of all the edges adjacent to each of the vertices v_i and v_j is not larger than E the new edge is formed. The instances used in the experiments described in this paper were generated with $N_v = 1000, 1250, 1500, 1750, 2000, 5000$ and 10000 vertices. For $N_v = 1000$ the values $R = 0.1$ and $S = 0.5$ were used and these parameters were decreased for larger graphs by multiplying by $\dfrac{1}{\sqrt{N_v/1000}}$ in order to avoid generating overly dense graphs. The energy budget was set to $E = 0.15$. An example of an REDS graph with $N_v = 5000$ vertices is presented in Fig. 1.

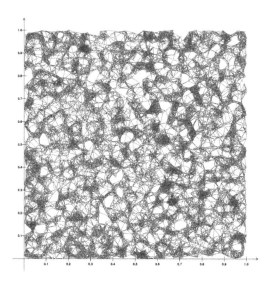

Fig. 1. An example of an REDS graph with $N_v = 5000$ vertices.

The initial state S_0 for the test instances was obtained by randomly selecting, with the uniform probability, $\alpha_{inf} = 1\%$ and 10% of the vertices in graph G. The state S_0' was obtained by randomly selecting, with the uniform probability, $\alpha_{known} = 10\%, 20\%, 50\%$ and 100% of the infected vertices from S_0. The generation of artificial disease cases was performed with $R_a = 0, 1, 2$ and 5 (obviously, for $R_a = 0$ the initial state S_0 did not contain any artificially added infected vertices). The parameters of the epidemic model were set to the transmission probability $\beta = 0.1$ and the recovery probability $\gamma = 0.5$.

3.2 Optimization Algorithm

In the experiments the MOEA/D algorithm [5] was used with Tchebycheff decomposition method, maximum number of neighbours replaced $n_r = 2$ and the probability of selecting parents from the neighbourhood $\delta = 0.9$. The number of neighbours was set to an odd number $T = 21$ according to the findings in the paper [8]. The stopping criterion was set to $max_{FE} = 10000$ solution evaluations.

Because of the non-deterministic nature of the studied problem, each solution was evaluated by performing $N_{sim} = 100$ simulations, the results of which were averaged to obtain the criterion $f_2^{(targ)}$. When comparing the solutions to the mass vaccination scheme the criterion $f_2^{(mass)}$ was also calculated by performing $N_{sim} = 100$ simulations.

Genetic Operators. Three crossover operators (single point, two-point and uniform) and six mutation operators (bit-flip, displacement, insertion, inversion, scramble and transpose) were used with an autoadaptation mechanism based on success rates of the operators [9].

Local Search. In the optimization algorithm an informed local search was used increasing and decreasing the number of vaccinated vertices using information about how frequently each vertex was infected. For each solution $v_0 \in \{0,1\}^{N_v}$ found by the MOEA/D algorithm the local search was performed with the probability P_{LS}. In the MOEA/D each solution v_0 is associated with a certain weight vector λ_0 used for scalarization of multiple objectives. The local search consisted of two steps in which two new solutions were tested. The first solution $v_0^{(-)}$ was generated by replacing at most $\alpha_{LS} \cdot N_v$ elements of the binary vector v_0 equal one by zeros (thereby decreasing the number of vaccinated vertices). For replacement by zeros the elements equal one and with the lowest infection frequencies were selected. The second solution $v_0^{(+)}$ was generated by replacing at most $\alpha_{LS} \cdot N_v$ elements of the binary vector v_0 equal zero by ones (thereby increasing the number of vaccinated vertices). For replacement by ones the elements equal zero and with the highest infection frequencies were selected. Each of the two new solutions was evaluated using the simulation procedure used for evaluating solutions in the optimization algorithm. All three solutions v_0, $v_0^{(-)}$ and $v_0^{(+)}$ were compared by scalarizing the objectives they attained using the weight vector λ_0. The result of the local search was the best of these three solutions.

Parameter Tuning. The population size N_{pop}, and the probabilities of the crossover P_{cross} and the mutation P_{mut} were tuned using the grid search approach. The ranges of tested values were $N_{pop} \in \{ 50, 100, 200, 500 \}$, $P_{cross} \in \{ 0.2, 0.4, 0.6, 0.8, 1.0 \}$ and $P_{mut} \in \{ 0.02, 0.04, 0.06, 0.08, 0.10 \}$. To avoid overfitting, the tuning was performed on a set of 30 optimization problem instances with $N_v = 1000$, separate from the instances used in the rest of the experiments. Results produced by the optimization algorithm with various settings were compared by calculating the hypervolume indicator [11] for the set of nondominated solutions found by the optimization algorithm within the budget of $max_{FE} = 10000$ solution evaluations. The best values found using the methodology described above were $N_{pop} = 50$, $P_{cross} = 0.2$ and $P_{mut} = 0.1$.

The local search method used in this paper is parameterized by the probability P_{LS} of performing the local search for a solution found by the evolutionary algorithm and the fraction of the solution vector α_{LS} that undergoes change in the local search procedure. Tuning of these two parameters was performed using the grid search approach with the search ranges $P_{LS} \in \{ 0.2, 0.4, 0.6, 0.8, 1.0 \}$

and $\alpha_{LS} \in \{ 0.02, 0.04, 0.06, 0.08, 0.10 \}$. The best values found were $P_{LS} = 0.2$ and $\alpha_{LS} = 0.08$.

Benefits of the Local Search. Using the results obtained in the parameter tuning phase of the experiments it is possible to determine what is the benefit of using the local search and if it is statistically significant. To this end the results obtained using no local search ($P_{LS} = 0.0$) and the local search with the best set of parameters ($P_{LS} = 0.2$ and $\alpha_{LS} = 0.08$) were compared. The median hypervolume obtained without the local search was 157798.09 and the median hypervolume obtained using the local search was 195730.41. Using results of the tests for 30 optimization problem instances used for parameter tuning a Wilcoxon statistical test was performed with the null hypothesis stating the equality of medians. The p-value obtained in the test was $1.73 \cdot 10^{-6}$ which confirms high statistical significance of the difference between the obtained results. Therefore, it can be concluded that the proposed local search procedure has a positive impact on the results and consequently the local search with $P_{LS} = 0.2$ and $\alpha_{LS} = 0.08$ was used in the experiments.

4   Results

In the experiments the performance of the optimized targeted vaccination scheme was compared to the mass vaccination strategy on optimization problem instances described in Sect. 3.1. Because the optimization problem tackled in this paper is a bi-objective one, the results were compared using the hypervolume indicator [11], which, in the bi-objective case, is equal to the area of the subset of the objective space that is dominated by a given set of solutions. Larger hypervolume values correspond to better Pareto fronts. In the experiments each optimized solution v with the objectives $f_1(v)$ and $f_2^{(targ)}(v)$ was compared with the mass vaccination scheme with the same number of vaccinated individuals $f_1(v)$ resulting in the number of infections $f_2^{(mass)}(v)$. A comparison between optimized targeted vaccinations and mass vaccinations with the same $f_1(v)$ can be performed using the ratio of $f_2^{(mass)}(v)$ to $f_2^{(targ)}(v)$ defined in Eq. (1). The larger this ratio, the bigger the advantage of optimized vaccinations.

Examples of Pareto fronts produced by the targeted and mass vaccination schemes for $N_v = 1000$ and 10000 and for $\alpha_{inf} = 0.01$ and 0.10 are presented in Fig. 2. Presented Pareto fronts were obtained for $\alpha_{known} = 1.0$ and $R_a = 0$, that is, when all initial cases of the disease were known and taken into account in simulations used by the optimization algorithm. Clearly, the optimization algorithm was able to produce better results than those obtained using mass vaccinations. It can be observed that for the instances with $N_v = 10000$ the improvement is smaller than for problem instances with $N_v = 1000$. This can be attributed to the fact that in the latter case the search space is much larger, making the optimization problem harder to solve. Also, the improvement is smaller for larger value of the fraction of initially infected individuals α_{inf}, because for a larger outbreak the epidemic is more difficult to contain. These observations are consistent with hypervolume values presented in Tables 1 and 2 for $\alpha_{known} = 1.0$ and $R_a = 0$. For the initial outbreak fraction $\alpha_{inf} = 1\%$ the improvement of the hypervolume ranges from 1.15795 (for $N_v = 10000$) to 1.87563 (for $N_v = 1000$) and for the initial outbreak fraction $\alpha_{inf} = 10\%$ it ranges from 1.07588 (for $N_v = 10000$) to 1.42968 (for $N_v = 1250$). Note, that with the exact knowledge of the initial outbreak ($\alpha_{known} = 1.0$), the optimization algorithm always produced results better than the mass vaccination scheme. The smallest improvement in terms of the hypervolume was 1.07588 for $N_v = 10000$ and the initial outbreak fraction $\alpha_{inf} = 10\%$.

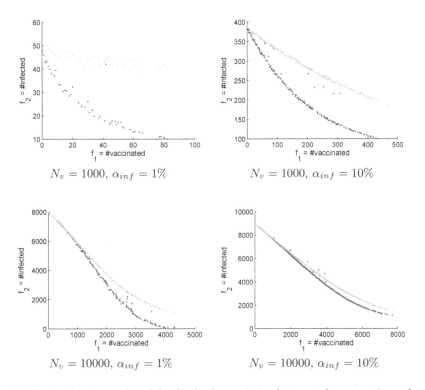

Fig. 2. Pareto fronts produced by both the optimized targeted vaccination scheme (blue) and the mass vaccination scheme (red). (Color figure online)

In order to assess the influence of the non-diagnosed cases on the optimization effectiveness, tests for different values of α_{known} were performed. Values of the ratio $\Delta(v)$ (Eq. (1)) were summarized in Figs. 3 and 4 for $N_v = 1000$ and 10000 respectively and for $\alpha_{inf} = 0.01$ and 0.10, separately for each value of α_{known}. The histograms on the left side show the fraction of solutions v found by the evolutionary algorithm (vertical axis) for which the improvement $\Delta(v)$ in a given range (horizontal axis) was obtained with respect to the corresponding mass vaccination. Graphs on the right side show the fraction of solutions v (vertical axis) for which the improvement $\Delta(v)$ was not larger than $\Delta(v)'$ (horizontal axis). Bars near the value of $\Delta(v) = 1$ represent cases when the optimized targeted vaccination scheme resulted in the same number of infections as the mass vaccination scheme with the same number of vaccinated vertices $f_1(v)$. On the other hand, bars at values of $\Delta(v) > 1$ represent cases when the optimization resulted in better vaccination plans than just the mass vaccination.

Plots in Figs. 3 and 4 show that smaller values of α_{known} make the problem difficult for the optimization algorithm. The bars at $\Delta(v) = 1$ in the histograms are higher and the curves are steeper for smaller values of α_{known}. This indicates that for smaller values of α_{known} it becomes more difficult for the optimization algorithm to find solutions v with $f_2^{(targ)}(v) < f_2^{(mass)}(v)$ resulting in $\Delta(v) > 1$. This observation can be confirmed by comparing values presented in Tables 1 and 2. Values in the column corresponding to $R_a = 0$ (no infected individuals created randomly) unequivocally show that the improvement obtained in the optimization process diminishes with decreasing α_{known}. For $N_v = 5000$ and 10000, and $\alpha_{known} = 0.1$ and 0.2 the optimized targeted vaccination scheme can even perform worse than the mass vaccination. This can be attributed to the fact that when only a small fraction of the actually infected individuals is used in the

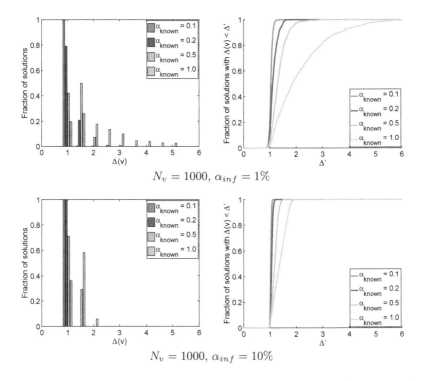

$$N_v = 1000,\ \alpha_{inf} = 1\%$$

$$N_v = 1000,\ \alpha_{inf} = 10\%$$

Fig. 3. Fraction of solutions v found by the evolutionary algorithm (vertical axis) for which the improvement $\Delta(v)$ in a given range (horizontal axis) was obtained with respect to the corresponding mass vaccination scenario ($N_v = 1000$).

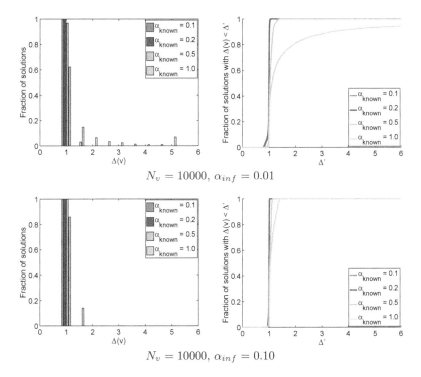

Fig. 4. Fraction of solutions v found by the evolutionary algorithm (vertical axis) for which the improvement $\Delta(v)$ in a given range (horizontal axis) was obtained with respect to the corresponding mass vaccination scenario ($N_v = 10000$).

simulations these simulations present a much less severe epidemic than the real one (see Fig. 5). Then, the optimizer prefers solutions with fewer vaccinations, good for smaller outbreaks, but inadequate for a much larger one.

From the results presented above it can be concluded that the optimization of vaccinations is beneficial, but detailed knowledge of the initially infected individuals may be required for the optimization to be successful. In order to compensate for the non-diagnosed cases of the disease, artificially generated cases are added to the simulations. The number of the additional cases is equal to the number of known cases $N_{known} = \alpha_{known} \cdot \alpha_{inf} \cdot N_v$ multiplied by the factor R_a. Figure 5 shows Pareto fronts obtained during the optimization with $\alpha_{known} = 0.1$ and 1.0, and with $R_a = 0$ and 5.

The Pareto front for $\alpha_{known} = 1.0$, $R_a = 0$ (blue) is the realistic one, that is, the one obtained for all initial disease cases known and none artificially generated. The Pareto front for $\alpha_{known} = 0.1$, $R_a = 0$ (red) is overly optimistic, because many disease cases are not taken into account when solutions are evaluated using simulations. The Pareto front for $\alpha_{known} = 0.1$, $R_a = 5$ (green) is much closer to the real one, because artificially generated disease cases make up for the unknown ones, at least partially. On the other hand, when all the

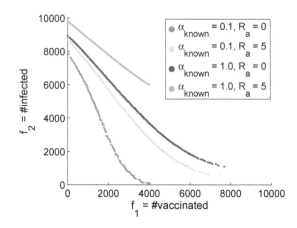

Fig. 5. Pareto fronts obtained during optimization with $\alpha_{known} = 0.1$ and 1.0, and with $R_a = 0$ and 5. (Color figure online)

disease cases are already known ($\alpha_{known} = 1.0$), but we add artificial disease cases nevertheless ($R_a = 5$), the Pareto front (orange) is overly pessimistic.

The final evaluation of the solutions found by the optimizer was performed using all the initial cases of the disease (both known and unknown) in order to simulate how these solutions would work in a real epidemic. From these real Pareto fronts hypervolume indicator was calculated. Table 1 presents results for the initial outbreak fraction $\alpha_{inf} = 0.01$ with the fraction of known disease cases $\alpha_{known} = 0.1, 0.2, 0.5$ and 1.0. Results obtained with the artificial disease cases multiplier $R_a = 0, 1, 2$ and 5 are compared. Table 2 presents results for the initial outbreak fraction $\alpha_{inf} = 0.10$.

Each value in the "Relative hypervolume change" column is calculated from tests on 30 problem instances with given values of N_v, α_{inf}, α_{known} in which simulations were performed using $R_a \cdot N_{known}$ artificially generated disease cases. The value is the median ratio between the hypervolume attained by the optimized solutions and solutions using the mass vaccination scheme. If the value is above 1.0 it means that the targeted vaccination produced larger hypervolume and thus a better Pareto front than the mass vaccination scheme. Value below 1.0 indicates that the optimizer did not produce a better Pareto front than the mass vaccination scheme. In order to statistically verify the results a Wilcoxon statistical test was performed on the results obtained for 30 problem instances which produced each median shown in the table. Results of the statistical testing are summarized in the column "Statistical significance w.r.t. mass vaccinations". If the calculated median is larger than 1.0 and the p-value obtained in the statistical test is not larger than 0.01 the symbol   is used to indicate a statistically significant improvement with respect to mass vaccinations. If the calculated median is smaller than 1.0 and the p-value obtained in the statistical test is not larger than 0.01 the symbol – is used to indicate a statistically significant worsening of the results with respect to mass vaccinations.

Table 1. Median relative change in the hypervolume for varying values of R_a. Initial outbreak fraction $\alpha_{inf} = 1\%$.

N_v	α_{known}	Relative hypervolume change				Statistical significance w.r.t. mass vaccinations				Statistical significance w.r.t. $R_a = 0$		
		$R_a=0$	$R_a=1$	$R_a=2$	$R_a=5$	$R_a=0$	$R_a=1$	$R_a=2$	$R_a=5$	$R_a=1$	$R_a=2$	$R_a=5$
1000	0.1	1.03038	1.04797	1.02195	1.01621				○	○	○	○
	0.2	1.07426	1.07191	1.08646	1.08596					○	○	○
	0.5	1.27560	1.28376	1.26180	1.20336					○		
	1.0	1.56273	1.45944	1.36449	1.23981							
1250	0.1	1.05720	1.05254	1.06644	1.07262					○	○	○
	0.2	1.09815	1.07282	1.10891	1.11645					○	○	○
	0.5	1.47489	1.43241	1.39121	1.26680					○		
	1.0	1.76882	1.59012	1.43712	1.30025							
1500	0.1	1.06242	1.09325	1.08951	1.12193					○	○	○
	0.2	1.12872	1.17781	1.21896	1.16958					○	○	○
	0.5	1.45181	1.43037	1.35225	1.26651							
	1.0	1.87563	1.67529	1.53455	1.36242							
1750	0.1	1.06354	1.07689	1.10458	1.07321					○	○	○
	0.2	1.16555	1.15163	1.17800	1.15094					○	○	○
	0.5	1.44326	1.40442	1.32503	1.22773							
	1.0	1.79990	1.57971	1.41697	1.28905							
2000	0.1	1.00577	0.99359	1.02918	1.03876	○	○	○		○	○	○
	0.2	1.15928	1.17403	1.16765	1.12480					○	○	○
	0.5	1.51157	1.43506	1.36149	1.24940							
	1.0	1.83255	1.59902	1.44911	1.30874							
5000	0.1	0.86113	0.85451	0.87382	0.92049					○	○	
	0.2	0.95608	0.95497	0.95905	0.98745				○	○	○	
	0.5	1.18669	1.12667	1.10486	1.07862							
	1.0	1.49199	1.27559	1.20099	1.12685							
10000	0.1	0.87416	0.88620	0.92703	0.94522					○		
	0.2	0.90431	0.93356	0.95223	0.97048							
	0.5	1.01865	1.01208	1.02275	1.02749					○	○	
	1.0	1.15795	1.09287	1.06896	1.05533							

If the p-value obtained in the statistical test is larger than 0.01 the symbol ○ is used to indicate that the difference between the optimized vaccination scheme and the mass vaccination scheme is not statistically significant. In the column "Statistical significance w.r.t. $R_a = 0$" a comparison is performed between the results obtained for $R_a = 1$, 2 and 5, and the results obtained for $R_a = 0$.

From the results presented in Tables 1 and 2 it can be concluded that evolutionary optimization produces better results than the mass vaccination scheme for instances up to $N_v = 2000$ even when only 10% of the initial disease cases are known ($\alpha_{known} = 0.1$) and when no disease cases are artificially generated ($R_a = 0.0$). However, for larger problem instances ($N_v = 5000$ and 10000) at least half of the initial cases of the disease have to be known ($\alpha_{known} \geq 0.5$) in order to produce results competitive with the mass vaccination scheme. Artificial generation of initial disease cases for the simulations seems to alleviate this problem to a certain extent, because for $\alpha_{known} = 0.1$ the results for $R_a = 5$ are overall better than for $R_a = 0$. Unfortunately this effect is accompanied by significant worsening of the results for $\alpha_{known} = 0.5$ and 1.0. These observations

Table 2. Median relative change in the hypervolume for varying values of R_a. Initial outbreak fraction $\alpha_{inf} = 10\%$.

N_v	α_{known}	Relative hypervolume change				Statistical significance w.r.t. mass vaccinations				Statistical significance w.r.t. $R_a = 0$		
		$R_a=0$	$R_a=1$	$R_a=2$	$R_a=5$	$R_a=0$	$R_a=1$	$R_a=2$	$R_a=5$	$R_a=1$	$R_a=2$	$R_a=5$
1000	0.1	1.08600	1.11978	1.11851	1.14652					o	o	
	0.2	1.16652	1.17257	1.17312	1.18536					o	o	o
	0.5	1.30521	1.24985	1.23312	1.20927					−	−	−
	1.0	1.38105	1.27104	1.23013	1.10445					−	−	−
1250	0.1	1.14430	1.13143	1.13418	1.16724					o	o	o
	0.2	1.25717	1.20756	1.21153	1.23373					−	−	o
	0.5	1.36285	1.28547	1.27181	1.23863					−	−	−
	1.0	1.42968	1.31663	1.27050	1.11842					−	−	−
1500	0.1	1.10309	1.10204	1.11359	1.12303					o	o	o
	0.2	1.17378	1.14599	1.15028	1.16856					−	−	o
	0.5	1.28663	1.23529	1.22677	1.19649					−	−	−
	1.0	1.35712	1.25994	1.21578	1.09628					−	−	−
1750	0.1	1.10573	1.10258	1.10538	1.12091					o	o	o
	0.2	1.17354	1.16648	1.16661	1.18555					o	o	o
	0.5	1.28270	1.22169	1.22562	1.19871					−	−	−
	1.0	1.35298	1.25990	1.21768	1.09890					−	−	−
2000	0.1	1.05959	1.07556	1.07146	1.11445					o	o	
	0.2	1.15095	1.13510	1.14612	1.16601					o	o	o
	0.5	1.25156	1.20874	1.19857	1.18017					−	−	−
	1.0	1.32577	1.23990	1.19762	1.08981					−	−	
5000	0.1	0.93636	0.97251	1.00170	1.04881	−	−	o				
	0.2	0.99553	1.03140	1.05830	1.09716	o						
	0.5	1.08812	1.10644	1.11318	1.09674							
	1.0	1.15849	1.12531	1.10199	1.04471					−		
10000	0.1	0.95674	0.97536	0.99635	1.03064	−	−	−				
	0.2	0.98163	1.01592	1.03494	1.05137	−						
	0.5	1.03901	1.05426	1.05802	1.04334							
	1.0	1.07588	1.06131	1.04670	1.01496					−		

can be explained by the fact that worse results produced by the optimizer for $\alpha_{known} = 0.1$ are caused by the simulated epidemic being less severe than the real one which makes the optimizer prefer solutions with fewer vaccinated individuals. This is remedied by adding artificially generated initial cases of the disease. On the other hand, the severity of the simulated epidemic for $\alpha_{known} = 1.0$ can be expected to match the real one and in such case adding artificially generated initial cases of the disease makes the optimizer choose solutions with more vaccinated individuals than necessary, thus producing worse results. Interestingly, for $\alpha_{inf} = 10\%$ the optimizer with $R_a = 5$ was the only one which produced results better than the mass vaccination scheme for all problem instance sizes and for all tested values of the α_{known} parameter. Admittedly, however, this improvement comes at the cost of worsening the results with respect to $R_a = 0$ in some cases. Nevertheless, in all tests for $\alpha_{inf} = 10\%$ the results obtained for $R_a = 5$ were better than the ones produced by the mass vaccination scheme and these improvements were statistically significant.

5   Conclusions

In this paper the multiobjective optimization of a targeted vaccination scheme was studied in the presence of non-diagnosed cases of a disease. It was observed that when all initial cases of the disease were known the optimized targeted vaccination scheme was better than the mass vaccination scheme. However, when only a fraction of initial cases was known, the performance of the optimizer deteriorated. To alleviate this problem an uncertainty-handling method was studied in this paper which added random infected individuals to the simulation of the epidemic outbreak. This modification improved the results in situations when the optimizer was badly affected by the lack of knowledge of the initial cases of the disease, however, it worsened the results when most of the disease cases were already known. Nevertheless, for larger initial fraction of infected individuals ($\alpha_{inf} = 0.1$) this modified optimization approach was the only one which consistently produced results statistically better than the ones obtained using the mass vaccination scheme. This is a very promising result. On the other hand, the results suggest that a more sophisticated mechanism may be needed, for example one based on the assessment of the fraction α_{known}, because adding many artificial cases ($R_a = 5$) helps counteracting the effects of limited knowledge when α_{known} is low, but deteriorates the results somewhat for $\alpha_{known} = 1$.

Acknowledgment. This work was supported by the Polish National Agency for Academic Exchange (NAWA) within the Bekker programme under grant PPN/BEK/2018/1/00430. Calculations have been carried out using resources provided by Wroclaw Centre for Networking and Supercomputing (http://wcss.pl), grant No. 407.

References

1. Antonioni, A., Bullock, S., Tomassini, M.: REDS: an energy-constrained spatial social network model. In: Lipson, H., Sayama, H., Rieffel, J., Risi, S., Doursat, R. (eds.) ALIFE 14: The Fourteenth International Conference on the Synthesis and Simulation of Living Systems. MIT Press (2014)
2. Bozzette, S.A., et al.: A model for a smallpox-vaccination policy. N. Engl. J. Med. **348**(5), 416–425 (2003)
3. Brauer, F.: Compartmental models in epidemiology. In: Brauer, F., van den Driessche, P., Wu, J. (eds.) Mathematical Epidemiology. Lecture Notes in Mathematics, vol. 1945, pp. 19–79. Springer, Heidelberg (2008). https://doi.org/10.1007/978-3-540-78911-6_2
4. Danila, R., Nika, M., Wilding, T., Knottenbelt, W.J.: Uncertainty in on-the-fly epidemic fitting. In: Horváth, A., Wolter, K. (eds.) EPEW 2014. LNCS, vol. 8721, pp. 135–148. Springer, Cham (2014). https://doi.org/10.1007/978-3-319-10885-8_10
5. Li, H., Zhang, Q.: Multiobjective optimization problems with complicated pareto sets, MOEA/D and NSGA-II. IEEE Trans. Evol. Comput. **13**(2), 284–302 (2009)
6. Li, S.L., et al.: Essential information: uncertainty and optimal control of Ebola outbreaks. Proc. Natl. Acad. Sci. **114**(22), 5659–5664 (2017)

7. Martcheva, M.: Introduction to epidemic modeling. In: Martcheva, M. (ed.) An Introduction to Mathematical Epidemiology. TAM, vol. 61, pp. 9–31. Springer, Boston (2015). https://doi.org/10.1007/978-1-4899-7612-3_2
8. Michalak, K.: The effects of asymmetric neighborhood assignment in the MOEA/D algorithm. Appl. Soft Comput. **25**, 97–106 (2014)
9. Michalak, K.: The Sim-EA algorithm with operator autoadaptation for the multiobjective firefighter problem. In: Ochoa, G., Chicano, F. (eds.) EvoCOP 2015. LNCS, vol. 9026, pp. 184–196. Springer, Cham (2015). https://doi.org/10.1007/978-3-319-16468-7_16
10. Nowzari, C., Preciado, V.M., Pappas, G.J.: Analysis and control of epidemics: a survey of spreading processes on complex networks. IEEE Control Syst. Mag. **36**(1), 26–46 (2016)
11. Zitzler, E., Thiele, L., Laumanns, M., Fonseca, C.M., da Fonseca, V.G.: Performance assessment of multiobjective optimizers: an analysis and review. IEEE Trans. Evol. Comput. **7**, 117–132 (2002)

Community Detection in Attributed Graphs with Differential Evolution

Clara Pizzuti$^{(\boxtimes)}$ ⓘ and Annalisa Socievole ⓘ

Institute for High Performance Computing and Networking (ICAR), National
Research Council of Italy (CNR), via P. Bucci 8-9C, 87036 Rende, CS, Italy
{clara.pizzuti,annalisa.socievole}@icar.cnr.it

Abstract. Detecting communities in networks, by taking into account
not only node connectivity but also the features characterizing nodes, is
becoming a research activity with increasing interest because of the information nowadays available for many real-world networks of attributes
associated with nodes. In this paper, we investigate the capability of
differential evolution to discover groups of nodes which are both densely
connected and share similar features. Experiments on two real-world networks with attributes for which the ground-truth division is known show
that differential evolution is an effective approach to uncover communities.

Keywords: Attributed networks · Community detection · Complex
networks · Differential evolution

1 Introduction

Complex networks are recognized as a powerful formalism to represent and study
the relationships of the objects constituting real-world systems. In the last two
decades, a lot of effort has been focused on studying network structure for identifying communities, i.e. groups of nodes densely connected with few external
connections. More recently, however, because of the availability of many real-
world networks whose nodes are enriched with attributes, providing important
information characterizing the network, the interest of researchers in investigating new methods to uncover community structure, taking into account the links
among nodes as well as their attributes, has notably increased. In fact, attribute
data characterizing each node coupled with relationship data between nodes has
been shown to provide a better understanding of community structure [1].

In the last years many methods to detect communities in attributed graphs
have been proposed [2]. Some of these approaches compute the similarity, with
respect to a defined function, between couples of nodes and consider this value as
a weight on the corresponding edge. The communities on the resulting weighted
graph are then obtained by using a community detection method for weighted
graphs [3–5]. Some methods combine structure and attributes in different ways

© Springer Nature Switzerland AG 2020
P. A. Castillo et al. (Eds.): EvoApplications 2020, LNCS 12104, pp. 323–335, 2020.
https://doi.org/10.1007/978-3-030-43722-0_21

[6, 7]. Other methods build an attribute-augmented graph by extending the original graph with new nodes representing the attributes [8–10].

In this paper, a method for finding communities in attributed graphs, named @NetDE, which is based on *Differential Evolution (DE)*, is proposed. The method optimizes a fitness function derived from the *unified distance measure* of Papadopoulos et al. [11], which simultaneously combines the similarity between nodes and their connections. The communities returned by the method have nodes densely connected and homogeneous attribute values. The method is compared with state-of-the-art methods on two real-world networks for which the true network division is known. The experiments show that @NetDE, though has the same accuracy of other two evolutionary based approaches, it is much more efficient since the same results are obtained by using a much smaller population size and few iterations than the other evolutionary methods. Moreover, when compared with other state-of-the-art methods, @NetDE sensibly outperforms these contestant methods.

The paper is organized as follows. In the next section we introduce the problem of community detection in attributed networks. In Sect. 3 a brief description of some methods proposed in the literature for attributed networks is given. In Sect. 4 the fitness function is described. In Sect. 5 a basic introduction to the Differential Evolution (DE) method is given and the DE-based algorithm @NetDE is described, along with the chromosome representation adopted by the method. Section 6 describes the two networks used for evaluating the methods, the measures adopted to evaluate them, and the results obtained by all the methods. Section 7 concludes the paper and discusses future developments.

2   Problem Definition

In the following, the definition of attributed graph and the concept of community over this kind of graph are given.

Definition. An *attributed graph* is a 4-tuple $G = (V, E, A, F)$ where $V = \{v_1, v_2, ..., v_N\}$ is a set of N nodes, $E = \{(v_i, v_j) : 1 \leq i, j \leq N, i \neq j\}$ is a set of M edges, $A = \{\alpha_1, \alpha_2, ..., \alpha_{\mathcal{A}}\}$ is the set of numerical and categorical attributes (features), and $F = \{a_1, a_2, ..., a_{\mathcal{A}}\}$ is a set of functions. The functions $a_\alpha : V \to D_\alpha$, $1 \leq \alpha \leq \mathcal{A}$, where D_α is the domain of attribute α, assign to each node $v \in V$ a vector of feature values.

The problem of community detection in attributed graphs consists in finding a partition $\mathcal{C} = \{C_1, ..., C_k\}$ of the nodes of V such that intra-cluster density is high and inter-cluster density is low, and nodes in the same community are highly similar, while nodes of different communities are rather dissimilar.

3   Related Work

In the last years a lot of methods to detect communities in attributed graphs have been proposed [2]. In the following we review some of the most recent approaches used for comparing the quality of the results obtained by @NetDE with respect to other state-of-the-art methods.

SA-Cluster [8] is an approach which introduced the concept of attribute-augmented graph, that is the original graph is extended with new nodes representing the attributes. An attribute vertex is connected with a graph vertex if this node has that attribute value. A unified distance measure between nodes is computed by combining structural closeness and attribute similarity and using a neighborhood random walk model on the graph augmented with attributes.

Jia et al. [9] proposed the method *kNN-enhance* which builds a *kNN* enhanced network by adding to the original network the *kNN* graph of node attributes, i.e. the graph of the k nearest neighbors of each node. The original graph is enriched with the links between nearest neighbors, if they have common node attributes. The method exploits an approach proposed in [12] to select the number of communities and the centers of these communities, and uses the two methods *kNN*-nearest and *kNN*-Kmeans to cluster nodes in groups. *kNN*-nearest assigns a node to the cluster of its nearest neighbor, while *kNN*-Kmeans clusters nodes analogously to the K-means method.

AGGMR [10] builds an augmented graph where, instead of adding dummy vertices corresponding to attribute values like *SA-Cluster*, it summarizes these values in attribute centers by clustering these attribute vertices. The attribute relationships are then transformed into edges in the augmented network. Finally, the new network is partitioned by using a modularity based method [13].

Regarding methods based on evolutionary computation, He and Chan [14] proposed *ECDA*, an algorithm that optimizes a fitness function based on the number of significant connections between nodes, where the significance is determined by a statistical measure based on the frequency of occurrences of edges connecting nodes labelled with the same topic.

Li *et al.* [15] proposed *MOEA-SA*, a multiobjective evolutionary algorithm which maximizes the concept of modularity of Newman and Girvan [13] as objective for obtaining dense link connections, and the attribute similarity function S_A, to have high values of feature node similarity. In [16], the method @NetGA, based on Genetic Algorithms, which introduces a fitness function based on the measure proposed by Papadopoulos et al. [11] is proposed. More recently, the multiobjective method MOGA-@Net, that optimizes both the structural quality as well as the node similarity has been proposed [17]. To maximize the first objective, three well known measures, modularity, conductance, and community score, are investigated. The second objective of feature homogeneity inside the same community is defined according to similarity measures between attributes, depending on the attribute type.

In the experimental result section we compare the differential evolution based method @NetDE with the described approaches and show the very good performance of the proposed approach.

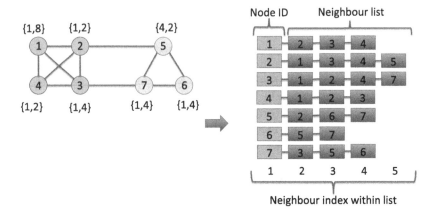

Fig. 1. A toy attributed network of 7 nodes with the adjacency list.

4   Clustering Unified Distance Measure

The *clustering unified distance measure* is a measure used in [16] as fitness function to minimize by a Genetic Algorithm to detect community structure in attributed networks. The measure is based on the *unified distance measure*, introduced by Papadopoulos et al. [11] that considers the graph structure and the node attributes, and adapted for Genetic Algorithms. This measure combines the two functions of *similar connectivity* and *attribute distance* which compute the dissimilarity of each couple of nodes with respect to the structure of the network and the information associated with nodes, respectively.

Given an attributed graph $G(V, E, A, F)$, the *similar connectivity* $SC(i, j)$ between the two nodes i and j measures how dissimilar they are with respect to their shared neighbors. Low values mean that the two nodes i and j should be grouped together. It is defined as

$$SC(i, j) = \frac{1}{N} \sum_{k=1}^{N} [w(i, k) - w(j, k)]^2 \tag{1}$$

where

$$w(i, j) = \begin{cases} 1 & if \ (i = j) \ or \ (i, j) \in E \\ 0 & otherwise \end{cases} \tag{2}$$

Consider the toy network in Fig. 1. The *similar connectivity* $SC(1, 3)$ between the two nodes 1 and 3 is computed as:

$$\begin{aligned}
\mathbf{SC(1, 3)} &= 1/7 * [(w(1, 1) - w(3, 1))^2 + (w(1, 2) - w(3, 2))^2 \\
&\quad + (w(1, 3) - w(3, 3))^2 + (w(1, 4) - w(3, 4))^2 + (w(1, 5) - w(3, 5))^2 \\
&\quad + (w(1, 6) - w(3, 6))^2 + (w(1, 7) - w(3, 7))^2)] \\
&= (1/7 * ((1 - 1)^2 + (1 - 1)^2 + (1 - 1)^2 + (1 - 1)^2 \\
&\quad + (0 - 0)^2 + (0 - 0)^2 + (0 - 1)^2)) = 0.1429
\end{aligned}$$

Table 1. Similar connectivity matrix of the toy network of Fig. 1.

	1	2	3	4	5	6	7
1	0	0.1429	0.1429	0	0.8571	1.0000	0.8571
2		0	0.2857	0.1429	0.7143	0.8571	0.7143
3			0	0.1429	0.7143	0.8571	0.7143
4				0	0.8571	1.0000	0.8571
5					0	0.1429	0.2857
6						0	0.1429
7							0

and that one between nodes 3 and 7 as

$$
\begin{aligned}
SC(3,7) &= 1/7 * [(w(3,1) - w(7,1))^2 + (w(3,2) - w(7,2))^2 \\
&+ (w(3,3) - w(7,3))^2 + (w(3,4) - w(7,4))^2 \\
&+ (w(3,5) - w(7,5))^2 + (w(3,6) - w(7,6))^2 \\
&+ (w(3,7) - w(7,7))^2)] \\
&= 1/7 * [(1-0)^2 + (1-0)^2 + (1-1)^2 + (1-0)^2 + (0-1)^2 \\
&+ (0--1)^2 + (1-1)^2)] = 0.7143
\end{aligned}
$$

Thus $SC(1,3) < SC(3,7)$, as expected, since node 3 shares the common neighbor nodes 2 and 3 with node 1, and no neighbors with node 7, then 3 and 7 are more dissimilar than 3 and 1. Table 1 reports the *similar connectivity* matrix of the network. We can notice that there is no dissimilarity between nodes 1 and 4 because their links are exactly the same.

The *attribute distance* between two nodes measures how dissimilar they are with respect to their attribute values. It is computed as:

$$
AD(i,j) = \sum_{\alpha \in A} W_\alpha \cdot \delta_\alpha(i,j), \quad \sum_{\alpha \in A} W_\alpha = 1 \tag{3}
$$

where W_α is the weight of attribute α, and $\delta_\alpha(i,j)$ is the attribute distance between nodes i and j for attribute α. For numerical attributes scaled in the interval $[0,1]$, $\delta_\alpha(i,j) = [a_\alpha(i) - a_\alpha(j)]^2$, while, for the categorical attributes

$$
\delta_\alpha(i,j) = \begin{cases} 0 & if \quad a_\alpha(i) = a_\alpha(j) \\ 1 & otherwise \end{cases} \tag{4}
$$

Consider again the network depicted in Fig. 1. The *attribute distance* between nodes 1 and 3, where the attributes values have been scaled in the interval $[0,1]$ and assuming equal weights of the attributes, is computed as

$$
AD(1,3) = 0.5 * \delta_{\alpha_1}(1,3) + 0.5 * \delta_{\alpha_2}(1,3) = 0.5 * 0 + 0.5 * (1-0.5)^2 = 0.1250
$$

while between nodes 3 and 7

$$
AD(3,7) = 0.5 * \delta_{\alpha_1}(3,7) + 0.5 * \delta_{\alpha_2}(3,7) = 0.5 * 0 + 0.5 * 0 = 0
$$

Table 2. Attribute distance matrix of the toy network of Fig. 1.

	1	2	3	4	5	6	7
1	0	0.2812	0.1250	0.2812	0.3516	0.1250	0.1250
2		0	0.0312	0	0.0703	0.0312	0.0312
3			0	0.0312	0.1016	0	0
4				0	0.0703	0.0312	0.0312
5					0	0.1016	0.1016
6						0	0
7							0	0

The *unified distance measure (udm)* combines the *attribute distance* (AD) and the *similar connectivity* (SC) between two nodes as follows:

$$d(i, j) = W_{attr} \cdot AD(i, j) + W_{links} \cdot SC(i, j) \tag{5}$$

where W_{attr} and W_{links} are weights representing the importance of attributes and edges, respectively.

The unified distance measure between nodes 1 and 3, giving equal weights to attributes and links, is

$$\mathbf{d(1, 3)} = W_{attr} * AD(1, 3) + W_{links} * SC(1, 3) = 0.5 * 0.1250 + 0.5 * 0.1429 = 0.1339$$

and that one between nodes 3 and 7 as

$$\mathbf{d(3, 7)} = W_{attr} * AD(3, 7) + W_{links} * SC(3, 7) = 0.5 * 0 + 0.5 * 0.7143 = 0.3571$$

Thus $d(1, 3) < d(3, 7)$ as expected. In fact, node 3, even if having the same attribute values of node 7, is more densely connected with node 1, sharing neighbors 2 and 4. Table 2 reports the *attribute distance* between all the pairs of nodes of the toy network.

Given a network division $\mathcal{C} = \{C_1, \ldots, C_k\}$, the *clustering unified distance measure cudm($\mathcal{C}$)* of the solution $\mathcal{C}$ is defined as

$$cudm(\mathcal{C}) = \frac{1}{k} \sum_{C \in \mathcal{C}} \sum_{\{i,j\} \in C \ i \neq j} d(i, j) \tag{6}$$

where k is the number of communities of the solution $\mathcal{C}$, i and j are nodes of a community $C \in \mathcal{C}$ and $d(i, j)$ is the *unified distance measure* between nodes i and j.

5   A Differential Evolution Based CD Method

In this section we first recall the basic principles of differential evolution and then describe the method based on DE for the detection of communities.

The basic schema to solve a problem with differential evolution consists of four steps: initialization, mutation, crossover, and selection [18]. A population $P = \{\boldsymbol{x}_1, \ldots, \boldsymbol{x}_{nPop}\}$ of $nPop$ N-dimensional target vectors is generated at random. Each target vector $\boldsymbol{x}_i^t$, at a generic generation t, generates a *mutant* vector by applying the mutation operator. The simplest operator is the *DE/rand/1*. The mutant vector

$$\boldsymbol{v}_i^t = \boldsymbol{x}_{r1}^t + F(\boldsymbol{x}_{r2}^t - \boldsymbol{x}_{r3}^t)$$

where $F \in [0, 1]$ is a scaling factor, is generated by combining three parameter vectors $\boldsymbol{x}_{r1}^t$, $\boldsymbol{x}_{r2}^t$, $\boldsymbol{x}_{r3}^t$, selected at random from the current population.

Many other operators have been defined. In this paper we use the *DE/current-to-rand/1* operator which computes the mutant vector by using the current target vector $\boldsymbol{x}_i^t$, besides the three random parameter vectors, as follows:

$$\boldsymbol{v}_i^t = \boldsymbol{x}_i^t + F * (\boldsymbol{x}_{r1}^t - \boldsymbol{x}_i^t) + F(\boldsymbol{x}_{r2}^t - \boldsymbol{x}_{r3}^t)$$

After mutation, the binomial crossover operator generates the trial vector $\boldsymbol{u}_i^t$ from the mutant vector $\boldsymbol{v}_i^t$ as

$$u_{i,j}^t = \begin{cases} v_{i,j}^t & if \ rand_j \leq CR \ or \ j = j_{rand} \\ x_{i,j}^t & otherwise \end{cases} \tag{7}$$

where $u_{i,j}^t$, $x_{i,j}^t$, and $v_{i,j}^t$ are the jth dimension of $\boldsymbol{u}_i^t$, $\boldsymbol{x}_i^t$, and $\boldsymbol{v}_i^t$, respectively, $rand_j$ is a random number between 0 and 1, CR is the crossover control parameter, j_{rand} is a random number between 1 and N. Finally, the target vector x_i^{t+1} at the $(t+1)th$ generation is obtained by applying the selection between $\boldsymbol{u}_i^t$ and $\boldsymbol{x}_i^t$:

$$x_i^{t+1} = \begin{cases} u_i^t & if \ f(u_i^t) \leq f(x_i^t) \\ x_i^t & otherwise \end{cases} \tag{8}$$

where f is the fitness function to optimize.

In order to detect communities, the differential evolution based method needs to define the representation of the problem, the fitness function to optimize, and the operators to use. Regarding the representation, it is worth pointing out that we have to deal with a discrete problem, where each target vector is a vector of N dimensions, corresponding to the N nodes of the graph.

@NetDE uses the *Indexed locus-based* representation, analogously to [19,20]. This representation is based on the *Relative Position Indexing* strategy [21], proposed for combinatorial problems. In this representation, the neighbors of each node are enumerated, as determined by the adjacency list of the graph G, i.e. the list of nodes which associates each vertex in the graph with the collection of its neighboring vertices. Then, to connect i and j, instead of directly using the identifier j of one of the neighbors of node i, the relative position of j is used.

Consider the network of Fig. 1 with the associated adjacency list. In Fig. 2 the locus-based representation of the network division in the two communities $\{1, 2, 3, 4\}, \{5, 6, 7\}$ and the corresponding indexed representation are shown. For instance, in the locus-based representation node 5 is connected with node 6, in

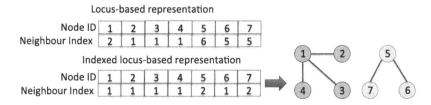

Fig. 2. Locus-based and Indexed locus-based representation of the network division $\{1, 2, 3, 4\}, \{5, 6, 7\}$ for the toy network of Fig. 1.

the indexed one, 6 is substituted with 2 since 6 is the second neighbor of 5, as shown in the adjacency list.

The fitness function minimized by the @NetDE method is the *cumd* measure, described in the previous section. As already explained, this measure allows to obtain a community division that takes into account both the similarity of node features, as well as the connections shared by pairs of nodes inside the network structure.

The method @NetDE receives in input the graph $G = (V, E, A, F)$, the weighting factors W_{attr} and W_{links} which give a score to attributes and links, respectively, and an importance weight to each attribute W_α. Then it performs the following steps:

1. for a fixed number of iterations, run the DE based method on G by using *cumd* as fitness function to optimize, the *DE/current-to-rand/1* as mutation operator, and the binomial crossover;
2. return the partition $\mathcal{C} = \{C_1, \ldots, C_k\}$ corresponding to the solution with the lowest fitness value $cumd(\mathcal{C})$;
3. merge a community C_i with a neighboring community C_j if the number of connections from nodes belonging to C_i to nodes of C_j is higher than the number of links among nodes inside C_i.

In the next section, we execute @NetDE on two real-world networks and compare it with other state-of-the-art methods.

6   Experimental Evaluation

We performed experiments to evaluate @NetDE on two real-world networks with attributes for which the ground-truth division is known. The algorithm has been implemented in Matlab 2015b by using the Global Optimization Toolbox. For each simulation, we assigned equal weight to attributes and links, thus setting $W_{attr} = W_{links} = 0.5$, and also $W_\alpha = 1/\mathcal{A}, \forall \alpha$. We did not investigate different settings of the weights because this problem is beyond the scope of the paper. MOGA-@Net, @NetGA, and *MOEA-SA* have been executed for 200 generations with a population size of 300. @NetDE, instead, used a population of size 10 for 10 generations.

Table 3. Features of the real-world datasets.

Dataset	Graph type	Nodes	Edges	Attributes
Cora	Citation	2708	5429	1433
Citeseer	Citation	1787	3285	3703

6.1 Datasets[1]

Cora is a citation network of scientific publications. An edge between two nodes is a citation from a publication to another. The dictionary, consisting of a set of unique words, represents the attributes' domain of this network. If a word appears in the paper, the attribute for that word is set to 1, otherwise it is set to 0. Publications have been classified into seven categories: (1) neural networks, (2) rule learning, (3) reinforcement learning, (4) probabilistic methods, (5) theory, (6) genetic algorithms, and (7) case-based reasoning.

Citeseer is also a dataset of publication citations with each node belonging to one of the following six classes: (1) agents, (2) information retrieval (IR), (3) databases (DB), (4) artificial intelligence (AI), (5) human-computer interaction (HCI), and (6) machine-learning (ML).

Table 3 summarizes the characteristics of these two networks.

6.2 Evaluation Measures

To evaluate the solutions obtained by the method, we used the following evaluation measures.

Normalized Mutual Information (NMI). Let A and B be two different partitions of a network. The normalized mutual information $NMI(A,B)$ [22] of the two divisions A and B is defined as follows. Let C be the confusion matrix whose element C_{ij} is the number of nodes of community i of the partition A that are also in the community j of the partition B.

$$NMI(A,B) = \frac{-2\sum_{i=1}^{c_A}\sum_{j=1}^{c_B}C_{ij}log(C_{ij}N/C_{i.}C_{.j})}{\sum_{i=1}^{c_A}C_{i.}log(C_{i.}/N) + \sum_{j=1}^{c_B}C_{.j}log(C_{.j}/N)} \tag{9}$$

where c_A (c_B) is the number of groups in the partition A (B), $C_{i.}$ ($C_{.j}$) is the sum of the elements of C in row i (column j), and N is the number of nodes. If $A = B$, $NMI(A,B) = 1$. If A and B are completely different, $NMI(A,B) = 0$.

Accuracy. Let $l_t(i)$ and $l_p(i)$ be the ground truth community label and the predicted cluster label of node i, respectively. The accuracy is defined as

$$ACC = \sum_{i=1}^{N}\delta(l_t(i), l_p(i))/N$$

where $\delta(.)$ is the Kroenecker function and N the number of nodes.

---

[1] https://linqs.soe.ucsc.edu/.

F-measure. Let T be the vector of the ground truth labels of each node and P that of the predicted labels obtained by a method. Then

$$F - measure = \frac{2 \times precision \times recall}{precision + recall}$$

where $precision = | T \cap P | / | P |$ and $recall = | T \cap P | / | T |$, $| . |$ denotes the cardinality of the sets.

6.3   Results

We compared @NetDE with the two multiobjective methods MOGA-@Net [17] and *MOEA-SA* [15], the @NetGA method [16] based on Genetic Algorithms using the same fitness function, the augmented graph based methods *kNN-nearest* and *kNN-Kmeans* [9], *AGGMMR* [10], *SA-cluster* [8], the popular topological based method *Louvain* [23] which does not consider the attributes, and the classical *K-means* clustering method, which does not consider the network structure. The values of the evaluation metrics are those reported in the referenced papers, thus not all the indexes are available for all the methods.

Table 4. Comparison of different methods on the Cora network.

Method	Cora		
	Accuracy	NMI	F-measure
@NetDE	1	1	1
MOGA-@Net	1	1	1
@NetGA	1	1	1
MOEA-SA	–	0.46 (0.001)	–
kNN-nearest	0.4878	0.3464	0.4403
kNN-Kmeans	0.6662	0.4569	0.5014
AGGMMR	–	–	0.8238
SA-cluster	0.2637	0.1190	0.2825
Louvain	–	0.603	–
K-means	0.4136	0.2334	0.3068

Tables 4 and 5 clearly show the superiority of the methods based on evolutionary computation over the contestant approaches. In fact, they are able to obtain the ground-truth division for both *Cora* and *Citeseer* networks. It is worth pointing out that, though @NetDE, MOGA-@Net, and @NetGA obtain the same result, @NetDE is much more efficient that the other two methods since it is able to find the perfect solution with a very small population size and running for only few generations. For instance, @NetGA with the same parameters

Table 5. Comparison of different methods on the Citeseer network.

Method	Citeseer		
	Accuracy	NMI	F-measure
@NetDE	1	1	1
MOGA-@Net	1	1	1
@NetGA	1	1	1
MOEA-SA	–	0.35 (0.004)	–
kNN-nearest	0.4955	0.2518	0.3819
kNN-Kmeans	0.6301	0.3703	0.4749
K-means	0.5344	0.2712	0.3727
AGGMMR	–	–	0.7501
SA-cluster	0.2325	0.0466	0.2984
Louvain	–	0.534	–

of @NetDE obtains an NMI value of just 0.182. Thus, the DE-based approach is promising on networks of large size.

7   Conclusion

Differential Evolution is a popular evolutionary algorithm because of its capabilities in successfully solving many real-world problems. The method proposed in this paper for detecting community structure over attributed graphs, where nodes are characterized by a set of features, confirmed its ability in dealing also with this kind of problem. A comparison with recently proposed methods on real-world networks with attributes and for which the ground-truth division is known, has highlighted the capability of differential evolution to detect more accurate divisions than all the other methods, and equal the performance when compared with the two evolutionary methods MOGA-@Net and @NetGA. However, @NetDE is much more efficient since it obtains the same results by using very few generations and small populations. Further investigation, however, is necessary for better understanding the advantages of @NetDE with respect to the other two evolutionary techniques. Future work aims at experimenting the method on other real-world attributed networks and on synthetic networks. Moreover, since the reported experiments used the $DE/current$-to-$rand/1$ mutation operator, other kinds of operators will be considered.

References

1. Newman, M.E.J., Clauset, A.: Structure and inference in annotated networks. Nat. Commun. **7**(11863), 1–11 (2016)
2. Bothorel, C., Cruz, J.D., Magnani, M., Micenkova, B.: Clustering attributed graphs: models, measures and methods. Netw. Sci. **3**(03), 408–444 (2015)

3. Neville, J., Adler, M., Jensen, D.: Clustering relational data using attribute and link information. In: Proceedings of the Text Mining and Link Analysis Workshop, 18th International Joint Conference on Artificial Intelligence, pp. 9–15 (2003)
4. Steinhaeuser, K., Chawla, N.V.: Community detection in a large real-world social network. In: Liu, H., Salerno, J.J., Young, M.J. (eds.) Social Computing, Behavioral Modeling, and Prediction, pp. 168–175. Springer, Boston (2008). https://doi.org/10.1007/978-0-387-77672-9_19
5. Cruz, J.D., Bothorel, C., Poulet, F.: Semantic clustering of social networks using points of view. In: CORIA, pp. 175–182 (2011)
6. Combe, D., Largeron, C., Egyed-Zsigmond, E., Géry, M.: Combining relations and text in scientific network clustering. In: 2012 IEEE/ACM International Conference on Advances in Social Networks Analysis and Mining (ASONAM), pp. 1248–1253. IEEE (2012)
7. Dang, T., Viennet, E.: Community detection based on structural and attribute similarities. In: International Conference on Digital Society (ICDS), pp. 7–12 (2012)
8. Zhou, Y., Cheng, H., Yu, J.X.: Graph clustering based on structural/attribute similarities. Proc. VLDB Endowment **2**(1), 718–729 (2009)
9. Jia, C., Li, Y., Carson, M.B., Wang, X., Yu, J.: Node attribute-enhanced community detection in complex networks. Sci. Rep. **2626**(7), 1–15 (2017)
10. Zhe, C., Sun, A., Xiao, X.: Community detection on large complex attribute network. In: International Conference on Knowledge Discovery and Data Mining, pp. 2041–2049 (2019)
11. Papadopoulos, A., Pallis, G., Dikaiakos, M.D.: Weighted clustering of attributed multi-graphs. Computing **99**(9), 813–840 (2016). https://doi.org/10.1007/s00607-016-0526-5
12. Li, Y., Jia, C., Yu, J.: Benchmark graphs for testing community detection algorithms. Phys. A: Stat. Mech. Appl. **438**, 321–334 (2015)
13. Newman, M.E., Girvan, M.: Finding and evaluating community structure in networks. Phys. Rev. E **69**(2), 026113 (2004)
14. He, T., Chan, K.C.C.: Evolutionary community detection in social networks. In: Proceedings of the IEEE Congress on Evolutionary Computation, CEC 2014, Beijing, China, 6–11 July 2014, pp. 1496–1503 (2014)
15. Li, Z., Liu, J., Wu, K.: A multiobjective evolutionary algorithm based on structural and attribute similarities for community detection in attributed networks. IEEE Trans. Cybern. **48**(7), 1963–1976 (2018)
16. Pizzuti, C., Socievole, A.: A genetic algorithm for community detection in attributed graphs. In: Sim, K., Kaufmann, P. (eds.) EvoApplications 2018. LNCS, vol. 10784, pp. 159–170. Springer, Cham (2018). https://doi.org/10.1007/978-3-319-77538-8_12
17. Pizzuti, C., Socievole, A.: Multiobjective optimization and local merge for clustering attributed graphs. IEEE Trans. Cybern. 1–13 (2019). https://doi.org/10.1109/TCYB.2018.2889413
18. Das, S., Suganthan, P.N.: Differential evolution: a survey of the state-of-the-art. IEEE Trans. Evol. Comput. **15**(1), 4–31 (2011)
19. Sun, H., Ma, S., Wangand, Z.: A community detection algorithm using differential evolution. In: IEEE International Conference on Computers and Communications, ICCC, Chengdu, China, 13–16 December 2017, pp. 1515–1519 (2017)
20. Pizzuti, C., Socievole, A.: Self-adaptive differential evolution for community detection. In: Sixth International Conference on Social Networks Analysis, Management and Security (SNAMS-2019), Granada, Spain, 22–25 October 2019, pp. 110–117 (2019)

21. Onwubolu, G.C. (ed.): Differential Evolution: A Handbook for Global Permutation-Based Combinatorial Optimization. Studies in Computational Intelligence. Springer, Heidelberg (2009). https://doi.org/10.1007/978-3-540-92151-6
22. Danon, L., Diaz-Guilera, A., Duch, J., Arenas, A.: Comparing community structure identification. J. Stat. Mech. Theor. Exp. **2005**(09), P09008 (2005)
23. Blondel, V.D., Guillaume, J.L., Lambiotte, R., Lefebvre, E.: Fast unfolding of communities in large networks. J. Stat. Mech. Theor. Exp. **2008**(10), P10008 (2008)

.

Applications of Deep Bioinspired Algorithms

Fake News Detection Using Time Series and User Features Classification

Marialaura Previti[1], Victor Rodriguez-Fernandez[2(✉)], David Camacho[3],
Vincenza Carchiolo[4], and Michele Malgeri[1]

[1] Dip. di Ingegneria Elettrica, Elettronica e Informatica (DIEEI),
Università degli Studi di Catania, Catania, Italy
`marialaura.previti@unict.it, michele.malgeri@dieei.unict.it`
[2] Universidad Autónoma de Madrid, Madrid, Spain
`victor.rodriguezf@uam.es`
[3] Departamento de Sistemas Informaticos,
Technical University of Madrid, Madrid, Spain
`david.camacho@upm.es`
[4] Dip. di Matematica e Informatica (DMI),
Università degli Studi di Catania, Catania, Italy
`vincenza.carchiolo@unict.it`

Abstract. In a scenario where more and more individuals use online social network platforms as an instrument to propagate news without any control, it is necessary to design and implement new methods and techniques that guarantee the veracity of the disseminated news. In this paper, we propose a method to classify true and false news, commonly known as fake news, which exploits time series-based features extracted from the evolution of news, and features from the users involved in the news spreading. Applying our methodology over a real Twitter dataset of precategorized true and false news, we have obtained an accuracy of 84.61% in 10-fold cross-validation, and proved experimentally that all the selected features are relevant for this classification task.

Keywords: Fake news detection · Random forest classification · Time series features · User information features

1 Introduction

In the last decades, due to the increasing amount of time spent by a large part of world population interacting through Online Social Networks (OSNs), more and more individuals tend to seek out and consume news from OSNs, instead of using traditional mass media, such as newspapers and television. There are several reasons for this change of behaviors:

- in cases where modern communication technologies are unavailable, OSNs users, not belonging to any category of journalists, can provide news in real time through these platforms (*gatewatching* [1]), often helping press agencies to collect information in order to provide breaking news. For example, they allow identifying the outbreaks of infectious diseases in real time [2], detecting the spread of seasonal epidemics, such as influenza, in order to organize

© Springer Nature Switzerland AG 2020
P. A. Castillo et al. (Eds.): EvoApplications 2020, LNCS 12104, pp. 339–353, 2020.
https://doi.org/10.1007/978-3-030-43722-0_22

containment measures [3–5], detecting and tracking discussion communities on vaccination [6], or detecting information about natural disasters in order to manage rescue and promptly warn affected populations [7–9];

- the access to OSNs is fast, always available and less expensive than traditional mass media and help users to select topics they are interested in;
- through OSNs, interactions with news (through like and repost) and with other users interested in the topic of posts (through exchange of comments) are possible. Instead, in traditional mass media communication is unidirectional.

Albeit these advantages, the quality of news in social media is often low, due to the lack of authoritative sources that check their veracity. This helps malicious users to propagate false news over the network. Moreover, the possibility of choice among many sources of information conducts some groups of individuals to seek out sources of information which reinforce their pre-existing point of view about a specific topic, generating the *echo chambers phenomenon* [10]. In this context, the credibility of news spreaders and the frequency of exposure to the same piece of news play an important role.

The intent of false (or *fake*) news is to manipulate news in order to add false information with purpose to create a damage (political, economical or reputational among others) to an adverse counterpart or to perform surreptitious advertising to their products or personal characteristics in order to gain an advantage in comparison with competitors. In order to help big companies and political parties in this intent, often behind OSNs accounts there are not physical users, but bots and cyborg users whose sole purpose is to propagate an idea reaching as many users as possible in a specific category of users [11].

A short and complete definition of fake news was provided by Allcott and Gentzkow [12], they established that fake news is *news intentionally and verifiably false that could mislead readers*. Typically, fake news is spread over OSNs in form of rumors, i.e., groups of posts related to the same topic propagate by different users and reposted several times.

In such a wide scenario with so many facets, it is necessary to find strategies to stop the proliferation of fake news on OSNs and, for this purpose, the early identification in true or false is a fundamental step. We propose a method to classify rumors exploiting their temporal evolution and information about user involved in rumor spreading.

The initial decision to exploit the temporal evolution of the rumors in classification was taken thanks to the studies done in [13], because the authors have shown that the temporal evolution of the true and false news are different, but at this starting point we added the information about users involved in each rumor, because from a similar study conducted on two OSNs dataset [14], the only use of time series produces poor results in the early stages of propagation that improve when more temporal information is acquired, while the information about users (e.g., user followers, followees and engagement) contains previous clues on the diffusion capacities of the involved individuals, making our method effective from the initial stages of propagation. Moreover, but not less important, our method does not require the use of tweet texts, so it requires reduced computing capacity to calculate the used features and reduced storage capacity, because it is not necessary to extract and store the entire tweets but only some basic information, in fact the elaborations of this paper were carried out with a simple mid-range notebook and a subset of tweets collected in the starting phase of propagation, while maintaining accuracy results consistent with the results currently existing in the literature.

The rest of the paper has been structured as follows. Next section provides a short introduction to the current state of the art in the area of fake news detection. In Sect. 3, we describe our methodology that consists in the classification of features extracted from time series representing temporal evolution of rumors (rumors are collections of tweets about the same topic and in the context of OSNs can be qualified as news) and information related to users involved in each rumor. In Sect. 4, we apply this methodology on a real dataset and perform an experimental analysis for each feature. Finally, in Sect. 5 the main conclusions and some future lines of work are outlined.

2 Related Work

In this section, we report only the most relevant attempts to identify fake news on OSNs, a simple taxonomy of those approaches can be organized in *content-based approaches* and *context-based approaches*:

The **content-based** approaches aim at finding clues in texts and images of OSNs posts useful to differentiate false and true news, hence the majority of them are linguistic approaches.

For example, in [15] the authors focused on mining particular linguistic cues as patterns of pronouns, conjunctions and words that arouse in readers negative emotions, while in [16], authors use Rhetorical Structure Theory (RST platform) to represent rhetorical relations among the words in the text and to extract style-based features of news by mapping the frequencies of rhetorical relations to a vector space, in [17] authors use Linguistic Inquiry and Word Count (LIWC platform) to extract the lexicons falling into psycholinguistic categories, exploiting a large set of words that represent psycholinguistic processes, summary categories, and part-of-speech categories. These two classifiers, usually used for long texts, were applied to Twitter messages by [18] obtaining accuracy respectively of 60% and 72%.

Considering the enormous amount of work needed to create good training sets, in the last years, many researchers use debunking agencies (i.e., organizations whose goal is to check the contents of news assigning them a "value of veracity") to construct their dataset of true/false news and, after the text preprocessing, they use traditional classifiers. For example, Ferreira and Vlachos [19] developed a stance classification approach based on multiclass logistic regression, using features extracted from the article headline and the claim, achieving an accuracy of 73% on their dataset Emergent, Wu et al. [20] proposed a graph-kernel based hybrid SVM classifier which captured the high-order propagation patterns in addition to semantic features such as topics and sentiments reaching a classification accuracy of 88% in false rumor early detection on Sina Weibo dataset.

The visual-based approaches try to identify fake images that are intentionally created or obtained by the capture of specific characteristics in larger images. These techniques are often used in combination with other ones in order to obtain good results, for example, in the case of faking image related to hurricane Sandy, Gupta et al. [21] performed a classification, not only of news contents, but also of users who posted fake tweets.

On the other hand, there are approaches based on **social context** that include relevant user social engagements in their analysis, capturing this information from various perspectives. These approaches can be: stance-based [22,23], that utilize users' viewpoints (e.g., provided in form of like and repost) from relevant post contents to infer the veracity of original news articles, or propagation-based, that reason about the interrelations of relevant social media posts to predict news credibility.

For instance, in [24], authors proposed a credibility analysis approach based on PageRank-like credibility propagation on a multi-typed network consisting of events, tweets and users. For each interaction, their algorithm updated the event credibility scores, and they proved that their approach is 14% more accurate than the decision tree classifier approach on the same dataset.

Another method to automatically assess credibility of news propagated through Twitter was provided by Castillo et al. [25], that exploited a TwitterMonitor to identify trend topics and analyzed the collected tweets to discard conversations and unsure tweets, keeping only tweets labeled as news, and considering message, user, topic and propagation features to assign a value of credibility to each topic. The value obtained was put into several classifiers obtaining, in the best case, 86% of accuracy. This platform was reused in [18] on BuzzFeed ad PoliFact datasets (two datasets of tweets verified by debunking organizations) obtaining an accuracy of 80% and 79.6% respectively.

Finally, Ma et al. [14] proposed an approach to capture the variations of social context features during the propagation of post over time exploiting Dynamic Time Series Structure model that use the features of rumor's life cycle. They obtained an accuracy that range from 78% to 89% after 25 h from the start of propagation on a Twitter dataset and from 77% to 86% in 49 h from the start of propagation on a Sina Weibo dataset. In this model the accuracy in the initial phase of propagation is lower respect to the end because it lacks of sufficient variation of social context.

3   Extraction of User Information and Time Series Features for Fake News Detection on Twitter

This work was inspired by the work of Vosoughi et al. [13]. They performed an investigation on differential diffusion of verified true and false news stories propagated on Twitter between 2006 and 2017 and, after a deep analysis of

126 thousand stories twitted by 3 million of individuals they concluded that: *"Falsehood diffuses significantly farther, faster, deeper, and more broadly than the truth in all categories of information."*.

According to these conclusions, our approach consists on extracting features from the *temporal evolution* of each rumor and features from the users involved in each rumor propagation, then, after a classifier pre-training phase, evaluate the quality of each feature by Gini-importance method and use only the most important ones for the specific dataset in the final classification through random forest classifier.

To perform this kind of analysis we need a dataset composed of several raw tweets belonging to specific rumors, whose veracity has already labelled as true or false in some way (e.g. by exploiting links to debunking website pages). In particular, we are interested in the following fields of each tweet:[1]

- created_at that is the datetime of the current tweet creation;
- id_str, that is the identification number of the current tweet;
- the following fields of user object of current tweet object:
  - id_str, that is the identification number of user who has posted the current tweet;
  - friends_count, that is number of followees;
  - followers_count, that is number of followers;
  - listed_count, that is the number of public lists a user is member of (e.g., when he receives a reply);
  - favorites_count, that is number of tweets the user has liked during his account's lifetime;
  - statuses_count, that is number of tweets and retweets issued by the user during his account's lifetime;
  - created_at, that is the datetime that the user account was created on Twitter;
- if the current tweet is a retweet, the following fields of original tweet object:
  - created_at, that is the datetime of the original tweet creation;
  - id_str, that is the identification number of the original tweet.

Below are detailed the two families of features that are proposed in this work for the characterization of news on Twitter. The combination of all of them comprises the feature set that will be used to feed the classification algorithm.

3.1   Extraction of Time Series-Based Features

Datetimes of original and subsequent tweets are used to construct the timeline of each rumor. We select the oldest tweet of each rumor as origin and calculate a timestamp for the remaining part of rumor tweets, as the difference (in seconds) between the tweet datetime and the origin. After this, we construct a time series for each rumor by computing how many tweets there are for each hour in the first 24 h, so each rumor time series is the sum of the time series of cascade that belong to rumor translate over the time axis, as explained in toy example of Fig. 1.

---

[1] The names of fields has been extracted from the Twitter developers documentation.

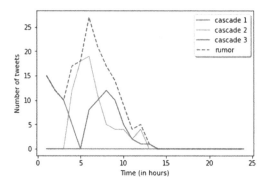

Fig. 1. Example of the construction of a rumor time series: there are 3 cascades (i.e. original tweets with all their retweet) with different starting time. The oldest tweet (belonging to the first cascade) marks the starting point of the rumor and the other 2 cascades are shifted on X axis respect to it. The sum of the 3 shifted curve points constitute the rumor curve.

The decision of taking into account just the first 24 h of propagation is based on some preliminary analyses on cascades of a subset of Vosoughi et al. dataset [26], and on the use of rumors in other works (e.g., [27]). These works confirm that the bulk of the news propagation happens in the first hours after carrying out of the event that generated news, and is drastically reduced in about a week. Therefore, it is useless to process the whole temporal evolution of news spreading in order to obtain a good classification. Moreover, the temporal evolution highlighted by these works led us to consider not seasonal time series equations to represent the temporal evolution of rumors, in fact, the final step consists in extracting numerical features from the time series of each rumor.

The collection of time series features has been performed through the `tsfeatures` tool (list of features for this type of analysis in [28]). We selected the most promising among the features proposed in [29] and [30], and after a pre-training of a random forest classifier, we computed the Gini-importance (i.e., the difference between a node's impurity and the weighted sum of the impurity measures of the two child nodes in tree [31]) to remove the unsuitable features for our dataset.

Thus, we consider our non-seasonal time series as $x_t = f_t + e_t$, where f_t is the smoothed trend component computed using the *smoother of Friedman* [32], and e_t is a remainder component. Based on this, the following features are extracted:

- Strength of trend, i.e., $1 - \frac{Var(e_t)}{Var(f_t + e_t)}$, where $Var(e_t)$ is the variation of e_t.
- Spike measures the *spikiness* of a time series, and it is computed as the variance of the leave-one-out variances of e_t.
- Linearity and curvature measures the linearity and curvature of a time series calculated based on the coefficients of an orthogonal quadratic regression.

– Autocorrelation function of e_t (e_acf1 and e_acf10), keeping the value of the first autocorrelation coefficient and the sum of the first ten squared autocorrelation coefficients.
– Shannon entropy, i.e., $-\int_{-\pi}^{\pi} f(x)logf(x)dx$ where $f(x)$ is an estimate of the spectral density of data.
– Stability and lumpiness are two features based on not overlapped tilled windows and means and variances are produced for all windows, the first one is the variance of means and the second one is the variance of variances.
– Crossing points, i.e. the number of time series crosses the mean line.
– Max level shift, max var shift and max Kullback-Leibler shift are features based on overlapping windows, they find respectively the sizes and the time indexes of the largest mean shift, the largest variance shift and the largest shift in Kullback-Leibler divergence between two consecutive windows.

3.2 Adding User Information to the Feature Set

Exploiting only the temporal evolution of the news is not enough to make a robust characterization and detection of their veracity, so, the feature set obtained from time series is extended with information about the users that participated in the rumor. More specifically, we calculate the average of user followers, followees and engagements for all the users involved in all the cascades of a rumor spread. The average of user followers and followees give us an idea of how connected the users of the rumor are within the Twitter network. Instead, the average of user engagement indicates how active the users were since the creation of their Twitter accounts, up to the time in which they tweeted or retweeted a piece of news. User engagement takes into account the number of tweets (T), retweets (Rt), replies (Rp) and favorites (F) of a user during the entire time he stayed on Twitter platform in days (D):

$$Eng = \frac{T + Rt + Rp + F}{D} \tag{1}$$

4 Experimentation

4.1 Dataset

For the experimental part of this paper, we used a partial Twitter dataset provided by Vosoughi, Roy and Aral [13]. They did not provide the *raw Twitter data* to comply with the Twitter policy on user privacy. Dataset contains the fields mentioned in the previous section for each tweet (properly anonymized), as well as, a rumor id and a cascade id, in order to identify the tweets belonging to the same rumor and cascade without the use of the tweet text (not provided by authors), and the veracity (true, false or mixed) of the news deriving from the analyzes carried out by 6 debunking agencies.

We removed tweets categorized as "mixed" to avoid uncertainty in the classification. Also, we split the tweets by rumor, in order to apply the method mentioned in the previous section to construct the rumor time series. Isolated tweets, i.e., tweets that do not contribute to the propagation of any rumor, were also removed from the dataset. Another reduction of the dataset was performed by truncating each rumor after 24 h of propagation, by removing rumors with less than 30 tweets and with a duration of less than 10 h, due to these rumors do not give a big picture of news spreading. At the end of this preprocessing, our dataset was composed of 1998 rumors (1582 false, 406 true) with a total of 1,503,990 tweets. In order to obtain a balanced dataset, we used 406 true rumors and 406 false rumors, randomly selected.

4.2   Features Extraction and Classification Results

For the training phase, we applied a random forest classifier with 500 trees, the rest of the parameters were set to the default values given by the implementation of random forest used in the R package `mlr` [33].

Table 1. Gini importances. The features in bold are kept for classification. Considering the great difference between the higher and lower value in table, we used as threshold the arithmetic average between these two values in order to decide which fields keep.

TS feature	Importance	TS feature	Importance	Dataset information	Importance
trend	**27.3315**	stability	**23.5289**	av_user_followers	**30.14687**
spike	**30.12765**	crossing_points	12.71993	av_user_followees	**29.24244**
linearity	**31.46726**	max_level_shift	**26.58879**	av_user_engagement	**29.24244**
curvature	**28.02144**	time_level_shift	2.166012	category	9.128586
e_acf1	**24.31782**	max_var_shift	**29.12224**		
e_acf10	**26.51979**	time_var_shift	3.463651		
entropy	**25.62444**	max_kl_shift	**24.04622**		
lumpiness	**21.41172**	time_kl_shift	1.747805		

After training the model, we applied the Gini-importance technique that calculates the importance of each feature. As explained before, this is calculated as the decrease of impurity for classification. The results are shown in Table 1.

We kept only the fields that surpass the mean value between the obtained minimum and maximum values. Considering the low importance of the features `crossing_points`, `time_level_shift`, `time_var_shift`, `time_kl_shift` and `category`, we removed these columns from the dataset and rerun training and, performing the 10-fold cross-validation, we obtained $84.61 \pm 5.96\%$ of accuracy.

4.3   Accumulated Local Effect Plot Analysis

In order to interpret the predictions of the resulting model, we will apply recent model-agnostic methods from the field of eXplainable AI (XAI) [34,35]. The advantage of these methods over model-specific ones is their flexibility, because they can be applied to any model, and provide different ways of representing the explanations.

First of all, we will analyze the interaction between features. If these features interact with each other, the prediction can not be expressed as the sum of the feature effects, because the effect of each feature is influenced by other ones, hence the way to estimate the interaction strength among features is to measure how much of the prediction variation depends on the interaction of the features. This goal can be reached using H-statistic measurement [36]:

$$H_j^2 = \frac{\sum\limits_{i=1}^{n}[f(x^{(i)}) - PD_j(x_j^{(i)}) - PD_{-j}(x_{-j}^{(i)})]}{\sum\limits_{i=1}^{n} f^2(x^{(i)})} \tag{2}$$

where $f(x)$ is the prediction function, $PD(x_j)$ is the partial dependence function of feature j, $PD(x_{-j})$ is the partial dependence function of all features except j and n is the number of data points used for measurement.

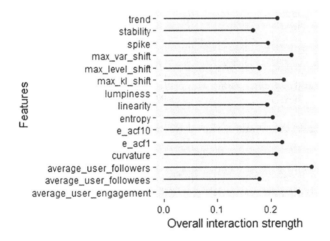

Fig. 2. Interaction strength of each feature versus the rest.

Figure 2 shows the application of this measure to each feature used in our dataset. All the features have weak interaction with other ones (ranging in [0.16, 0.28]). The average user followers has the highest relative interaction effect, followed by average user engagement, hence features deriving from time series are interacting with user features.

Finally, in order to interpret the resulting model, we analyze its Accumulated Local Effects (ALE) plot [37]. ALE is a common technique in the field of explainable machine learning. ALE plots are a faster and unbiased alternative to Partial Dependence Plots (PDP) and Individual Conditional Expectation (ICE), since they overcome the problems of model interpretation when the features are correlated as in this case.

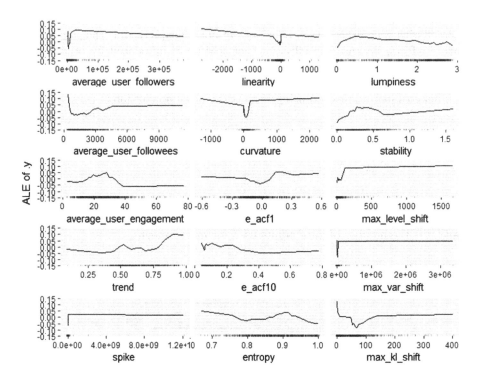

Fig. 3. Accumulated Local Effects (ALE) for each feature.

To estimate local effects, ALE method implementation divides the feature into many intervals and computes the differences in the predictions, that is the effect each feature has for each individual instance in a certain interval. All the effects of each interval are summed and after divided for the number of instances in each interval in order to obtain an average, the *local effect*. To accumulate the effects, the contributions of each interval are summed, giving the ALE value for a certain feature. More detail about the theory behind this estimation in [38].

In Fig. 3 the effect of each feature in the prediction of false news is shown. The corresponding charts for true news has been omitted because, in a binary classification, the curves are mirrored with respect to the X axis.

Looking at the effect of **user-based features** (*average user followers, average user followees* and *average user engagement*), we see that false news spreaders usually have a large number of followers, a low number of followees and a low user engagements. This probably means that their accounts were created ad hoc to reach a particular category of users and only become active when a particular idea must be propagated, remaining inactive for the rest of the time.

Looking at the ALE curves of **time series-based features**, we observe that, for values close to 0 of *linearity* and *curvature*, the prediction is often true, while it is false for the rest of values of these features. That indicates that, unlike false rumors, true news tend to have a constant diffusion. Considering the above mentioned formula for *strength of trend*, for high variations of the f_t component the rumor is classified as false, which hints that most of the false news have an higher variation of spreading over time with respect to true news. Finally, regarding the *max_level_shift* and *max_var_shift* we see that, except for low value of these two features, the classifier gives false news prediction. True rumors tend to have fewer shifts in the evolution of number of tweets than fake news.

Observing the whole figure, we can see that there are no features with high ALE value for all the value of each feature. This means that there is not a feature with predominant importance that alone can help to easily classify the news, but each feature contribute in the formation of the result, this means that removing one or more features the accuracy will decrease.

4.4   Tuning the Level of Aggregation of the Rumor Time Series

In the above experiment, the tweet counts needed for creating the rumor time series were calculated on an hourly basis. However, it is interesting to study whether the use of shorter levels of aggregation (also known as unit of analysis or sampling rate) can obtain better values of classification accuracy. Thus, we aggregated the tweets with a range of levels of aggregation, from 10 to 60 min, in 10-min increments and re-apply our methodology (Table 2).

Table 2. Average accuracy and standard deviation for different levels of aggregation of the rumor time series.

Level of aggregation	Average accuracy
10 min	$84.97 \pm 3.16\%$
20 min	$85.46 \pm 5.6\%$
30 min	$84.11 \pm 2.02\%$
40 min	$82.76 \pm 4.14\%$
50 min	$83.75 \pm 3.84\%$
60 min	$84.61 \pm 5.96\%$

4.5   Studying the Evolution of the Classification Accuracy over Time

Considering that the best result found in the previous experiment is that using a 20-min level of aggregation maximizes the accuracy on 24-h length rumor time series, we carried out a study of the evolution of the accuracy with this level of aggregation, in order to understand if the overall time of 24 h of spreading is necessary to obtain a good classification, or instead, a smaller time can be considered without losing too much accuracy. This is really important because an early detection of false news is always most desirable that a higher classification accuracy in a later time, when fake news have already become viral.

Taking into account that some of the time series-based features (e.g., linearity and curvature) cannot be calculated if the time series are too short, we started our analysis with 21 points (which correspond, in 20-min steps, to 7 h of propagation after the publication of the first tweet about a rumor) and re-executed the proposed methodology with 10-fold cross-validation resampling strategy, just as in the previous experiments. The average and deviation of the accuracy values found after this experiment are reported in Fig. 4. There are not high variations in accuracy: the lowest values of accuracy in average is $82.02 \pm 4.06\%$ at 7 h and 20 min, the highest $86.95 \pm 2.9\%$ at 10 h. This shows that, by reducing the length of time series to 8 h instead of the initial 24, the accuracy remains over 82%, which is a fair value, specially if we take into account the earliness of that classification. This is due to we did not exploit just the information about the propagation, but also the information about the involved users. So, unlike similar approaches that use time series (e.g., [14]) and need hours before to reach a stable values of accuracy, we have quite constant results in classification.

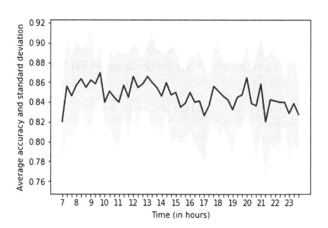

Fig. 4. Accuracy and standard deviation chart in 20 min time steps classifications.

5   Conclusions

In this work, we presented a method to classify true and false news spread on Twitter, exploiting both time series-based features and information about users involved in news spreading. We applied the feature set to a dataset of precategorized news, obtaining an accuracy in ten-fold cross-validation of 84.61% for 24 h time series with tweets sampling of 1 h. In order to obtain this result, we studied the importance of each feature after a pre-training process, and we used only the most important ones to perform the best classification possible for our dataset. The relevance of these features was also proved by a posterior study about the effect of each feature in the classification. Finally, we re-performed the same methodology on time series of the same dataset but with different level of aggregation, in order to find the one that allow the highest accuracy result, and, in this case, we performed a study of the evolution of accuracy over the time and, considering that the accuracy vary between 82% and 87% in all the cases, we reached to the conclusion that time series can be truncated at 8 h with a low loss of classification accuracy.

As future work, an important extension of the proposed methodology lies in the combination of the current set of features with others derived from the tweet metadata (e.g., tags, geographic locations). This new extension will be compared against other techniques and algorithms currently used in the area of fake news detection using more datasets.

Acknowledgements. This work has been supported by several research grants: Spanish Ministry of Science and Education under TIN2014-56494-C4-4-P grant (Deep-Bio), European Union, under ISFP-POLICE ACTION: 823701-ISFP-2017-AG-RAD grant (YoungRes), and Comunidad Autónoma de Madrid under P2018/TCS-4566 grant (CYNAMON).

References

1. Bruns, A.: The active audience: transforming journalism from gatekeeping to gate-watching (2008)
2. Chunara, R., Andrews, J.R., Brownstein, J.S.: Social and news media enable estimation of epidemiological patterns early in the 2010 Haitian cholera outbreak. Am. J. Trop. Med. Hyg. **86**(1), 39–45 (2012)
3. Lee, K., Agrawal, A., Choudhary, A.: Real-time disease surveillance using twitter data: demonstration on flu and cancer. In: Proceedings of the 19th ACM SIGKDD International Conference on Knowledge Discovery and Data Mining, pp. 1474–1477. ACM (2013)
4. Christakis, N.A., Fowler, J.H.: Social network sensors for early detection of contagious outbreaks. PLoS ONE **5**(9), e12948 (2010)
5. Schmidt, C.W.: Trending now: using social media to predict and track disease outbreaks. Environ. Health Perspect. **120**(1), a30 (2012)
6. Bello-Orgaz, G., Hernandez-Castro, J., Camacho, D.: Detecting discussion communities on vaccination in twitter. Future Gen. Comput. Syst. **66**, 125–136 (2017)
7. Sakaki, T., Okazaki, M., Matsuo, Y.: Earthquake shakes twitter users: real-time event detection by social sensors. In: Proceedings of the 19th International Conference on World Wide Web, pp. 851–860. ACM (2010)
8. Guy, M., Earle, P., Ostrum, C., Gruchalla, K., Horvath, S.: Integration and dissemination of citizen reported and seismically derived earthquake information via social network technologies. In: Advances in Intelligent Data Analysis IX, pp. 42–53 (2010)
9. Spence, P.R., Lachlan, K.A., Griffin, D.R.: Crisis communication, race, and natural disasters. J. Black Stud. **37**(4), 539–554 (2007)

10. Barberá, P., Jost, J.T., Nagler, J., Tucker, J.A., Bonneau, R.: Tweeting from left to right: is online political communication more than an echo chamber? Psychol. Sci. **26**(10), 1531–1542 (2015)

11. Varol, O., Ferrara, E., Davis, C.A., Menczer, F., Flammini, A.: Online human-bot interactions: detection, estimation, and characterization. In: Eleventh International AAAI Conference on Web and Social Media (2017)

12. Allcott, H., Gentzkow, M.: Social media and fake news in the 2016 election. J. Econ. Perspect. **31**(2), 211–236 (2017)

13. Vosoughi, S., Roy, D., Aral, S.: The spread of true and false news online. Science **359**(6380), 1146–1151 (2018)

14. Ma, J., Gao, W., Wei, Z., Lu, Y., Wong, K.-F.: Detect rumors using time series of social context information on microblogging websites. In: Proceedings of the 24th ACM International on Conference on Information and Knowledge Management, pp. 1751–1754. ACM (2015)

15. Feng, V.W., Hirst, G.: Detecting deceptive opinions with profile compatibility. In: Proceedings of the Sixth International Joint Conference on Natural Language Processing, pp. 338–346 (2013)

16. Rubin, V.L., Lukoianova, T.: Truth and deception at the rhetorical structure level. J. Assoc. Inf. Sci. Technol. **66**(5), 905–917 (2015)

17. Pennebaker, J.W., Boyd, R.L., Jordan, K., Blackburn, K.: The development and psychometric properties of LIWC2015. Technical report (2015)

18. Shu, K., Wang, S., Liu, H.: Beyond news contents: the role of social context for fake news detection. In: Proceedings of the Twelfth ACM International Conference on Web Search and Data Mining, pp. 312–320. ACM (2019)

19. Ferreira, W., Vlachos, A.: Emergent: a novel data-set for stance classification. In: Proceedings of the 2016 Conference of the North American Chapter of the Association for Computational Linguistics: Human Language Technologies, pp. 1163–1168 (2016)

20. Wu, K., Yang, S., Zhu, K.Q.: False rumors detection on Sina Weibo by propagation structures. In: 2015 IEEE 31st International Conference on Data Engineering, pp. 651–662. IEEE (2015)

21. Gupta, A., Lamba, H., Kumaraguru, P., Joshi, A.: Faking Sandy: characterizing and identifying fake images on twitter during Hurricane Sandy. In: Proceedings of the 22nd International Conference on World Wide Web, pp. 729–736. ACM (2013)

22. Mohammad, S.M., Sobhani, P., Kiritchenko, S.: Stance and sentiment in tweets. ACM Trans. Internet Technol. (TOIT) **17**(3), 26 (2017)

23. Qazvinian, V., Rosengren, E., Radev, D.R., Mei, Q.: Rumor has it: identifying mis-information in microblogs. In: Proceedings of the Conference on Empirical Methods in Natural Language Processing, pp. 1589–1599. Association for Computational Linguistics (2011)

24. Gupta, M., Zhao, P., Han, J.: Evaluating event credibility on twitter. In: Proceedings of the 2012 SIAM International Conference on Data Mining, pp. 153–164. SIAM (2012)

25. Castillo, C., Mendoza, M., Poblete, B.: Information credibility on twitter. In: Proceedings of the 20th International Conference on World Wide Web, pp. 675–684. ACM (2011)

26. Carchiolo, V., Longheu, A., Malgeri, M., Mangioni, G., Previti, M.: Terrorism and war: twitter cascade analysis. In: Del Ser, J., Osaba, E., Bilbao, M.N., Sanchez-Medina, J.J., Vecchio, M., Yang, X.-S. (eds.) IDC 2018. SCI, vol. 798, pp. 309–318. Springer, Cham (2018). https://doi.org/10.1007/978-3-319-99626-4_27

27. De Domenico, M., Lima, A., Mougel, P., Musolesi, M.: The anatomy of a scientific rumor. Sci. Rep. **3**, 2980 (2013)
28. Introduction to the tsfeatures package. https://cran.r-project.org/web/packages/tsfeatures/vignettes/tsfeatures.html. Accessed 11 Nov 2019
29. Hyndman, R.J., Wang, E., Laptev, N.: Large-scale unusual time series detection. In: 2015 IEEE International Conference on Data Mining Workshop (ICDMW), pp. 1616–1619. IEEE (2015)
30. Fulcher, B.D., Jones, N.S.: Highly comparative feature-based time-series classification. IEEE Trans. Knowl. Data Eng. **26**(12), 3026–3037 (2014)
31. Nembrini, S., König, I.R., Wright, M.N.: The revival of the Gini importance? Bioinformatics **34**(21), 3711–3718 (2018)
32. Friedman, J.H.: A variable span scatterplot smoother (1984). http://www.slac.stanford.edu/cgi-wrap/getdoc/slac-pub-3477.pdf
33. Bischl, B., et al.: mlr: machine learning in R. J. Mach. Learn. Res. **17**(170), 1–5 (2016)
34. Ribeiro, M.T., Singh, S., Guestrin, C.: Model-agnostic interpretability of machine learning (2016). arXiv preprint arXiv:1606.05386
35. Puri, N., Gupta, P., Agarwal, P., Verma, S., Krishnamurthy, B.: Magix: model agnostic globally interpretable explanations (2017). arXiv preprint arXiv:1706.07160
36. Friedman, J.H., Popescu, B.E., et al.: Predictive learning via rule ensembles. Ann. Appl. Stat. **2**(3), 916–954 (2008)
37. Apley, D.W.: Visualizing the effects of predictor variables in black box supervised learning models (2016). arXiv preprint arXiv:1612.08468
38. Accumulated local effects plot. https://christophm.github.io/interpretable-ml-book/ale.html. Accessed 11 Nov 2019

Social Learning vs Self-teaching in a Multi-agent Neural Network System

Nam Le[✉], Anthony Brabazon, and Michael O'Neill

Natural Computing Research & Applications Group, University College Dublin, Dublin, Ireland
namlehai90@ucdconnect.ie

Abstract. Learning has been shown to be beneficial to in creating more adaptive algorithms, and also in evolving neural networks. Moreover, learning can be classified into two types, namely social learning, or learning from others (e.g., imitation), and individual trial-and-error learning. A *"social learning strategy"* – a rule governing whether and when to use social or individual learning, is often said to be more beneficial than relying on social or individual learning alone. In this paper we compare the effect on evolution of social learning in comparison with that of individual learning. A neural architecture called a "self-taught neural network" is proposed in order to allow an agent to learn on its own, without any supervision. We simulate a multi-agent system in which agents, each controlled by a neural network, have to develop adaptive behaviour and compete with each other for survival. Experimental results show that evolved self-teaching presents the most effective behaviour in our simulated world. We conclude this paper with some indications for future work.

Keywords: Meta-learning · Multi-agent · Baldwin Effect · Neural networks · Hybrid algorithms

1 Introduction

The idea that lifetime learning can influence evolution in a Darwinian framework was introduced over one hundred years ago in the famous paper *'A new factor in evolution'* [1]. The described phenomenon was later termed the **Baldwin Effect** [2]. Following the classic paper of [3] which demonstrated an instance of the Baldwin effect in a computer simulation a significant related literature has emerged including, [4,5], and recently [6]. The so-called *effect* in computation can simply be understood as a *hybrid* algorithm combining an evolutionary algorithm (EA) with some form of local-search at the phenotypic level. This line of research motivated the idea of evolving neural networks, or *neuroevolution* (NE), in which one can observe learning and evolution interacting with each other in creating adaptive neural networks with [7] and [8] being two exemplar studies. Most recently, authors in [9,10] proposed a self-teaching neural architecture

© Springer Nature Switzerland AG 2020
P. A. Castillo et al. (Eds.): EvoApplications 2020, LNCS 12104, pp. 354–368, 2020.
https://doi.org/10.1007/978-3-030-43722-0_23

which can learn without requiring any supervisory or external reinforcement signals.

Learning can generally be classified into two types, namely *social learning* (SL) and *individual (asocial) learning* (IL). IL can be broadly understood as learning when the learner directly interacts with its environment, e.g., via trial-and-error, without the presence of others or their information. SL, on the other hand, can be interpreted as learning from others, e.g., imitation, through observation or interaction. Several studies have shown that social learning in combination with asocial learning by some *strategy* can outperform individual or social learning alone [11–13]. This line of thought has also been employed in hybridising EA in which a phenotypic local search combining both social and individual learning presents an adaptive effect to keep an evolving population on track in dynamic environments [13,14]. However, this still leaves an open challenge as these findings can be problem-specific, and the results may not generalise beyond the specific modelling of each learning mechanism.

This paper addresses the question of how effectively social and individual learning influence evolution in evolving self-taught neural networks. We simulate a situated multi-agent system in which each agent, controlled by a neural network, seeks to find and absorb resources from its environment, thereby competing for survival with other agents. In this simulation, agents have limited 'visibility' of their environment. As the environment is dynamically generated, the solution cannot be defined in advance. These factors make it harder for an agent to develop an *intelligent* behavioural policy.

In the remainder of the paper we present a brief overview of research on learning and evolution in neural networks, social learning and related concepts. In turn we describe simulations used to investigate our research question and then analyse and discuss the results obtained. Through the rest of paper, we use the terms *observer/learner/student*, and *teacher/demonstrator/teacher*, interchangeably, in order to keep our terminology in line with that used in the prior literature that we discuss.

2   Related Work

Evolution and learning are complementary forms of adaptation by which an organism can modify its behaviour in response to environmental challenges. Indeed, evolution and lifetime learning are closely intertwined, as a capability for lifetime learning can only arise as a result of an evolutionary process. Perhaps less evidently, the linkage also goes the other way and learning can influence the evolutionary process, enhancing the adaptivity of a species over time. This phenomenon is termed the **Baldwin Effect** and was demonstrated in a classic simulation paper [3]. The so-called Baldwin Effect in evolutionary computation (EC) means a combination of an evolutionary search over genotypic space and a local search process over phenotypic space, provided that what is found from phenotypic search is not directly encoded back into the genotype. This paper stimulated a number of important follow-on studies in which learning has been shown to help and guide evolution in different domains, including cases of search on NK-landscapes [15], and search in neuroevolution-controlling robots [7].

Learning and evolution in neural network learning has been studied in several papers following the original work of Hinton and Nowlan [3]. Notable studies include [16] in which the authors used a genetic algorithm to evolve the initial weights of a digit classifier neural network which then can be further adapted by backpropagation (life time learning). This study found that learning can take advantage of starting weights produced by evolution to further the classification performance.

Nolfi and his colleagues made a simulation of *animats*, or robots, controlled by neural networks situated in a grid-world, with discrete state and action spaces [7]. Each agent lives in its own copy of the world, hence there is no mutual interaction. The evolutionary task is to evolve action strategies to collect food effectively, while each agent learns to predict the sensory inputs to neural networks for each time step. Learning was implemented using backpropagation, based on the error between the actual and the predicted sensory inputs, to update the weights of a neural network. It was shown that learning to predict the sensory inputs can enhance the evolutionary search, hence increasing the performance of the robot.

Researchers at Google DeepMind also employed the Baldwin Effect, using a genetic algorithm to evolve the initial weights for deep neural networks [17]. By combining the advantage of searching over a vast distribution of weights using evolutionary search, and the exploitative power of gradient descent learning, they reported a *meta-learner* that can solve a multiple tasks including regression and physical robot environments. This result is an indication to create meta-learning, another step towards Artificial General Intelligence (AGI).

More recently, authors in [9] proposed a technique called evolving self-taught neural networks (ESNN) which are used to control agents living within a food-patch for survival. Unlike those mentioned above, an ESNN is capable of teaching itself without external supervision or reinforcement. Evolution plus self-teaching was shown to provide a way to generate better self-reinforced signals over time, and to generate more adaptive behaviour than evolution or self-teaching in isolation. An ENSS can be understood as a form of meta-learning towards AGI.

Generally learning in neural networks can be thought of as part of neural plasticity. There have been some other ideas, like evolving local learning rules to update the weights [18], evolution of neuromodulation which facilitates the information transfer between neurons in hopes of creating meta-learning. Please refer to [8] for more recent studies on evolving plastic neural networks. In short, neural networks in most of these work still require some sort of supervisory or external reinforcement signals to guide the learning process.

Delving a little deeper into the term lifetime learning, it can be subdivided into *asocial* (or individual) learning (IL), and *social* learning (SL). Each is a plausible way for an individual agent to acquire information from the environment at the phenotypic level. By SL, we mean *learning that is influenced by the observation of, or the interaction with, another animal or its products* [19].

Several models have been proposed to investigate how to use SL effectively, both in biology [20] and in EC [12]. A key finding of these studies is that social learning should be combined with individual learning in a strategic way, and such a strategy can potentially outperform both social and individual learning alone. Social learning strategies consist of rules specifying the way an individual relies on social learning by answering three questions: when SL should be used, from whom an agent should learn, and what an agent should learn or copy[1] from others. As an example of a social learning strategy, *critical social learning* proposed by [21] and also adopted in recent EC studies [13,14], suggests a strategy as follows: first learn socially, then learn individually. Prima facie, this bears loose analogy with the way highly cognitive animals like humans learn in nature, since we copy significantly from others then innovate ourselves to make progress. Results obtained from these studies present an effect of a learning strategy on evolution better than that of social or individual learning alone, promoting evolutionary optimisation in dynamic environments [14].

Interestingly, an important strand of research in Artificial Life adopts a related approach in both simulation studies and robotics in which neural networks are mostly used to control the behaviour of a robot (for a brief recent survey please refer to [22]). For example, [23] showed that social learning when combined with individual learning can provide a better way for neural network-controlled robot to learn and adapt to its environment compared to robots which possessed either social or individual learning alone.

In this paper, we extend previous research on evolving self-taught neural networks [9] by investigating the effect of social learning, or social learning strategy, might have on evolving autonomous intelligence in a multi-agent system. Unlike previous work, we do not allow agents live within the food-patch, but force them do two tasks: first to find resources, and second to compete for food. The self-taught agent can be considered to be autonomous. Social learning is implemented in the simulations as the student (agent) seeks to copy the process that has produced "good" behaviour in its teacher. In the next section, we describe our simulation model in more detail.

3   Simulation Setup

3.1   The Simulated World of Food and Agents

Suppose that 20 agents are situated in a continuous 640×640 2D-world, called **MiniWorld**. Agents seek to find resources to feed themselves in order to survive. In MiniWorld, 50 food particles are randomly dispersed and each particle is represented by a square image with size 10×10. Each agent in MiniWorld also has a similar size. We use two world maps (map A, and map B) in our simulations as described in Fig. 2. In the simualtions we implement a *toroidal* environment – so that when an agent moves beyond an "edge", it appears on the opposite "side" of the environment.

---

[1] The term *copy* is often used to stand for any form of social learning, not just copying.

Initially agents have to forage to find the food sources. A visualisation of an agent and its relationship with food particles in MiniWorld is shown in Fig. 2. Through the visualisation, based on our assumption on initial heading, it can be seen that map B is likely to be more difficult than map A from an agent perspective.

All agents in the population live in the same MiniWorld and their behaviours interact. As an agent finds and consumes food particles, it changes the environment faced by the other agents. This creates *mutual-competition-within-patch* between the agents (Fig. 1).

a) Map A   b) Map B

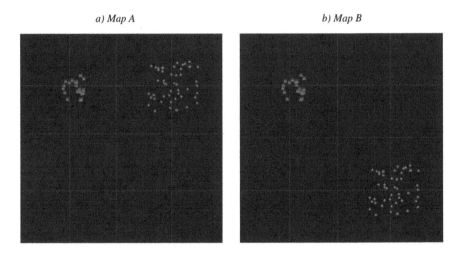

Fig. 1. MiniWorld – The environment of agents and food, 640×640. (a) and (b) Denote w and h as the width and the height of MiniWorld. In both map A and B, initially all agents are located in a radius of 40 (4 times the size of an agent) around a central point: $(w/4, h/4)$. Food particles in map A have horizontal and vertical dimensions randomly chosen in the range $(5w/8, 7w/8)$ and $(h/8, 3h/8)$, respectively. The food region in map A is the square that has the same central point as the top right quarter, and each side of that square has the length of $w/4$. In map B, the food has its horizontal and vertical dimensions randomly chosen in the range $(5w/8, 7w/8)$ and $(5h/8, 7h/8)$, accordingly. The food region in map B is the square that has the same center as the bottom right quarter, and each side of that square has the length of $w/4$. When an agent's body happens to collide with a food particle, the food particle is "eaten", the energy level of the agent increases by 1, and another food piece is randomly spawned in the **same region** but at a different location. The collision detection criterion is specified by the distance between the two bodies (of the agent and of the food particle). The environment changes as an agent eats a particle.

The default velocity (or speed) of each agent is 1. Every agent has three basic movements: Turn left by 9° and move; move forward by double speed; or turn right by 9° and move. For simplicity, these rules are pre-defined by the system designer of MiniWorld. We can imagine a perfect scenario such as if an agent

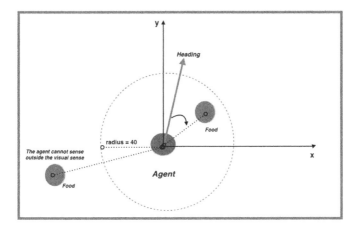

Fig. 2. Each agent has a heading (in principle) of movement in the environment. Rather than initialising all agents with random headings, all the agents are initialised with a **horizontal heading** (i.e., with a heading of 0°). This somewhat explains the purpose of the design of map A and map B. In map A, all agents are initially created with a tendency to move forwards the food source. On the contrary, agents in map B are born with facing away from the food source resulting in a more difficult environment. Assume that every agent has an a priori ability to sense the angle between its current heading and the food if this appears in its visual range. The visual range of each agent is a circle with radius 40. Each agent takes as inputs, three pieces of sensory information. The three bits (left, front, right) are set to 0 or 1 depending on whether the substance appears (in the left, front, and right) or not. Let θ (in degrees) be the angle between the agent and the substance in its visual sense. An agent determines whether a food appears in the left, front, or right side in its visual range using the following rule: Right if $15 < \theta < 45$; Front if $\theta < 15$ or $\theta > 345$; and Left if $315 < \theta < 345$.

sees a food in front of its current location, it doubles its speed and moves forward to the food particle. If an agent sees the food on the left (right), it will turn to the left (right) and move forward to the food particle. The motor action of an agent is guided by its neural network as described below.

3.2   The Neural Network Controller

Each agent is controlled by a fully-connected neural network to determine its movements in the environment. What an agent decides to do changes the next sensory information it receives, and hence its future behaviour. This forms a sensory-motor dynamic, and the neural network acts as a situated cognitive module, guiding an agent to behave adaptively.

The architectural design of the neural network controller is visualised in Fig. 3. All neurons except the inputs use a sigmoidal activation function. All connections (or synaptic strengths) are initialised as Gaussian (0, 1). These weights are first initialised as *innate*, or merely specified by the genotype of an agent, but also have the potential to change during the lifetime of that agent.

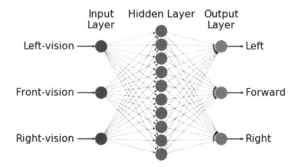

Fig. 3. Basic network without learning. Each neural network includes 3 layers with 3 input nodes, 10 hidden nodes, and 3 output nodes. The first layer takes as input what an agent senses from the environment in its visual range. The output layer produces 3 values in which the max value is chosen as a motor-guidance.

Note that the neural architecture as shown in Fig. 3 has no ability to learn, or to teach itself. In the following section, we extend this architecture to allow for self-taught learning agents.

3.3   The Self-taught Neural Architecture

To allow for self-teaching, two modules are implemented in the neural controller for each agent. One is called the **Action Module**, and the other is called the **Reinforcement Module**. The action module has the same network as previously shown in Fig. 3. This module takes as inputs the relevant sensory information and produces reinforcement outputs in order to guide the motor action of the agent. The reinforcement module has the same set of inputs as the action module, but possesses separate sets of hidden and output neurons.[2] The goal of reinforcement network is to provide *reinforcement signals* to guide the behaviour of each agent. The topology of a neural network in this case is visualised in Fig. 4.

In the following sections we describe the simulations we use to investigate the evolutionary consequence of lifetime learning, including self-taught learning and social learning.

3.4   Simulation 1: Evolution Alone (EVO)

In this simulation, we evolve a population of agents which do not have a lifetime learning capability. The neural network controller for each agent is as described in Fig. 3, without any learning capability. The *genotype* of each agent is the

---

[2] The reinforcement and the action modules need not have the same topology. In our simulation, the reinforcement module possesses the same neuronal structure as the action module, but has 10 hidden neurons separate from the hidden neurons of the action module.

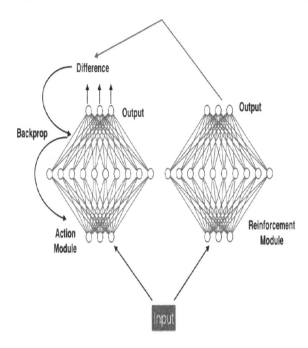

Fig. 4. Self-taught neural architecture. The difference between the output of the reinforcement module and the action module is used to update the weights in action modules through backpropagation. Through this self-learning process, the action module approximates its output activation towards the output of the reinforcement module. The learning rate is 0.01.

weight matrix of its neural network, and the evolutionary process takes place as we evolve a population of weights.

Selection chooses individuals based on the number of food particles consumed. The higher the number of particles eaten, the higher the agent's fitness value. For crossover, two individuals are selected to produce one offspring. We implement crossover as follows. The more successful a parent, the greater the likelihood that its weights are copied to the child. Each weight element in the matrix of the child network is copied from the fitter parent if the random probability is greater than 0.5, and vice versa.

Once a child has been created, that child will be mutated based on a predefined *mutation rate*. In our work, the *mutation rate* is set at 0.05. A random number is generated, and if that number is less than the *mutation rate*, a mutation occurs. If a mutation occurs for a weight in the child, a random number is added to that weight. After that, the newly born individual is placed in the next generation. This process is repeated until the new population is filled with 100 new individual agents. No elitism is employed in our evolutionary algorithm.

The population goes through a total of 100 generations, with 5000 time steps per generation. At each time step, an agent undertakes the following activities:

Perceiving MiniWorld through its sensors, computing its motor outputs from its sensory outputs, moving in the environment which then updates its new heading and location. In the 'evolution alone' simulation, the agent cannot perform any kind of learning during its lifetime. After that, the population undergoes selection and reproduction processes.

3.5   Simulation 2: Evolution of Self-taught Agents (EVO+IL)

In this simulation, we allow lifetime learning, in addition to the evolutionary algorithm, to update the weights of neural network controllers when agents interact with the environment. We evolve a population of **Self-taught** agents – agents that can teach themselves. The self-taught agent has a self-taught neural network architecture as described previously and as shown in Fig. 4. During the lifetime of an agent, the reinforcement modules produce outputs in order to guide the weight-updating process of the action module. Only the weights of action modules can be changed by learning, the weights of reinforcement module are genetically specified in the same evolutionary process as specified above in the evolution alone simulation. We use the same parameter settings for evolution as in EVO simulation above.

At each time step, an agent does the following activities: Perceiving Mini-World through its sensors, computing its motor outputs from its sensory outputs, moving in the environment which then updates its new heading and location, and updating the weights in action module by **self-teaching**. After one step, the agent updates its fitness using the number of food particles consumed. After that, the population undergoes selection and reproduction processes as in the evolution alone simulation.

In these experiments, we implement learning and evolution in a Darwinian, not a Lamarckian framework. This means that the lifetime learning of an agent (the weights in its action module) is not passed down to its offspring.

3.6   Simulation 3: Evolution + Social Learning Alone (EVO+SL)

In simulation 3, we use social learning, instead of individual learning (self-taught learning), in combination with evolution. In order to implement social learning, we first propose the supervised learning-based imitation procedure by which an individual student learns from its teacher. The process of social learning by imitation between two agents is depicted in Fig. 5. Please note that, imitation learning here happens between two action networks. The reinforcement module which is related to self-learning is untouched.

In this simulation, only social learning is implemented, there is no individual learning. The type of social transmission adopted is called *Oblique transmission*, which was also used in previous successful social learning applications in EC [13,14]. The *Who strategy* specifies the most successful agent in terms of fitness from the previous generation as the teacher for all individuals in the current population. It is assumed that at each step, each agent keeps its input-output

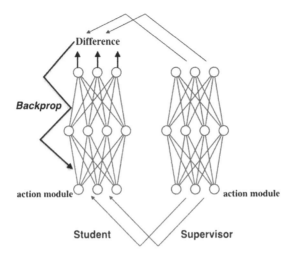

Fig. 5. Social learning process in the form of imitation learning between a student and its teacher. The teacher provide its input-output pairs during its lifetime, as a training set of experiences, to its student. Thus, the student is exposed to the same inputs as the teacher. The output difference between them is used to guide the student to approximate the teacher's output. The weight-updating in student's action network is carried out using a backpropagation learning algorithm, with a learning-rate of 0.01.

pair, in which the input includes three sensory values while the output comprises of three movement values as shown in the neural controller architecture (Fig. 3).

For each social learning agent, the social learning strategy (i.e., the answers to the three questions of *When*, *Who*, and *What*) is defined as follows:

(i) When: a student learns socially at birth before experiencing its own environment. We can interpret this scenario so that a newborn agent is naive, and learns from the most successful individual at birth.
(ii) Who: learn from the most successful individual in the previous generation.
(iii) What: learn the teacher's sensory-motor experience.

After undertaking social learning, every individual agent returns to and experiences its own environment using the same procedure as described in the previous simulations. Since we employ *Oblique transmission*, social learning does not appear at the initial generation, but starts from the second generation.

3.7 Simulation 4: Evolution in Combination with Social and Individual Learning (EVO+SL+IL)

In this simulation, we incorporate both social and asocial learning (self-teaching) in combination with evolution. Each type of learning is as already described above. In the initial generation, there is no social learning, only self-learning is performed. From the second generation, every agent performs social learning at birth, as described above, before experiencing its lifetime in its environment.

4 Results and Analysis

We compare agent performance across the various experimental setups, in terms of the best and the average amounts of food eaten, of the population in the four simulation settings as above. All results are averaged over 30 independent runs.

A similar trend can be observed in Figs. 6 and 7 in that all experiments produce higher performance in map A than in map B. This is as expected for the reasons already set out: Map B is designed to be more difficult than map A as the agents' initial trajectory is away from the food sources.

4.1 EVO Alone vs EVO+Self-taught

We initially compare the performance between the baseline experiment of evolution alone with the performance of evolution of self-taught agents. In all maps, EVO+Self-taught outperforms EVO alone in terms of both best and the average fitness. This could be explained by the effect of individual learning on evolution, or the *Baldwin Effect*. One more notable point here is that EVO alone cannot absorb any energy at all in map B, while evolved self-taught agents can.

Simply speaking, an agent that cannot learn can only use its *innate* ability, hardwired in its brain, to search the environment. However, as analysed above, in map B the agent in EVO alone is born without any tendency to sense relevant information (about food) in the environment, and also has no ability to change its motor program hardwired in its brain. Its sensory-motor experience cannot be changed since it cannot sense relevant information (i.e. information to find the food source).

Conversely, with an ability to teach oneself by leveraging the difference between the action and the reinforcement modules, the weights of the action module of some self-taught agent can alter to produce a wider range of movement. By undertaking some initial random movement, the sensory-motor experience of an agent can be expanded, and there may have been some agents that reached the food sources. The agents that reach food sources have a higher chance of being selected to leave offspring. Thus, its *good* genetic information, consisting of the *initial* weights of both the action and the reinforcement modules, is more likely to proliferate, hence its self-supervising or self-teaching ability. It is this ability that has made future evolved self-supervised agents better at teaching themselves in order to develop more effective movement in MiniWorld. This process repeats, as what has given advantage during lifetime of the self-taught agent is preserved and promoted by the evolutionary process. This can be considered the interaction between learning and evolution.

4.2 Social Learning vs Self-teaching

We can see that in all maps, EVO+Self-taught also outperforms both EVO+SL and EVO+SL+IL in terms of both average and best fitness. The difference is bigger in the harder map B than in map A.

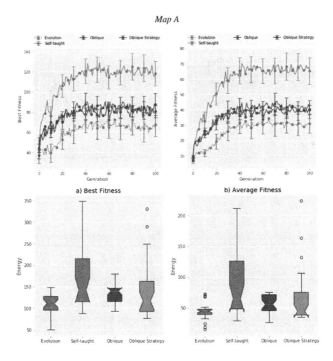

Fig. 6. Fitness comparison in Map A.

One interesting behaviour that can be observed here that EVO+SL alone failed to eat anything in map B. Social learning is a form of *information-parasitism*, and cannot produce new information about the environment. Importantly, because there is no individual learning permitted, what social learners can learn is just what the evolutionary process has provided to them. More specifically, as of the second generation, social learners learn from the best agent of the preceding generation and with no agent performing well, there is nothing useful to learn.

Even when coupled with self-learning, social learning produces poorer results than self-learning alone in all maps. What is presented in Fig. 7 shows that EVO+SL+IL can produce *good enough* behaviour (agents can find food), but not as good as EVO+Self-taught – without the presence of social learning. This means the employment of social learning here is not promoting, but rather reducing the power of self-learning.

There are several factors contributing to what we can call the *discouraging-effect* of social learning. First, unlike previous studies as mentioned in Sect. 2, here there is no *pre-defined optimal solution* in MiniWorld. Thus, social learning here cannot simply copy a *known* optimal solution.

Secondly, through the supervisory-based social learning process, the student has to develop its own policy based on the previous sensory-motor experience of its teacher as *off-line* training-samples. The experience of the teacher can make more sense if the student would be likely to face the same experience in *its own*

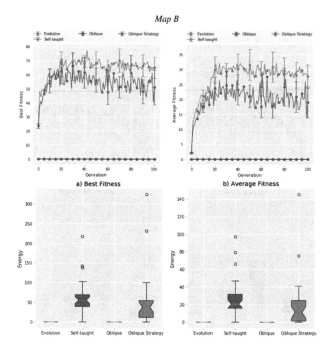

Fig. 7. Fitness comparison in Map B.

world like what it has learned from the teacher. However, the nature of the multi-agent in MiniWorld is that the sensory-motor experience of an agent depends on not only its own actions, but also on those of others which might change the world the agent is experiencing. What the student is going to experience depends on what other agents in the same world are doing which can be different from what the teacher and the other agents were doing in the teacher's world. This creates a variety of dynamics dependent on **space and time**. This is what can make the world the student agent is experiencing dynamically different from the world the supervisor has experienced. Social learning, or cultural learning, from any previous generation is more likely to produce outdated information, thus *discouraging effect* as we have seen. Approximating an action network based on outdated information, even from the *best teacher*, is not promising.

One more factor which can be added is the fact that an agent in MiniWorld has little knowledge about its environment.

5   Conclusion

We have investigated the effect of different forms of learning (social and individual learning) on evolving self-taught neural networks in a situated multi-agent system in which knowledge of the environmental state is dynamic and cannot be completely accessed by the agent. Experimental results have shown that the combination of self-teaching and evolution is most effective in evolving intelligent agents as the agent develops its own policy based on its evolved self-teaching capability. When self-teaching is powerful enough, social learning even when being used selectively reduces the power of self-teaching.

This work continues to consolidate the power of hybrid algorithms by combining the metaphor of evolution and learning. Learning has been again shown to facilitate evolution in developing intelligent behaviour, even when the *good* behaviour is unknown and dynamic over time and space. Previous studies have shown the power of the combination of both social and individual learning in evolutionary dynamic optimisation [13,14]. While this finding does not concord with that of some previous studies, we note that the experiments undertaken in this work implement a more complex environment and hence, are likely to be more generalisable to "harder" real world environments.

Indeed, what can be extracted here is that if a learner is good at *self-teaching*, self-learning can sometimes result in a better outcome than learning from external supervisory signals.

Another philosophical point here is that a constructive approach towards social learning via the synthesis of artificial agents can yield important insights into mechanisms that can inform biologists, psychologists and Artificial Intelligence researchers by fleshing out theory. From the computational side, another contribution is the use of an evolved self-taught neural network. This provides a framework for building intelligent autonomous adaptive systems in the environment without engineered rewards and where the state of this environment is only partially observable [24]. The evolved ability to teach oneself produces a form of autonomous intelligence, without any kind of *external supervision*. Building adaptive autonomous multi-agent system is potentially a promising way to reach general intelligence. In future work, both weights and topology could be evolved rather than assuming a fixed architecture. MiniWorld can also be extended into more complex environmental settings by incorporating for example, food & poison, and via the inclusion of obstacles which would add further complexity to the learning task, potentially forcing a stronger learning/evolutionary response from agents.

References

1. Baldwin, J.M.: A new factor in evolution. Am. Nat. **30**(354), 441–451 (1896)
2. Le, N.: Organic selection and social heredity: the original Baldwin effect revisited. In: The 2019 Conference on Artificial Life. MIT Press (2019)
3. Hinton, G.E., Nowlan, S.J.: How learning can guide evolution. Complex Syst. **1**, 495–502 (1987)
4. Ackley, D., Littman, M.: Interactions between learning and evolution. In: Langton, C.G., Taylor, C., Farmer, J.D., Rasmussen, S. (eds.) Artificial Life II. SFI Studies in the Sciences of Complexity, vol. X, pp. 487–509. Addison-Wesley, Reading (1992)
5. Harvey, I.: Is there another new factor in evolution? Evol. Comput. **4**(3), 313–329 (1996)
6. Le, N.: Evolving self-taught neural networks: the Baldwin effect and the emergence of intelligence. In: 2019 AISB Annual Convention - 10th Symposium on AI & Games, Falmouth, UK, 16–18 April 2019

7. Nolfi, S., Parisi, D., Elman, J.L.: Learning and evolution in neural networks. Adapt. Behav. **3**(1), 5–28 (1994)
8. Soltoggio, A., Stanley, K.O., Risi, S.: Born to learn: the inspiration, progress, and future of evolved plastic artificial neural networks. Neural Netw. **108**, 48–67 (2018)
9. Le, N., Brabazon, A., O'Neill, M.: The evolution of self-taught neural networks in a multi-agent environment. In: Kaufmann, P., Castillo, P.A. (eds.) EvoApplications 2019. LNCS, vol. 11454, pp. 457–472. Springer, Cham (2019). https://doi.org/10.1007/978-3-030-16692-2_31
10. Le, N.: Evolution and self-teaching in neural networks. In: Proceedings of the Genetic and Evolutionary Computation Conference Companion (GECCO 2019). ACM Press (2019)
11. Laland, K.N.: Social learning strategies. Anim. Learn. Behav. **32**(1), 4–14 (2004). https://doi.org/10.3758/BF03196002
12. Le, N., O'Neill, M., Brabazon, A.: Adaptive advantage of learning strategies: a study through dynamic landscape. In: Auger, A., Fonseca, C.M., Lourenço, N., Machado, P., Paquete, L., Whitley, D. (eds.) PPSN 2018. LNCS, vol. 11102, pp. 387–398. Springer, Cham (2018). https://doi.org/10.1007/978-3-319-99259-4_31
13. Le, N., O'Neill, M., Brabazon, A.: How learning strategies can promote an evolving population in dynamic environments. In: 2019 IEEE Congress on Evolutionary Computation (CEC), June 2019, pp. 2284–2291 (2019)
14. Le, N., O'Neill, M., Brabazon, A.: Evolutionary consequences of learning strategies in a dynamic rugged landscape. In: Proceedings of the Genetic and Evolutionary Computation Conference (GECCO 2019), pp. 812–819. ACM, New York (2019). https://doi.org/10.1145/3321707.3321741
15. Suzuki, R., Arita, T.: Repeated occurrences of the Baldwin effect can guide evolution on rugged fitness landscapes. In: 2007 IEEE Symposium on Artificial Life. IEEE, April 2007
16. Keesing, R., Stork, D.G.: Evolution and learning in neural networks: the number and distribution of learning trials affect the rate of evolution. In: NIPS 1990 (1990)
17. Fernando, C.T., et al.: Meta-learning by the Baldwin effect. CoRR, vol. abs/1806.07917 (2018). http://arxiv.org/abs/1806.07917
18. Bengio, S., Bengio, Y., Cloutier, J., Gecsei, J.: On the optimization of a synaptic learning rule. In: Levine, D.S., Elsberry, W.R. (eds.) Optimality in Biological and Artificial Networks. Lawrence Erlbaum, New York (1995)
19. Heyes, C.M.: Social learning in animals: categories and mechanisms. Biol. Rev. **69**(2), 207–231 (1994)
20. Feldman, M.W., Aoki, K., Kumm, J.: Individual versus social learning: evolutionary analysis in a fluctuating environment. Working Papers, Santa Fe Institute (1996)
21. Enquist, M., Eriksson, K., Ghirlanda, S.: Critical social learning: a solution to Rogers' paradox of nonadaptive culture. Am. Anthropol. **109**(4), 727–734 (2007). https://doi.org/10.1525/aa.2007.109.4.727
22. Marriott, C., Borg, J.M., Andras, P., Smaldino, P.E.: Social learning and cultural evolution in artificial life. Artif. Life **24**(1), 5–9 (2018)
23. Acerbi, A., Nolfi, S.: Social learning and cultural evolution in embodied and situated agents. In: 2007 IEEE Symposium on Artificial Life. IEEE, April 2007
24. Le, N.: Evolving self-supervised neural networks: autonomous intelligence from evolved self-teaching. CoRR, vol. abs/1906.08865 (2019). http://arxiv.org/abs/1906.08865

Evolving Instinctive Behaviour in Resource-Constrained Autonomous Agents Using Grammatical Evolution

Ahmed Hallawa[1]([⊠]), Simon Schug[1], Giovanni Iacca[2], and Gerd Ascheid[1]

[1] Chair for Integrated Signal Processing Systems, RWTH Aachen University,
52056 Aachen, Germany
{hallawa,schug,ascheid}@ice.rwth-aachen.de
[2] Department of Information Engineering and Computer Science,
University of Trento, 38123 Povo, Italy
giovanni.iacca@unitn.it

Abstract. Recent developments in the miniaturization of hardware have facilitated the use of robots or mobile sensory agents in many applications such as exploration of GPS-denied, hardly accessible unknown environments. This includes underground resource exploration and water pollution monitoring. One problem in scaling-down robots is that it puts significant emphasis on power consumption due to the limited energy available online. Furthermore, the design of adequate controllers for such agents is challenging as representing the system mathematically is difficult due to complexity. In that regard, *Evolutionary Algorithms* (EA) is a suitable choice for developing the controllers. However, the solution space for evolving those controllers is relatively large because of the wide range of the possible tunable parameters available on the hardware, in addition to the numerous number of objectives which appear on different design levels. A recently-proposed method, dubbed as *Instinct Evolution Scheme* (IES), offered a way to limit the solution space in these cases. This scheme uses *Behavior Trees* (BTs) to represent the robot behaviour in a modular, re-usable and intelligible fashion. In this paper, we improve upon the original IES by using *Grammatical evolution* (GE) to implement a full BT evolution model integratable with IES. A special emphasis is put on minimizing the complexity of the BT generated by GE. To test the scheme, we consider an environment exploration task on a virtual environment. Results show 85% correct reactions to environment stimuli and a decrease in relative complexity to 4.7%. Finally, the evolved BT is represented in an if-else on-chip compatible format.

Keywords: Grammatical Evolution · Behavior Tree · Autonomous agents

1 Introduction

Resource-constrained miniaturized autonomous robots (or sensory agents) are becoming available on a wide scale. Their compact dimensions enable flexible

© Springer Nature Switzerland AG 2020
P. A. Castillo et al. (Eds.): EvoApplications 2020, LNCS 12104, pp. 369–383, 2020.
https://doi.org/10.1007/978-3-030-43722-0_24

usage in a wide range of applications ranging from monitoring of underground infrastructure [1] and exploration of natural resources, such as oil and gas, to human body diagnostics [2]. However, the available energy on these robots is restricted by their scaled-down size, which puts a special emphasis on the reduction of power consumption. In many cases, the agents are kinetically passive and exposed to noisy and dynamically changing environments, thus requiring robust behaviors capable of dealing with uncertainty [3]. Consequently, sophisticated methods are required in order to develop adaptive behaviors that empower these robots to collaboratively achieve a given set of objectives with such limited hardware resources. Evolvable hardware addresses this problem by autonomously reconfiguring hardware using *Evolutionary Algorithms* (EAs) [4]. Inspired by the biological process of evolution, EAs are a class of meta-heuristics which are well-suited for dealing with complex search spaces. They have proven to be useful in a wide range of applications [5], especially in situations where conventional optimization techniques can not find satisfactory solutions due to a lack of a priori knowledge of the problem under investigation. Broadly speaking, two kinds of approaches have been proposed to apply EA to reconfigurable hardware, namely *extrinsic* and *intrinsic* evolution. In extrinsic evolution, candidate solutions are evaluated using a virtual simulation of the corresponding hardware behavior. Consequently, a static hardware configuration is generated by the algorithm and, subsequently, flashed onto the target device. By contrast, intrinsic evolution refers to approaches that conduct fitness measurements by implementing each candidate solution on the device and observe its behavior. As this eliminates the need for complex simulation environments, the validity of this method is enhanced [6]. However, both extrinsic and intrinsic evolution show some limitations when it comes to the learning process of an agent's behavior. Extrinsic evolution suffers from the inability to adapt the final solution to changes in the problem definition after it has been deployed on the hardware. Though intrinsic evolution is capable to overcome this drawback by continuously adapting the agent, it requires extensive computational power that is not available in miniaturized robots, due to their scaled-down size. In this work we progress on this research area by proposing and verifying a Behaviour Trees (BTs) evolution model integratable with an EA recently proposed in the literature, the Instinctive Evolution Scheme (IES) [7], with the purpose of evolving a behaviour suitable for resource-constrained autonomous robots or sensory agents. The rest of the paper is structured as follows: in Sect. 2 a background on different behaviour schemes in robotics is given, followed by an introduction to IES. Section 3 introduces the proposed model based on BTs and IES. Finally, Sects. 4, 5 and 6 discuss the case study used to verify the model, the results from our experiments, and conclusion respectively.

2   Background

Representing Behaviour: Representation of a behaviour is critical for its development and optimization. In many applications in robotics, *Artificial Neural Networks* (ANNs) are used to encode adaptive behavior. ANNs are capable of performing complex computational tasks and can easily be combined with EAs. Consequently, there have been numerous successful attempts of evolving robot controllers using ANNs, e.g. [8]. Though ANNs are powerful, they are generally treated as a black box. Understanding and validating the inner workings of a successfully evolved controller, thus becomes a very difficult task. Furthermore, even subtle changes in the specifications of the controller require retraining algorithms as it is unfeasible to manually adapt a completed controller. On the other hand, one alternative is *Finite State Machines* (FSMs). In FSMs, the behavior is abstracted by means of states and transitions that define the response of the agent to a given external output. FSMs lend themselves well for user-defined autonomous behaviors but have also seen successful application with EAs e.g. [9]. Compared to ANNs, they are easier to understand/explain and therefore support the analysis of the behavioral spectrum of an evolved controller. Despite their usefulness in simple action sequences, FSMs quickly become illegible for complex tasks, as the amount of states grows exponentially, a phenomenon termed *state explosion* [10]. Behavior Trees (BTs) represent a promising alternative to FSMs as a mathematical model of plan execution. Based on a hierarchical network of actions and conditions, BTs are capable of describing complex behaviors readily intelligible for users, and allow for easy decomposition and reuse of encapsulated sub-behaviors [11]. Furthermore, there have been attempts of adopting EAs to automatically generate BTs for a given task [12]. Though the general feasibility of the procedure has been shown, several parts of the design process were done manually. As BTs allow for flexible design of actions and conditions specifically tailored to the platform they are deployed on, they do not necessarily require

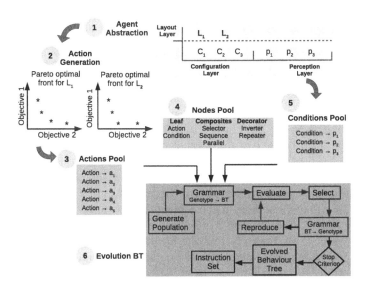

Fig. 1. Instinct Evolution Scheme as proposed by [7]

hardware with extensive computational resources. Therefore, they are suited to be used with resource-constrained miniaturized robots.

Instinct Evolution Scheme: The Instinct Evolution Scheme (IES), introduced in [7], attempts to mimic the instinctive behaviour found in nature, where biological entities react to environment stimuli in a fast-reflexive way, with no complex processing. This is adequate for resource constrained robots or sensory agents. The main idea is to use extrinsic evolution, but after minimizing the solution space using "lower-level" objectives. The reduced solution space is then set as the new solution space for the evolution of the behaviour using GE on BTs. In other words, the scheme provides a methodology to limit the solution space for evolving an optimum instinctive behaviour represented by a BT via identifying a set of "interesting" actions and conditions to be used for evolving the behaviour. The scheme consists of six steps as shown in Fig. 1: Firstly, an agent is abstracted as a *layout layer*, then each element in the layout layer (L_1, L_2 ...) includes a set of possible tunable configurations in the *configuration layer* (C_1, C_2 ...) and finally, there is a *perception layer*, which is the set of all perception interfaces with the environment, e.g. sensors. In other words, the layout layer consists of configurable modules that are provided by the hardware architecture of the robot, e.g. a communication module, a compression module ... etc. For each of these modules, a set of configurations are possible, which can be found in the configuration layer, e.g. the Variable Gain Amplifier (VGA) voltage. In step 2, the solution space is minimized, i.e. a multi-objective optimization algorithm is used to identify the Pareto front of the variables in the configuration layer relative to "local" objectives. For example, in case of communication module, the local objectives might be the Signal-to-Noise Ratio (SNR) vs. power consumption. This is done for each element in the layout layer (L_1, L_2 ...) using, for example, R2-indicator based Evolutionary Multi-objective Optimization Algorithm (EMOA). This optimization process will lead to a set of Pareto fronts for each module in the layout layer, relative to its local objectives. In addition, each solution in these Pareto fronts is a configuration, which is "interesting" as it is already dominating other solutions that are not on this Pareto front. In other words, the solution space has shrunk to only solutions that would offer a gain relative to the local objectives for each of the modules in the layout layer. In the next step (step 3), these solutions in the generated Pareto fronts are used to produce a pool dubbed as an *action pool*. This is now the new solution space of possible reactions from the robot to the environment, and it will be used in step 6 to evolve a BT, i.e. all actions in the evolved BT in step 6 are from this action pool. On the other hand, in step 4, a set of possible types of nodes are defined in the *nodes pool*. This basically sets the hardware allowable types of nodes in the BT, e.g. if the hardware allow *parallel* nodes, which can check multiple conditions or actions at the same time, then it is added to the nodes pool. This is done for all types of possible nodes, e.g. invert nodes, repeaters nodes ... etc. In step 5, the *perception pool* is generated. This is done via defining all possible sensors (or any points of interaction between the robot and the environment).

Then, possible conditions to be checked for each of these sensors are set. Obviously, in an unknown environment, defining exactly what are the conditions to be checked is not possible, however, if the robot swarm conduct one real experiment in the environment before the evolution of BT, the data extracted can be statistically studied and a set of "interesting" conditions for each sensor in the perception layer can be defined. This paper is based on IES, hence, in our work the objective is to evolve a BT given an action, condition and nodes pools.

3   Methodology

Implementation of Behavior Trees: The literature offers multiple implementations of BT, such as in [13,14]. The main differences are mainly in the execution logic and the possible node types. These two factors play an important role in the performance of any BT. As mentioned in Sect. 2, the BTs' main strengths are their modularity and re-usability. These are possible because all node types used in a BT return one of the three possible states: *Success, Failure* and *Running*. Furthermore, a *tick* function is used as an intermediate layer that selects the appropriate routine based on the node type which has been called. In our work, four possible nodes were implemented: selector node, sequence node, action node and condition node. These nodes are sufficient to achieve a wide range of behaviors. Furthermore, a parsing function was implemented to produce an instruction set using if-else conditions only, which is more hardware-friendly. And as stated earlier, this work is based on the IES described in Sect. 2. Accordingly, the actions pool is considered as an input to the GE process presented in this work. Furthermore, it is assumed that the number of available sensors is also given (the perception layer). For the conditions pool, each given sensor is fed a set of environment data during the initialization of the virtual environment used in the evolution process of the BT, then thresholds are defined by $threshold = M_i \pm n \cdot \sigma_i$, based on the statistical analysis of the sensed data by the virtual environment. A condition node in the evolved BT then checks whether the current sensor readings are located within the range defined by two neighboring thresholds. The resulting condition pool for the ith sensor can be seen in Table 1. Finally, to facilitate the BT evaluation, each executed BT has an action log and condition log, where all actions and conditions that were triggered at all time steps are recorded and later used for its evaluation.

Table 1. Condition pool for the ith sensor

Condition 1	$x < M_i - \sigma_i$
Condition 2	$M_i - \sigma_i \leq x < M_i$
Condition 3	$M_i \leq x < M_i + \sigma_i$
Condition 4	$M_i + \sigma_i \leq x$

Representation in a Context-Free Grammar: A central task of incorporating BTs into the framework of GE is to find a grammatical representation that can be used in the genotype-to-phenotype mapping. Therefore, a formal language needs to be abstracted from the syntax and semantics of BTs transforming the two-dimensional hierarchical structure of a BT into a one-dimensional string representation. The final language L_{BT} was derived based on the alphabet $\Sigma_{BT} = \{a, c, s, q, \langle, \rangle, \circ, 0, 1, ..., 9\}$ (See Table 2).

Table 2. Symbols of the language L_{BT} designed for BTs description

Notation	Meaning
s	Selector node
q	Sequence node
a_i	Action node with the identifier i
c_k	Condition node with the identifier k
$\langle\ \rangle$	Encapsulation of a subtree
$\circ$	Separation of two nodes/subtrees with the same parent

In the next step, we develop a context-free grammar $G_{BT} = (V, \Sigma_{BT}, P, S)$ capable of describing the language L_{BT}. Given the variables $V = \{A, C, N, T\}$ and the start symbol $S = \{<N><<T> \circ <T>>\}$ the following production rules P were created:

$$<T> ::= a<A> \mid <T> \circ <T> \mid \tag{1}$$
$$c<C> \mid <N><<T> \circ <T>>$$
$$<N> ::= s \mid q \tag{2}$$
$$<A> ::= 1 \mid 2 \mid ... \mid \mathcal{N}_A \tag{3}$$
$$<C> ::= 1 \mid 2 \mid ... \mid \mathcal{N}_C \tag{4}$$

The variable $<T>$ represents a subtree, while the variable $<N>$ is a placeholder for a composite node that controls the flow of its respective subtree. Composite nodes are required to have at least two child nodes. Hereby the useless nesting of single composite nodes within each other is prohibited. Hence, the start symbol already includes two subtrees for the root node and further composite nodes can only be inserted with two respective subtrees. Furthermore, the variables $<A>$ and $<C>$ can be replaced by a number representing their unique identifier, where $\mathcal{N}_A$ is the number of possible actions and $\mathcal{N}_C$ is the number of possible conditions to choose from.

Selection: Early tests showed that roulette selection method suffered from premature convergence, thus rank-based selection and tournament selections were implemented instead. Rank-based offered a better solution than the roulette, however, while the tournament selection did not add any further benefits despite its relative higher computational costs. Therefore, rank-based selection was adopted in the implementation. Furthermore, *elitism* was also implemented.

Crossover: After two parents have been chosen by rank-based selection, they are subject to crossover with the probability $p_{crossover}$, where $p_{crossover}$ denotes the *crossover rate*. The well established one-point crossover is implemented as it represents the *de facto* standard for GE and has proven to provide good performance in different applications [15]. For each parent, a random crossover point is drawn from the discrete uniform distribution $\mathcal{U}\{2, k_{end,i} - 1\}$, where $k_{end,i}$ denotes the end of the coding region of the genotype of parent i. If the length of the resulting genotype exceeds $l_{genotype}$, the excess codons are discarded and the last codon is replaced by the escape character '0' to properly define the end of the coding region. If, on the other hand, the length of the resulting genotype underruns $l_{genotype}$, the missing codons are generated from the discrete uniform distribution $\mathcal{U}\{1, c_{max}\}$, similarly to the initialization process. As the one-point crossover is applied to the genotype without access to phenotypic information, it does not respect the tree structure of the phenotype. As a result, changes on the genotype with one-point crossover can lead to drastic differences in the phenotypic appearance. As an alternative, a more sophisticated crossover operation has been implemented that allows for the protection of the integrity of the BT by exchanging arbitrary subtrees between the parents. Moreover, to realize a more general procedure that can be applied to arbitrary grammars, the extension to GE proposed by [16] can be used. In this regard, two new variables $<X>$ and $<Y>$ are introduced to the grammar marking the beginning and ending of a subtree. Consequently, the extended grammar $G_{BT+} = (\tilde{V}, \Sigma_{BT}, \tilde{P}, \tilde{S})$ with the variables $\tilde{V} = \{A, C, N, T, X, Y\}$ and the start symbol $\tilde{S} = \{<N>\langle<X><T><Y> \circ <X><T><Y>\rangle\}$ is created. The production rules $\tilde{P}$ were extended to denote possible crossover points encapsulating subtrees:

$$<T> ::= \; <X><T><Y> \circ <X><T><Y> \; | \tag{5}$$
$$<N>\langle<X><T><Y> \circ <X><T><Y>\rangle \; |$$
$$a<A> \; | \; c<C>$$
$$<N> ::= \; s \; | \; q \tag{6}$$
$$<A> ::= \; 1 \; | \; 2 \; | \; ... \; | \; \mathcal{N}_A \tag{7}$$
$$<C> ::= \; 1 \; | \; 2 \; | \; ... \; | \; \mathcal{N}_C \tag{8}$$

The crossover points for each individual can then be generated during the parsing process. When the parser encounters $<X>$ during execution it will not use the currently active codon. Instead, it creates a new row in the $N \times 2$ matrix $XOSites$ that is kept for each individual. It stores the current position within the genotype in the first column and adds a placeholder value in the second column. Afterwards the variable $<X>$ is removed from the phenotype and the parsing process continues as usual. When $<Y>$ is encountered the last row of $XOSites$ which contains a placeholder value in the second column is searched. The placeholder value is then replaced by the index one before the current position within the genotype and the variable $<Y>$ is removed from the phenotype. For a valid BT, each row of $XOSites$ denotes a section of the genotype that can be exchanged without disrupting the integrity of the BT. The crossover operation can then randomly pick a pair of crossover points from the $XOSites$ matrix of each parent and exchange the respective sections of the gene to create the genotypes for the two children.

Mutation: Mutation is realized by iterating through the genotype of an individual until the escape character '0' is reached. With the predefined probability $p_{mutation}$, commonly referred to as the *mutation rate*, a single codon is replaced by a new codon drawn from the discrete uniform distribution $\mathcal{U}\{1, c_{max}\}$. Thus, only the non-coding region of the genotype is subject to mutation.

Fitness Function: The fitness function can be split into two components: the first component includes the primary objective that should be solved by the BT. Naturally, it is dependent on the problem domain and varies in its concrete implementation. This part can get computationally expensive, as each BT in the population needs to be executed for a certain amount of time within the simulated environment in order to evaluate the embodied behavior. The second component of the fitness function deals with the complexity of the BT. As seen in [12] evolving BTs often results in cluttered trees with a high amount of redundancy. In this regard, the number of certain node types in the BT are calculated. This can be done by counting the number of occurrences of the corresponding symbol in the phenotype. Thus, the complexity measurement is set as follows:

$$C_i = \frac{n_i}{N_{max,i}} \ \forall \ i \in \{1, 2, 3\} \tag{9}$$

where C_i is the complexity with regard to node type i, n_i is the number of nodes of type i present in the BT and $N_{max,i}$ is the maximum amount of nodes of type i that can be encoded within a single genotype of size $l_{genotype}$. The subindices denote the node types considered in this work: 1 stands for action node, 2 for condition node and 3 for composite nodes. Consequently, it holds $C_i \in [0, 1)$. The

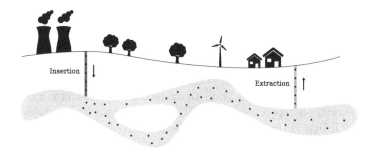

Fig. 2. GPS-denied, hardly accessible environment scenario

maximum amount of nodes of a certain type strongly depends on the structure of the production rules of the grammar. For a given genotype length, it can be approximated by determining the number of codons that are typically needed to create a certain node type:

$$N_{max,1} = N_{max,2} = \frac{l_{genotype}}{4} \quad (10) \qquad N_{max,3} = \frac{l_{genotype}}{2} \quad (11)$$

For $N_{max,1}$ and $N_{max,2}$ it is assumed that one codon is needed in order to create a new subtree $<T>$ by applying the rule $<T> ::= <T> \circ <T>$. Additionally, three codons are necessary to generate an action or condition node and its respective node identifier. Furthermore, for $N_{max,3}$, typically only two codons are needed. First a general composite node with two child subtrees is created with one codon by applying the rule $<T> ::= <N>\langle<T> \circ <T>\rangle$. Subsequently, another codon is used to replace $<N>$ and decide on the type of the composite node. As this sequence cannot generate leaf nodes, $N_{max,3}$ represents an upper bound.

4   Case Study

To be able to test the proposed GE framework, a virtual environment inspired by a real-world problem is set such as in Fig. 2. Typically, in a real-world case of exploring a GPS-denied, hardly accessible unknown environment, a swarm of robots or sensory agents are injected from one point to be later extracted from another point. Due to their limited resources, the agents need to minimize their power consumption while simultaneously guaranteeing that the collected data obtained from the environment are sufficient to identify the environmental properties of interest. The robot will under go all five steps in IES, thus we assume that all pools of IES are already generated, because the focus of this work is the evolution of the behaviour tree given these pools (Step 6 in IES). The objective here is to evolve a BT given a virtual environment. To achieve this, the environmental properties which the agents are exposed to are created artificially, this will help us to define deterministically identifiable zones, and thus test the ability of the evolved behaviour to correctly identify a zone. Furthermore, in order to assess how good an evolved BT is, each environment zone introduced artificially has a score for each of the n possible actions available in the action pool. In addition, to make the test more challenging, the environment zones where designed such that it is not possible to identify a zone using only a single sensor, or using all sensors (i.e. some sensor readings are redundant). And since running the controller itself involves computational costs, we set a special emphasis on decreasing the complexity of the behaviour tree representation on the robot.

Therefore, to evaluate an evolved BT, firstly the BT is executed within the simulation of a virtual environment, and an action log is created, which contains the identifiers of the invoked actions for each time step. Afterwards, the action log is analyzed in order to rate the quality of the embodied behavior of an agent by comparing it to the predefined optimum solution, and the distance to that optimal solution. The latter is realized by calculating the Hamming distances d_i for each zone i between the identifier of the action invoked by an agent and the corresponding optimum action identifier defined by the virtual environment. i.e. each possible action from the action pool has a fitness distance from the optimal action for each zone. Furthermore, as mentioned earlier the complexity of the BT is important to consider, BTs with more nodes are penalized. This is achieved by incorporating the weighted complexity with regard to different node types into the fitness function as follows:

$$F = D - \Theta \cdot \underbrace{\sum_{i=1}^{3} \phi_i \cdot C_i}_{C} \qquad (12)$$

where F is the fitness, D can be interpreted as the relative quality of the embodied behavior of an agent and $D \in [0,1]$ holds. Finally, $\Theta, \phi_i \in [0,1]$ are weighting coefficients: Θ specifies the extent of the penalty on complex individuals. $\phi_i \in [0,1]$ are weighting coefficients determining the portion of the individual complexity measurements on the combined complexity measurement C. Therefore, it must hold $\sum_{i=1}^{3} \phi_i = 1$. The values for ϕ_1, ϕ_2, ϕ_3 should reflect the costs of the node types, e.g. action or condition or composite. In this work action nodes are regarded as the most resource demanding, followed by condition nodes, while composite nodes have the smallest impact on performance. Accordingly, the weighting coefficients were set to $\phi_1 = 0.5$, $\phi_2 = 0.3$ and $\phi_3 = 0.2$.

5   Results

Scenario A: 4 Zones: The first tests investigating the ability of the GE to create adaptive BTs in a zone identification task were conducted with 4 zones and 6 sensors. For each zone two properties have been defined that can be detected with two separate sensors. As a property is always shared by two zones, two condition nodes need to be checked in order to unambiguously identify an individual zone (Table 3).

Table 3. Settings for the GE with 4 zones and 6 sensors.

Parameter	Value
Population Size ($N_{population}$)	100
Mutation Rate ($p_{mutation}$)	0.1
Crossover Rate ($p_{crossover}$)	0.1
Complexity Penalty (Θ)	0.5
Genotype Size ($l_{genotype}$)	300
Number of Zones (n)	4

(a) Parameters

	Zone 1	Zone 2	Zone 3	Zone 4
Sensor 1	1	1	-1	-1
Sensor 2	-1	-1	1	1
Sensor 3	1	-1	1	-1
Sensor 4	-1	1	-1	1
Sensor 5	0	0	0	0
Sensor 6	0	0	0	0

(b) Distribution of sensor properties

Scenario B: 8 Zones: To investigate the ability of the proposed scheme to evolve adaptive BTs, a zone identification task were conducted on an environment with 8 zones and with 8 available sensors on the robot. As shown in Table 4b, for each zone, four properties have been defined that can be detected with four separate sensors out of the eight available ones. Since two environment properties are always shared by two zones, at least two conditions are needed to unambiguously identify an individual zone, which is challenging for the grammatical evolution scheme. Furthermore, four sensors are redundant in the zone identification, requires the GE to check only the relevant ones and discard the rest. The used settings are summed up in Table 4a. Figure 3a presents the average identification performance over 25 runs. Moreover, the average complexity of the BTs shown in Fig. 3b, as shown, it increases considerably when compared with the one influenced with complexity penalty. Moreover, looking at a single run of the GE for the 8 zones scenario as shown in Fig. 4, the zone identification task performance shows a consistent convergence throughout the whole run, while the complexity of the underlying BTs is subject to substantial changes indicating a proper exploration of more complex trees regardless of the involved penalty. Moreover, the corresponding BT is shown in Fig. 6a, in total 4 composite nodes, 4 condition nodes and 4 action nodes are used by the tree. Note that it would require 8 actions to perfectly identify each zone. Finally, Fig. 6b shows the generated if-else control flow (Fig. 5).

Table 4. Settings for the GE with 8 zones and 8 sensors.

Parameter	Value
Population Size	200
Mutation Rate	0.1
Crossover Rate	0.9
Complexity Penalty	0.5
Genotype Size	300
Number of Zones	8

(a) GE tuning parameters

	Z1	Z2	Z3	Z4	Z5	Z6	Z7	Z8
Sensor 1	1	1	-1	-1	0	0	0	0
Sensor 2	-1	-1	1	1	0	0	0	0
Sensor 3	1	-1	1	-1	0	0	0	0
Sensor 4	-1	1	-1	1	0	0	0	0
Sensor 5	0	0	0	0	1	1	-1	-1
Sensor 6	0	0	0	0	-1	-1	1	1
Sensor 7	0	0	0	0	1	-1	1	-1
Sensor 8	0	0	0	0	-1	1	-1	1

(b) Virtual environment zone properties

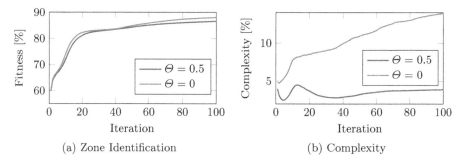

(a) Zone Identification

(b) Complexity

Fig. 3. Fitness convergence over 25 runs for 8 zones and 8 sensors.

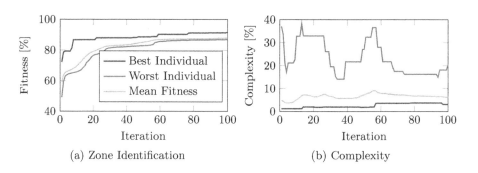

(a) Zone Identification

(b) Complexity

Fig. 4. Fitness convergence over a single run for 8 zones and 8 sensors.

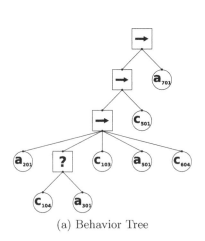

(a) Behavior Tree

```
 1  state = action(201);
 2  if state ! = FAILURE
       then
 3    |   state = condition(104);
 4    |   if state == FAILURE
          then
 5    |   |   state =
          |       action(301);
 6    |   end
 7  end
 8  if state ! = FAILURE
       then
 9    |   state = condition(103);
10  end
11  if state ! = FAILURE
       then
12    |   state = action(501);
13  end
14  if state ! = FAILURE
       then
15    |   state = condition(604);
16  end
17  if state ! = FAILURE
       then
18    |   state = condition(501);
19  end
20  if state ! = FAILURE
       then
21    |   state = action(701);
22  end
```

(b) Control Flow

Zone	1	2	3	4	5	6	7	8
Actual Solution	201	201	301	301	501	501	701	701
Optimum Solution	101	201	301	401	501	601	701	801

(c) Action Log

Fig. 5. Best BT solution for 8 zones environment and 8 sensors.

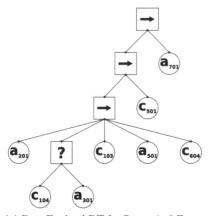

(a) Best Evolved BT for Scenario 8 Zones

```
1  state = action(201);
2  if state ! = FAILURE then
3  |    state = condition(104);
4  |    if state == FAILURE
        then
5  |    |    state = action(301);
6  |    end
7  end
8  if state ! = FAILURE then
9  |    state = condition(103);
10 end
11 if state ! = FAILURE then
12 |    state = action(501);
13 end
14 if state ! = FAILURE then
15 |    state = condition(604);
16 end
17 if state ! = FAILURE then
18 |    state = condition(501);
19 end
20 if state ! = FAILURE then
21 |    state = action(701);
22 end
```

(b) Control Flow of 6a

Fig. 6. Best evolved BTs and corresponding control flow

6   Conclusion

In this work, a Grammatical Evolution (GE) learning model for Behavior Trees (BTs) was successfully integrated into the Instinct Evolution Scheme (IES), thereby providing an offline framework for evolving an online behavior to resource-constrained autonomous robots. A special emphasis was put on minimizing the complexity of the evolved BTs. Furthermore, tests on virtually developed environments showed the effectiveness of the used fitness function and grammar.

References

1. Stoianov, I., Nachman, L., Madden, S., Tokmouline, T.: PIPENET a wireless sensor network for pipeline monitoring. In: Proceedings of the 6th International Conference on Information Processing in Sensor Networks - IPSN 2007, p. 264 (2007)
2. Nelson, B.J., Kaliakatsos, I.K., Abbott, J.J.: Microrobots for minimally invasive medicine. Annu. Rev. Biomed. Eng. **12**(1), 55–85 (2010)

3. Fister, I., Fister Jr., I. (eds.): Adaptation and Hybridization in Computational Intelligence. ALO, vol. 18. Springer, Cham (2015). https://doi.org/10.1007/978-3-319-14400-9
4. Higuchi, T., Liu, Y., Yao, X.: Evolvable Hardware. Springer, Heidelberg (2006). https://doi.org/10.1007/0-387-31238-2
5. Mattiussi, C., Floreano, D.: Analog genetic encoding for the evolution of circuits and networks. IEEE Trans. Evol. Comput. **11**(5), 596–607 (2007)
6. Glackin, B., Maguire, L.P., McGinnity, T.M.: Intrinsic and extrinsic implementation of a bio-inspired hardware system. Inf. Sci. **161**(1–2), 1–19 (2004)
7. Hallawa, A., De Roose, J., Andraud, M., Verhelst, M., Ascheid, G.: Instinct-driven dynamic hardware reconfiguration: evolutionary algorithm optimized compression for autonomous sensory agents. In: Proceedings of the 2017 Annual Conference on Genetic and Evolutionary Computation. ACM (2017)
8. Pintér-Bartha, Á., Sobe, A., Elmenreich, W.: Towards the light - comparing evolved neural network controllers and finite state machine controllers. In: 10th International Workshop on Intelligent Solutions in Embedded Systems (2012)
9. König, L., Mostaghim, S., Schmeck, H.: Decentralized evolution of robotic behavior using finite state machines. Int. J. Intell. Comput. Cybern. **2**(4), 695–723 (2009)
10. Valmari, A.: The state explosion problem. In: Reisig, W., Rozenberg, G. (eds.) ACPN 1996. LNCS, vol. 1491, pp. 429–528. Springer, Heidelberg (1998). https://doi.org/10.1007/3-540-65306-6_21
11. Colledanchise, M., Ogren, P.: How behavior trees modularize hybrid control systems and generalize sequential behavior compositions, the subsumption architecture, and decision trees. IEEE Trans. Robot. **33**(2), 372–389 (2017)
12. Nicolau, M., Perez-Liebana, D., O'Neill, M., Brabazon, A.: Evolutionary behavior tree approaches for navigating platform games. IEEE Trans. Comput. Intell. AI Games **9**(3), 227–238 (2016)
13. Bagnell, J.A., et al.: An integrated system for autonomous robotics manipulation. In: IEEE International Conference on Intelligent Robots and Systems, pp. 2955–2962 (2012)
14. Marzinotto, A., Colledanchise, M., Smith, C., Ögren, P.: Towards a unified behavior trees framework for robot control. In: 2014 IEEE International Conference on Robotics and Automation (ICRA), pp. 5420–5427. IEEE (2014)
15. Keijzer, M., Ryan, C., O'Neill, M., Cattolico, M., Babovic, V.: Ripple crossover in genetic programming. In: Miller, J., Tomassini, M., Lanzi, P.L., Ryan, C., Tettamanzi, A.G.B., Langdon, W.B. (eds.) EuroGP 2001. LNCS, vol. 2038, pp. 74–86. Springer, Heidelberg (2001). https://doi.org/10.1007/3-540-45355-5_7
16. Nicolau, M., Dempsey, I.: Introducing grammar based extensions for grammatical evolution. In: Proceedings of the 2006 IEEE Congress on Evolutionary Computation, pp. 2663–2670, April 2006 (2006)

Adversarial Optimization Approach for Development of Robust Controllers

Mohammed Baraq Mushtaq[1] and Tobias Rodemann[2(✉)]

[1] Technical University of Darmstadt, Karolinenplatz 5,
64289 Darmstadt, Germany
mohammed_baraq.mushtaq@stud.tu-darmstadt.de
[2] Honda Research Institute Europe, Carl-Legien-Strasse 30,
63073 Offenbach/Main, Germany
tobias.rodemann@honda-ri.de

Abstract. Due to increasing popularity of electric vehicles there is rising demand for smart controller solutions that optimize the flow of energy between buildings and electric vehicles. Simple rule-based controllers are (often manually) developed and tuned for specific use case scenarios, for example a specific building, mobility usage patterns and country-specific regulations. However, it is often very difficult to correctly anticipate the exact conditions the controller has to work on so that a high performance under worst-case conditions is a very important target. In this work we use an adversarial optimization approach in order to find both challenging scenarios and controller parameterizations that perform well in those scenarios. We can show that in comparison to a standard controller, our approach can find challenging scenarios for a standard controller and controllers that outperform the baseline on those worst-case scenarios.

Keywords: Adversarial optimization · Controller · Robustness · Smart Grid

1 Introduction

Tuning controller parameters using evolutionary algorithms is a well-known approach [7]. However, over-fitting to specific settings is a constant danger, as with machine learning approaches in general. It is therefore essential to tune the controller on a representative set of probable scenarios. Unfortunately, this is not possible in many practical instances, when there is a large variety of possible scenarios. An example we investigate in this work is a smart charging controller that needs to deal with different situations at the customers' location, which are difficult to anticipate. Instead of performing a random sampling of potential scenarios we therefore propose an adversarial optimization approach, where two antagonistic optimization processes are working in parallel. One optimization process is trying to maximize the performance of a controller on a set of scenarios, while the other optimization process is aiming to find worst-case scenarios for the current controller. We find that through this approach we can tune

P. A. Castillo et al. (Eds.): EvoApplications 2020, LNCS 12104, pp. 384–399, 2020.
https://doi.org/10.1007/978-3-030-43722-0_25

controllers that can cope with worst-case scenarios and randomly sampled scenarios. After laying out an overview of recent research, the application domain is described. Subsequently, an iterative co-evolutionary optimization approach is introduced. Enhancing the previous approach an archive-based optimization method is proposed. Finally, the obtained results for the system model are discussed.

2   Related Work

To cope with uncertainties for the system's design, the concept of robust optimization is applied, where objective functions are optimized considering a confined set of feasible use-case scenarios [3]. Going further, there has been research on determining worst-case robust solutions. This problem can be described from a game theoretic perspective, where two optimization procedures for controller and scenario space are competing against each other [8]. Evolutionary optimization methods have been employed for such worst-case optimization problems. A nested minimax optimization is proposed in [16]. A neural net controller for a highly uncertain and safety critical plant is optimized with evolutionary algorithms using a bi-level optimization loop. In the lower level, for a controller configuration the worst possible plant is identified for every iteration in the upper loop. The goal of the upper level optimization loop is to identify a controller, which optimizes the fitness for the worst possible plant. This approach yields robust controllers with the best worst-case performance. In [1,2], an iterative co-evolutionary optimization approach is presented. In this approach, in an iterative manner one population is frozen while the other population evolves for a given number of iterations. To avoid a cycling effect, where both populations follow local optima without yielding significantly better individuals, a *hall of fame* is proposed in [11]. The authors suggest to store and utilize previously identified worst-case scenarios for the fitness assignment. The competitive co-evolutionary optimization approaches have mainly been evaluated on test problems, the application on real world problems is yet to be done. Fundamental limits to worst-case or adversarial robustness for classifiers have been introduced in [10]. Although the paper focuses on different types of classifiers, there might be similar difficulties in finding a single adversarial robust control strategy for an arbitrary scenario space.

3   Methods

3.1   Application Domain: Smart Charging

Smart charging strategies are a key factor to optimally control power flows in energy supply systems with renewable energy sources (RES). In this work a rule-based energy management strategy (EMS) is implemented to enable sustainable and cost-efficient power flows within the energy supply system of a building complex and an attached charging station for electric vehicles (EV). The system model investigated is characterized by use of RES and utilization of an energy storage component. A predictive control strategy for efficient charging of EVs is introduced in [15]. Moreover, in [5] a predictive control strategy for a stationary battery is proposed. The realized EMS in this work combines and extends these previous approaches. In the following, the overall system configuration is introduced. The implemented EMS is subsequently described, including a scenario description for the control strategy. Finally, the objective or fitness function for the optimization of the EMS is defined.

3.2 System Configuration

The energy supply system can be divided into demand and supply side, additionally a storage component enables power flexibility for the system. The supply side comprises photovoltaic power modules (PV) and the external electricity grid, as the energy system is connected to the grid. Whereas, the demand side consists of the building power demand profile and the energy demand for EV charging. While the demand profile of the building complex can be estimated quite well based on measured data, the charging behavior of EVs and the respective power demand, however, holds higher uncertainty. The main sources of uncertainty stem from the state of charge (SoC) of EVs to be charged, charging time duration, arrival time of EVs at the charging station or the price of electricity.

The stationary battery within the system provides flexibility during a net surplus of PV power. The excess power is transferred into the battery storage. When there is net shortage of power, the battery can be discharged. The EMS controls the power flow of the EV charging station and the stationary battery. Both, energy supply system and EMS are parameterized. Figure 1 gives an overview on the configuration of the system model. The model is set up in SimulationX and is composed of modules of the GreenCity Library [9,17].

Control Strategy and Scenario Description. The implemented EMS, as described before, is comprised of predictive EV and battery charging strategies. The control strategy tries to mitigate peak power demand for the charging process and to maximize self-consumption of the power generated by the PV module. The EMS can be illustrated using decision trees. Different operating modes are activated when certain threshold values are exceeded or not. For instance, at a certain value for the required power of the building complex, the charging power for electric vehicles is reduced. Accordingly, the thresholds parameterize and describe the control strategy. These parameters can then be optimized for specific objective functions. Figure 2 shows the structure of an implemented EV charging strategy.

As mentioned before, the energy supply system is parameterized. The parameters define the system behavior and comprise, amongst others, the load profile for the building power demand, the averaged arrival time of EVs at the charging station and the standard deviation of the SoC of arriving EVs. These parameters are termed scenario parameters in the following.

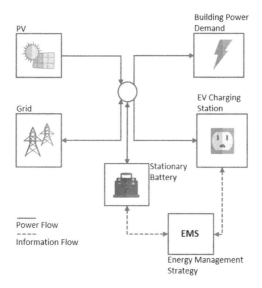

Fig. 1. Configuration of the analyzed energy supply system. The power supply within the system is provided by PV modules and the external grid. Building power demand and charging power demand from the EV charging station constitute the demand side. The energy system contains a stationary battery. The energy management strategy controls the power flow of the stationary battery and the EV charging station. Note the legend for the different connection types. (Figure has been designed using resources from Freepik.com)

3.3   Objective Function Formulation

The three objectives for the EMS are cost efficiency, resilience and customer satisfaction for EV charging. Hence, energy costs, time duration of grid independent operation and a customer satisfaction indicator (α) for EV charging are calculated. Equations 1 to 3 show these three objective functions. Energy costs (f_{cost}) are calculated by the sum of a base price (c_{bel}) and electric energy bought from (E_{supply}) and sold to (E_{feed}) the external grid over the simulation time. The price for bought energy c_{grid} holds a higher value than the remuneration c_{feed} for sold energy. Resilience for the energy system is measured by the minimum time duration (in minutes) in which the system can supply the power load P_{load} only using stored energy E_{bat} of the stationary battery. As indicated in Eq. 2, the quotient of stored energy and power load is a function of time, the minimum of this function over the simulation time determines the resilience value f_{res}. The function of the customer satisfaction index α is shown in Fig. 3. When the final *SoC* value after a charging process moves towards the desired *SoC* value ($SoC_{desired}$) for a charging process, α rapidly increases. Charging beyond $SoC_{desired}$ yields small increases of α. For a detailed description of the customer satisfaction index, it is referred to [15].

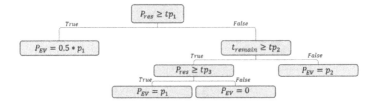

Fig. 2. Structure of the EV charging strategy within the EMS. P_{EV} denotes the EV charging power, which equals to p_i depending on the operating mode. Different operating modes are activated when the threshold parameters tp_i are exceeded for the remaining charge duration t_{remain} at the EV charging station and the residual power P_{res} between building power demand and PV power generation.

$$f_{cost} = c_{grid} * E_{supply} - c_{feed} * E_{feed} + c_{bel} \tag{1}$$

$$f_{res} = \min \frac{E_{bat}}{P_{load}}(t_{sim}) * 60 \tag{2}$$

$$f_{EV} = \alpha(SoC) \tag{3}$$

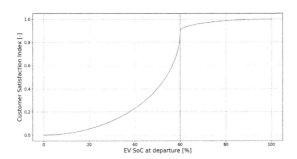

Fig. 3. Customer satisfaction index for the EV charging process [15]. Note the change in the function curve at the desired state of charge of 60% for a charging process ($SoC_{desired}$).

Desirability Function. The introduced objective functions have different value ranges. One approach to obtain an aggregated objective is to average over the objective functions [19]. However, varying scales of the objective functions impede the balanced optimization of the aggregated objective. Since, larger scale objective functions may have stronger weights on the overall objective. Therefore, desirability functions are employed [14,18]. Desirability functions allow for uniform scaling of objective functions. This uniform scaling allows for proper aggregation of objective functions with various value ranges. The aggregated function can subsequently be utilized in an optimization framework. The desirability function $d(f)$ for a given objective function f is determined by a nonlinear transformation according to Eq. 4 (with $b0, b1$ as manually tuned parameters).

$$d(f) = \exp\left(-\exp\left(-(b_0 + b_1 * f)\right)\right) \qquad (4)$$

The desirability function is scaled to the interval $I = [0, 1]$. High desirability values correspond to objective values of high quality. For a detailed description of desirabilities, it is referred to [18]. The three resulting desirabilities are aggregated by calculating the arithmetic mean. The optimization is formulated as a minimization problem. Hence, the aggregate desirability function is internally defined as $1 - d(f)$.

4   Adversarial Optimization

4.1   Optimization Problem

For the development of robust control strategies, a certain performance level ought to be ensured even for failures in the system or unpredicted scenarios. Therefore, discrete scenarios can be sampled from the scenario space S. The aim here is to identify controller parameterizations, which exhibit low sensitivity to uncertainties in the scenario space. This approach establishes to some extent robustness against scenario variations. However, the robustness strongly depends on the sampled scenarios. To establish worst-case robustness of solutions, worst-case scenarios need to be specifically considered in the optimization process. For larger scenario spaces with many possible scenario configurations, the identification of worst-case scenarios is itself an optimization problem. Equation 5 shows the formulation of the adversarial optimization problem [13]. Formulating the problem gives conceptual insights into adversarial optimization. Essentially, adversarial optimization unites two optimization problems. Since the objective function for both problems is identical, a strongly coupled problem results. Moreover, considering a game theoretic perspective, both optimization problems act as antagonistic players. The goal of the first player is to identify a worst-case scenario $s*$, for that the second player tries to find a respective worst-case robust solution $x*$. Where the vector s comprises all scenario parameters for the energy supply system and x consists of all threshold parameters for the control strategy.

$$\min f_{\text{agg}}(x, s) \qquad \max f_{\text{agg}}(x, s)$$
$$x_{\text{l}} \leq x \leq x_{\text{u}} \qquad s_{\text{l}} \leq s \leq s_{\text{u}} \qquad (5)$$
$$g(x, s) = P_{\text{res}} - P_{\text{gmax}} \leq 0$$

Here, f_{agg} denotes the aggregated objective function. The inequality restriction $g(x, s)$ ensures that the power supply satisfies the power demand. Hence,

$g(\boldsymbol{x}, \boldsymbol{s})$ restricts the residual power P_{res} to be less than or equal to the maximum grid power supply P_{gmax}.

Co-evolutionary optimization methods can be employed to solve such adversarial problem structures. In this approach, scenario and controller populations are optimized or evolved iteratively [1,2]. In the following, the applied co-evolutionary optimization method is presented. Subsequently, enhancing the co-evolutionary approach, an archive-based optimization method is proposed.

4.2   Archives

Optimization Archives are commonly used in dynamic optimization to store good solutions and retrieve them, when the objective space changes [6]. This can enable efficient optimization of a dynamically changing objective function. As mentioned in Sect. 2, fundamental limits to adversarial robustness may exist. Based on the insight, that robustness of a single solution against all possible or even multiple worst-case scenarios might not be feasible, optimization archives for adversarial optimization are proposed in this work. It is assumed, that for enabling a level of robustness against different worst-case scenarios, a set of robust controllers is necessary. Such robust controllers ought to be stored in an archive during the optimization. Hence, in this work, optimization archives are adopted for adversarial optimization to obtain a set of optimal controllers at the end of an optimization run. The remaining question is, how individuals of the controller population are stored in the archive. It is important to maintain a diversity of good control strategies throughout the optimization. Therefore, a variance-based method is adopted from [6]. The individual k in the archive is removed, which maximizes the variance Var of the remaining control strategies (Eq. 6). The current best control strategy from the controller population is subsequently stored in the archive.

$$\mathrm{Var}(k) = \sum_{l=1}^{m} \sum_{a \in A/\{k\}} (x_{la} - \overline{x}_l)^2 \tag{6}$$

Here, m denotes the length of the control strategy or decision variable $\boldsymbol{x}$, A the archive and k the currently dismissed controller in the archive. Var is determined by summing up the variance of all elements of $\boldsymbol{x}$. The mean value of element l over all variables in the archive is given by $\overline{x}_l$, x_{la} represents the value of element l for the a_{th} variable in the archive. In summary, the current best control strategy replaces the strategy k in each iteration, maintaining a diverse archive of a given size.

4.3   Co-evolutionary Approach

First, the iterative coevolutionary optimization (Coevol) is introduced. The optimization method for Coevol is illustrated in Fig. 4. In this approach, iteratively one population is optimized for the previous best individual of the other population. Precisely, the controller population is optimized for the worst scenario identified in the previous scenario optimization. The scenario population is likewise optimized for the best previously identified controller. Utilizing the optimization archives mentioned in the previous section, a diverse set of robust control strategies is stored over the optimization run.

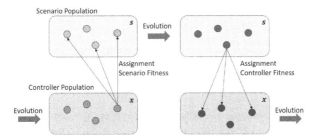

Fig. 4. Iterative co-evolutionary optimization (CoevoI). The controller population is optimized for the best scenario configuration s_i, identified in the previous scenario optimization loop. The scenario population is optimized vice versa. The current best control strategies x_i of the controller population are stored in the controller archive using the variance-based storage scheme.

4.4 Nested, Archive-Based Optimization

Co-evolutionary optimization methods have to cope with intransitive behavior, where the optimization continuously moves towards different local optima [8]. As described in Sect. 2, in [11] it is suggested to store identified worst-case scenarios and utilize them for the controller optimization. However, this goes along with rising computational costs, since in every iteration an additional worst-case scenario needs to be considered. In this work, to enhance the co-evolutionary optimization methods it is proposed to apply the concept of optimization archives for the scenario optimization. This ought to maintain a diverse set of worst-case scenarios, while limiting computational costs. It is assumed that a variety of identified worst-case scenarios can be represented by an archive of a given size n. The archive in each outer iteration is generated by determining the subset of n scenarios, with the highest variance, drawn from the whole set of identified worst-case scenarios over the optimization run. Equivalent to the variance calculation for the controller archives, the variance of the scenario archive is determined using Eq. 6. Hence, a nested, archive-based optimization method (NAOpt) is proposed. Using a nested approach, the worst-case scenario for each current best control strategy can be determined. The nested approach allows more iterations for the scenario optimization, since a premature convergence of the scenario optimization is not an issue as opposed to the iterative approach.

Convergence is rather favorable for each scenario optimization. The proposed optimization method is shown in Fig. 5. Similar to the iterative approach, a set of robust control strategies is also archived over the optimization run.

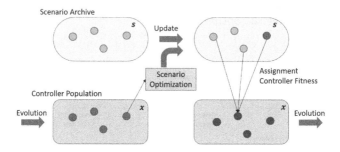

Fig. 5. Nested, Archive-based optimization (NAOpt). In each outer iteration, the nested scenario optimization identifies the worst-case scenario for the current best control strategy. The subset of previously identified worst-case scenarios with maximum variance is stored in the scenario archive. For the controller population a minimax fitness assignment is utilized. Each controller individual is evaluated against all individuals in the scenario archive. The current best control strategies are stored in the controller archive using the variance-based storage scheme.

5   Results

5.1   Performance Evaluation

This section begins with a detailed description of the evaluation procedure for the analysis of the worst-case robustness for the optimized control strategies. Subsequently, the results for the iterative and archive-based optimization methods are compared. The concept of Evolutionary Trajectories is then introduced for further analysis of the adversarial optimization methods.

Since the objective function $f(x, s)$ is evaluated via an engagement of control strategy x and scenario configuration s, the performance or fitness for either populations is relative. A good fitness function value for a controller can only be considered as such, when the corresponding scenario is a challenging one. The fitness of each scenario itself depends on the controller population it is evaluated against. Hence, for a better evaluation of the results, a baseline control strategy is employed. The employed reference EMS (REMS) is similar to a reference control strategy described in [7]. The charging power of the EV charging station is set to a constant value. The battery is charged when the residual power P_{res}, which equals to the difference between building power demand and PV power generation, exceeds a threshold parameter tp_{charge}. The battery is discharged when P_{res} is below the threshold value tp_{charge}.

The baseline controller is evaluated against all worst-case scenarios identified during an optimization run and against randomly sampled scenario configurations. Similarly, the archive of optimized controllers from an optimization run is evaluated. The performance of the baseline controller can then be compared to the averaged performance of the corresponding archive. By evaluating the performance of the baseline controller against the identified worst-case scenarios, the severity of these scenarios can be analyzed. Comparing the performance of baseline to optimized control strategies gives insight into the robustness of the latter. For each controller in an optimization archive the worst performances for the worst-case scenarios and the randomly sampled scenarios are determined. The performance of a specific controller is determined by averaging these two performance values. Subsequently, the performances of the archives' controllers are averaged. The performance of the baseline is similarly calculated by averaging the performances for the worst-case scenarios and the randomly sampled scenarios. In the last step, the performance of the controller archives for each optimization run is then averaged. Similarly, the performance of the reference controller is averaged. Figure 6 visualizes the evaluation procedure. The performance over the worst-case scenario $f_{\text{worst case}}$ is calculated as in Eq. 7. The performance for the randomly chosen scenarios f_{random} is calculated according to Eq. 8. As mentioned above, both calculated values for $f_{\text{worst case}}$ and f_{random} are averaged to determine overall performance.

$$f_{\text{worst case}} = \max_{s \in S_{\text{worst case}}} f(x_{\text{archive}}, s) \tag{7}$$

$$f_{\text{random}} = \max_{s \in S_{\text{random}}} f(x_{\text{archive}}, s) \tag{8}$$

5.2   Fitness Gap Analysis

In this section the optimization methods are evaluated and compared regarding the severity of the identified worst-case scenarios as well as the robustness of the optimized control strategies.

Both optimization methods are implemented utilizing the CMA-ES framework [12]. Considering computational costs, the population size for controller and scenario optimization is chosen to be 10. Initial value for mutation rate is specified to 0.2 for the scenario population and 0.25 for the controller population, these values correspond to mutation rates recommended for the used framework. The robustness of control strategies for severe scenarios is determined by the desirability of the objective function value. The robustness of the control strategies is better for higher desirability values, worse robustness is indicated by lower desirability values. Likewise, analyzing the severity of identified worst-case scenarios, lower desirabilities for the baseline strategy indicate higher severity and vice versa.

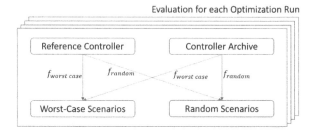

Fig. 6. Evaluation procedure. For each optimization run, the reference controller and the identified controller archive are evaluated against the worst-case scenarios, collected over all iterations, and against randomly sampled scenario configurations. The performance of the controller archives over all optimization runs is subsequently averaged. Similarly, the average performance of the reference controller is determined.

Iterative Co-evolutionary Optimization. For the iterative co-evolutionary optimization method (CoevoI), the number of inner iterations for the scenario optimization is set to 50 and for the controller optimization to 25. The outer iteration number is set to 20. More iteration steps are allocated to the scenario optimization loop. This ought to ensure, that scenarios with certain severity are identified. The controller population may slowly move towards better performance. Table 1 shows the averaged desirability values for baseline and optimized controllers. The baseline controller with a rather low mean desirability of 0.338 does not perform well for the identified worst-case scenarios. The optimized controller performs better with a mean value of 0.737. The results indicate, that the control strategies optimized by CoevoI show higher robustness compared to the baseline with a desirability difference (Δ Desirability) of approximately 0.4.

Nested, Archive-Based Optimization. Table 2 shows averaged desirability values for baseline and optimized control strategies for the Nested, Archive-based Optimization approach (NAOpt). The outer iteration number is set to 20. The number of inner iterations for controller optimization is set to 25. The number of inner nested iterations for scenario optimization is set to 70. The iteration steps for the scenario optimization in this nested approach are set higher compared to the iterative approach, since here for every iteration the worst-case scenario for the current best controller is searched. The mean desirability value of 0.148 for the baseline controller shows poor performance of the baseline for the worst-case scenarios identified by NAOpt. The Δ Desirability value between baseline and optimized controllers amounts to approximately 0.6.

The severity of the identified scenarios is higher than for CoevoI by a difference in mean baseline desirability of 0.19. The difference in Δ Desirability between NAOpt and CoevoI amounts to 0.209. This indicates higher robustness of the controllers optimized by NAOpt. Higher severity of the identified scenarios is indicated by the lower mean desirability of the baseline control strategy.

Table 1. Comparing averaged desirability values of baseline and optimized controller for the Iterative Co-evolutionary Optimization (CoevoI). Number of inner iterations for scenario optimization is set to 50 and for controller optimization to 25. The number of outer iterations is set to 20. A total of 20 optimization runs are analyzed.

Control strategy	Mean	Std. deviation
Baseline	0.338	0.170
CoevoI	0.737	0.162
Δ Desirability	0.399	

Table 2. Comparing averaged desirability values of baseline and optimized controller for the Nested, Archive-based Optimization (NAOpt). Number of iterations for the nested scenario optimization is set to 70 and for controller optimization to 25. The number of outer iterations is set to 20. A total of 20 optimization runs are analyzed.

Control strategy	Mean	Std. deviation
Baseline	0.148	0.106
NAOpt	0.756	0.170
Δ Desirability	0.608	

5.3 Evolutionary Trajectories

As indicated in Sect. 2, adversarial optimization approaches can be described by predator-prey dynamics [8]. Figure 7 shows a converging trajectory for a biologic predator-prey relation with competition within both populations [4]. Here, the variation in overall population size of predators and prey is reduced till there is almost no variation. Applied on adversarial optimization the convergence point bears similarities to a worst-case optimal solution, since from this point the population size or fitness value would not be reduced or worsened anymore. Evolutionary trajectories (ET) give insight into co-evolutionary dynamics during the optimization. Note that there is a key distinction between the displayed predator-prey dynamics and ET for adversarial optimization. The mean of the trajectory in Fig. 7 remains the same. However, for adversarial optimization this behavior is not necessary, rather a spiralling curve towards an optimal area in the objective space may be observed.

Figures 8 and 9 show ETs for the implemented iterative and archive-based optimization methods. The ETs show the relation between controller and scenario optimization. The trajectories consist of current best individuals for both optimization loops. For the controller optimization higher desirability or better performance and for the controller optimization lower desirability or worse performance is desired.

For the iterative approach (CoevoI) a rather straight trajectory towards higher controller and scenario desirability can be observed. CoevoI quickly start to converge similar to the predator-prey characteristic mentioned above. The iterative method reaches a local optimal area. The optimization then seems to follow local scenarios and controllers, this is indicated by the rather high variance of the convergence phase.

The nested, archive-based optimization method (NAOpt) displays a different trajectory. In this approach worst-case scenarios, identified in previous iteration loops, are considered in the controller optimization. A key distinction of NAOpt compared to the previous method is the search path towards the convergence phase. Since a diversity of solutions is considered, utilizing scenario archives, the trajectory shows direction changes. This indicates proper searching for optimal areas. During the convergence phase there is low variance for the scenario fitness, however the variance of the controller fitness is a bit higher than for the iterative optimization approaches. In addition, the convergence phase shows decreasing variance. This is indicated by the sub-area with higher density within the convergence area. The final solution has worse controller desirability, but also better scenario desirability than for the iterative optimization method. Here, the desirability values for controller and scenario population seem to be balanced out more. This is opposed to the previous approaches, where for controller desirability or performance a rather direct increase is observed.

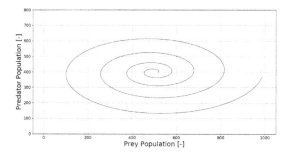

Fig. 7. Evolutionary trajectory of a biologic predator and prey population with intraspecies competition, adapted from [4]

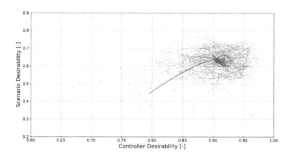

Fig. 8. Spline interpolated evolutionary trajectory of CoevoI. The trajectories consist of the current best individuals for both optimization loops. The mark at each trajectory indicates the starting point of the optimization run, the thicker line represents the averaged trajectory. A total of 20 optimization runs are analyzed. Higher variance of the convergence phase indicates low convergence for scenario and controller optimization.

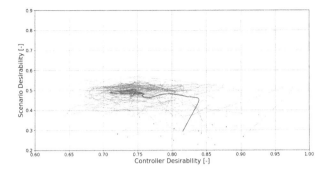

Fig. 9. Spline interpolated evolution trajectory of NAOpt. The trajectories consist of the current best individuals for both optimization loops. The mark at each trajectory indicates the starting point of the optimization run, the thicker line represents the averaged trajectory. A total of 20 optimization runs are analyzed. The trajectory shows a proper search path towards better performance areas in the objective space. Decreasing variance of the convergence phase can be observed.

6   Summary and Outlook

In this work we have implemented an adversarial optimization concept to identify robust controller parameters even for severe scenarios. Our analysis has shown that our approach can find scenarios more difficult than randomly sampled scenarios, and controllers that outperform baseline controllers on the evolved scenarios and also randomly sampled scenarios. The approach was tested on the problem of smart charging of EVs in private homes under optimal self-consumption of PV power generation, energy costs, and customer satisfaction for EV charging.

We compared two different approaches for adversarial optimization, namely the Iterative Co-evolutionary Optimization (CoevoI) and the Nested, Archive-based Optimization (NAOpt). The results showed that the utilization of scenario archives considerably improves the robustness of the optimized control strategies. This goes along with increased severity of the identified scenarios during the optimization path.

An analysis based on the concept of predator-prey dynamics showed that the adoption of evolutionary trajectories can give additional insights into adversarial optimization. Evolutionary trajectories show the relation between scenario and controller optimization, this allows to analyze the co-evolutionary dynamics of the adversarial optimization problem. The rather intuitive iterative optimization structure (CoevoI) exhibits negative co-evolutionary dynamics, where both optimization loops follow local optima. This manifests in the lack of finding severe scenarios and respective robust controllers. Whereas, NAOpt proves to identify more severe scenarios and respective robust controllers, considering an archive of worst-case scenarios identified over the course of optimization. The Evolutionary Trajectories for NAOpt accordingly display a different progress and convergence behavior compared to CoevoI. In particular, a proper search path towards optimal areas in the objective space can be observed. Additionally, the results show, that the chosen size of the scenario archive for NAOpt is able to represent worst-case scenarios identified during the optimization run, while reducing computational costs.

It is suggested to utilize the concept of Evolutionary Trajectories to further analyze and improve adversarial optimization methods. Improvement could be made by directly utilizing the Evolutionary Trajectory during the optimization, for instance in the fitness assignment. A more detailed analysis of the convergence behavior for controller and scenario optimization could give additional insights into the optimization methods. Better convergence might also narrow down the worst-case optimal area in the controller parameter space. For further research, the size of the controller archive might be analyzed. The assumption of needing a variety of optimal controller configurations to enable worst-case robustness could be further confirmed this way.

Acknowledgments. Baraq Mushtaq acknowledges the financial support from the Honda Research Institute Europe.

References

1. Al-Dujaili, A., Srikant, S., Hemberg, E., O'Reilly, U.M.: On the application of Danskin's theorem to derivative-free minimax optimization. arXiv preprint arXiv:1805.06322 (2018)
2. Barbosa, H.J.: A coevolutionary genetic algorithm for constrained optimization. In: Proceedings of the 1999 Congress on Evolutionary Computation-CEC99 (Cat. No. 99TH8406), vol. 3, pp. 1605–1611. IEEE (1999)
3. Ben-Tal, A., El Ghaoui, L., Nemirovski, A.: Robust Optimization, vol. 28. Princeton University Press, Princeton (2009)
4. Bischof, R., Zedrosser, A.: The educated prey: consequences for exploitation and control. Behav. Ecol. **20**(6), 1228–1235 (2009)
5. Braam, F., Hollinger, R., Engesser, M.L., Müller, S., Kohrs, R., Wittwer, C.: Peak shaving with photovoltaic-battery systems. In: IEEE PES Innovative Smart Grid Technologies, Europe, pp. 1–5. IEEE (2014)
6. Branke, J.: Evolutionary Optimization in Dynamic Environments, vol. 3. Springer, Heidelberg (2012)
7. Cheng, R., Rodemann, T., Fischer, M., Olhofer, M., Jin, Y.: Evolutionary many-objective optimization of hybrid electric vehicle control: from general optimization to preference articulation. IEEE Trans. Emerg. Top. Comput. Intell. **1**(2), 97–111 (2017)
8. Cramer, A.M., Sudhoff, S.D., Zivi, E.L.: Evolutionary algorithms for minimax problems in robust design. IEEE Trans. Evol. Comput. **13**(2), 444–453 (2008)
9. ESI-ITI: SimulationX 4.0. http://www.simulationx.com/
10. Fawzi, A., Fawzi, O., Frossard, P.: Fundamental limits on adversarial robustness. In: Proceedings of ICML, Workshop on Deep Learning (2015)
11. Halck, O.M., Dahl, F.A.: Asymmetric co-evolution for imperfect-information zero-sum games. In: López de Mántaras, R., Plaza, E. (eds.) ECML 2000. LNCS (LNAI), vol. 1810, pp. 171–182. Springer, Heidelberg (2000). https://doi.org/10.1007/3-540-45164-1_18

12. Hansen, N., Müller, S., Koumoutsakos, P.: Reducing the time complexity of the derandomized evolution strategy with covariance matrix adaptation. Evol. Comput. **11**, 1–18 (2003). http://www.lri.fr/ hansen/publications.html
13. Herrmann, J.W.: A genetic algorithm for minimax optimization problems. In: Proceedings of the 1999 Congress on Evolutionary Computation-CEC99 (Cat. No. 99TH8406), vol. 2, pp. 1099–1103. IEEE (1999)
14. Ogino, Y., Iida, R., Rodemann, T.: Using desirability functions for many-objective optimization of a hybrid car controller. In: GECCO 2017 Conference Companion (2017)
15. Rodemann, T., Kitamura, K.: Simulation-based design and evaluation of a smart energy manager. In: Computer Aided Systems Theory - EUROCAST (2019, to appear)
16. Sebald, A.V., Schlenzig, J.: Minimax design of neural net controllers for highly uncertain plants. IEEE Trans. Neural Netw. **5**(1), 73–82 (1994)
17. Unger, R., Mikoleit, B., Schwan, T., Bäker, B., Kehrer, C., Rodemann, T.: Green building - modeling renewable building energy systems with emobility using Modelica. In: Proceedings of Modelica 2012 Conference. Modelica Association, Munich, Germany (2012)
18. Wagner, T., Trautmann, H.: Integration of preferences in hypervolume-based multiobjective evolutionary algorithms by means of desirability functions. IEEE Trans. Evol. Comput. **14**(5), 688–701 (2010)
19. Zhu, L., Deb, K., Kulkarni, S.: Multi-scenario optimization using multi-criterion methods: a case study on byzantine agreement problem. In: 2014 IEEE Congress on Evolutionary Computation (CEC), pp. 2601–2608. IEEE (2014)

Soft Computing Applied to Games

Efficient Heuristic Policy Optimisation for a Challenging Strategic Card Game

Raúl Montoliu[1(✉)], Raluca D. Gaina[2], Diego Pérez-Liebana[2],
Daniel Delgado[1], and Simon Lucas[2]

[1] Institute of New Imaging Technologies,
University Jaume I, Castellón, Spain
{montoliu,delgadod}@uji.es
[2] Queen Mary University of London, London, UK
{r.d.gaina,diego.perez,simon.lucas}@qmul.ac.uk

Abstract. Turn-based multi-action adversarial games are challenging scenarios in which each player turn consists of a sequence of atomic actions. The order in which an AI agent runs these atomic actions may hugely impact the outcome of the turn. One of the main challenges of game artificial intelligence is to design a heuristic function to help agents to select the optimal turn to play, given a particular state of the game. In this paper, we report results using the recently developed N-Tuple Bandit Evolutionary Algorithm to tune the heuristic function parameters. For evaluation, we measure how the tuned heuristic function affects the performance of the state-of-the-art evolutionary algorithm Online Evolution Planning. The multi-action adversarial strategy card game *Legends of Code and Magic* was used as a testbed. Results indicate that the N-Tuple Bandit Evolutionary Algorithm can effectively tune the heuristic function parameters to improve the performance of the agent.

Keywords: Game artificial intelligence · Board and card games solving · Learning in games · Multi-action games · Heuristic policy optimisation

In turn-based multi-action adversarial games, each player turn consists of several atomic actions and the order in which the agent plays those actions has a significant influence in the game. Evolutionary algorithms are the current state of the art in this kind of games. They need a heuristic function (also known as fitness function) to estimate a score about how good or bad it is to be in a particular state of the game. Heuristic functions tend to have several parameters that should be tuned to obtain good results. Most of the previous works manually tuned the parameters using expert knowledge and experience playing the game [1,6]. An alternative solution is to use an evolutionary algorithm to find the best parameter combination.

This work has been partially supported by the grant CAS18/00207 from the Spanish Ministry of Education, culture and sports.

© Springer Nature Switzerland AG 2020
P. A. Castillo et al. (Eds.): EvoApplications 2020, LNCS 12104, pp. 403–418, 2020.
https://doi.org/10.1007/978-3-030-43722-0_26

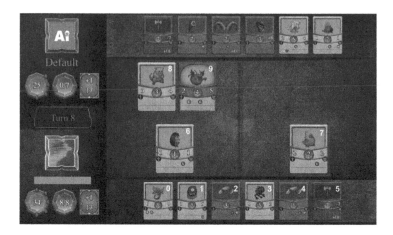

Fig. 1. A screenshot of the *Legend of Code and Magic* game during the battle phase (https://www.codingame.com). The cards in the opponent player hand (top) are unknown during the match.

Recently, the N-Tuple Bandit Evolutionary algorithm (*NTBEA*) [9] was presented as an effective method for parameter tuning. It is very useful when the evaluation function of the game is noisy and fairly expensive in CPU time, as is the case in multi-action adversarial games. Hence, it is desirable to have an evolutionary algorithm that can operate very efficiently, making the best possible use of the available fitness evaluation budget, and also one that is robust to noise. *NTBEA* satisfies both criteria. It has successfully been used to tune agent parameters [8]. The main novelty of the paper is that, in this paper, *NTBEA* is used to tune the parameters of the heuristic function. As far as we know, this is the first research paper performing this task using *NTBEA*.

The performance of the state-of-the-art evolutionary algorithm Online Evolutionary Planning (OEP) [6], with the heuristic function parameters tuned using *NTBEA*, was assessed. It has been previously tested on the game *HeroAIcademy*. Instead, in this paper, the multi-action adversarial strategy card game Legends of Code and Magic (*LOCM*) [7] was used as testbed. *LOCM* is a game with some similarities to the popular *Hearthstone*[1]. Some of the more challenging features of the game are: (1) a variable number of actions can be played in each turn, (2) some parts of the game are unknown in the state, (3) the order in which the cards are played is very relevant, and (4) the game has a very large branching factor.

One challenging difference of *LOCM* with respect to *Hearthstone* is that, in the former, the time budget to obtain the next turn is just 200 ms in contrast to 60000 ms of a typical *Hearthstone* game. In addition, in the *LOCM* game, the board is divided into two lanes (left and right) instead of just one as in *Hearthstone*. This adds an even higher branching factor since the agents have to

---

[1] https://playhearthstone.com.

deal with the problem of having to decide in which part of the board each card should be played. Figure 1 shows a screenshot of this game.

Summarising, this paper presents three main novelties:

- We apply the N-Tuple Bandit Evolutionary algorithm to adjust the parameters of the heuristic function used by an evolutionary agent. As far as we know, this is the first paper applying *NTBEA* for this purpose.
- This is the first research paper using the multi-action adversarial game *Legends of Code and Magic* as a testbed. This game has as principal challenging characteristics its very low time budget to obtain player actions in a turn (200 ms) and a very large branch factor. In addition, this is the first time that *NTBEA* is used in a game as challenging as *LOCM*.
- We assess the performance of the Online Evolution Planning algorithm, with the parameters of their heuristic function tuned using *NTBEA*. As far as we know, this is the first paper applying this type of evolutionary algorithm to a strategy card game.

1   Definitions, Notation and Problem Formulation

This section introduces the terminology and the notation that will be used throughout this paper and formulates the problem to be solved. The notation follows the one exposed by Cowling et al. in [4]. More detail on the game theory concepts can be found in standard textbooks on this subject, e.g. [10].

A *game* is defined as a direct graph (S, Λ) where S are the nodes and Λ the edges of the graph. The nodes S are called *states* of the game. The leaf nodes are called *terminal states* and the other nodes *non-terminal states*. In general, a game has a positive number of k players. Some games also have an *environment player* (player 0). Each state s is associated with a number $\rho(s) \in \{0, \ldots, k\}$, that represents the player about to act. Each terminal state s_T is associated with a vector $\mu(s_T) \in \mathbb{R}^k$, which represents the *reward* vector. In some games, the non-terminal states can also be associated with an *immediate* reward vector that gives an idea of how well the players are doing. A heuristic function $\lambda(s)$ can be used to estimate the reward vector $\mu(s)$, given the state (terminal or not).

The game starts at time $t = 0$ in the initial state s_0. At time $t = 0, 1, 2, \ldots$, if state s_t is non terminal, player $\rho(s_t)$ chooses an edge $(s_t, s_{t+1}) \in \Lambda$ and the game transitions though that edge to the state s_{t+1}. This continues until a terminal state is reached at time $t = T$. Then, each player receives a reward equal to their corresponding entry in the vector $\mu(s_T)$ and the game ends. If the game allows immediate rewards, players receive the immediate reward $\mu(s_{t+1})$ after reaching the state s_{t+1}.

Players typically do not choose edges directly, but choose *actions*. In the simplest case, each outgoing edge of a state s corresponds to an action that player $\rho(s)$ can play. The set of actions from a state s is denoted $A(s)$. Note that, given a state s, the player $\rho(s)$ can play just one action (i.e. choose an edge (s_t, s_{t+1})) from the ones included in $A(s)$.

The *transition function* Φ maps a (state, action) pair (s_t, a) to a resulting state s_{t+1} by choosing an edge (s_t, s_{t+1}).

A *policy* for player i maps each state s with $\rho(s) = i$ to a probability distribution over $A(s)$. This distribution specifies how likely the player i is to choose each action from that state. One fundamental problem to be solved in adversarial game AI is to find the policy that leads to the highest expected reward, given that all other players are trying to do the same.

The terms *action* and *atomic action* can be confused in multi-action games. In this paper, we will refer to *turn* as every edge outgoing a state (i.e. the actions) and to *atomic action* to every element that can be part of a turn. The set of all possible atomic actions given a state s is denoted $\Gamma(s) = \{\gamma_1, \gamma_2, \ldots, \gamma_{q_s}\}$. The edges outgoing the state s, are all the possible permutations of the elements of $\Gamma(s)$ which, depending on the number of elements, can be a very large number. Therefore, there are as many different turns that can be played from a state s, as possible permutations in $\Gamma(s)$. In most games, the number of atomic actions q_s included in the set $\Gamma(s)$ depends on the state s.

We denote $\tau(s) = [\gamma_1, \gamma_2, \ldots, \gamma_{p_s}]$ as the list of ordered atomic actions, included in $\Gamma(s)$, that are played for player $\rho(s)$. Note that each atomic action can be played just once in a turn and that not all atomic actions included in $\Gamma(s)$ must be played, i.e. $p_s \leq q_s, \forall s$. The number of elements included in the list $\tau(s)$ can be different depending on the game and the policy used.

The problem that the agents have to solve is, given a state s, to find the list $\tau(s)$ that leads to the highest immediate expected reward, i.e. to find the best subset of atomic actions allowed from the state s and the appropriate order to play them.

The heuristic function $\lambda(s)$ is frequently defined as a linear combination of some features included in the state as follows:

$$\lambda(s) = \sum_{f=1}^{F} \omega_f * \theta_f \tag{1}$$

where F is the number of features of the state being taken into account when estimating the reward vector. Therefore, the problem to be solved in this paper is to find the correct value of each weight ω_f. In this paper, we proposed to use *NTBEA* for this purpose.

In the *LOCM* game, there are only two players $(k = 2)$ and there is no *environment player*. The number of atomic actions q_s included in $\Gamma(s)$ can vary along with the state. Preliminary experiments have shown that this number can vary from 1 to 35, with two peaks around 5 and 15 actions as most common cases. These statistics have been calculated after running 100 matches where the *OEP* agent (explained in detail in Sect. 2.3) has played versus itself. Similar results can be obtained when using other agents. In addition, there is no fixed number of atomic actions q_s.

2   Related Work and Background

2.1   Related Work on Strategy Card Games

Most of the previous works on Strategy Card Game AI deal with the *Hearthstone* game. Since the cards in the opponent's deck should be unknown in this type of games, some authors have developed methods to predict them. Dockhorn et al. [5] used the knowledge gathered from a database of human replays to create a knowledge-base of frequent player card combinations. Bursztein presented in [2] a similar work where a bag-of-words of card co-occurrence bi-gram was used for training a prediction system for the next upcoming card.

Santos et al. [12] proposed a modified version of the Monte Carlo Tree Search (*MCTS*) algorithm which integrates expert knowledge in the algorithm's search process through a database of decks that the algorithm uses to cope with the imperfect information and through the inclusion of a heuristic that guides the *MCTS* rollout phase. Zhang and Buro [13] improved the effectiveness of MCTS by reducing search complexity in the selection phase and by improving the rollout phase, in which *MCTS* will sample action sequences according to a rollout policy. Choe and Kim [3] presented an MCTS-based approach to reduce the complexity of the search space and decide on the best strategy. They used state abstraction to present the search space as a Directed Acyclic Graph (DAG) and introduced a variant of Upper Confidence Bound for Trees algorithm for the DAG. In addition, they applied a sparse sampling algorithm to handle imperfect information and randomness and reduce the stochastic branching factor.

2.2   N-Tuple Bandit Evolutionary Algorithm

The N-Tuple Bandit Evolutionary algorithm (*NTBEA*) [9] combines multi-armed bandits with an evolutionary algorithm to provide a sample-efficient optimization algorithm. *NTBEA* was developed to handle noisy optimization problems in a sample-efficient way. The algorithm analyses the contribution of each individual parameter value, together with combinations of parameter values. Each combination is referred to as an N-Tuple. A modified form of the bandit equation is used to balance exploiting apparently good parameter settings with exploring those that have not yet been sampled much.

The algorithm starts sampling a single solution point uniformly at random in the search space. The fitness of this solution is evaluated once, in the problem domain, using the noisy evaluator. This solution is then stored in the bandit fitness landscape model, together with its fitness value. The model is then searched within the neighbourhood for a new solution. *NTBEA* assumes that the execution time of querying the bandit landscape model is negligible compared to evaluating a candidate solution on the target problem.

The neighbourhood is defined using the number of neighbours and the proximity distribution to the current solution, which is controlled by a mutation operator. The neighbouring solution with the highest estimated Upper Confidence Bounds aggregated value ($\widehat{UCB}$) is then selected and the process repeats until the evaluation budget is used up, or some other termination condition is met.

For a problem with F parameters to be tuned, $NTBEA$ is typically configured using F 1-Tuple bandits, $\frac{F*(F-1)}{2}$ 2-Tuples bandits and one F-Tuple macro-arm bandit.

A key part of the algorithm is the value function used to sample in a large search space. The UCB value of any arm i is defined as:

$$UCB_a = X_a + C * \sqrt{\frac{\log n}{n_a + \epsilon}} \tag{2}$$

where X_a is the mean reward for playing arm a. This is the exploitation term. The right-hand term controls the exploration, where n is the total number of times this bandit has been played, and n_a is the number of times the arm a has been played. The term C is called the exploration factor: higher values of C lead to exploratory search, low values lead to a more greedy or exploitative search. The ϵ value is used to control whether each arm should be pulled at least once. In the standard UCB formula, ϵ is set to zero ensuring that each arm is pulled once in turn, but for $NTBEA$ purposes, this would be impractical, as the macro-arm consisting of the entire N-Tuple would force an exhaustive exploration of the search space.

The UCB aggregate value for all arms used, given a solution x is defined as follows:

$$\widehat{UCB}(x) = \frac{\sum_{j=1}^{m} UCB_{N_j(x)}}{m} \tag{3}$$

where m is the total number of bandits used and N is the N-Tuple indexing function such that $N_j(x)$ indexes the j-th bandit for search space point x.

2.3   Online Evolutionary Planning

Online Evolutionary Planning (OEP) [6] is an evolutionary approach that can be applied to multi-action adversarial games. It optimises the action sequence of the current turn, without looking ahead to future turns of the player or the opponent. OEP begins its search by creating an initial population of genomes. Each genome represents a complete turn, a fixed-length sequence of atomic actions. These atomic actions can be sampled randomly, or another initialisation strategy can be used. The population is then improved from generation to generation until computation time runs out or the allowed budget is depleted.

The crossover step of the evolutionary algorithm used can lead to an illegal action in some of the created offspring. A repair strategy is needed, for instance by picking random legal actions or using a greedy approach [1]. A proportion of the offspring undergoes mutation. One randomly chosen action of the sequence is changed to another action randomly chosen from all legal actions. If this leads to illegal actions later in the sequence, they are replaced using the repair strategy as well.

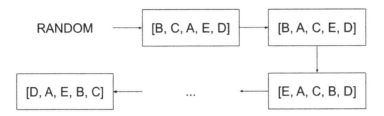

Fig. 2. An example of the *OEP* algorithm in a turn with 5 possible atomic actions: A, B, C, D and E. In this example, a 1+1 evolutionary algorithm is used.

When the time budget is exhausted, *OEP* returns the action sequence represented by the current best genome, so it can be executed, one atomic action at a time. It can, therefore, be seen as doing one iteration of rolling horizon evolutionary algorithm (RHEA) [11] at the beginning of each turn, and with a search horizon of one turn. Figure 2 shows an example of the OEP operation where $\Gamma(S) = \{A, B, C, D, E\}$.

3 Methods

3.1 Legend of Code and Magic

Legends of Code and Magic (*LOCM*) [7] is an implementation of a multi-action adversarial Strategy Card Game, designed to perform AI research. Its advantage over real card game AI engines is that it is much simpler to handle by the agents, and thus allows testing more sophisticated algorithms and quickly implementing theoretical ideas. The most similar commercial game is *Hearthstone*. One important difference is that the time budget in *LOCM* is just 200 ms in contrast to 60000 ms used in *Hearthstone*. Therefore, some algorithms frequently used in *Hearthstone*, such as *MCTS*, do not perform as well here.

LOCM is based on the fair arena mode, i.e., before every game, both players create their decks secretly from symmetrical yet limited choices. Because of that, the deck building phase cannot be simply reduced to using human-created top-meta decks as in *Hearthstone*. All cards effects are deterministic. The non-determinism is introduced by the ordering of cards in the decks.

The game has two phases. First, in the draft phase, for 30 turns, both players are given a choice between 3 different cards. Players select the card they want to add to their deck. Both players can select the same card. Players do not know which cards have been selected by the opponent. Once the draft phase is over, both decks (consisting of 30 cards each) are shuffled. The second phase is the battle, where each player plays cards from their hand on the two lanes, on their side of the board. Each player starts with 30 health points (HP). To reduce the health points of an opponent, the player must make use of cards to deal damage. The game is over once any player reaches 0 or less HP.

There are two different types of cards: Creatures and Items. Placing a Creature (similar to minions in *Hearthstone*) on the board is called summoning. A player summons Creatures to their side of the board by paying their cost in *mana*. They are used to attack the opponent and also serve as a defence against the Creatures of the opposing player. When a Creature attacks the opponent directly (and not their cards), it reduces the HP of the opponent according to its attack strength. When a Creature attacks another Creature, they both deal damage equal to their attack strength to the defence of the other creature. Creatures are removed from play when their defence reaches 0 or less. Creatures can have different abilities. One of the most important ones is *Guard*, which enforces that enemy creatures from the same lane must attack creatures with *Guard* first.

The other type of card is Items (similar to spells in *Hearthstone*). When played, Items have an immediate and permanent effect on the board or the players. There are three types of Items: (1) green Items must target the active player's creatures and have beneficial effects to them. (2) red Items must target the opponent's creatures and have a negative effect on them. (3) blue Items can be played to give the active player a positive effect or cause damage to the opponent, depending on the card.

Mana is necessary to play cards from the hand. Each turn, the number of mana units that each player can use increases. Each player can spend as much mana units per turn as they have. For instance, if the player starts the turn with 6 mana units, it is possible to summon two cards with cost 3 each, or summon only one with 6 mana cost. The cost of the cards varies from 0 to 12.

To run a turn the agent must provide to the environment a list of atomic actions. The complete rules of the game can be found in [7].

Valid and Possible Atomic Actions. As shown in Fig. 1, the valid atomic actions that can be played in the actual state of the game are as follows (yellow numbers in the top-right corner of each card show their ID): {*Summon 1 L; Summon 1 R; Summon 3 L; Summon 3 R; Use 2 6; Use 2 7; Use 4 6; Use 4 7; Use 5 8; Use 5 9; Attack 6 9, Attack 7 −1*}. Note that card 6 cannot attack either to opponent card 8 or directly to the opponent since opponent card 9 has the *Guard* property.

But, if the agent decides to play first the atomic action *Use 5 9*, then two new atomic actions can be played for card 6 since now the opponent card 9 will no longer be on the board and no other card with the *Guard* ability remains on the board. These two new possible atomic actions are: *Attack 6 8* and *Attack 6 −1*.

To give to the agents the opportunity to discover this kind of interesting behaviours, all the possible atomic action that can be played (taking into account any possible order of playing the atomic actions) and not only the valid ones, should be included in the set $\Gamma[s]$.

3.2 Agents

All the agents tested in this paper, start from the list of all possible actions that can be played in a state s (i.e. the list $\Gamma(s)$) and attempt to find an optimal turn $\tau(s)$. In all cases, before playing an atomic action, the agent checks if the atomic action is a valid one. If not, this atomic action is ignored and the agent tries to play the next one in the list $\tau(s)$.

Random Agent. The random agent just shuffles the initial list of atomic actions $\Gamma(s)$. They are then played in the resulting order. The heuristic function is not used.

NoAI Agent. This agent directly plays the list of initial atomic actions in the original order. This order follows a simple strategy which aims to directly attack the opponent whenever possible. Similarly to the *Random agent*, *NoAI* does not use the heuristic function.

OEP-Based Agent. The original version of the *OEP* algorithm has to select 5 atomic actions (in the game *HeroAIcademy* $q_s = 5, \forall s$) to be played from the set of all valid actions that can be played. Therefore, the genome is a list of five atomic actions. In our case, the genome is the list of all possible (not only valid) atomic actions (i.e. $\Gamma(s)$) that can be played given the state of the game. The agent plays the atomic actions following the order in the list $\Gamma(s)$. If an action is not valid, given the current state of the game, it is ignored and play continues with the next one.

Mutation consists of changing the order of the atomic actions on the list. This allow to discover interesting sequence of actions that can maximise the immediate rewards.

Since the time budget of *LOCM* is very small (200ms), a simple 1+1 evolutionary algorithm has been used. Therefore, no crossover step is needed. In cases where the time budget is higher, a more sophisticated evolutionary algorithm could be used.

3.3 Heuristic Function Design

The heuristic function $\lambda(s)$ has been designed as a linear combination of several features, balanced by a set of weights (see Eq. 1). Five different features are proposed:

- θ_1: The objective of the game is to reduce the health points of the opponent to zero. This feature is the difference between the opponent health points after playing the turn (i.e. at state s_{t+1}), and their initial health points (i.e. at state s_t). A larger value means that the agent is reducing more health points from the opponent.

– θ_2: Agents have to also pay attention to the opponent cards on the board, since, in the next turn, they can be used to attack the player. Therefore, it is very important to balance the attacks between the opponent cards and the opponent directly. This feature is the possible loss of health points if the opponent decides to directly attack the player using all its cards. In this case, small values are preferable.
– θ_3: This feature is used to help the agent to decide which card should be played, as not all the cards are equally useful in each turn. The feature sums the values of all cards on the player's board. The better the cards on the board, the higher the value.
– θ_4: Sometimes it is better not to play some items, in order to allow them to be used in the future. This feature is the sum of the values of all Item cards in the player's hand. The better Item cards in the hand, the higher the value.
– θ_5: Some cards increase the number of cards that are going to be drawn in the next player turn. This feature is the number of cards that will be drawn in the next player turn.

In this paper, we propose to use *NTBEA* to adjust the weights $[\omega_1, \ldots, \omega_5]$. The noisy evaluator needed for *NTBEA* consists of playing several games between the *OEP* agent using the tuned heuristic function and the *NoAI* agent. The fitness of a set of weights is determined by the win rate of the *OEP* agent in the evaluation games played. Several plays are needed since the results of a game between two agents strongly depend on the decks used.

3.4   The Deck Problem

The outcome of the agents strongly depends on the deck used and on the order of the cards. To deal with this problem, and therefore to allow a fair comparison of the agents, several decks have been built in advance.

The draft step of the game has been run 10 times. Each time, 3 different strategies have been used to select one of the 3 cards proposed by the system. The first strategy (employed by the winner in the CEC19 *LOCM* competition) selects the card with the best score based on a hand-designed estimation of the value of each card. The second strategy (employed by the runner up in the CEC19 competition) tries to obtain a certain number of cards with low mana cost (useful for the beginning of the game), and a certain amount of moderate and high cost (useful for the middle and last turns of the game). The third strategy is a combination of both ideas: when the system provides 3 cards falling in the same mana cost group, the best according to the first strategy is selected. Once the 3 decks have been obtained, they are shuffled 10 times, producing 10 different orders to play each deck.

In total, a database of $3 * 10 * 10 = 300$ different decks was obtained. The battle phase of the game was then modified to replace the draft phase with direct use of the pre-built decks.

4   Experiments and Results

4.1   Experimental Set up

In this paper, we use terminology adopted from tennis to compare the performance of the agents. A *game* is a play between two agents using a particular deck and a particular order. The result of a game is 1 if the first player is the winner or 0 if the second player wins.

A *set* is a collection of 12 games between two agents. In a set, 3 decks $\mathcal{D}_1^{d,o}$, $\mathcal{D}_2^{d,o}$ and $\mathcal{D}_3^{d,o}$ are used (where d and o stand for the $d-th$ draft used to generate the 3 decks and the o-th order) to produce a fair comparison between agents, since all possible combination of games using the 3 decks are taken into account. Additionally, each agent plays half the games as first player, and half as second player.

Finally, a *match* is to play several sets varying the draft (d) from where the 3 decks and their order (o) are selected. In total, a match consists of 100 sets, or 1200 games between two agents. The result of a match is the mean win rate per deck for the first agent.

NTBEA was used to tune the weights of the heuristic function (i.e. $[\omega_1, \ldots, \omega_5]$). For all features, less ϕ_2, six different values were tested: $[0, 1, 2, 3, 4, 5]$. In the case of the feature ϕ_2 the following values were used instead: $[-5, -4, -3, -2, -1, 0]$. 100 neighbours and a mutation probability of 10% were used.

For the noisy evaluator, a set was played using the *OEP* agent, with the solution being the current one in *NTBEA*, versus the *NoAI* agent. Each time the noisy evaluator was used, d and o were randomly obtained, so as to prevent overfitting the result to a particular deck. Note that a brute force algorithm needs to play $6^5 * 1200 \approx 0.9 * 10^7$ games to explore the complete search space. The use of *NTBEA* can drastically reduce the number of times that a game is played.

The number of calls to the heuristic function was used as a time budget for the agents, therefore, the agents performance is independent of the speed of the computer used to run the experiments. All the experiments reported in this paper limit the agent budget to 500 calls.

As an average, the *OEP* agent needed 54.98 ms (with $\sigma = 19.74$) to complete the budget. The experiments were run in a Dell XPS 15 9570 computer with an Intel(R) Core(TM) I9-8590HK CPU @ 2.9 GHz processor and 32 MB of RAM.

4.2   Preliminary Experiments

The main objective of the game is to reduce the health points of the opponent to 0. As a first experiment, we conducted a match between the agents *OEP(1s)* and *OEP([1, 0, 0, 0, 0])*. The first is an agent with the same weights for all features (i.e. $\omega_f = 1, \forall f$). The second agent has all weights set to zero less the first one, i.e. an agent that only take into account the reduction of opponent health points (feature θ_1).

Table 1. Win rate mean and standard deviation (for all decks) of matches between two agents. μ and σ stand for mean and standard deviation, respectively.

1st agent	2nd agent	μ	σ
$OEP([1, 1, 0, 0, 0])$	$OEP([1, 0, 0, 0, 0])$	0.68	0.12
$OEP([1, 0, 1, 0, 0])$	$OEP([1, 0, 0, 0, 0])$	0.81	0.11
$OEP([1, 0, 0, 1, 0])$	$OEP([1, 0, 0, 0, 0])$	0.55	0.12
$OEP([1, 0, 0, 0, 1])$	$OEP([1, 0, 0, 0, 0])$	0.50	0.11

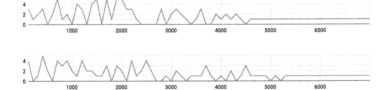

Fig. 3. Evolution of the parameters when using *NTBEA*. From top to bottom, the figures show the evolution of the 5 parameters (starting with θ_1). The x-axis is the number of iterations. The y-axis shows the parameter value.

The results obtained show the first agent winning 85.6% of the games. Thus we can conclude that only taking into account θ_1 does not produce the best results and a combination of all features is suggested to work better.

Table 1 shows the results of several matches where the first agent is *OEP* taking into account various combinations of two features, versus the *OEP(1s)* agent. This aims to study how important the features $\theta_2, \theta_3, \theta_4, \theta_5$ are.

The results obtained suggest that feature θ_3 (related to the value of the cards on the board) has a strong relevance. Furthermore, θ_2 (related to the opponent damage threat), seems to also be important. However, features θ_4 and θ_5 appear to have less influence.

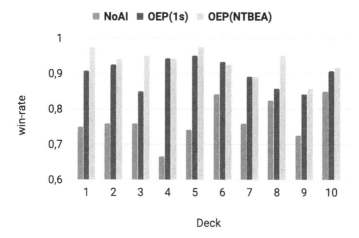

Fig. 4. Mean win rate for each deck for matches played by *NoAI*, *OEP(1s)* and *OEP(NTBEA)* versus Random.

4.3   *NTBEA* Evolution and Recommend Solution

Figure 3 shows the evolution of the parameters tuned by *NTBEA*. Every 100 iterations the recommended solution given the actual state of the *NTBEA* process has been estimated. At the beginning of the process, the parameters vary a lot, since *NTBEA* had not had enough time to find a good solution in a so noisy scenario as *LOCM*. Around 5000 iterations, the algorithm converges for all parameters.

The final solution recommended by *NTBEA* is $[3, 2, 5, 1, 1]$. In the recommended solution, all features are considered important (none were set to 0) with θ_3 and θ_1 being given most importance.

According to the results obtained, it is not only important to reduce the health of the opponent (θ_1) as the *NoAI* agent tries to do. To have good cards on the board is the most important feature (θ_3) and it is also relevant to take

Table 2. Win rate mean and standard deviation (for all decks) of matches between two agents. μ and σ stand for mean and standard deviation, respectively.

1st agent	2nd agent	μ	σ
NoAI	*Random*	0.767	0.057
OEP(1s)	*Random*	0.901	0.039
OEP(NTBEA)	*Random*	0.933	0.036
OEP(1s)	*NoAI*	0.803	0.057
OEP(NTBEA)	*NoAI*	0.825	0.058
OEP(1s)	*EMCTS*	0.505	0.022
OEP(NTBEA)	*EMCTS*	0.560	0.021

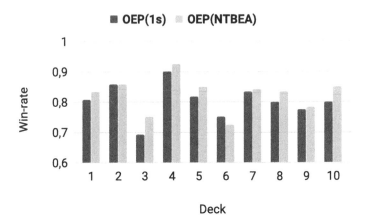

Fig. 5. Mean win rate for each deck for matches played by *OEP(1s)* and *OEP(NTBEA)* against *NoAI*.

into account the amount of damage that the opponent can produce in the next turn (θ_2). The solution obtained using *NTBEA* agrees with the results obtained in Sect. 4.2.

4.4 *OEP* Agent Performance

In this section, several matches have been tested to study the performance of the *OEP* agent when using the heuristic function tuned by *NTBEA* (we call this agent *OEP(NTBEA)*) versus some baselines.

We first test the performance of the *NoAI*, *OEP(1s)* and *OEP(NTBEA)* agents versus *Random*. Figure 4 shows the result obtained for each deck. First three rows of Table 2 show the mean (and standard deviation) across all decks.

Results shows that *NoAI* can win a lot of games against *Random* (76.7%) since it uses a sensible strategy. Using all the cards on the board to directly attack the opponent is a successfully and aggressive strategy that requires the opponent player to develop an appropriate defence. Results also show that *OEP(1s)* clearly outperforms *NoAI* winning the 90% of the games. Finally, *OEP(NTBEA)* obtains even better results than *OEP(1s)*, suggesting that the combination found by *NTBEA* improves the performance of *OEP*. *OEP(NTBEA)* has better win rate for all decks less one.

For a second experiment, we test *OEP(1s)* and *OEP(NTBEA)* agents versus *NoAI*. Figure 5 and the fourth and fifth rows of Table 2 show the results of those matches. *OEP(NTBEA)* outperforms the original algorithm with almost all decks, with a better mean win rate.

The last experiment aims to study whether the tuned heuristic is also useful when playing against a different agent to the one used during training. For this purpose, both *OEP(1s)* and *OEP(NTBEA)* agents played a match against an agent that uses the Evolutionary Monte Carlo Tree Search algorithm (EMCTS) [1].

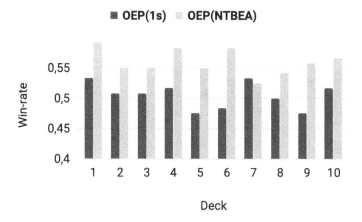

Fig. 6. Mean win rate for each deck for matches played by *OEP(1s)* and *OEP(NTBEA)* against *EMCTS*.

EMCTS combines some of the ideas of tree search from *MCTS* with the genome-based approach of evolutionary algorithms. *EMCTS* starts from a complete sequence of atomic actions, just like the genomes of *OEP*. *EMCTS* grows a tree by mutating the current sequence, using the same mutation operator as *OEP*. *EMCTS* does not use rollouts to complete the game, it simply evaluates the sequences at the leaf nodes. The backpropagation step is unchanged from MCTS. When the time budget is exhausted, the tree is traversed until a node without descendants is found. The best sequence of atomic actions in the path is the one returned by the algorithm, to be played by the agent. We have used the same heuristic function design as in the *OEP* algorithm and all the weights have been set to 1.

Figure 6 and last two rows of Table 2 show the results obtained. They show that the training of *OEP(NTBEA)* was robust enough to also obtain better results for almost all decks against the different opponent. As Fig. 6 and Table 2 show, *OEP(1s)* has a very similar performance to *EMCTS*, winning close to 50% of matches, i.e. none of the two agents clearly outperforms the other one. However, when using the weights tuned by *NTBEA*, the win rate increases such that the *OEP*-based agent is preferable in almost all decks.

5   Conclusions

This paper presented the use of the N-Tuple Bandit Evolutionary Algorithm (*NTBEA*) to optimise the parameters of the heuristic function. The challenging strategic card game *Legends of Code and Magic* was used to test the proposed approach. The results obtained demonstrate that *NTBEA* can effectively tune the heuristic function weights to improve the performance of the evolutionary algorithm used, Online Evolutionary Planning (*OEP*), even when playing against opponents different to those used during training.

Future work must be focused on studying whether the parameters obtained with *NTBEA* can be applied when other decks are used. In addition, some other N-tuple configurations could also be studied.

Acknowledgements. The authors want to thank J. Kowalski for his help solving doubts about the *LOCM* rules and N. Justensen and H. Baier for their help in better understanding their algorithms.

References

1. Baier, H., Cowling, P.I.: Evolutionary MCTS for multi-action adversarial games. In: Preceedings of the 2018 IEEE Conference on Computational Intelligence and Games, CIG 2018 (2018). https://doi.org/10.1109/CIG.2018.8490403
2. Bursztein, E.: I am a legend: hacking hearthstone using statistical learning methods. In: 2016 IEEE Conference on Computational Intelligence and Games (CIG) (2016). https://doi.org/10.1109/CIG.2016.7860416
3. Choe, J.S.B., Kim, J.K.: Enhancing Monte Carlo tree search for playing hearthstone. In: Proceedings of the 1st Conference on Games, GOG 2019 (2019)
4. Cowling, P., Powley, E., Whitehouse, D.: Information set Monte Carlo tree search. IEEE Trans. Comput. Intell. AI Games **4**, 120–143 (2012). https://doi.org/10.1109/TCIAIG.2012.2200894
5. Dockhorn, A., Frick, M., Akkaya, Ü., Kruse, R.: Predicting opponent moves for improving hearthstone AI. In: Medina, J., et al. (eds.) IPMU 2018. CCIS, vol. 854, pp. 621–632. Springer, Cham (2018). https://doi.org/10.1007/978-3-319-91476-3_51
6. Justesen, N., Mahlmann, T., Togelius, J.: Online evolution for multi-action adversarial games. In: Squillero, G., Burelli, P. (eds.) EvoApplications 2016. LNCS, vol. 9597, pp. 590–603. Springer, Cham (2016). https://doi.org/10.1007/978-3-319-31204-0_38
7. Kowalski, J., Miernik, R.: Legends of code and magic (2019). https://jakubkowalski.tech/Projects/LOCM/. Accessed 26 May 2019
8. Lucas, S.M., et al.: Efficient evolutionary methods for game agent optimisation: model-based is best. In: AAAI Workshop on Games and Simulations for Artificial Intelligence (2019)
9. Lucas, S.M., Liu, J., Perez-Liebana, D.: The n-tuple bandit evolutionary algorithm for game agent optimisation. In: Proceedings of IEEE Congress on Evolutionary Computation, CEC 2018 (2018)
10. Myerson, R.: Game Theory: Analysis of Conflict. Harvard University Press, Cambridge (1997)
11. Perez Liebana, D., Samothrakis, S., Lucas, S., Rohlfshagen, P.: Rolling horizon evolution versus tree search for navigation in single-player real-time games. In: Proceedings of the 15th Annual Conference on Genetic and Evolutionary Computation, GECCO 2013, pp. 351–358 (2013). https://doi.org/10.1145/2463372.2463413
12. Santos, A., Santos, P.A., Melo, F.S.: Monte Carlo tree search experiments in hearthstone. In: 2017 IEEE Conference on Computational Intelligence and Games, CIG 2017, pp. 272–279 (2017)
13. Zhang, S., Buro, M.: Improving hearthstone AI by learning high-level rollout policies and bucketing chance node events. In: 2017 IEEE Conference on Computational Intelligence and Games, CIG 2017, pp. 309–316 (2017)

Finding Behavioural Patterns Among League of Legends Players Through Hidden Markov Models

Alberto Mateos Rama[1] , Victor Rodriguez-Fernandez[1($\boxtimes$)] ,
and David Camacho[2]

[1] Universidad Autónoma de Madrid, Madrid, Spain
alberto.mateosr@estudiante.uam.es, victor.rodriguezf@uam.es
[2] Universidad Politécnica de Madrid, Madrid, Spain
david.camacho@upm.es

Abstract. This work is aimed at finding behavioural patterns among professional players of League of Legends, one of the greatest recent phenomena in the world of video games. For that purpose, Hidden Markov Models (HMM) are used to model the sequence of events produced by a gameplay. First, the set of interesting game events for analysis is defined, and based on that, each gameplay of the dataset is transformed into a sequences of events. Then, four HMMs will be trained with the data from four different groups of sequences, according to the team that produces the events of the sequence (red/blue) and to whether that sequence led to a victory of the team or not. Finally, the resulting HMMs will be visualized and compared in order to achieve some conclusions about the macro game strategy in League of Legends, which will help to understand the game at the highest level of its competition.

Keywords: League of Legends · Hidden Markov Model ·
Macro-game · Behavioural patterns

1 Introduction

The industry of videogames has been one of the most relevant and profitable in the last decade, earning way more money than film or music industries [3]. On the top of that industry there is a videogame released in 2009, *League of Legends (LoL)*[1], that has reached the number of 100 million active players in 2016 [2]. The importance of League of Legends is not only about the record of users, but it is also the most relevant game in e-sports right now and in streaming sites like *Twitch* [1]. The tournaments that Riot (the creators of League of Legends) organize throughout the entire year are the most followed by the users by far.

Apart from all of this, League of Legends is a valuable source of study in the field of data analysis, and more specifically, in the task of finding behavioural

---

[1] League of Legends official website: https://euw.leagueoflegends.com/.

© Springer Nature Switzerland AG 2020
P. A. Castillo et al. (Eds.): EvoApplications 2020, LNCS 12104, pp. 419–430, 2020.
https://doi.org/10.1007/978-3-030-43722-0_27

patterns among players. This is not just due to the utility that this information can have for professional players, but also to the free availability of large datasets of gameplays, and to the fact that League of Legends is a game based in strategy and not just in skill, which means that finding the right behaviours in the games would be extremely beneficial.

This work proposes a way to help the growing industry of competitive games with the use of machine learning and data science into a dataset of League of Legend gameplays. In particular, we will study and analyze behavioural patterns among professional League of Legends players with a higher abstraction level than the one offered by the raw dataset. In League of Legends, there are tons of variables, and it can be difficult to determine with precision the state of the game with just what you can see on the screen at once.

In order to obtain a better level of abstraction in the data, we have found that Hidden Markov Models (HMMs) are a great tool, mainly because they provide the possibility to find hidden patterns that are not visible in the raw sequence of events. This way, it is possible to find some conducts that even the professional players do unconsciously, and that could help them to improve their success. Also, HMMs have both interpretable and predictive capabilities, which allow us not only to understand the patterns within the model, but also to use it for predicting the result of a gameplay.

In summary, the different goals accomplished in this work are:

1. Obtaining the data of a relevant amount of professional gameplays, and determine which variables can give us the most important information to understand the strategical decisions.
2. Fitting different HMMs and determine which of them achieve the best ratio between the quality and complexity.
3. Visualize the selected models and compare them.
4. Analyze the behaviour of the players to achieve a better understanding of the game, and settle some bases for a theory of League of Legends behaviour and for a potential predictive model.

The rest of the work is structured as follows: Sect. 2 gives some backgrounds with respect to the main topics of this work: League of Legends and Hidden Markov Models. In Sect. 3, we describe all the steps carried out to create the HMM-based behavioural models from a war dataset of LoL gameplays. Then, in Sect. 4 that methodology is applied to a popular Kaggle dataset of professional gameplays, and the resulting models are visualized, compared and analyzed properly using the author's knowledge of this game. Finally, Sect. 5 summarises the results achieved and proposes some future lines of work in this field.

2   Background

2.1   League of Legends

League of Legends, also known as LoL, is a Multiplayer Online Battle Arena (MOBA). It is a videogame developed by Riot Game and released in 2009. This game faces 5 allied players versus 5 enemies in two teams (blue and red). Each team has the main objective of destroying the enemy main structure, the nexus, while defending the own one.

To achieve this, every single player has the control of a character with different abilities and items, that can gain more power over the enemies when you get more experience (to develop the abilities) or gold (to buy items). This resources are obtained in different ways, but the most relevant ones, and the ones that we study, are the *macro game* decisions.

Macro game is a term used to refer the big strategical decisions of the game, like grouping a whole team to take a tower. This kind of objectives gives a team a big buff in gold and in power. The ones that we study in this work can be seen in Fig. 1, placed on top of the map of the game. There we can find:

1. The nexus of each team (blue and red circles in the figure).
2. Basic structures of each team (crosses of their respective colors). The 3 closer to each nexus are the inhibitors and the rest are towers.
3. The spawn point of the dragons (orange cross in the figure).
4. The spawn of the herald and the Baron Nashor (purple cross in the figure).

Each one of this objectives is relevant in a strategical level because, on their own, they suppose a great benefit for the team that achieves them. In some way, studying this moves is like studying the ones in a grand master's chess game.

2.2 Hidden Markov Models

HMMs are statistical models where the underlying states cannot be observed directly during the process, but what we see is the *emission* of that state [9]. Although the observations that a HMM emit can be both continuous and discrete, only discrete observations will be considered in this work. In words of Rabiner and Juang: "A HMM is a doubly stochastic process with an underlying stochastic process that is not observable (it is hidden), but can only be observed through another set of stochastic processes that produce the sequence of observed symbols." [6]. The term *Markov* in a HMM pertains to the time-dependence between the consecutive states, which follows a Markov process. This means that the current state only depends on the previous state and not on earlier states. HMMs are composed of the following parameters:

1. A dictionary of observable states.
2. An underlying sequence of hidden states.
3. A vector of initial probabilities with the odds of starting in a certain hidden state.
4. A transition matrix, with the odds of moving between hidden states.
5. An emission, or output matrix, with the odds of finding a certain element of the observable sequence when you are in the different hidden states.

In the majority of applications, the set of parameters of a HMM cannot be inferred analytically but need to be estimated from recorded sample data.

Fig. 1. League of Legends map with the main macro objectives marked. (Color figure online)

Although there are classical supervised learning techniques for HMM, in many applications the hidden data is missing, so we no longer know which state to assign for each observation. The solution is to use *unsupervised learning* techniques, among which the *Baum-Welch* algorithm stands out for being the first to address the problem for classical HMM [4]. In brief, it is a form of Expectation-Maximization (EM) which tries to maximize the likelihood of a set of observation sequences to be produced by a model.

One important aspect to consider when fitting a HMM to a given dataset is that the number of hidden states must be known in advanced, which is unrealistic in our case. To choose an optimal number of states without prior knowledge about the model topology, several statistical measures are used to compare and select models, (and sometimes the selection depends on a combination of all of them) [8], of which BIC is the best known [7,10]. This metric is defined as:

$$BIC(H) = -2(logLik(H)) + P \log K,$$

where *logLik* is the (log)-likelihood that the model has produced the data with which it has been trained on, P is the number of parameters in the model, and K the number of observations used to train the model. The less the BIC scores, the better the model is considered. As it can be seen, BIC penalizes the likelihood of a model by a complexity factor proportional to number of parameters in the model and the number of training observations, so it gives advantages to simple and general models.

3 Methodology

3.1 Data Preprocessing

Using the API that Riot Games provides, every user can find a lot of information of the games, so is not hard to get a big enough dataset. However, not all the information is relevant or is given in an useful way, so some processing is required.

The starting dataset is formed by thousand of professional gameplays with different variables, specified in different formats, that should be transformed to be more manageable. The workflow used to achieve that transformation and select the required information can be found in Fig. 2.

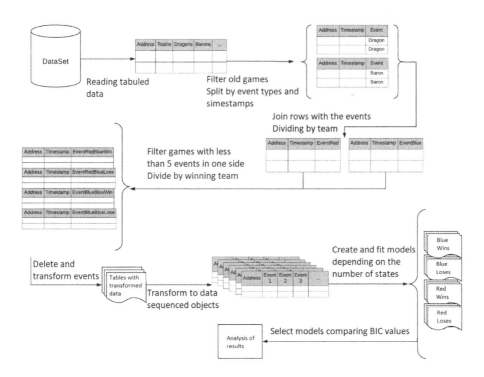

Fig. 2. Basics of the data processing

From all the possible events recorded in each gameplay, we have selected the ones considered to be more informative from a strategical (macro game) perspective. In that selection we decided to discard gameplays where one of both teams had made less than a certain number of events, because they are not representative. Another filter was to discard the gameplays that were too old, due to League of Legends is a changing game with a ton of patches per year that exclude or include different features.

Taking these facts into consideration we have selected the following game events for this project:

1. *Elemental dragon slain*: Every dragon offers a different buff for the entire game to the team that kills it. In the models it is represented as ELEMENTALDRAGON.
2. *Outer tower destroyed* (for each lane): The first tower of each lane is the outer one. After taking it, the team achieves a lot of gold for each member, and also privates the enemy from a security zone, mitigating their influence on that part of the map. In the models is represented as TOPLANEOUTERTURRET, BOTLANEOUTERTURRET (Bot is the short version of "Bottom"), MIDLANEOUTER-TURRET.
3. *Inner tower destroyed* (for each lane): Is the next available when the outer one is taken, and the impact in the game is similar. In the models it is represented as TOPLANEINNERTURRET, BOTLANEINNERTURRET, MIDLANEINNERTURRET.
4. *Nexus tower destroyed*: This ones are the last defenses of the nexus itself. Losing this ones exposes the nexus to the enemy team and that usually is a sentence for the game. In the models is represented as NEXUSTURRET.
5. *Herald*: It gives a temporal buff to the team that allows them to do a lot of damage to one or more towers if used properly. In the models is represented as HERALD.
6. *Elder dragon*: This one spawns for the first time 35 min into the game, and temporally powers all the other dragon buffs for the team, and gives another powerful buff to the damage. In the models is represented as ELDERDRAGON.
7. *Baron Nashor*: Spawns for the first time at the minute 20 of the game, and temporally gives a buff to the team that empowers the allied minions with more damage and sustain and also powers some stats of the characters. With the elder one, is considered the biggest buff a team can get to help them to finish a game. In the models is represented as BARON.

All of these events are computed and sequenced separately for the each team, so we can determine which ones are performed by the blue team or the red team, and then compare their behaviours. Moreover, in order to find the behaviour that gives a team the victory, the event sequences are also annotated by the winning/losing team. As a result, after preprocessing the dataset in this way, we obtain four groups of event sequences:

1. Event sequences of the blue team, when the blue team wins the match.
2. Event sequences of the blue team, when the blue team loses the match.
3. Event sequences of the red team, when the red team wins the match.
4. Event sequences of the red team, when the red team loses the match.

3.2   Model Training and Selection

Once the data is processed and properly structured, we can start working with it to create the HMMs. Each group of event sequences mentioned above will have its own Hidden Markov Model modelling them. That means that we created 4 different models with the combination of winning/losing red/blue team.

As we mentioned in the Sect. 2, to train the models we use the Baum-Welch algorithm. This algorithm ensures the convergence to a local optimal model giving a set of initial parameters for the model. To facilitate getting the global optimal model, the algorithm is executed several times using random values for the initial parameters.

For each run of the Baum-Welch algorithm we need to fix the number of states of the model. To compare different possibilities and find the best one for each group of event sequences, we tried a different number of states from a range, and scored them with the BIC. Finally, we will pick the models with the smallest (or close to the smallest) BIC.

4 Experimentation

4.1 Experimental Setup

In order to implement this project we have used the R language[2], because it offers a lot of useful packages for data science. More specifically, we have used the package seqHMM for modelling the event sequences using HMMs [5]. Rstudio has been the main tool for the project, and we have followed patterns to ease the reproducibility of the experiments, like the standard package organization in R, in order to publish the code in Github[3].

4.2 Dataset

The dataset used was extracted from Kaggle[4], and comprises a total of 7620 professional gameplays. The data was restructured in order to use it in this project, following these steps:

1. Remove the old gameplays that are not representative anymore.
2. Split the dataframes by type of event (with an identifier, timestamp and the type).
3. Remove the gameplays with less than 5 events from each of the teams.
4. Join the rows of the event tables according to the team that carried them out and the team that won.

The next step consisted in using that structured data to create and fit the models as we described earlier, specifying the number of states and with the Baum-Welch algorithm. After that, the BIC values were calculated and compared to select the right models.

---

[2] R project for statistical computing: https://www.r-project.org/.

[3] LoLBehaviouralPatternsPublic: https://github.com/AlbertoMateosR/LoLBehaviouralPatternsPublic.

[4] Link to the dataset: https://www.kaggle.com/chuckephron/leagueoflegends.

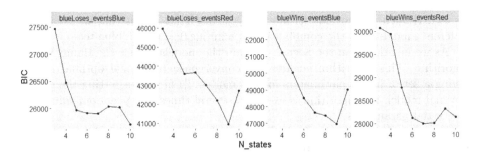

Fig. 3. BIC values with respect to the number of states, for each group of events considered in this work.

4.3   Experimental Results

Model Selection. First we will detail the selected models for the different groups of event sequences considered. We can find the right number of states rounded with a red circle in the Fig. 3.

As we can see, the selected models are not always the ones with the smallest BIC. Instead, in one group of events (the events of the red team when they lose), we have selected the model that presented a better relation between complexity and information. That selected models are:

1. For the channel in charge of the blue events in a victory of the red team (blueLoses-eventsBlue in the figure), the model with 10 states. Hereafter, we will refer to this model as *blue/losers*.
2. For the channel in charge of the red events in a victory of the red team (blueLoses-eventsRed in the figure), the model with 9 states. We will refer to this model as *red/winners*.
3. For the channel in charge of the blue events in a victory of the blue team (blueWins-eventsBlue in the figure), the model with 9 states. We will refer to this model as *blue/winners*.
4. For the channel in charge of the red events in a victory of the blue team (blueWins-eventsRed in the figure), the model with 6 states. We will refer to this model as *red/losers*.

The selected models are visualized and analyzed in the next section. We decided to use a personalized layout in order to make the flow of the model and events clearer.

Analysis of the Selected Models. We started analysing the behavioural patterns contained in the blue/winners model, and then compare it to blue/losers model. Both models are shown in Fig. 4. We enumerated the hidden states of the model in order to refer to them easier (see the top-left of each node on the graph). The width of the edges represent the probability of transition between states. We can also see the initial probability of each hidden state at the bottom of each node in the graph. We added a legend with the color of the events to identify them. The slices in the pie chart inside the nodes represent the probability distribution of each event. Events with a probability below a threshold of 0.1 will be gathered into the same category (represented with the colour white).

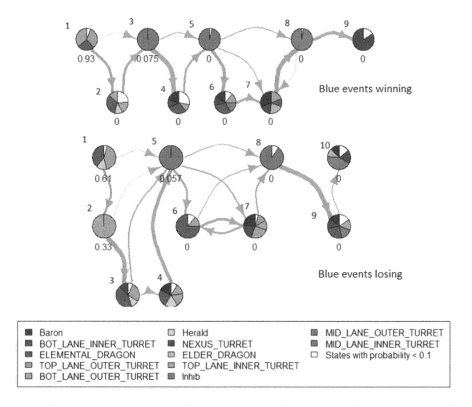

Fig. 4. Comparative between blue/winners and blue/losers HMMs (Color figure online)

In both cases we can find the initial states quite easily. It seems like it is the most common for the teams to start taking a dragon or one of the towers in the sides (Bottom or Top) (State 1).

With this, they seek to establish his domain on either side. This is due to, by taking the rival's tower, its influence in that area of the map is weakened, and so it is on nearby objectives.

The tower of the Bottom seems, in both cases, more important because the dragon provides a permanent benefit relatively simple to achieve. In the case of blue/losers model, we find one more state (state 2) but still is quite similar. This makes sense, due to the gameplay has just begun at that stage. The fact that Bot (Bottom) appears as the second event, explains the dance that occurs in many games: a team takes the tower from one side, and in response the opponent takes the one from the other side.

Following the blue/winners model, two paths are observed. First, they take another objective to increase their advantage, such as a dragon, the tower that is still standing, or the herald (winners-state 2); and in second place or as a third step, they take the Mid outer tower (winners-state3).

This denotes the importance of the Mid, since it is vital strategically. It is the central and shorter line, and so, the most direct path to the rival's nexus. It is also safer than taking one of the inner towers, as it exposes the allied team less to the enemy zone of influence.

In the blue/losers model it can be seen that, except in exceptional cases, this sequence is not so clear, and they take intermediate steps that slow down their game. It seems then that materializing the quick advantage is of utmost importance.

After that, the winners again choose to take another objective to become stronger (winners-state 4), and later, they take another vital objective at a strategic level such as the next mid tower, the inner one (winners-state 5). Meanwhile, the losers take more intermediate steps and even cycles between states without strategic events.

In the next step of the winner option, the same thing happens again, they take an objective that strengthens them (winners-state 6). Depending on their power they take another (winners-state 7), or go straight to materialize its advantage, this time with an inhibitor (winners-state 8), and after that they can either proceed the same for another inhibitor, or more likely, to finish the game (winners-state 9).

There is therefore a clear pattern that the winning teams follow, and that losers fail to perpetrate. Strengthen with an intermediate objective, and quickly materialize such strength at a strategic level. And repeat that until win. In the behavior of the red teams in this circumstance, the observations are the same, so there is not more interest on reanalyzing it. The next relevant comparison that can be made is between the behaviours of the winning teams when they play on the blue team or in the red one. These models can be found in Fig. 5.

It is clearly noted that the aforementioned sequence is also present, but this time, the number of states is distributed differently. First, in the case of the red teams model, the initial state is divided and the herald's event appears. Also, in the third state we can find the Baron's event. Finally, between the second tower of the Mid and the Inhibitors, there is only one state to strengthen.

From all this and the early appearance of late game events in the model, it can be deduced that the red teams benefit from maintaining a more passive profile, and get the victory in long gameplays.

In the late game, players take longer to respawn after death, so it is common that, with presence of a baron at that time, the gameplay can be finished at once. This, together with the map asymmetry, which favors the red team in the barons (because they do not have to overextend in the map to take it, and also a wall protects them in case of steal), would explain this fact. Indeed, this asymmetry could explain the lack of elder dragons in the red model. The patterns that the model shows are pretty similar because they have a similar plan that the models represented.

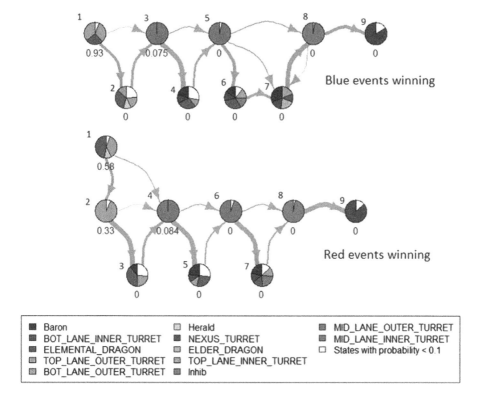

Fig. 5. Comparative between the blue/winners and red/winners models (Color figure online)

5   Conclusions

Although League of Legends is a game with a lot of variables and possibilities, by using Hidden Markov Models we have found some of the strategical bases that the professional players follow in order to win games, and what can prevent them from doing it, also comparing the differences when you play in one team or the other.

Both teams seem to start taking control of one side of the map, preferably on the bottom side, because it gives more control over the dragons. Once they get that advantage, it is important to materialize it as fast as possible, so if the strength is enough they can go to Mid to take an strategical objective. For the next one, or in the case the power is not enough, the team should try to get an objective that gives them more advantage, and as soon as possible, go for the next strategical objective in the Mid lane.

The difference between the teams provided by the map asymmetry has resulted also relevant. This proves that with a deeper research this game can be perfected and studied like chess. As future work, we plan to develop predictive models based on he behavioural models shown in this work, in order to be able to predict, beforehand, whether a team is going to lose or win a gameplay.

Ackowledgements. This work has been supported by several research grants: Spanish Ministry of Science and Education under TIN2014-56494-C4-4-P grant (DeepBio) and Comunidad Autónoma de Madrid under P2018/TCS-4566 grant (CYNAMON).

References

1. League of legends twitch channel becomes first to reach 1 billion views. https://www.cnet.com/news/league-of-legends-twitch-channel-becomes-first-to-reach-1-billion-views/. Accessed 30 Oct 2019
2. Riot games reveals league of legends has 100 million monthly players. https://www.forbes.com/sites/insertcoin/2016/09/13/riot-games-reveals-league-of-legends-has-100-million-monthly-players/. Accessed 30 Oct 2019
3. Baltezarević, R., Baltezarević, B., Baltezarević, V.: The video gaming industry: from play to revenue. Int. Rev. **3–4**, 71–76 (2018)
4. Baum, L.E., Petrie, T.: Statistical inference for probabilistic functions of finite state Markov chains. Ann. Math. Stat. **37**, 1554–1563 (1966)
5. Helske, S., Helske, J.: Mixture hidden Markov models for sequence data: the seqHMM package in R. arXiv preprint arXiv:1704.00543 (2017)
6. Rabiner, L.R., Juang, B.H.: An introduction to hidden Markov models. IEEE ASSP Mag. **3**(1), 4–16 (1986)
7. Rodríguez-Fernández, V., Gonzalez-Pardo, A., Camacho, D.: Finding behavioral patterns of UAV operators using multichannel hidden Markov models. In: 2016 IEEE Symposium Series on Computational Intelligence (SSCI), pp. 1–8. IEEE (2016)
8. Rodriguez-Fernandez, V., Gonzalez-Pardo, A., Camacho, D.: Modelling behaviour in UAV operations using higher order double chain Markov models. IEEE Comput. Intell. Mag. **12**(4), 28–37 (2017). https://doi.org/10.1109/MCI.2017.2742738
9. Visser, I.: Seven things to remember about hidden Markov models: a tutorial on markovian models for time series. J. Math. Psychol. **55**(6), 403–415 (2011)
10. Vrieze, S.I.: Model selection and psychological theory: a discussion of the differences between the akaike information criterion (AIC) and the Bayesian information criterion (BIC). Psychol. Methods **17**(2), 228 (2012)

Learning the Designer's Preferences to Drive Evolution

Alberto Alvarez[✉] and Jose Font

Malmö University, Nordenskiöldsgatan 1, 21119 Malmö, Sweden
{alberto.alvarez,jose.font}@mau.se

Abstract. This paper presents the Designer Preference Model, a data-driven solution that pursues to learn from user generated data in a Quality-Diversity Mixed-Initiative Co-Creativity (QD MI-CC) tool, with the aims of modelling the user's design style to better assess the tool's procedurally generated content with respect to that user's preferences. Through this approach, we aim for increasing the user's agency over the generated content in a way that neither stalls the user-tool reciprocal stimuli loop nor fatigues the user with periodical suggestion handpicking. We describe the details of this novel solution, as well as its implementation in the MI-CC tool the Evolutionary Dungeon Designer. We present and discuss our findings out of the initial tests carried out, spotting the open challenges for this combined line of research that integrates MI-CC with Procedural Content Generation through Machine Learning.

Keywords: Procedural Content Generation · Machine Learning · Mixed-Initiative Co-Creativity · Evolutionary Computation

1 Introduction

As game production grows, so does the usage of computer-aided design (CAD) tools to develop various facets of games. CAD tools enable users to create new content or refine previously created content with the assistance of some type of technology that focuses on reducing the workload of the developer. Procedural Content Generation (PCG) denotes the use of algorithms to generate different types of game content, such as levels, narrative, visuals, or even game rules, with limited human input [24]. Search-based PCG is the subset of techniques whose approach generates content by using a search algorithm, a content representation mechanism, and a set of evaluation functions to drive the content creation process towards near-optimal solutions [32].

Mixed-initiative co-creativity (MI-CC) [31] is a branch of PCG through which a computer and a human user create content by engaging into an iterative reciprocal stimuli loop [9,15,19,20,25,27]. This approach addresses the design process with insight and understanding of the affordances and constraints of the human process for creating and designing games [17]. MI-CC helps designers to either optimize their current design towards a specific goal (thus exploiting the search

© Springer Nature Switzerland AG 2020
P. A. Castillo et al. (Eds.): EvoApplications 2020, LNCS 12104, pp. 431–445, 2020.
https://doi.org/10.1007/978-3-030-43722-0_28

space) or foster their creativity by proposing unexpected suggestions (exploring the search space). To these ends, diversity has been an important feature for the research community to focus on during the past decade, including novelty search [13], surprise [8], curiosity [28] and, more recently, quality-diversity approaches [10].

PCG through Quality-Diversity (PCG-QD) [7] is a subset of search-based PCG, which uses quality-diversity algorithms [22] to explore the search space and produce high quality and diverse suggestions. MAP-Elites [21] is a successful quality-diversity algorithm that maintains a map of good suggestions distributed along several feature dimensions. A constrained MAP-Elites implementation was presented by Khalifa et al. [10], combining MAP-Elites with a feasible-infeasible (FI2Pop) genetic algorithm [11] for the procedural generation of levels for bullet hell games. The first implementation of a PCG-QD algorithm for MI-CC was presented by Alvarez et al. [1], elaborating on the combined MAP-Elites and FI2Pop approach by introducing a continuous evolution process that benefits from the multidimensional discretization of the search space performed in MAP-Elites.

In all the above MI-CC approaches, the designers play an active role in the procedurally generated content while struggling between the expressiveness of the automatic generation and the control that they want to exert over it [3]. Having this as motivation, this paper takes the work in [1] one step forward by adding an underlying interactive PCG via machine learning algorithm [29], the Designer Preference Model, that models the user's design style, to be able to predict future designer's choices and thus, driving the content generation with a combination of the designer's subjectivity and the search for quality-diverse content.

2   Previous Work

2.1   Mixed-Initiative Co-Creativity

Similar to user or player modeling, designer modeling for content creation tools (CAD and MI-CC tools) was suggested by Liapis et al. [18], where it is proposed the use of designers models that capture their styles, preferences, goals, intentions, and interaction processes. In their work, they suggest methods, indications, and advice on how each part can be model to be integrated into a holistic designer model, and how each game facet can use and benefit from designer modeling. Moreover, in [16] the same authors discuss their implementation of designer modeling and the challenges of integrating all together in their MI-CC tool, Sentient Sketchbook, which had a positive outcome on the adaptation of the tool towards individual "artificial" users.

Furthermore, Lehman et al. [12] presented Innovation Engines that combine the capabilities and advantages of machine learning and evolutionary algorithms to produce novel 3D graphics with the use of Compositional Pattern-Producing Networks (CPPN) evolved with MAP-Elites, and evaluated by the confidence a deep neural network had on the models belonging to a specific object category.

2.2   Procedural Content Generation via Machine Learning

Summerville et al. [29] define Procedural Content Generation via Machine Learning (PCGML) as the generation of game content by models that have been trained on existing game content. The main approaches to PCGML are: autonomous content generation, content repair, content critique, data compression, and mixed-initiative design.

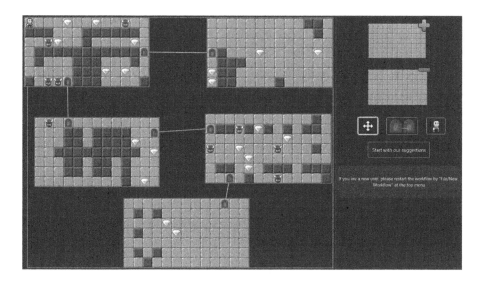

Fig. 1. Screenshot of the dungeon editor screen in EDD, displaying a sample dungeon composed by five rooms.

In the latter case and, as appointed by Treanor et al. [30], AI may engage with a human user participating in the creation of content, so that new gameplay emerges from this shared construction. This emerging relationship between the user and the AI system, when implemented through a trained machine learning algorithm, has the potential to reduce user frustration, error, and training time. This is due to the capacity of a machine learning solution to adapt to the design preferences of the user that interacts with the MI-CC tool by learning from the user-generated dataset of previous choices.

2.3   The Evolutionary Dungeon Designer

The Evolutionary Dungeon Designer (EDD) is an MI-CC tool for designers to build 2D dungeons. EDD allows designers to manually edit the overall dungeon and its composing rooms (see Fig. 1), as well as to use procedurally generated suggestions either as inspiration to work on or as a finished design (see Fig. 2). Both options fluently alternate during the creation process by means of a workflow of mutual inspiration, through which all manual editions performed by the user are fed into the underlying continuous Evolutionary Algorithm, accommodating them into the procedural suggestions. A detailed description of EDD and its features can be found in [2–5].

Subsequent user studies [3,5] carried out with game designers on EDD raised the following areas of improvement: (1) the designers struggled with EDD's capability of understanding the designer's intentions and preserving custom designs; (2) the tool was unable to generate aesthetically pleasing suggestions since the fitness function only accounted for functionality, but not aesthetics, of design patterns; (3) the designers wanted to keep certain manual editions from being altered by the procedural suggestions.

With the aims of addressing these limitations as well as fostering the user's creativity with quality-diverse proposals, EDD was improved with the Interactive Constrained MAP-Elites (IC MAP-Elites) [1], an implementation of MAP-Elites into the continuous evolutionary process in EDD. With this addition, the user drives the generation of procedural suggestions by modifying at any moment the areas of the search space where the evolution should put the focus on. This is done by selecting among the available dimensions: symmetry, similarity, design patterns, linearity, and leniency. Additionally, the designers have now the chance to limit the search space by locking map areas and thus preserving manually edited content.

This paper contributes by building on top of EDD's IC MAP-Elites, adding a data-driven Designer Preference Model that adapts and personalizes the design experience, as well as balances the expressivity of the tool and the controllability of the designer over the tool. Other researchers have pursued a similar goal by biasing the search space through having the user perform a manual selection after every given number of generations [13,14,23]. Nevertheless, this approach leads to an increase in user fatigue by repeatedly asking for user input and thus, stalling the evolutionary process until such input is received. Moreover, this staged process seems incompatible with the dynamic reciprocal workflow of MI-CC tools, where the focus is on the designer proactively creating content rather than passively browsing a set of suggestions.

The remaining sections of the paper are structured as follows: Sect. 3 describes the data-driven Designer Preference Model; Sect. 4 presents the initial experimental results, and Sect. 5 discusses the results and future lines of research of this novel approach.

3   Designer Preference Model

The Designer Preference Model is a data-driven intelligent system that learns the user's design style by training and testing over a continuously growing dataset composed of the user's actions and choices while operating EDD. The underlying evolutionary algorithm (EA) uses this model to assess the generated suggestions according to the predicted preference of the designer. This is a complementary assessment to EDD's original fitness function, which evaluates individuals first based on the presence and distribution of spatial and meso-patterns

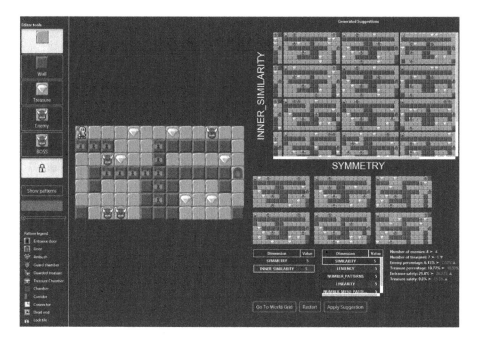

Fig. 2. The room editor screen in EDD. The top-right pane shows the suggestions provided by the IC MAP-Elites algorithm. Below are the six top-raked suggestions by the Designer Preference Model. The left pane contains the manual edition features.

(Fig. 3), and then based on their degree of adaptation to the user-selected quality-diversity dimensions [1]. The relevance of the Designer Preference Model gradually increases over EDD's fitness function as long as the model gains confidence in its assessments.

3.1 Model Update and Usage

The proposed model is a relatively small neural network M with as many input neurons as the number of tiles composing each room, two hidden layers (100 and 50 neurons respectively), and six output neurons, one per each discrete preference value assigned to the individuals by the designer. When the designer starts EDD, the neural network is created with random initialization and without any prior training (i.e. cold start). While the designer creates and modifies rooms, on the background, the EA produces and presents individuals to the designer using the MAP-Elite's cells (Fig. 2), while it adapts to the designer's design. Following a proactive learning approach [6], anytime the designer chooses one suggestion to replace her current design, a training session is requested for a model M with a dataset S created with the current cells and their populations based on the designer's chosen suggestion. The loop, depicted in Fig. 4, can be described in the following two steps:

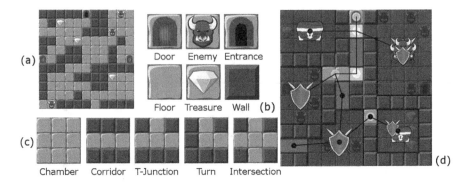

Fig. 3. A sample room in EDD (a) compose by tiles (b), spatial patterns (c) and meso-patterns (d). Detailed descriptions for these components can be found in [4].

Dataset Creation: The designer chooses a suggestion to replace her current design, which in turn, requests a training session using all the current individuals (i.e. the elites and the rest of the feasible populations) to create a new dataset to train the model closer to the "actual" preference of the designer. As shown in Fig. 4b, an ad-hoc matrix is created, based on the position of the applied suggestion, to calculate the estimated preference, starting with the applied suggestion (1.0 preference value), and reducing the preference value by 0.2 per each step that was taken away from the applied suggestion in the matrix until a minimum of 0.0.

Once all the individuals are given an estimated preference value based on their grid position by the ad-hoc matrix, they are all used to compose a general dataset S where each individual is transformed to match the network input. Finally, we divide the set into a training set (90%) and test set (10%) with the same label distribution. Through this process, we end up having a maximum of $M \times N \times feasible_{population}$ tuples, which relates to the granularity of each presented dimension times the maximum amount of feasible individuals per cell.

Training and Usage: The model is then trained for a limited set of epochs (i.e. 20 epochs) and later incorporated into the evolutionary loop to further evaluate individuals. As mentioned above, the model tries to slowly fit towards the designer's preference, and as it becomes more confident in predictions, the more weight W_1 it has in the final fitness of an individual. Confidence is calculated based on the output of the softmax layer, which limits the output of all the neurons into the range 0 to 1, as the sum of all the neurons' output must be 1.0. This characteristic of the softmax layer enables us to interpret the results as the probabilities for each of the classes. For instance, if the network predicts that an individual is going to be preferred to the designer with a 1.0 preference with a probability of 0.9, it means that the remaining 0.1 is distributed among the other output classes, and as a consequence, the network has high confidence. The resulting weights (Eq. 1) and weighted sum (Eq. 2) to evaluate each of the individuals in the EA were the following:

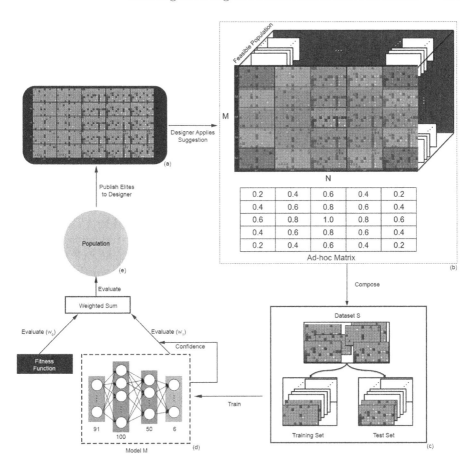

Fig. 4. Overview of the Designer Preference Model integrated into the fitness function of EDD. Elites are published and shown to the designer in a grid fashion (a), and once the designer chooses and applies one of the suggestions, an ad-hoc matrix is created based on the position of the selected suggestion to estimate the preference of suggestions (b). The ad-hoc matrix is then applied to all the elites in the grid, and the feasible populations within the EA cells to compose a general dataset S with rooms labeled by the estimated preference. The composed dataset S is then subdivided into a training set (90%) and test set (10%), both with the same label distribution (c). The dataset is used to train a model M, which is a relatively small neural network, for 20 epochs (d). The model is then used to evaluate the population of the EA together with the current fitness function in a weighted sum, with the weight of the model M conditioned by the confidence of the network (e).

$$w_1 = \min(M_{conf} \cdot M_{TestAcc}, 0.5),$$
$$w_0 = 1.0 - w_1 \tag{1}$$

$$weightedSum = (w_0 \cdot objective) + (w_0 \cdot predicted_{pref}) \tag{2}$$

Finally, the loop continues and the model awaits for the next training session that will be triggered the next time that the user applies a suggestion. In the meantime, the trained model is used as part of the combined individual evaluation process.

4   Evaluation

4.1   Model Performance, Integration, and Setup

We conducted a set of experiments to test the extent to which the Designer Preference Model learns from the user-generated data and fits into the previously existing MI-CC workflow in EDD. These experiments also aimed for finding the hyperparameter configuration for the model that better suited its goals.

This resulted in a fully connected neural network with two hidden layers with 100 and 50 neurons respectively. Bigger and deeper networks, as well as longer training epochs, did result in higher accuracy but it was not worth the time-complexity/accuracy tradeoff since it obstructed the dynamic and high-paced workflow of the tool. Finally, the network had six output nodes related to the different preference values a suggestion could have (i.e. from 0.0 to 1.0 in 0.2 intervals, both ends inclusive) with a softmax layer, which was used to account for the confidence on the network.

Additionally, we decided to train the model's network under independent episodes every time the designer applied a suggestion using the most up-to-date data (the dataset that was created each time a selection was applied). We evaluated and through experimentation later discarded a more continuous approach, since continuously training between episodes led to the generation of large noisy datasets that distorted the training process.

As a result, the Designer Preference Model is smoothly integrated into EDD's workflow. User-wise, it runs in a completely transparent way, neither breaking the reciprocal stimuli loop nor slowing down the performance of the EA in a perceptible way.

4.2   User Study

A user study was also conducted to collect preliminary results that assess the relevance of the Designer Preference Model. We aimed for gathering feedback from game designers on how the model would be used, as well as their perception of the adaptive capabilities of the model.

Fifteen game design students (i.e. novice designers) participated in the study; all of them were introduced to all the features of the tool and were tasked to create a dungeon with interconnected rooms for as long as they were satisfied with their design. At the end of each test session, the participants were asked to fill a brief questionnaire assessing their understanding of the suggestions, its usability, pros, and constraints.

For the purposes of the user study and to test the new model's assessment capabilities in contrast to EDD's original fitness function, we presented the suggestions as displayed in Fig. 2. The top-right pane displays EDD's IC-MAP-Elites as described in [1]. The bottom-right pane shows a smaller grid displaying the top raked individuals assessed by the Designer Preference Model. As the designer applied the top suggestions, the lower grid would get trained with the expected preference, as explained in Sect. 3 and, as a consequence, the lower grid would become more adapted.

This system was designed to validate the hypothesis that users would prefer to make use of the suggestions in the bottom-right pane in the long run, after the Designer Preference Model had been trained a sufficient amount of times, thus gaining confidence in its assessment. A total of 105 rooms were created and the designers applied 43 times suggestions to their designs, with most of the cases happening once the designers had manually created most of the dungeon. Unfortunately, this did not generate enough activity in EDD's procedural content generation system to be able to draw accurate conclusions from the study.

5   Open Problems and Future Work

This paper presents the first MI-CC tool with quality-diversity that explores the usage of a data-driven designer preference model, and its implementation into the EA loop as a complementary evaluation of individuals. Through this model, we searched to cope with some of the limitations presented in previous work, mainly, the user fatigue when queried to choose solutions for the EA, and the stalling of the evolutionary process, thus, adapting the control of the user in the search-space to the dynamic workflow of MI-CC tools.

In this section, we present the multiple challenges that arose when trying to use the designer preference model from our first experiments and preliminary study and the open areas for active research. Through our user study, we were able to test the behavior of our preference model adapted to each of the designers and the performance of such in the wild. While the model, in general, was less used than expected, it was indeed able to learn to certain extent characteristics of the preferred suggestions.

5.1   Dataset

The dataset S created each discrete step the designer applied a suggestion, had a set of intrinsic attributes that while positive and interesting to learn from, they could have been counterproductive and could potentially explain the low and fluctuating accuracy of the model. Firstly, as mentioned in Sect. 3, each generated dataset had a maximum number of samples of $M \times N \times feasible_{population}$, capped to 625 samples in our study, which might not be enough data to accurately learn or would require more training epochs, which ultimately would result in overfitting. This aligns with the open problems presented in [29], where the authors discuss that games will always be constrained by the amount of data, and even though we can generate many samples with our EA, it still might not be enough to cope with the amount of data that ML-approaches require.

Secondly, by taking advantage of the grid visualization of the MAP-Elites, we also inherited the behavioral relation among the different elites, and consequently, each independent training session would intrinsically represent such relation. While our objective was indeed to learn this behavior relationship, which could reveal interesting relations and perspectives by the model, the differences that each pair of behavioral dimensions have could potentially disrupt the whole model between training sessions. For instance, if we train with symmetry and similarity as dimensions, and subsequently change them to symmetry and leniency, what before could be 0.8 in preference in the dataset (i.e. a neighbor of the previously applied suggestion), could now be 0.0 in preference for this dataset, since the pair of dimensions would sort individuals completely different.

Finally, the fact that we automatically assigned an estimated preference value to all individuals based on their grid position, and as pointed out in the previous point, relations could fluctuate dramatically, which could arise a potential issue with the dataset. For instance, a challenge with estimating the preference can be observed in the aesthetic aspects of the rooms, where two rooms can be quite aesthetically similar (i.e. have a single different tile) and yet, due to the way we assign the preference values to train, have a very different preference, thus, enabling confusion in the model. Nevertheless, we did not want the assigned preference value to be based on the similarity between suggested rooms since what the model would end up just learning is to classify based on aesthetic similarity. Therefore, there would not be any need to train any model and through just composing a similarity table and comparing new rooms to the ones already included we would probably achieve the same result.

5.2 Preference Modality

We chose the suggestion grid of the MAP-Elites as an inflection point for the training of the model since it felt more appropriate and natural to the workflow of the tool, and more of a pointer to the actual preference of a designer. The suggestion grid is a reflection of the EA search for quality solutions and having the designer proactively choosing solutions that were interesting for them seemed like an indicator of the preference and interest of the designer.

Based on when the designers actually started applying suggestions and their reason why, indicates that they were not as representative of the preference of the designer as expected. Instead, suggestions were seen as an in-between step to help shape the final room, after creating a first draft of the room and before actually reaching a satisfactory room. This opens up the investigation on what design processes or combinations of processes could be captured to accurately represent the designers' preferences with higher fidelity.

Firstly, we need to consider the level of the designer that is using the tool. The design process, the objectives when designing, the vision on what to do, and the ideas on what to design and what is expected from an interactive tool as ours, could vary quite drastically between designer levels, as it is concluded in [19].

Considering our previous studies with game designers that are more experienced and the one done for this study, we realize that novice designers come with many different ideas that they would like to try, as well as experimenting with very different designs, which in turn means that their preferences and intentions change in very short periods. Understanding this, and adding it as a constraint on the design of preference models is vital since we would want to recognize this key changes to probably discard the model and start fresh since what the model had learned might not be useful anymore.

Secondly, choosing what and when to gather information to create the model is a key aspect. Besides the EA suggestions on the designer's design, we could use the designer's history of changes through their design as well as their current designs. In our case, constantly analyzing the composition of the dungeon and the rooms could bring some insight on the stage of the design process of the designer, which could be used to further understand what to use, if we should keep using the same model, and how to train.

It might even be relevant to have a set of models per set of rooms that have some qualitative similarities to avoid confusion in the model, and updating the model that is relevant to the specific objectives of the designer. In counterpart, this would break the aspect of generalization (i.e. learning the preference of the designer throughout their design process) that could enable us to learn more from the designer.

5.3   Dynamic-Dynamic System vs. Dynamic-Static System

In our experiments, we designed a system where the model would move through the solution space (i.e. the preference-space of the designer) as the designer moves as well, which we call a dynamic-dynamic system. In such a system, the designers drift in many dimensions as they develop, understand better the tool, get deeper in the creative process, have different objectives, and such on. Further, designers might have drifted quite drastically in between training sessions, which ultimately makes the dynamic model harder to move with the designers, resulting in a deficient model.

Therefore, we can conclude that to have some stability and be more robust to an ever-changing designer and creative process, we need some part of the approach to be static. Yet, the designer will never stop being a dynamic component, thus, it is the model that needs to be static. An exciting and interesting open area of research is then in the notion of community models, which would be models fed with several designers' designs, clustered together by their qualitative similarities creating archetypes of designers or archetypes of designs. Such a set of group models would adapt to the dynamic designer by placing the models in the solution space, where a designer instead of drifting together with their model, they would traverse such a space of models as she drifts through the many dimensions of her creative process.

5.4 Future Work

Taking as a starting point the big amount of data (i.e. handmade rooms) collected from all the user studies done to date, and as abovementioned, we believe that a community model formed through clustering is a more realistic model. The envisioned system would follow exactly the same approach and core concept presented in this paper, i.e. a model that as it becomes more confident on the preference of the designer, the more weight it has to evaluate newly generated individuals by the IC-MAP-Elites, as a complementary evaluation to the objective function.

Such a system could be created by using the data of each designer (i.e. a list of created rooms), then those could be arranged in different clusters that would represent archetypical designers or archetypical designs. From this point, we would have a foundation from which we would categorize new designers and we could, on the one hand, create a model from the data in the cluster and start adapting it to the current designer, avoiding the cold start problem. On the other hand, we could as well just keep trying to assign the designer, based on her designs, to different clusters, using each cluster as a model to infer what the "community" of designers would prefer, and since, the designer is part of that community at the moment, what she would prefer. Therefore, creating a model that could be more robust for evaluating designers' preferences by means of having more or less stable clusters that designers could navigate as they go deeper into the design process.

Furthermore, we could go a step further and conceptualize a layered model that on the top layer could represent the community models of the designers, and on the bottom layer, specific designer's models. The bottom layer would then be created in a more classical training session outside our MI-CC tool, with the designer being queried a set of models and she explicitly labeling what she likes and whatnot. Such a model could be used to communicate the expected design style and preference among a group of designers working together or to train new designers based on senior designers' preferences, intentions, and style.

We would also like to explore different steps on the tool where we could collect relevant and crucial data of the designers that could bring us a step closer to a more accurate model of their preferences. Furthermore, accounting for the designer level could have a very impactful result on an effective model, and on how we handle them and their relevance.

Finally, exploring and using different representations of the data, such as images of the rooms in a Convolutional Neural Network (CNN), or qualitative and more processed information of the room (e.g. tiles density, sparsity, and amount, room complexity, connected rooms information, etc.) is an interesting future line. We believe that CNNs could perform better but required even larger amounts of data, and creating 625 images of the suggestion (i.e. our maximum number of data tuples) and then training the model could be cumbersome and have a significant impact on the workflow.

6   Conclusion

In this paper, we have presented the Designer Preference Model, which is a data-driven system that learns an individual designer's preference through the designer's proactive choosing of generated suggestions without disrupting the continuous reciprocal workflow in MI-CC. We implemented our approach in the Evolutionary Dungeon Designer, a Quality-Diversity MI-CC tool, where designers can create dungeons and rooms while the underlying evolutionary system provides suggestions adapted to their current design.

We used the model as a complementary evaluation system to the fitness function of the suggestions in a weighted sum, where the model gained more weight as it became more confident and performed better. Therefore, we aimed at better assessing these provided suggestions with the use of the Designer Preference Model, for them to be interesting and preferable but still usable for designers.

Through our experiments and preliminary studies on using the model to adapt to different designers, we identified a set of challenges and open areas for active research that integrates MI-CC with PCG through Machine Learning. Those challenges relate to the amount of user data needed to accurately learn from the user's preferences, what type of data is needed from the process, the cold start problem, the seldom collection of data to train, the quality of the dataset, and the designer-model setup. Moreover, we wanted to come closer to machine teaching [26] approaches where the human provides fewer data points but with higher quality (i.e. the necessary data to correctly learn) rather than classic approaches to ML (i.e. offline training with a substantial amount of data). In our approach, while the designer has the decision on when to train the algorithm and to a certain extent, with what data to train, we are still missing certain granularity to empower designers to give the right information to the algorithm.

The combination of MI-CC tools with PCG through Machine Learning is a promising area of research that has the potential to enhance content creation. Specifically, designer modeling and our approach to model the designer's preference can have a great impact on the creative process of designers by considering their preferences, intentions, and objectives into the loop, by adapting the workflow to their requirements, or by smoothing the communication among various designers.

Finally, by adding the preference model as a complementary evaluation to the generated suggestions of the evolutionary algorithm, we can give more control, to a certain extent, to the designers over the evaluation of the individuals. In consequence, we can generate higher quality suggestions that better fit a specific designer.

Acknowledgements. The Evolutionary Dungeon Designer is part of the project *The Evolutionary World Designer*, supported by The Crafoord Foundation.

References

1. Alvarez, A., Dahlskog, S., Font, J., Togelius, J.: Empowering quality diversity in dungeon design with interactive constrained MAP-Elites. In: 2019 IEEE Conference on Games (CoG), pp. 1–8 (2019)
2. Alvarez, A., Dahlskog, S., Font, J., Holmberg, J., Johansson, S.: Assessing aesthetic criteria in the evolutionary dungeon designer. In: Proceedings of the 13th International Conference on the Foundations of Digital Games, FDG 2018 (2018)
3. Alvarez, A., Dahlskog, S., Font, J., Holmberg, J., Nolasco, C., Österman, A.: Fostering creativity in the mixed-initiative evolutionary dungeon designer. In: Proceedings of the 13th International Conference on the Foundations of Digital Games, FDG 2018 (2018)
4. Baldwin, A., Dahlskog, S., Font, J.M., Holmberg, J.: Mixed-initiative procedural generation of dungeons using game design patterns. In: Proceedings of the IEEE Conference Computational Intelligence and Games (CIG), pp. 25–32 (2017)
5. Baldwin, A., Dahlskog, S., Font, J.M., Holmberg, J.: Towards pattern-based mixed-initiative dungeon generation. In: Proceedings of the 12th International Conference on the Foundations of Digital Games, FDG 2017, pp. 74:1–74:10. ACM, New York (2017)
6. Donmez, P., Carbonell, J.G.: Proactive learning: cost-sensitive active learning with multiple imperfect oracles. In: Proceedings of the 17th ACM Conference on Information and Knowledge Management, pp. 619–628. ACM (2008)
7. Gravina, D., Khalifa, A., Liapis, A., Togelius, J., Yannakakis, G.N.: Procedural content generation through quality diversity. In: 2019 IEEE Conference on Games (CoG), pp. 1–8 (2019)
8. Gravina, D., Liapis, A., Yannakakis, G.: Surprise search: beyond objectives and novelty. In: Proceedings of the Genetic and Evolutionary Computation Conference 2016, GECCO 2016, pp. 677–684. ACM, New York (2016)
9. Guzdial, M., Liao, N., Riedl, M.: Co-creative level design via machine learning. In: Joint Proceedings of the AIIDE 2018 Workshops Co-Located with 14th AAAI Conference on Artificial Intelligence and Interactive Digital Entertainment (AIIDE 2018), Edmonton, Canada, 13–14 November 2018 (2018)
10. Khalifa, A., Lee, S., Nealen, A., Togelius, J.: Talakat: bullet hell generation through constrained map-elites. In: Proceedings of The Genetic and Evolutionary Computation Conference, pp. 1047–1054. ACM (2018)
11. Kimbrough, S.O., Koehler, G.J., Lu, M., Wood, D.H.: On a feasible-infeasible two-population (FI-2Pop) genetic algorithm for constrained optimization: distance tracing and no free lunch. Eur. J. Oper. Res. $190(2)$, 310–327 (2008)
12. Lehman, J., Risi, S., Clune, J.: Creative generation of 3D objects with deep learning and innovation engines. In: Proceedings of the 7th International Conference on Computational Creativity (2016)
13. Lehman, J., Stanley, K.O.: Abandoning objectives: evolution through the search for novelty alone. Evol. Comput. $19(2)$, 189–223 (2011)
14. Liapis, A., Yannakakis, G.N., Togelius, J.: Adapting models of visual aesthetics for personalized content creation. IEEE Trans. Comput. Intell. AI Games $4(3)$, 213–228 (2012)
15. Liapis, A., Yannakakis, G.N., Togelius, J.: Generating map sketches for strategy games. In: Esparcia-Alcázar, A.I. (ed.) EvoApplications 2013. LNCS, vol. 7835, pp. 264–273. Springer, Heidelberg (2013). https://doi.org/10.1007/978-3-642-37192-9_27

16. Liapis, A., Yannakakis, G.N., Togelius, J.: Designer modeling for sentient sketch-book. In: 2014 IEEE Conference on Computational Intelligence and Games, pp. 1–8, August 2014. https://doi.org/10.1109/CIG.2014.6932873
17. Liapis, A., Yannakakis, G.N., Alexopoulos, C., Lopes, P.: Can computers foster human users' creativity? Theory and praxis of mixed-initiative co-creativity. Digit. Cult. Educ. **8**(2), 136–153 (2016)
18. Liapis, A., Yannakakis, G., Togelius, J.: Designer modeling for personalized game content creation tools. In: Artificial Intelligence and Game Aesthetics - Papers from the 2013 AIIDE Workshop, Technical Report, vol. WS-13-19, pp. 11–16. AI Access Foundation (2013)
19. Lucas, P., Martinho, C.: Stay awhile and listen to 3buddy, a co-creative level design support tool. In: Goel, A.K., Jordanous, A., Pease, A. (eds.) Proceedings of the Eighth International Conference on Computational Creativity, Atlanta, Georgia, USA, 19–23 June 2017, pp. 205–212 (2017)
20. Machado, T., Gopstein, D., Nealen, A., Togelius, J.: Pitako-recommending game design elements in Cicero. In: 2019 IEEE Conference on Games (CoG), pp. 1–8. IEEE (2019)
21. Mouret, J.B., Clune, J.: Illuminating search spaces by mapping elites. arXiv preprint arXiv:1504.04909 (2015)
22. Pugh, J.K., Soros, L.B., Stanley, K.O.: Quality diversity: a new frontier for evolu-tionary computation. Front. Robot. AI **3**, 40 (2016)
23. Secretan, J., Beato, N., D'Ambrosio, D., Rodriguez, A., Campbell, A., Stanley, K.: Picbreeder: evolving pictures collaboratively online. In: Proceedings of Computer Human Interaction Conference, pp. 1759–1768, April 2008
24. Shaker, N., Togelius, J., Nelson, M.J.: Procedural Content Generation in Games: A Textbook and an Overview of Current Research. Springer, Cham (2016). https://doi.org/10.1007/978-3-319-42716-4
25. Shaker, N., Shaker, M., Togelius, J.: Ropossum: an authoring tool for designing, optimizing and solving cut the rope levels. In: AIIDE (2013)
26. Simard, P.Y., et al.: Machine teaching: a new paradigm for building machine learn-ing systems (2017)
27. Smith, G., Whitehead, J., Mateas, M.: Tanagra: reactive planning and constraint solving for mixed-initiative level design. IEEE Trans. Comput. Intell. AI Games **3**(3), 201–215 (2011)
28. Stanton, C., Clune, J.: Curiosity search: producing generalists by encouraging indi-viduals to continually explore and acquire skills throughout their lifetime. PLOS ONE **11**(9), 1–20 (2016)
29. Summerville, A., et al.: Procedural content generation via machine learning (PCGML). IEEE Trans. Games **10**(3), 257–270 (2018)
30. Treanor, M., et al.: AI-based game design patterns. In: Proceedings of the 10th International Conference on the Foundations of Digital Games 2015. Society for the Advancement of Digital Games (2015)
31. Yannakakis, G.N., Liapis, A., Alexopoulos, C.: Mixed-initiative co-creativity. In: Proceedings of the 9th Conference on the Foundations of Digital Games (2014)
32. Yannakakis, G.N., Togelius, J.: Artificial Intelligence and Games, vol. 2. Springer, Cham (2018). https://doi.org/10.1007/978-3-319-63519-4

Testing Hybrid Computational Intelligence Algorithms for General Game Playing

A. E. Vázquez-Núñez[1], A. J. Fernández-Leiva[1] , P. García-Sánchez[2] ,
and A. M. Mora[3(✉)]

[1] Department of Languages and Computer Sciences, University of Málaga,
Málaga, Spain
eduardo.vazquezn@gmail.com, afdez@lcc.uma.es
[2] Department of Computer Science and Engineering, University of Cádiz,
Cádiz, Spain
pablo.garciasanchez@uca.es
[3] Department of Signal Theory, Telematics and Communications,
University of Granada, Granada, Spain
amorag@ugr.es

Abstract. General Videogame Playing is one of the hottest topics in the research field of AI in videogames. It aims at the implementation of algorithms or autonomous agents able to play a set of unknown games efficiently, just receiving the set of rules to play in real time. Thus, this work presents the implementation of eight approaches based on the main techniques applied in the literature to face this problem, including two different hybrid implementations combining Montecarlo Tree Search and Genetic Algorithms. They have been created within the General Video Game Artificial Intelligence (GVGAI) Competition platform. Then, the algorithms have been tested in a set of 20 games from that competition, analyzing its performance. According to the obtained results, we can conclude that the proposed hybrid approaches are the best approaches, and they would be a very competitive entry for the competition.

Keywords: Artificial Intelligence · Videogames · Evolutionary algorithms · MCTS · Hybrid algorithm · General Videogame Playing · GVGAI

1 Introduction

General Game Playing (GGP) [8] is a part of Artificial Intelligence (AI) whose goal is to build a program (also called an agent or *bot*) that can effectively play different types of games without needing to make changes to its source code and without previously training it to play them. The only information provided to the agent/bot are the game rules, and from there it is assumed that it must be able to play by himself (which is actually what humans do). GGP presents us

P. A. Castillo et al. (Eds.): EvoApplications 2020, LNCS 12104, pp. 446–460, 2020.
https://doi.org/10.1007/978-3-030-43722-0_29

a problem that falls into the category of obtaining Artificial Intelligence that shows human behavior (a sort of human-like agents).

Following a classic approach, playing each game would require the implementation of a different algorithm, in which a strategy is planned depending on the domain of the game. Due to the specialization of the implementation, it is not easy to use the same program in different games, or moreover, it might even be useless within the same game, if the rules are modified. For example, a program could be very good playing chess, but it would be disastrous facing any of the multiple variations of this game.

Among the games that are used as a framework for the study of the GGP we can consider the classic games of the ATARI 2600 console, including titles known worldwide such as Pac-Man, Asteroids, or Space Invaders.

One of the pioneers in General Game Playing is the Stanford Logic Group at Stanford University, California. With the aim of deepening this field, they created their own platform for the GGP. In this platform, the representation of the games is made by means of a series of rules, defined under a language called Game Description Language (GDL) [10]. In this way, the representation of the games is unified under a single language so that any (autonomous) player can get the complete information of the game through its rules.

In addition, using this platform, they are organizing an annual competition in which the participants present their own, competing controllers: The General Video Game AI Competition (GVGAI Competition) [6,9].

In this paper we will review the main concepts related to the General Game Playing, whose knowledge helps to understand the state of this research and the scope of this work.

Then, eight different controllers have been implemented using the Framework of the General Video Game AI Competition (GVGAI), applying techniques such as Monte Carlo Tree Search, Genetic Algorithms, and two hybrid versions of these. Then, the agents have been tested and evaluated in 20 games.

After the implementation, several experiments have been carried out and the results obtained by the different algorithms have been analysed, comparing their performances in the different games.

2   Background

Essentially, GGP is a problem which aims to generate agents able to behave as humans when they face a new game (most of times unknown), i.e. the objective if to create human-like bots in that sense [12]. Thus, this is a branch of the so-called Artificial General Intelligence (AGI) [14] which tries to implement an autonomous player good in playing several different games.

In order to study in depth the field of General Video Game Playing, the classic Atari 2600 console and its games have been chosen as the standard framework on which to carry out development and experimentation. This is an ideal framework as these games are easy to understand and model, and require little processing for execution.

This makes it possible to generate large and varied batteries of games on which launching the different agents. Due to these reasons, there are currently several development frameworks based on Atari 2600 available so that anyone interested in General Game Playing can create an agent without having to worry about emulating and modeling the games. Among them, we can find the Atari 2600 Learning Environment (A.L.E) [1] and the GVGAI Framework. The latter will be studied in detail and used for the implementation proposed in this project. Some of these frameworks have ended up inspiring some competitions in which participants are faced to get the agent with better results in a series of games, as is the case of the aforementioned General Video Game Playing AI Competition (GVGAI)[1].

One of the main characteristics of General Game Playing is the ignorance of game rules beforehand. Indeed the rules are communicated at run time, and the agents/bots must be able to interpret them correctly. In order to do so, game spaces must be defined using a Game Description Language (GDL) [10], which would be interpreted by a separated engine.

Moreover there is an approach focused on videogames, VGDL, which would be the focus of this paper, as well as the famous General Video Game AI Competition [9]. The Game Description Language (VGDL) [4], is a language designed by Michael Genesereth as part of the General Game Playing project at Stanford University. Using this language all video games can be represented as sets of rules. It is a logical programming language, similar to Prolog, although it presents important differences such as:

- The semantics of GDL are purely declarative.
- GDL has restrictions to ensure that all issues are resolvable.
- There are reserved words to allow and ease the definition of games.

Following this line, the Video Game Description Language (VGDL) is a high-level language designed by Tom Schaul [13] and originally implemented in Python using the py-game framework. VGDL allows the user to define games concisely with just a few lines of flat code. In this way one can generate large portfolios of games that allow the evaluation of algorithms oriented to General Game Playing. A game is described using two different components:

- *Game*: The dynamics and interactions between objects are described (See Fig. 1).
- *Level*: Positions of objects, represented as characters in a plain-text matrix/file (See Fig. 2).

Supported by this language, the General Video Game AI Competition (GVGAI Competition) is a competition originally created by the Stanford Logic Group [6] in 2005 and still active nowadays. In it participants compete for designing and implementing the controller able to reach the best score after playing a series of games unknown at the time of the competition.

---

[1] http://www.gvgai.net/index.php.

```
BasicGame frame_rate=30
    SpriteSet
        hole   > Immovable color=DARKBLUE img=hole
        avatar > MovingAvatar #cooldown=4
        box    > Passive img=box
    LevelMapping
        0 > hole
        1 > box
    InteractionSet
        avatar wall > stepBack
        box avatar  > bounceForward
        box wall    > undoAll
        box box     > undoAll
        box hole    > killSprite scoreChange=1
    TerminationSet
        SpriteCounter stype=box    limit=0 win=True
```

Fig. 1. Example of definition of Sokoban game, where the player can push boxes through holes in order to get to the exit of a maze.

```
wwwwwwwwwwwww
wA             w    w
w   w               w
w       w    w +ww
www  w1    wwwww
w            w G w
w  1            ww
w        1     ww
wwwwwwwwwwwww
```

Fig. 2. Example of definition of a level for the game Zelda. Avatar ('A'), Key ('+') Exit ('G'), and Enemies ('1')

The goal of the GVGAI is to explore the problem of creating drivers (or agents) for General Video Game Playing, so that they can play any game. It is, in short, to program an agent that can play a wide variety of games without previously knowing what games will be.

This work will be focused on the implementation and test of a set of agents which will be evaluated following similar rules as in the competition. They will be presented several unknown games (by means of their VGDL definition) and must try to obtain the highest score as possible.

3   Implemented Algorithms (Agents)

There are a huge number of possible algorithms applicable when exploring and choosing the next action in a game. The majority of existing approaches are mainly based on different types of tree search, as well as neural networks or evolutionary algorithms. Currently, the algorithms that have obtained the best results in this field are implementations of Monte Carlo Tree Search (MCTS) [2]. It is a best-first search technique that does not require an evaluation function like other algorithms such as minimax. It is based on building a tree of future states and simulate different simulations of the game and learn from these results. Its behavior is based on the stages of selection, expansion, simulation and back-propagation. It can be stopped at any moment, and return the most promising movement found up to that instant.

The other Computational Intelligence technique applied in this paper is a Genetic Algorithm (GA) [7]. GAs are inspired by the *natural selection* process, using the concept of *fitness* to score each solution (also called *individual*). Fittest individuals have a higher probability to reproduce and generate new solutions that will inherit part of their structure. After a certain number of iterations, where individuals will recombine between them to form new individuals, it is expected that the selective pressure will produce better solutions. At each iteration, or *generation*, different operators are applied to parent individuals to recombine them and generate new offspring (*crossover*), or to modify existent ones (*mutation*). At the end of each generation, the least fit individuals are removed. The process continues until a termination criterion is met [5].

In this paper, 8 different algorithms have been implemented (and later compered) to face GGP problem. These have been grouped in two basic methods, two variants of MCTS, two configurations of a GA and two hybrid models combining MCTS + GA. Their description is:

- **Random:** This is one of the simplest algorithms. It just selects a random action from the available ones.
- **One Step Ahead:** Another algorithm of great simplicity. Its operation consists of observing the state following the application of each of the available actions and choosing the one that produces the best result. This algorithm can be modified to look at the following N steps (N Step Ahead).
- **Montecarlo Tree Search:** In order to apply the MCTS algorithm to the problem dealt with in this paper, the following considerations must be taken into account:
  - A tree is built in which each node represents a state of the game.
  - Each node of the tree will have as children the states resulting from applying each of the available actions.
  - Due to the stochastic nature of the games and the lack of knowledge of the depth of the whole tree, as well as the time limitation for each play, the game is only simulated up to a certain depth.
  - The score of a node is simulated as follows: If the node is terminal, a large positive number is returned in case the player wins, and a large negative number in case he loses. For intermediate nodes, the game score is returned.
  - For each step, the root of the tree is placed in the current state of the game, and the best action resulting from the execution of the algorithm for that state is returned.

For this paper, two different variants of the MCTS algorithm have been implemented, which especially affect the selection policy

- **Montecarlo Tree Search (Greedy Variant):** In this approach, a Greedy selection is used, in which the value of a node is simply its cumulative score.
- **Montecarlo Tree Search (UCT Variant):** In this approach of MCTS, the selection function has been modified, as well as the propagation methods to apply the formula Upper Confidence Bounds for Trees (UCT) as the estimated value of a node.

– **Genetic Algorithms:** The genetic algorithms that have been implemented have the following characteristics:

- *Individuals:* Each individual is made up of a series of genes, which correspond to a sequence of actions up to a given depth.
- *Population:* The population is generated in the following way: Starting from an initial state, a certain number of individuals is generated for each of the available actions.
- *Initialization:* Individuals are generated randomly, except for the first action, which corresponds to the main action to which they belong.
- *Fitness:* A normalized evaluation function is used. It is the score obtained after simulating the sequence of actions of the individual, weighted with respect to depth and normalized with respect to the scores of other individuals.
- *Selection*: The selection of parents is made by means of a binary tournament. Thus, two individuals are selected randomly and their scores are compared. The loser will be replaced by the new individual.
- *Crossover:* The generation of the new individual is carried out by means of an uniform crossover. Each of its genes will belong to one of the parents according to a random probability.
- *Mutation:* There is a probability that the new individual will undergo some mutation in their genes, generating a random action in their place.
- *Main loop*: The algorithm executes a certain number of iterations as long as there is enough time available. For each iteration, the complete process is performed for the population corresponding to each of the actions.
- *Return:* At the end of the main loop, it returns the action that has obtained the highest score in one of its individuals.

In this paper, two variants of the genetic algorithm have been implemented, varying the depth of exploration (number of actions) for each individual, i.e., the length of its genome. The main difference lies in the fact that the greater the depth, the greater the capacity to predict the result, but nevertheless, the time required for simulation increases, with fewer iterations being carried out.

- **Genetic Algorithm (Depth Variant 7).**
- **Genetic Algorithm (Depth Variant 10).**

– **Hybrid algorithms of GA and MCTS:** One of the main objectives of this study is to design and test some hybrid algorithms combining the MCTS algorithm and the genetic algorithms. To this end, modifications have been made to both algorithms in order to evaluate in the same way the possible actions obtained after their execution.

- **Collaborative approach (SEQ):** In this proposal, the algorithms are executed collaboratively (or sequentially). For each game step, one of the two algorithms is executed alternately, using as base the result of the previous algorithm.
- **Competitive method (PAR):** In the competitive (or parallel) hybrid algorithm, both algorithms are executed at each step of the game (with half the time available to each). Their results are evaluated and the result that produces the highest score is chosen.

4   Experiments

4.1   Experimental Setup

In order to be able to analyse and compare the effectiveness of the different algorithms, several tests will be carried out running them on different games. Due to the stochastic components of these games, the algorithms will be executed 10 times for each of the games, so that the results obtained will be more robust.

Moreover, the parameters configuration used for the algorithms during the experimentation are listed in Table 1.

Table 1. Parameters used in the experiments for MCTS and GAs.

Parameter	Value
MCTS parameters	
Scanning depth	10
Balancing constant in UCT (K)	$sqrt(2)$
GA parameters	
Depth weighting constant (GAMMA)	0.90
Minimum time available to allow execution (Break_MS)	35
Number of actions of individuals (SIMULATION_DEPH)	Depending on the variant, it will be worth 7 or 10
Size of the population for each action (POPULATION_SIZE)	5
Probability of substituting a gene of the individual losing the tournament with that of the winner (RECPROB)	0.1
Probability of mutation (MUT)	1/SIMULATION_DEPH

4.2   Experiment 1: First Set of Games

The first set of games selected for experimentation are those corresponding to the Validation Set of the CIG15 GVGAI Competition[2] (IEEE Conference on Computational Intelligence and Games). The games corresponding to this list are:

- *(G1) Camel Race:* The player controls a camel and must get to the finish line (on the right of the screen) before any other camel does.
- *(G2) Dig Dug:* The player moves in a cave, collecting gems and gold coins, digging into it. There are also enemies who will kill the player by touching him, however the player can throw rocks to defeat the enemies.
- *(G3) Firestorms:* The player must find the exit of each level avoiding flames created in portals around the screen. He can use water to protect himself.
- *(G4) Infection:* The player aims to infect a number of animals in the level by touching them. There are also doctors in the level who can cure infected animals, but we can defeat them with a sword.
- *(G5) Firecaster:* The aim is to get the avatar to an exit in a maze made of wooden boxes. The avatar can use fire to burn (and remove) them, however, we must be careful for not to damage our character.
- *(G6) Overload:* The avatar must reach an exit with an exact number of coins, otherwise, it will be trapped. He can collect a sword to defeat enemies and cut plants.
- *(G7) Pac-Man:* The avatar moves in a maze full of regular and power pills and 4 ghosts chasing him. The objective is to clean the level bu eating all these pills. The ghosts will kill Pac-Man if they touch him, however, Pac-Man could eat them after collecting a power pill.
- *(G8) Seaquest:* The player controls a submarine that must rescue divers by bringing them to the surface, while avoiding enemies or eliminate them using its torpedoes. The submarine must return to surface from time to time before oxygen capacity is empty.
- *(G9) Whack A Mole:* There are a set of holes from which moles appear. The aim is to pick up them while avoiding a cat who is also arising from the holes.

Table 2. Table of obtained scores for the algorithms (agents) in the 10 games of the Validation Set of CIG15 (GVGAI Competition). Each cell represents the average score obtained as well as its standard deviation after executing them 10 times.

	Random	One Step Ahead	MCTS UCT	MCTS GREEDY	AG D7	AG D10	MCTS+AG SEQ	MCTS+AG PAR
G1	-1 ± 0	1 ± 0	-1 ± 0	-1 ± 0	-1 ± 0	-1 ± 0	-1 ± 0	-1 ± 0
G2	0.3 ± 1.34	4 ± 0	16.6 ± 6.93	12.6 ± 4.27	1.7 ± 3.5	0.2 ± 1.03	23.7 ± 6.13	21.6 ± 9.31
G3	2.1 ± 0.32	0 ± 0	-2.7 ± 1.77	-2.4 ± 1.43	0 ± 0	0 ± 0	0.2 ± 2.75	0 ± 0
G4	7.2 ± 20.18	10.6 ± 49.34	26.3 ± 30.32	36.7 ± 55.47	34.6 ± 30.8	7.7 ± 27.41	41.1 ± 31.36	63.8 ± 24.12
G5	7.9 ± 3.35	2 ± 0	10.6 ± 3.5	9.1 ± 2.88	11.6 ± 3.68	15.4 ± 2.12	14.3 ± 2.67	17.7 ± 2.79
G6	7.6 ± 2.32	1 ± 0	11.9 ± 1.6	10.8 ± 2.1	11 ± 3.68	15.4 ± 2.12	14.3 ± 2.67	17.7 ± 2.79
G7	68.3 ± 30.53	6 ± 0	164.9 ± 46.75	128.5 ± 65.6	19.4 ± 24.52	88.2 ± 88.42	234.9 ± 48.01	225.1 ± 48.85
G8	5.2 ± 4.8	0 ± 0	135.6 ± 315.34	237.5 ± 418.23	634.1 ± 997.59	105.4 ± 320.32	643.7 ± 534.87	865.5 ± 941.4
G9	-7.2 ± 1.93	0.15 ± 0	-1.1 ± 4.15	10.4 ± 3.37	3 ± 6.85	.1.4 ± 3.84	-3.3 ± 6.83	1.7 ± 8.79
G10	0.9 ± 1.66	1 ± 0	2.7 ± 2.45	1.7 ± 0.67	2.8 ± 2.82	1.8 ± 1.23	1.5 ± 1.08	1.4 ± 1.35

---

[2] http://www.gvgai.net/training_set.php?rg=2.

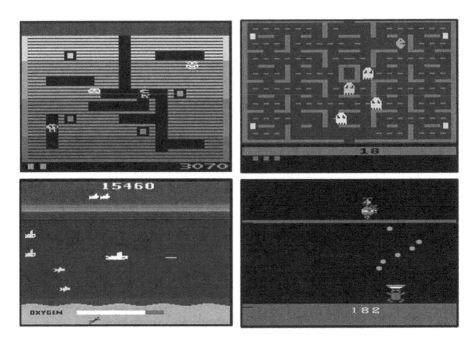

Fig. 3. Atari games which inspired some of the GVGAI competition games. From top to down and from left to righ: Dig Dug, Pac-Man, Seaquest, Eggomania.

- *(G10) Eggomania:* The player must catch several eggs thrown by a hen from the top of the screen before they are broken on the floor.

Some of the original Atari games on which these implementations were inspired can be seen in Fig. 3.

Table 2 shows the average result of the 10 runs, as well as the standard deviation of the game score.

Analyzing the results, we can observe that, depending on the game, the same algorithms obtain quite different values, although a tendency can be appreciated in which the genetic and hybrid algorithms obtain the best scores. Being the *competitive hybrid version (MCTS+AG PAR)* the one that seems to obtain the maximum score in a greater number of games.

Due to the large number of algorithms and problems that have been considered, it is difficult to compare them just observing the numerical results. To improve this aspect, a comparison has been made based on rankings [3], assigning r_{ij} rankings to the results obtained by each algorithm j on each problem i. That is, for every problem, a ranking is assigned $1 \leq r_{ij} \leq k$, where k is the number of algorithms to compare. These rankings are assigned in an ascending way, that is, 1 to the best result, 2 to the second, and so on (if there are ties, average rankings are assigned).

Observing the comparison by ranking, both in Table 3 and in the distribution graph of Fig. 4, it is easier to notice the dominion of the competitive hybrid

Table 3. Average rank position for the 10 runs of each algorithm facing each of the 10 games of the Validation Set of CIG15 (GVGAI Competition).

	Random	One Step Ahead	MCTS UCT	MCTS GREEDY	AG D7	AG D10	MCTS+AG SEQ	MCTS+AG PAR
G1	3.85	1	3.85	3.85	3.85	3.85	3.85	3.85
G2	7.5	6	3	5	7.5	1	1	2
G3	8	4	4	4	4	1	1	4
G4	7	2	6	5	8	4	4	3
G5	5.5	8	5.5	3	3	3	3	1
G6	7	8	6	1.5	2.5	2.5	2.5	1.5
G7	6	8	5	7	1	3	3	2
G8	7	8	5	2	6	3	3	1
G9	6	7	5	3	4	2	2	1
G10	3	8	2	1	4.5	6	6	4.5

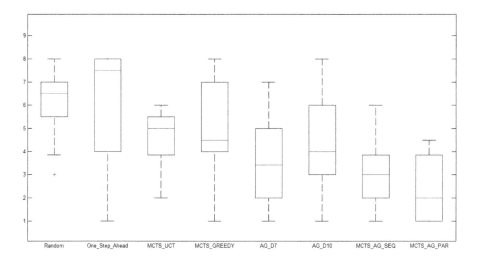

Fig. 4. Diagram of boxplots representing the distribution of positions in the ranking of each of the algorithms (lower is better).

algorithm (PAR) over the others, obtaining the first position in 4 out of the 10 games, sharing one of those positions (Game 6) with the genetic algorithm of depth 7. In addition, their distribution of values, as well as the value of the median, are in the lowest positions.

Before a victory of the competitive hybrid algorithm (MCTS+AG PAR) over the others can be concluded, it is necessary to carry out a series of statistical tests to verify that the distributions of values of the algorithms are independent, so that they validate the conclusions obtained previously. To this end, the Friedman test [3] will be performed, which, based on the algorithm rankings, establishes a null hypothesis that all algorithms behave equally. A p-value associated with the distribution is then calculated. In Table 4 we can see the result of the test, which

Table 4. Friedman statistic distributed according to chi-square with 7 degrees of freedom: 20.858444. P-value computed by Friedman Test: 0.00398558.

Algorithm	Ranking
Random	6.25
One Step Ahead	6.1
MCTS-UCT	4.65
MCTS-GREEDY	5.05
AG-D7	3.65
AG-D10	4.65
MCTS-AG-SEQ	3.15
MCTS-AG-PAR	2.5

presents the ranking of each algorithm, in addition to the p-values calculated by the Friedman test.

As it can be seen, the p-value obtained is less than 0.01, so we can safely state that the null hypothesis is false. This implies that the comparison made previously on the algorithms is still valid.

4.3   Experiment 2: Second Set of Games

Although in principle a set of 10 games should offer sufficient variety, it has been considered appropriate to repeat the tests on a new set of 10 games, in order to verify that the results have not been affected by the specific circumstances of the games on which they have been played.

The new list of games on which the experiments have been repeated are those corresponding to the Training Set of the CIG14 (GVGAI Competition)[3]:

- *Alien:* The player controls a starship at the bottom of the screen shooting aliens at the upper part.
- *Boulder Dash*: The player must move the avatar through a cave, collecting diamonds, and searching for the exit, while avoiding the enemies.
- *Butterflies:* The player must hunt butterflies.
- *Chase:* The player has to chase goats and kill them, but they could also attack the avatar.
- *Frogs:* A frog must traverse the level (from down to top) avoiding obstacles and dangers.
- *Missile Command*: The aim is to destroy several missiles which have been shot to cities that the player must defend.
- *Portals:* The player must move the avatar from an entrance to an exit traversing several doors which translate it to an unpredictable position in the screen.

---

[3] http://www.gvgai.net/training_set.php?rg=1.

Table 5. Table of maximum scores of the algorithms in each of the 10 games of the Training Set CIG14 (GVGAI Competition). Each cell represents the maximum score obtained for each algorithm obtained after executing them 10 times.

	Random	One Step Ahead	MCTS UCT	MCTS GREEDY	AG D7	AG D10	MCTS_A G SEQ	MCTS_A G PAR
G1	66	45	74	78	80	80	80	84
G2	3	2	22	6	7	5	26	22
G3	52	26	72	16	62	74	64	40
G4	7	1	7	3	7	7	7	7
G5	0.2	1	1	0.2	1	1	1	1
G6	0.1	0.3	2	2	8	5	2	5
G7	0	0	0	0	1	1	1	1
G8	0	0	0	0	1	0	0	1
G9	16	4	32	10	34	34	45	43
G10	7	1	4	6	8	8	8	8

- *Sokoban:* The avatar must get to an exit in a maze with several boxes, where it can to push these boxes to move them or to make them fall down by holes.
- *Survive Zombies:* The avatar must avoid being touched by zombies, because otherwise it will be transformed in another one.
- *Zelda:* The player must move the avatar in a dungeon with several enemies, he must find a key in order to open the exit door.

Table 6. Average rankings for the 10 runs of each algorithm facing each of the 10 games of the Training Set CIG14 (GVGAI Competition).

	Random	One Step Ahead	MCTS UCT	MCTS GREEDY	AG D7	AG D10	MCTS_A G SEQ	MCTS_A G PAR
G1	7	8	6	5	3	3	3	1
G2	7	8	2.5	5	4	6	1	2.5
G3	5	7	2	8	4	1	3	6
G4	3.5	8	3.5	7	3.5	3.5	3.5	3.5
G5	7.5	3.5	3.5	7.5	3.5	3.5	3.5	3.5
G6	7	8	5	5	1	2.5	5	2.5
G7	6.5	6.5	6.5	6.5	2.5	2.5	2.5	2.5
G8	5.5	5.5	5.5	5.5	1.5	5.5	5.5	1.5
G9	6	8	5	7	3.5	3.5	1	2
G10	5	8	7	6	2.5	2.5	2.5	2.5

In this case, we will present only the table of maximum scores (Table 5) and the comparison of rankings obtained by the algorithms (Table 6 and Fig. 5).

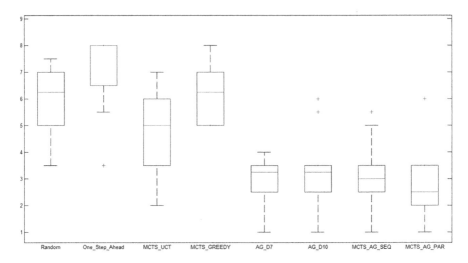

Fig. 5. Diagram of boxplots representing the distribution of positions with respect to the ranking of each of the algorithms for the new experimental setup. In this case we try to minimize its values.

Tables 5 and 6, together with Fig. 5 show the obtained average maximum scores, average rank and distribution of ranks in the 10 runs for every algorithm on the new set of games. Although in this case the difference is somewhat minor, it is still observable that the competitive hybrid algorithm (MCTS+AG PAR) gets an average maximum score and rank position slightly better than the rest, demonstrating that even in a framework of 10 completely different games, the conclusions previously obtained are still valid.

5 Conclusions and Future Work

This paper presents a research study conducted on the scope of General Game Playing. To this end, 8 different algorithms (agents) have been implemented inside the framework of General Video Game AI Competition, in order to test their performance in a set of 20 different videogames. The algorithms include two basic approaches, 2 Montecarlo Tree Search (MCTS) implementations, 2 Genetic Algorithms configurations and 2 Hybrid methods combining MCTS and GA, collaborative (or Sequential) and competitive (or Parallel).

Obtained scores as well as reached ranking position for every algorithm have been compared in two different experiment. After analyzing the results, we can conclude that, from the compared algorithms, there is not a method outperforming the rest. Although there is a trend towards the victory of the competitive hybrid algorithm over the others, in some of the games its performance falls far below that of its competitors.

The diversity in the obtained scores lays on the fact that different games have produced different winners, so it is still very difficult to find an algorithm that becomes an expert player of any possible type of game. This is derived from the intrinsic nature of General Game Playing, whose objective is to imitate human behavior when facing new unknown games. Indeed it is really hard to find a human player who really excels in any type of game.

For future work, it would be of great interest to continue deepening techniques related to the MCTS algorithm, as it offers great opportunities for expansion, such as adding learning about the state of the game or pattern recognition [11], as well as continue working on advanced hybridization proposals that combine the advantages of different algorithms. In addition, new sets of games could be considered for the experiments, or comparisons could be made with human players, as well as with other agents from the state of the art (competition winners or other entries for instance). In general, research on General Game Playing is at an early stage, so it could be expanded so that it is not only limited to single-player games, or simple classic games, but applied to multiplayer games, with physics in real time, or partially observable games.

Acknowledgements. This work has been supported by Ministerio español de Ciencia, Innovación y Universidades (MINECO) with project DeepBio (TIN2017-85727-C4-1-P) with Universidad de Málaga, DeepBio (TIN2017-85727-C4-2-P) with Universidad de Granada, and KNOWAVES (TEC2015-68752), also funded by FEDER. Together with project 5G-CLOPS (RTI2018-102002-A-I00) granted by Ministerio español de Ciencia, Innovación y Universidades and project EVO5G (B-TIC-402-UGR18) supported by Junta de Andalucáa and FEDER.

References

1. Bellemare, M.G., Naddaf, Y., Veness, J., Bowling, M.: The arcade learning environment: an evaluation platform for general agents (extended abstract). In: Yang, Q., Wooldridge, M.J. (eds.) Proceedings of the Twenty-Fourth International Joint Conference on Artificial Intelligence. IJCAI 2015, Buenos Aires, Argentina, 25–31 July 2015, pp. 4148–4152. AAAI Press (2015)
2. Chaslot, G., Bakkes, S., Szita, I., Spronck, P.: Monte-Carlo tree search: a new framework for game AI. In: Darken, C., Mateas, M. (eds.) Proceedings of the Fourth Artificial Intelligence and Interactive Digital Entertainment Conference, Stanford, California, USA, 22–24 October 2008. The AAAI Press (2008)
3. Derrac, J., García, S., Hui, S., Suganthan, P.N., Herrera, F.: Analyzing convergence performance of evolutionary algorithms: a statistical approach. Inf. Sci. **289**, 41–58 (2014). https://doi.org/10.1016/j.ins.2014.06.009
4. Ebner, M., Levine, J., Lucas, S.M., Schaul, T., Thompson, T., Togelius, J.: Towards a video game description language. In: Lucas, S.M., Mateas, M., Preuss, M., Spronck, P., Togelius, J. (eds.) Artificial and Computational Intelligence in Games, Dagstuhl Follow-Ups, vol. 6, pp. 85–100. Schloss Dagstuhl - Leibniz-Zentrum fuer Informatik (2013)
5. García-Sánchez, P., Tonda, A., Fernández-Leiva, A.J., Cotta, C.: Optimizing hearthstone agents using an evolutionary algorithm. Knowl.-Based Syst. (2019)
6. Genesereth, M.R., Love, N., Pell, B.: General game playing: overview of the AAAI competition. AI Mag. **26**(2), 62–72 (2005)

7. Goldberg, D.E.: Genetic Algorithms in Search, Optimization and Machine Learning. Addison Wesley, Boston (1989)
8. Levine, J., et al.: General video game playing. In: Lucas, S.M., Mateas, M., Preuss, M., Spronck, P., Togelius, J. (eds.) Artificial and Computational Intelligence in Games, Dagstuhl Follow-Ups, vol. 6, pp. 77–83. Schloss Dagstuhl - Leibniz-Zentrum fuer Informatik (2013)
9. Liebana, D.P., et al.: The 2014 general video game playing competition. IEEE Trans. Comput. Intell. AI Games **8**, 229–243 (2016)
10. Love, N., Hinrichs, T., Haley, D., Schkufza, E., Genesereth, M.: General game playing: game description language specification. Technical report LG-2006-01, Stanford University, March 2008. http://logic.stanford.edu/classes/cs227/2013/readings/gdl_spec.pdf
11. Lucas, S.M., Samothrakis, S., Pérez, D.: Fast evolutionary adaptation for Monte Carlo tree search. In: Esparcia-Alcázar, A.I., Mora, A.M. (eds.) EvoApplications 2014. LNCS, vol. 8602, pp. 349–360. Springer, Heidelberg (2014). https://doi.org/10.1007/978-3-662-45523-4_29
12. Mnih, V., et al.: Human-level control through deep reinforcement learning. Nature **518**(7540), 529–533 (2015)
13. Schaul, T.: A video game description language for model-based or interactive learning. In: 2013 IEEE Conference on Computational Intelligence in Games (CIG), Niagara Falls, ON, Canada, 11–13 August 2013, pp. 1–8. IEEE (2013)
14. Schaul, T., Togelius, J., Schmidhuber, J.: Measuring intelligence through games. CoRR abs/1109.1314 (2011). http://arxiv.org/abs/1109.1314

Evolutionary Computation in Digital Healthcare and Personalized Medicine

Accelerated Design of HIFU Treatment Plans Using Island-Based Evolutionary Strategy

Filip Kuklis, Marta Jaros⬭, and Jiri Jaros$^{(\boxtimes)}$⬭

Faculty of Information Technology, Centre of Excellence IT4Innovations,
Brno University of Technology, Bozetechova 2, 612 66 Brno, Czech Republic
`jarosjir@fit.vutbr.cz`

Abstract. High Intensity Focused Ultrasound (HIFU) is an emerging technique for non-invasive cancer treatment where malignant tissue is destroyed by thermal ablation. Such a treatment consists of a series of short sonications destroying small volumes of tissue. High-quality treatment plans allow to precisely target malignant tissue and protect surrounding healthy tissue. Recently, we developed an evolutionary strategy to design such HIFU treatment plans using patient-specific material properties and a realistic thermal model. Unfortunately, the execution time was prohibitive for routine use. Here, we present an optimized evolutionary strategy based on island model parallelization and a revised fitness function implementation. The proposed improvements allow to develop a good treatment plan 4 times faster and with 5% higher success rate.

Keywords: Evolutionary strategy · Island model · HIFU · Treatment planning · k-Wave toolbox

1 Introduction

In last years, High-Intensity Focused Ultrasound (HIFU) has been used to treat a variety of solid malignant tumors in a well-defined volume, including the pancreas, liver, prostate, breast, uterine fibroids, and soft-tissue sarcomas. The main benefits of HIFU over the conventional tumor/cancer treatment modalities, such as open surgery, radio- and chemo-therapy, is its non-invasiveness. Furthermore, it is non-ionizing and has fewer complications after treatment. To this day, over 100,000 cases have been treated throughout the world with great success [24].

The basic principle of thermal HIFU treatment is to raise the temperature by several tens of degrees so that the tissue is destroyed via coagulative necrosis with delivering adequate ultrasound energy to the targeted area. The HIFU beam focusing results in cytotoxic levels of temperature only at a specific location within a small volume (e.g., about 1 mm in diameter and about 10 mm in length), which minimizes the potential for thermal damage to tissue outside the

© Springer Nature Switzerland AG 2020
P. A. Castillo et al. (Eds.): EvoApplications 2020, LNCS 12104, pp. 463–478, 2020.
https://doi.org/10.1007/978-3-030-43722-0_30

focal region. Large tumors can be destroyed by producing a contiguous lesion lattice encompassing the tumor and appropriate margins of surrounding tissue. However, complications may develop if vital blood vessels adjacent to the tumors are severely damaged. Blood perfusion may also carry away a significant amount of energy and deteriorate the treatment outcome [12].

Despite the advantages of HIFU, this method still suffers from delivery precision in contrast to other established therapies such as radiotherapy. With recent advances in numerical methods and high performance computing, detailed simulations accurately capturing the relevant physical behavior of focused ultrasound waves and temperature distribution in heterogeneous tissue are now possible [21]. However, model-based treatment planning (determining the best transducer position and sonication parameters to deliver the ultrasound energy to the planning target volume) is still currently performed in a relatively rudimental way based on heuristics rather than physical models of the therapy. This leads to rather poor quality of the treatment plans.

Recently, first steps towards the automated design of precise HIFU treatment plans have been made via the use of Covariance Matrix Adaptation Evolutionary Strategy (CMA-ES) [8] in combination with a physically relevant fitness function [4]. The planning algorithm achieved promising results by producing treatment plans with negligible mistreated and undertreated areas. Unfortunately, the evolution process often took more than one day, even on very powerful computing servers integrating two processors with 24 cores in total.

This paper presents our effort in reducing the evolution run time. It was decided to adopt the island model of EA [1,2,20] where the population is split into several sub-populations assigned to particular computational resources. These sub-populations mostly evolve independently, which ensures higher diversity of the evolutionary process, yet share some collective knowledge about promising areas in the search space, which improves the convergence towards global optima. Furthermore, since the fitness function evaluation is extremely time-consuming, considerable time has been spent in the code optimization.

The rest of the paper is organized as follows. The next section recapitulates the structure of the evolutionary algorithm, its encoding and fitness function. Section 3 details the optimization of the fitness function. Section 4 describes the island model implementation. The parameters of the island model and the quality of proposed optimizations are elaborated in Sect. 5. The last section concludes the paper and draws future work directions.

2   Proposed Algorithm

This section first describes the optimization algorithm based on the Matlab implementation of the Covariance Matrix Adaptation (CMA) Evolutionary Strategy (ES) developed by Hansen [7]. Then, the treatment plan encoding is outlined. Finally, the fitness function based on the tissue-realistic heat diffusion developed as part of the k-Wave toolbox is introduced [21,22].

2.1 Evolutionary Strategy

The CMA-ES [7,8] is a very popular stochastic method for real-parameter (continuous domain) optimization of nonlinear, non-convex objective functions. The CMA [9] describes the pairwise dependencies between variables/genes on the top of the classic ES.

In CMA-ES, a population of λ new search points (individuals, offspring) is generated by sampling a multivariate normal distribution $\mathcal{N}(\boldsymbol{m}, \boldsymbol{C})$ determined by its mean $\boldsymbol{m} \in \mathbb{R}^N$ and its symmetric and positive defined covariance matrix $\boldsymbol{C} \in \mathbb{R}^{N \times N}$, which determines the shape of the distribution ellipsoid. The length of the step is controlled by the so-called step-size parameter $\sigma \in \mathbb{R}^N$:

$$x_i \sim \boldsymbol{m} + \sigma \mathcal{N}_i(0, \boldsymbol{C}) \text{ for } i = 1, ..., \lambda. \tag{1}$$

The newly generated individuals are first ranked according to their fitness and then the best μ individuals are selected. The elitism is not used. Next, the mean value, step size and the covariance matrix are updated. The mean value $\boldsymbol{m}$ is updated by weighted intermediate recombination where the weight of every selected individual is proportional to its rank. The CMA-ES utilizes an evolution path to control the step size σ. Conceptually, the evolution path is the search path the strategy takes over a number of generation steps. The adaptation of the covariance matrix follows a natural gradient approximation of the expected fitness. The adaptation procedure first learns all pairwise dependencies between all variables. Then, it conducts a principal components (eigenvectors) analysis (PCA) of steps sequentially in time and space. Finally, a new rotated problem representation is determined using the Mahalanobis metric [3].

The main benefit of the CMA-ES is a very small population and fast convergence for real-valued problems compared to Genetic Algorithms (GA) [2] or Estimation of Distribution Algorithms (EDA) [14]. The step-size control facilitates fast (log-linear) convergence and possibly linear scaling with the dimension. The covariance matrix adaptation increases the likelihood of previously successful steps and can improve performance by orders of magnitude [8].

2.2 Treatment Plan Encoding

The ablation of large target areas using HIFU requires multiple sonications to effectively cover this area. The candidate solution I describes the trajectory the HIFU transducer follows in the tissue during the treatment. The treatment is not continuous but proceeds at precisely defined points in the tissue where the HIFU focus is placed. The number of sonications is limited to N, usually low tens. The amount of energy delivered during a single sonication is given by the length of the sonication t_{on} and the length of the subsequent cooling interval t_{off}. One sonication can thus be defined as a 4-tuple S_i composed of two spatial coordinates of the beam focus (only 2D problems are considered), and sonication and cooling intervals t_{on} and t_{off}, respectively:

$$I = (S_1, S_2, ..., S_N), \text{ where } S_i = (x_i, y_i, t_{on, i}, t_{off, i}) \tag{2}$$

2.3 Fitness Function

Generally, the treatment planning problem is defined as the search for suitable positions and sonication times for the specified number sonications to cover the target area and minimize the volume of mistreated areas. The assessment of the treatment plan quality is composed of several stages, detailed in [4]. First, the heat deposition for every sonication is determined using the predicted shape and position of the ultrasound focus and the sonication length. Physically, they can be determined by complex numerical models [11,15,22]. However, since their execution times are often prohibitive for applications in evolutionary algorithms, several simplifications had to be made: (1) the centre of the focus can be placed at coordinates given by the sonication $S_i = [x_i, y_i]$, and (2) the distribution of the energy in the focus follows the Gaussian distribution [5,23].

Second, the numerical thermal model is executed on the whole sequence of sonications to calculate the temperature distribution in the domain during the treatment. The heat diffusion is modelled by the Pennes' bioheat equation [18] which has a corresponding ultrasound energy absorption term as a source term, incorporates various tissue properties and effects of blood perfusion.

Figure 1 shows the spatial temperature distribution along the main focus axis at the end of the first sonication, and then every 20 s during the cooling period. Without the proximity of a large blood vessel, the spatial temperature distribution follows the Gaussian distribution. The temperature magnitude declines from a peak of 72 °C at the end of the sonication down to about 46 °C at the end of the cooling interval. On the other hand, the area with temperature exceeding 37 °C is slowly growing.

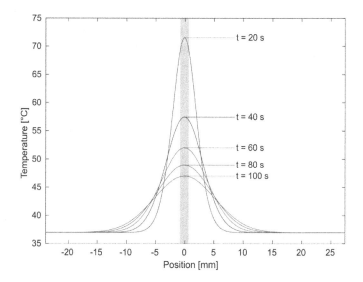

Fig. 1. Heat distribution along the main focus axis during a sonication with $t_{on} = 20$ s and $t_{off} = 100$ s at time $t = 20$ s, 40 s, 60 s, 80 s, 100 s. (Color figure online)

Thermal damage is computed using the Sapareto-Dewey iso-effect thermal dose relationship [19] which is expressed in seconds and represents the equivalent time which would produce the same biological effects at a temperature of 43 °C. This metric is called cumulative equivalent minutes at 43 °C (CEM_{43}). CEM_{43} is calculated for every point in the tissue and summed up over all sonications. Thermal doses of 240 min at 43 °C irreversibly damage and coagulate critical cellular protein, tissue structural components and the vasculature leading to immediate tissue destruction [24]. The area with the dose exceeding 240 CEM_{43} is depicted in Fig. 1 by a yellow bar.

The output of the thermal model is a spatial map of CEM_{43} accumulated over the whole treatment. This map is thresholded by a value of 240 to produce a binary mask of destroyed tissue. The evaluation of the quality of the HIFU treatment is based on the assumption that all tissue in the target area is destroyed while all tissue in the prohibited area (organs at risk) is left unharmed. In order to give the optimization algorithm some freedom, do not care areas can be specified as well.

The fitness function for a 2D case can be written as

$$f = \int_0^Y \int_0^X ((D * \overline{C}) + (P * C))dxdy$$

$$C = \begin{cases} 0 & \text{for } CEM_{43} \le 240 \\ 1 & \text{for } CEM_{43} > 240 \end{cases} \qquad (3)$$

$$D \in \mathbb{R}^+, P \in \mathbb{R}^+,$$

where X, Y are domain sizes along the x and y axes, respectively, C is a binary mask representing the actually treated area, $\overline{C}$ is a complementary mask representing the non-treated area, D is a target map specifying the area to be treated and P represents prohibited area. Since D and P are defined as functions over 2D space, users can specify the level of urgency a given point in the space shall be treated or protected with. The goal is then to minimize the fitness function.

3   Acceleration of Fitness Function

The probability of finding the optimal solution by CMA-ES is known to increase with the population size [10]. However, a larger population usually implies a much higher number of evaluations. As can be seen in Table 1, the fitness function is very complex due to the realistic simulation of heat diffusion which consumes over 99% of the computational time. That only allows populations with at most 40 individuals to be used due to a time constraint of 48 h. Therefore, the first step towards a more robust EA is to analyze and optimize the fitness function.

3.1   Analysis of the Matlab Implementation

The fitness function consists of the calculation of the heat diffusion followed by the assessment of the treated area. We only focused on the heat diffusion since the treated area assessment is computationally trivial.

Table 1. Time profile of the whole evolution process executed by Matlab.

Code	Calls	Total time	% Time
Fitness evaluation	2,990	47,998 s	99.9%
Population initialization	1	13.87 s	0.1%
Final solution evaluation	1	12.53 s	0.0%
Writes to log file	140	1.21 s	0.0%
Other		3.34 s	0.0%
Total		48,029 s	100%

The heat diffusion code was originally implemented in Matlab using the k-Wave toolbox [22]. Its pseudocode can be seen in Listing 1.1. This code supports precise tissue parameter settings derived from patient-specific models of the tissue anatomy discretized into a grid with spatial and temporal resolutions set according to the convergence testing, see Sect. 5.

The computation is based on a k-space pseudospectral scheme in which spatial gradients are calculated using the Fourier collocation spectral method and temporal gradients are calculated using a k-space corrected finite difference scheme. The precomputations of the k-space term and the heat source term are based on simple matrix operations and two Fourier transforms. Since being executed only once, this part of computation is negligible. On the other hand, the functions inside the loop are called between 50 and 200 times for typical sonication lengths. The computation of the divergence term uses 3 forward and 4 inverse 2D Fourier transforms. Hence, 350–1400 FFTs are executed. This causes the computation of divergence term to take almost 85% of the computation time of the whole simulation. The update of the damage integral takes about 10% and the rest of the operations amount to last 5%.

Listing 1.1. Pseudocode of the heat deposition calculation for one sonication.

```
Precompute k-space derivative term;
Precompute heat source term;

Loop through the sonication time span
begin
   Compute perfusion term;
   Compute divergence term;
   Update tissue temperature;
   Update damage integral;
end
```

3.2   Optimized Implementation

In order to maximize computational efficiency, the fitness function was rewritten from Matlab to C++ with several low-level optimizations. First, the Matlab FFT [6] taking about 75% of the execution time was replaced with the Intel MKL [13] version which offers 89% faster execution on the domain sizes of interest. Second, the element-wise matrix-matrix operations were parallelized and vectorized using the C++ OpenMP 4.5 library [17] to exploit multiple processor cores and vector instructions such as Intel AVX. Multiple mathematical operations were applied to each grid point where possible to maximize temporal data locality. Finally, the C++ code was compiled with the highest optimization level tuned for the CPUs being used in our experiments.

Since the medical data processing and the CMA-ES itself was implemented in Matlab, the optimized fitness function was wrapped by a MEX function to be directly invoked from within Matlab without any additional overhead.

3.3   Performance Evaluation

The optimization of the fitness function itself brought more than twofold reduction of the execution time. In order to use an appropriate level of parallelism a scaling test was performed, see Fig. 2. The question to be answered was whether it is better to evaluate multiple individuals at the same time, or use multiple processor cores to evaluate a single one. Since CMA-ES uses a very small population and every individual may take a considerably different time, an even usage of all cores may become an issue. In the scaling test, the number of cores collaborating to evaluate a single individual was progressively increased from 1 to 24. The execution time of a single individual decreases almost linearly up to 12 cores (a single processor). When both processors are used, the performance deteriorates significantly. This can be attributed to the scaling of the Intel FFTs and the inter-CPU interconnect.

This measurement opens three almost equal possibilities how the population evaluation can be parallelized while keeping a reasonable level of load balance:

1. 6 individuals at the same time, each using 4 cores,
2. 3 individuals at the same time, each using 8 cores,
3. 2 individuals at the same time, each using 12 cores.

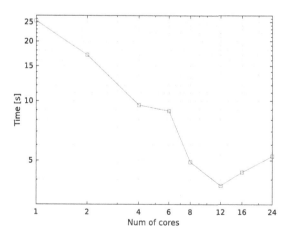

Fig. 2. Execution time of the fitness function on a dual-socket server with 24 cores.

4 Island Model

Faster evolution can be achieved by concurrent evaluation of multiple individuals. One possibility is to keep the evolutionary algorithm unchanged and only parallelize the evaluation. We, however, decided to split the population into multiple ones and run a parallel island-based CMA-ES with a subset of cores assigned to each island. These cores can be used either to evaluate multiple individuals concurrently, or to accelerate the evaluation of a single individual. The updated execution profile revealed only a 1.5% overhead introduced by the island model.

The pseudocode displayed in Listing 1.2 shows the island CMA-ES workflow. First, the algorithm is initialized. Then the evolution runs in a loop until the stop condition is met. The loop starts with generation and evaluation of *lambda* new individuals from the local island CMA-ES model. The islands migrate individuals every M-th generation. During the migration, the population on each island is sorted according to the fitness values and N best individuals are broadcast to other islands. The other islands accept these individuals only if the acceptance condition is satisfied. Next, some of the immigrants are selected by a roulette wheel to replace N worst individuals in the local population. At the end of the loop, the local CMA-ES models are updated based on the newly formed population and the loop repeats.

Listing 1.2. Pseudocode of the island-based CMA-ES.

```
1   init_params(params);
2   while(stopflag)
3     % Generate and evaluate local population
4     for k = 1:lambda
5       ind = create_new_individual(params);
6       fitness(k) = eval_thermal_model(ind);
7     end
8
9     % Perform migration
10    if(mod(gen, M) == 0)
11      sort(fitness);
12      for i = 1:N                    % Islands perform migration in turn
13        if(i == current_island)      % Who broadcasts individuals
14          broadcast(i, fitness(1:n_best));
15        else if (accept_cond)        % Shall I accept migrants
16          rcv(i) = broadcast(i);
17        end
18        if(glob_select)              % Global or per island selection
19          sel(:) = roulette(rcv(:));
20        else if(isl_select)
21          for i = 1:size(rcv)
22            sel(i) = roulette(rcv(i));
23          end
24        end
25      end
26      % Replace worst part of population
27      fitness(lambda - n_sel:lambda) = sel(:);
28    end
29
30    % Update local model
31    select_parents;
32    update_params(params, fitness);
33    gen = gen + 1;
34  end
```

5 Experimental Results

The experimental work presented in this paper investigates the benefits of several different versions of the island based CMA-ES and compares them with a pan-population (PP) version. To allow statistical evaluation, 15 independent runs for each version were executed with the maximum execution time per run limited to 48 h. To compare the original CMA-ES treatment planning with the island-based CMA-ES, two main metrics were examined: (1) success rate, (2) total number of fitness evaluations to converge. Success rate represents the percentage of runs which found the optimal solution with the fitness value of zero. In such a case, the treated area covers the whole desired area and the prohibited area is unharmed. The total number of fitness evaluations to converge is straightforward for the pan-population model. In the case of the island model, the total number of evaluation is the sum over all islands.

During the evaluation of the proposed algorithm we strove to work under as realistic conditions as possible. The same benchmark as in the paper by Cudova [4] was used. The HIFU treatment plans were designed for a representative map of the biological materials acquired from the open-source AustinWoman voxel model [16]. As a case study, one abdominal target within the right lobe of the liver was used. Two levels of D were chosen, a higher one ($D_{x,y} = 2$) in the middle of the target area, and a lower one ($D_{x,y} = 1$) close to the boundaries. The prohibited area P was marked by three different levels of importance. The highest one ($P_{x,y} = 5$) covered the rib and the tendon. The middle one ($P_{x,y} = 2$) covered the fat layers and the areas further from the treated areas. The lowest level ($P_{x,y} = 1$) was used for areas neighboring the treated areas. To make the interface between treated and prohibited areas smooth, a thin don't care area was used ($D_{x,y} = 0$ and $P_{x,y} = 0$). The size of the heat source was based on a single element transducer using the nominal properties of the HAIFU JC-200. The spatial peak of the volume rate of heat deposition was set to 100 W/cm^2, which approximately matches the values used for clinical treatments.

The parameters of the numerical heat diffusion model were set according to convergence testing as follows:

- Discretized simulation domain size 495×495 grid points, periodic boundary condition.
- Spatial resolution 0.2 mm.
- Temporal resolution 0.1 s.
- The total length of the simulation $\sum_{i=0}^{N}(t_{on,i} + t_{off,i})$.
- Allowed positions of the ultrasound focus center limited to the bounding box at grid positions $[270, 230] \times [345, 295]$.
- Maximum sonication and cooling periods $t_{on} = [0, 20\,\text{s}]$, $t_{off} = [0, 20\,\text{s}]$.
- Number of sonications considered $N = 6$.

The success rate and evolution time is highly dependent on the number of sonications used in the treatment. Generally, the more the sonications is used, the easier the job to design an optimal treatment plan is. Naturally, it is easier to cover a given area with a higher number of smaller dots. On the other hand, the applicaiton of the treatment takes much longer as well as the fitness function evaluation. This is given by a rising number of thermal model invocation in the simulation, and heating od distant points in the real treatment. In our previous paper [4], treatment plans with 4, 5, 6, 8 and 10 sonications have been deeply investigated. Six and eight sonications were concluded to be the best. Since shorter treatments poses a harder problem, we decided to use 6 sonications in the rest of the paper.

5.1 Examined Parameters of Island Model

Apart from CMA-ES related parameters, the proposed island model introduces several parameters influencing the behavior of the evolution. The following list elaborates the parameters of interest along with their examined values.

1. *Number of islands* - Having 24 computers cores and considering the scalability of the fitness function, we investigate the island CMA-ES with 3 and 6 islands and compared them with the original pan-population version.
2. *Total number of individuals* - The number of individuals per island is $\lambda_{\text{island}} = 13$, which is a default population size for CMA-ES with 6 sonications. The total population size for 3 and 6 islands reaches 39 and 78, respectively.
3. *Migration interval* - The number of generations between two migrations M remains constant during the evolution and is set to 1, 2 or 3 generations.
4. *Migration selection strategy* - Depending on the strategy, one or three best individuals are migrated.
5. *Island topology* - The island topology is a fully connected graph.
6. *Acceptance policy* - Each island has a predefined probability determining whether the immigrants are accepted or refused. This probability is progressively decreased along with the increasing quality of local individuals.
7. *Replace strategy* - Each island replaces R worst individuals in its population with R migrants. The migrants are selected using a roulette wheel.

5.2 Pan-Population Model

The results of the original PP model with the Matlab fitness function evaluation for with the population size $\lambda = 13, 20, 40$ were taken from the previous paper [4]. Since the optimized fitness function enables to shorten the computation time by a factor of two, another case with a population of $\lambda = 78$ individuals is added into the comparison.

5.3 CMA-ES with 6 Islands

In this section, four examined variants of the 6-island model with the total population of 78 individuals are explained.

1. *Send 1 Best - Accept All (6ISB)* - Every island broadcasts its best individual to the others. The others accept all migrants and replace the worse part of local populations.

2. *Send 3 Best - Select Roulette (6IS3)* - Three best individuals are broadcast but only a single immigrant from each island selected by a roulette wheel is accepted.
3. *Send 1 or 3 Best - Select Roulette - Acceptance Policy (6IS1AP or 6IS3AP)* - The strategy tries to maximize the diversity among islands by introducing the acceptance probability that decreases with the quality of local solutions, see Table 2. This allows the islands to converge to different optimal solutions which then can be displayed to the clinicians for deeper evaluation.

Table 2. The probability to accept immigrant individuals.

Fitness value	>200	>100	>50	>30	<30
Probability	0.75	0.4	0.1	0.05	0

5.4   CMA-ES with 3 Islands

The 3-island model is equivalent to the pan-population model with the population size of 39 individuals. The strategies used in this variant are the same as for the 6-island model, however, since most of them produces significantly worse results, they are excluded from the plots for the sake of clarity.

5.5   Success Rate Comparison

Figure 3 shows the success rate of examined versions of CMA-ES. Here, the influence of the population size, as well as the island model strategies, are shown. In green, pan-population CMA-ES is shown. There can be seen a strong influence of the population size on the success rate. By optimizing the fitness function in C++, which enabled an increase of the population size up to 78 individuals, the success rate increased from 53% to 87.5%.

Splitting the global population into 6 islands, shown in blue, brings another significant improvement to the success rate. When 3 best individuals are broadcast from each island (6IS3), the success rate reaches 93.3%. To reach a 100% success rate, the acceptance policy has to be turned on. The migration of 3 individuals appears to bring to much genetic material that prevents the CMA-ES to explore local neighborhoods. There are also two cases which are worse than the PP model. In the case of 6ISB, the exchange of genetic material is not sufficient to explore the search space efficiently. This strategy thus reaches about 1% worse success rate. When the acceptance policy is tightened, the success rate of this 6-island CMA-ES drops to 77.4%

Interesting results were achieved with a 3-island version of CMA-ES, shown in yellow. When broadcasting only a single individual and even having a half of the total population, the success rate remains the same as for the 6 islands with migration of 3 individuals per island. The 3-island model thus seems to be more efficient in terms of computational requirements, which was further confirmed in Fig. 4.

5.6 Number of Evaluations Comparison

Figure 4 presents the difference in the total number of evaluations before the algorithms converge. The simplest 6-island strategies (6IBS and 6IS3) are considerably worse than an equivalent PP version with 78 individuals. Both strategies using the acceptance policy require about the same number of evaluations to converge, however, the superiority of 6IS3AP is emphasized by the best success rate. This version also reaches the most stable performance with only a low variance in the measured number of evaluations.

The PP model with smaller populations needs a significantly lower number of evaluations to converge, but that is redeemed by a poor success rate. The fastest variant uses only 3 islands. Even if the PP model with 40 individuals may sometimes be faster, the 3-island version on average produces the treatment plans in a shorter time, and with much higher quality. The detailed comparison of the best variants can be seen in Fig. 5.

5.7 Acceptance Policy

The acceptance policy defines the probability the immigrants are incorporated into the local population. In this investigation, we calculated the success rate over all islands to see what percentage of the islands could converge to the global optimum and if we can get multiple different optimal solutions. This strategy has shown to be very beneficial for 6-island modes. The highest benefit was

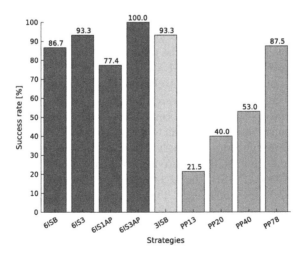

Fig. 3. Success rate of different evolution strategies. (Color figure online)

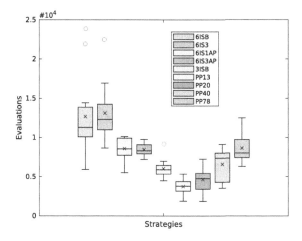

Fig. 4. Number of evaluations before CMA-ES converges.

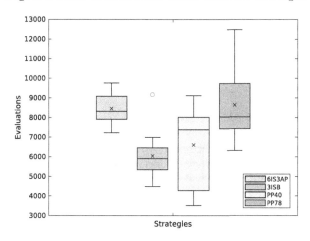

Fig. 5. Comparison of the performance of the best variants of CMA-ES.

brought to S3AP where 2.5 islands out of 6 usually converged to the optimum while the number of evaluations also increased. On the other side, this technique deteriorates the success rate for three-island modes. Most of the trials for 3 islands did not converge to the global optimum, even after a great number of generations, see Table 3.

5.8 Migration Interval

The influence of different migration interval was also tested. The impact of the prolonged migration interval appears to be rather negative. The increase in the migration interval yields an increase in the number of evaluations, and even degradation of the success rate. The modification of migration interval behaves

Table 3. The number of evaluations needed to find one optimal plan and average success rate for different acceptance policies.

	Evaluations/success rate		
Strategy	SB	S1AP	S3AP
6-island	12,900/86.7%	8,430/230%	8,320/252%
3-island	6,220/93.3%	12,500/82.1%	13,600/84.5%

differently for 3-island and 6-island model. The results are shown in Table 4. The reason is much slower convergence which can be clearly seen from Fig. 6. The leftmost plots show a rapid decrease of the best individual fitness values followed by the average and worst individual. Contrary the rightmost plots with prolonged migration interval show much slower convergence.

Table 4. The influence of the migration interval on the average number of evaluations/ success rate.

	Number of evaluations/success rate		
Interval	1	2	3
6-island	11,076/86.7%	17,472/73.3%	13,416/86.7%
3-island	5,811/93.3%	8,541/93.3%	7,800/53.3%

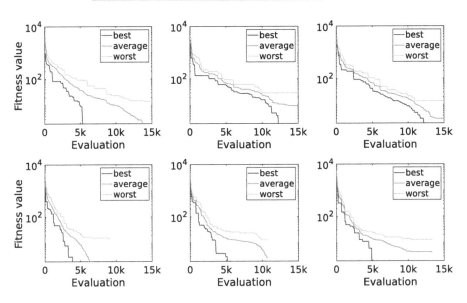

Fig. 6. Convergence of 6ISB on the top and 3ISB strategy on the bottom, for migration interval 1, 2 and 3 from left to right, respectively.

6 Conclusion

This study has presented an acceleration of the CMA-ES algorithm for the design the HIFU treatment plans by the island model. Since the fitness function evaluation took prohibitively long, low-level optimization, parallelization and vectorization in C++ were conducted. This optimization enabled to use twice as big population while fitting into the same maximal time period of 48 h. Next, the effort was put into the parallelization using the island model. Several different parameters on three and six islands were investigated including the number of migrating individuals, the acceptance policy and the length of the migration interval.

The highest success rate was achieved by a 6-island model migrating three best individuals every generation with decreasing acceptance ratio towards the end of the evolution. Comparing the original algorithm with the fastest variant, a 3-island model migrating a single best individual every generation but without the acceptance policy, the evolution was accelerated more than 4 times on the same computer. This allows us to deliver an optimal patient specific treatment plan within 6 h. Practically, the patient can be scanned during the day, and the treatment plan will be computed overnight.

The proposed island model also allows the parallelization of the evolutionary strategy on more interconnected computers, which will be used in the future work to further accelerate the evolution and incorporate a realistic ultrasound model.

Acknowledgment. This work was supported by The Ministry of Education, Youth and Sports from the National Programme of Sustainability (NPU II) project IT4Innovations excellence in science - LQ1602" and by the IT4Innovations infrastructure which is supported from the Large Infrastructures for Research, Experimental Development and Innovations project IT4Innovations National Supercomputing Center - LM2015070.

References

1. Alba, E., Tomassini, M.: Parallelism and evolutionary algorithms. IEEE Trans. Evol. Comput. **6**(5), 443–462 (2002)
2. Cantú-Paz, E.: Efficient and Accurate Parallel Genetic Algorithms. Kluwer Academic Publishers, Dordrecht (2000)
3. Chen, S., Ma, B., Zhang, K.: On the similarity metric and the distance metric. Theor. Comput. Sci. **410**(24–25), 2365–2376 (2009)
4. Cudova, M., Treeby, B.E., Jaros, J.: Design of HIFU treatment plans using an evolutionary strategy. In: Proceedings of the Genetic and Evolutionary Computation Conference Companion on - GECCO 2018, pp. 1568–1575. ACM Press, New York (2018). https://doi.org/10.1145/3205651.3208268
5. Dillon, C., Vyas, U., Payne, A., et al.: An analytical solution for improved HIFU SAR estimation. Phys. Med. Biol. **57**(14), 4527–4544 (2012)
6. Frigo, M., Johnson, S.: The Design and Implementation of FFTW3. Proc. IEEE **93**(2), 216–231 (2005)

7. Hansen, N.: The CMA evolution strategy: a comparing review. In: Towards a New Evolutionary Computation, vol. 192, pp. 75–102. Springer, Heidelberg (2006). https://doi.org/10.1007/3-540-32494-1_4

8. Hansen, N.: The CMA Evolution Strategy: A Tutorial. Technical report (apr 2016)

9. Hansen, N., Ostermeier, A.: Adapting arbitrary normal mutation distributions in evolution strategies: the covariance matrix adaptation. In: Proceedings of IEEE International Conference on Evolutionary Computation, pp. 312–317. IEEE (1996)

10. Hansen, N., Kern, S.: Evaluating the CMA evolution strategy on multimodal test functions. In: Yao, X., et al. (eds.) PPSN 2004. LNCS, vol. 3242, pp. 282–291. Springer, Heidelberg (2004). https://doi.org/10.1007/978-3-540-30217-9_29

11. Huijssen, J., Verweij, M.: An iterative method for the computation of nonlinear, wide-angle, pulsed acoustic fields of medical diagnostic transducers. J. Acoust. Soc. Am. **127**(1), 33–44 (2010)

12. Ichihara, M., Sasaki, K., Umemura, S., et al.: Blood flow occlusion via ultrasound image-guided high-intensity focused ultrasound and its effect on tissue perfusion. Ultrasound Med. Biol. **33**(3), 452–459 (2007)

13. Intel Corporation: Intel® 64 and IA-32 Architectures Optimization Reference Manual (2011)

14. Madera, J., Dorronsoro, B.: Estimation of Distribution Algorithms. Metaheuristic Procedures for Training Neutral Networks, pp. 87–108, December 2006

15. Marquet, F., Perndoiot, M., Aubry, J.F., et al.: Non-invasive transcranial ultrasound therapy based on a 3D CT scan: protocol validation and in vitroresults. Phys. Med. Biol. **54**(9), 2597–2613 (2009)

16. Massey, J., et al.: AustinMan and AustinWoman: High fidelity, reproducible, and open-source electromagnetic voxel models. In: 34th Meeting of the Bioelectromagnetics Society (2012)

17. van der Pas, R., Stotzer, E., Terboven, C.: Using OpenMP-The Next Step: Affinity, Accelerators, Tasking, and SIMD. MPI Press, Kuala Lumpur (2017)

18. Pennes, H.: Analysis of tissue and arterial blood temperatures in the resting human forearm. J. Appl. Physiol. **1**(2), 93–122 (1948)

19. Sapareto, S., Dewey, W.: Thermal dose determination in cancer therapy. Int. J. Radiat. Oncol. Biol. Phys. **10**(6), 787–800 (1984)

20. Sudholt, D.: Parallel evolutionary algorithms. In: Kacprzyk, J., Pedrycz, W. (eds.) Springer Handbook of Computational Intelligence, pp. 929–959. Springer, Heidelberg (2015). https://doi.org/10.1007/978-3-662-43505-2_46

21. Suomi, V., Jaros, J., Treeby, B., Cleveland, R.: Full modelling of high-intensity focused ultrasound and thermal heating in the kidney using realistic patient models. IEEE Trans. Biomed. Eng. **PP**(99), 1–12 (2017)

22. Treeby, B., Jaros, J., Rendell, A., Cox, B.: Modeling nonlinear ultrasound propagation in heterogeneous media with power law absorption using a k-space pseudospectral method. J. Acoust. Soc. Am. **131**(6), 4324–36 (2012)

23. Ye, G., Smith, P., Noble, J.: Model-based ultrasound temperature visualization during and following HIFU exposure. Ultrasound Med. Biol. **36**(2), 234–249 (2010)

24. Zhou, Y.F., Syed Arbab, A., Xu, R.: High intensity focused ultrasound in clinical tumor ablation. World J. Clin. Oncol. **2**(1), 8–27 (2011)

Using Genetic Algorithms for the Prediction of Cognitive Impairments

Nicole Dalia Cilia, Claudio De Stefano, Francesco Fontanella$^{(\boxtimes)}$,
and Alessandra Scotto Di Freca

Department of Electrical and Information Engineering (DIEI),
Università di Cassino e del Lazio Meridionale,
Via G. Di Biasio, 43, 03043 Cassino, FR, Italy
{nicoledalia.cilia,destefano,fontanella,a.scotto}@unicas.it

Abstract. Cognitive impairments affect millions of persons worldwide, and especially elderly ones. These impairments may be one of the first signs of the arising of neurodegenerative diseases, such as Alzheimer's and Parkinson's, and it is expected that the incidence of this kind of diseases will dramatically increase worldwide in the near future. For this reason, the improvement of the tools currently used to diagnose these diseases is becoming crucial. Handwriting is one of the human skills affected by this kind of impairments, and anomalies such as micrographia have been adopted as diagnosis sign for the Parkinson's disease. In a previous paper, we presented a study in which the handwriting of the subjects involved was recorded while they were performing some elementary tasks, such as the copy of simple words or the drawing of elementary forms. Then we extracted the features characterizing the dynamics of the handwriting and used them to train a classifier to predict whether the subject analyzed was affected by a cognitive impairment or not. In this paper, we present a system that uses a genetic algorithm to improve of the performance of the system previously presented. The genetic algorithm has been used to select the subset of tasks that allow improving the prediction ability of the previous system. The experimental results confirmed the effectiveness of the proposed approach.

Keywords: Genetic algorithms · Handwriting · Alzheimer's disease · Parkinson's disease · Neurodegenerative disorders

1 Introduction

Cognitive impairments are defined as cognitive decline greater than expected for an individual's age and education level but that does not interfere deeply with activities of daily life. Their symptoms can remain stable or even disappear, but for more than half of the cases they evolve into dementia diseases [10], thus their early identification could lead to the prevention of dementia diseases. Moreover, some types of cognitive impairments have a high risk of progression to Alzheimer's disease (AD), and then they can be considered as prodromal

© Springer Nature Switzerland AG 2020
P. A. Castillo et al. (Eds.): EvoApplications 2020, LNCS 12104, pp. 479–493, 2020.
https://doi.org/10.1007/978-3-030-43722-0_31

symptoms of this disorder. The risk of being affected by Alzheimer's increases strongly with age thus it is expected that in the next decades the incidence of cognitive impairments will dramatically increase [19]. To date, Alzheimer's clinical diagnosis is performed by physicians that, in most cases, in addition to cognitive tests, perform some invasive biomarker tests, e.g. cerebrospinal fluid tests. This creates a strong need for the improvement of the approaches currently being used for diagnosis of these diseases.

One of the basic skills compromised by cognitive impairments is certainly the handwriting [3,16,17,24]. In fact, it has been observed that some handwriting anomalies can be used as diagnostic signs. For example, has been found that the handwriting of Alzheimer's patients shows alterations in spatial organization and poor control of movement [18,20]. Most of the studies which analyze the effects of cognitive impairments on handwriting have been conducted in the medical field, with few studies adopting classification algorithms to analyze people's handwriting to detect those affected by cognitive impairments. Moreover, almost all of these studies have involved a few dozens of subjects, thus limiting the effectiveness of classification algorithms. To try to overcome these problems, in [8] the authors proposed a protocol consisting of twenty five handwriting tasks, with the aim of investigating how cognitive impairments affect the different motor and cognitive skills involved in the handwriting process. The protocol has been then adopted to collect handwriting data from about one hundred seventy-five subjects, both cognitive impaired or healthy. This data has been then used to build a system in which two kinds of pen traits were distinguished, i.e. on-paper and on-air. With the former representing the movements in which the pen is touching the paper, whereas the latter are those in which the pen is on air during the handwriting process. It is worth noting that in the literature has been found that this distinction allows a better characterization of the handwriting anomalies caused by cognitive impairments [9,13,14]. For each task, the features extracted have been employed to train two classifiers, both for on-paper and on-air features [6,7]. Finally, in order to predict the cognitive state of a subject (healthy or impaired) the fifty responses provided by the classifiers trained on the single tasks were combined according to the Majority-vote rule.

In the scenario outlined above, it arises the need to optimize system performance. The need is twofold: from one hand we want to maximize the prediction performance of the system; on the other hand, we want to reduce the number of tasks to be performed. This optimization problem can be seen as a combinatorial one, in which given the set $T = \{t_1, t_2, \ldots, t_n\}$, the best subset must be found, according to a given evaluation function (the prediction performance in our case). Though the best subset can be found by exhaustively evaluating all the possible solutions, this search strategy is impracticable in our case, where the total number of possible solutions is $2^{50} \approx 10^{15}$. For this reason, a heuristic search is needed. Since Genetic Algorithms (GAs) are well-known for their global search ability without using any domain knowledge or assumptions about the search space, they have been widely used for this kind of combinatorial problems. This is because GA binary vectors provide a natural and straightforward representation for item subsets: the value 1 or 0 of the chromosome i-th element indicates whether the i-th item is included or not in the subset represented by the chromosome.

Because of their search-ability Evolutionary algorithms have been also used for health applications. In particular, GA and GP have been mostly used. As concerns the GP-based approaches, they have been used in a wide range of applications. For example, in [2], the authors proposed a constrained-syntax GP-based algorithm for discovering classification rules in medical data. The authors tested their approach on five datasets and achieved better results than decision trees. In [4], instead, the authors tackled a problem related to the physio-chemical properties of proteins, involving the prediction on these properties in tertiary structure. The authors proved that the proposed approach was more effective than artificial Neural Networks and Support Vector Machines. More recently, the Cartesian GP approach has been used to automatically identify subjects affected by the Parkinson's disease through the analysis of their handwriting [22,23]. GP algorithms have been also used as a tool to support medical decisions for treating rare diseases [1].

Also GA has been widely used in medical applications, in most of the medical specialities, e.g., medical imaging, rehabilitation medicine, and health care management [11]. As concerns neurodegenerative diseases, in [25] the authors used a GA with Multi-Objective fitness function to find the relevant volumes of the brain related to the Alzheimer's disease, whereas in [15] the authors used a GA to search the optimal set of neuropsychological tests, to be used to build a system for the prediction of the Alzheimer's disease.

Note that, to the best of our knowledge, there are no other studies in which a GA has been used to improve the performance of a system for the prediction of cognitive impairments, based on handwriting analysis.

In this paper, we present a GA-based system for the improvement of the prediction performance of the system described above. In particular, the devised system selects the subset of tasks, both on-air and on paper, that allows improving the performance of the proposed system in predicting the cognitive impairments of the subjects involved. The final prediction of the cognitive state of a subject is made applying the majority vote rule to the responses collected from the selected tasks. The system has been trained by using the dataset made of the responses provided by the classifier used to predict the cognitive impairment of a subject for a given task. A part of it has been used as a training set, to implement the fitness function for evaluating the individuals to be evolved, whereas the remaining part has been used as a test set to assess the performance of the system on unseen data.

We tested our approach taking into account four well-known classifiers: decision trees, random forests, neural networks, and support vector machines. Moreover, in the first set of experiments, we analyzed the generalization ability of the system as well as its capability in reducing the number of tasks needed to correctly predict cognitive impairments. Then, by counting the occurrences of the tasks in the solutions found in the several runs performed, we tried to figure out the more relevant tasks. Finally, we compared the proposed approach with the majority-vote and the weighted majority rules, which are well-known and widely used strategies for combining the responses provided by several classifiers. Moreover, since the problem in hand is a combinatorial one in which the best subset must be found, as is the case of feature selection problems [5], we compared our results with those achieved by a state-of-the-art algorithm for feature selection. The comparison results confirmed the effectiveness of the proposed approach.

The remainder of the paper is organized as follows: Sect. 2 describes the data collection and the protocol developed to collect handwriting data. Section 3 details the proposed system. Section 4 displays the experiments and presents the results achieved. Finally, Sect. 5 is devoted to some concluding remarks.

2   Data Collection and Protocol

In the following subsections, the data collection procedure, the protocol designed for collecting handwriting samples, the segmentation and feature extraction methods, are detailed.

2.1   Data Collection

The one hundred seventy five subjects who participated in the experiments, namely eighty six cognitively impaired patients and eighty nine healthy controls, were recruited with the support of the geriatric ward, Alzheimer unit, of the University hospital Federico II in Naples. As recruiting criteria we have took into account clinical tests (such as PET, TAC and enzymatic analyses) and standard cognitive tests (such as MMSE). As for the healthy controls, in order to have a fair comparison, demographic as well as educational characteristics were considered and matched with the patient group.

The data were collected by using a graphics tablet, which allowed the subjects to write on standard A4 white sheets using an apparently normal pen: such a pen produces both the ink trace on the sheet and the digital information, which are recorded on the tablet in the form of spatial coordinates and pressure for each point, acquired at a frequency of 200 Hz. The tablet also records the in-air movements (up to a maximum of three centimetres in height). In this condition, the subject should not change his natural writing movements as it happens, for instance, when the writing is produced with a stylus on the surface of a tablet.

2.2   Protocol

The aim of the protocol is to record the dynamics of the handwriting, in order to investigate whether there are specific features that allow us to distinguish cognitively impaired subjects from the healthy ones. The goal of these tasks is to test the patients' abilities in repeating simple as well as complex graphic gestures, which have a semantic meaning, such as letters and words of different lengths and with different spatial organizations. The tasks considered for this

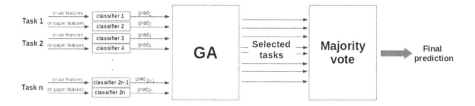

Fig. 1. The layout of the proposed system. Note that in our case $n = 25$.

study are been presented in [8], and they are arranged in increasing order of difficulty, in terms of the cognitive functions required. Taking into account their objectives, we have grouped the tasks as follows:

- *Graphic* tasks, whose objective is to test the patient's ability in: (i) writing elementary traits; (ii) joining some points; (iii) drawing figures (simple or complex and scaled in various dimensions).
- *Copy* and *Reverse Copy* tasks, whose objective is to test the patient's abilities in repeating complex graphic gestures, which have a semantic meaning, such as letters, words and numbers (of different lengths and with different spatial organizations).
- *Memory* tasks, whose objective is to test the variation of the graphic section, keeping in memory a word, a letter, a graphic gesture or a motor planning.
- *Dictation*, whose purpose is to investigate how the writing in the task varies (with phrases or numbers) in which the use of the working memory is necessary.

3   The Proposed System

The following subsections details the steps performed to implement the proposed system (see Fig. 1).

3.1   Segmentation and Feature Extraction

We extracted both on-paper and on-air features by considering their segmentation in elementary strokes assuming as segmentation points both pen-up and pen-down, as well as the zero-crossing of the vertical velocity profile. The feature values were computed for each stroke and averaged over all the strokes relative to a single task. In particular, from each task, we have extracted the following types of features:

(i) Static features: Start time; Duration; Initial vertical position; Vertical dimension; Initial horizontal position; Horizontal dimension; Inclination from the initial point to the final point; Loop surface; Absolute size.

(ii) Dynamic features: Vertical speed peak; Peak of vertical acceleration; Straightness error; Relative initial inclination; Time relative to the vertical speed peak; Relative duration of the on-paper sections; Average speed; Absolute Jerk: the Root Mean Square (RMS) value of the absolute jerk on all samples of a stroke or segment; Normalized Jerk; Number of points of acceleration peaks; Average pen pressure.

Note that we have separately redefined and computed the features over on-paper and on-air traits since in the literature has been found that the two conditions exhibit significant differences in characterizing the handwriting anomalies caused by cognitive impairments [9].

3.2   Classification

Once the features were extracted, for each task, two classifiers were trained (both for on-paper and on-air features), and the test predictions obtained using the 5-fold cross-validation was stored. As a consequence, at the end of this step, for each classification algorithm considered, a dataset containing one hundred seventy-five samples was available, one for each subject, with each sample consisting of fifty predictions. The datasets so built were used to train and test the GA module detailed in the next subsection. In particular, a part of it was used as the training set (T_r in the following), to implement the fitness function for evaluating the individuals to be evolved, whereas the remaining part was used as test set (T_s) to assess the performance of the system on unseen data.

3.3   GA for Task Selection

To optimize the performance of the system in predicting the cognitive state of the involved subjects, we used a GA to select the subset of fifty tasks (both on-air and on-paper) that allows the system to achieve the best prediction performance. As mentioned in the introduction, we used a GA because this algorithm is well-known for its global search ability and also because it provides a natural and straightforward representation of item (tasks in our case) subsets: the value 1 or 0 of the chromosome i-th element indicates whether the i-th item (task) is included or not in the subset represented by the chromosome. Given the i-th individual to be evaluated, representing the task subset s_i, its fitness was computed by considering in the majority-vote rule only the tasks included in s_i (see Fig. 1).

The GA was implemented by using a generational evolutionary algorithm, which starts by generating a population of P individuals, randomly generated. Afterwards, the fitness of the generated individuals is evaluated by computing the prediction accuracy on T_r. After this preliminary evaluation phase, a new population is generated by selecting $P/2$ couples of individuals using the tournament method, of size t. The one point crossover operator is then applied to each of the selected couples, according to a given probability factor p_c. Afterwards, the mutation operator is applied with a probability p_m. The value of p_m was set to 1/50, where 50 is the chromosome length, i.e. the total number of available tasks. This probability value allows, on average, the modification of only one chromosome element. This value has been suggested in [21] as the optimal mutation rate below the error threshold of replication. Finally, these individuals are added to the new population. The process just described is repeated for N_g generations.

4   Experimental Results

We tested our approach by training four well-known and widely-used classifiers: decision trees (DT), random forests (RF), neural networks (NN), and support vector machines (SVM). Thus, according to the procedure detailed in Subsect. 3.2, we built up four datasets, where each sample contained the responses provided by the given classifier on the fifty tasks, i.e. twenty five for the on-paper features and twenty five for the on-air features (see Fig. 1). Each dataset was split into two parts, statistically independent: a training set T_r, made of the 80% of the available samples, and a test set T_s, made of the remaining samples. T_r was used to evaluate the individuals' fitness, whereas T_s was used to assess the performance of the best individual on unseen data. For each dataset, we performed fifty runs and at the end of each run, the task subset encoded by the individual with the best fitness was stored as the solution provided by that run. The results reported in the following were computed by averaging those obtained by the fifty best individuals stored. As for the parameters of the GA, we performed some preliminary trials to set them. These parameters were used for all the experiments described below and are reported in Table 1. We performed three sets of experiments. In the first set, we analyzed the generalization ability of the GA-based system as well as its capability in reducing the number of tasks needed to correctly predict cognitive impairments. To this aim, we have plotted the training and test accuracy of the best individual as well as the population's average number of selected tasks and the number of the selected tasks of the best individual during the fifty runs performed. As concerns the second set of experiments, we analyzed the number of occurrences of the selected tasks in order to figure out which are the most relevant ones. Finally, we compared the results

Table 1. The values of the parameters used in the experiments.

Parameter	Symbol	Value
Population size	P	100
Crossover probability	p_c	0.6
Tournament size	t	5
Elitism	e	2
Mutation probability	p_m	0.02
Number of Generations	N_g	1000

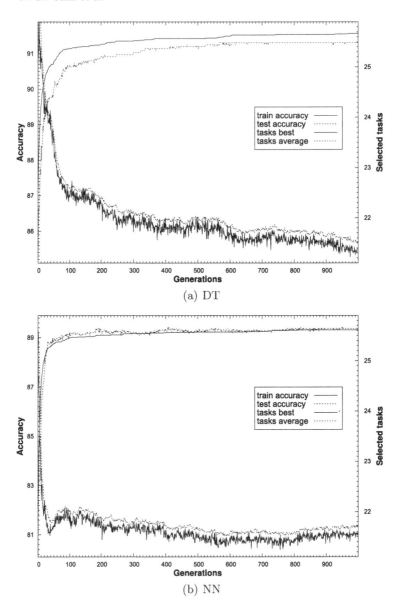

Fig. 2. Evolution of accuracy and average number of selected tasks for DT and NN classifiers.

achieved by the proposed approach with those obtained by the majority-vote and weighted majority rules as well as those achieved by the floating Forward Selection (FFS) algorithm.

The plots obtained from the first set of experiments are shown in Figs. 2 and 3. The plots show the evolution of: (i) the average training and test accuracy

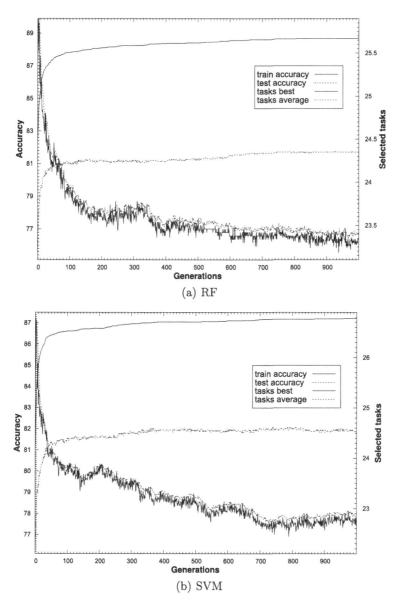

Fig. 3. Evolution of accuracy and average number of selected tasks for RF and SVM classifiers.

of the best individual; (ii) the average number of selected tasks for the best individual and the whole population, computed by averaging the values of the fifty run performed. From the plots, it can be seen that, for every classifier, the GA did not suffer overfitting, because the test and train curves show similar trends, although train and test accuracies differ a lot among the classifiers. Most probably, these differences depend on the generalization ability of the classifiers, with the DT and NN exhibiting very good results, whereas RF and SVM achieved poor generalization results. A common, and very interesting, trend emerging from the plots is that as the number of iterations increases the fitness function increases, even if only slightly, and the number of selected tasks, both average and best, decreases. At the end of the run, for every classifier, about less than half of the tasks were selected. Moreover, it is worth noting that the number of selected tasks of the best individual is always less than the average one. This seems to confirm our assumption that better prediction performance can be achieved by suitably selecting a subset of the whole set of available tasks.

The histograms of the second set of experiments are shown in Figs. 4 and 5. They show the number of occurrences of the selected tasks, computed on the fifty runs performed. Gray and white bars represent on-air and on-paper tasks, respectively. The histograms does not show a common pattern, with some tasks more selected for a given classifier and less or even far less for the remaining ones, as is the case, for example, for the task 1 (signature), which was selected about twenty times for the DT and far less for the remaining classifiers. This depends on the fact that for a given task the classifiers achieved different prediction performances. The only aspect shared by the four histograms is that for the same task the number of occurrences of the on-paper and on-air tasks differs little. This is due to the fact that, for every task, for a given classifier, the prediction performance of on-air and on-paper features are very similar.

In order to test the effectiveness of our system, we compared its results with those achieved by the majority-vote and the weighted majority rules, which are well-known and widely used strategies for combining the responses provided by several classifiers. The first rule, given a set of responses to be combined, in our case the prediction provided by the classifiers for the single tasks, assigns an unknown sample (a subject in our case) to the class (CI or HC) that has the highest occurrence among those provided by the whole set of classifiers. As for the second rule, it takes into account the prediction performance of the single classifiers by multiplying each response with the training accuracy achieved by the related classifier. Finally, since the problem in hand is a combinatorial one in which the best subset must be found, as is the case of feature selection problems, we compared our results with those achieved by the Sequential Forward Floating Search Algorithm (SFS in the following). This strategy searches the solution space by using a greedy hill-climbing technique. It starts with the empty set of features and, at each step, selects the best feature according to the subset evaluation function. SFS stops when the addition of a new feature does not produce any improvement. Further details can be found in [12]. To statistically validate the comparison results, we performed the non-parametric Wilcoxon rank-sum test ($\alpha = 0.05$). Comparison results are shown in Table 2, where the values in bold are the best ones, for a given classifier, according to the Wilcoxon test. From the table, it can be seen that the DT achieved the best overall prediction performance. Moreover, the GA achieved much better results than those of the combination rules. The GA largely outperforms SFS, on all the four classifiers

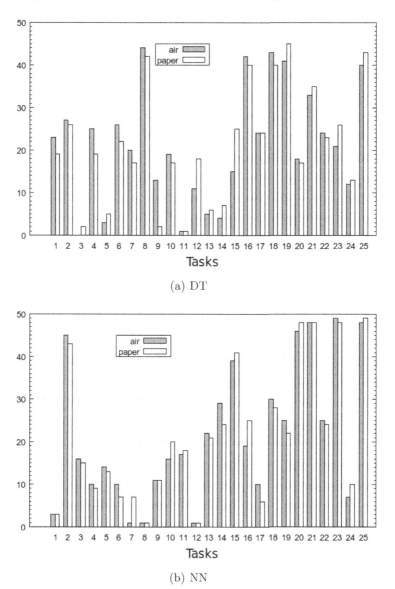

(a) DT

(b) NN

Fig. 4. Number of occurrences of the selected tasks for DT and NN classifiers.

considered, confirming its effectiveness. Finally, it is worth noting that the standard deviations exhibited by the GA results are significantly lower than those of the other results confirming the average good quality of solutions found by our system.

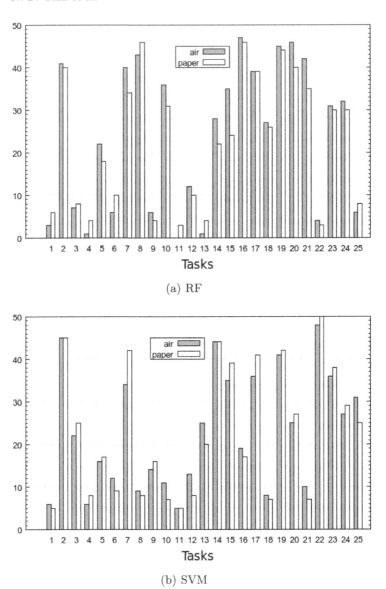

(a) RF

(b) SVM

Fig. 5. Number of occurrences of the selected tasks for RF and SVM classifiers.

Table 2. Comparison results. For each classifier the best result is highlighted in bold.

Classifier	GA		MjV		WMjV		FFS	
	Avg	Dev	Avg	Dev	Avg	Dev	Avg	Dev
DT	**91.26**	**1.75**	83.40	5.89	83.43	5.8	68.86	7.1
NN	**89.20**	**2.23**	72.00	6.93	73.34	6.3	77.02	3.6
RF	**81.71**	**2.29**	67.83	5.68	68.13	5.68	76.69	2.0
SVM	**82.11**	**2.05**	79.09	5.98	79.14	5.92	70.05	7.3

5   Conclusions

Cognitive impairments are one the first signs of the arising of neurodegenerative diseases and it is expected their incidence will increase in the near feature. Thus, the improvement of the tools currently available to diagnose these diseases is becoming crucial. Since handwriting is one of the human skills affected by cognitive impairments, it can be analyzed to detect this kind of diseases.

In this paper, we presented a GA-based approach for the improvement of the performance of a system that record and analyze the handwriting of the involved subjects in performing some simple tasks, in order to detect those that are cognitively impaired. In particular, the system selects the subset of tasks that allow the maximization of the prediction performance.

In the experiments performed we tested the generalization ability of the system as well as its capability in reducing the number of tasks needed to correctly predict cognitive impairments. Moreover, we also tried to figure out which are the more relevant tasks, i.e. those most frequently selected by the GA in the performed runs. Finally, we compared our results with those of the majority-vote and the weighted majority rules, as well as the sequential floating search algorithm. The experimental results showed that the proposed system has a good generalization ability, by selecting only half of the available tasks. As concerns the relevance of the single tasks, the results showed that it varies greatly among the different classifiers considered; most probably, this depends on the fact that, for a given task, they exhibit a wide performance variability. As concerns the comparison results, they confirmed the effectiveness of our system.

Acknowledgement. This work is supported by the Italian Ministry of Education, University and Research (MIUR) within the PRIN2015-HAND project.

References

1. Bakurov, I., Castelli, M., Vanneschi, L., Freitas, M.J.: Supporting medical decisions for treating rare diseases through genetic programming. In: Kaufmann, P., Castillo, P.A. (eds.) EvoApplications 2019. LNCS, vol. 11454, pp. 187–203. Springer, Cham (2019). https://doi.org/10.1007/978-3-030-16692-2_13

2. Bojarczuk, C.C., Lopes, H.S., Freitas, A.A., Michalkiewicz, E.L.: A constrained-syntax genetic programming system for discovering classification rules: application to medical data sets. Artif. Intell. Med. **30**(1), 27–48 (2004)
3. Carmona-Duarte, C., Ferrer, M.A., Parziale, A., Marcelli, A.: Temporal evolution in synthetic handwriting. Pattern Recogn. **68**(Suppl. C), 233–244 (2017)
4. Castelli, M., Vanneschi, L., Manzoni, L., Popovič, A.: Semantic genetic programming for fast and accurate data knowledge discovery. Swarm Evol. Comput. **26**, 1–7 (2016)
5. Cilia, N., De Stefano, C., Fontanella, F., di Freca, A.S.: A ranking-based feature selection approach for handwritten character recognition. Pattern Recognit. Lett. (2018)
6. Cilia, N.D., De Stefano, C., Fontanella, F., Molinara, M., Di Freca, A.S.: Handwriting analysis to support alzheimer's disease diagnosis: a preliminary study. In: Vento, M., Percannella, G. (eds.) CAIP 2019. LNCS, vol. 11679, pp. 143–151. Springer, Cham (2019). https://doi.org/10.1007/978-3-030-29891-3_13
7. Cilia, N.D., De Stefano, C., Fontanella, F., Molinara, M., Di Freca, A.S.: Using handwriting features to characterize cognitive impairment. In: Ricci, E., Rota Bulò, S., Snoek, C., Lanz, O., Messelodi, S., Sebe, N. (eds.) ICIAP 2019. LNCS, vol. 11752, pp. 683–693. Springer, Cham (2019). https://doi.org/10.1007/978-3-030-30645-8_62
8. Cilia, N., De Stefano, C., Fontanella, F., Di Freca, A.S.: An experimental protocol to support cognitive impairment diagnosis by using handwriting analysis. In: Proceeding of The 8th International Conference on Current and Future Trends of Information and Communication Technologies in Healthcare (ICTH), pp. 1–9. Elsevier (2019). Procedia Comput. Sci
9. De Stefano, C., Fontanella, F., Impedovo, D., Pirlo, G., di Freca, A.S.: Handwriting analysis to support neurodegenerative diseases diagnosis: a review. Pattern Recognit. Lett. **121**, 37–45 (2019)
10. Elbaz, A., Carcaillon, L., Kab, S., Moisan, F.: Epidemiology of Parkinson's disease. Revue Neurologique **172**(1), 14–26 (2016)
11. Ghaheri, A., Shoar, S., Naderan, M., Hoseini, S.S.: The applications of genetic algorithms in medicine. Oman Med. J. **30**(6), 406–416 (2015)
12. Gütlein, M., Frank, E., Hall, M., Karwath, A.: Large scale attribute selection using wrappers. In: Proceedings of the IEEE Symposium on Computational Intelligence and Data Mining (CIDM 2009) (2009)
13. Impedovo, D., Pirlo, G.: Dynamic handwriting analysis for the assessment of neurodegenerative diseases: a pattern recognition perspective. IEEE Rev. Biomed. Eng., 1–13 (2018)
14. Impedovo, D., Pirlo, G., Vessio, G., Angelillo, M.T.: A handwriting-based protocol for assessing neurodegenerative dementia. Cogn. Comput. **11**(4), 576–586 (2019). https://doi.org/10.1007/s12559-019-09642-2
15. Johnson, P., et al.: Genetic algorithm with logistic regression for prediction of progression to Alzheimer's disease. BMC Bioinform. **15**(S11) (2014). https://doi.org/10.1186/1471-2105-15-S16-S11
16. Marcelli, A., Parziale, A., Santoro, A.: Modeling handwriting style: a preliminary investigation. In: 2012 International Conference on Frontiers in Handwriting Recognition, pp. 411–416, September 2012
17. Marcelli, A., Parziale, A., Santoro, A.: Modelling visual appearance of handwriting. In: Petrosino, A. (ed.) ICIAP 2013. LNCS, vol. 8157, pp. 673–682. Springer, Heidelberg (2013). https://doi.org/10.1007/978-3-642-41184-7_68

18. Marcelli, A., Parziale, A., Senatore, R.: Some observations on handwriting from a motor learning perspective. In: 2nd International Workshop on Automated Forensic Handwriting Analysis (2013)
19. James, M., Wimo, A., Guerchet, M., Ali, G., Wu, Y.T., Prina, M.: World Alzheimer report 2015-the global impact of dementia: an analysis of prevalence, incidence, cost and trends. Alzheimer's Disease International, August 2015
20. Neils-Strunjas, J., Groves-Wright, K., Mashima, P., Harnish, S.: Dysgraphia in Alzheimer's disease: a review for clinical and research purposes. J. Speech Lang. Hear. Res. $49(6)$, 1313–30 (2006)
21. Ochoa, G.: Error thresholds in genetic algorithms. Evol. Comput. $14(2)$, 157–182 (2006)
22. Senatore, R., Della Cioppa, A., Marcelli, A.: Automatic diagnosis of neurodegenerative diseases: an evolutionary approach for facing the interpretability problem. Information $10(1)$, 30 (2019)
23. Senatore, R., Della Cioppa, A., Marcelli, A.: Automatic diagnosis of Parkinson disease through handwriting analysis: a Cartesian genetic programming approach. In: 2019 IEEE 32nd International Symposium on Computer-Based Medical Systems (CBMS), pp. 312–317, June 2019
24. Tseng, M.H., Cermak, S.A.: The influence of ergonomic factors and perceptual-motor abilities on handwriting performance. Am. J. Occup. Ther. $47(10)$, 919–926 (1993)
25. Valenzuela, O., Jiang, X., Carrillo, A., Rojas, I.: Multi-objective genetic algorithms to find most relevant volumes of the brain related to Alzheimer's disease and mild cognitive impairment. Int. J. Neural Syst. $28(09)$ (2018)

Short and Medium Term Blood Glucose Prediction Using Multi-objective Grammatical Evolution

Sergio Contador[3], J. Manuel Colmenar[3], Oscar Garnica[1],
and J. Ignacio Hidalgo[1,2(✉)]

[1] Universidad Complutense de Madrid, Madrid, Spain
absys@ucm.es
[2] Instituto de Tecnología del Conocimiento, Madrid, Spain
[3] Universidad Rey Juan Carlos, Móstoles, Spain
s.contador.2019@alumnos.urjc.es, josemanuel.colmenar@urjc.es

Abstract. In this paper we investigate the benefits of applying a multi-objective approach for solving a symbolic regression problem by means of grammatical evolution. In particular, we continue with previous research about finding expressions to model the glucose levels in blood of diabetic patients. We use here a multi-objective Grammatical Evolution approach based on NSGA-II algorithm, considering the root mean squared error and an ad-hoc fitness function as objectives. This ad-hoc function is based on the Clarke Error Grid analysis, which is useful for showing the potential danger of mispredictions. Experimental results show that the multi-objective approach improves previous results in terms of Clarke Error Grid analysis reducing the number of dangerous mispredictions.

Keywords: Grammatical Evolution · Multi-objective optimization · Glucose prediction · Diabetes

1 Introduction

Symbolic Regression (SR) is one of the most well known applications of Genetic Programming (GP) and its variants such as, Grammatical Evolution (GE). The purpose of SR is to obtain close forms that represent a set of data points, i.e. to get an equation that best adjusts its shape to the data representation. The applications of SR are uncountable, since this process involves a lot of areas in the data analysis, modeling, classification and identification domains.

Health care is one of the fields where the mentioned domains are becoming more and more important. In this regard, one of the diseases with higher increases in prevalence is Diabetes Mellitus (DM), or simply Diabetes[1]. Diabetes

---

[1] The International Diabetes Federation estimates around 415 million diabetic patients [17] (rising from 108 million since 1980), which is about 8–10% of prevalence on adults over 18 years, and it is the seventh leading cause of death in 2016, with 1.6 million deaths directly caused by diabetes and 2.2 million additional deaths attributable to high blood glucose.

© Springer Nature Switzerland AG 2020
P. A. Castillo et al. (Eds.): EvoApplications 2020, LNCS 12104, pp. 494–509, 2020.
https://doi.org/10.1007/978-3-030-43722-0_32

is a chronic disease caused by a defect either in the production or in the action of the insulin generated by the pancreatic system, corresponding to the two main types of Diabetes: Type 1 (T1DM) and Type 2 (T2DM).

The pancreas in patients with T1DM is not able to produce enough insulin to process the sugar produced after the food ingestion. Hence, the patients need to inject some additional artificial insulin with each meal, and sometimes between meals, to maintain healthy levels of glucose. In the case of T2DM patients, the insulin produced by the pancreas is not working properly, in a phenomena known as insulin resistance. In advanced stages of the disease, many T2DM patients need also to inject some insulin.

This task can be performed following two different alternatives. The first one is through a Continuous Subcutaneous Insulin Infuser (CSII) device, also known as *insulin pump*. This device can be programmable and adjusted to administrate the desired amount of insulin on different instant times. The other option are Multiple Insulin Doses (MID). In both alternatives, the decisions about the amount of insulin to be injected are challenging and have to consider many factors. Selecting the right amount of insulin is critical. If too much insulin is injected, hypoglycemia may occur, while insufficient injections keep glucose levels too high. The goal is to maintain the blood glucose levels within the target range most of the time, usually between 70 and 180 mg/dl [20]. It has been shown that when these values are not maintained or there is high variability then both short-term and long-term complications can emerge.

Control of blood glucose in insulin-dependent patients requires predicting the future glucose values to determine the amount of insulin to inject. This amount depends on many factors, but, above all, the patient should account for four of them: (i) the glucose value at the time of injection; (ii) the estimate of the amount of food ingested, usually measured in carbohydrate rations; (iii) the insulin previously injected; and (iv) the estimate of the ratio of how much is still active in the body. Making all these estimates manually is a complicated process that has to be done several times every day. Fortunately, recent advances, in both devices and algorithms, allow automating some parts of this control process. There are different kinds of blood glucose control strategies [11]: manual, semi-automated [24] and automated solutions based on the artificial pancreas [1]. For all of them, it is extremely important to develop mathematical models or artificial intelligence systems to describe the interaction between the glucose system and the insulin using the measurements and stored data.

In this paper we investigate a multi-objective approach for modeling glucose and construct predictive models from the short term (30 min) to the medium term (120 min) time horizons. We use GE with two objectives: Root Mean Squared Error (RMSE) and an adapted fitness, which is based on the Clarke Error Grid (CEG) metric [2]. The main contribution of the paper is to show that the development of a problem-specific fitness function considerably improves the quality and the robustness of the GE algorithm as a SR tool. Experimental results show how our proposal improves previous works that also apply GE.

The rest of the paper is organized as follows. In Sect. 2, we review the previous work. In Sect. 3 we explain the multi-objective approach. Section 4 gives details about the data set and discuss the results, comparing with previous work and analyzing the contribution of the multi-objective approach. We finish the paper with the conclusions, in Sect. 5.

2   Related Work

The problem of modeling and predicting glucose levels and glucose-insulin inter-action modeling has been an intensive area of research for the last ten years. We will focus in predicting glucose levels for a forecasting horizon of up to two hours, to be an aid in the daily management of insulin. Two hours is usually the time needed to decide if the dose of insulin after a meal was correct. Hidalgo *et al.* proposed the application of GE to obtain customized models of patients. The proposal has been tested using in-silico patient and real patients data [11]. The work has been extended recently on [23] and [12], where it is shown that data augmentation and structured GE increases the quality of the prediction results.

Inspired by Hidalgo's group works, Contreras *et al.* presented a hybrid model for predicting glucose in the mid-term (120 min) for T1DM patients [4]. The system uses synthetic data generated by the UVA/PADOVA simulator [13]. Both the fitness function of the evolutionary grammar and the performance metrics use a penalty factor to take into account the physical damage caused by deviations in blood glucose prediction according to the CEG. The authors generate four models for each patient corresponding to different phases of the day: night, breakfast, lunch, and dinner. The data obtained for the night phase are quite good; however, results with data of real patients have not been reported. In this work, we use a multi-fitness approach instead of a penalization function, which is more appropriate for a multi-objective problem.

Although more centered in the classification, i.e. prediction of a class instead of a glucose value, there are other interesting works. For instance, in [18], the authors developed a method for predicting postprandial hypoglycemia using a classification approach with machine learning techniques personalized to each patient. They show the process to generate a hypoglycemic prediction model by Support Vector Classifier machines (SVC) for bi-class classification, trained and tested using *scikit-learn*. They use the hypoglycemia risk as a feature and as a class-labeling factor. The results demonstrate an acceptable performance for all patients (in terms of specificity an sensitivity) and the feasibility of predicting postprandial hypoglycemic events from a classification perspective. In [22], dual mode adaptive basal-bolus advisor based on reinforcement learning is presented. Authors proposed and Adaptive Basal-Bolus Algorithm (ABBA) which provides personalised recommendation for the daily insulin doses using the information of the previous day. Regarding the level of customization of the models, some proposals provide models for the average case [14], and others model the par-ticularities of each patient. Several papers apply classical modeling techniques, resulting in models or profiles defined by linear equations with a limited set of inputs [15].

The treatment for subjects with T1DM uses rates of basal insulin delivery, insulin to carbohydrate ratios and individual correction factors, typically from observations of the endocrinologist. However, those models are often inaccurate, since clinical data in T1DM are not extensive enough to identify the exact models [25]. There are also some models, used in artificial pancreas systems or closed-loop control models, that try to emulate the action of the pancreas [5]. They are based on the assumption that it is possible to reach a reasonable control with approximate models, provided that the model is related to the control objective [8]. Experimental results suggest that these approaches, due to the lack of accurate individualized models, have a significant risk of an excessive insulin administration and, therefore, the possibility that blood glucose levels fall to hypoglycemia zone. Our evolutionary models try to avoid this situation.

De Falco *et al.* [6] presented a work on GP-based induction of a glucose-dynamics model for telemedicine. The work aims to create a regression model that allows the determination of the blood glucose value from the interstitial glucose in patients with T1DM with the idea of using it in a telemedicine portal. The work is divided into two parts. In the first part, the aim is to expand the blood glucose values in the database using the *Steil-Rebrin* model [21]. To make the most accurate estimation, the parameters of this equation are adjusted using an evolutionary algorithm with the RMSE as the fitness function. Since there are many more estimated blood glucose values than actual values, a correction factor must be applied to avoid deviations in the extraction of the model.

The work that we present here extends those works based on GE, and explores the use of a multi-objective approach, based on the Non-dominated Sorting Genetic Algorithm (NSGA-II) [7], applied to real data from diabetic patients. We are interested not only in the specific problem, but also in the performance of the multi-objective implementation. We expect with this work to integrate the different possibilities of using GE for short term and medium term glucose prediction in diabetic people.

3   Description of the Problem

Our objective is to construct an insulin-carbohydrates recommendation tool. So, we construct predictive models that help us on evaluating those recommendations. Predictive models should use information that we can collect in standard daily conditions. More precisely, we collect the following data:

- Interstitial glucose using a Medtronic Continuous Glucose Monitor System (CGMS) the device which gives us observations every five minutes.
- Notes of estimated carbohydrate units ingested, taken by each patient.
- Insulin injected using an insulin infuser device from Medtronic, which registers injections of both basal and bolus insulin every five minutes.

Once all the information has been collected, we process the data to fill up gaps using cubic splines and to match all the events to the closest timestamp in order to construct a set of matched time series, corresponding to glucose, insulin, and carbohydrates values. We also process the set of features available at the time of modelling. At each time point, t, data from up to two hours before are available for prediction and we use also the information of the meals and insulin injected from the time of prediction to the prediction horizon H. From them, we define the following set of features[2], as we made in [11]:

- Actual glucose value at prediction time, t: $G(t)$,
- Glucose measured 15 min before t: $G_{t-15}(t)$,
- Glucose measured 30 min before t: $G_{t-30}(t)$,
- Glucose measured 45 min before t: $G_{t-45}(t)$,
- Glucose measured 60 min before t: $G_{t-60}(t)$,
- Glucose measured 75 min before t: $G_{t-75}(t)$,
- Glucose measured 90 min before t: $G_{t-90}(t)$,
- Glucose measured 105 min before t: $G_{t-105}(t)$,
- Glucose measured 120 min before t: $G_{t-120}(t)$,
- Actual grams of carbohydrates ingested at prediction time, t: $C(t)$,
- Sum of grams of carbohydrates ingested in the last 30 min: $C_{t-30}(t)$,
- Sum of grams of carbohydrates ingested from time $t-31$ to $t-60$: $C_{t-60}(t)$,
- Sum of grams of carbohydrates ingested from time $t-61$ to $t-90$: $C_{t-90}(t)$,
- Sum of grams of carbohydrates ingested from time $t-91$ to $t-120$: $C_{t-120}(t)$,
- Actual units of insulin injected at prediction time, t: $I(t)$,
- Units of insulin injected in the last 30 min: $I_{t-30}(t)$,
- Units of insulin injected from time $t-31$ to $t-60$: $I_{t-60}(t)$,
- Units of insulin injected from time $t-61$ to $t-90$: $I_{t-90}(t)$,
- Units of insulin injected from time $t-91$ to $t-120$: $I_{t-120}(t)$,
- Sum of grams of carbohydrates ingested from t to $t+H$: $C_{t+H}(t)$, and
- Units of insulin injected from t to $t+H$: $I_{t+H}(t)$.

For each time horizon $H \in \{30, 60, 90, 120\}$, find an expression for $\widehat{G}_{t+H}(t)$ given by Eq. (1), that minimizes the objective functions RMSE and F_{CLARKE}.

$$\widehat{G}_{t+H}(t) = f_{t+H}(G_{t-120}(t), G_{t-105}(t), G_{t-90}(t), G_{t-75}(t), G_{t-60}(t), G_{t-45}(t),$$
$$G_{t-30}(t), G_{t-15}(t), G(t), I_{t-120}(t), I_{t-90}(t), I_{t-60}(t), I_{t-30}(t), I(t),$$
$$I_{t+H}(t), C_{t-120}(t), C_{t-90}(t), C_{t-60}(t), C_{t-30}(t), C(t), C_{t+H}(t))$$
$$(1)$$

RMSE is a usual fitness function when adjusting data by SR, shown in Eq. (2). As a second objective function, we have defined F_{CLARKE} as shown in Eq. 3, which follows the CEG criterion used to test the clinical significance of differences between a glucose measurement technique and the venous blood glucose reference measurements [2].

In this regard, CEG considers a grid divided into five zones (A to E) depending on the severity of the misprediction. The values that fall within zones A and B are clinically exact and/or acceptable and thus the clinical treatment will be correct. We consider A and B as a unique category with no contribution to

---

[2] When constructing prediction models that help in the recommendation, we can use variables (features) that include the information involved in the recommendation process and thus be able to use them effectively. This does not mean that we use information from the future.

Eq. 3. In zone C values can be dangerous in some situations. Although less dangerous as D and E zones, we should try also to minimize predictions in these zones, so predicted points in these zones contribute a value of 1 to Eq. 3. Finally Zones D and E represent potentially dangerous areas, since the prediction is far from being acceptable and the indicated treatment will be different from the correct treatment. Each prediction in zone D adds 10 to Eq. 3, while predictions in zone E add 100. The inequalities and conditions of Eq. 4 delimit these zones accordingly to [2].

$$\text{RMSE} = \sqrt{\frac{1}{N}\sum_{i=1}^{N}(G_{t+H}(t_i) - \widehat{G}_{t+H}(t_i))^2} \tag{2}$$

$$F_{CLARKE} = \sum_{i=1}^{N} w_i \tag{3}$$

where $w_i =$ is computed by:

$$w_i = \begin{cases} 100 & \text{if } (\widehat{G}_{t+H}(t_i) \geq 180) \wedge (G_{t+H}(t_i) \leq 70) \\ 100 & \text{if } (\widehat{G}_{t+H}(t_i) \leq 70) \wedge (G_{t+H}(t_i) \geq 180) \\ 10 & \text{if } (180 \geq \widehat{G}_{t+H}(t_i) \geq 70) \wedge (G_{t+H}(t_i) \geq 240) \\ 10 & \text{if } ((180 \geq \widehat{G}_{t+H}(t_i) \geq 70) \wedge (G_{t+H}(t_i) \leq \frac{175}{3})) \vee \\ & ((\widehat{G}_{t+H}(t_i) \geq \frac{6}{5} \times G_{t+H}(t_i)) \wedge (70 \geq G_{t+H}(t_i) \geq \frac{175}{3})) \\ 1 & \text{if } (\widehat{G}_{t+H}(t_i) \geq G_{t+H}(t_i) + 110) \wedge (290 \geq G_{t+H}(t_i) \geq 70) \\ 1 & \text{if } (\widehat{G}_{t+H}(t_i) \leq \frac{7}{5} \times G_{t+H}(t_i) - 182) \wedge (180 \geq G_{t+H}(t_i) \geq 130) \end{cases} \tag{4}$$

Our proposal is a multi-objective approach of GE [19]. We use the same approximation and grammars of [23], where the interested reader can find more details about applying GE for the creation of models. As it is well known, the GE method is powered by an evolutionary computation algorithm, usually an adapted implementation of a genetic algorithm or a particle swarm optimization algorithm. There exist some other multi-objective implementations as [9]. However, we have used our own library, which is publicly available through GitHub, as we will later explain.

Here we use also a bi-objective approach, using Eqs. 2 and 3 as fitness functions. As evolutionary engine we have applied NSGA-II, which is perhaps the most effective way of optimizing and searching solutions to multi-objective problems with evolutionary computation when dealing with 2 or 3 objectives. One of the important questions for selecting a multi-objective approach is to study the fitness functions, i.e. the objectives. Although the objectives may work in the same direction, it is not desirable that both measure similar features. Fitness functions should guide the algorithm through the search space in different manners, although with a common search. This is the case for Eqs. 2 and 3 where both try to minimize the error and to obtain solutions with a 100% of predictions in zones A and B.

Figure 1 represents an extract of the grammar in Backus-Naur Form (BNF) format designed for finding a predictive model of future glucose levels. This is a typical grammar for symbolic regression adapted to the variables and features explained above. It is a recursive grammar and the operators are reduced to addition, subtraction and multiplication based on the conclusions of [16] an our previous experimental experience.

```
func> ::= <expr>

<expr> ::= (<expr> <op> <expr>) | (<cte> <op> <expr>) | <var>

<var> ::= <varch> | <varins> | <vargl>

<op> ::= + | - | *

# Glucose
<vargl> ::= G_{t-120}(t) | G_{t-105}(t) | G_{t-90}(t) | G_{t-75}(t) | G_{t
    -60}(t) | G_{t-45}(t) | G_{t-30}(t) | G_{t-15}(t) | G(t)

# CH
<varch> ::= C_{t-120}(t) | C_{t-90}(t) | C_{t-60}(t) | C_{t-30}(t) | C(t) |
    C_{t+H}(t)

# Insulin:
<varins> ::= I_{t-120}(t) | I_{t-90}(t) | I_{t-60}(t) | I_{t-30}(t) | I(t) |
    I_{t+H}(t)

<cte> ::= <factor> * <digit>
<factor> ::= 0.1 | 0.01 | 0.001 | 0.0001 | 1
<digit> ::= 0 | 1 | 2 | 3 | 4 | 5 | 6 | 7 | 8 | 9 | 10
```

Fig. 1. Grammar for glycemic modeling.

4   Experimental Results

The implementation of the multi-objective GE (MO-GE) algorithm was made in Java, and the code is publicly available at the GitHub repository called JECO, which stands for Java Evolutionary Computation library, described in [10]. As stated before, we have created this multi-objective approach by integrating NSGA-II as optimization engine. Table 1 summarizes the configuration of the evolutionary engine for the MO-GE approach.

Ten T1DM patients ($n = 10$) have been selected for the observational study, based on conditions of good glucose control. Data from patients were acquired over multiple weeks using the devices explained in Sect. 3. Log entries were stored in five-minute intervals. In this data set we have at least 10 complete days of data for each patient. These days are not necessarily consecutive nor the same days for all the patients. Each log entry contains the date and time, the blood glucose value, the amount of insulin (injected via pump), and the amount of carbohydrate intakes as estimated by the patients. The population characterization is female (80%), average age 42.30 ± 11.07, years of disease 27.20 ± 10.32,

Table 1. Configuration of the evolutionary engine.

Properties for the multi-objective GE algorithm	
Grammar	gr120bvr.bnf
Objectives = 2	# F_{CLARKE} # RMSE
Normalized data	No
Genetic operators	
Tournament size	2
Population size	400
Crossover probability	0.75
Mutation probability	0.01
Chromosome length	300
Number of generations	400
Maximum number of wraps	5

years with pump therapy 10.00 ± 4.98, weight 64.78 ± 13.31 kg, HbA1c average of $7.27 \pm 0.50\%$. The average number of days with data is 44.80 ± 30.73. Table 2 shows the number of data points and the main descriptive statistics for the data set. Statistics include the percentages of time that patient's glucose are in a healthy range ([70–180] mg/dl), on hyperglycemia values (>250 mg/dl) and in hypoglycemia (<70 mg/dl). This a common way of evaluating the quality of the management of glucose in diabetics. The greater the time in range ([70–180] mg/dl), the better.

In Figs. 2, 3, 4, and 5 we analyze the differences of the multi-objective approach (MO-GE) when compared to the mono objective (GE), using the results of all 10 patients. All figures represent solutions in the multi-objective space. Each point represents a solution referenced by its pair (RMSE vs Number of points in zones C, D and E). First, Fig. 2 shows the solutions obtained with both a single-objective GE evolution approach using the RMSE value as fitness function (red points) and the solutions obtained with the MO-GE approach (green points) for two selected patients (Patients 2 and 10). As it can be seen, the use of the proposed fitness function F_{CLARKE} as an additional objective improves the fitness of the solutions, not only for the new fitness function, but also in terms of RMSE. We can also observe that all the solutions generated by GE are dominated by solutions generated with MO-GE. Moreover, the distribution of the solutions suggest that our MO-GE is more robust than the GE, since we find most of the solutions close to the approximation to the Pareto front. This is observed for all the 4 time predictions horizons. Similar results were obtained with the rest of the patients.

Table 2. Descriptive statistics for the data sets for all ten patients. Values in range 180–250 are (100% − Time glucose$_{<70}$ −Time glucose$_{>250}$ − Time in range$_{70-180}$).

Patient	Data points	Average (mg/dl)	Std. deviation (mg/dl)	Time glucose <70 mg/dl	Time glucose >250 mg/dl	Time in range [70–180] mg/dl
1	4018	157.67	62.25	4.48%	7.31%	37.57%
2	23534	145.44	64.02	8.33%	6.18%	41.83%
3	23821	143.46	45.45	2.14%	2.26%	49.18%
4	20090	150.47	56.70	4.12%	5.14%	41.29%
5	8036	139.17	67.93	14.17%	7.10%	41.89%
6	12628	142.58	60.08	10.08%	4.44%	41.21%
7	6888	176.33	68.35	3.65%	14.28%	27.07%
8	6027	135.34	46.11	4.85%	1.84%	54.06%
9	5740	146.82	59.82	7.54%	5.20%	39.49%
10	4305	166.13	86.12	9.33%	16.16%	35.69%

Figures 3 and 4 show the distribution of the solutions in the multi-objective with both approaches. As expected the error and the number of points in dangerous predictions zones increases with the horizon of prediction. However, solutions are restricted to a limited area of the graph (maximum RMSE by maximum number of points in zones C, D and E). It is also important to note that, although there are some non dominated solutions with a very low number of points in zones CDE, those are not necessarily the best ones. Let us for example analyse the solutions for a 120 min horizon, patient 5, with the lowest value of CDE in the graph (the magenta colored points close to the y axis around the point [71, 7]). Of course this solution is very precise, however the predictions that are bad could be very dangerous for the patients, since as the RMSE indicates, the deviation from the correct prediction should be very high. When selecting the final model or predictor, the decision maker should take these particularities into account. Another interesting feature that can be extracted from Figs. 3 and 4 is that the longer the prediction horizon, the worse the RSME value, which is consistent with the intuitive idea of difficulty of prediction for long horizons. However, this situation is not happening with CEG. Notice, for instance, that a small set of solutions from the 120 min horizon are located close to the CDE value of 10, which is really small. This means that, despite those solutions having a high RSME value (around 70), the predictions are well located in terms of the grid defined by CEG, which provides a good CDE value. Besides, it can be seen that the width of the solutions set from the 120 prediction horizon is the highest, and the width is reduced as the prediction horizon is shortened. This means that good CDE values can be reached in every horizon (as well as bad ones), and this variability is reduced with the reduction of the prediction horizon. These facts prove that both objectives are not proportional and hence, the multi-objective approach is correct.

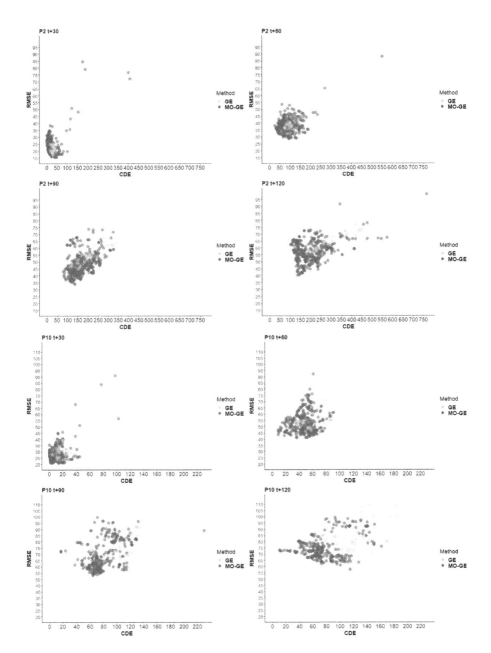

Fig. 2. Distribution of the solutions in the multi-objective space for solutions obtained with both a single-objective GE evolution approach using the RMSE value as fitness function (red points) and the solutions obtained with the MO-GE approach (green points) for two selected patients (Patients 2 and 10), for all time horizons. (Color figure online)

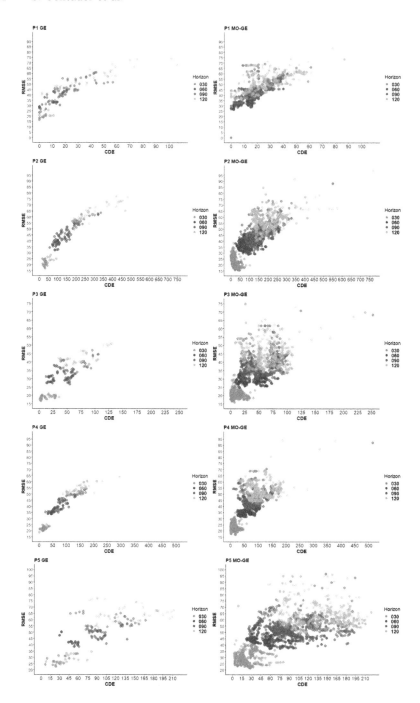

Fig. 3. Distribution of the solutions in the multi-objective space for the different solutions obtained for Patients 1 to 5 with the MO-GE and GE approaches. Each color represents a time Horizon. (Color figure online)

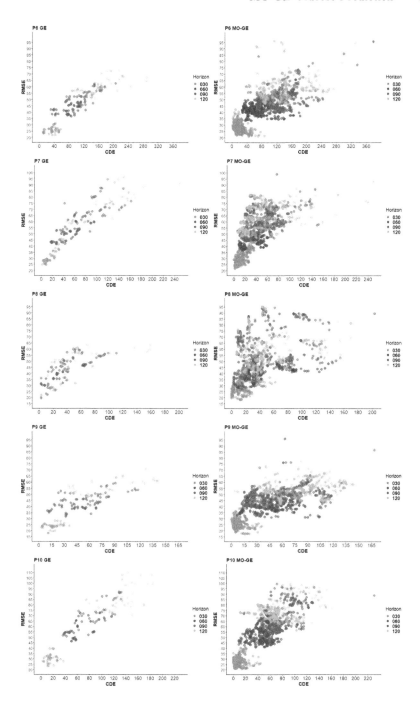

Fig. 4. Distribution of the solutions in the multi-objective space for the different solutions obtained for Patients 6 to 10 with the MO-GE and GE approaches. Each color represents a time Horizon. (Color figure online)

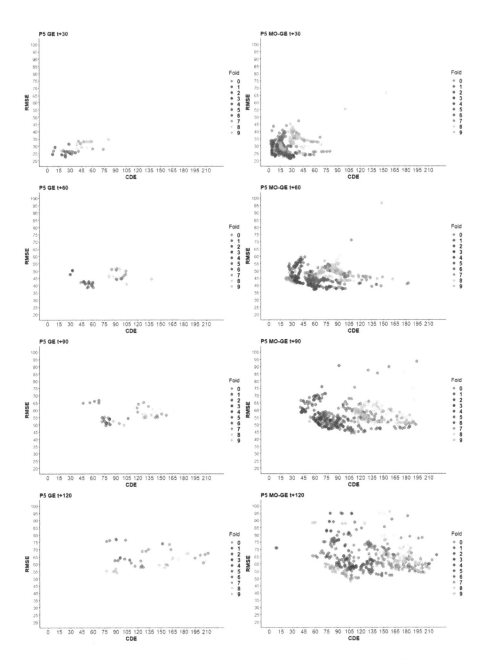

Fig. 5. Distribution of the solutions in the multi-objective space for the different solutions obtained for Patient 5 with the MO-GE and GE approaches. Each color represents the solutions obtained with one of the folds of the 10 folds cross validation strategy. (Color figure online)

An additional analysis is made on Fig. 5 where we can see the distribution of the solutions in the multi-objective space for Patient 5 with both approaches, mono (GE) and multi-objective (MO-GE). Each color represents the solutions obtained with one of the folds of the 10 folds cross validation strategy for a prediction horizon. Two questions arise from them. First, some of the fold are more difficult to solve than others, and a deeper study of the data should be done in order to improve the algorithm, for instance, detecting some kind of pattern and seeing when the MO-GE works better as proposed in [3]. In addition, MO-GE was able to find very good solutions for one of the folds, which seem to be one of the most difficult having in consideration the solutions reported by the GE algorithm. Table 3 shows the aggregated results for both the single-objective and multi-objective approaches, GE and MO-GE, respectively. For each time horizon, the percentage of predictions that go into zones A or B (A+B column), C, D and E is depicted. Again, the MO-GE algorithm reaches the best performance, reducing predictions in the most dangerous zones D and E for short term predictions, 30 and 60 min. For medium term predictions (90 and 120 min), sum of D and E points are very similar on average, however MO-GE finds better global solutions. Results were tested for statistical significance and we found differences in the number of points in zones D and E, where the multi-objective approach reduces the most dangerous predictions. Experiments were performed on an Intel(R) Core (TM) i7-7700CPU at 3.60 GHz with 16 GB RAM Memory under Windows 10. Experiments were launched with 8 threads in parallel to benefit from all the cores-threads of the computer without affecting performance and no other task running at the same time. The average time for obtaining a model with GE is 390.37 s and 11164.61 s for the MO-GE approach, almost 29 times slower.

Table 3. Percentage of predictions for each zone of the CEG metric. Aggregated data of all the patients in the four time horizons.

Algorithm	Horizon	A+B	C	D	E	Horizon	A+B	C	D	E
GE	30	92.81	**1.26**	5.31	**0.60**	90	**92.96**	1.24	5.22	**0.56**
MO-GE	30	**95.70**	2.38	**0.95**	0.97	90	91.77	2.37	**4.66**	1.20
GE	60	93.19	**1.23**	5.00	0.59	120	**90.76**	**1.35**	6.96	**0.91**
MO-GE	60	**94.39**	1.85	**3.24**	**0.52**	120	90.35	2.93	**5.01**	1.70

5   Conclusions

In this paper we investigated the benefits and drawbacks of a multi-objective implementation of grammatical evolution for constructing models of glucose. In particular we implemented a GE algorithm combined with NSGA-II guided by two fitness functions: RMSE and another designed to follow the principles of

Clarke Error Grid. Results shows that the multi-objective approach gives better models reducing the number of predictions in the most dangerous zones.

Acknowledgments. This work has been supported by: Fundación Eugenio Rodriguez Pascual 2019 grant -*Desarrollo de sistemas adaptativos y bioinspirados para el control glucémico con infusores subcutáneos continuos de insulina y monitores continuos de glucosa (Development of adaptive and bioinspired systems for glycaemic control with continuous subcutaneous insulin infusors and continuous glucose monitors)*; The Spanish Ministerio de Innovación Ciencia y Universidad - grant RTI2018-095180-B-I00; Madrid Regional Government-FEDER grants B2017/BMD3773 (GenObIA-CM); and Y2018/NMT-4668 (Micro-Stress- MAP-CM).

References

1. Bakhtiani, P.A., Zhao, L.M., El Youssef, J., Castle, J.R., Ward, W.K.: A review of artificial pancreas technologies with an emphasis on bi-hormonal therapy. Diab. Obes. Metab. **15**(12), 1065–1070 (2013)
2. Clarke, W., Cox, D., Gonder-Frederick, L., Carter, W., Pohl, S.: Evaluating clinical accuracy of systems for self-monitoring of blood glucose. Diab. Care **10**(5), 622–628 (1987)
3. Contador, S., Hidalgo, J.I., Garnica, O., Velasco, J.M., Lanchares, J.: Can clustering improve glucose forecasting with genetic programming models? In: Proceedings of the Genetic and Evolutionary Computation Conference Companion, pp. 1829–1836. ACM (2019)
4. Contreras, I., Oviedo, S., Vettoretti, M., Visentin, R., Vehí, J.: Personalized blood glucose prediction: a hybrid approach using grammatical evolution and physiological models. PLoS ONE **12**(11), e0187754 (2017)
5. Dassau, E., et al.: Artificial pancreatic beta-cell protocol for enhanced model identification. In: Diabetes, vol. 58, pp. A105–A106. American Diabetes Association, Alexandria (2009)
6. De Falco, I., Della Cioppa, A., Koutny, T., Krcma, M., Scafuri, U., Tarantino, E.: Genetic programming-based induction of a glucose-dynamics model for telemedicine. J. Netw. Comput. Appl. **119**, 1–13 (2018)
7. Deb, K.: Multi-objective Optimization Using Evolutionary Algorithms, vol. 16. Wiley, Hoboken (2001)
8. Gevers, M.: Identification for control: from the early achievements to the revival of experiment design*. Eur. J. Control **11**(4), 335–352 (2005)
9. Hemberg, E., Ho, L., O'Neill, M., Claussen, H.: A comparison of grammatical genetic programming grammars for controlling femtocell network coverage. Genet. Program Evolvable Mach. **14**(1), 65–93 (2013)
10. Hidalgo, J.I., et al.: Identification of models for glucose blood values in diabetics by grammatical evolution. In: Ryan, C., O'Neill, M., Collins, J.J. (eds.) Handbook of Grammatical Evolution, pp. 367–393. Springer, Cham (2018). https://doi.org/10.1007/978-3-319-78717-6_15
11. Hidalgo, J.I., Colmenar, J.M., Kronberger, G., Winkler, S.M., Garnica, O., Lanchares, J.: Data based prediction of blood glucose concentrations using evolutionary methods. J. Med. Syst. **41**(9), 142 (2017)
12. Lourenço, N., Colmenar, J.M., Hidalgo, J.I., Garnica, Ó.: Structured grammatical evolution for glucose prediction in diabetic patients. In: Proceedings of the Genetic and Evolutionary Computation Conference, pp. 1250–1257. ACM (2019)

13. Man, C.D., Micheletto, F., Lv, D., Breton, M., Kovatchev, B., Cobelli, C.: The UVA/PADOVA type 1 diabetes simulator: new features. J. Diab. Sci. Technol. **8**(1), 26–34 (2014)
14. Mays, L.: Diabetes mellitus standards of care. Nurs. Clin. North Am. **50**(4), 703–711 (2015). Pathophysiology and Care Protocols for Nursing Management
15. Messori, M., Toffanin, C., Favero, S.D., Nicolao, G.D., Cobelli, C., Magni, L.: Model individualization for artificial pancreas. Comput. Methods Programs Biomed. **171**, 133–140 (2016)
16. Moreno-Salinas, D., Besada-Portas, E., López-Orozco, J., Chaos, D., de la Cruz, J., Aranda, J.: Symbolic regression for marine vehicles identification. IFAC-PapersOnLine **48**(16), 210–216 (2015)
17. Ogurtsova, K., et al.: IDF diabetes atlas: global estimates for the prevalence of diabetes for 2015 and 2040. Diab. Res. Clin. Pract. **128**, 40–50 (2017)
18. Oviedo, S., Contreras, I., Quirós, C., Giménez, M., Conget, I., Vehi, J.: Risk-based postprandial hypoglycemia forecasting using supervised learning. Int. J. Med. Inform. **126**, 1–8 (2019)
19. Ryan, C., Collins, J.J., Neill, M.O.: Grammatical evolution: evolving programs for an arbitrary language. In: Banzhaf, W., Poli, R., Schoenauer, M., Fogarty, T.C. (eds.) EuroGP 1998. LNCS, vol. 1391, pp. 83–96. Springer, Heidelberg (1998). https://doi.org/10.1007/BFb0055930
20. Sparacino, G., Zanderigo, F., Corazza, S., Maran, A., Facchinetti, A., Cobelli, C.: Glucose concentration can be predicted ahead in time from continuous glucose monitoring sensor time-series. IEEE Trans. Biomed. Eng. **54**(5), 931–937 (2007)
21. Steil, G., et al.: Interstitial fluid glucose dynamics during insulin-induced hypoglycaemia. Diabetologia **48**(9), 1833–1840 (2005)
22. Sun, Q., et al.: A dual mode adaptive basal-bolus advisor based on reinforcement learning. IEEE J. Biomed. Health Inform. **23**, 2633–2641 (2018)
23. Velasco, J.M., et al.: Enhancing grammatical evolution through data augmentation: application to blood glucose forecasting. In: Squillero, G., Sim, K. (eds.) EvoApplications 2017. LNCS, vol. 10199, pp. 142–157. Springer, Cham (2017). https://doi.org/10.1007/978-3-319-55849-3_10
24. Weissberg-Benchell, J., Antisdel-Lomaglio, J., Seshadri, R.: Insulin pump therapy. Diab. Care **26**(4), 1079–1087 (2003)
25. Yu, C., Zhao, C.: Rapid model identification for online glucose prediction of new subjects with type 1 diabetes using model migration method. IFAC Proc. Vol. **47**(3), 2094–2099 (2014). 19th IFAC World Congress

Evolutionary Machine Learning

A Greedy Iterative Layered Framework for Training Feed Forward Neural Networks

L. L. Custode[5], C. L. Tecce[1], I. Bakurov[3], M. Castelli[4], A. Della Cioppa[1,2(✉)], and L. Vanneschi[3,4(✉)]

[1] Natural Computation Lab, DIEM, University of Salerno, Fisciano, Italy
adellacioppa@unisa.it
[2] ICAR-CNR, Via P. Castellino, 111, 80131 Naples, Italy
[3] NOVA Information Management School (NOVA IMS),
Universidade Nova de Lisboa, Campus de Campolide, 1070-312 Lisbon, Portugal
lvanneschi@novaims.unl.pt
[4] LASIGE, Departamento de Informática, Faculdade de Ciências,
Universidade de Lisboa, 1749-016 Lisbon, Portugal
[5] Department of Information Engineering and Computer Science,
University of Trento, Trento, Italy

Abstract. In recent years neuroevolution has become a dynamic and rapidly growing research field. Interest in this discipline is motivated by the need to create ad-hoc networks, the topology and parameters of which are optimized, according to the particular problem at hand. Although neuroevolution-based techniques can contribute fundamentally to improving the performance of artificial neural networks (ANNs), they present a drawback, related to the massive amount of computational resources needed. This paper proposes a novel population-based framework, aimed at finding the optimal set of synaptic weights for ANNs. The proposed method partitions the weights of a given network and, using an optimization heuristic, trains one layer at each step while "freezing" the remaining weights. In the experimental study, particle swarm optimization (PSO) was used as the underlying optimizer within the framework and its performance was compared against the standard training (i.e., training that considers the whole set of weights) of the network with PSO and the backward propagation of the errors (backpropagation). Results show that the subsequent training of sub-spaces reduces training time, achieves better generalizability, and leads to the exhibition of smaller variance in the architectural aspects of the network.

Keywords: Neuroevolution · Particle swarm optimization · Artificial neural networks

1 Introduction

An artificial neural network (ANN) is a biologically-inspired computer system that simulates the biological neural networks (BNNs) and their biochemical

© Springer Nature Switzerland AG 2020
P. A. Castillo et al. (Eds.): EvoApplications 2020, LNCS 12104, pp. 513–529, 2020.
https://doi.org/10.1007/978-3-030-43722-0_33

processes [10]. As such, an ANN consists of a set of interconnected layers of basic processing units, called neurons, which, altogether, comprise a powerful and versatile computing system that can solve numerous complex problems, including, but not limited to automatic speech and image recognition, natural language processing, autonomous car driving, bio-informatics, fraud-detection [24].

Several properties of ANNs make them an appropriate technique to solve supervised machine-learning (SML) problems. First, ANNs are data-driven, self-adaptive, real-time learning methods, that rely on few *a priori* assumptions about the models for problems under study [23,33]. Thus, the ANNs are suitable for problems with solutions requiring knowledge that may be difficult to specify, but for which there are sufficient data to do so. Second, ANNs are universal function approximators. More specifically, ANNs have been proven to be capable, with some limitations, of approximating any continuous function to any desired level of accuracy [12–14]. The effectiveness of ANNs derives from the neurons' mode of interacting with each other, i.e. their interconnections. Traditionally, such interconnections are assigned random weights to initialize a network. Then, a training algorithm is executed to identify the optimal set of weights, thereby allowing the network to achieve *satisfactory* performance, given the problem at hand. Typically, within the context of SML, such a training algorithm consists of the backward propagation of the errors, known as *backpropagation*. This is an optimization algorithm, based on the gradient of a loss function in the weight space [22,31].

Backpropagation is one of the most popular training algorithms for ANNs. In practice, however, backpropagation presents significant limitations related to multi-modal and non-differentiable cost functions. Moreover, backpropagation is particularly inefficient and time-consuming in the face of problems with a huge number of local optima and *plateaus* in the error surface [11].

In the context of deep learning (DL), the backpropagation is known to suffer from vanishing/exploding gradients. This phenomenon refers to a situation in which the gradient of a cost function can become exceedingly large or extremely small. More specifically, the backpropagation performs very small/big updates to the set of weights, thereby rendering the training process imprecise and time-consuming [15].

This work introduces a novel population-based framework for training ANNs. The proposed technique optimizes the weights of an ANN, one layer per step, while freezing all remaining weights in the other layers. This approach forces the optimization algorithm to work in a subspace of the original search space. This choice boasts two main advantages compared with the more traditional approach, which is aimed at optimizing the whole network at once: (i) it increases the effectiveness of the exploration and (ii) reduces the time needed for the optimization process. To investigate the capability of the technique proposed in this work, particle swarm optimization (PSO) was used as the underlying optimizer in our experiments. However, the framework is flexible to a point, to allow for the use of any optimization heuristic. In the following discussion, we present results, obtained on a set of well-known benchmark problems, which demonstrate the capacity of the proposed system to produce results better than (or comparable to) those yielded by backpropagation and to produce them more quickly, in terms of training time, than traditional approaches.

It is important to note here that the main purpose of this paper is to present our preliminary results concerning the ability of the proposed layered paradigm to optimize an ANN, but that there has been no special effort expended to identify the most suitable optimizer for the problem at hand. For this reason, only standard versions of the PSO and backpropagation algorithms have been used, despite the existence of several well-known variants of these algorithms that may be able to achieve better performance.

For the same reason, only feed-forward fully-connected networks have been considered in the performed experiments, even if, in principle, the proposed technique applies to recurrent networks as well.

The paper is organized as follows: Sect. 2 reviews prior related work, aimed at defining techniques for optimizing the weights of ANNs; Sect. 3 describes the proposed approach; while Sect. 4 presents the experimental settings and discusses the obtained results; and finally, Sect. 5 summarizes the main findings of this paper and suggests ideas for future research.

2   Prior Related Work

It is challenging to train an ANN to find an optimal, or at least a satisfactory, set of synaptic weights for a given problem. We refer to this task as WEANN (Weight Evolving Artificial Neural Networks), which is a simplified version of the standard Neuroevolution problem. The difficulty is associated mainly with the non-linearity of the problem that the network is meant to solve, the lack of knowledge regarding the best set of weights and biases, and the dependency of the performance of the training algorithm on the architectural aspects of the network (specifically, the topology and activation functions of the neurons). Hence, given their utility as alternatives to backpropagation and its variants [21], heuristic search algorithms were used to optimize ANNs [3,18,26,28].

Within this research track, evolutionary algorithms (EAs) were assigned a special role, due to their recognized advantages over gradient-based techniques [23,31]. EAs are better at handling a global search in a vast, complex, multimodal and non-differentiable surface, and especially useful when the gradient of the cost function is expensive to calculate. Moreover, EAs can be used to train many types of ANNs, including feed-forward, recurrent and higher-order. Finally, EAs can easily incorporate special characteristics, such as regularization. Among the many existing references that report on the use of EAs to optimize ANNs, we refer the reader to [23,31].

Given our selection of PSO as the underlying optimization algorithm to conduct our experiments, in this section, we focus on prior contributions studying the application of PSO to training ANNs. In [9,16,32] PSO was used to evolve the weights and topology of the network. In particular, in [16], authors presented a multi-dimensional particle swarm optimization (MD-PSO) technique to automatically design ANNs through a process of evolution to the optimal network configuration (consisting of connections, weights, and biases) within an architecture space. Similarly, in [9], the study consisted of performing a simultaneous evolution of an ANN's three principal components: the set of synaptic weights, the architecture, and the transfer functions of each neuron. The main topic of the paper was to find the optimal design of an ANN, using eight proposed fitness functions to evaluate the quality of each solution. In [32], the authors introduced a new evolutionary system, constrained to the use of PSO, for feed-forward ANNs. The architecture and the weights of ANNs were adjusted adaptively according to the quality of the network.

All of these approaches differ substantially from the one presented in this paper, because their performance is not directly comparable with standard training algorithms, such as backpropagation. In fact, the objective of standard training algorithms is "only" to find an optimal set of synaptic weights, and that is also the objective of the system presented here. Another chief and distinctive feature of this work is its lack of *apriori* considerations regarding the extent to which the standard PSO was effective at training an ANN to solve a given optimization problem. In this paper, we show it is possible to achieve a better performance by reducing the search space by constraining the evolutionary process within a subspace of the whole solution space, without reducing the exploratory power of the selected optimization technique.

In [1] and [25], the authors applied PSO in the context of using cooperative learning (CL) to train ANNs. The training process was conducted within a multi-swarm architecture, such that each swarm optimized a subset of the solution's vector, which was previously split and distributed across swarms according to a given rule. To identify an optimal solution to the original problem, it was necessary to combine particles from all swarms to form the candidate solution vector, which was then passed to the fitness function. In [1], the authors presented three splitting rules to train ANNs for classification problems. Each time a new global best solution was found, the fitness value of the best particles in all the swarms was updated to reflect that value, because of all these particles participated in the creation of the global best. A similar idea was proposed in [25], in which the authors sought to improve the performance of the basic PSO by halving the solution vector (Esplit) and allocating each on its swarm. Then, a plain swarm, containing the entire solution vector, was used as an "attractor" for other two swarms. Both approaches suffer from problems related to selection of which particles to bind for composition of the solution, and the assignment of fitness within the evolutionary process. Regarding the latter, the question discussed in [1] is: How much credit should each swarm be awarded when the combined vector (constructed from all the swarms) results in a better solution? It is not, in fact, an easy task, to define a proper way to split the value of the fitness so as to give the bulk of it to the best swarm involved in representing the final solution. A precise answer to this question, supported by experimental results, was not provided.

Given the nomenclature assigned to the CL framework, the technique presented in this paper uses Lsplit (or Layer-split) architecture to distribute the network's weights across different swarms. However, unlike the approaches described above, the swarms are not evolved simultaneously, but rather sequentially, one after another, layer after layer.

Our approach does not suffer from any of the aforementioned problems, because the optimization phase of a given layer is constrained to the remaining part of the network. In fact, the main objective is to maximize the performance of the whole network by adapting the behavior of each layer to the ones that follow.

In [34], the authors presented a hybrid algorithm (called PSO-BP), combining PSO with backpropagation, to train the weights of feedforward ANNs. The main idea is to combine the rapid converge of PSO during the initial stages of a global search (as the PSO search process is likely to slow considerably as it approaches a global optimum) with the gradient descent method that can achieve faster convergence around global optima. The proposed PSO-BP algorithm presents a heuristic way to give a transition from particle swarm search to gradient descent. The experimental results showed that the PSO-BP algorithm is better than the backpropagation algorithm in terms of convergence speed and accuracy.

3   The Proposed Method

Due to the nature of gradient descent optimization, the backpropagation suffers from certain drawbacks that can, in some cases, compromise its effectiveness. For instance, the backpropagation can get stuck in local optima or have problems optimizing error surfaces with vast neutral *plateaus*. Furthermore, non-differentiability and vanishing/exploding gradients can be other possible sources of difficulties. These problems have been solved partially by stochastic gradient descent with momentum [19], but they remain an issue.

Evolutionary ANNs (EANNs) rely on the use of evolutionary and nature-inspired algorithms and can represent an alternative to gradient-based techniques. Although EANNs are characterized by their adaptability, broad range of applications and flexibility, they usually require significant amounts of computational power to perform the training task. Considering a population-based optimization heuristic and that each individual in the population represents the whole set of synaptic weights, as the network grows bigger and deeper, so increases the computational power required to train the system [27,30].

The purpose of the algorithm proposed in this paper is to use a population-based heuristic to overcome the exploratory shortcomings of the backpropagation, while reducing the computational effort required during training of ANNs. The proposed system is characterized by two main elements: (i) it is a population-based heuristic algorithm, which allows us to conduct a global optimization in a potentially huge, rugged, multi-modal and non-differentiable search space, avoiding *plateaus* in the error surface and eliminating the vanishing/exploding gradient problem; and (ii) considering a n-dimensional search space, where each dimension represents a weight in a given ANN, and a candidate solution is an n-dimensional vector of candidate weights, the algorithm severs the layers, splitting the search space into subspaces that are then optimized sequentially.

In recent years, deep learning has become very popular and state-of-the-art networks usually contain many layers. Therefore, to reduce the computational time needed for their optimization, it makes sense to avoid using population-based heuristics to achieve a simultaneous optimization of the whole network. For this reason, we considered splitting the solution vector into semantically different subsets of the search space, each optimized within its population.

Our solution to the problem of ANN weights optimization is called greedy iterative layered training (GILT) algorithm and is described in the next section. It is worth noting here that, in theory, GILT can use any optimization heuristic. However, given that, in our experiments, we have chosen to use PSO as the optimization algorithm for GILT, the method will hereinafter be referred to as GILT-PSO.

3.1 Greedy Iterative Layered Training

The GILT algorithm conducts a greedy training of an ANN using an arbitrary population-based heuristic algorithm. By greedy, we mean that the algorithm does not seek to train the whole network at the same time. Instead, it searches, one layer at a time, for an optimal set of weights, while freezing the other layers. Each layer is optimized in its turn, and the whole procedure is iterated until the satisfaction of a stopping criterion or through a predefined number of epochs. During the optimization of a given layer, the algorithm's objective is to find a set of weights for the current layer that maximizes the performance of the whole network. In GILT, after the optimization of a given layer, the final population is stored for later use in seeding the new population that will optimize the same layer in the subsequent epoch. In other words, throughout this framework, a layer can be viewed as a point in an n-dimensional space and, at the end of the optimization process, we will have not only one single point representing the layer, but for each layer we will have a cloud of available points. If a sufficient number of iterations is given to the optimization technique, even after the first epoch, the population optimizing each layer is likely to reach a good degree of convergence. Thus, it is expected that the populations will be made of the best individual and a certain number of its perturbations. We expect this training framework to provide higher exploratory power than the backpropagation, while maintaining good exploitability. At the same time, semantically splitting the solution space by ANN layers forces the heuristic algorithm to conduct the optimization within a subspace of the search space, which is unlike the simultaneous optimization of all layers. In conclusion, it is important to note that the final solution is constrained to the initial setting of the network because all adjustments to the weights are influenced by the way the neurons in the other layers perceive them. Moreover, repeating this process for more than one epoch only serves to fine-tune the solution obtained on the first one. It is worth noting that our methodology does not make use of minibatches, which means that, for each

---

Algorithm 1. Network Training

Input : O - Optimizer, l - Layout, X - Training set, y - Training labels,
max_epochs - Number of epochs,
$stopping\_criterion$ - A stopping criterion method

Output: w - Set of weights for the whole network that minimizes loss

1 $current\_epoch \leftarrow 0$
2 $w \leftarrow Random()$
3 $seeds \leftarrow$ 2-dimensional array with initial weights
4 **while** $current\_epoch < max\_epochs$ **and not** $stopping\_criterion()$ **do**
5 $\quad$ **foreach** *(l_index, layer)* **in** w **do**
6 $\quad\quad$ $layer \leftarrow O.optimize\ (\ seeds[l\_index],\ l\_index,\ w,\ X,\ y\ )$
7 $\quad\quad$ $seeds[l\_index] \leftarrow O.get\_population()$
8 $\quad\quad$ $w \leftarrow replace(w, l\_index, layer)$
9 $\quad$ **end**
10 $\quad$ $current\_epoch \leftarrow current\_epoch + 1$
11 **end**
12 **return** w

---

fitness evaluation, all contents of the dataset are fed to the ANN. The mean squared error between the expected output and the current one has been used as a fitness metric. The proposed method is described in Algorithm 1.

4 Experimental Study

4.1 Test Problems

The performance of GILT-PSO has been tested on four different classification problems and with several network topologies for each problem. The reason behind this choice is to prove the general suitability of GILT-PSO; thus, we preferred to test the algorithm under different (although simple) test cases instead of focusing on a single complex task.

The datasets used have been taken from the UCI repository [5] and they are:

1. **Iris:** This dataset consists of measurements related to three classes of the iris plant, and it contains 50 instances for each class. One class is linearly separable from the other two; the latter is not. Each sample is described in terms of four features: sepal length in cm, sepal width in cm, petal length in cm, petal width in cm [8].
2. **Seeds:** Data belonging to three varieties of wheat: Kama, Rosa, and Canadian; 70 elements of each, randomly selected for the experiment. High-quality visualization of the internal kernel structure was detected, using a soft x-ray technique. The images were recorded on 13×18 cm x-ray KODAK plates. Studies were conducted using combine harvested wheat grain originating from experimental fields, explored at the Institute of Agrophysics of the Polish Academy of Sciences in Lublin. Each sample is described in terms of seven

features: area, perimeter, compactness, length of the kernel, width of the kernel, asymmetry coefficient, length of the kernel groove [2].

3. **Breast Cancer Wisconsin (Diagnostic):** Features are computed from a digital image of fine needle aspirate (FNA) of a breast mass. They refer to characteristics of the cell nuclei that are visible in the image. The dataset consists of two classes (malignant and benign) and 569 total samples. Each sample is described in terms of 30 features: mean, standard error and worst of radius, texture, perimeter, area, smoothness, compactness, concavity, concave points, symmetry, fractal dimension [17,29].

4. **Wine:** Results of a chemical analysis of wines grown in the same region in Italy, but derived from three cultivates. The dataset is characterized by three classes and 178 total observations. Each sample is described in terms of 13 features: alcohol, malic acid, ash, alkalinity of ash, magnesium, total phenols, flavonoids, non-flavonoid phenols, proanthocyanidins, color intensity, hue, OD280/OD315 of diluted wines, proline.

4.2   Experimental Setting

For each of the above datasets, several topologies for the hidden layers have been used, while the number of input and output neurons are set according to the number of features and classes for the specific problem. The ANNs used are fully connected and they present the following topologies: (in, 3, out), (in, 20, out), (in, 30, 20, out), (in, 50, 30, out), (in, 40, 40, 30, out), where *in* and *out* stand respectively for the number of input features and target classes of the underlying problem. All hidden neurons have the same activation function, which is the hyperbolic tangent, while the output layer's activation is Softmax.

The results obtained using GILT-PSO have been compared with the ones obtained by the standard backpropagation algorithm, and implemented in the SciKit framework [20] through the class MLPClassifier. The parameters have been chosen after a coarse-grained grid search and are shown below:

- activation = 'tanh': Hyperbolic tangent
- solver = 'sgd': Stochastic gradient descent
- alpha = 0: L2 regularization parameter
- shuffle = True: Shuffling of the dataset for each epoch
- learning_rate = 'constant'
- learning_rate_init = 0.03
- validation_fraction = 0
- early_stopping = False
- tol = 0: Used for the early stopping
- momentum = 0.9
- batch_size = size of the training set

It should be noted here that using a batch size equal to the entire dataset "guarantees" the convergence for the MLP classifier, thereby complicating the comparison with respect to GILT-PSO.

To offer empirical proof of the effectiveness of GILT-PSO, we performed a comparison with the standard PSO; in this context, we use the term "standard PSO" to indicate a PSO with the objective of optimizing all the weights in the ANN at once, i.e. without splitting them into layers. The hyperparameters for PSO and GILT-PSO are the following: $w = 0.73$, $c_1 = 1.5$, $c_2 = 1.5$, and they have been chosen according to [6]. The version of the PSO algorithm used is the classical one described in [7].

Because this work aims to prove the effectiveness of the proposed layered approach without depending on low-level details of the underlying optimizers, we decided to use basic variants of both backpropagation and PSO.

During the experiments, the goal was to perform a fair evaluation across all algorithms under investigation; thus, the number of epochs for the backpropagation was calculated according to the following formula:

$$n_{\text{BPepochs}} = n_{\text{particles}} \cdot n_{\text{iterations}} \cdot n_{\text{epochs}} \cdot (n_{\text{hidden layers}} + 1)$$

where $n_{\text{hidden layers}}$ represents the number of hidden layers of a given network. However, for the standard PSO, the number of iterations was calculated by:

$$n_{\text{pso\_it}} = n_{\text{iterations}} \cdot n_{\text{epochs}} \cdot (n_{\text{hidden layers}} + 1)$$

These equations ensure the same number of fitness evaluations for all the algorithms under comparison.

The major objective of our experiments was to compare the performance of different training algorithms for different ANN architectures across different problems. For each layout and each dataset, 30 independent runs were performed and final classification accuracy on the training and validation set, for each network, was stored. The validation accuracy was then used to select the best network in order to evaluate it on the test set. It is worth to note that, for each run, a new set of random weights are generated and used as a starting point for all the algorithms under comparison. Based on these results, we performed a statistical analysis to validate our conclusions. For the first experiment, the used parameters were the following: number of epochs equal to 2, number of iterations equal to 17 and number of particles equal to 15.

Using only two epochs was found to be sufficient to evaluate the performance of the network after a first rough optimization by GILT-PSO and, thus, to understand its effectiveness.

4.3   Experimental Results

Table 1 reports a broad perspective of the experimental results that we obtained using 2 epochs. Here, the reader can find the average classification accuracy on the validation set, and the respective standard deviation, for each training algorithm, calculated using the best solutions found (in terms of training accuracy), at the end of each run, across all studied problems and topologies. From the table, the competitive advantage of GILT-PSO over backpropagation and standard PSO is clear: GILT-PSO is not only, in average terms, more accurate, but also more stable (in fact, it has a lower standard deviation).

Table 1. Summary of the validation accuracy in terms of mean and standard deviation across all the problems under examination.

Algorithm	Mean	Std deviation
BP	0.889	0.096
GILT-PSO	0.903	0.034
PSO	0.898	0.040

Table 2. Median accuracy on the test set of the best networks evaluated on the validation set - 2 epochs.

Dataset	Layout	BP	GILT-PSO	PSO
Iris	[4, 3, 3]	0.889	**0.944**	0.861
	[4, 20, 3]	**0.889**	0.833	0.833
	[4, 30, 20, 3]	**0.889**	**0.889**	**0.889**
	[4, 50, 30, 3]	**0.889**	**0.889**	**0.889**
	[4, 40, 40, 30, 3]	**0.944**	0.889	0.889
Seeds	[7, 3, 3]	**0.913**	0.870	**0.913**
	[7, 20, 3]	0.870	**0.913**	0.826
	[7, 30, 20, 3]	0.870	0.870	**0.913**
	[7, 50, 30, 3]	0.739	**0.913**	**0.913**
	[7, 40, 40, 30, 3]	0.652	**0.957**	0.870
Wine	[13, 3, 3]	0.824	0.853	**0.882**
	[13, 20, 3]	0.824	0.882	**0.941**
	[13, 30, 20, 3]	**0.882**	**0.882**	0.706
	[13, 50, 30, 3]	0.824	0.824	**0.912**
	[13, 40, 40, 30, 3]	**0.882**	**0.882**	0.853
Breast	[30, 3, 2]	0.482	0.786	**0.804**
	[30, 20, 2]	0.482	**0.875**	0.795
	[30, 30, 20, 2]	0.411	**0.696**	0.482
	[30, 50, 30, 2]	0.411	**0.688**	0.607
	[30, 40, 40, 30, 2]	0.634	0.554	**0.732**

If we study the results obtained by the different algorithms on each of the studied problems, we can see that, in the majority of the cases, GILT-PSO outperforms both backpropagation and PSO or returns a result comparable to the best of them. More specifically, when selecting the best solution (in terms of training accuracy) from the 30 runs, the highest validation accuracy, for most of the problems and topologies, is obtained using GILT-PSO. These results, considering 2 epochs, are summarized in Table 2, where the best accuracy values for each row are highlighted in bold.

Table 3. Median accuracy on the test set of the best networks evaluated on the validation set - 3 epochs.

Dataset	Layout	BP	GILT-PSO	PSO
Iris	[4, 3, 3]	0.889	**0.917**	0.889
	[4, 20, 3]	**0.889**	0.833	**0.889**
	[4, 30, 20, 3]	**0.889**	**0.889**	**0.889**
	[4, 50, 30, 3]	**0.889**	**0.889**	**0.889**
	[4, 40, 40, 30, 3]	0.833	**0.889**	**0.889**
Seeds	[7, 3, 3]	**0.913**	0.870	0.826
	[7, 20, 3]	**0.913**	0.891	0.870
	[7, 30, 20, 3]	0.826	**0.913**	0.891
	[7, 50, 30, 3]	0.870	**0.913**	**0.913**
	[7, 40, 40, 30, 3]	0.739	**0.913**	0.870
Wine	[13, 3, 3]	0.824	0.882	**0.941**
	[13, 20, 3]	0.824	0.882	**0.912**
	[13, 30, 20, 3]	0.882	0.882	**0.941**
	[13, 50, 30, 3]	0.824	0.912	**0.941**
	[13, 40, 40, 30, 3]	**0.882**	**0.882**	0.765
Breast	[30, 3, 2]	0.464	**0.804**	0.661
	[30, 20, 2]	0.464	**0.661**	0.446
	[30, 30, 20, 2]	0.429	**0.804**	0.607
	[30, 50, 30, 2]	0.420	**0.536**	0.500
	[30, 40, 40, 30, 2]	0.643	**0.750**	0.634

Here, we can observe that, 11 times out of 20, GILT-PSO outperforms or furnishes comparable results to both backpropagation and standard PSO; more specifically, it outperforms the backpropagation 16 times.

The same experiments were repeated for when the number of epochs was equal to three. The results are shown in Table 3. In this case, GILT-PSO outperforms the other algorithms or returns a result that is comparable to the best of them, in 13 cases out of 20.

4.4 Execution Time Comparison

Another advantage of the layered approach used by GILT-PSO is its efficiency, in terms of the running time needed for the training phase. As already discussed, optimizing only one layer at a time allows the chosen optimizer to reduce the dimensionality of the search space. First, working with smaller candidate solutions reduces the computational time needed to perform the mathematical operations involved in the optimization process. Second, having smaller candidate solutions also means working with smaller amounts of data, thereby reducing the consequent overhead.

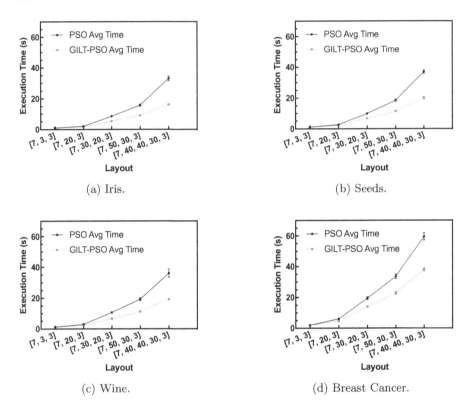

(a) Iris.

(b) Seeds.

(c) Wine.

(d) Breast Cancer.

Fig. 1. Comparison of the average execution times between the GILT-PSO algorithm and the PSO algorithm. The error bars account for the standard deviations.

It is worth to notice that only the running times regarding the standard PSO and GILT-PSO are presented in this paper because both algorithms rely on the framework which was created in the context of this research, i.e., we can guarantee the implementation compatibility for both PSO-based approaches, while the used implementation of the backpropagation relies on the external library [20]. However, GILT-PSO and PSO were the methods that returned the best results in terms of accuracy, as reported in the previous section. As such, it makes sense to compare those two systems as well, in terms of running time. The comparison is reported in Fig. 1. Based on this figure, it is clear that GILT-PSO is faster than PSO, and that the difference between these two methods grows increasingly visible as the size of the network increases.

4.5   Non-parametric Statistical Test with Control Method

To evaluate whether the previously presented results differ from each other in a statistically significant way, a statistical analysis, based on a non-parametric test [4] has been performed. In particular, given that the data are not normally

Table 4. Adjusted p-values for the post-hoc procedures for Aligned Friedman test (backpropagation is the control method) for 2 epochs.

Algorithm	p	z	Bonferroni	Holm	Holland	Rom	Finner	Li
GILT-PSO	0.056	1.915	0.056	0.025	0.025	0.025	0.025	0.032
PSO	0.385	0.869	0.385	0.050	0.050	0.050	0.050	0.050

Table 5. Adjusted p-values for the post-hoc procedures for Aligned Friedman test (backpropagation is the control method) for 3 epochs.

Algorithm	p	z	Bonferroni	Holm	Holland	Rom	Finner	Li
GILT-PSO	0.182	1.335	0.182	0.025	0.025	0.025	0.025	0.037
PSO	0.298	1.041	0.298	0.050	0.050	0.050	0.050	0.050

distributed, an aligned Friedman test was executed for multiple comparisons. The null hypothesis H_0 for this test states that the medians between the different algorithms are identical. The goal of the test is to confirm this hypothesis or reject it, with the level of confidence $\alpha = 0.05$. The p-value we have obtained applying the Aligned Friedman method is equal to 0.0005. This value is lower than the chosen level of confidence, which confirms the existence of statistically significant differences among the results returned by the studied algorithms. Given that H_0 is rejected, we can proceed with the *post-hoc* procedures to investigate whether the results returned by the PSO-based methods (PSO and GILT-PSO) are statistically different from the ones returned by the backpropagation. To this end, a new null hypothesis H_0' is used. H_0' states that the performance of a PSO-based algorithm is identical to the one of the backpropagation, which is used as a control method. Table 4 reports the adjusted p-values for the post-hoc procedures for Aligned Friedman test, in case the number of epochs is equal to 2. In the table, the generic (i, j) adjusted p-value represents the smallest level of significance that results in the rejection of H_0' between algorithm i and the control method j, i.e., the lowest value for which the algorithm i and the control method are not statistically equivalent, for the j-th *post-hoc* procedure. The lower a value, the more likely the null hypothesis can be rejected. A very important feature of such a table is that it is not tied to a pre-set level of significance α. Rather, depending on the value of α we choose, the *post-hoc* procedures will either accept or reject H_0'. Considering the value used for α, the table says that the statistical equivalence between backpropagation and GILT-PSO can be statistically rejected by all of the *post-hoc* procedures, except for Bonferroni since the adjusted p-values for those methods are lower than 0.05. Furthermore, the statistical equivalence between PSO and backpropagation cannot be rejected by all the procedures.

For the number of epochs equal to 3, the results of the *post-hoc* analysis are reported in Table 5. Considering the value used for α, this analysis suggests that the statistical equivalence between backpropagation and GILT-PSO can be rejected by all of the *post-hoc* procedures except for Bonferroni, as all the adjusted p-values for those methods are smaller than 0.05. Moreover, the statistical equivalence between PSO and backpropagation cannot be statistically rejected by all the procedures.

5   Conclusions

A new greedy optimization algorithm, called greedy iterative layered training (GILT), to optimize the synaptic weights of an artificial neural network (ANN), was proposed in this paper. GILT uses a population-based optimization heuristic and works by optimizing the weights by layers. At each step, the synaptic weights of one layer are optimized, without modifying the weights of all the other connections in the network. Given that in this study we used particle swarm optimization (PSO), the system was referred to as GILT-PSO.

According to the presented results, GILT-PSO outperforms backpropagation when considering the best networks trained among a set of 30 runs; it also outperforms PSO in terms of training time, while maintaining a comparable exploratory power. The presented statistical analysis shows that there is a significant difference between the results returned by GILT-PSO and the ones of backpropagation. Furthermore, the results returned by GILT-PSO in the different runs possess a smaller standard deviation than the ones of backpropagation, which seems to indicate that GILT-PSO may exhibit more stable (and thus more reliable) behavior.

These achievements are important and encourage us to pursue the study, particularly considering that GILT benefits from other potential advantages: it is not bounded to a specific optimization technique or fitness measure. In other words, in principle, it can be used not only with the PSO but also with any other population-based optimization heuristic. Moreover, when defining a new fitness measure and a new representation for the individuals, GILT can also be used to evolve the structure of the network as well as the neurons activation functions.

In the future, we plan to extend the study by using other types of optimization techniques, instead of PSO, and by extending the representation of the solutions and the fitness in such a way that GILT can be used to optimize the synaptic weights, the structure of the network and the activation functions of the neurons at the same time. Moreover, we plan to implement minibatch learning to increase the efficiency of our methodology. Furthermore, to better assess the capabilities and limitations of the proposed algorithm, more (and more complex) test cases must be considered.

Finally, we are currently working on the development of strategies to further improve the efficiency (in terms of training time) of the proposed algorithm. In the current version, in fact, to calculate fitness we need to perform a certain number of matrix operations, that involve the evaluation of the whole network.

But considering that at each step only one layer at a time can change, the process can be significantly optimized. In particular, each time that a layer is considered, it is possible to store the results of the partial evaluations of the previous layers. In this way, we could perform only the matrix operations of the current and following layers. It makes sense to expect that, particularly for deep networks, this will represent a considerable performance improvement.

Acknowledgements. This work was partially supported by FCT, Portugal through funding of LASIGE Research Unit (UID/CEC/00408/2019), and projects PREDICT (PTDC/CCI-CIF/29877/2017), BINDER (PTDC/CCI-INF/29168/2017), GADgET (DS-AIPA/DS/0022/2018) and AICE (DSAIPA/DS/0113/2019) and by the financial support from the Slovenian Research Agency (research core funding No. P5-0410).

This work is the result of the collaboration between the University of Salerno and Nova IMS. The first two authors contributed equally to this work.

References

1. Van den Bergh, F., Engelbrecht, A.P.: Cooperative learning in neural networks using particle swarm optimizers. South Afr. Comput. J. **2000**(26), 84–90 (2000)
2. Charytanowicz, M., Niewczas, J., Kulczycki, P., Kowalski, P.A., Łukasik, S., Żak, S.: Complete gradient clustering algorithm for features analysis of x-ray images. In: Piętka, E., Kawa, J. (eds.) Information Technologies in Biomedicine. AINSC, vol. 69, pp. 15–24. Springer, Heidelberg (2010). https://doi.org/10.1007/978-3-642-13105-9_2
3. De Falco, I., Cioppa, A.D., Natale, P., Tarantino, E.: Artificial neural networks optimization by means of evolutionary algorithms. In: Chawdhry, P.K., Roy, R., Pant, R.K. (eds.) Soft Computing in Engineering Design and Manufacturing, pp. 3–12. Springer, London (1998). https://doi.org/10.1007/978-1-4471-0427-8_1
4. Derrac, J., García, S., Molina, D., Herrera, F.: A practical tutorial on the use of nonparametric statistical tests as a methodology for comparing evolutionary and swarm intelligence algorithms. Swarm Evol. Comput. **1**, 3–18 (2011)
5. Dheeru, D., Karra Taniskidou, E.: UCI machine learning repository (2017). http://archive.ics.uci.edu/ml
6. Eberhart, Shi, Y.: Particle swarm optimization: developments, applications and resources. In: Proceedings of the 2001 Congress on Evolutionary Computation (IEEE Cat. No.01TH8546), vol. 1, pp. 81–86, May 2001
7. Eberhart, R., Kennedy, J.: A new optimizer using particle swarm theory. In: Proceedings of the Sixth International Symposium on Micro Machine and Human Science, MHS 1995, pp. 39–43, October 1995. https://doi.org/10.1109/MHS.1995.494215
8. Fisher, R.A.: The use of multiple measurements in taxonomic problems. Ann. Eugenics **7**(7), 179–188 (1936)
9. Garro, B.A., Vázquez, R.A.: Designing artificial neural networks using particle swarm optimization algorithms. Comput. Intell. Neurosci. **2015**, 61 (2015)
10. Haykin, S.: Neural Networks: A Comprehensive Foundation. Prentice Hall PTR, Upper Saddle River (1994)
11. Hochreiter, S.: Untersuchungen zu dynamischen neuronalen netzen. Diploma, Technische Universität München **91**(1) (1991)

12. Hornik, K.: Approximation capabilities of multilayer feedforward networks. Neural Netw. **4**(2), 251–257 (1991)
13. Hornik, K., Stinchcombe, M., White, H.: Multilayer feedforward networks are universal approximators. Neural Netw. **2**(5), 359–366 (1989)
14. Irie, B., Miyake, S.: Capabilities of three-layered perceptrons. In: IEEE International Conference on Neural Networks, vol. 1, p. 218 (1988)
15. Kolbusz, J., Rozycki, P., Wilamowski, B.M.: The study of architecture MLP with linear neurons in order to eliminate the "vanishing gradient" problem. In: Rutkowski, L., Korytkowski, M., Scherer, R., Tadeusiewicz, R., Zadeh, L.A., Zurada, J.M. (eds.) ICAISC 2017. LNCS (LNAI), vol. 10245, pp. 97–106. Springer, Cham (2017). https://doi.org/10.1007/978-3-319-59063-9_9
16. Kiranyaz, S., Ince, T., Yildirim, A., Gabbouj, M.: Evolutionary artificial neural networks by multi-dimensional particle swarm optimization. Neural Netw. **22**(10), 1448–1462 (2009)
17. Mangasarian, O.L., Street, W.N., Wolberg, W.H.: Breast cancer diagnosis and prognosis via linear programming. Oper. Res. **43**(4), 570–577 (1995)
18. Montana, D.J., Davis, L.: Training feedforward neural networks using genetic algorithms. In: IJCAI, vol. 89, pp. 762–767 (1989)
19. Moreira, M., Fiesler, E.: Neural networks with adaptive learning rate and momentum terms. Idiap-RR Idiap-RR-04-1995, IDIAP, Martigny, Switzerland, October 1995
20. Pedregosa, F., et al.: Scikit-learn: machine learning in python. J. Mach. Learn. Res. **12**, 2825–2830 (2011)
21. Rashid, T.: Make Your Own Neural Network. CreateSpace Independent Publishing Platform (2016)
22. Rumelhart, D.E., Hinton, G.E., Williams, R.J.: Learning internal representations by error propagation. Technical report, California Univ San Diego La Jolla Inst for Cognitive Science (1985)
23. Ding, S., Li, H., Su, C., Yu, J., Jin, F.: Evolutionary artificial neural networks: a review. Artif. Intell. Rev. **39**, 251–260 (2013)
24. Samarasinghe, S.: Neural Networks for Applied Sciences and Engineering: From Fundamentals to Complex Pattern Recognition. Auerbach Publications (2016)
25. Settles, M., Rylander, B.: Neural network learning using particle swarm optimization. In: Advances in Information Science and Soft Computing, pp. 224–226 (2002)
26. Shaw, D., Kinsner, W.: Chaotic simulated annealing in multilayer feedforward networks. In: Canadian Conference on Electrical and Computer Engineering, vol. 1, pp. 265–269. IEEE (1996)
27. Sher, G.I.: Handbook of Neuroevolution Through Erlang. Springer, New York (2013). https://doi.org/10.1007/978-1-4614-4463-3
28. Si, T., Hazra, S., Jana, N.D.: Artificial neural network training using differential evolutionary algorithm for classification. In: Satapathy, S.C., Avadhani, P.S., Abraham, A. (eds.) Proceedings of the International Conference on Information Systems Design and Intelligent Applications 2012 (INDIA). AINSC, vol. 132, pp. 769–778. Springer, Heidelberg (2012). https://doi.org/10.1007/978-3-642-27443-5_88
29. Street, W.N., Wolberg, W.H., Mangasarian, O.L.: Nuclear feature extraction for breast tumor diagnosis. Proc. Soc. Photo-Opt. Inst. Eng. **1993** (1999)
30. Whitley, D., Starkweather, T., Bogart, C.: Genetic algorithms and neural networks: optimizing connections and connectivity. Parallel Comput. **14**, 347–361 (1990)
31. Yao, X.: Evolving artificial neural networks. Proc. IEEE **87**(9), 1423–1447 (1999)

32. Zhang, C., Shao, H., Li, Y.: Particle swarm optimisation for evolving artificial neural network. In: IEEE International Conference on Systems, Man, and Cybernetics, vol. 4, pp. 2487–2490. IEEE (2000)
33. Zhang, G., Patuwo, B.E., Hu, M.Y.: Forecasting with artificial neural networks: the state of the art. Int. J. Forecast. **14**(1), 35–62 (1998)
34. Zhang, J.R., Zhang, J., Lok, T.M., Lyu, M.R.: A hybrid particle swarm optimization-back-propagation algorithm for feedforward neural network training. Appl. Math. Comput. **185**(2), 1026–1037 (2007)

Evolution of Scikit-Learn Pipelines with Dynamic Structured Grammatical Evolution

Filipe Assunção[1,2](✉)[iD], Nuno Lourenço[1][iD], Bernardete Ribeiro[1][iD], and Penousal Machado[1][iD]

[1] CISUC, Department of Informatics Engineering,
University of Coimbra, Coimbra, Portugal
{fga,naml,bribeiro,machado}@dei.uc.pt
[2] LASIGE, Department of Informatics, Faculdade de Ciencias,
Universidade de Lisboa, Lisbon, Portugal

Abstract. The deployment of Machine Learning (ML) models is a difficult and time-consuming job that comprises a series of sequential and correlated tasks that go from the data pre-processing, and the design and extraction of features, to the choice of the ML algorithm and its parameterisation. The task is even more challenging considering that the design of features is in many cases problem specific, and thus requires domain-expertise. To overcome these limitations Automated Machine Learning (AutoML) methods seek to automate, with few or no human-intervention, the design of pipelines, i.e., automate the selection of the sequence of methods that have to be applied to the raw data. These methods have the potential to enable non-expert users to use ML, and provide expert users with solutions that they would unlikely consider. In particular, this paper describes AutoML-DSGE – a novel grammar-based framework that adapts Dynamic Structured Grammatical Evolution (DSGE) to the evolution of Scikit-Learn classification pipelines. The experimental results include comparing AutoML-DSGE to another grammar-based AutoML framework, Resilient Classification Pipeline Evolution (RECIPE), and show that the average performance of the classification pipelines generated by AutoML-DSGE is always superior to the average performance of RECIPE; the differences are statistically significant in 3 out of the 10 used datasets.

Keywords: Automated Machine Learning · Scikit-Learn · Dynamic Structured Grammatical Evolution

1 Introduction

Nowadays, with the ever-growing amount of collected information the challenge is not concerned with the lack of information, but rather on how to design efficient Machine Learning (ML) models that can extract useful knowledge, or

P. A. Castillo et al. (Eds.): EvoApplications 2020, LNCS 12104, pp. 530–545, 2020.
https://doi.org/10.1007/978-3-030-43722-0_34

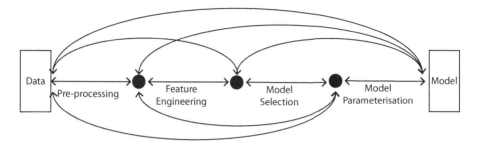

Fig. 1. From data to ML model deployment.

aid in the automation of daily-life tasks. Typically, to deploy a Machine Learning (ML) system we need to follow a pre-defined number of steps: (i) pre-process the data; (ii) design, extract, and select features, i.e., data characteristics; (iii) select the most appropriate ML model; and (iv) parameterise the ML model. The flow of the iterative steps that one must traverse from the data to the model is depicted in Fig. 1: the multiple steps are all interconnected, which means that for example in case we have already a model, but we acknowledge that the set of features is not the most adequate one we may be thrown back to the beginning of the process again. In addition, even when the practitioner is a ML expert, and is well aware of which models are more adequate for particular tasks, it still needs to design features, which are domain-dependent, and therefore often require domain-expertise, and sometimes multidisciplinary teams.

To overcome the difficulty caused by the correlation between the multiple choices that have to be made prior to deploying a ML system we can resort to Automated Machine Learning (AutoML). In brief words Automated Machine Learning (AutoML) concerns searching for the most effective ML models for a particular task. One of the key-advantages of AutoML is that it does not require human input, and consequently the gain is twofold: (i) on the one hand it empowers non-expert users with the ability to apply ML models to their problems; (ii) on the other hand, it opens the door to novel solutions, that a human-expert would potentially neglect.

The current work focuses on AutoML applied to classification datasets. The common approach of AutoML to this sort of problems is to evolve a classification pipeline, i.e., an ordered sequence of tasks that are performed to accurately distinguish between the different classes of the problem. The pipeline tasks can be any known form of data pre-processing; feature design, extraction, or selection; or ML algorithm. In particular, we evolve Scikit-Learn [1] pipelines with Dynamic Structured Grammatical Evolution (DSGE) [2]. Our main contributions are:

- The proposal of a new grammar-based AutoML framework based on Dynamic Structured Grammatical Evolution (DSGE): AutoML-DSGE;
- The release of the framework as open-source, available on GitHub: https://github.com/fillassuncao/automl-dsge;

- The performance of a wide set of experiments on multiple classification tasks;
- The comparison of AutoML-DSGE to previous AutoML methods. The results show that the results of AutoML-DSGE are always superior to those reported by other grammar-based AutoML methods, and are statistically superior in 3 out of the 10 used datasets.

The remainder of the paper is structured as follows. Section 2 surveys multiple AutoML methods; Sect. 3 describes DSGE; Sect. 4 details the evolution of Scikit-Learn classification pipelines with DSGE; Sect. 5 analyses the experimental results; and Sect. 6 draws conclusions and addresses future work.

2   Related Work

The most common and widely used form of AutoML is grid search: the best parameterisation of a ML model is discovered by an exhaustive search of all the combinations of a grid of parameters. However, grid search suffers from the curse of dimensionality, i.e., the explosion in the number of parameters drastically increases the amount of setups that need to be tested. To deal with the previous we can instead use grid search methods that seek to narrow the number of setups, for example by adapting the resolution of the grid in run-time [3]. Nonetheless, grid search has the advantage that it is highly parallelisable. To overcome the issue of having to explore the entire grid of hyper-parameters we may instead apply random search. While grid search performs an exhaustive enumeration of the domain, random search selects the combinations of the hyper-parameters in a stochastic manner. Random search is as parallelisable as grid search. Nonetheless, it is non-adaptive [4], and with very high dimensional search spaces it also struggles to find near-optimal solutions. According to Bergstra et al., given the same computational time, random search is able to discover better parameterisations for Artificial Neural Networks (ANNs) than grid search [5,6].

An alternative to grid and random search are Bayesian methods [7], which model probabilistically the behaviour of the system, in order to drive search towards regions of the domain that are prone to generate good parameterisations. Snoek et al. applied Bayesian optimisation to tune the parameters of the Branin-Hoo function, Logistic Regression, Online Linear Discriminant Analysis, Latent Structured Support Vector Machines, and Convolutional Neural Networks [8]. Bergstra et al. have demonstrated that statistical methods can perform better at hyper-parameter optimisation [9] than manual tuning or random search. Other class of heuristic approach is Evolutionary Computation (EC), which has also been widely used to optimise ML algorithms (e.g., [10,11]).

The majority of the methods mentioned until now focus on the optimisation of a specific ML model. Nonetheless, the ultimate goal of AutoML is to fully automate the entire process: from the data pre-processing, and feature design and selection up to the model choice and parameterisation. Recently, there have been competitions seeking to promote such systems; an example is ChaLearn [12]. The challenge is organised into 6 increasingly difficult levels (preparation, novice, intermediate, advanced, expert, and master), where the ultimate goal is to "create the perfect black box eliminating the human in the loop" [13].

Weka [14] and Scikit-learn [1] are examples of two ML libraries that enable users to explore their data and easily deploy learning models. They make available stable implementations of the vast majority of ML methods, but despite providing default parameterisation they are not suit for effectively solving all problems. Auto-WEKA [15,16], Tree-based Pipeline Optimization Tool (TPOT) [17], Hyperopt-Sklearn [18], Auto-Sklearn [19], and Resilient Classification Pipeline Evolution (RECIPE) [20], are examples of methods that aim at evolving the pipelines for the Weka and Scikit-learn libraries, from the pre-processing of the raw data to the parameterisation of the model to be used (in essence they automate the flow-chart depicted in Fig. 1). Except for TPOT and Resilient Classification Pipeline Evolution (RECIPE), all the previous methodologies are based on Bayesian optimisation; TPOT and RECIPE use Genetic Programming (GP). The goal is to search for Weka or Scikit-Learn pipelines, i.e., sequences of the libraries' primitives that perform feature selection and classification. The frameworks are not only responsible for selecting the primitives but also promote their parameterisation. Auto-Weka, Hyperopt-Sklearn, Auto-Sklearn and RECIPE generate pipelines of fixed size; TPOT allows the generation of pipelines of unrestricted size, i.e., it does not have a fixed number of pre-processors, and multiple copies of the dataset can be used in simultaneous, so that multiple methods are applied to it, and then the features combined. Whilst the majority of these approaches target the maximisation of the classification performance, in addition TPOT also seeks for compact pipelines.

The focus of the current work is on AutoML approaches based on EC. In particular, we are interested in grammar-based methods, such as RECIPE. The main advantage of grammar-based methods over others is that they facilitate the definition of the search space, and thus in case we have a-priori knowledge about the problem we can bias the grammar. On the other hand, the grammar enables the framework to be easily extended: to add more methods to the search space we just require the definition of new production rules. To the best of our knowledge, RECIPE is the only grammar-based AutoML framework that aims at optimising classification pipelines. The current paper introduces AutoML-DSGE and compares it to RECIPE. AutoML-DSGE is based on DSGE, which is detailed next.

3   Dynamic Structured Grammatical Evolution

To properly introduce DSGE [2] we must start by detailing Structured Grammatical Evolution (SGE) [21], which is a variant of Grammatical Evolution (GE) [22]. The three methods are grammar-based GP approaches, and thus the search space is defined by means of a Context-Free Grammar (CFG). CFGs are rewriting systems, and thus the grammar, G, can be formally defined by a 4-tuple $G = (N, T, P, S)$, where: (i) N is the set of non-terminal symbols; (ii) T is the set of terminal symbols; (iii) P is the set of production rules of the form

$x ::= y$, $x \in N$ and $y \in \{N \cup T\}^*$; and (iv) S is the start symbol (or axiom). An example of a CFG is shown in Fig. 2. The main difference between the methods lies on the encoding of the individuals, and thereby on the genotype decoding procedure.

The individuals in GE are encoded as linear ordered sequences of integers; each integer represents a derivation step and is called a codon. The genotype to phenotype mapping works by reading the codons sequentially, from left to right. Starting from the axiom the mapping procedure iteratively decides which production rule should be applied to expand the leftmost non-terminal symbol. To select the production rule the modulo mathematical operation (%) is used to find the remainder after the division of the codon by the number of possibilities for expanding the leftmost non-terminal symbol. The remainder defines the expansion possibility that should be applied to the leftmost non-terminal symbol. No codon is read when there is only a possibility for expanding a non-terminal symbol. On the other hand, grammars can be recursive, and thus the number of codons may be insufficient; in such cases the sequence of codons is re-used from the start (wrapping). To avoid entering an infinite wrapping loop, or generating solutions that are too complex to be evaluated, a maximum number of wrappings is set, and when this bound is reached the mapping procedure is halted, and the individual is assigned the worst possible fitness value.

The drawbacks commonly pointed to GE are low locality and high redundancy [23,24]. The locality measures how the changes in the genotype impact the phenotype. In GE there is not a one-to-one mapping between the codons and the non-terminal symbols, and therefore it is easy for a change in one of the codons to affect all the derivation steps from that point on-wards (low locality). On the other hand, the redundancy is concerned to the fact that in GE it is possible that different genotypes generate the same phenotype because of the modulo operation used on the decoding procedure.

SGE solves the limitations of GE by introducing a new genotypic representation that defines a one-to-one mapping between the codons and the non-terminal symbols, i.e., instead of a single ordered sequence of codons the genotype is composed by multiple independent ordered sequences of codons, one for each non-terminal symbol. The size of each sequence of codons is of the maximum number of possible expansions for the non-terminal symbol it encodes, and thus there is no wrapping. The use of the modulo operation is not required as we know exactly which non-terminal symbol the codon encodes.

In SGE the genotypes encode more codons than the ones used in the decoding procedure, and consequently the genetic operators may easily act upon non-coding genes. This under some circumstances can slow down evolution. To prevent this effect, the genotype of DSGE is similar to those of SGE with one main difference: it only encodes the codons strictly required for decoding the individual. In case mutations affect the amount of necessary codons, the genotype is expanded. In this paper we use DSGE; the code for DSGE can be found in the GitHub repository https://github.com/nunolourenco/sge3.

Table 1. Scikit-Learn classes that are allowed to be part of the pipelines.

Pre-processing	Feature manipulation	Classification
Imputer	VarianceThreshold	ExtraTreeClassifier
Normalizer	SelectPercentile	DecisionTreeClassifier
MinMaxScaler	SelectFpr	GaussianNB
MaxAbsScaler	SelectFwe	BernouliNB
RobustScaler	SelectFdr	MultinominalNB
StandardScaler	RFE	SVC
	REFCV	NuSVC
	SelectFromModel	KNeighborsClassifier
	IncrementalPCA	RadiusNeighborsClassifier
	PCA	NearestCentroid
	FastICA	LDA
	GaussianRandomProjection	QDA
	SparseRandomProjection	LogisticRegression
	RBFSampler	LogisticRegressionCV
	Nystroem	PassiveAggressiveClassifier
	FeatureAgglomeration	Perceptron
	PolynomialFeatures	Ridge
		RidgeCV
		AdaBoostClassifier
		GradientBoostingClassifier
		RandomForestClassifier
		ExtraTreesClassifier

4 AutoML-DSGE

The goal of this paper is to introduce a new framework, to which we call AutoML-DSGE, that adapts DSGE to the evolution of classification pipelines. In particular, we optimise Scikit-Learn [1] pipelines. Next, we define pipelines (Sect. 4.1), the used grammar (Sect. 4.2), and detail the evolution of pipelines using DSGE (Sect. 4.3). The code for AutoML-DSGE is released as open-source software, and can be found in the GitHub repository https://github.com/fillassuncao/automl-dsge.

4.1 Pipelines

In the field of ML a classification pipeline is defined as an ordered set of operations that are performed to the data instances in order to accurately separate them in the multiple classes of the dataset. The operations in the pipeline can be grouped into 3 disjoint sets: (i) data pre-processing; (ii) feature design and

$$\langle\text{pipeline}\rangle ::= \langle\text{preprocessing}\rangle \langle\text{algorithm}\rangle \tag{1}$$
$$| \langle\text{algorithm}\rangle \tag{2}$$
$$\langle\text{preprocessing}\rangle ::= \langle\text{imputation}\rangle \mid \langle\text{bounding}\rangle \mid \langle\text{dimensionality}\rangle \mid \tag{3}$$
$$| \langle\text{binarizer}\rangle \mid \langle\text{imputation}\rangle \langle\text{bounding}\rangle \tag{4}$$
$$| \langle\text{imputation}\rangle \langle\text{binarizer}\rangle \tag{5}$$
$$| \ldots \tag{6}$$
$$\langle\text{imputation}\rangle ::= \text{preprocessing:imputer} \langle\text{strategy\_imp}\rangle \tag{7}$$
$$\langle\text{strategy\_imp}\rangle ::= \text{strategy:mean} \mid \text{strategy:median} \mid \text{strategy:most\_frequent} \tag{8}$$
$$\ldots \tag{9}$$
$$\ldots \tag{10}$$
$$\langle\text{algorithm}\rangle ::= \langle\text{strong}\rangle \mid \langle\text{weak}\rangle \mid \langle\text{tree\_ensemble}\rangle \tag{11}$$
$$\ldots \tag{12}$$
$$\ldots \tag{13}$$
$$\langle\text{weak}\rangle ::= \langle\text{nearest}\rangle \mid \langle\text{discriminant}\rangle \mid \ldots \tag{14}$$
$$\ldots \tag{15}$$
$$\ldots \tag{16}$$
$$\langle\text{nearest}\rangle ::= \text{classifier:radius\_neighbors} \langle\text{radius}\rangle \langle\text{weights}\rangle \tag{17}$$
$$\langle\text{k\_algorithm}\rangle \langle\text{leaf\_size}\rangle \langle\text{p}\rangle \langle\text{d\_metric}\rangle \tag{18}$$
$$\langle\text{radius}\rangle ::= \text{radius:RANDFLOAT(1.0,30.0)} \tag{19}$$
$$\langle\text{weights}\rangle ::= \text{weights:uniform} \mid \text{weights:distance} \tag{20}$$
$$\langle\text{k\_algorithm}\rangle ::= \text{algorithm:auto} \mid \text{algorithm:brute} \mid \ldots \tag{21}$$
$$\langle\text{leaf\_size}\rangle ::= \text{leaf\_size:RANDINT(5,100)} \tag{22}$$
$$\ldots \tag{23}$$
$$\ldots \tag{24}$$

Fig. 2. CFG used by AutoML-DSGE for optimising Scikit-Learn pipelines.

selection; and (iii) classification. Table 1 enumerates the methods that are considered to form the pipelines in the current work. Recall that we focus on classification pipelines, and thus only classification algorithms are taken into account. Nonetheless, the extension of the approach to regression algorithms is straightforward. We will optimise Scikit-Learn pipelines, and thus the methods in the table are Scikit-Learn implementations. Further details can be found in https://scikit-learn.org/stable/user_guide.html.

4.2   Grammar

The grammar used by AutoML-DSGE describes the search space of the Scikit-Learn classification pipelines. The grammar is shown in Fig. 2. The production rules are only partially shown because of space constraints: the grammar is comprised of 89 production rules that encode the different pipeline methods and their parameterisation. The complete grammars can be found in https://github.com/fillassuncao/automl-dsge/tree/master/sge/grammars. There is a separate grammar for each dataset because of specific dataset parameters, e.g., number of features. The used grammars are adapted from the grammars used by RECIPE, which is the method we compare AutoML-DSGE to.

The axiom of the grammar is the pipeline non-terminal symbol, and consequently the pipeline can be found by either pre-processing and classification methods (line 1) or just by the classification method (line 2). The current version of AutoML-DSGE does not consider ensembles. The extension of AutoML-DSGE to enable the optimisation of ensembles could be easily introduced by adding a recursive production rule to build pipelines with more than one classifier algorithm, each a voter of the ensemble. The pre-processing methods manipulate the dataset and features (lines 3–6), and the classification methods cover a wide range of ML approaches, amongst which, are clustering methods, Support Vector Machines (SVMs), trees, or ANNs (lines 11–18). In more detail, the pipeline methods are encoded as follows: the pre-processing and classification methods are encoded respectively by the preprocessing and classifier tags, that are placed before the method name (e.g., classifier:radius_neighbors in line 17). The method name must match the name of the function that is used in the mapping from the phenotype to the Scikit-Learn interpretable code (see Sect. 4.3). The same rationale is applied to the method parameters, where the parameter name precedes the parameter value. The parameters can be of three types: (i) closed choice, e.g., the weights parameter, in line 20, that can assume the values uniform or distance; (ii) random integer, e.g., the leaf size parameter in line 22; or (iii) random float, e.g., the radius parameter in line 19.

The search space of AutoML-DSGE, i.e., the number of possible combinations of the grammar is greater than 9.39×10^{17}. The continuous parameters can generate an infinite number of possibilities, and thus are not considered in the search space size. In addition, the parameters related to the number of features are also not taken into account because they are problem dependent.

4.3   Evolution of Pipelines

The pipelines are evolved using DSGE, and therefore, a population of individuals is continuously evolved throughout a given number of generations, until a stop criteria is met. Each individual encodes a different pipeline. The core of the representation of the individuals in AutoML-DSGE is similar to the representation scheme used in DSGE, with one main difference related to the need to directly keep real values in the genotype. Otherwise, they would have to be encoded by production rules, such as:

Table 2. Description of the used datasets.

Dataset	#Inst.	#Feat.	Feat. types	#Classes	Missing
Breast Cancer	699	9	Integer	2	Yes
Car Evaluation	1728	5	Categorical	4	No
Caenorhabditis Elegans	478	765	Binary	2	No
Chen-2002	179	85	Real	2	No
Chowdary-2006	104	182	Real	2	No
Credit-G	1000	20	Real/Categorical	2	No
Drosophila Melanogaster	119	182	Real	2	No
DNA-No-PPI-T11	135	104	Real/Categorical	2	Yes
Glass	214	9	Real	7	No
Wine Quality-Red	1599	11	Real	10	No

$$\langle \text{randfloat} \rangle ::= \langle \text{signal} \rangle \langle \text{rec-number} \rangle . \langle \text{rec-number} \rangle$$
$$\langle \text{signal} \rangle ::= - \mid +$$
$$\langle \text{rec-number} \rangle ::= \langle \text{number} \rangle \mid \langle \text{number} \rangle \langle \text{number-recursive} \rangle$$
$$\langle \text{number} \rangle ::= 0 \mid 1 \mid 2 \mid 3 \mid 4$$
$$5 \mid 6 \mid 7 \mid 8 \mid 9$$

The encoding of real values by means of production rules has two main disadvantages. On the one hand it enlarges the search space. On the other hand there is no easy way to control the limits (minimum and maximum) of the generated real values. In case the search space encompasses two or more real values with different ranges there would be the need for different production rules, one for each real value range. Because of the aforementioned we encode the integers and floats directly, as real values. When expanding the grammar, when we reach a terminal symbol that is either RANDINT or RANDFLOAT we store a tuple in the genotype. The tuple has the format (rand-type, rand-min, rand-max, rand-value), where rand-type can assume integer of float, the rand-min and rand-max are the minimum and maximum limits of the range, and the rand-value is the randomly generated value of the type rand-type, and within the [rand-min, rand-max] range. The tuple is necessary for performing the mutation, i.e., when a mutation is applied to an individual and it is required to generate a new random value for a specific parameter we must know its type and allowed range.

DSGE is a grammar-based approach, and thus the genotype is completely separate from the phenotype. The phenotype does not directly represent a trainable pipeline. Consequently, for assessing the fitness of the individuals we have to perform two sequential steps: (i) map the genotype to the phenotype; (ii) map the phenotype to Scikit-Learn interpretable model. To map the genotype to the phenotype the decoding procedure of DSGE is adapted: the only difference lies in the decoding of the real-values, where the value in the last position of the tuple is read. The phenotype of AutoML-DSGE is readable, despite not

Table 3. Experimental parameters.

Parameter	Value
Number of runs	30
Number of generations	100
Population size	100
Mutation rate	10%
Crossover rate	90%
Elitism	5 individuals
Tournament size	2
Max. pipeline train time	5 min
Max. #generations without improvement	5

being Scikit-Learn executable code. The readability of the phenotype is facilitated by the fact that each parameter has the parameter name associated to the value; an example of a phenotype is "classifier:random_forest criterion:gini max_depth:None n_estimators:50 min_weight_fraction_leaf:0.01 ... ".

To map the phenotype to a Scikit-Learn interpretable pipeline we have to traverse the phenotype linearly from left to right and for each pre-processing or classifier method create the corresponding Scikit-Learn object. Therefore, for each method in the grammar we have to build a function that creates the Scikit-Learn object: the function receives all the parameters that are encoded in the grammar and outputs the Scikit-Learn object. Whenever the grammar is extended to include more methods we have to create the corresponding functions.

To evaluate the evolved pipelines we use cross-validation (with 3 folds). In the current paper the fitness is the average of the performances on the cross-validation. The metric used to evaluate the performance is the F-measure. We decide for this metric because some of the datasets where we will be conducting the experiments are highly unbalanced.

The goal of AutoML is to generate (automatically) effective Scikit-Learn classification pipelines that non-expert ML users can deploy in their problems and domains. With this in mind, similarly to other approaches, we limit the train time of each pipeline to a maximum CPU time, that in this paper is set to five minutes. For the same reason evolution is halted when there is no improvement for five generations.

5   Experimentation

To investigate the ability of AutoML-DSGE to generate effective classification Scikit-Learn pipelines we apply it to the classification of 10 datasets, which are described in Sect. 5.1. The experimental setup is detailed in Sect. 5.2, and the analysis of the evolutionary results, and comparison to the pipelines generated by RECIPE is carried out in Sect. 5.3.

Table 4. AutoML-DSGE, and RECIPE comparative performance. The results are averages of 30 independent runs.

Dataset	AutoML-DSGE	RECIPE	p-value
Breast Cancer	**0.9568 ± 0.0296**	0.9311 ± 0.0798	**0.0264** (++)
Car Evaluation	**0.9964 ± 0.0068**	0.9962 ± 0.0079	0.9761
Caenorhabditis Elegans	**0.6140 ± 0.0644**	0.6049 ± 0.0681	0.7948
Chen-2002	**0.9451 ± 0.0413**	0.9292 ± 0.0618	0.3371
Chowdary-2006	**0.9970 ± 0.0163**	0.9812 ± 0.0514	0.0679
Credit-G	**0.7400 ± 0.0370**	0.7075 ± 0.0359	**0.0008** (+++)
Drosophila Melanogaster	**0.6679 ± 0.1001**	0.6353 ± 0.1518	0.2585
DNA-No-PPI-T11	**0.7114 ± 0.1194**	0.7021 ± 0.0761	0.9681
Glass	**0.7628 ± 0.1095**	0.7325 ± 0.1021	0.0524
Wine Quality-Red	**0.6600 ± 0.0387**	0.6430 ± 0.0422	**0.0257** (++)

5.1   Datasets

To enable a fair comparison between AutoML-DSGE and RECIPE we conduct the experiments on the same datasets used by RECIPE: 10 datasets – 5 from the University of California Irvine (UCI) ML repository [25], and 5 from bioinformatics [26–28]. A summary of the dataset characteristics is shown in Table 2. The table provides information on the number of instances (#Inst.), number of features (#Feat.), type of features (Feat. types), number of classes (#Classes), and if there are or not missing values in the dataset (Missing).

5.2   Experimental Setup

The parameters required for performing the experiments contained in this article are described in Table 3. The parameters are the same for AutoML-DSGE and RECIPE. The maximum CPU train time is measure in minutes, and thus it is important to mention that the experiments are performed in a dedicated server with an Intel(R) Core(TM) i7-5930K CPU @ 3.50 GHz, and 32 GB of RAM.

The code used for AutoML-DSGE, and RECIPE can be found, respectively, in the GitHub repositories github.com/laic-ufmg/Recipe/, and github.com/fillassuncao/automl-dsge. The code of RECIPE was modified to include the evolution stop criteria based on a maximum number of generations without improvement, which despite described in the framework paper [20], is not included in the current code version.

To enable the comparison of results we apply the same dataset partitioning scheme used in RECIPE: all datasets are split using a 10-fold cross-validation strategy; and thus as we perform 30 evolutionary runs each fold is kept as the test set three times, and the remaining used for training the pipelines. During each run, the test set is kept aside from evolution, and the train set is used to train the pipelines with cross-validation (3 folds). By the end of evolution, the

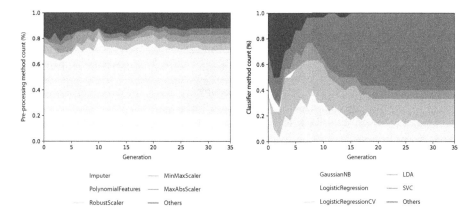

Fig. 3. Stacked area charts of the AutoML-DSGE evolution of the pre-processing (left) and classification (right) methods on the Car dataset. The results reflect the percentage of the best pipelines that use each of the methods.

best pipeline is trained using all the train data and applied to the test set. The evolution is conduced using the grammar of Fig. 2.

To establish the pair-wise comparison of the results, and check whether or not the differences between AutoML-DSGE and RECIPE are statistically significant we use the Wilcoxon Signed-Rank test, with a significance level of 5%. Further, for the statistically significant differences we compute the effect size.

5.3   Experimental Results

To compare the pipelines generated by AutoML-DSGE and RECIPE we conduct evolution for the same datasets, and using equivalent grammatical formulations, i.e., the search space is the same for both frameworks. The test performance (f-measure), for each dataset is presented in Table 4. The results are averages of 30 independent runs. A f-measure marked in bold indicates the approach that reports the highest average performance. In addition, the table also reports the p-values for the pair-wise comparisons between the two approaches, and bold p-values indicate statistically significant differences. The effect-size is denoted in brackets after the p-value, with +, ++, and +++ denoting small ($0.1 \leq r < 0.3$), medium ($0.3 \leq r < 0.5$), and large ($r \geq 0.5$) effect sizes, respectively.

The analysis of the results indicates that AutoML-DSGE reports results that are always superior to those obtained by RECIPE. In addition to the higher average, the standard deviation is lower in the AutoML-DSGE results in 7 out of 10 datasets, i.e., for the considered datasets AutoML-DSGE generates more consistently higher results. These differences are statistically significant in 3 datasets (Breast Cancer, Credit-G, and Wine Quality-Red). The effect size is medium twice, and high once. AutoML-DSGE is never worse than RECIPE.

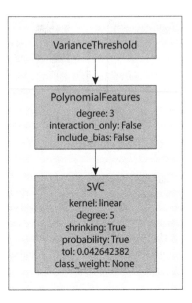

Fig. 4. Best pipeline generated for classifying the Car dataset. Each box represents a pipeline method and its parameterisation.

The results of Table 4 report the average performance of the 30 evolutionary runs, for each dataset. Nonetheless, as we are optimising ML methods we investigate the generalisation ability of the generated pipelines. To this end, we compute the average difference between the evolutionary, and test performances for the 10 datasets. Except for the Chowdary-2006 and Car datasets, the average difference between the evolutionary and test performance is lower in AutoML-DSGE than in RECIPE. Considering all datasets, the average difference between the evolutionary and test set performance is of approximately 0.0328 in AutoML-DSGE and of 0.0589 in RECIPE. This proves that the tendency to overfit is lower in AutoML-DSGE, as it reports more often than RECIPE evolutionary performances that are closer to the test ones.

To analyse the structure of the pipelines evolved by AutoML-DSGE we inspect the methods that compose them. Due to space constraints we focus on the Car dataset, as it is the dataset where, on average, more generations are performed. Figure 3 shows the evolution of the pre-processing and classification methods of the best individuals as generations proceed. The results show the evolution of the percentage of the runs that use each of the pre-processing and classification methods. Recall that the different evolutionary runs can differ in the number of performed generations, and therefore to avoid a misleading representation of the evolution of the methods that compose the pipelines we consider that all runs have the same number of generations. That is, we consider that all runs evolve for the same number of generations as the longer run (in this case 35 generations). For the evolutionary runs that perform less generations we keep the last generation (which is the best found solution) for the remainder of the generations. The results show that, for the Car dataset, the pre-processing methods distribution does not change as evolution proceeds. On the other hand, a different behaviour is noticeable on the classifier methods, that converge to the SVC, and LogisticRegression (or LogisticRegressionCV) method. The evolution also shows that evolution is focused on the methods that are more effective for that specific dataset. Otherwise, the used methods would be more diverse, and the percentage of the Others would be higher. In particular, we plot in Fig. 4 the best pipeline found for classifying the Car dataset. We also inspect the evolutionary patterns in the remaining datasets and acknowledge similar conclusions. It is however important to point out that for the different datasets evolution focuses on different pre-processing and classification methods.

Ultimately, AutoML-DSGE generates no invalid pipelines. After investigating the pipelines that were assigned with the worse possible fitness we conclude that their train is halted because they are unable to train in the maximum granted CPU time of five minutes, or because they run out of memory.

6   Conclusions and Future Work

Prior to the deployment of a ML model there are a number of choices that have to be made. There is the need to pre-process the dataset, design, extract and select features, and decide which ML model is the most adequate. On top of that, all this sequential choices are correlated, meaning that one affects multiple others. The choices that have to be made require both domain-specific, and ML expertise. In an effort to facilitate the widespread use of ML models we introduce a novel AutoML framework: AutoML-DSGE.

AutoML-DSGE is a grammar-based AutoML approach, and thus the search space is defined in a human-readable CFG. This key-point of the framework enables the easy adaptation of AutoML-DSGE to tackle different problems using a wide set of methods. Further, it eases the introduction of a-priori knowledge in the search and tuning of the pipelines. The current version of the framework focuses on the optimisation of Scikit-Learn classification pipelines. The code is released as open-source software, and can be found in the GitHub repository: https://github.com/fillassuncao/automl-dsge.

We compare the performance AutoML-DSGE to RECIPE, which to the best of our knowledge is the only grammar-based AutoML framework. The methods are compared on 10 datasets from different domains. The results show that the pipelines generated by AutoML-DSGE surpass in performance the ones obtained by RECIPE; the average performances of AutoML-DSGE are always superior to RECIPE, and are statistically superior in 3 datasets (with medium and large effect sizes). Moreover, AutoML-DSGE is less prone to overfitting than RECIPE.

Future work will be divided into 4 independent research lines: (i) apply AutoML-DSGE to a wider set of benchmarks; (ii) extend the framework to regression problems; (iii) introduce ensembling and stacking methods; and (iv) enable the user to select between the Weka and Scikit-Learn ML libraries, or even own implemented methods.

Acknowledgments. This work is partially funded by: Fundação para a Ciência e Tecnologia (FCT), Portugal, under the PhD grant agreement SFRH/BD/114865/2016, the project grant DSAIPA/DS/0022/2018 (GADgET), and is based upon work from COST Action CA15140: ImAppNIO, supported by COST (European Cooperation in Science and Technology): www.cost.eu. We also thank the NVIDIA Corporation for the hardware granted to this research.

References

1. Pedregosa, F., et al.: Scikit-learn: machine learning in Python. J. Mach. Learn. Res. **12**, 2825–2830 (2011)
2. Lourenço, N., Assunção, F., Pereira, F.B., Costa, E., Machado, P.: Structured grammatical evolution: a dynamic approach. In: Ryan, C., O'Neill, M., Collins, J.J. (eds.) Handbook of Grammatical Evolution, pp. 137–161. Springer, Cham (2018). https://doi.org/10.1007/978-3-319-78717-6_6
3. Jiménez, Á.B., Lázaro, J.L., Dorronsoro, J.R.: Finding optimal model parameters by deterministic and annealed focused grid search. Neurocomputing **72**(13–15), 2824–2832 (2009)
4. Young, S.R., Rose, D.C., Karnowski, T.P., Lim, S., Patton, R.M.: Optimizing deep learning hyper-parameters through an evolutionary algorithm. In: MLHPC@SC, pp. 4:1–4:5. ACM (2015)
5. Bergstra, J., Bardenet, R., Bengio, Y., Kégl, B.: Algorithms for hyper-parameter optimization. In: NIPS, pp. 2546–2554 (2011)
6. Bergstra, J., Bengio, Y.: Random search for hyper-parameter optimization. J. Mach. Learn. Res. **13**, 281–305 (2012)
7. Shahriari, B., Swersky, K., Wang, Z., Adams, R.P., de Freitas, N.: Taking the human out of the loop: a review of Bayesian optimization. Proc. IEEE **104**(1), 148–175 (2016)
8. Snoek, J., Larochelle, H., Adams, R.P.: Practical Bayesian optimization of machine learning algorithms. In: NIPS, pp. 2960–2968 (2012)
9. Bergstra, J., Yamins, D., Cox, D.D.: Making a science of model search: hyperparameter optimization in hundreds of dimensions for vision architectures. In: ICML (1). JMLR Workshop and Conference Proceedings, vol. 28, pp. 115–123. JMLR.org (2013)
10. Chunhong, Z., Licheng, J.: Automatic parameters selection for SVM based on GA. In: Fifth World Congress on Intelligent Control and Automation, WCICA 2004, vol. 2, pp. 1869–1872. IEEE (2004)
11. Friedrichs, F., Igel, C.: Evolutionary tuning of multiple SVM parameters. Neurocomputing **64**, 107–117 (2005)
12. Guyon, I., et al.: A brief review of the ChaLearn AutoML challenge: any-time anydataset learning without human intervention. In: AutoML@ICML. JMLR Workshop and Conference Proceedings, vol. 64, pp. 21–30. JMLR.org (2016)
13. Guyon, I., et al.: Design of the 2015 ChaLearn AutoML challenge. In: IJCNN, pp. 1–8. IEEE (2015)

14. Frank, E., Hall, M.A., Holmes, G., Kirkby, R., Pfahringer, B.: WEKA - a machine learning workbench for data mining. In: Maimon, O., Rokach, L. (eds.) The Data Mining and Knowledge Discovery Handbook, pp. 1305–1314. Springer, Cham (2005). https://doi.org/10.1007/0-387-25465-X_62

15. Thornton, C., Hutter, F., Hoos, H.H., Leyton-Brown, K.: Auto-WEKA: combined selection and hyperparameter optimization of classification algorithms. In: KDD, pp. 847–855. ACM (2013)

16. Kotthoff, L., Thornton, C., Hoos, H.H., Hutter, F., Leyton-Brown, K.: Auto-WEKA 2.0: automatic model selection and hyperparameter optimization in WEKA. J. Mach. Learn. Res. **18**, 25:1–25:5 (2017). http://jmlr.org/papers/v18/16-261.html

17. Olson, R.S., Bartley, N., Urbanowicz, R.J., Moore, J.H.: Evaluation of a tree-based pipeline optimization tool for automating data science. In: GECCO, pp. 485–492. ACM (2016)

18. Komer, B., Bergstra, J., Eliasmith, C.: Hyperopt-sklearn: automatic hyperparameter configuration for scikit-learn. In: ICML Workshop on AutoML (2014)

19. Feurer, M., Klein, A., Eggensperger, K., Springenberg, J.T., Blum, M., Hutter, F.: Efficient and robust automated machine learning. In: NIPS, pp. 2962–2970 (2015)

20. de Sá, A.G.C., Pinto, W.J.G.S., Oliveira, L.O.V.B., Pappa, G.L.: RECIPE: a grammar-based framework for automatically evolving classification pipelines. In: McDermott, J., Castelli, M., Sekanina, L., Haasdijk, E., García-Sánchez, P. (eds.) EuroGP 2017. LNCS, vol. 10196, pp. 246–261. Springer, Cham (2017). https://doi.org/10.1007/978-3-319-55696-3_16

21. Lourenço, N., Pereira, F.B., Costa, E.: Unveiling the properties of structured grammatical evolution. Genet. Program. Evolvable Mach. **17**(3), 251–289 (2016). https://doi.org/10.1007/s10710-015-9262-4

22. O'Neill, M., Ryan, C.: Grammatical evolution. IEEE Trans. Evol. Comput. **5**(4), 349–358 (2001)

23. Keijzer, M., O'Neill, M., Ryan, C., Cattolico, M.: Grammatical evolution rules: the mod and the bucket rule. In: Foster, J.A., Lutton, E., Miller, J., Ryan, C., Tettamanzi, A. (eds.) EuroGP 2002. LNCS, vol. 2278, pp. 123–130. Springer, Heidelberg (2002). https://doi.org/10.1007/3-540-45984-7_12

24. Thorhauer, A., Rothlauf, F.: On the locality of standard search operators in grammatical evolution. In: Bartz-Beielstein, T., Branke, J., Filipič, B., Smith, J. (eds.) PPSN 2014. LNCS, vol. 8672, pp. 465–475. Springer, Cham (2014). https://doi.org/10.1007/978-3-319-10762-2_46

25. Dua, D., Graff, C.: UCI machine learning repository (2017). http://archive.ics.uci.edu/ml

26. Chen, X., et al.: Gene expression patterns in human liver cancers. Mol. Biol. Cell **13**(6), 1929–1939 (2002)

27. Chowdary, D., et al.: Prognostic gene expression signatures can be measured in tissues collected in RNAlater preservative. J. Mol. Diagn. **8**(1), 31–39 (2006)

28. Wan, C., Freitas, A.A., De Magalhães, J.P.: Predicting the pro-longevity or anti-longevity effect of model organism genes with new hierarchical feature selection methods. IEEE/ACM Trans. Comput. Biol. Bioinform. (TCBB) **12**(2), 262–275 (2015)

An Empirical Exploration of Deep Recurrent Connections Using Neuro-Evolution

Travis Desell[✉], AbdElRahman ElSaid, and Alexander G. Ororbia

Rochester Institute of Technology, Rochester, NY 14623, USA
{tjdvse,aae8800}@rit.edu, ago@cs.rit.edu

Abstract. Neuro-evolution and neural architecture search algorithms have gained significant interest due to the challenges of designing optimal artificial neural networks (ANNs). While these algorithms possess the potential to outperform the best human crafted architectures, a less common use of them is as a tool for analysis of ANN topologies and structural components. By performing these techniques while varying the allowable components, the best performing architectures for those components can be found and compared to best performing architectures for other components, allowing for a best case comparison of component capabilities – a more rigorous examination than simply applying those components in some standard fixed topologies. In this work, we utilize the Evolutionary eXploration of Augmenting Memory Models (EXAMM) algorithm to perform a rigorous examination and comparison of recurrent neural networks (RNNs) applied to time series prediction. Specifically, EXAMM is used to investigate the capabilities of recurrent memory cells as well as various complex recurrent connectivity patterns that span one or more steps in time, i.e., deep recurrent connections. Over 10.56 million RNNs were evolved and trained in 5, 280 repeated experiments with varying components. Many modern hand-crafted RNNs rely on complex memory cells (which have internal recurrent connections that only span a single time step) operating under the assumption that these sufficiently latch information and handle long term dependencies. However, our results show that networks evolved with deep recurrent connections perform significantly better than those without. More importantly, in some cases, the best performing RNNs consisted of only simple neurons and deep time skip connections, *without any memory cells*. These results strongly suggest that utilizing deep time skip connections in RNNs for time series data prediction not only deserves further, dedicated study, but also demonstrate the potential of neuro-evolution as a means to better study, understand, and train effective RNNs.

Keywords: Neuro-evolution · Recurrent neural networks · Time series data prediction · Aviation · Power systems

© Springer Nature Switzerland AG 2020
P. A. Castillo et al. (Eds.): EvoApplications 2020, LNCS 12104, pp. 546–561, 2020.
https://doi.org/10.1007/978-3-030-43722-0_35

1   Introduction

Neural architecture search poses a challenging problem since the possible search space for finding optimal or quasi-optimal architectures is massive. For the case of recurrent neural networks (RNNs), this problem is further confounded by the fact that every node in its architecture can be potentially connected to any other node via a recurrent connection which passes information stored in a vector history to the current time step. Complexity is further increased when one considers that recurrent connections could explicitly connect information from any time step $< t$ in the history of the sequence processed so far to step t, improving memory retention through time delays. Figure 1 illustrates this challenge, showing the different types of potential recurrent connections that can exist even within a simple network with one input, two hidden and one output node, allowing connections with a time skip up to 3.

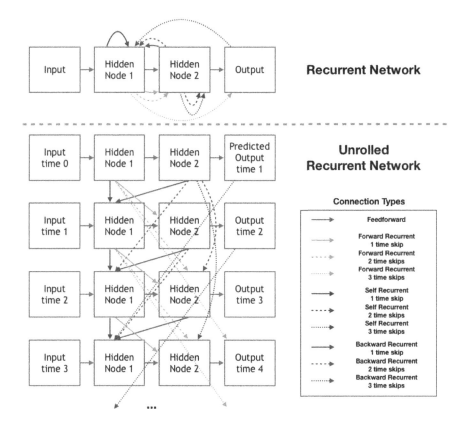

Fig. 1. RNNs can have a wide variety of connections. Most RNNs consist of feed forward, self recurrent, and backward recurrent connections with a single time step; however it is also possible to also have forward recurrent connections and recurrent connections which span/skip multiple time steps.

Most modern-day RNNs simplify the recurrent connectivity structure and instead improve retention by utilizing memory cells such as Δ-RNN units [1], gated recurrent units (GRUs) [2], long short-term memory cells (LSTMs) [3], minimal gated units (MGUs) [4], and update gate RNN cells (UGRNNs) [5]. The use of memory cells, as opposed to investigating the use of denser temporal/recurrent connectivity structures, is popular largely due to the assumption that while the recurrent synapses that define a cell only explicitly connect $t-1$ to t, their latch-like behavior is sufficient for capturing enough information about the sequence observed so far when making predictions of what will come next. Nonetheless, RNNs still struggle to effectively learn long-term dependencies in temporal data [1, 6–10].

There also exists a body of literature that suggests that recurrent connections which skip more than a single time step, which we will coin as *deep recurrent connections*, can play an important role in allowing an RNN to more effectively capture long-term temporal dependencies. This research dates back to Lin *et al.*'s development of NARX (Nonlinear AutoRegressive eXogenous Model) neural networks with increasing embedded memory orders (EMOs) or time windows [11,12], which involved adding recurrent connections up to a specified number time skips. Further work went on to show that the order of a NARX network is crucial in determining how well it will perform – when the EMO of a NARX model matches the order of an unknown target recursive system strong and robust generalization is achieved [13,14]. Diaconescu later utilized these EMO-based NARX networks to predict chaotic time series data, with best results found in the EMO ranges of 12 to 30, which are significantly large time skips [15]. More generally, it has been expressed in classical literature that skip connections can substantially express the computational abilities of artificial neural networks (ANNs) [16]. Yet, modern popular ANNs have only taken advantage of feedforward skip connections [17], including RNNs [18,19], with a few notable exceptions [20].

Findings for RNNs with deep recurrent connections are also not limited to Lin *et al.*'s EMO NARX networks. Chen and Chaudhari developed a segmented-memory recurrent neural network (SMRNN) [21], which utilizes a two layer recurrent structure which first passes input symbols to a symbol layer, and then connects the symbol layers to a segmentation layer. This work showed that intervals $10 \leq d \leq 50$ provided the best results on this data, as a lower d required more computation each iteration (the segmentation was used too frequently) slowing convergence, and at higher values of d it approximated a conventional RNN (that did not use a segmentation layer). The segment interval d operates similarly to a deep recurrent connection; it passes information from past states further forward along the unrolled network. It was shown that SMRNN outperformed both LSTM and Elman RNNs on the latching problem. ElSaid *et al.* later utilized time-windowed LSTM RNNs to predict engine vibration in time series data gathered from aircraft flight data recorders [22,23]. This work investigated a number of architectures and found that a two-level system with an EMO/time window of order 10 provided good predictions of engine vibration up to 20 s in the future. This was a challenging problem due to the spiking nature of engine vibration, yet this architecture significantly outperformed time-windowed NARX models, Nonlinear Output Error (NOE), and the Nonlinear Box–Jenkins (NBJ) models.

In this work, we further investigate the power of deep recurrent connections in comparison to memory cells by taking a rather unconventional approach to the analysis, using an neuro-evolutionary algorithm we call EXAMM (Evolutionary eXploration of Augmenting Memory Models) [24]. Instead of simply testing a few hand-crafted RNNs with and without deep recurrent connections composed of different kinds of memory cells, neuro-evolution was used to select and mix the architectural components as well as decide the depth and density of the connectivity patterns, facilitating an exploration of the expansive, combinatorial search space when accounting for the many different components and dimensions one could explore – yielding a more rigorous, comprehensive yet automated examination. A variety of experiments were performed evolving RNNs consisting of simple neurons or memory cells, $e.g.$, LSTM, GRU, MGU, UGRNN, Δ-RNN cells, as well as exploring the option of using deep recurrent connections or not, of varying degree and intensity. RNNs were evolved with EXAMM to perform time series data prediction on four real world benchmark problems. In total, 10.56 million RNNs were trained to collect the results we report in this study.

The findings of our EXAMM-driven experimentation uncovered that networks evolved with deep recurrent connections perform significantly better than those without, and, notably, in some cases, the best performing RNNs consisted of only simple neurons with deep recurrent connections ($i.e.$, no memory cells). These results strongly suggest that utilizing deep recurrent connections in RNNs for time series data prediction not only warrants further study, but also demonstrates that neuro-evolution is a potentially powerful tool for studying, understanding, and training effective RNNs.

2   Evolving Recurrent Neural Networks

Neuro-evolution, or the use of artificial evolutionary processes (such as genetic algorithms [25]) to automate the design of artificial neural networks (ANNs), has been well applied to feed forward ANNs for tasks involving static inputs, including convolutional variants [26–31]. However, significantly less effort has been put into exploring the evolution of recurrent memory structures that operate with complex sequences of data points.

Despite the current lack of focus on RNNs, several neuro-evolution methods have been proposed evolving RNN topologies (along with weight values themselves) with NeuroEvolution of Augmenting Topologies (NEAT) [30] perhaps being the most well-known. Recent work by Rawal and Miikkulainen investigated an information maximization objective [32] strategy for evolving RNNs, which essentially operates similarly to NEAT except with LSTM cells being used instead of simple (traditional) neurons. Research centered around this line of NEAT-based approaches has also explored the use of a tree-based encoding [33] to evolve recurrent cellular structures within fixed architectures composed of multiple layers of the evolved cell types. More recently, work by Camero *et al.* has shown that a Mean Absolute Error (MAE) random sampling strategy can provide good estimates of RNN performance [34], successfully incorporating it into an LSTM-RNN neuro-evolution strategy [35]. However, none of this prior work has investigated the evolution deep recurrent connectivity structures nor focused on using a powerful evolutionary strategy such as EXAMM as an empirical analysis tool for RNNs.

With respect to other nature-inspired metaheuristic approaches for evolving RNNs, ant colony optimization (ACO) has also been investigated [36] as a way to select which connections should be used but only for single time-step Elman RNNs. ACO has also been used to reduce the number of trainable connections in a fixed time-windowed LSTM architecture by half while providing significantly improved prediction of engine vibration [37].

For this study, EXAMM was selected as the RNN analysis algorithm for a number of reasons. First, this procedure progressively grows larger ANNs in a manner similar to NEAT which stands in contrast to current ACO-based approaches, which have been often restricted to operating within a fixed neural topology. Furthermore, in contrast to the well-known NEAT, EXAMM utilizes higher order node-level mutation operations, Lamarckian weight initialization (or the reuse of parental weights), and back-propagation of errors (backprop) [38] to conduct local search, the combination of which has been shown to speed up both ANN training as well as the overall evolutionary process. Unlike the work by Rawal and Miikkulainen, EXAMM operates with an easily-extensible suite of memory cells, including LSTM, GRU, MGU, UGRNN, Δ-RNN cells and, more importantly, has the natural ability to evolve deep recurrent connections over large, variable time lags. In prior work it has also been shown to more quickly and reliably evolve RNNs in parallel than training traditional layered RNNs sequentially [39]. For detailed EXAMM implementation details we refer the reader to [24].

3   Experimental Data

This experimental study utilized two open-access real-world data sets as benchmark problems for evolving RNNs that can predict four different time series parameters. The first dataset comes from a selection of 10 flights worth of data taken from the National General Aviation Flight Information Database (NGAFID) and the other comes from data collected from 12 burners of a coal-fired power plant. Both datasets are multivariate (with 26 and 12 parameters, respectively), non-seasonal, and the parameter recordings are not independent. Furthermore, the underlying temporal sequences are quite long – the aviation time series range from 1 to 3 h worth of per-second data while the power plant data consists of 10 days worth of per-minute readings. To the authors' knowledge, other real world time series data sets of this size and at this scale are not freely available. These datasets are freely provided in the EXAMM github repository.

3.1   Aviation Flight Recorder Data

Each of the 10 flight data files last over an hour and consist of per-second data recordings from 26 parameters, including engine parameters such as engine cylinder head temperatures, gasket temperatures, oil temperature and pressure, and rotations per minute (RPM); flight parameters such as altitude above ground level, indicated air speed, lateral and normal acceleration, pitch, and roll; and environmental parameters such as outside air temperature and wind speed. The data is provided raw and without any normalization applied.

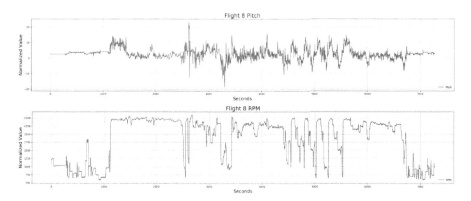

Fig. 2. Example parameters pitch (top) and RPM (bottom) of Flight 8 from the NGAFID dataset.

RPM and *pitch* were selected as prediction parameters from the aviation data since RPM is a product of engine activity, with other engine-related parameters being correlated. Pitch itself is directly influenced by pilot controls. As a result, both of these target variables are particularly challenging to predict. Figure 2 provides an example of the RPM and pitch time series from Flight 8 of this dataset. In addition, the pitch parameter represents how many degrees above or below horizontal the aircraft is angled. As a result, the parameter typically remains steady around a value of 0, however, it increases or decreases depending on whether or not the aircraft is angled to fly upward or downward, based on pilot controls and external conditions. On the other hand, RPM will mostly vary between an idling speed, i.e., if the plane is on the ground, and a flight speed, with some variation between takeoff and landing. Since the majority of the flights in NGAFID (and, by extension, all of the flights in the provided sample) are student training flights, multiple practice takeoffs and landings can be found. This results in two different types of time series, both of which are dependent on the other flight parameters but each with highly different characteristics – creating excellent time series benchmarks for RNNs.

3.2   Coal-Fired Power Plant Data

This dataset consists of 10 days of per-minute data readings extracted from 12 out of a coal plant's set of burners. Each of these 12 data files contains 12 parameters of time series data: Conditioner Inlet Temp, Conditioner Outlet Temp, Coal Feeder Rate, Primary Air Flow, Primary Air Split, System Secondary Air Flow Total, Secondary Air Flow, Secondary Air Split, Tertiary Air Split, Total Combined Air Flow, Supplementary Fuel Flow, and Main Flame Intensity. This data was normalized to the range [0, 1], which serves furthermore as a data anonymization step.

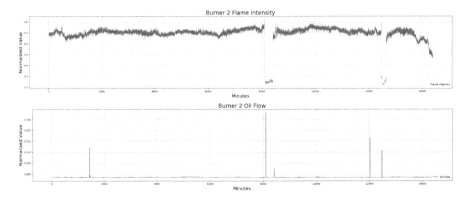

Fig. 3. Example parameters for Burner #2 from the coal plant dataset: flame intensity (top) and fuel flow (bottom).

For the coal plant data, *main flame intensity* and *supplementary fuel flow* were selected as parameters of interest. Figure 3 provides examples of these two parameters from Burner # 2 found in the dataset. Main flame intensity is mostly a product of conditions within the burner and parameters related to coal quality which causes it to vary over time. However sometimes planned outages occur or conditions in the burner deteriorate so badly that it is temporarily shut down. In these cases, sharp spikes occur during the shutdown, which last for an unspecified period of time before the burner turns back on again and the parameter (value) sharply increases. The burners can also potentially operate at different output levels, depending on power generation needs. As a result, step-wise behavior is observed.

On the other hand, supplementary fuel flow remains fairly constant. Nonetheless, it yields sudden and drastic spikes in response to decisions made by plant operators. When conditions in the burners become poor due to coal quality or other effects, the operator may need to provide supplementary fuel to prevent the burner from going into shutdown. Of particular interest is if an RNN can successfully detect these spikes given the conditions of the other parameters. Similar the key parameters (RPM and pitch) selected in the NGAFID data, main flame intensity is mostly a product of conditions within the (coal) burner while supplementary fuel flow is more directly controlled by human operators. Despite these similarities, however, the characteristics of these time series are different from each other as well as from the NGAFID flight data, providing additional, unique benchmark prediction challenges.

4   Results

4.1   Experiments

The first set of (5) experiments only permitted the use of a single memory cell type, *i.e.*, exclusively Δ-RNN, GRU, LSTM, MGU, or UGRNN (one experiment per type), and no simple neurons. All of these experiments only allowed the generation of feedforward connections between cells (these experiments were denoted as *delta*, *gru*, *lstm*, *mgu* or *ugrnn*). The second set of (2) experiments were conducted where the first one only permitted the use of simple neurons and feedforward connections (denoted as *simple*) while the second permitted EXAMM to make use of feedforward connections and simple neurons as well as the choice of any memory cell type (denoted as *all*). The next set of experiments (5) were identical to the first set with the key exception that EXAMM could choose either between simple neurons and one specified specific memory cell type (these experiments are appended with a *+simple*, i.e., *lstm+simple*). The final set of (12) experiments consisted of taking the setting of each of the prior 12 $(5 + 2 + 5)$ runs and re-ran them but with the modification that EXAMM was permitted to generate deep recurrent connections of varying time delays (these runs are appended with a *+rec*).

   This full set of (24) experiments was conducted for each of the four prediction parameters, i.e., RPM, pitch, main flame intensity, and supplementary fuel flow. K-fold cross validation was carried out for each prediction parameter, with a fold size of 2. This resulted in 5 folds for the NGAFID data (as it had 10 flight data files), and 6 folds for the coal plant data (as it has 12 burner data files). Each fold and EXAMM experiment was repeated 10 times. In total, each of the 24 EXAMM experiments were conducted 220 times (50 times each for the NGAFID parameter k-fold validation and 60 times each for the coal data parameter k-fold validation), for a grand total of 5, 280 separate EXAMM experiments/simulations.

4.2   EXAMM and Backpropagation Hyperparameters

All RNNs were locally trained with backpropagation through time (BPTT) [40] and stochastic gradient descent (SGD) using the same hyperparameters. SGD was run with a learning rate of $\eta = 0.001$, utilizing Nesterov momentum with $mu = 0.9$. No dropout regularization was used since, in prior work, it has been shown to reduce performance when training RNNs for time series prediction [37]. For the LSTM cells that EXAMM could make use of, the forget gate bias had a value of 1.0 added to it, as [41] has shown that doing so improves training time significantly. Otherwise, RNN weights were initialized by EXAMM's Lamarckian strategy. To prevent exploding gradients, gradient clipping (as described by Pascanu *et al.* [9]) was used when the norm of the gradient was above a threshold of 1.0. To improve performance on vanishing gradients, gradient boosting (the opposite of clipping) was used when the norm of the gradient was below a threshold of 0.05.

Each EXAMM neuro-evolution run consisted of 10 islands, each with a population size of 5. New RNNs were generated via intra-island crossover (at a rate of 20%), mutation at a rate 70%, and inter-island crossover at 10% rate. All of EXAMM's mutation operations (except for *split edge*) were utilized, each chosen with a uniform 10% chance. The experiments labeled *all* were able to select any type of memory cell or Elman neurons at random, each with an equal probability. Each EXAMM run generated 2000 RNNs, with each RNN being trained locally (using the BPTT settings above) for 10 epochs. Recurrent connections that could span a time skip between 1 and 10 could be chosen (uniformly at random). These runs were performed utilizing 20 processors in parallel, and, on average, required approximately 0.5 compute hours. In total, the results we report come from training $10,560,000$ RNNs which required ~$52,800$ CPU hours of compute time.

4.3   Experimental Results

Figure 4 shows the range of the fitness values of the best found neural networks across all of the EXAMM experiments, sorted by their average case performance. This combines the results from all folds and all trial repeats – each box in the box plots represent 110 different fitness values. The box plots are ordered according to mean fitness (calculated as mean absolute error, or MAE) of the RNNs for that experiment/setting (across all folds), with the top being the highest average MAE, i.e., the worst performing simulation setting, and the bottom containing the lowest average MAE, i.e., the best performing setting. Means are represented by green triangles and medians by orange bars. Run type names with deep recurrent connections are highlighted in red.

How well the different experiments performed was also analyzed by calculating the mean and standard deviation of all best evolved fitness scores from each repeated experiment across each fold. This was done since each fold of the test data had a different range of potential best results. It was then possible to rank/order the experiments/simulations in terms of their deviation from the mean (providing a less biased metric of improvement). Table 1 presents how well each experiment performed as an average of how many standard deviations they were from the mean in their best case performance. Search types which utilized deep recurrent connections (*+rec*) are highlighted in bold.

4.4   Effects of Deep Recurrent Connections

Table 2 provides measurements for how the addition of deep recurrent changed the performance of the varying memory cell types, as well as the *all* and *simple*

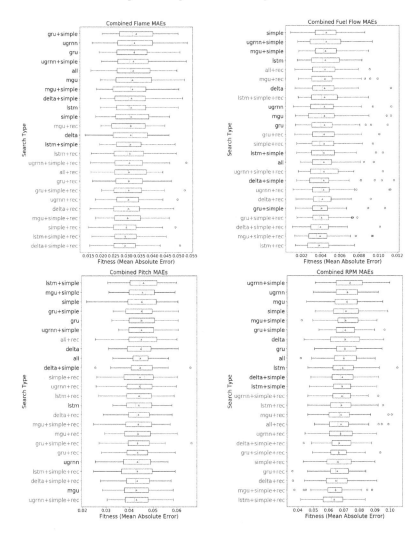

Fig. 4. Consolidated range of fitness (mean absolute error) of the best found RNNs for the two datasets' (flame intensity and fuel flow for the coal plant dataset, and pitch and RPM for the aviation dataset) target prediction parameters. Results are for the 24 experiments across all 6 folds, with 10 repeats per fold. Run types are ordered top-down by mean. (Color figure online)

runs. In it, we show how many standard deviations from the mean the average case moved when averaging the differences of a run type to the version of that run type with *+rec* over all four prediction parameters. For example, *mgu* to *mgu+rec* and *mgu+simple* to *mgu+simple+rec* in the mgu row. Adding the *+rec* setting showed significant differences, improving deviations from the mean by −0.2 overall. In addition, for each of the prediction parameters, the best found

Table 1. Best fitness performance values reported for each EXAMM experimental setting. Experimental settings are ranked by their number of standard deviations from the mean of all experiments. Lower values had better performance.

Type	Devs from Mean
gru+simple	-1.02844
mgu+rec	-1.15701
ugrnn+simple	-1.21079
mgu	-1.24655
mgu+simple	-1.26880
gru	-1.29390
simple	-1.30901
lstm+simple	-1.35475
lstm	-1.35496
delta+simple	-1.37473
ugrnn+rec	-1.42362
ugrnn	-1.43371
delta	-1.48912
mgu+simple+rec	-1.55717
gru+simple+rec	-1.58618
lstm+simple+rec	-1.63655
all+rec	-1.64301
all	-1.66893
lstm+rec	-1.70057
ugrnn+simple+rec	-1.71172
gru+rec	-1.73098
delta+rec	-1.95685
simple+rec	-1.97756
delta+simple+rec	-2.08205

(a) σ_{Flame}: Best MAE

Type	Devs from Mean
gru+rec	-1.10116
ugrnn+simple	-1.18567
lstm+simple	-1.18625
mgu+rec	-1.18778
lstm+simple+rec	-1.21500
mgu+simple	-1.21509
all	-1.22138
gru+simple	-1.27796
gru+simple+rec	-1.29070
simple+rec	-1.29699
simple	-1.30479
ugrnn	-1.30559
ugrnn+simple+rec	-1.31366
delta	-1.33034
delta+rec	-1.35481
all+rec	-1.37338
lstm	-1.38003
delta+simple	-1.38368
lstm+rec	-1.38510
ugrnn+rec	-1.42369
mgu	-1.45259
mgu+simple+rec	-1.50962
gru	-1.53812
delta+simple+rec	-1.54667

(b) $\sigma_{FuelFlow}$: Best MAE

Type	Devs from Mean
ugrnn+simple	-0.99073
gru	-1.01889
lstm+simple	-1.09707
gru+simple	-1.10143
delta	-1.19651
lstm	-1.24966
all	-1.25872
delta+rec	-1.42943
mgu+simple	-1.48976
all+rec	-1.55755
ugrnn+rec	-1.58235
mgu+rec	-1.60397
lstm+rec	-1.63888
ugrnn+simple+rec	-1.64192
mgu	-1.67690
ugrnn	-1.70299
delta+simple+rec	-1.77567
delta+simple	-1.78042
gru+rec	-1.81352
lstm+simple+rec	-1.89858
simple	-2.05128
mgu+simple+rec	-2.09451
gru+simple+rec	-2.09545
simple+rec	-2.24764

(c) σ_{Pitch}: Best MAE

Type	Devs from Mean
gru	-0.94516
simple	-0.99991
gru+simple	-1.08121
mgu	-1.17371
ugrnn+simple	-1.19714
all+rec	-1.34347
ugrnn	-1.36917
ugrnn+simple+rec	-1.44366
gru+simple+rec	-1.49508
mgu+simple	-1.49991
lstm	-1.50167
delta+simple+rec	-1.51271
delta+simple	-1.51795
mgu+rec	-1.52494
delta	-1.57259
lstm+simple	-1.64965
all	-1.69526
lstm+simple+rec	-1.71450
ugrnn+rec	-1.72680
lstm+rec	-1.74024
simple+rec	-1.74335
gru+rec	-1.88070
mgu+simple+rec	-1.89718
delta+rec	-2.05063

(d) σ_{RPM}: Best MAE

RNN utilized deep recurrent connections. Looking at the top 3 best and top 3 average case RNNs, 11 out of 12 utilized deep recurrent connections. Similarly, in the bottom 3 best, +rec occurs twice and does not appear at all in the bottom

3 average case run types. For the Flame and RPM parameters, on the average case, even the worst performing run type with *+rec* performs better than any experiments without it.

5   Discussion

The results presented in this work contribute some significant and interesting insights for RNN-based time series data prediction. Deep recurrent connections yielded the most significant improvements in RNN generalization, and, in some cases, were more important than the use of memory cells, with the *simple+rec* experiments performing quite strongly. For all four benchmark datasets, the best found RNNs utilized deep recurrent connections. As a whole, adding deep recurrent connections to the evolutionary process resulted in large shifts of

Table 2. Performance improvement (in std. devs from the mean) for resulting from adding deep recurrent connections.

Type	Dev for avg	Dev for best
all	−0.09113	−0.01828
simple	−0.27842	−0.40014
delta	−0.25571	−0.30079
gru	−0.31534	−0.43257
lstm	−0.14463	−0.24462
mgu	−0.11507	0.01901
ugrnn	−0.19291	−0.08625
overall	−0.19903	−0.20909

improvement in the standard deviations from mean measurement. These results are particularly significant given that the commonly accepted practice is that one should primarily use LSTM or other gated neural structures in order to stand a chance at capturing long term time dependencies in temporal data (despite the fact that internal connections only explicitly traverse a single time step) when classically it has been known that time delays and temporal skip connections can vastly improve generalization over sequences.

Another very interesting finding was that only using simple neurons and deep recurrent connections, without any memory cells, (the *simple+rec* experiment) led to quite good performance. This found the best RNN with respect to the Pitch prediction problem (aviation), the second best on the Flame prediction problem dataset (coal), and the fourth best on the RPM prediction problem (aviation). This shows that, in some cases, it may be more important to have deep recurrent connections than more complicated memory cells.

We also found that the newer Δ-RNN memory cell did consistently stand out as one of the better-performing memory cells. In three out of the four datasets, EXAMM found it to be the best performing RNN cell-of-choice, and for the average case performance, the Δ-RNN made it into the top 3 experiments for all four datasets. Furthermore, unlike the other memory cell experiments Δ-RNN did not appear in the bottom 3 *for any of the experiments, either in the average or best cases*. The only other experiment setting/configuration to boast top 3 best performance and no bottom 3 performance was the *simple+rec* experiment. However this did not perform as well in the average case, only appearing in the top 3 twice. Our results showing that the Δ-RNN consistently outperforms more complex cells such as the LSTM corroborates the findings of [1], which presented early findings in the domain of language modeling. While a newer memory cell, our results indicate that, while deep recurrence and time delay are critical for robustly modeling sequences, simpler gated cells like the Δ-RNN cell should also be strongly considered when designing RNNs, especially for time series forecasting.

6   Future Work

The choice of selecting time skip depths uniformly at random between the hyperparameter range $[1, 10]$ was a somewhat arbitrary choice. We hypothesize that an adaptive approach to selecting the depth skip (or length of the time delay) based on previously well-performing configurations/model candidates might provide better accuracy and remove the need for choosing the bounds of time delay range. Perhaps the most interesting direction to pursue is to develop memory cells that efficiently and effectively use recurrent connections that explicitly span more than one step in time, *i.e.*, perhaps more intelligent/powerful gating mechanisms could be design to properly mix together the information that flows from multiple time delays. In addition, perhaps EXAMM can be used to automatically incorporate or design better variations of highway connections as well, given the potential expressive power that recurrent highway networks [20] offer.

The strong performance of the *simple+rec* experiment might also suggest that generating and training RNNs using an evolutionary process with Lamarckian weight initialization may make training RNNs with non-gated recurrent connections easier. This naturally happens since neuro-evolution process such as EXAMM will discard poor RNN solutions that occur in the search space, *i.e.*, poor minima/regions that result from exploding or vanishing gradients when using backpropagation through time (BPTT), and not add them to its candidate solution population, preventing the generation of at least offspring that generalize too poorly. As a result, the evolutionary process will tend to preserve RNNs which have been training well (or at least, when trained with BPTT, have well-behaved gradients). Future investigation can explore if this is truly the case by retraining the best found architectures from scratch and comparing their performance across various sequence modeling settings.

7   Conclusion

While most work in the field of neuro-evolution focuses on the evolution of neural architectures that can potentially outperform hand-crafted designs, this work showcases the potential of neuro-evolution for a different use: a robust analysis and investigation of the performance and capabilities of different artificial neural network components. Specifically, we demonstrate EXAMM as powerful tool for analyzing/designing recurrent networks, focused on the choice of internal memory cells and the density and complexity of recurrent connectivity patterns. Rigorously investigating a new neural processing component can be quite challenging given that, often, its performance is tied to the overall architecture it is used within. For most work, new architectural components or strategies are typically only investigated within a few select architectures which may not necessarily represent how well the processing mechanism would perform given a much wider range of potential architectures it could be integrated into. Neuroevolution helps alleviate this problem by allowing the structural components themselves to play a key role in determining the architecture/systems they will most likely work well within. This facilitates a far more fair comparison of their capabilities and, perhaps, allows us to draw more general insights in our quest to construct robust neural models that generalize well.

Acknowledgements. This material is in part supported by the U.S. Department of Energy, Office of Science, Office of Advanced Combustion Systems under Award Number #FE0031547 and by the Federal Aviation Administration National General Aviation Flight Information Database (NGAFID) award. We also thank Microbeam Technologies, Inc., Mark Dusenbury, James Higgins, Brandon Wild for their help in collecting and preparing the data.

References

1. Ororbia II, A.G., Mikolov, T., Reitter, D.: Learning simpler language models with the differential state framework. Neural Comput. **29**(12), 3327–3352 (2017)
2. Chung, J., Gulcehre, C., Cho, K.H., Bengio, Y.: Empirical evaluation of gated recurrent neural networks on sequence modeling. arXiv preprint arXiv:1412.3555 (2014)
3. Hochreiter, S., Schmidhuber, J.: Long short-term memory. Neural Comput. **9**(8), 1735–1780 (1997)
4. Zhou, G.-B., Wu, J., Zhang, C.-L., Zhou, Z.-H.: Minimal gated unit for recurrent neural networks. Int. J. Autom. Comput. **13**(3), 226–234 (2016). https://doi.org/10.1007/s11633-016-1006-2
5. Collins, J., Sohl-Dickstein, J., Sussillo, D.: Capacity and trainability in recurrent neural networks. arXiv preprint arXiv:1611.09913 (2016)
6. Bengio, Y., Frasconi, P., Simard, P.: The problem of learning long-term dependencies in recurrent networks. In: IEEE International Conference on Neural Networks, pp. 1183–1188. IEEE (1993)
7. Bengio, Y., Simard, P., Frasconi, P.: Learning long-term dependencies with gradient descent is difficult. IEEE Trans. Neural Netw. **5**(2), 157–166 (1994)
8. Hochreiter, S., Bengio, Y., Frasconi, P., Schmidhuber, J., et al.: Gradient flow in recurrent nets: the difficulty of learning long-term dependencies (2001)
9. Pascanu, R., Mikolov, T., Bengio, Y.: On the difficulty of training recurrent neural networks. In: International Conference on Machine Learning, pp. 1310–1318 (2013)
10. Jing, L., et al.: Gated orthogonal recurrent units: on learning to forget. Neural Comput. **31**(4), 765–783 (2019)
11. Lin, T., Horne, B.G., Tino, P., Giles, C.L.: Learning long-term dependencies in NARX recurrent neural networks. IEEE Trans. Neural Netw. **7**(6), 1329–1338 (1996)
12. Lin, T., Horne, B.G., Giles, C.L.: How embedded memory in recurrent neural network architectures helps learning long-term temporal dependencies. Neural Netw. **11**(5), 861–868 (1998)

13. Lin, T., Horne, B.G., Giles, C.L., Kung, S.-Y.: What to remember: how memory order affects the performance of NARX neural networks. In: 1998 IEEE International Joint Conference on Neural Networks Proceedings. IEEE World Congress on Computational Intelligence (Cat. No. 98CH36227), vol. 2, pp. 1051–1056. IEEE (1998)
14. Giles, C.L., Lin, T., Horne, B.G., Kung, S.-Y.: The past is important: a method for determining memory structure in NARX neural networks. In: 1998 IEEE International Joint Conference on Neural Networks Proceedings. IEEE World Congress on Computational Intelligence (Cat. No. 98CH36227), vol. 3, pp. 1834–1839. IEEE (1998)
15. Diaconescu, E.: The use of NARX neural networks to predict chaotic time series. Wseas Trans. Comput. Res. **3**(3), 182–191 (2008)
16. McClelland, J.L., Rumelhart, D.E., PDP Research Group, et al.: Parallel Distributed Processing, vol. 2. MIT Press, Cambridge (1987)
17. He, K., Zhang, X., Ren, S., Sun, J.: Deep residual learning for image recognition. In: Proceedings of the IEEE Conference on Computer Vision and Pattern Recognition, pp. 770–778 (2016)
18. Graves, A.: Generating sequences with recurrent neural networks. arXiv preprint arXiv:1308.0850 (2013)
19. Srivastava, R.K., Greff, K., Schmidhuber, J.: Highway networks. arXiv preprint arXiv:1505.00387 (2015)
20. Zilly, J.G., Srivastava, R.K., Koutník, J., Schmidhuber, J.: Recurrent highway networks. In: Proceedings of the 34th International Conference on Machine Learning, vol. 70, pp. 4189–4198. JMLR.org (2017)
21. Chen, J., Chaudhari, N.S.: Segmented-memory recurrent neural networks. IEEE Trans. Neural Netw. **20**(8), 1267–1280 (2009)
22. ElSaid, A., Wild, B., Higgins, J., Desell, T.: Using LSTM recurrent neural networks to predict excess vibration events in aircraft engines. In: 2016 IEEE 12th International Conference on e-Science (e-Science), pp. 260–269. IEEE (2016)
23. ElSaid, A., Jamiy, F.E., Higgins, J., Wild, B., Desell, T.: Using ant colony optimization to optimize long short-term memory recurrent neural networks. In: Proceedings of the Genetic and Evolutionary Computation Conference, pp. 13–20. ACM (2018)
24. Ororbia, A., ElSaid, A., Desell, T.: Investigating recurrent neural network memory structures using neuro-evolution. In: Proceedings of the Genetic and Evolutionary Computation Conference, GECCO 2019, pp. 446–455. ACM, New York (2019)
25. Goldberg, D.E., Holland, J.H.: Genetic algorithms and machine learning. Mach. Learn. **3**(2), 95–99 (1988)
26. Salama, K., Abdelbar, A.M.: A novel ant colony algorithm for building neural network topologies. In: Dorigo, M., et al. (eds.) ANTS 2014. LNCS, vol. 8667, pp. 1–12. Springer, Cham (2014). https://doi.org/10.1007/978-3-319-09952-1_1
27. Suganuma, M., Shirakawa, S., Nagao, T.: A genetic programming approach to designing convolutional neural network architectures. In: Proceedings of the Genetic and Evolutionary Computation Conference, GECCO 2017, pp. 497–504. ACM, New York (2017)
28. Sun, Y., Xue, B., Zhang, M.: Evolving deep convolutional neural networks for image classification. CoRR, abs/1710.10741 (2017)
29. Miikkulainen, R., et al.: Evolving deep neural networks. arXiv preprint arXiv:1703.00548 (2017)
30. Stanley, K., Miikkulainen, R.: Evolving neural networks through augmenting topologies. Evol. Comput. **10**(2), 99–127 (2002)

31. Stanley, K.O., D'Ambrosio, D.B., Gauci, J.: A hypercube-based encoding for evolving large-scale neural networks. Artif. Life **15**(2), 185–212 (2009)
32. Rawal, A., Miikkulainen, R.: Evolving deep LSTM-based memory networks using an information maximization objective. In: 2016 Proceedings of the Genetic and Evolutionary Computation Conference, pp. 501–508. ACM (2016)
33. Rawal, A., Miikkulainen, R.: From nodes to networks: evolving recurrent neural networks. CoRR, abs/1803.04439 (2018)
34. Camero, A., Toutouh, J., Alba, E.: Low-cost recurrent neural network expected performance evaluation. arXiv preprint arXiv:1805.07159 (2018)
35. Camero, A., Toutouh, J., Alba, E.: A specialized evolutionary strategy using mean absolute error random sampling to design recurrent neural networks. arXiv preprint arXiv:1909.02425 (2019)
36. Desell, T., Clachar, S., Higgins, J., Wild, B.: Evolving deep recurrent neural networks using ant colony optimization. In: Ochoa, G., Chicano, F. (eds.) EvoCOP 2015. LNCS, vol. 9026, pp. 86–98. Springer, Cham (2015). https://doi.org/10.1007/978-3-319-16468-7_8
37. ElSaid, A., Jamiy, F.E., Higgins, J., Wild, B., Desell, T.: Optimizing long short-term memory recurrent neural networks using ant colony optimization to predict turbine engine vibration. Appl. Soft Comput. **73**, 969–991 (2018)
38. Rumelhart, D.E., Hinton, G.E., Williams, R.J., et al.: Learning representations by back-propagating errors. Cogn. Model. **5**(3), 1 (1988)
39. ElSaid, A., Benson, S., Patwardhan, S., Stadem, D., Travis, D.: Evolving recurrent neural networks for time series data prediction of coal plant parameters. In: The 22nd International Conference on the Applications of Evolutionary Computation, Leipzig, Germany, April 2019
40. Werbos, P.J.: Backpropagation through time: what it does and how to do it. Proc. IEEE **78**(10), 1550–1560 (1990)
41. Jozefowicz, R., Zaremba, W., Sutskever, I.: An empirical exploration of recurrent network architectures. In: International Conference on Machine Learning, pp. 2342–2350 (2015)

Using Skill Rating as Fitness
on the Evolution of GANs

Victor Costa[(✉)], Nuno Lourenço[(✉)], João Correia[(✉)],
and Penousal Machado[(✉)]

CISUC, Department of Informatics Engineering, University of Coimbra,
Coimbra, Portugal
{vfc,naml,jncor,machado}@dei.uc.pt

Abstract. Generative Adversarial Networks (GANs) are an adversarial model that achieved impressive results on generative tasks. In spite of the relevant results, GANs present some challenges regarding stability, making the training usually a hit-and-miss process. To overcome these challenges, several improvements were proposed to better handle the internal characteristics of the model, such as alternative loss functions or architectural changes on the neural networks used by the generator and the discriminator. Recent works proposed the use of evolutionary algorithms on GAN training, aiming to solve these challenges and to provide an automatic way to find good models. In this context, COEGAN proposes the use of coevolution and neuroevolution to orchestrate the training of GANs. However, previous experiments detected that some of the fitness functions used to guide the evolution are not ideal.

In this work we propose the evaluation of a game-based fitness function to be used within the COEGAN method. Skill rating is a metric to quantify the skill of players in a game and has already been used to evaluate GANs. We extend this idea using the skill rating in an evolutionary algorithm to train GANs. The results show that skill rating can be used as fitness to guide the evolution in COEGAN without the dependence of an external evaluator.

Keywords: Neuroevolution · Coevolution · Generative Adversarial Networks

1 Introduction

Generative models have gained a lot of interest in the past years. The recent advances in the field contributed with impressive results, mainly in the context of images. Generative Adversarial Networks (GANs) [9] presented a relevant advance in this context, producing realistic results in several domains. In the original GAN model, two neural networks, a generator and a discriminator, are competing in a unified training process. The generator fabricates samples and the discriminator detects if these samples are fake or from an input distribution.

© Springer Nature Switzerland AG 2020
P. A. Castillo et al. (Eds.): EvoApplications 2020, LNCS 12104, pp. 562–577, 2020.
https://doi.org/10.1007/978-3-030-43722-0_36

Despite the high-quality results, GANs are hard to train and a trial-and-error strategy is frequently followed to get the expected results. The challenges with GAN training are commonly related to the balance between the discriminator and the generator. In this context, the vanishing gradient and the mode collapse are two common problems affecting GANs. The vanishing gradient leads to stagnation of the training, caused by an imbalance between the forces of the generator and the discriminator. The mode collapse problem is characterized by the lack of representation of the target distribution used in training.

In order to solve these issues and to achieve better results, different strategies were proposed. A relevant effort was spent on the design of alternative loss functions to use in the GAN training, originating the proposal of alternative models such as WGAN [3], LSGAN [16], and RGAN [12]. Other proposals target the improvement of the architecture used in GANs, defining new modules like in SAGAN [34] or a set of recommendations as in DCGAN [21]. However, problems like the mode collapse and the vanishing gradient are still present in the training.

The use of evolutionary algorithms to train GANs was recently proposed [1,5–7,29,32]. Techniques such as neuroevolution, coevolution, and Pareto set approximations were used in their models. The application of evolutionary algorithms in GANs takes advantage of the evolutionary pressure to guide individuals toward convergence, often discarding problematic individuals.

Coevolutionary GAN (COEGAN) proposes the use of neuroevolution and coevolution to orchestrate the training of GANs. Despite the advances in the training stability, there is still room for improvement in the model. The experimental evaluation identified that the fitness function can be enhanced to better guide the evolution of the components, mainly regarding the discriminator. Currently, the discriminator uses the loss function of the respective GAN component. However, this function displayed a high variability behavior, disrupting the evolution of the population. The generator uses the Fréchet Inception Distance (FID) score, which introduces an external evaluator represented by a trained Inception Network [27,28]. Although the good results introduced by the FID score as fitness, the drawbacks are the execution cost and the dependence of an external evaluator.

The FID score is currently the most used metric, but several other metrics were proposed to evaluate the performance of GANs [4,33]. Metrics such as skill rating was successfully used to evaluate GANs in some contexts [20]. Skill rating uses a game rating system to assess the skill of generators and discriminators. Each generator and discriminator is considered as a player in a game and the pairing between them is designed as a match. The outcome of the matches is used as input to calculate the skill of each player.

We took inspiration from the use of skill rating to quantify the performance of generators and discriminators in GANs to design a fitness function to be used within COEGAN. Therefore, we replace the regular fitness used in COEGAN with the skill rating, i.e., the discriminator and the generator use the skill rating metric instead of the loss function and the FID score. We present an experimental study on the use of this metric, comparing the results with the previous approach used in COEGAN, a random search approach, and with a non-evolutionary model based on DCGAN. The results evidenced that skill rating provides useful information to guide the evolution of GANs when used in combination with the COEGAN model. The skill rating is more efficient with respect to execution time and does not compromise the quality of the final results.

The remainder of this paper is organized as follows: Sect. 2 introduces the concepts of GANs and evolutionary algorithms, presenting state-of-the-art works using these concepts; Sect. 3 presents COEGAN and our approach to use skill rating as fitness; Sect. 4 displays the experimental results using this approach; finally, Sect. 5 presents our conclusions and future work.

2   Background and Related Works

Generative Adversarial Networks (GANs) [9] are an adversarial model that have became relevant for presenting high-quality results in generative tasks, mainly on the image domain. In summary, a GAN is composed of a generator and a discriminator, trained as adversaries by a unified algorithm. Each component is represented by a neural network and has a role guided by its specific loss function. The generator has to produce synthetic samples that should be classified as real by the discriminator. The discriminator should distinguish between fake samples and samples originated from an input distribution. For this, the discriminator receives a real input distribution for training, such as an image dataset. The generator is fed with a latent distribution, usually with a lower dimension than the real input distribution, and never directly looks into the real distribution.

In the original GAN model, the loss function of the discriminator is defined as follows:

$$J^{(D)}(D, G) = -\mathbb{E}_{x \sim p_{data}}[\log D(x)] - \mathbb{E}_{z \sim p_z}[\log(1 - D(G(z)))]. \tag{1}$$

For the generator, the non-saturating version of the loss function is defined by:

$$J^{(G)}(G) = -\mathbb{E}_{z \sim p_z}[\log(D(G(z)))]. \tag{2}$$

In Eq. 1, p_{data} is the real data used as input to the discriminator. In Eqs. 1 and 2, z is the latent space used to feed the generator, p_z is the latent distribution, G is the generator, and D represents the discriminator.

Despite the quality of the results, GANs are hard to train and the presence of stability issues on the training process is frequent. The vanishing gradient and the mode collapse are two of the most common problems that affect the training of GANs. The vanishing gradient issue is characterized by a disequilibrium between the forces of the GAN components. For example, the discriminator becomes too powerful and does not make mistakes when detecting fake samples produced by the generator. In this case, the progress on the training stagnates. The mode collapse problem occurs when the generator only partially captures the input distribution used on the discriminator training. This issue affects the variability and the quality of the created samples.

Several approaches were used to minimize these issues and leverage the quality of the results. In this context, alternative loss functions were proposed to replace the functions used in the classical GAN model, such as WGAN [3], LSGAN [16], and RGAN [12]. Another strategy is to propose architectural changes to the GAN model. DCGAN [21] proposed a reference architecture for the discriminator and the generator in GANs, describing a set of constraints and rules to achieve better results. On the other hand, a predefined strategy to progressively grow a GAN during the training procedure was proposed in [13]. SAGAN [34] proposed the use of a self-attention module in order to capture the relationship between spatial regions of the input sample. Although these approaches tried to minimize the problems and produce better results, issues still affect the training of GANs [3,10,23]. Besides, the discovery of efficient models and hyperparameters for the models is not a trivial task, requiring recurrent empirical validation.

Recently, research was conducted to propose the use of evolutionary algorithms to train and evolve GANs [1,5–7,29,32]. Evolutionary algorithms take inspiration on the mechanism found in nature to evolve a population of potential solutions on the production of better outcomes for a given problem [24]. E-GAN [32] uses an evolutionary algorithm to combine three different types of loss functions in the training. An approach based on the Pareto set approximations was used in [7] to model the GAN problem. Lipizzaner [1] proposes the use of spatial coevolution to match generators and discriminators in the training process. Mustangs [29] unifies the concepts of E-GAN and Lipizzaner in a single model, using different loss functions and spatial coevolution in the solution.

COEGAN uses neuroevolution and coevolution on the training and evolution of GANs. Despite the advances identified by the experiments, the results also showed that the fitness functions used in the model can be improved. COEGAN uses the loss function (Eq. 1) as the fitness for discriminators and the FID score for generators. The use of better fitness can be helpful for the creation of better models and also avoid the common stability issues when training GANs. Furthermore, as specified in the FID score, COEGAN uses an external evaluator to quantify the fitness for generators.

Several strategies were proposed to quantify the performance of GANs [4,33]. Although the FID score is the most used metric to evaluate and compare GANs, alternative approaches can be successfully applied, such as skill rating [20]. The skill rating metric for GANs uses the Glicko-2 [8] rating system to calculate the performance. Glicko-2 was also used as comparison criteria between different evolutionary algorithms [30,31].

3   Our Approach

We present in this section our approach to applying skill rating as fitness in an evolutionary algorithm. For this, we make use of the previously introduced method called COEGAN [5,6], adapting the model for our proposal in this paper. Thus, we firstly introduce in this section the COEGAN algorithm. After that, we describe the skill rating method and its application in COEGAN.

3.1   COEGAN

COEGAN [5,6] proposes the use of neuroevolution and coevolution to train and evolve GANs. The motivations of COEGAN are to solve the stability issues frequently found when training GANs and also to automatically discover efficient models for different applications.

COEGAN is inspired by DeepNEAT [17] to design the model, also using coevolution techniques presented in NEAT applied to competitive coevolution [26]. The genome of COEGAN is represented by a sequential array of genes. This genome is transformed into a neural network, where each gene directly represents a layer in this network. The evolution occurs on the architecture and the internal parameters of each layer. Therefore, the mutation operators were used to add a layer, remove an existing layer, and mutate the internal parameters of a layer. For the sake of simplicity, in this work we only use convolutional layers in the addition operator. As in the original COEGAN proposal, crossover was not used in the final model because it introduced instability in the system.

Two separated populations are used in COEGAN: a population of discriminators and a population of generators. Thus, competitive coevolution was used to design the environment. In the evaluation phase, individuals are matched following an *all vs. all* strategy, i.e., each generator G_i will be matched against each discriminator D_j. Other strategies can be used, such as *all vs. best*. However, the *all vs. all* approach achieved the best results, despite the high execution cost with the application.

The selection phase uses a strategy based on NEAT [25]. Therefore, a speciation mechanism is used to promote innovation when evolving the populations. Fitness sharing adjusts the fitness of the individuals, making the selection proportional to the average fitness of each species. The species are grouped following the similarity on the genome of the individuals.

The fitness for the discriminator is the respective loss function of the classical GAN model, given by Eq. 1. The fitness of the generator is represented by the Fréchet Inception Distance (FID) [11], given by:

$$FID(x,g) = ||\mu_x - \mu_g||_2^2 + Tr(\Sigma_x + \Sigma_g - 2(\Sigma_x \Sigma_g)^{1/2}). \tag{3}$$

where μ_x, Σ_x, μ_g, and Σ_g represent the mean and covariance estimated for the real dataset x and fake samples g, respectively. The FID score uses the Inception Network [27,28], usually trained with the ImageNet dataset [22], to transform images into a feature space, which is interpreted as a continuous multivariate Gaussian. The mean and covariance of the two resulting Gaussians for the transformation of real and fake images are applied in Eq. 3.

3.2   Skill Rating

In games like chess, it is common to use a rating system to quantify the skill of players. In this context, the Glicko-2 [8] rating system can be used to measure the performance of players given a history of matches. The Glicko-2 system associates to each player three variables: the rating r, the deviation RD, and the volatility σ. The rating r indicates the actual skill of player after a sequence of matches with other players in a game. The volatility σ represents the expected variability on the rating of a player. The deviation RD represents the confidence in the player's rating. A system constant τ is also used to control the rate of change on the volatility σ. Different from r, RD, and σ, this parameter is associated with the whole rating system.

All players are initialized with the recommended values of 1500 for the rating r, 350 for the deviation RD and 0.06 for the volatility σ. These values can be tuned according to the characteristics of the application. At a fixed time period, the results of all matches between players are stored and used to update the rating r, deviation RD, and volatility σ. It is recommended to use a time span large enough to contain at least 10 to 15 games for each player.

The Glicko-2 rating system was previously used on the comparison of evolutionary algorithms [30,31]. In this case, different algorithms are executed on a given problem and the solutions found by them are matched to produce the outcome used as input to the Glicko-2 system. Thus, the algorithms are ranked according to the rating score.

Another application of the Glicko-2 system was to evaluate the performance of GANs [20]. In this case, the rating was applied between discriminators and generators of different epochs to calculate the progressive skills of them. The authors found that skill rating provides a useful metric to relatively compare GANs.

We took inspiration on these use cases of Glicko-2 to apply the system in COEGAN. The fitness function for discriminators and generators in the COEGAN algorithm was changed to use the skill rating metric computed using Glicko-2. Therefore, each generator G_i and discriminator D_j have an associated skill rating, represented by r, RD, and σ.

At the evaluation phase of the evolutionary algorithm, discriminators and generators are matched to be trained with the GAN algorithm and also to be evaluated for selection and reproduction. We modeled each evaluation step between a generator and a discriminator as a game to be quantified and applied to the skill rating calculation, composing a tournament of generators against discriminators. Therefore, as we use the *all vs. all* pairing strategy, each outcome of the match between (G_i, D_j) is stored and used to update the skill rating at the end of each generation. Inspired by the approach in [20], we use the following equations to calculate the outcome of a match for the discriminator:

$$D_j^{real} = \sum_{x \sim p_{data}} th\left(D_j(x) > 0.5\right) \tag{4}$$

$$D_{ij}^{fake} = \sum_{z \sim p_z} th\left(D_j(G_i(z)) < 0.5\right) \tag{5}$$

$$D_{ij}^{wr} = \frac{D_j^{real} + D_{ij}^{fake}}{m + n} \tag{6}$$

where D_j^{real} is the win rate of the discriminator with respect to the real data, D_{ij}^{fake} is the rate related to the fake data, D_{ij}^{WR} is the overall win rate of the discriminator D_j, th is a threshold function that outputs 1 when the threshold is met and 0 otherwise, D_j outputs the probability of the sample to be real, G_i is the generator, p_{data} is the input distribution, x is a sample drawn from the input distribution, p_z is the latent distribution, z is the latent input for the generator, m is the number of real samples, and n is the number of fake samples. In summary, the win rate for the discriminator is based on the number of mistakes made by it with the real input batch (Eq. 4) and fake data produced by the generator (Eq. 5).

For the generator, the result is calculated as:

$$G_{ij}^{wr} = 1 - D_{ij}^{wr} \tag{7}$$

where D_{ij}^{wr} is the discriminator win rate given by Eq. 6.

The win rates of each generator and discriminator are used as input to update the skill rate of the individuals. Each individual G_i and D_j has a set of outcomes T^{wr}, containing the win rate of each match and the skill of the adversarial. Thus, a generator G_i has a set $T_{G_i}^{wr}$ containing each pair (G_{ij}^{wr}, D_j^{sk}) for a generation. A discriminator D_j has a set $T_{D_j}^{wr}$ containing each pair (D_{ij}^{wr}, G_i^{sk}). The sets $T_{G_i}^{wr}$ and $T_{D_j}^{wr}$ are used to calculate the new skill rating at the end of the generation, represented by G_i^{sk} and D_j^{sk}, respectively. It is important to note that the update of the skill rating of a player depends on the skill of the adversary, i.e., win a game from a strong player is more rewarding than to win from a weak player.

We propose in this work the use of skill rating as fitness in COEGAN, represented by the use of D_j^{sk} instead of Eq. 1 for discriminators and G_i^{sk} instead of Eq. 3 for generators. Therefore, the fitness functions for discriminators and generators are defined as:

$$F_{D_j} = r_{D_j^{sk}}, \qquad F_{G_i} = r_{G_i^{sk}}, \tag{8}$$

where $r_{D_j^{sk}}$ and $r_{G_i^{sk}}$ are the rating r for discriminators and generators, respectively. At each generation, individuals update the skill rating following these rules. In the breeding process, the offspring carry the skill rating of their parent. In this way, we keep track of the progress of individuals through generations, even when mutations occur to change their genome.

Besides the matches between each pair (G_i, D_j), individuals in the current generation can also be matched against individuals from previous generations. The algorithm can keep track of the best individuals from the last generations to match them against the current individuals in order to ensure the progression of them. This is also a strategy to avoid the intransitivity problem that occurs in competitive coevolution algorithms. The intransitivity problem means that a solution a is better than other solution b and b is better than c, but it is not guaranteed that a is better than c, leading to cycling between solutions during the evolutionary process and harming the progress toward optimal outcomes [2, 18]. However, this work does not use previous generations in the skill rating calculation. We leave the evaluation of this strategy for future work.

4   Experiments

To evaluate the use of skill rating with COEGAN, we conducted an experimental study using the Street View House Numbers (SVHN) dataset [19]. The SVHN dataset is composed of digits from 0 to 9 extracted from real house numbers. Therefore, it is a dataset with a structure similar to the MNIST dataset [15] used in previous COEGAN experiments, but with more complexity introduced by the use of real images, presenting digits with a variety of backgrounds. The experiments compare the results of the original COEGAN approach (with the FID score and the loss function as fitness for generators and discriminators), COEGAN with skill rating applied as fitness, a random search approach, and a DCGAN-based architecture. We also present a comparison between the FID score and the skill rating metric in experiments with the MNIST dataset.

4.1   Experimental Setup

Table 1. Experimental parameters.

Evolutionary parameters	Value
Number of generations	50
Population size (generators and discriminators)	10
Add layer rate	20%
Remove layer rate	10%
Change layer rate	10%
Output channels range	[32, 256]
Tournament k_t	2
FID samples	2048
Genome limit	4
Species	3
Skill rating parameters	**Value**
r, RD, σ	1500, 350, 0.06
Constant τ	1.0
GAN parameters	**Value**
Batch size	64
Batches per generation	20
Optimizer	Adam
Learning rate	0.001
Betas	0.5, 0.999

Table 1 lists the parameters used in our experiments. These parameters were chosen based on preliminary experiments and the results presented in our previous works [5,6]. All experiments are executed for 50 generations. The number of individuals in the populations of generators and discriminators is 10. This number of individuals is enough to achieve the recommended matches to feed the Glicko-2 rating system. For the variation operators, we use the rates 20%, 10%, and 10% for the add layer rate, remove layer rate, and change layer rate, respectively. The number of output channels is sampled using the interval [32,256]. A tournament with $k_t = 2$ is applied inside each species to select the individuals for reproduction and the algorithm self-adjust to contains 3 species for the population of generators and discriminators. The number of samples used to calculate the FID score is 2048. To make the experiments comparable, each individual has a genome limited to 4 genes, the same number of layers used in the DCGAN-based experiments. Besides, as the DCGAN-based model does not use an evolutionary algorithm, these evolutionary parameters described above are not applied to it.

The initial skill rating parameters used in the experiments are the same suggested by the Glicko-2 system [8], i.e., the rating r, deviation RD, and the volatility σ are initialized with 1500, 150, and 0.06, respectively. The system constant τ was set to 1.0. We conduct previous experiments to choose the best τ for our context. We found no relevant changes with respect to this parameter. Nevertheless, experiments focused on the tuning of τ should be executed to evaluate its effect on our proposal.

All experiments used the original GAN model, i.e., the neural networks are trained with the classical loss functions defined by Eqs. 1 and 2. The GAN parameters were chosen based on preliminary experiments and the setup commonly used on the evaluation of GANs [10,13,21]. The batch size used in the training is 64. The Adam optimizer [14] is used with the learning rate of 0.001, beta 1 of 0.5, and beta 2 of 0.999. Each pairing between generators and discriminators is trained by 20 batches per generation. As the *all vs. all* is used, each generator and discriminator will be trained for a total of 200 batches. For the DCGAN-based experiments, we have a single generator and discriminator. Therefore, we train them for 200 batches to keep the results comparable with the COEGAN experiments.

The results are evaluated using the FID score and the skill rating. For the SVHN dataset, the FID score is based on the Inception Network trained with the SVHN dataset instead of the ImageNet dataset, the same strategy used in the experiments of [20]. For the MNIST results, we use the Inception Network trained with the ImageNet dataset. All results presented in this work are obtained by the average of five executions, with a confidence interval of 95%.

4.2   Results

Figure 1 presents the results of the best FID score per generation for the experiments with the SVHN dataset. We can see that the results for the original COEGAN proposal, i.e., COEGAN guided by the FID and the loss as fitness functions, are still better than the results for COEGAN with the skill rating metric. However, COEGAN guided by skill rating presented better FID scores than the random search approach. Thus, this evidences that skill rating provides useful information to the system, presenting evolutionary pressure to the individuals in the search of efficient models. Moreover, COEGAN with the FID score as fitness outperforms the DCGAN-based approach, illustrating the advantages of COEGAN.

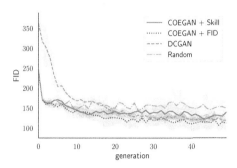

Fig. 1. Best FID score for generators with a 95% confidence interval

We found in the experiments that skill rating sometimes overestimates the score for bad individuals, affecting the final results of the training. A dataset with the complexity of SVHN may require more training epochs to achieve better outcomes, and the variability introduced by the *all vs. all* pairing may be too much for complex datasets. Therefore, another approach such as spatial coevolution used in [1, 29] will be considered in further experiments. Furthermore, the calculation of the match outcome, given by Eqs. 4–7, can be improved to overcome this problem.

Table 2. FID score of the algorithms used in the experiments with SVHN.

Algorithm	FID score
COEGAN + Skill	135.1 ± 9.8
COEGAN + FID	111.7 ± 22.1
DCGAN-based	119.0 ± 10.1
Random search	148.9 ± 30.7

Table 2 shows the average FID of the best scores at the last generation for each experiment with the SVHN dataset. We can see the difference between the FID of the solutions experimented in this work. As expected, the results for the random search approach is unstable and worse than the others, presenting a high standard deviation. However, the difference is not big due to the limitations we impose on the experimental parameters. Experiments adding the possibility of larger networks for COEGAN should be performed to assess the capacity to outperform both the random search and DCGAN approaches by a larger margin.

Despite the inferior results when compared to COEGAN with FID as fitness, the advantage with the skill rating is that we can avoid the use of an external evaluator as in the FID calculation, represented by the Inception Network. The execution cost of the skill rating metric is also lower than the FID score. The FID score requires a high number of samples to have a good representation of the data. In our experiments, we use 2048 against 64 on the skill rating calculation (64 represents the batch size used in Eq. 6). Furthermore, the Inception Network has a complex architecture and the FID score uses slow procedures in the calculation. Skill rating uses the own neural network of individuals in the experiments, and the Glicko-2 system is fast to execute.

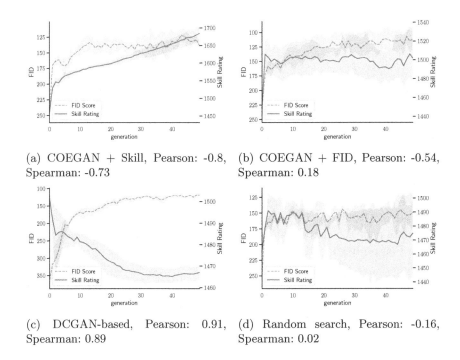

(a) COEGAN + Skill, Pearson: -0.8, Spearman: -0.73

(b) COEGAN + FID, Pearson: -0.54, Spearman: 0.18

(c) DCGAN-based, Pearson: 0.91, Spearman: 0.89

(d) Random search, Pearson: -0.16, Spearman: 0.02

Fig. 2. Comparison between the best FID score and the respective skill rating of generators trained with the SVHN dataset.

Figure 2 shows the progression of the skill rating through generations compared with the best FID scores. We can see in COEGAN guided by skill rating a clear improvement of the rating, as this is the same function used to provide evolutionary pressure in the individuals. In the experiments of COEGAN with FID, the progress also exists but is less relevant. The random approach presented an erratic behavior of the skill rating, showing that the individuals do not improve in this approach. In the DCGAN-based experiments, the skill rating behaves differently, showing a decreasing pattern. As there is only a single discriminator and generator, the number of matches per generation is only one. Therefore, we do not meet the recommendations of the Glicko-2 system of having at least ten matches per time period and the rating is not useful for this case.

Except for the DCGAN experiments, we can also see in Fig. 2 some level of correlation between the best FID score and the respective skill rating among the generators in the populations. The results demonstrated that skill rating follows the tendency of the FID score, evidencing that it can be used to guide the evolution of GANs. We computed the Pearson correlation and the Spearman rank correlation between FID and skill rating to support this analysis. We found a relevant negative correlation for the experiments with COEGAN guided by skill rating, achieving a Pearson correlation coefficient of -0.8 and a Spearman rank correlation of -0.73. As FID is a distance measurement (lower is better) and skill rating is a score (high is better), the negative correlation is expected.

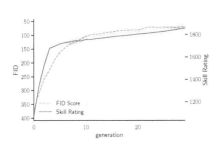
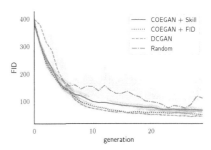

(a) Best FID score and the respective skill rating for COEGAN + Skill. Pearson: -0.96, Spearman: -0.99

(b) Best FID score for all solutions

Fig. 3. Results for the experiments with the MNIST dataset.

We experienced high variability on the FID score in the experiments with the SVHN dataset, both for the Inception Network trained with the ImageNet and SVHN datasets. Therefore, we conduct a study using the MNIST dataset to enhance the relationship between the FID score and skill rating. We followed the same parameters presented in Table 1, but limiting the number of generations to 30. Figure 3(a) shows a smoother progression of skill rating and FID, illustrating a more clear relation between them, which is evidenced by the Pearson's correlation coefficient of -0.96 and the Spearman's rank correlation of -0.99. We also show in Fig. 3(b) that COEGAN guided by skill rating achieves performance similar to COEGAN guided by FID, outperforming the random search approach.

Figure 4 presents the average number of parameters in generators and discriminators from the experiments with the SVHN dataset. As there is no evolutionary algorithm applied to DCGAN, the number of parameters is constant. It is important to note that the average number of parameters on the individuals in the COEGAN experiments is much lower than the parameters in

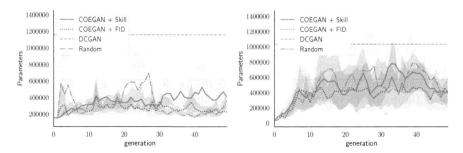

(a) Number of parameters for generators (b) Number of parameters for discriminators

Fig. 4. Average number of parameters in the neural networks of generators and discriminators at each generation. Note that the number of parameters for the DCGAN-based
experiments is constant, as there is not an evolutionary algorithm applied to this case.

DCGAN. Despite this, the results of COEGAN are still better than DCGAN.
Therefore, the experiments evidenced that the evolutionary algorithm applied in
COEGAN was able to find more efficient models. We limited in the experimental
setup the complexity and the number of layers in the genome. Experiments with
an expanded setup should be conducted to assess the possibility of even better
results.

(a) COEGAN with skill rating as fitness

(b) COEGAN with the FID score and
loss function as fitness

Fig. 5. Samples produced by the best generator after the COEGAN training.

Figure 5 shows samples produced by the generator after the COEGAN training with FID and skill rating as fitness. In order to achieve better quality, we
trained the algorithms using 200 batches at each generation (instead of 20). We
can see that the quality of the samples is similar, with both strategies presenting
variability on the samples.

5   Conclusions

Generative Adversarial Networks (GANs) represented a relevant advance in generative models, producing impressive results in contexts such as the image domain. In spite of this, the training of a GAN is challenging and often requires a trial-and-error approach to achieve the desired outcome. Several strategies were used in order to improve training stability and produce better results. Proposals modified the original GAN model to introduce alternative loss functions and architectural changes. On the other hand, the use of evolutionary algorithms in the context of GANs was recently proposed. COEGAN combines neuroevolution and coevolution on the training and evolution of GANs. However, experiments identified that the fitness used in COEGAN can be improved to better guide the evolution of discriminators and generators in the populations.

We propose the use of a game rating system, based on the application of Glicko-2 introduced in [20], to design a new fitness strategy for COEGAN. Thus, we changed the fitness functions used by discriminators and generators to use the skill rating metric instead of the loss function and the FID score. We conducted experiments to evaluate this proposal and compare the results with the previous COEGAN fitness proposal, a DCGAN-based approach, and a random search model.

The results evidenced that, although the FID score as fitness provides better results, the skill rating method also contribute with useful information in the evolution of GANs. The use of COEGAN with skill rating outperforms the random search approach, demonstrating the effectiveness of this fitness function. When compared to the FID score, the advantages when using skill rating is the lower execution cost and the self-contained solution, i.e., skill rating does not need to use an external component such as in the FID score. The calculation of the FID requires a trained Inception Network, making the score highly dependent on the context where it was trained and applied. Therefore, skill rating has the potential to be used in more domains. Besides, the skill rating does not require a neural network to interpret images produced by generators. Instead, the output of the discriminator is used in the calculation, resulting in a lower execution cost when compared to the FID score. We also show that there is a correlation between the FID score and the skill rating metric when using the latter as fitness with COEGAN. However, skill rating worked better with the MNIST dataset, making this correlation more evident. The SVHN dataset is more complex and sometimes lead to disagreement between FID and skill rating. The strategy to obtain the results of matches between generators and discriminators can be improved to better represent the player's skill.

As future work, we aim to expand the strategies evaluated in this paper regarding the use of skill rating as fitness. We will evaluate changes in the skill tournament to take into account individuals from previous generations. Besides, different strategies to calculate the outcome of matches can be used to improve the results. We will investigate the use of strategies that bring information about the variability of the samples produced by generators, in order to approximate the information provided by the FID score.

Acknowledgments. This article is based upon work from COST Action CA15140: ImAppNIO, supported by COST (European Cooperation in Science and Technology).

References

1. Al-Dujaili, A., Schmiedlechner, T., Hemberg, E., O'Reilly, U.M.: Towards distributed coevolutionary GANs. In: AAAI 2018 Fall Symposium (2018)
2. Antonio, L.M., Coello, C.A.C.: Coevolutionary multiobjective evolutionary algorithms: survey of the state-of-the-art. IEEE Trans. Evol. Comput. **22**(6), 851–865 (2018)
3. Arjovsky, M., Chintala, S., Bottou, L.: Wasserstein generative adversarial networks. In: International Conference on Machine Learning, pp. 214–223 (2017)
4. Borji, A.: Pros and cons of GAN evaluation measures. Comput. Vis. Image Underst. **179**, 41–65 (2019)
5. Costa, V., Lourenço, N., Correia, J., Machado, P.: COEGAN: evaluating the coevolution effect in generative adversarial networks. In: Proceedings of the Genetic and Evolutionary Computation Conference, pp. 374–382. ACM (2019)
6. Costa, V., Lourenço, N., Machado, P.: Coevolution of generative adversarial networks. In: Kaufmann, P., Castillo, P.A. (eds.) EvoApplications 2019. LNCS, vol. 11454, pp. 473–487. Springer, Cham (2019). https://doi.org/10.1007/978-3-030-16692-2_32
7. Garciarena, U., Santana, R., Mendiburu, A.: Evolved GANs for generating pareto set approximations. In: Proceedings of the Genetic and Evolutionary Computation Conference, GECCO 2018, pp. 434–441. ACM, New York (2018)
8. Glickman, M.E.: Example of the Glicko-2 system, pp. 1–6. Boston University (2013). http://www.glicko.net/glicko/glicko2.pdf
9. Goodfellow, I., et al.: Generative adversarial nets. In: NIPS. Curran Associates, Inc. (2014)
10. Gulrajani, I., Ahmed, F., Arjovsky, M., Dumoulin, V., Courville, A.C.: Improved training of wasserstein GANs. In: Advances in Neural Information Processing Systems, pp. 5769–5779 (2017)
11. Heusel, M., Ramsauer, H., Unterthiner, T., Nessler, B., Hochreiter, S.: GANs trained by a two time-scale update rule converge to a local Nash equilibrium. In: Advances in Neural Information Processing Systems, pp. 6629–6640 (2017)
12. Jolicoeur-Martineau, A.: The relativistic discriminator: a key element missing from standard GAN. In: International Conference on Learning Representations (2019)
13. Karras, T., Aila, T., Laine, S., Lehtinen, J.: Progressive growing of GANs for improved quality, stability, and variation. In: International Conference on Learning Representations (2018)
14. Kingma, D.P., Ba, J.: Adam: a method for stochastic optimization. In: International Conference on Learning Representations (ICLR) (2015)
15. LeCun, Y.: The MNIST database of handwritten digits (1998). http://yann.lecun.com/exdb/mnist/
16. Mao, X., Li, Q., Xie, H., Lau, R.Y., Wang, Z., Smolley, S.P.: Least squares generative adversarial networks. In: 2017 IEEE International Conference on Computer Vision (ICCV), pp. 2813–2821. IEEE (2017)
17. Miikkulainen, R., et al.: Evolving deep neural networks. arXiv preprint arXiv:1703.00548 (2017)
18. Mitchell, M.: Coevolutionary learning with spatially distributed populations. In: Computational Intelligence: Principles and Practice (2006)

19. Netzer, Y., Wang, T., Coates, A., Bissacco, A., Wu, B., Ng, A.Y.: Reading digits in natural images with unsupervised feature learning (2011)
20. Olsson, C., Bhupatiraju, S., Brown, T., Odena, A., Goodfellow, I.: Skill rating for generative models. arXiv preprint arXiv:1808.04888 (2018)
21. Radford, A., Metz, L., Chintala, S.: Unsupervised representation learning with deep convolutional generative adversarial networks. arXiv preprint arXiv:1511.06434 (2015)
22. Russakovsky, O., et al.: ImageNet large scale visual recognition challenge. Int. J. Comput. Vis. **115**(3), 211–252 (2015). https://doi.org/10.1007/s11263-015-0816-y
23. Salimans, T., Goodfellow, I., Zaremba, W., Cheung, V., Radford, A., Chen, X.: Improved techniques for training GANs. In: Advances in Neural Information Processing Systems, pp. 2234–2242 (2016)
24. Sims, K.: Evolving 3D morphology and behavior by competition. Artif. Life **1**(4), 353–372 (1994)
25. Stanley, K.O., Miikkulainen, R.: Evolving neural networks through augmenting topologies. Evol. Comput. **10**(2), 99–127 (2002)
26. Stanley, K.O., Miikkulainen, R.: Competitive coevolution through evolutionary complexification. J. Artif. Intell. Res. **21**, 63–100 (2004)
27. Szegedy, C., et al.: Going deeper with convolutions. In: Proceedings of the IEEE Conference on Computer Vision and Pattern Recognition, pp. 1–9 (2015)
28. Szegedy, C., Vanhoucke, V., Ioffe, S., Shlens, J., Wojna, Z.: Rethinking the inception architecture for computer vision. In: Proceedings of the IEEE Conference on Computer Vision and Pattern Recognition, pp. 2818–2826 (2016)
29. Toutouh, J., Hemberg, E., O'Reilly, U.M.: Spatial evolutionary generative adversarial networks. arXiv preprint arXiv:1905.12702 (2019)
30. Veček, N., Črepinšek, M., Mernik, M., Hrnčič, D.: A comparison between different chess rating systems for ranking evolutionary algorithms. In: 2014 Federated Conference on Computer Science and Information Systems, pp. 511–518. IEEE (2014)
31. Veček, N., Mernik, M., Črepinšek, M.: A chess rating system for evolutionary algorithms: a new method for the comparison and ranking of evolutionary algorithms. Inf. Sci. **277**, 656–679 (2014)
32. Wang, C., Xu, C., Yao, X., Tao, D.: Evolutionary generative adversarial networks. arXiv preprint arXiv:1803.00657 (2018)
33. Xu, Q., et al.: An empirical study on evaluation metrics of generative adversarial networks. arXiv preprint arXiv:1806.07755 (2018)
34. Zhang, H., Goodfellow, I., Metaxas, D., Odena, A.: Self-attention generative adversarial networks. arXiv preprint arXiv:1805.08318 (2018)

A Local Search with a Surrogate Assisted Option for Instance Reduction

Ferrante Neri$^{(\boxtimes)}$ and Isaac Triguero

Computational Optimisation and Learning (COL) Lab, School of Computer Science,
University of Nottingham, Nottingham, UK
{ferrante.neri,isaac.triguero}@nottingham.ac.uk

Abstract. In data mining, instance reduction is a key data pre-processing step that simplifies and cleans raw data, by either selecting or creating new samples, before applying a learning algorithm. This usually yields to a complex large scale and computationally expensive optimisation problem which has been typically tackled by sophisticated population-based metaheuristics. Unlike the recent literature, in order to accomplish this target, this article proposes the use of a simple local search algorithm and its integration with an optional surrogate assisted model. This local search, in accordance with variable decomposition techniques for large scale problems, perturbs an n-dimensional vector along the directions identified by its design variables one by one.

Empirical results in 40 small data sets show that, despite its simplicity, the proposed baseline local search on its own is competitive with more complex algorithms representing the state-of-the-art for instance reduction in classification problems. The use of the proposed local surrogate model enables a reduction of the computationally expensive objective function calls with accuracy test results overall comparable with respect to its baseline counterpart.

Keywords: Instance reduction · Instance generation ·
Computationally expensive problems · Surrogate assisted algorithms ·
Local search · Pattern Search

1 Introduction

Data science is a discipline that studies methods to store and manage data with the aim of extracting knowledge from it [6]. A typical problem in data science is to have a very large raw data set which requires pre-processing to enable data mining techniques to learn from a more manageable data set that is free of noise, redundant or irrelevant samples. In order to overcome this issue, a normal practice consists of selecting some instances and discarding others, or creating artificial samples that better represent the original training data.

However, it is fundamental to properly select or generate those instances. *Instance reduction* techniques, either selection [7] or generation [28], have to

© Springer Nature Switzerland AG 2020
P. A. Castillo et al. (Eds.): EvoApplications 2020, LNCS 12104, pp. 578–594, 2020.
https://doi.org/10.1007/978-3-030-43722-0_37

allow still to extract the required knowledge. In other words, we would like to simplify the original data set and keep it as informative as it is when it contains all the data, or even better if noisy data is removed appropriately [14].

Instance reduction can be formulated as an optimisation problem and be addressed by search algorithms. The pure selection of instances can be seen as a binary space search problem [1]. The generation of new representative instances, however, can be expressed as a continuous space search problem. The latter approach turned out to be more flexible, but also more complex [30]. In both cases, Evolutionary Algorithms (EAs) have excelled in comparison with other approaches [7,28]. EAs for instance generation are based on optimising the location of a subset of instances [18,30].

Note that most instance reduction algorithm were originally designed to enhance the performance of the Nearest Neighbour classifier (NN) [5], but the resulting pre-processed data set could be used, in principle, by any classifier [1]. In this work, we are focused on instance generation for NN classification, also known as prototype generation.

Two major challenges are associated to the instance reduction problem: the high dimensionality of the problem and the high cost of each objective function evaluation, which typically consists of classifying the training data. The first challenge is addressed by using an exploitative operator which can be embedded within heuristic frameworks. Some examples under the umbrella name of Memetic Algorithms are proposed in [8,9]. A comparison reporting the advantages of the extra local search is reported in [20]. In the recent literature, these problems are currently being addressed by using distributed approaches in big data platforms [33], but population-based approaches keep taking a long time to pre-process the data. Thus, there is a need for simpler and faster, yet powerful, search algorithms.

This article also explicitly addresses the second challenge by proposing a technique to limit the cost of instance reduction within the optimisation process. More specifically, this article proposes the use of a local search algorithm for large scale problems and a surrogate (approximated) local model to reduce the number of objective function calls. To the best of our knowledge, this is the first local search proposed for instance generation, and the use of surrogate models has been often neglected. The proposed local search samples the points in its neighbourhood and makes use of them to build a multi-variable (local) linear model. The resulting surrogate assisted local search [11,22,25,26] alternates the use of the true objective function with the approximation given by the surrogate model. A mechanism to ensure that wrong search directions are suggested by the surrogate model has been implemented: the algorithm checks the promising points provided by the surrogate model before accepting a new base point.

The remainder of this article is organised in the following way. Section 2 describes the instance reduction as an optimisation problem and provides an explanation why the problem is unavoidably large scale and why calculation of the objective function is computationally expensive. Section 3 describes and justifies the proposed method. Details about the implementation and linear regression model are also included. Section 4 displays the algorithmic results. Finally, Sect. 5 provides the conclusion of this study.

2 Problem Formulation

Let **TR** be a training data set and **TS** a test set for a supervised classification problem. Both data sets can be viewed as a matrix whose rows are the instances and columns are the features:

$$\mathbf{TR} = \begin{pmatrix} \mathbf{F_1} \ \mathbf{F_2} \ \dots \ \mathbf{F_m} \\ \mathbf{I_1} \ a_{11} \ a_{12} \ \dots \ a_{1m} \\ \mathbf{I_2} \ a_{21} \ a_{22} \ \dots \ a_{2m} \\ \dots \ \dots \ \dots \ \dots \ \dots \\ \mathbf{I_l} \ a_{l1} \ a_{l2} \ \dots \ a_{lm} \end{pmatrix}$$

Each instance belongs to a class ω. For the **TR** set the class ω is known, while it is unknown for **TS**. The objective of an instance reduction algorithm is to provide a reduced set **RS** of instances, which are either selected or generated from the examples of **TR**,

$$\mathbf{RS} = \begin{pmatrix} \mathbf{F_1} \ \mathbf{F_2} \ \dots \ \mathbf{F_m} \\ \mathbf{I_1} \ b_{11} \ b_{12} \ \dots \ b_{1m} \\ \mathbf{I_2} \ b_{21} \ b_{22} \ \dots \ b_{2m} \\ \dots \ \dots \ \dots \ \dots \ \dots \\ \mathbf{I_i} \ b_{i1} \ b_{i2} \ \dots \ b_{im} \end{pmatrix}$$

with $i \ll l$ that still allows the data representation of **TR**. **RS** should be created to efficiently represent the distributions of the classes. The size of RS should be significantly reduced to minimise the information that requires storing, and speed up the posterior classification phase.

We may, equivalently, represent the matrix **RS** as a vector **x** of length $n = i \times m$ whose elements are the rows of **TR** arranged sequentially

$$\mathbf{x} = (b_{11}, b_{12}, \dots, b_{1m}, b_{21}, b_{22}, \dots, b_{2m}, \dots, b_{i1}, b_{i2}, \dots, b_{im}) = (x_1, x_2, \dots, x_n)$$

The objective function $f(\mathbf{x})$ will measure how well the resulting RS exemplifies the original training data TR. To do so, in the literature, RS is inferred using the TR matrix as representative information of the problem, assuming that this will allow us to classify the elements of TS. In particular, this objective function simply calculates the classification accuracy (i.e. number of correct classifications regarding the total number of instances classified) using RS as training data, and TR as test data.

2.1 Computational Cost of the Objective Function

The exact computational cost of the objective function depends on the particular classifier that is being used. Most of the instance reduction literature focused their efforts on improving the well-known NN classifier, because it is one of the most affected classifiers by the size of the training data.

Focusing on the NN rule as base classifier, calculating the accuracy of RS consists of computing the Euclidean distance between all elements of TR against all elements of RS and determine which is the closest instance in RS for each element of TR. The class label of the closest instance is used as prediction.

This intuitively shows that the cost of the objective function will be very high when the size of TR is very big. The complexity of instance reduction models is $O((i \cdot m)^2)$ or higher, and best performing methods are based on EAs [30].

Current research is typically focused on the use of divide-and-conquer approaches, implemented with big data technologies, to parallelise the execution of instance reduction approaches. We can also find an approximation strategy, called windowing [31], which estimates the fitness value of RS using a random subset of TR at every iteration of the search (this reduces significantly the cost, but could mislead the search). However, the use of more sophisticated surrogate models to reduce the number of evaluations for instance reduction algorithms has been neglected.

3   A Local Search for Instance Reduction

This section presents the proposed method, outlines its theoretical and implementation aspects and justifies the choices made. More specifically, Subsect. 3.1 presents the structure of the baseline Local Search, Subsect. 3.2 describes the multivariable linear model used in this study, Subsect. 3.3 outlines the surrogate assisted technique to build and use the surrogate model with the original objective function, and finally, Subsect. 3.4 provides a justification of the algorithmic choices made.

3.1   Baseline Local Search

The proposed algorithm is based on a greedy local search [13,21] of the family of Pattern Search algorithms [27]. The algorithm perturbs each variable (of $\mathbf{x}$) at the time and replaces the current best point with a better one as soon as an improved solution is found. Along the directions identified by each variable, the algorithm attempts to move one step in one oriented direction and then half step in the opposite oriented direction if the first attempt fails. More specifically, the algorithm explores at first

$$\mathbf{x^t} = \mathbf{x} - \rho \cdot \mathbf{e^i}$$

where the scalar ρ is the step-size (exploratory radius) defined by the user and $\mathbf{e^i}$ is the ith versor, i.e. a vector composed of zeros and only a one in the ith position. Then if this exploration fails, the algorithm attempts to explore

$$\mathbf{x^t} = \mathbf{x} + \frac{\rho}{2} \cdot \mathbf{e^i}.$$

Algorithm 1. Baseline Local Search used for Instance Reduction (LSIR)

1: **INPUT x**
2: **while** local budget condition **do**
3:     $\mathbf{x^t} = \mathbf{x}$
        {****Exploration****}
4:     **for** $i = 1 : n$ **do**
5:         $\mathbf{x^t} = \mathbf{x} - \rho \cdot \mathbf{e^i}$
6:         **if** $f(\mathbf{x^t}) \leq f(\mathbf{x})$ **then**
7:             $\mathbf{x} = \mathbf{x^t}$
8:         **else**
9:             $\mathbf{x^t} = \mathbf{x} + \frac{\rho}{2} \cdot \mathbf{e^i}$
10:             **if** $f(\mathbf{x^t}) \leq f(\mathbf{x})$ **then**
11:                 $\mathbf{x} = \mathbf{x^t}$
12:             **end if**
13:         **end if**
14:     **end for**
15:     **if** $\mathbf{x}$ has **not** been updated **then**
16:         $\rho = \frac{\rho}{2}$
17:     **end if**
18: **end while**
19: **RETURN x**

Algorithm 1 shows the pseudocode of the baseline Local Search for Instance Reduction (LSIR) used in this study.

For the experiments carried out in this paper, on the basis of preliminary tests we employed a toroidal handling of the bounds, i.e. for $x_i \in [x_{low}, x_{high}]$, if $x_i > x_{high}$ it is reinserted by reassignment

$$x_i = x_{low} + (x_i - x_{high}) - \lfloor \frac{(x_i - x_{high})}{(x_{high} - x_{low})} \rfloor (x_{high} - x_{low})$$

while if $x_i < x_{low}$ it is reinserted by reassignment

$$x_i = x_{high} - \left((x_{low} - x_i) - \lfloor \frac{(x_{low} - x_i)}{(x_{high} - x_{low})} \rfloor (x_{high} - x_{low}) \right)$$

$\forall i$. The parentheses $\lfloor \rfloor$ indicate the truncation to the lower integer.

3.2 Linear Multivariable Surrogate Model

In order to approximate the objective function f and generate a surrogate function $\tilde{f}$, a multivariable linear regression with least square method is implemented, see [10,12]. For the sake of clarity, we built a local surrogate linear model

$$\tilde{f}(\mathbf{x}) = c_0 + c_1 x_1 + c_2 x_2 + c_n x_n = \sum_{j=1}^{n} c_j x_j + c_0.$$

In order to identify the $n + 1$ parameters $c_0, c_1, c_2, \ldots c_n$ the least square method has been applied.

The method processes a sample of $n + 1$ observation vectors

$$\mathbf{x^1}, \mathbf{x^2}, \ldots \mathbf{x^{n+1}}$$

where

$$\mathbf{x^j} = (x_{j1}, x_{j1}, \ldots, x_{jn})$$

and the corresponding function values

$$y_1 = f\left(\mathbf{x^1}\right)$$
$$y_2 = f\left(\mathbf{x^2}\right)$$
$$\ldots$$
$$y_j = f\left(\mathbf{x^j}\right)$$
$$\ldots$$

In order to find the parameters $c_0, c_1, c_2, \ldots c_n$ we have to minimise the following function Δ

$$\Delta = \sum_{j=1}^{n+1} \left(y_j - \left(c_0 + \sum_{i=1}^{n} c_i x_{ji} \right) \right)^2.$$

Thus, we have to calculate the partial derivatives of Δ with respect to $c_0, c_1, \ldots c_n$. The derivative with respect to c_0 and c_1 are, respectively

$$\frac{\partial \Delta}{\partial c_0} = -2 \left(\sum_{j=1}^{n+1} y_j - \left(c_0\,(n+1) + c_1 \sum_{j=1}^{n+1} x_{j1} + \ldots + c_n \sum_{j=1}^{n+1} x_{jn} \right) \right)$$

$$\frac{\partial \Delta}{\partial c_1} = -2 \left(\sum_{j=1}^{n+1} x_{j1} y_j - \left(c_0 \left(\sum_{j=1}^{n+1} x_{j1} \right) + \ldots + c_1 \left(\sum_{j=1}^{n+1} x_{j1}^2 \right) + \ldots + c_n \left(\sum_{j=1}^{n+1} x_{j1} x_{jn} \right) \right) \right)$$

The derivative with respect to the generic coefficient c_i is

$$\frac{\partial \Delta}{\partial c_i} = -2 \left(\sum_{j=1}^{n+1} x_{ji} y_j - \left(c_0 \left(\sum_{j=1}^{n+1} x_{ji} \right) + \ldots + c_i \left(\sum_{j=1}^{n+1} x_{ji}^2 \right) + \ldots + c_k \left(\sum_{j=1}^{n+1} x_{ji} x_{jk} \right) + \ldots \right) \right).$$

By simultaneously equating the derivatives to 0, we obtain the system of linear equations $\mathbf{Lc} = \hat{\mathbf{y}}$, that is

$$
\begin{pmatrix}
(n+1) & \sum_{j=1}^{n+1} x_{j1} & \sum_{j=1}^{n+1} x_{j2} & \cdots & \sum_{j=1}^{n+1} x_{jn} \\
\sum_{j=1}^{n+1} x_{j1} & \sum_{j=1}^{n+1} x_{j1}^2 & \sum_{j=1}^{n+1} x_{j1} x_{j2} & \cdots & \sum_{j=1}^{n+1} x_{j1} x_{jn} \\
\sum_{j=1}^{n+1} x_{j2} & \sum_{j=1}^{n+1} x_{j2} x_{j1} & \sum_{j=1}^{n+1} x_{j2}^2 & \cdots & \sum_{j=1}^{n+1} x_{j2} x_{jn} \\
\cdots & \cdots & \cdots & \cdots & \cdots \\
\sum_{j=1}^{n+1} x_{jn} & \sum_{j=1}^{n+1} x_{jn} x_{j1} & \sum_{j=1}^{n+1} x_{jn} x_{j2} & \cdots & \sum_{j=1}^{n+1} x_{jn}^2
\end{pmatrix}
\begin{pmatrix}
c_0 \\ c_1 \\ c_2 \\ \cdots \\ c_n
\end{pmatrix}
=
\begin{pmatrix}
\sum_{j=1}^{n+1} y_j \\
\sum_{j=1}^{n+1} x_{j1} y_j \\
\sum_{j=1}^{n+1} x_{j2} y_j \\
\cdots \\
\sum_{j=1}^{n+1} x_{jn} y_j
\end{pmatrix}.
$$

The solution of this system of linear equation is the set of parameters $\mathbf{c}$ which allow the construction of the surrogate model $\tilde{f}(\mathbf{x})$.

3.3   The Proposed Surrogate Local Search for Instance Reduction

With reference to Algorithm 1, each exploration in the **for** loop samples at least n and at most $2n$ trial points $\mathbf{x}^t$ in the neighbourhood of the current best point $\mathbf{x}$. The proposed Surrogate Assisted Local Search for Instance Reduction (SALSIR) exploits this logic by storing the visited points in a data structure $Surr$, that is a list where each entry is a point $\mathbf{x}$ and the corresponding $f(\mathbf{x})$:

$$Surr(k) = (\mathbf{x}, f(\mathbf{x})).$$

The data structure $Surr$ is filled until it contains n entries. Since the starting point is also inserted in $Surr$, $(n+1)$ points are available. These points are used to build a surrogate model $\tilde{f}(\mathbf{x})$.

For the remaining function calls, the LS uses the surrogate model $\tilde{f}(\mathbf{x})$ instead of the computationally expensive objective function $f(\mathbf{x})$. However, to ensure that wrongly estimated search directions do not jeopardise the functioning of the algorithm, when a solution estimated by the surrogate model outperforms the current best solution, its actual objective function value is checked. This increases the cost of the algorithm (reduces the advantages of the surrogate model [19]). On the other hand, this strategy enhances the reliability of the search.

If the moves failed in all directions, the exploratory radius is halved and the search repeated in a closer neighbourhood of $\mathbf{x}$. The pseudocode of this algorithm is shown Algorithm 2. We highlighted that the main loop of the algorithm is divided into parts: in the first the surrogate model is built while in the second the surrogate model is used as an alternative to the objective function.

3.4   Motivation of the Proposed Design

This section justifies the algorithmic choices and in particular answers to the following two questions.

1. *Why did we choose this algorithmic structure for this problem?*
2. *Why did we choose a multivariable linear model as a surrogate?*

To address the first question, we have to consider that the optimisation problem under examination besides being computationally expensive is large scale. In data science, it is very likely to have a large volume of data and matrix **RS** above can easily have still hundreds if not thousands of rows.

For this reason, we selected a LS component that is especially suited for large problems as it is the main element of the algorithm proposed in [34] and then used as a LS in [36] and modified as a stand-alone LS within other frameworks, see e.g. [3,4].

Techniques that perturb the variables separately, just like that used in this article, are known to be effective for large scale problems, see [15,17,24]. This observation was reported in the experimental study in [2]. Large scale problems are by no means easier than low-dimensional problems. However, since in practice the computational budget cannot grow exponentially with the problem dimensionality only a very limited portion of the decision space is explored.

Under these experimental conditions, the algorithm "sees" the problem as separable: average Pearson and Spearman coefficients of the variables approach zero independently on the problem when the dimensionality grows, see [2].

This study is one of the reasons behind the decision of using a linear surrogate model (second question above).

Algorithm 2. The Proposed Surrogate Assisted Local Search for Instance Reduction (SALSIR) Algorithm

---

1: **INPUT** x
2: **while** local budget condition **do**
3:     $k = 1; i = 1$
4:     $Surr = []$ {**Initialise the surrogate list**}
5:     $\mathbf{x^t} = \mathbf{x}$
    {**Build the surrogate**}
6:     **while** $k \leq (n+1)$ **do**
7:         $\mathbf{x^t} = \mathbf{x} - \rho \cdot \mathbf{e^i}$
8:         $Surr(k) = (\mathbf{x^t}, f(\mathbf{x^t}))$
9:         $k = k + 1$
10:         **if** $f(\mathbf{x^t}) \leq f(\mathbf{x})$ **then**
11:             $\mathbf{x} = \mathbf{x^t}$
12:         **else**
13:             $\mathbf{x^t} = \mathbf{x} + \frac{\rho}{2} \cdot \mathbf{e^i}$
14:             $Surr(k) = (\mathbf{x^t}, f(\mathbf{x^t}))$
15:             $k = k + 1$
16:             **if** $f(\mathbf{x^t}) \leq f(\mathbf{x})$ **then**
17:                 $\mathbf{x} = \mathbf{x^t}$
18:             **end if**
19:         **end if**
20:         $i = i + 1$
21:     **end while**
22:     Use $Surr$ to build the multivariable linear model $\tilde{f}(\mathbf{x}) = \sum_{j=1}^{n} c_j x_j + c_0$
    {**Use   the   surrogate   model   to   reduce   the   function   calls**}
23:     **for** i=i:n **do**
24:         $\mathbf{x^t} = \mathbf{x} - \rho \cdot \mathbf{e^i}$
25:         **if** $\tilde{f}(\mathbf{x^t}) \leq f(\mathbf{x})$ **then**
26:             Calculate $f(\mathbf{x^t})$
            {**Ensure that the surrogate does not mislead the search**}
27:             **if** $f(\mathbf{x^t}) \leq f(\mathbf{x})$ **then**
28:                 $\mathbf{x} = \mathbf{x^t}$
29:             **end if**
30:         **else**
31:             $\mathbf{x^t} = \mathbf{x} + \frac{\rho}{2} \cdot \mathbf{e^i}$
32:             **if** $\tilde{f}(\mathbf{x^t}) \leq f(\mathbf{x})$ **then**
33:                 Calculate $f(\mathbf{x^t})$
                {**Ensure that the surrogate does not mislead the search**}
34:                 **if** $f(\mathbf{x^t}) \leq f(\mathbf{x})$ **then**
35:                     $\mathbf{x} = \mathbf{x^t}$
36:                 **end if**
37:             **end if**
38:         **end if**
39:     **end for**
40:     **if** x has **not** been updated **then**
41:         $\rho = \frac{\rho}{2}$
42:     **end if**
43: **end while**
44: **RETURN** x

From the perspective of the interaction among variables, a complex model is unnecessary in the highly multivariate domain since both the objective functions and surrogate model (for the limited budget) would appear separable. The second reason is that, to our knowledge, there are no studies on the fitness landscape of the instance reduction problem. Although many studies propose many algorithms to achieve the reduction of instances, we do not know yet the features of the problem, e.g. how multimodal it is, and we do not know how the landscape depends on the specific data set. Hence, the simplistic approach of using a local linear model is a natural choice, see [16,22]. In the present paper, we propose a local surrogate model that is designed to work in a limited portion of the decision space by using the neighbour points visited by the local search algorithm, see [11,23,35,37].

4   Experimental Study

This section describes the experimental setup and presents the numerical results of our study. Subsection 4.1 provides a description of the experimental framework while Subsect. 4.2 displays, analyses, and interprets the results achieved against a number of algorithms for instance reduction previously proposed in the literature. Finally Subsect. 4.3 analyses the benefits and drawbacks of SALSIR with respect to its baseline counterpart.

4.1   Experimental Framework

For the proposed study, in order to test the viability of the use of a local search for instance reduction, we have chosen 40 small data sets from the KEEL data set repository [32] with less than 2,000 instances (based on [7,28]). Table 1 outlines the main features of these data sets. For each data set, the total number of examples (#Ex.), number of attributes (#Atts.), and number of classes (#ω.) are shown. These data sets are partitioned using a ten fold cross-validation scheme (10-fcv). For each data set, n can be computed as $n = 0.9 \times \#\text{Ex.} \times \#\text{Atts.}$

In order to evaluate the proposed methods, the following two measures have been used:

Classification accuracy:

$$Acc = \frac{N_{cc}}{N_I}$$

where N_{cc} is the number of correct classifications and N_I is the total number of instances. The classification is performed by the NN classifier using the resulting RS. The results in training ($TrainAcc$) and test ($TestAcc$) partitions are reported.

Reduction rate:

$$Red = 1 - \frac{size(\mathbf{RS})}{size(\mathbf{TR})}$$

Table 1. Brief description of the classification data sets used in this study

Data set	#Ex.	#Atts.	#ω	Data set	#Ex.	#Atts.	#ω
appendicitis	106	7	2	housevotes	435	16	2
australian	690	14	2	iris	150	4	3
autos	205	25	6	led7digit	500	7	10
balance	625	4	3	lymphography	148	18	4
bands	539	19	2	mammographic	961	5	2
breast	286	9	2	monks	432	6	2
bupa	345	6	2	movement_libras	360	90	15
car	1,728	6	4	newthyroid	215	5	3
cleveland	297	13	5	pima	768	8	2
contraceptive	1,473	9	3	saheart	462	9	2
crx	125	15	2	sonar	208	60	2
dermatology	366	33	6	spectheart	267	44	2
ecoli	336	7	8	tae	151	5	3
flare-solar	1,066	9	2	tic-tac-toe	958	9	2
german	1,000	20	2	vehicle	846	18	4
glass	214	9	7	vowel	990	13	11
haberman	306	3	2	wine	178	13	3
hayes-roth	133	4	3	wisconsin	683	9	2
heart	270	13	2	yeast	1484	8	10
hepatitis	155	19	2	zoo	101	17	7

where $size(RS)$ and $size(TR)$ are the sizes of reduced and training sets, respectively, that is the number of rows of the two matrices. This index measures the reduction of storage requirements achieved by an instance reduction algorithm.

Various instance reduction methods representing the state-of-the-art have been used for comparison with the proposed LSIR and SALSIR. In this study, We focused on the family of positioning adjustment methods (see [28]), which are the best performing instance reduction methods in the literature and follow a working logic similar to that of the proposed local search algorithms.

In order to compare the methods, we used as a benchmark the NN rule employing the entire TR set for training. In addition, we compared against the entire set of the positioning adjustment-based methods reviewed in [28]. We also included two advanced instance reduction algorithms: an incremental Differential Evolution (IPADE) [29], and a hybrid instance selection and instance generation algorithm (SSMA-SFLSDE) which is the current state-of-the-art according to [30]. Hence, 17 algorithms in total are considered in this study.

For the proposed LSIR method, and its surrogate variant, the search is started with a random subset of 5% of the rows of **TR** as suggested in [28]. Both LSIR and SALSIR are stopped either when $\rho < 10^{-5}$ or when $100 \times n$ objective function calls have been performed. Table 2 presents in greater detail the configuration parameters for IPADE, SSMA-SFLSDE and the proposed methods. Regarding the other comparison methods and related parameters we used the setup suggested in https://sci2s.ugr.es/pr/pgtax/experimentation.

Table 2. Parameters of the optimisation algorithms used for instance reduction.

Algorithm	Parameters
LSIR	Evaluations $= 100 \times n$, $\rho = 0.4$ Reduction rate $= 0.95$
SALSIR	Evaluations $= 100 \times n$, $\rho = 0.4$ Reduction rate $= 0.95$
IPADE	PopulationSize $= 50$, iterations of basic DE $= 500$ iterSFGSS $= 8$, iterSFHC $= 20$, Fl $= 0.1$, Fu $= 0.9$
SSMA-SFLSDE	PopulationSFLSDE $= 40$, IterationsSFLSDE $= 500$, iterSFGSS $= 8$, iterSFHC $= 20$, Fl $= 0.1$, Fu $= 0.9$
NN	Number of neighbors $= 1$, Euclidean distance

4.2   Results

Table 3 provides the average results of reduction rate, training and test accuracy on the 40 data sets used in this paper. For each type of result, the algorithms are ranked from the best to the worst. The NN algorithm is highlighted in bold as the benchmark method.

Table 3 shows that the proposed LSIR and SALSIR achieve the best and the third best training accuracy result, and are ranked forth and fifth in terms of test accuracy. The reduction rates of LSIR and SALSIR are comparable with those of the other methods that use a reduction rate parameter of 5%. It must be remarked that despite the low number of evaluations and a simple local search strategy, the proposed LSIR algorithm provides the highest train accuracy. This indicates that LSIR may be incurring in overfitting of the training data sets. Particularly interesting is the comparison with PSO, which also starts off from the same random set of instances (5%). PSO does not seem to find an RS that fits that well the training data. This turns out to be in its favour as it reduces the overfitting of the training data, providing a higher test result. This may suggest that an even lower number of evaluations may prevent our algorithm from overfitting the data.

Table 4 presents the average test classification accuracy results (from the 10-fcv), for the proposed methods and the NN rule. The best result for each data set is highlighted in the bold face.

We can observe that for the majority of the datasets (29 out of 40), both proposed methods outperform the benchmark NN. This means that the methods are not only able to reduce the size the training data by 95%, but also are also able to improve the performance of the NN classifier. In the remaining cases the data reduction process may deteriorate the performance of the NN algorithm (e.g. on aut data set). This may be due to overfitting of the training data, or

Table 3. Average Results on 40 small data sets

Red		TrainAcc		TestAcc	
PSCSA	0.9858	LSIR	0.8667	SSMASFLSDE	0.7845
IPADE	0.9798	SSMASFLSDE	0.8651	PSO	0.7501
AVQ	0.9759	SALSIR	0.8410	IPADE	0.7446
LVQTC	0.9551	HYB	0.8309	LSIR	0.7415
SSMASFLSDE	0.9547	ENPC	0.8247	SALSIR	0.7346
MSE	0.9520	PSO	0.8238	**NN**	**0.7326**
LVQPRU	0.9503	IPADE	0.7883	MSE	0.7237
DSM	0.9491	MSE	0.7566	ENPC	0.7167
VQ	0.9491	**NN**	**0.7369**	HYB	0.7153
PSO	0.9491	LVQTC	0.7327	LVQPRU	0.6997
LSIR	0.9488	LVQPRU	0.7304	LVQTC	0.6981
SALSIR	0.9488	AMPSO	0.7227	AMPSO	0.6903
LVQ3	0.9488	DSM	0.7036	DSM	0.6810
AMPSO	0.9430	LVQ3	0.6931	LVQ3	0.6763
ENPC	0.7220	AVQ	0.6869	PSCSA	0.6682
HYB	0.4278	PSCSA	0.6787	AVQ	0.6672
NN	**0.0000**	VQ	0.6614	VQ	0.6549

when the (random) original selection of instances per class was not suitable for these data sets. Thus, our local search strategy could benefit from a preliminary instance selection step before optimising the location of the instances, as proposed in [30].

In order to understand the significance of the provided results, we applied the Wilcoxon test to establish a fair comparison with the state-of-the-art. Table 5 displays the result of this comparison.

Table 5 highlights that the hybrid SSMA-SFLSDE algorithm remains to be the best algorithm, outperforming all the other methods. However, it should be remarked that SSMA-SFLSDE is composed of two population-based metaheuristics (a binary search to select relevant instances, and an adjustment of the position based on differential evolution). The selection of an appropriate number of instances per class is a well-known issue for instance generation techniques [29, 30], and the instance selection mechanism of SSMA-SFLSDE helps it to reduce overfitting and improve test accuracy. In this preliminary study, LSIR and SALSIR are naively used without a careful selection of instances per class.

More generally, LSIR and SALSIR are remarkably simpler than all the metaheuristic-based algorithms used in this study, and perform only a local search of the decision space. Despite these limitations, we observe that the proposed methods are competitive with a way more complex population-based meta-

Table 4. Classification accuracy in test of the proposed methods against the NN benchmark rule

Data set	NN	LSIR	SALSIR	Data set	NN	LSIR	SALSIR
appendicitis	0.7936	**0.8118**	0.8018	housevotes	**0.9216**	0.9149	0.9147
australian	0.8145	0.8261	**0.8464**	iris	0.9333	0.9467	**0.9733**
aut	**0.7474**	0.5434	0.49	led7digit	0.4020	**0.704**	0.688
bal	0.7904	**0.8718**	0.8463	lym	0.7387	0.7491	**0.755**
bands	0.6309	0.6811	**0.6848**	mammographic	0.7368	0.794	**0.8013**
bre	0.6535	**0.6896**	0.6789	monks	0.7791	**0.869**	0.8505
bupa	0.6108	**0.6452**	0.6143	movement_libras	0.8194	0.5778	0.5639
car	0.8565	**0.9143**	0.8762	newthyroid	**0.9723**	0.9632	0.9584
cleveland	0.5314	0.5483	**0.5644**	pima	**0.7033**	0.6903	0.6488
contraceptive	0.4277	**0.48**	0.4657	saheart	0.6449	**0.6926**	0.6687
crx	0.7957	**0.8362**	0.8217	sonar	**0.8555**	0.7776	0.706
dermatology	**0.9535**	0.9209	0.91	spectfheart	0.6970	**0.7943**	0.7862
ecoli	**0.8070**	0.7917	0.798	tae	0.4050	0.5188	**0.525**
flare-solar	0.5554	0.6473	**0.6594**	tic-tac-toe	0.7307	**0.7641**	0.7349
german	0.7050	**0.706**	0.677	vehicle	**0.7010**	0.6868	0.681
glass	0.7361	0.6071	**0.628**	vowel	**0.9939**	0.6253	0.5677
haberman	0.6697	0.686	**0.7384**	wine	**0.9552**	0.933	0.9333
hayes-roth	0.3570	0.4687	0.5701	wisconsin	0.9557	0.9313	**0.9571**
heart	0.7704	**0.8111**	0.7778	yeast	0.5047	**0.5552**	0.5546
hepatitis	**0.8075**	0.8054	0.7608	zoo	**0.9281**	0.8786	0.905

heuristics such as PSO and IPADE. This study can be viewed as a stepping stone towards the generation of a hybrid algorithm that employs LSIR and SALSIR.

4.3   The Effect of the Surrogate

Regarding the performance of LSIR and SALSIR, we should make two considerations. On the one hand, Table 3 shows that LSIR appears to outperform SALSIR on both test and training accuracy. On the other hand, training results suggest that the surrogate variant suffers from overfitting less than the its baseline counterpart. However, the Wilcoxon test finds significant differences between the two algorithms (in the test phase) at a level of significance $\alpha = 0.9$ and that LSIR tends to outperform SALSIR. As an example of this fact, Fig. 1 shows the convergence plot on a single partition of the Bupa data. We can observe that both algorithms progress steadily but LSIR marginally outperforms SALSIR. This result was expected since a surrogate assisted algorithm often deteriorates the performance of its counterpart that uses only the true objective function, see e.g. [11, 19].

Table 5. Summary of the Wilcoxon test. The symbol • indicates that the method in the row outperforms the method in the column. The symbol ○ indicates that the method in the column outperforms the method of the row. Upper and diagonal of level significance 0.9 and 0.95, respectively

	(1)	(2)	(3)	(4)	(5)	(6)	(7)	(8)	(9)	(10)	(11)	(12)	(13)	(14)	(15)	(16)	(17)
NN (1)	–	•		•		•	•	•	•	•	○		•	○	○	○	
LVQ3 (2)	○	–	○		○	•			○		○	○		○	○	○	○
MSE (3)		•	–	•	•	•	•		•		○	•	•	○	○	○	
DSM (4)	○		○	–	○	•			○		○	○		○	○	○	○
LVQTC (5)		•		•	–	•	•				○			○	○	○	○
VQ (6)	○	○	○	○	○	–		○	○	○	○	○	○	○	○	○	○
AVQ (7)	○		○		○		–	○	○	○	○	○		○	○	○	○
HYB (8)	○				•			–			○			○	○	○	○
LVQPRU (9)	○	•	○	•		•	•		–		○			○	○	○	○
ENPC (10)	○				•					–	○			○	○	○	○
PSO (11)	•	•	•	•	•	•	•	•	•	•	–	•	•		○		•
AMPSO (12)		•	○		•						○	–	•	○	○	○	○
PSCSA (13)			○								○		–	○	○	○	○
IPADE (14)	•	•	•	•	•	•	•	•	•	•		•	•	–	○		•
SSMA-SFLSDE (15)	•	•	•	•	•	•	•	•	•	•	•	•	•	•	–	•	•
LSIR (16)		•		•	•	•	•	•	•	•		•	•		○	–	•
SALSIR (17)		•		•	•	•	•	•	•	•	○	•	•	○	○		–

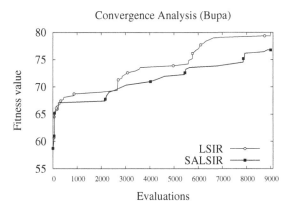

Fig. 1. Convergence plot example on one partition of Bupa data set

From the perspective of the computational saving, in the case depicted in Fig. 1, SALSIR saved 1991 evaluations with respect to LSIR. Since the purpose of a surrogate assisted algorithm is to reduce the number of objective function calls, we reported in Fig. 2 a histogram displaying the total number of evaluations and

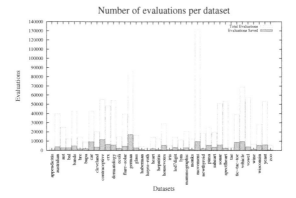

Fig. 2. Objective function calls saved by SALSIR (average 15%)

the number of saved evaluations by the surrogate variant. On average, around 15% of the evaluations have been saved.

5   Conclusion

This paper proposed a local search algorithm for addressing the large scale challenges imposed by instance reduction problems. The proposed local search is also endowed with a local surrogate model to mitigate the computational cost generated by objective function calls. The proposed local search algorithm can potentially be used within optimisation frameworks, such as portfolios, hyperheuristics, and memetic algorithms. Numerical results indicate that the use of local search algorithms is a promising subfield of optimisation for addressing instance reduction problems. The proposed local search, despite its algorithmic naivety, outperformed numerous classical algorithms for instance reductions and is competitive with sophisticated population-based metaheuristics representing the state-of-the-art. The comparison between the versions with and without surrogate assisted model shows that the proposed surrogate design/implementation allows for an approximately 15% saving on the number of objective function calls, with a relatively small loss in accuracy. As a future work, we will investigate the integration of the proposed local search within advanced instance reduction algorithms to address larger classification problems.

References

1. Cano, J.R., Herrera, F., Lozano, M.: Using evolutionary algorithms as instance selection for data reduction in KDD: an experimental study. IEEE Trans. Evol. Comput. **7**(6), 561–575 (2003)
2. Caraffini, F., Neri, F., Iacca, G.: Large scale problems in practice: the effect of dimensionality on the interaction among variables. In: Squillero, G., Sim, K. (eds.) EvoApplications 2017. LNCS, vol. 10199, pp. 636–652. Springer, Cham (2017). https://doi.org/10.1007/978-3-319-55849-3_41

3. Caraffini, F., Neri, F., Iacca, G., Mol, A.: Parallel memetic structures. Inf. Sci. **227**, 60–82 (2013)
4. Caraffini, F., Neri, F., Picinali, L.: An analysis on separability for memetic computing automatic design. Inf. Sci. **265**, 1–22 (2014)
5. Cover, T.M., Hart, P.E.: Nearest neighbor pattern classification. IEEE Trans. Inf. Theory **13**(1), 21–27 (1967)
6. Dhar, V.: Data science and prediction. Commun. ACM **56**(12), 64–73 (2013)
7. García, S., Derrac, J., Cano, J., Herrera, F.: Prototype selection for nearest neighbor classification: taxonomy and empirical study. IEEE Trans. Pattern Anal. Mach. Intell. **34**(3), 417–435 (2012)
8. García, S., Cano, J.R., Herrera, F.: A memetic algorithm for evolutionary prototype selection: a scaling up approach. Pattern Recogn. **41**(8), 2693–2709 (2008)
9. García-Pedrajas, N., de Haro-García, A., Pérez-Rodríguez, J.: A scalable memetic algorithm for simultaneous instance and feature selection. Evol. Comput. **22**(1), 1–45 (2014)
10. Hidalgo, B., Goodman, M.: Multivariate or multivariable regression? Am. J. Public Health **103**, 39–40 (2013)
11. Jin, Y.: Surrogate-assisted evolutionary computation: recent advances and future challenges. Swarm Evol. Comput. **1**(2), 61–70 (2011)
12. Jobson, J.D.: Multiple linear regression. In: Jobson, J.D. (ed.) Applied Multivariate Data Analysis. STS, pp. 219–398. Springer, New York (1991). https://doi.org/10.1007/978-1-4612-0955-3_4
13. Krasnogor, N.: Towards robust memetic algorithms. In: Hart, W.E., Krasnogor, N., Smith, J.E. (eds.) Recent Advances in Memetic Algorithms. STUDFUZZ, vol. 166, pp. 185–207. Springer, Berlin (2004). https://doi.org/10.1007/3-540-32363-5_9
14. Krawczyk, B., Triguero, I., García, S., Woźniak, M., Herrera, F.: Instance reduction for one-class classification. Knowl. Inf. Syst. **59**(3), 601–628 (2018). https://doi.org/10.1007/s10115-018-1220-z
15. Li, X., Yao, X.: Cooperatively coevolving particle swarms for large scale optimization. IEEE Trans. Evol. Comput. **16**(2), 210–224 (2012)
16. Lim, D., Jin, Y., Ong, Y.S., Sendhoff, B.: Generalizing surrogate-assisted evolutionary computation. IEEE Trans. Evol. Comput. **14**(3), 329–355 (2010)
17. Lin, S.F., Cheng, Y.C.: A separability detection approach to cooperative particle swarm optimization. In: Proceedings of the International Conference on Natural Computation, pp. 1141–1145 (2011)
18. Nanni, L., Lumini, A.: Particle swarm optimization for prototype reduction. Neurocomputing **72**(4–6), 1092–1097 (2008)
19. Neri, F., del Toro Garcia, X., Cascella, G.L., Salvatore, N.: Surrogate assisted local search on PMSM drive design. COMPEL: Int. J. Comput. Math. Electr. Electron. Eng. **27**(3), 573–592 (2008)
20. Nguyen, P.T.H., Sudholt, D.: Memetic algorithms beat evolutionary algorithms on the class of hurdle problems. In: Proceedings of the Genetic and Evolutionary Computation Conference, GECCO 2018, pp. 1071–1078. ACM (2018)
21. Resende, M.G.C., Ribeiro, C.C.: Local search. In: Resende, M.G.C., Ribeiro, C.C. (eds.) Optimization by GRASP, pp. 63–93. Springer, New York (2016). https://doi.org/10.1007/978-1-4939-6530-4_4
22. Ong, Y.S., Nair, P.B., Lum, K.Y.: Max-min surrogate-assisted evolutionary algorithm for robust design. IEEE Trans. Evol. Comp. **10**(4), 392–404 (2006)

23. Regis, R.G.: Surrogate-assisted particle swarm with local search for expensive constrained optimization. In: Korošec, P., Melab, N., Talbi, E.-G. (eds.) BIOMA 2018. LNCS, vol. 10835, pp. 246–257. Springer, Cham (2018). https://doi.org/10.1007/978-3-319-91641-5_21

24. Ros, R., Hansen, N.: A simple modification in CMA-ES achieving linear time and space complexity. In: Rudolph, G., Jansen, T., Beume, N., Lucas, S., Poloni, C. (eds.) PPSN 2008. LNCS, vol. 5199, pp. 296–305. Springer, Heidelberg (2008). https://doi.org/10.1007/978-3-540-87700-4_30

25. Pilato, C., Loiacono, D., Tumeo, A., Ferrandi, F., Lanzi, P.L., Sciuto, D.: Speeding-up expensive evaluations in high-level synthesis using solution modeling and fitness inheritance. In: Tenne, Y., Goh, C.-K. (eds.) Computational Intelligence in Expensive Optimization Problems. ALO, vol. 2, pp. 701–723. Springer, Heidelberg (2010). https://doi.org/10.1007/978-3-642-10701-6_26

26. Tong, H., Huang, C., Liu, J., Yao, X.: Voronoi-based efficient surrogate-assisted evolutionary algorithm for very expensive problems. In: IEEE Congress on Evolutionary Computation, pp. 1996–2003 (2019)

27. Torczon, V.: On the convergence of pattern search algorithms. SIAM J. Optim. **7**(1), 1–25 (1997)

28. Triguero, I., Derrac, J., García, S., Herrera, F.: A taxonomy and experimental study on prototype generation for nearest neighbor classification. IEEE Trans. Syst. Man, Cybern.-Part C **42**(1), 86–100 (2012)

29. Triguero, I., García, S., Herrera, F.: IPADE: iterative prototype adjustment for nearest neighbor classification. IEEE Trans. Neural Netw. **21**(12), 1984–1990 (2010)

30. Triguero, I., García, S., Herrera, F.: Differential evolution for optimizing the positioning of prototypes in nearest neighbor classification. Pattern Recogn. **44**(4), 901–916 (2011)

31. Triguero, I., Peralta, D., Bacardit, J., Garcia, S., Herrera, F.: A combined mapreduce-windowing two-level parallel scheme for evolutionary prototype generation. In: IEEE Congress on Evolutionary Computation, pp. 3036–3043 (2014)

32. Triguero, I., et al.: KEEL 3.0: an open source software for multi-stage analysis in data mining. Int. J. Comput. Intell. Syst. **10**, 1238–1249 (2017)

33. Triguero, I., Peralta, D., Bacardit, J., García, S., Herrera, F.: MRPR: a MapReduce solution for prototype reduction in big data classification. Neurocomputing **150**, 331–345 (2015)

34. Tseng, L.Y., Chen, C.: Multiple trajectory search for large scale global optimization. In: Proceedings of the IEEE Congress on Evolutionary Computation, pp. 3052–3059 (2008)

35. Wang, Y., Yin, D., Yang, S., Sun, G.: Global and local surrogate-assisted differential evolution for expensive constrained optimization problems with inequality constraints. IEEE Trans. Cybern. **49**(5), 1642–1656 (2019)

36. Zhao, S.Z., Suganthan, P.N., Das, S.: Self-adaptive differential evolution with multitrajectory search for large-scale optimization. Soft. Comput. **15**(11), 2175–2185 (2011). https://doi.org/10.1007/s00500-010-0645-4

37. Zhou, Z., Ong, Y.S., Lim, M.H., Lee, B.S.: Memetic algorithm using multi-surrogates for computationally expensive optimization problems. Soft. Comput. **11**(10), 957–971 (2007). https://doi.org/10.1007/s00500-006-0145-8

Evolutionary Latent Space Exploration of Generative Adversarial Networks

Paulo Fernandes, João Correia$^{(\boxtimes)}$, and Penousal Machado

CISUC, Department of Informatics Engineering,
University of Coimbra, Coimbra, Portugal
pcastillo@student.dei.uc.pt, {jncor,machado}@dei.uc.pt

Abstract. Generative Adversarial Networkss (GANs) have gained popularity over the years, presenting state-of-the-art results in the generation of samples that follow the distribution of the input training dataset. While research is being done to make GANs more reliable and able to generate better samples, the exploration of its latent space is not given as much attention. The latent space is unique for each model and is, ultimately, what determines the output from the generator. Usually, a random sample vector is taken from the latent space without regard to which output it produces through the generator. In this paper, we move towards an approach for the generation of latent vectors and traversing the latent space with pre-determined criteria, using different approaches. We focus on the generation of sets of diverse examples by searching in the latent space using Genetic Algorithms and Map Elites. A set of experiments are performed and analysed, comparing the implemented approaches with the traditional approach.

Keywords: Evolutionary Computation · Generative Adversarial Networks · Machine learning · MAP-Elites · Latent space · Image generation

1 Introduction

GANs have been presenting state-of-the-art results in the generation of samples that follow the distribution of the input training dataset [1]. In general, this model of adversarial learning works by having a generator and a discriminator training together and competing against each other in a min-max game. The discriminator is trained with real data as well as fake data created by the generator from latent space. The generator evolves from the feedback given by the discriminator on the generated data Fig. 1. Although able to produce results with high quality, GANs are often really hard to train, requiring a lot of fine-tuning through trial and error.

While a lot of research is being made in order to make GANs more reliable and able to generate better samples, the exploration of its latent space does not have as much attention. The latent space is unique for each model and

© Springer Nature Switzerland AG 2020
P. A. Castillo et al. (Eds.): EvoApplications 2020, LNCS 12104, pp. 595–609, 2020.
https://doi.org/10.1007/978-3-030-43722-0_38

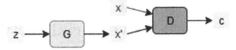

Fig. 1. Base model of a Generative Adversarial Network. G - generator; D - discriminator; z - latent vector; x - real samples; x' - generated samples

is, ultimately, what determines the output from the generator since, in simple terms, we have $g(z) = x'$, being x' the output of a latent vector z through the generator g. Typically we use the trained model to draw random samples from the latent space without any particular criteria.

In this work, we move towards the search and exploration of solutions from the latent space according to pre-determined criteria. The overall idea is to enable the search and generation of sets of latent vectors that accomplish a certain objective. We will start from exploring approaches that enable us to draw samples and traverse the latent space moved by a certain objective function. We will use Genetic Algorithms (GAs) and Multi-dimensional Archive of Phenotypic Elites (MAP-Elites) to assist on such task. Thus, the contributions of this paper are the following: (i) modelling of the latent space exploration as a search problem, enabling the use Genetic Algorithms and Map Elites (ii) a generalised approach to generate sets of images from a GAN according to with different objectives, e.g. generate diverse sets of images; (iii) a comparison analysis of the implemented latent space search algorithms with the conventional approach. Without lacking generalisation, we apply the ideas of this paper to the image domain, using Deep Convolutional Generative Adversarial Networkss (DCGANs) [2].

The remaining of the paper goes as follows: in the next Section, we cover approaches relate to this work (Sect. 2). In Sect. 3, we describe our approaches to this search problem. We describe the experimental setup in Sect. 4 and analyse and discuss the results in Sect. 5. In Sect. 6 we draw overall conclusions.

2   Related Work

GANs are generative models that are trained through a face-off between a generator and a discriminator, mostly used to train a generator that can produce realistic images. In order to generate an image, the generator is usually given a random noise vector, a high dimensional vector that, in training, is randomly sampled from a distribution, for example, a gaussian distribution, called the prior. The high dimensional space from which images are created is called latent space. Some work has already been made in this area, and not only with GANs, which is the type of model that we are going to work within this work. For instance, latent space exploration was performed in generative models using Kernel Principal Component Analysis (KPCA) [3], showing navigation through image features and novelty detection; but also in Variational Autoencoders (VAE), in, for example, mapping genes into a lower-dimensional space in order uncover underlying gene expression features in cases of tumour or cancer [4].

There are different ways that we can explore generative models latent space. White, T. shows three different arithmetical ways we can use to navigate in it [5]. The first, interpolation, is used to disclose the path between 2 samples in the space. Usually, a linear interpolation is used, but White suggests a new way, the spherical linear interpolation - slerp - which takes into account its prior distribution used for sampling noise. Analogy, the second approach, can be simplified as "King − Man + Woman = Queen", meaning that it is possible to perform operations between images to form new images with generally predictable results. Finally, Manifold Interpolated Neighbor Embedding (MINE), is an exploration model which makes use of nearest neighbours and interpolation to construct a manifold of the space. Also worth noting is that the authors showed that by combining generative models with labelled data, attribute vectors can be computed using simple arithmetic, like, for example, a smile vector which, by traversing uncovers several states of smiling in an image.

As for the use of Evolutionary Computation (EC) in order to evolve images, some works can be mentioned. For example, evolving master print templates [6] that, like a master key, could be able to open multiple fingerprints closed locks. In their work, Roy et al. compared four different Evolutionary Algorithms (EA), namely Hill-Climbing, Covariance Matrix Adaptation Evolution Strategy, Differential Evolution and Particle Swarm Optimization to evolve Synthetic MasterPrints according to the metric proposed by them, the Modified Marginal Success Rate. The samples were generated from two datasets, namely Authentec AES3400, with latter algorithm getting the best results, and FVC 2002 DB1-A, for which the second approach had the most success. Moreover, and with a two-stage workflow similar to what we implemented in this paper which includes first the unsupervised training of GANs and second the evolution of latent space, there are two works. One that implements Interactive Evolutionary Computation [7] for image generation and the other, in the topic of video-games that uses GANs and latent space evolution to learn and improve Mario Levels [8] using Covariance Matrix Adaptation Evolution Strategy.

There is also a new approach to generative models which was inspired by GANs, the Generative Latent Optimization [9]. This approach takes away the adversarial discriminator and replaces it with simple reconstruction losses where the focus is to evolve the latent space to match the one learnable noise vector to each one of the images in the training dataset.

3   The Approach

Our goal in this paper is to use approaches that can explore the latent space and create a set of latent vectors towards an objective. In particular, we set the objective to: find a set of images that can maximize a diversity measure. We pursuit the objective by exploring the latent space of GAN models using EC. Therefore, this experiment was separated into two main parts:

– Training of the GANs - develop a generative model that can produce images
  which follow the distribution of a certain training input
– Exploration of the latent space via EC - navigate the latent space of the
  generative model in order to find a possible solution for our problem.

The exploration of the latent space and set of latent vectors has the potential
to promote the generation of samples according to pre-determined criteria to
solve and adapt to other problems. It could be used during the training of the
GAN, to have a few latent vectors generated that maximize the loss of the model,
instead of randomly generating all of them. It could be used to generate samples
of a particular type. Some metrics of evaluation of GANs must draw samples
from the latent space, generate the samples and test them on another model
[10]– "what if we guide that generation?" We can use this approach to spot
problems on the training of models.

Also, this problem was applied to 3 distinct sets of images in order to com-
prehend how well our approach would work for different situations:

– handwritten digits – MNIST
– clothing – Fashion – MNIST
– faces – Facity.

3.1 Model Definition

We are using a type of GANs suitable for generating images, the DCGAN [2].
They make use of deep convolutional layers to better explore space correlation
in images, producing more realistic images. For every GAN, the latent space,
which is the input for all generators, is an array of floats of shape 1×100. The
generators used in both MNIST datasets are built with the following model,
generating output with shape $28 \times 28 \times 1$:

```
 1  Dense((7, 7, 128), activation="relu")
 2  UpSampling2D()
 3  Conv2D(128, kernel_size=3, padding="same"))
 4  BatchNormalization(momentum=0.8))
 5  Activation("relu"))
 6  UpSampling2D())
 7  Conv2D(64, kernel_size=3, padding="same"))
 8  BatchNormalization(momentum=0.8))
 9  Activation("relu"))
10  Conv2D(1, kernel_size=3, padding="same"))
11  Activation("tanh"))
```

The generator used with the facity dataset, has an output shape of $128 \times 128 \times 3$ and is built with the following model:

```
 1  Dense((8, 8, 128), activation="relu")
 2  UpSampling2D()
 3  Conv2D(256, kernel_size=3, padding="same")
```

```
4   BatchNormalization(momentum=0.8)
5   Activation("relu")
6   UpSampling2D()
7   Conv2D(128, kernel_size=3, padding="same")
8   BatchNormalization(momentum=0.8)
9   Activation("relu")
10  UpSampling2D()
11  Conv2D(64, kernel_size=3, padding="same")
12  BatchNormalization(momentum=0.8)
13  Activation("relu")
14  Conv2D(3, kernel_size=3, padding="same")
15  Activation("tanh")
```

The discriminators used for each GAN, all follow the same model, having an input shape defined by the output of the generators.

```
1   Conv2D(32, kernel_size=3, strides=2, padding="same")
2   LeakyReLU(alpha=0.2)
3   Dropout(0.25)
4   Conv2D(64, kernel_size=3, strides=2, padding="same")
5   ZeroPadding2D(padding=((0, 1), (0, 1)))
6   BatchNormalization(momentum=0.8)
7   LeakyReLU(alpha=0.2)
8   Dropout(0.25)
9   Conv2D(128, kernel_size=3, strides=2, padding="same")
10  BatchNormalization(momentum=0.8))
11  LeakyReLU(alpha=0.2))
12  Dropout(0.25))
13  Conv2D(256, kernel_size=3, strides=1, padding="same")
14  BatchNormalization(momentum=0.8)
15  LeakyReLU(alpha=0.2)
16  Dropout(0.25)
17  Flatten()
18  Dense(1, activation='sigmoid')
```

After building both the model of the discriminator and of the generator, they are combined into a single, combined, model which receives the same input as the generator and has the output of the discriminator.

3.2 GAN Training

The adversarial neural networks are trained by having the discriminator learn to distinguish the real samples, which come from the input datasets, from the fake samples, that are generated by the generator, and by having the generator learn to produce images that successfully trick the discriminator into classifying them as real samples [1].

The input datasets used Fig. 2, were the following:

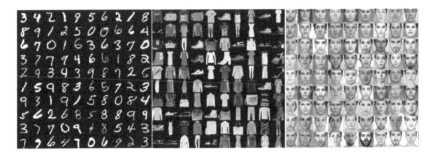

Fig. 2. Samples from the datasets used for training. From left to right: MNIST, Fashion-MNIST, Facity

- MNIST – dataset of handwritten digit with 70000 (60000 for training and 10000 for testing) $28 \times 28 \times 1$ (black and white) images, divided into 10 classes [11].
- Fashion MNIST – dataset of pieces of clothing with 70000 (60000 for training and 10000 for testing) $28 \times 28 \times 1$ (black and white) images, divided into 10 classes [12].
- Facity – dataset of faces with 4024 $128 \times 128 \times 3$ (rgb) images, not divided by training or classes.

3.3   Latent Space Exploration

In order to traverse the latent space, we require to generate sets of individuals. To pursuit our objectives, we used the following approaches:

- Random Sampling (RS)
- GA
- MAP-Elites

The three approaches were thought to evolve set of individuals, but they vary in the way they promote change along with iterations.

In the RS approaches a completely new random set of individuals is created at the beginning of each generation and evaluated by an evaluation function, as shown in Algorithm 1.

Algorithm 1. Random Sampling

1: **procedure** RANDOMSAMPLING(iterations, popsize, objective, fitnessfunc)
2:     **for** $i \leftarrow 1$ to *iterations* **do**
3:         population = RANDOMPOPULATION(popsize)
4:         population = FITNESSFUNC(population)
5:         best = BEST(population, objective)
       return BEST(population)

Algorithm 2. Genetic Algorithm

1: **procedure** GENETICALGORITHM(generations, popsize, problemargs)
2:      population = RANDOMPOPULATION(popsize)
3:      **for** $i \leftarrow 1$ to generations **do**
4:          population = VARIATIONOPERATORS(popsize, problemargs)
5:          population = problemargs.FITNESSFUNC(population)
6:          population = problemargs.SORT(objective)
     return BEST(population)

The GA is an EC approach where we start with a randomly generated population of individuals, but a new population is created trough variation operators (mutation and crossover) which are applied to the individuals of the old population evaluated by a certain fitness function (refer to Algorithm 2).

The last algorithm, the MAP-Elites, works a little bit differently. It is an illumination algorithm, and it was made for exploring the search space of solutions as much as possible [13]. A map of plausible combinations of feature dimensions for the individual's phenotype, which is previously defined, is maintained throughout the training. The algorithm starts by generating a random number of individuals and placing them on the feature map. Afterwards, MAP-Elites runs by iterations. At each iteration, a single new individual is created from applying variation operators to individuals already placed in the map. Each new individual is then evaluated and placed in the map according to its features, though in each cell of the map, only the best is kept according to the fitness function.

Algorithm 3. MAP-Elites

1: **procedure** MAPELITES(iterations, initpopsize, map, problemargs)
2:      **for** $i \leftarrow 1$ to initpopsize **do**
3:          newind = RANDOMINDIVIDUAL(problemargs)
4:          PLACEINMAP(newind, map)
5:      **for** $i \leftarrow 1$ to iterations **do**
6:          newind = VARIATIONOPERATORS(map, problemargs)
7:          PLACEINMAP(newind, map)
     return BEST(map)

Individuals, Initialization. For this problem, we the decided to work with sets of 50 images, meaning that, since we are working with a latent dimension of size 100, each individual has a genotype of size 5000 that is represented in an 1×5000 array. In order to maintain consistency, The initialization of individuals follows the same Gaussian distribution as the prior used to generate fake images in the training of the generative models.

Evaluation, Metrics and Variation Operators. All algorithms use the same method to evaluate the fitness of the individuals, an average similarity function. Through the use of the specified GAN generator, the genotype of the individuals is transformed into a set of images. Afterwards the images are compared to one another using a similarity metric, averaging between all values at the end. Since we want the most diversity possible, we have modelled the problem for minimization. In terms of the feature dimensions for MAP-Elites, both the average similarity and max similarity are used map individuals.

To measure similarity, 2 distinct metrics were used, namely Root-Mean-Squared Error (RMSE) and Normalized Cross-Correlation (NCC) [14]. The RMSE metric is calculated as

$$\text{RMSE} = 1 - \sqrt{\frac{\sum((A - B) \odot (A - B))}{\text{size}}} \tag{1}$$

while NCC is calculated as

$$\text{NCC} = \frac{\sum(A - B) \odot (A - B)}{\sqrt{(\sum A \odot A) \times (\sum B \odot B)}} \tag{2}$$

Where A and B are images, size is a function that measures the size of the images and $\odot$ is the Hadamard product. We selected these metrics for their fast calculation time and to observe the impact of both since they work in different ways. With RMSE we have a strict and direct pixel by pixel comparison whereas with NCC we are looking for certain contrast in the pixel intensities. These are options out of a number of different similarity metrics [14], but covering all of them is out of the scope of.

Two variation operators were used for the experiments: crossover and mutation. In the crossover, the two individuals are chosen from the set of available individuals using tournament selection in the GA and random choice in the MAP-Elites. In both algorithms, the algorithm used is the uniform crossover [15].

In the case of the mutation operator, it was used a random reset mutation, where each gene has a probability of being mutated. The mutation resets the selected genes with completely new values that are taken from the same Gaussian distribution used in the initialization of the individuals.

4   Experimental Setup

The experimental setup was thought to analyse how different algorithms and distinct metrics affect, for different situations, the end result in terms of diversity, which is the main goal. Moreover, by analysing the observable characteristics of the sets of images obtained, we also wanted to see if the diversity measured by an algorithm, is consistent to what we, as humans, perceive as a diverse.

To perform the experiments three generative models were trained, 1 for each dataset to be used Fig. 3. Most of the parameters are the same Table 1, the only

Table 1. GAN parameters

Parameter	Setting
Optimizer	Adam
Beta1	0.5
Beta2	0.999
Learn rate	0.0002
Batch size	32
Loss function	Binary cross-entropy
Noise distribution	N(0, 1)

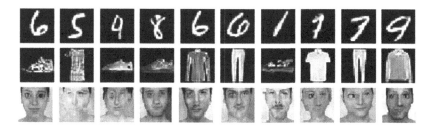

Fig. 3. Random sample of images generated from the 3 generative models

thing that changes is the number of epochs of training: (i) MNIST - 200; (ii) Fashion-MNIST - 800; (iii) Facity - 1000.

So that the results would be comparable, we keep the conditions of the algorithms as close as possible Table 2, for instance, performing a number of iterations on MAP-Elites that would produce the same number of evaluations as in the GA, maintaining the same number of generated images and attempts to reach the diverse set of images.

5   Experimental Results

In this section, we analyse the results from the experiments in terms of optimisation of the fitness function and the visual outputs from each algorithm. In order to analyse the results for comparison, we provide graphics with aggregated the values of evaluations. We group the values for Random Sampling and Map Elites in iterations, that corresponds to 50 evaluations. This way, it is possible to compare with the information of the GA. Basically, one iteration is equivalent to a generation on the GA, which in turn is equivalent to 50 evaluations on Random Sampling and Map Elites algorithms. We also separate the analysis of image diversity in two groups based on the similarity metric: RMSE and NCC.

Table 2. GA and MAP-Elites parameters

Parameter	Setting
Population size	50 in RS/GA, initial $\leq$ 50 in MAP-Elites
Number of generations	500 in GA, 25K in RS/MAP-Elites
Genotype length	50× size of latent space
Elite size	1
Tournament size	3
Crossover operator	Uniform crossover
Crossover rate	0.7 in GA/MAP-Elites
Mutation operator	Gene replacement
Mutation rate per gene	0.02 in GA/MAP-Elites
Feature dimensions	Avg similarity: bins = [0:0.01:1], Max similarity bins = [0:0.01:1] in MAP-Elites

In Fig. 4, we can observe the results of the different algorithms across the iterations. It is clear that the GA is able to optimise the fitness function. The same does not happen with MAP-Elites though, we get little improvement compared to the random sampling, and that does not change when working with different datasets, the difference between the actually gets narrower the more complex is the type of images.

When analysing the Map Elites algorithm, we are also concerned with the mapping of the individuals. As such, we analysed the heatmaps of the algorithm across iterations for the datasets and metrics, as presented in Fig. 5, to understand how much of the space was being explored by the algorithm, which helps us to understand the distribution of samples along with the iterations.

We can observe that space exploration is limited and that it generally seems to take increasingly more time to expand and, therefore, more time to find better solutions. It is noticeable the existence of a cluster of solutions in this approach and that the expansion is easier for less fit (dark blue) zones, which corroborates the evolution graphs. Here we clearly see how much MAP-Elites struggles to find better solutions when the mapping is not favourable to the problem. With the facity dataset and the NCC metric, the random initialisation values were clustered into a very small area, which made it really difficult for the algorithm to expand. Even the variation operations caused changes so small that they still fall in the same area.

The results suggest that this algorithm is not suitable for this type of problem. However, it could be related to the selection of feature descriptor and algorithm's parametrisation. The mapping functions tend to be simplistic and become a bottleneck that does not allow the ideal exploration of the search space and expansion of the mapped area, something that we will further investigate.

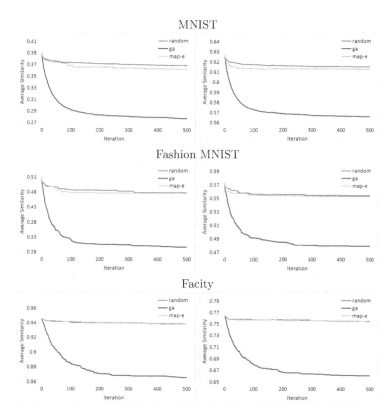

Fig. 4. Average Maximum values across iterations for the different datasets and similarity metrics: on the left NCC and on the right RMSE. The values are averages of 10 runs.

In terms of visuals the outputs from Figs. 6 and 7 showcase the best set of images that maximize the pre-determined criteria. For this last analysis, we only focused on the NCC metric and RMSE metric, respectively. It is noticeable the differences between the different approaches and metrics. In general, every approach, for each metric, ended up having a different set of images at the end.

Between the NCC and RMSE results, one aspect is noticeable, and it showcases the particularity of each similarity metric. In the RMSE, we observe that it tended to pick a set of variables that generated images which minimize the overlap of elements and with a dissimilar background (facity). The NCC, on the other hand, tended to promote contrast between the different images. This is a clear example of the success of the approach of searching and achieving the pre-determined objective. Among the different approaches, we can observe that the GA was able to generate the most visually diverse set of images.

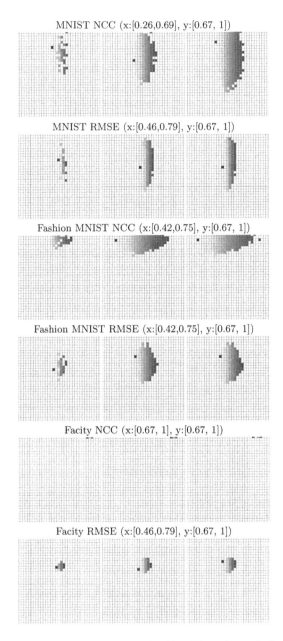

Fig. 5. Heatmap of the Map constructed with MAP-Elites for each dataset and similarity metric. Images correspond to 0th, 12000th and 25000th iterations of the algorithm. The color represent fitness, yellow for better fitness and blue for worse, while the red represents the best individual. The x axis corresponds to the average similarity and the y axis to the maximum similarity. (Color figure online)

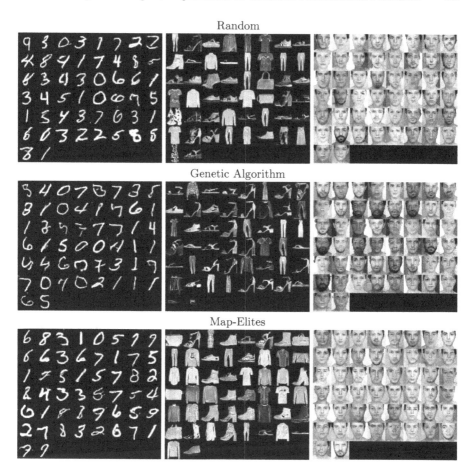

Fig. 6. The best individual of one of the evolutionary seeds for each dataset per type of approach in the last iteration using the NCC metric.

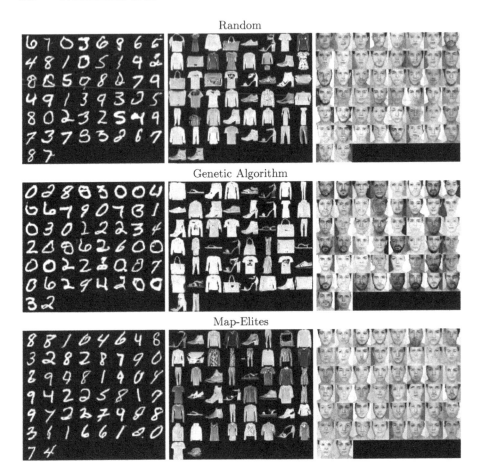

Fig. 7. The best individual of one of the evolutionary seeds for each dataset per type of approach in the last iteration using the RMSE metric.

6   Conclusions

This work presents multiple methods that enable the user to explore the latent space with a pre-determined objective. We have implemented Genetic Algorithms and Map Elites and compared with the traditional approach of random sampling from the latent space. Some of the results obtained with were unexpected but suggested that we are able to generate diverse sets of latent variables that translate into samples that correspond to certain criteria. The conducted experiments, in the image domain, with different datasets, point out that it is possible to apply our approach to GANs of different types of datasets, ranging from grayscale to colour images. The overall results worked as a proof of concept that is possible to guide the generation of latent variables towards certain criteria.

Future work could include other strategies and objectives for navigation, such as the usage of different metrics; fine-tuning of parameters, application of different criteria for illuminating the latent space in map-elites, which may include working with more than 2, usage of multiple seeds per set as well as adding a pre-processing layer that could help focus on the regions of interest in the images (for example the removal of the background). Moreover, the generation of groups of images uncovers problems of generalization. Therefore research could be done in order to explore reinforcement of training datasets.

Acknowledgments. This work is partially supported by national funds through the Foundation for Science and Technology (FCT), Portugal, within the scope of the project UID/CEC/00326/2019 and it is based upon work from COST Action CA15140: Improving Applicability of Nature-Inspired Optimisation by Joining Theory and Practice (ImAppNIO).

References

1. Goodfellow, I.J., et al.: Generative adversarial nets. In: NIPS, pp. 2672–2680 (2014)
2. Radford, A., Metz, L., Chintala, S.: Unsupervised representation learning with deep convolutional generative adversarial networks (2015)
3. Winant, D., Schreurs, J., Suykens, J.: Latent space exploration using generative kernel PCA. In: Proceedings of the 28th Belgian Dutch Conference on Machine Learning (Benelearn2019). BNAIC/Benelearn (2019)
4. Way, G.P., Greene, C.S.: Extracting a biologically relevant latent space from cancer transcriptomes with variational autoencoders, pp. 80–91 (2018)
5. White, T.: Sampling generative networks. CoRR abs/1609.04468 (2016). http://arxiv.org/abs/1609.04468
6. Roy, A., Memon, N., Togelius, J., Ross, A.: Evolutionary methods for generating synthetic masterprint templates: dictionary attack in fingerprint recognition. In: 2018 International Conference on Biometrics (ICB), pp. 39–46, February 2018
7. Bontrager, P., Lin, W., Togelius, J., Risi, S.: Deep interactive evolution. In: Liapis, A., Romero Cardalda, J.J., Ekárt, A. (eds.) EvoMUSART 2018. LNCS, vol. 10783, pp. 267–282. Springer, Cham (2018). https://doi.org/10.1007/978-3-319-77583-8_18
8. Volz, V., Schrum, J., Liu, J., Lucas, S.M., Smith, A., Risi, S.: Evolving mario levels in the latent space of a deep convolutional generative adversarial network (2018)
9. Bojanowski, P., Joulin, A., Lopez-Paz, D., Szlam, A.: Optimizing the latent space of generative networks (2017)
10. Heusel, M., Ramsauer, H., Unterthiner, T., Nessler, B., Hochreiter, S.: GANs trained by a two time-scale update rule converge to a local nash equilibrium. In: Advances in Neural Information Processing Systems, pp. 6626–6637 (2017)
11. LeCun, Y., Cortes, C.: MNIST handwritten digit database (2010)
12. Xiao, H., Rasul, K., Vollgraf, R.: Fashion-MNIST: a novel image dataset for benchmarking machine learning algorithms (2017)
13. Mouret, J.B., Clune, J.: Illuminating search spaces by mapping elites (2015)
14. Goshtasby, A.A.: Similarity and dissimilarity measures. In: Goshtasby, A.A. (ed.) Image Registration, pp. 7–66. Springer, London (2012). https://doi.org/10.1007/978-1-4471-2458-0_2
15. Eiben, A.E., Smith, J.E.: Introduction to Evolutionary Computing. Natural Computing Series. Springer, Heidelberg (2015). https://doi.org/10.1007/978-3-662-05094-1

Neuro-Evolutionary Transfer Learning Through Structural Adaptation

AbdElRahman ElSaid, Joshua Karnas, Zimeng Lyu, Daniel Krutz,
Alexander G. Ororbia, and Travis Desell[⊠]

Rochester Institute of Technology, Rochester, NY 14623, USA
{aae8800,dxkvse,tjdvse}@rit.edu, {josh,zimenglyu}@mail.rit.edu,
ago@cs.rit.edu

Abstract. Transfer learning involves taking an artificial neural network (ANN) trained on one dataset (the source) and adapting it to a new, second dataset (the target). While transfer learning has been shown to be quite powerful and is commonly used in most modern-day statistical learning setups, its use has generally been restricted by architecture, i.e., in order to facilitate the reuse of internal learned synaptic weights, the underlying topology of the ANN to be transferred across tasks must remain the same and a new output layer must be attached (entailing removing the old output layer's weights). This work removes this restriction by proposing a neuro-evolutionary approach that facilitates what we call *adaptive structure transfer learning*, which means that an ANN can be transferred across tasks that have different input and output dimensions while having the internal latent structure continuously optimized. We test the proposed optimizer on two challenging real-world time series prediction problems – our process adapts recurrent neural networks (RNNs) to (1) predict coal-fired power plant data before and after the addition of new sensors, and to (2) predict engine parameters where RNN estimators are trained on different airframes with different engines. Experiments show that not only does the proposed neuro-evolutionary transfer learning process result in RNNs that evolve and train faster on the target set than those trained from scratch but, in many cases, the RNNs generalize better even after a long training and evolution process. To our knowledge, this work represents the first use of neuro-evolution for transfer learning, especially for RNNs, and is the first methodological framework capable of adapting entire structures for arbitrary input/output spaces.

Keywords: Neuro-evolution · Recurrent neural networks · Time series data prediction · Transfer learning

1 Introduction

Transfer learning has proven to be a powerful tool for training artificial neural networks (ANNs), allowing them to re-use knowledge gained after training

© Springer Nature Switzerland AG 2020
P. A. Castillo et al. (Eds.): EvoApplications 2020, LNCS 12104, pp. 610–625, 2020.
https://doi.org/10.1007/978-3-030-43722-0_39

on one task in order to better, more quickly generalize on a new target task. However, one of the key limitations of ANN-based transfer learning is that the process typically requires the neural architecture being transferred to remain fixed so that the previously its trained weights to be reused or tuned. Furthermore, transfer learning is generally only utilized for classification-based tasks, where the underlying neural structure is feedforward or convolutional in nature, with little to no attention paid to transferring knowledge across recurrent neural networks (RNNs) aside from the notable exception of partial knowledge transfer through the use of pre-trained embeddings of (sub)words and phrases [1,2]. In addition, to our knowledge, no work exists on developing a transfer learning framework for RNNs for the far harder task of time series forecasting.

Why is time series forecasting so important? We argue that countless real-world systems would benefit from the ability to forecast or predict data. A cloud-based self-adaptive hosting system will benefit from being able to anticipate future resource needs. The ability to predict user loads and the time necessary to allocate the required resources to handle these loads would enable the system to proactively begin the adaptation process in advance. This would enable the system to account for the *tactic latency* [3] when invoking additional resources and appropriately support increased user levels. Conversely, being able to anticipate reduced user loads would enable such a system to proactively begin to deactivate resources; thus enabling the system to reduce costs [4,5]. Mechanical systems, such as self-driving cars and UASs would also benefit from the ability to more accurately predict the need for preventative maintenance which is critically important for cost and safety reasons. RNNs have proven to be powerful predictors of these types of complicated and correlated time series data. Furthermore, transfer learning, the kind of which we described earlier, could potentially empower these systems even further, allowing them to readily internally-used ANNs/RNNs in the event that new sensors become available or are corrupted/destroyed or when mechanical structures are modified or upgraded.

A major use of transfer learning has been for specialization. Gupta *et al.* used RNNs to make predictions of phenotypes – an RNN is trained to predict 20 different phenotypes based on clinical time series data and then this trained network is retrained to predict previously unseen phenotypes for which there are varying amounts of labeled data [6]. Zhang *et al.* made use of this same principle when predicting the remaining useful life (RUL) of various systems when data was scarce [7]. They show that training a model with related source data and then "specializing" the model by tuning it to available target data leads to significantly better performance when compared to a model only trained on target data. There have been a number of variants and improvements built on this general idea [7–10], also known as "pre-training". However, none of these works alter the structure of the ANNs being transferred.

Transfer learning with minor structural changes has been investigated, where mid-level features are transferred from a source task to a target task. In these cases, new output layers are fine-tuned on target data. Mun *et al.* derived mid-level features (parameters) from the hidden layers of an ANN trained on a source task and then transferred those features to a target task. The ANN for the target task was constructed by removing the output layer from the source ANN and then augmented with two new additional hidden layers, *i.e.*, "adaptation layers", as well as a new output layer [11]. Along similar lines, Taylor *et al.* utilize NEAT to evolve inter-task mappings to translate trained neural network policies from a source to a target network [12]. Yang *et al.* took this concept further to designing designing networks for cross-domain, cross-application, and cross-lingual transfer settings [13]. Vierbancsics *et al.* used a different approach where an indirect encoding is evolved which can be applied to neural network tasks different structures [14].

Hinton *et al.* proposed the concept of "knowledge distillation", where an ensemble of teacher models are "compressed" (or the knowledge of which is transferred) to a single pupil model [15]. In their experiments a distilled single model performed nearly as well as the ensemble itself (also outperforming a single baseline model). Tang *et al.* have also conducted the converse of this experiment – they train a complex pupil model using a simpler teacher model [16]. Their findings demonstrate that knowledge gathered by a simple teacher model can effectively be transferred to a more complex pupil model (which has greater generalization capability). Deo *et al.* also concatenated mid-level features from two datasets as input yo a target feed forward network [17].

Ultimately, none of the above transfer learning strategies have involved any significant architectural changes to the networks being transferred. This work overcomes this limitation by proposing a neuro-evolutionary approach. Previously trained neural networks can be adapted to new tasks with different inputs and outputs by allowing the system to alter the input and output layers and only generating new minimal connectivity to these new components. Following this, a neuro-evolutionary process can then be used to adapt the internal structure of the ANN/RNN, reusing all applicable internal architectural components and weights. We have expanded the Evolutionary eXploration of Augmenting Memory Models (EXAMM) algorithm [18] to facilitate this kind of "adaptive structure transfer learning" and apply it to time series data prediction problems in two real world domains: power systems and aviation. Our results indicate that this process yields good RNN estimators faster when new sensors are added to a coal-fired power plant, resulting in predictors with more accurate predictive ability than those trained from scratch. We show that in some cases it is even possible to the transfer knowledge of the RNNs trained to predict engine parameters between aircraft and airframes with different engines and structural designs.

2   Evolutionary eXploration of Augmenting Memory Models (EXAMM)

EXAMM progressively evolves larger RNNs through a series of mutation operations and crossover (reproduction), as shown in Fig. 1. Mutations can occur at the edge level, *e.g.*, *split edge*, *add edge*, *enable edge*, *add recurrent edge*, and *disable edge* operations, or as higher-level node mutations, *e.g.*, *add node*, and *split node*. The type of an added node is selected uniformly at random from a suite of simple neurons, Δ-RNN units [19], gated recurrent units (GRUs) [20], long short-term memory cells (LSTMs) [21], minimal gated units (MGUs) [22], and update gate RNN cells (UGRNNs) [23], which allows EXAMM to select for the best performing recurrent memory units. Recurrent edges are added with a time-skip selected uniformly at random, $i.e.$, $\sim U(1, 10)$. For more details on these operations we refer the reader to [18].

To speed up the neuro-evolution process, EXAMM utilizes an asynchronous, distributed computing strategy incorporating islands to promote speciation, which promotes both exploration and exploitation of the (massive) search space. A master process maintains a population for each island and generates new RNN candidate models from the islands in a round-robin manner. Candidate models are locally trained, via back-propagation of errors (backprop), upon request by workers. When a worker completes the training of an RNN, that RNN is inserted into the island it was generated from if and only if its fitness, $i.e.$, validation set mean squared error, is better than the worst fitness score in the island. The insertion of this RNN is then followed by removal of the worst RNN in the island. This asynchrony is particularly important as the generated RNNs will have different architectures, each taking a different amount of time to train. It allows the workers to complete the training of the generated RNNs at whatever speed they can, yielding an algorithm that is naturally load-balanced. Unlike synchronous parallel evolutionary strategies, EXAMM easily scales up to any number of available processors, allowing population sizes that are independent of processor availability. The EXAMM codebase has a multi-threaded implementation for multi-core CPUs as well as an MPI [24] implementation which allows EXAMM to operate using high performance computing resources.

3   Adaptive Structure Transfer Learning

EXAMM typically initializes each island population with the minimal network configuration/topology possible for the given inputs and outputs, $i.e.$, each input has a single feedforward connection to each output (as shown in Fig. 1a). Each island population starts with this minimal configuration, which is sent to the first worker requesting an RNN to be trained. Subsequent requests for work from that island create new RNN candidates from mutations of the minimal network until the population is full. After an island population is full, EXAMM will start generating new RNNs utilizing both intra-island crossover and mutation. When all islands are full, then EXAMM will generate new RNNs from inter-island crossover in addition to the aforementioned intra-island crossover and mutation.

To enable transfer learning, this work extends EXAMM by allowing it to accept any ANN in place of the initial minimal network configuration. To fill the island populations, mutations of the provided initial ANN are made and intra-island and inter-island crossover continue as described earlier. In addition, we extend EXAMM to adjust the network in the face of different numbers of inputs and outputs, *a capability not yet demonstrated in any other transfer learning technique or application*. To accomplish this, EXAMM first adjusts the network's

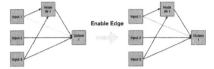

(a) The edge between Input 1 and Output 1 is split, adding two edges and a new node with innovation number (IN) 1.

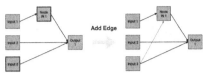

(b) Input 3 and Node IN 1 are selected to have an edge added between them.

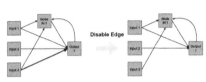

(c) The edge between Input 3 and Output 1 is enabled.

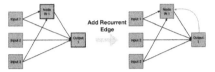

(d) A recurrent edge is added between Output 1 and Node IN 1

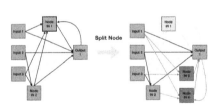

(e) The edge between Input 3 and Output 1 is disabled.

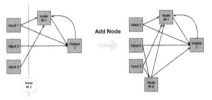

(f) A node with IN 2 is added at a random depth. Edges are added to randomly selected inputs/outputs.

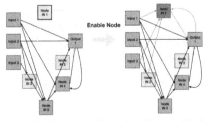

(g) Node IN 1 is split into Nodes IN 3 and 4, which get half, but at least 1, of the inputs and outputs.

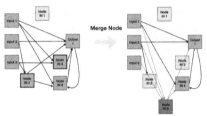

(h) Node IN 2 and 3 are selected to be merged. They are disabled along and Node IN 5 is created with edges between all their inputs and outputs.

(i) Node IN 1 is selected to be enabled, along with all its input and output edges.

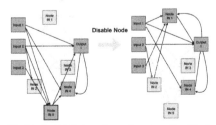

(j) Node IN 5 is selected to be disabled, along with all its input and output edges.

Fig. 1. Edge and node mutation operations.

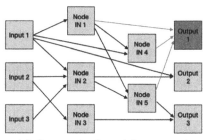

(a) Output 1 selected for removal.

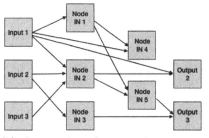

(b) Output 1 and connections are removed.

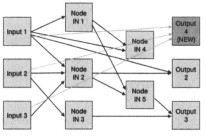

(c) Output 4 is added and connected to all inputs.

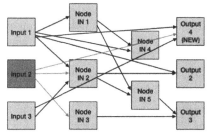

(d) Input 2 is selected for removal.

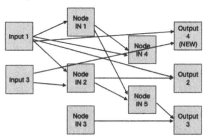

(e) Input 2 and connections are removed.

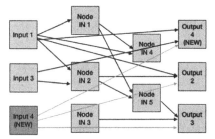

(f) Input 4 is added and connected to all outputs.

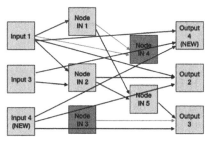

(g) Nodes 3 and 4 are not forward and backward reachable, they are selected for removal.

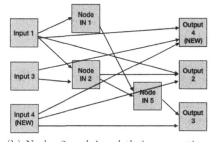

(h) Nodes 3 and 4 and their connections are removed.

Fig. 2. The adaptive structure transfer learning process.

output nodes and then its input nodes (see Fig. 2 for an example of this process). If outputs need to be removed, their respective output nodes are removed along with any edges incoming to those particular output nodes. If outputs need to be added, they are connected to each existing input. Similarly, if inputs need to be removed, their respective input nodes are removed along with all of the respective outgoing edges. Finally, if input nodes need to be added, they are added and connected with a synapse connecting them to each output.

Removing inputs and outputs potentially disconnect parts of the RNN's graph such that they are either never reached from either a backprop pass or their output never effects the final output of the RNN. To safeguard against this, after a mutation or crossover operation is completed, EXAMM checks that all edges and nodes to ensure both forward reach-ability, *i.e.*, there is a path to the edge or node from an enabled input node, and their backward reach-ability, *i.e.*, there is a path from the node or to any output. Nodes and edges that are neither forward nor backward reachable (by any path of enabled nodes and edges) are disabled and no longer utilized in the backprop-adjustment process. They can however later be reconnected and enabled via EXAMM's mutation and crossover operations.

Following this, the EXAMM neuro-evolution process can continue as normal, adapting the transferred neural structures to the new inputs and outputs by adding new internal nodes and edges via EXAMM's mutation and crossover operations. This allows the learning process to be bootstrapped by reusing of the previously learned structure and potentially all of the (source) weights.

4   Transfer Learning Examples

This work examines two case studies of real-world transfer learning involving large-scale system sensor data. The first involves prediction of coal fired power plant parameters transferring RNNs trained before the addition of new sensor capabilities to new RNNs including the new sensor inputs. The second involves predicting engine parameters of three different aircraft with different airframes and engines. While the coal fired power plant data used in this study is propri-etary and could not be made public, the aviation data has been made openly available to ensure reproducibility of our results and to encourage further study[1].

4.1   Coal-Fired Power Plant Transfer Learning

The source dataset for training RNNs consisted of four data files, each containing approximately 24.5 h of per-minute data readings from one of the coal plant's burners. This time series was characterized by 12 parameters: (1) *Conditioner Inlet Temp*, (2) *Conditioner Outlet Temp*, (3) *Coal Feeder Rate*, (4) *Primary Air Flow*, (5) *Primary Air Split*, (6) *System Secondary Air Flow Total*, (7) *Secondary Air Flow*, (8) *Secondary Air Split*, (9) *Tertiary Air Split*, (10) *Total Combined Air*

---

[1] https://github.com/travisdesell/exact/tree/master/datasets.

Flow, (11) *Supplementary Fuel Flow*, and (12) *Main Flame Intensity*. From this dataset, the *Main Flame Intensity* parameter was the one selected for prediction due to its practical use in determining potential plant issues and performance optimization. It is mostly a product of internal burner conditions and parameters related to coal quality which makes it challenging to predict.

The target dataset consisted of another four data files, each containing 24.5 h of per-minute data from the same burner, which also included fuel quality parameters from a newly-installed full stream elemental analyzer (FSEA) sensor. This data set added 8 new parameters: (1) *Base Acid Ratio*, (2) *Ash Content*, (3) *Na (Sodium) Content*, (4) *Fe (Iron) Content*, (5) *BTU*, (6) *Ash Flow*, (7) *Na (Sodium) Flow*, and (8) *Fe (Iron) Flow*. RNNs evolved by EXAMM on the source data were transferred to this dataset, making use of these additional 8 inputs.

4.2 Aviation Transfer Learning

The source data for the aviation transfer learning problem consisted of 36 flights gathered from the National General Aviation Flight Information Database[2]. This flight data comes from three different airframes, 12 of these flights are from Cessna 172 Skyhawks (C172s), 12 are from Piper PA-28 Cherokees (PA28s) and the last 12 from Piper PA-44 Seminoles (PA44s). Each of the 36 flights came from a different aircraft. The duration of each flight ranged from 1 to 3 h, with data coming from 26 sensors for PA28s, 31 sensors for C172s, and 39 sensors for PA44s. These different airframes have significant design differences, as shown in Fig. 3. C172s have a single engine and are "high wing", *i.e.*, wings are on the top, PA28s have a single engine and are "low wing", *i.e.*, wings are on the bottom, and PA44s have dual engines and are low wing.

(a) Cessna 172 Skyhawk   (b) Piper PA-288 Cherokee   (c) Piper PA-44 Seminole

Fig. 3. The three different airframes used for aviation transfer learning in this work (images under creative commons licenses).

These aircraft share 18 common sensor parameters: (1) *Altitude Above Ground Level (AltAGL)*, (2) *Barometric Altitude (AltB)*, (3) *GPS Altitude (Alt-GPS)*, (4) *Altitude Miles Above Sea Level (AltMSL)*, (5) *Fuel Quantity Left (FQtyL)*, (6) *Fuel Quantity Right (FQtyR)*, (7) *Ground Speed (GndSpd)*, (8)

---

[2] http://ngafid.org.

Indicated Air Speed (IAS), (9) *Lateral Acceleration (LatAc)*, (10) *Normal Acceleration (NormAc)*, (11) *Outside Air Temperature (OAT)*, (12) *Pitch*, (13) *Roll*, (14) *True Airspeed (TAS)*, (15) *Vertical Speed (VSpd)*, (16) *Vertical Speed Gs (VSpdG)*, (17) *Wind Direction (WndDir)*, and (18) *Wind Speed (WndSpd)*.

Since each of these airframes have different engines, they have different sets of engine sensor parameters. The C172 and PA44 have an absolute barometric pressure sensor which the PA28 does not. PA28s add the following 8 parameters: (1) *Engine 1 Exhaust Gas Temperature 1 (E1 EGT1)*, (2) *Engine 1 Exhaust Gas Temperature 2 (E1 EGT2)*, (3) *Engine 1 Exhaust Gas Temperature 3 (E1 EGT3)*, (4) *Engine 1 Exhaust Gas Temperature 4 (E1 EGT4)*, (5) *Engine 1 Fuel Flow (E1 FFlow)*, (6) *Engine 1 Oil Pressure (E1 OilP)*, (7), *Engine 1 Oil Temperature (E1 OilT)*, and (8) *Engine 1 Rotations Per minute (E1 RPM)*.

C172s add the following 13 parameters: (1) *Absolute Barometric Pressure (BaroA)*, (2) *Engine 1 Cylinder Head Temperature 1 (E1 CHT1)*, (3) *Engine 1 Cylinder Head Temperature 2 (E1 CHT2)*, (4) *Engine 1 Cylinder Head Temperature 3 (E1 CHT3)*, (5) *Engine 1 Cylinder Head Temperature 4 (E1 CHT4)*, (6) *Engine 1 Exhaust Gas Temperature 1 (E1 EGT1)*, (7) *Engine 1 Exhaust Gas Temperature 2 (E1 EGT2)*, (8) *Engine 1 Exhaust Gas Temperature 3 (E1 EGT3)*, (9) *Engine 1 Exhaust Gas Temperature 4 (E1 EGT4)*, (10) *Engine 1 Fuel Flow (E1 FFlow)*, (11) *Engine 1 Oil Pressure (E1 OilP)*, (12) *Engine 1 Oil Temperature (E1 OilT)* and 13) *Engine 1 Rotations Per minute (E1 RPM)*.

Finally, PA44s add the following 21 parameters: (1) *Absolute Barometric Pressure (BaroA)*, (2) *Engine 1 Cylinder Head Temperature 1 (E1 CHT1)*, (3) *Engine 1 Exhaust Gas Temperature 1 (E1 EGT1)*, (4) *Engine 1 Exhaust Gas Temperature 2 (E1 EGT2)*, (5) *Engine 1 Exhaust Gas Temperature 3 (E1 EGT3)*, (6) *Engine 1 Exhaust Gas Temperature 4 (E1 EGT4)*, (7) *Engine 1 Fuel Flow (E1 FFlow)*, (8) *Engine 1 Oil Pressure (E1 OilP)*, (9) *Engine 1 Oil Temperature (E1 OilT)*, (10) *Engine 1 Rotations Per minute (E1 RPM)*, (11) *Engine 1 Manifold Absolute Pressure (E1 MAP)*, (12) *Engine 2 Cylinder Head Temperature 1 (E1 CHT1)*, (13) *Engine 2 Exhaust Gas Temperature 1 (E1 EGT1)*, (14) *Engine 2 Exhaust Gas Temperature 2 (E1 EGT2)*, (15) *Engine 2 Exhaust Gas Temperature 3 (E1 EGT3)*, (16) *Engine 2 Exhaust Gas Temperature 4 (E1 EGT4)*, (17) *Engine 2 Fuel Flow (E1 FFlow)*, (18) *Engine 2 Oil Pressure (E1 OilP)*, (19) *Engine 2 Oil Temperature (E1 OilT)*, (20) *Engine 2 Rotations Per minute (E1 RPM)*, and (21) *Engine 2 Manifold Absolute Pressure (E1 MAP)*.

The underlying task for these problems was to predict all the EGT parameters from the engines, so RNNs predicting on PA28 or C172 data would predict E1 EGT1-4, and RNNs predicting on PA44 data would predict both E1 EGT1-4 and E2 EGT1-4. We examine transferring RNNs trained and evolved by EXAMM on each of these 3 airframe sources to each of other airframes as a target. Inputs are added or removed by the evolutionary transfer process to make the most of available sensor inputs. Likewise, outputs are added or removed to predict the EGTs of either 1 or 2 engines depending on the airframe. This transfer problem is particularly interesting given that it requires evolved/trained RNNs must learn to transfer useful knowledge between aircraft with different airframes and engines.

5   Results

5.1   EXAMM and Backpropagation Hyperparameters

Each EXAMM neuro-evolution run consisted of 4 islands, each with a population size of 10. New RNNs were generated via intra-island crossover (at rate of 20%), mutation at rate 70%, and inter-island crossover at 10% rate. All of EXAMM's mutation operations (except for *split edge*) were utilized, each chosen with a uniform 10% chance. EXAMM generated new nodes by selecting from simple neurons, Δ-RNN, GRU, LSTM, MGU and UGRNN memory cells (uniformly at random). Each EXAMM run on the plant data generated 2000 RNNs and each on the aviation data generated 4000 RNNs. Recurrent connections could span any time-skip between 1 and 10, chosen uniformly at random.

All RNNs were locally trained for 4 epochs with backpropagation through time (BPTT) [25] and stochastic gradient descent (SGD) using the same hyperparameters. SGD was run with a learning rate of $\eta = 0.001$, utilizing Nesterov momentum with $mu = 0.9$. No dropout regularization was used as it was shown in prior work to reduce performance when training RNNs for time series prediction [26]. For the LSTM cells that EXAMM could make use of, the forget gate bias had a value of 1.0 added to it (motivated by [27]). Otherwise, RNN weights were initialized by EXAMM's Lamarckian strategy. To prevent exploding gradients, gradient clipping (as described by Pascanu *et al.* [28]) was used when the norm of the gradient was above a threshold of 1.0. To improve performance on vanishing gradients, gradient boosting (the opposite of clipping) was used when the norm of the gradient went a threshold of 0.05.

5.2   Experiments

For each transfer experiment, EXAMM was repeated 10 times on the source data. For the coal plant data, data files 1–3 were used as training data and data file 4 was used as testing data. For the aviation data, the first 9 flights were used as training data, with the last 3 flights used as testing data. The RNNs with the best mean squared error (MSE) from each of the 10 EXAMM runs on the source data were used as the initial genomes for EXAMM when it was run on the target data.

Coal Plant Transfer Learning. EXAMM was trained on the source coal plant data (without fuel quality parameters) 10 times as described above. EXAMM was then trained 10 times from scratch using the target data (the coal plant data including the fuel quality parameters), as well as 10 times using the best RNN generated from each of the 10 source data EXAMM runs. Figure 4 presents the convergence of the MSE of the best found RNNs of each EXAMM run started

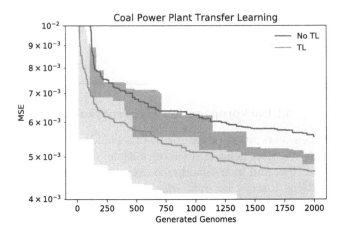

Fig. 4. Convergence rates (in terms of best MSE) for the EXAMM runs starting from scratch on the target coal plant data (No TL), and the EXAMM runs starting with RNNs transferred from the source data (TL).

from scratch on the target data, as well as the convergence of the 10 EXAMM runs starting from the RNNs transferred from the source runs.

For the coal plant transfer learning scenario, the EXAMM runs using adaptive structure transfer learning showed significant improvements in performance. The MSE of predictions for the transfer learning runs started with lower MSEs and the non-transfer learning EXAMM runs never reached similar performance even after 2000 RNNs were evolved and trained.

Aviation Transfer Learning. Figure 5 shows the performance of adaptive structure transfer learning using each of the airframes (C172, PA28 and PA44) as a source transferred to each other airframe as a target, *i.e.*, RNNs evolved and trained using EXAMM on C172 data were transferred to EXAMM runs with PA28 and PA44 data, PA28 source RNNs were transferred to C172 and PA44 targets, and PA44 source RNNs were transferred to C172 and PA28 RNNs. Since each airframe type had different input parameters, and the PA44 runs had additional outputs, this problem served as a useful case where adding and removing inputs and outputs from the RNN structures during transfer was necessary.

The aviation transfer learning problem proved to be more challenging than the coal plant problem. While the coal plant data all came from the same system, with the transfer target adding new sensor data; each of the flights used as training and testing data came from different aircraft, and the three different airframes transferred between had significant design and engine differences. Additionally, while the RNNs were predicting similar engine parameters they were transferred from different engine designs.

The simplest airframe with the least number of parameters (PA28) proved to be the easiest to transfer to. Using both C172 and PA44 source data, the transfer

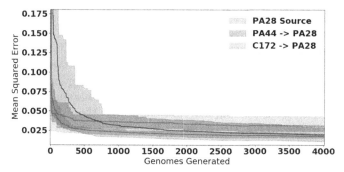

(a) Convergence rates (in terms of best MSE) for the EXAMM runs first using C172 and PA44 flights as source data and then transferred to PA28 data and EXAMM runs trained on PA28 flight data from scratch.

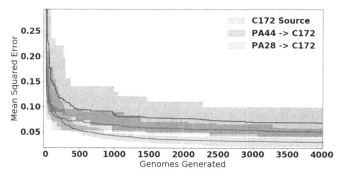

(b) Convergence rates (in terms of best MSE) for the EXAMM runs first using PA28 and PA44 flights as source data and then transferred to C172 data, and EXAMM runs trained on C172 flight data from scratch.

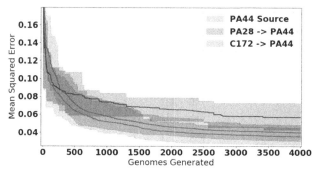

(c) Convergence rates (in terms of best MSE) for the EXAMM runs first using C172 and PA28 flights as source data and then transferred to PA44 data, and EXAMM runs trained on PA44 flight data from scratch.

Fig. 5. Aviation transfer learning experiments.

learning-based EXAMM runs swiftly outperformed the EXAMM runs trained on PA28 data from scratch while the runs from scratch never caught up to the transfer learning runs. Transferring from the most complicated PA44 source took longer to perform better than the runs from scratch, however it eventually reached similar performance to the C172 transfer learning runs. Interestingly, the runs from scratch never converged to the transfer learning runs, indicating that performing transfer learning may have improved the generalization ability of the evolved RNNs (in addition to faster learning).

For C172 predictions, using PA28 as a source for transfer had similar results as above with the transfer learning runs swiftly performing better than those trained from scratch on C172 data (with the from scratch runs never catching up). However, the transfer learning runs with PA44 data as a source never reached similar performance. This is potentially due to the difference between both the airframes, the number engines and a change in the number of outputs. PA44 transferred to PA28 may have performed better due to similarities in their engines and airframes, coming from the same manufacturer; whereas the C172 airframe and engine may have been too different for the transfer process to work.

Lastly, transfer learning struggled when PA28 and C172 data was used as a source with the most complicated PA44 data as a target. While the runs with C172 data came close to runs on the PA44 data from scratch they never quite reached the same performance. The PA28 source runs did not perform nearly as well, most likely due to the large difference in both inputs and outputs (26 inputs and 4 outputs vs. 39 inputs and 8 outputs). In general, this may indicate that adding outputs results in a more challenging knowledge transfer problem.

Table 1. Size of the evolved and transferred RNNs.

Group	Nodes			Edges			Recurrent edges		
	Min	Max	Avg	Min	Max	Avg	Min	Max	Avg
C172 Source	35	38.4	43	124	156.2	198	1	6.0	21
PA28 Source	30	32.2	38	103	124.1	179	0	4.1	21
PA44 Source	54	59.2	70	465	541.5	680	16	43.5	75
C172 to PA28	32	39.3	50	130	181.3	225	10	22.4	42
C172 to PA44	56	71.3	92	511	704.8	1014	28	83.6	171
PA28 to PA44	48	52.7	59	331	385.6	462	3	12.2	45
PA28 to C172	35	44.4	75	136	214.7	506	8	30.1	125
PA44 to PA28	46	75.7	128	351	716.9	1499	42	178.4	409
PA44 to C172	46	53.2	66	267	346.5	466	22	42.4	62

Table 1 provides a closer investigation of the evolved and transferred RNNs. The table demonstrates that the PA44 prediction problem is significantly more complicated than that of the PA28 and C172 airframes. The number of nodes, edges, and recurrent edges in the RNNs trained from scratch on the PA44 source data (see the PA44 Source row) are an order of magnitude larger than those trained from scratch on the PA28 and C172 data. It appears that EXAMM runs with RNNs transferred from C172 and PA28 source data to PA44 target data were unable to reach the required complexity swiftly enough (causing issues).

6   Discussion

This work demonstrates initial findings in utilizing neuro-evolution as a strategy to speed up transfer learning of RNNs applied to time series data forecasting. This research is particularly novel in that it is not only the first work to utilize neuro-evolution for transfer learning (to our knowledge) but also that it is the first transfer learning strategy that is capable of structural adaptation. Our approach modifies the input and output layers by adding and removing nodes as needed to transfer potential structures between different prediction tasks, continuing to evolve network structures beyond the initial network structure transfer.

The results are both promising and raise interesting directions for future work. With respect to data from a coal-fired power plant scenario where new sensor capabilities for determining fuel quality became available, RNNs trained on prior data without the new sensors serving as the transfer source were able to evolve and train on the target task faster in the short term and also continued to outperform RNNs only trained on the target dataset with the new sensor data; indicating that the transfer learning process improves generalization. Furthermore, using aviation data from three different airframes, it was shown that it is possible to successfully transfer knowledge from RNNs trained on aircraft with different airframes and engines when predicting engine parameters. This was particularly impressive given that we were transferring predictive ability from engine parameters from *different engine designs and different airframe designs*. When conducting transfer learning from the most complicated airframe type (PA44) to simpler airframe types (PA28 and C172) or between the simpler airframe types (PA28 and C172) we showed similar improvement in generalization – the RNNs generated via our transfer learning process performed better than those trained from scratch on target data.

Nonetheless, the aviation data did present some challenges. Transferring to the more complicated PA44 airframe with two engines proved to be challenging. The experiments transferring to PA44 as a target did not perform as well as those trained on the PA44 data from scratch. An analysis of the transferred and evolved RNNs showed that this could possibly be due to the additional target outputs from the additional engine compounded by the additional complexity of the prediction task (RNNs evolved for the PA44 data were an order of magnitude larger in size). Determining if it is possible to transfer to a more complicated system remains an area of future work and might potentially be enabled by utilizing different strategies for adding/removing the output/input nodes.

In conclusion, this work presents a novel and promising direction for neuro-evolution research. Compared to other transfer learning strategies that simply reuse weights and architectures on target data with minimal modification, using a adaptive structure methodology driven by neuro-evolution allows modification of inputs in the case of sensor data and could even allow the modification of input layer size if applied to the adaptation of convolutional neural networks. In addition, this approach allows the internal structure of the transferred networks to continue to be adapted, providing even better performance. This work provides a new opportunity to allow ANNs to quickly learn when exposed to different data and more quickly transfer learned knowledge to across prediction tasks.

Acknowledgements. This material is based upon work supported by the U.S. Department of Energy, Office of Science, Office of Advanced Combustion Systems under Award Number #FE0031547.

References

1. Mikolov, T., Sutskever, I., Chen, K., Corrado, G.S., Dean, J.: Distributed representations of words and phrases and their compositionality. In: Advances in Neural Information Processing Systems, pp. 3111–3119 (2013)
2. Devlin, J., Chang, M.W., Lee, K., Toutanova, K.: BERT: pre-training of deep bidirectional transformers for language understanding. arXiv preprint arXiv:1810.04805 (2018)
3. Moreno, G.A., Cámara, J., Garlan, D., Schmerl, B.: Proactive self-adaptation under uncertainty: a probabilistic model checking approach. In: Proceedings of the 2015 10th Joint Meeting on Foundations of Software Engineering, ESEC/FSE 2015, pp. 1–12. ACM, New York (2015). http://doi.acm.org/10.1145/2786805.2786853
4. Moreno, G.A.: Adaptation timing in self-adaptive systems. Ph.D. thesis, Carnegie Mellon University (2017)
5. Palmerino, J., Yu, Q., Desell, T., Krutz, D.: Accounting for tactic volatility in self-adaptive systems for improved decision-making. In: Proceedings of the 34th ACM/IEEE International Conference on Automated Software Engineering. ASE 2019. ACM, New York (2019)
6. Gupta, P., Malhotra, P., Vig, L., Shroff, G.: Transfer learning for clinical time series analysis using recurrent neural networks. arXiv preprint arXiv:1807.01705 (2018)
7. Zhang, A., et al.: Transfer learning with deep recurrent neural networks for remaining useful life estimation. Appl. Sci. **8**(12), 2416 (2018)
8. Yoon, S., Yun, H., Kim, Y., Park, G.T., Jung, K.: Efficient transfer learning schemes for personalized language modeling using recurrent neural network. In: Workshops at the Thirty-First AAAI Conference on Artificial Intelligence (2017)
9. Zarrella, G., Marsh, A.: MITRE at SemEval-2016 task 6: transfer learning for stance detection. arXiv preprint arXiv:1606.03784 (2016)
10. Mrkšić, N., et al.: Multi-domain dialog state tracking using recurrent neural networks. arXiv preprint arXiv:1506.07190 (2015)
11. Mun, S., Shon, S., Kim, W., Han, D.K., Ko, H.: Deep neural network based learning and transferring mid-level audio features for acoustic scene classification. In: 2017 IEEE International Conference on Acoustics, Speech and Signal Processing (ICASSP), pp. 796–800. IEEE (2017)

12. Taylor, M.E., Whiteson, S., Stone, P.: Transfer via inter-task mappings in policy search reinforcement learning. In: Proceedings of the 6th International Joint Conference on Autonomous Agents and Multiagent Systems, p. 37. ACM (2007)
13. Yang, Z., Salakhutdinov, R., Cohen, W.W.: Transfer learning for sequence tagging with hierarchical recurrent networks. arXiv preprint arXiv:1703.06345 (2017)
14. Verbancsics, P., Stanley, K.O.: Evolving static representations for task transfer. J. Mach. Learn. Res. **11**(May), 1737–1769 (2010)
15. Hinton, G., Vinyals, O., Dean, J.: Distilling the knowledge in a neural network. arXiv preprint arXiv:1503.02531 (2015)
16. Tang, Z., Wang, D., Zhang, Z.: Recurrent neural network training with dark knowledge transfer. In: 2016 IEEE International Conference on Acoustics, Speech and Signal Processing (ICASSP), pp. 5900–5904. IEEE (2016)
17. Deo, R.V., Chandra, R., Sharma, A.: Stacked transfer learning for tropical cyclone intensity prediction. arXiv preprint arXiv:1708.06539 (2017)
18. Ororbia, A., ElSaid, A., Desell, T.: Investigating recurrent neural network memory structures using neuro-evolution. In: Proceedings of the Genetic and Evolutionary Computation Conference, GECCO 2019, pp. 446–455. ACM, New York (2019). http://doi.acm.org/10.1145/3321707.3321795
19. Ororbia II, A.G., Mikolov, T., Reitter, D.: Learning simpler language models with the differential state framework. Neural Comput. **29**(12), 1–26 (2017). https://doi.org/10.1162/neco_a_01017. PMID: 28957029
20. Chung, J., Gulcehre, C., Cho, K., Bengio, Y.: Empirical evaluation of gated recurrent neural networks on sequence modeling. arXiv preprint arXiv:1412.3555 (2014)
21. Hochreiter, S., Schmidhuber, J.: Long short-term memory. Neural Comput. **9**(8), 1735–1780 (1997)
22. Zhou, G.-B., Wu, J., Zhang, C.-L., Zhou, Z.-H.: Minimal gated unit for recurrent neural networks. Int. J. Autom. Comput. **13**(3), 226–234 (2016). https://doi.org/10.1007/s11633-016-1006-2
23. Collins, J., Sohl-Dickstein, J., Sussillo, D.: Capacity and trainability in recurrent neural networks. arXiv preprint arXiv:1611.09913 (2016)
24. Message Passing Interface Forum: MPI: A message-passing interface standard. The International Journal of Supercomputer Applications and High Performance Computing 8(3/4), 159–416 (Fall/Winter 1994)
25. Werbos, P.J.: Backpropagation through time: what it does and how to do it. Proc. IEEE **78**(10), 1550–1560 (1990)
26. ElSaid, A., El Jamiy, F., Higgins, J., Wild, B., Desell, T.: Optimizing long short-term memory recurrent neural networks using ant colony optimization to predict turbine engine vibration. Appl. Soft Comput. **73**, 969–991 (2018)
27. Jozefowicz, R., Zaremba, W., Sutskever, I.: An empirical exploration of recurrent network architectures. In: International Conference on Machine Learning, pp. 2342–2350 (2015)
28. Pascanu, R., Mikolov, T., Bengio, Y.: On the difficulty of training recurrent neural networks. In: International Conference on Machine Learning, pp. 1310–1318 (2013)

Ant-based Neural Topology Search (ANTS) for Optimizing Recurrent Networks

AbdElRahman ElSaid, Alexander G. Ororbia, and Travis J. Desell[✉]

Rochester Institute of Technology, Rochester, NY 14623, USA
{aae8800,tjdvse}@rit.edu, ago@cs.rit.edu

Abstract. Hand-crafting effective and efficient structures for recurrent neural networks (RNNs) is a difficult, expensive, and time-consuming process. To address this challenge, we propose a novel neuro-evolution algorithm based on ant colony optimization (ACO), called Ant-based Neural Topology Search (ANTS), for directly optimizing RNN topologies. The procedure selects from multiple modern recurrent cell types such as Δ-RNN, GRU, LSTM, MGU and UGRNN cells, as well as recurrent connections which may span multiple layers and/or steps of time. In order to introduce an inductive bias that encourages the formation of sparser synaptic connectivity patterns, we investigate several variations of the core algorithm. We do so primarily by formulating different functions that drive the underlying pheromone simulation process (which mimic L1 and L2 regularization in standard machine learning) as well as by introducing ant agents with specialized roles (inspired by how real ant colonies operate), i.e., *explorer ants* that construct the initial feed forward structure and *social ants* which select nodes from the feed forward connections to subsequently craft recurrent memory structures. We also incorporate communal intelligence, where best weights are shared by the ant colony for weight initialization, reducing the number of backpropagation epochs required to locally train candidate RNNs, speeding up the neuro-evolution process. Our results demonstrate that the sparser RNNs evolved by ANTS significantly outperform traditional one and two layer architectures consisting of modern memory cells, as well as the well-known NEAT algorithm. Furthermore, we improve upon prior state-of-the-art results on the time series dataset utilized in our experiments.

Keywords: Ant colony optimization · Swarm intelligence · Neuro-evolution · Recurrent neural networks · Time series data prediction

1 Introduction

Given their success across a wide swath of pattern recognition tasks, artificial neural networks (ANNs) have become a popular tool to use when attempting to

---

A. G. Ororbia and T. J. Desell—Indicates equal advising.

© Springer Nature Switzerland AG 2020
P. A. Castillo et al. (Eds.): EvoApplications 2020, LNCS 12104, pp. 626–641, 2020.
https://doi.org/10.1007/978-3-030-43722-0_40

solve data-driven problems. However, in order to solve increasingly more complicated problems, neural architectures are becoming vastly more complex. Increasing the complexity of an ANN entails having to operate with more layers of neural processing elements required, most of which are usually wider and more densely-connected, greatly complicating the model design process. The resulting increase in complexity introduces new challenges and complications when fitting these ANN models to actual data. These problems are further compounded when ANNs are meant to process temporal data, entailing recurrent connections which can span varying periods of time. As a result, crafting performant ANNs becomes expensive and incredibly difficult for engineers, highlighting a grand challenge facing the domain of machine learning – the automation of ANN architecture design, which includes selecting the form of the underlying synaptic topology as well as the values of the weights themselves. The key to this automation might lie in developing optimization procedures that can effectively explore the vast, combinatorial search space of possible topological structures that could be constructed from a large set of neuronal units and the wide variety of synaptic connectivity patterns that relate them to one another.

Recent interest in automated architecture search has resulted in many proposed ideas related to deep feed forward and convolutional networks, including those based on nature-inspired metaheuristics [1]. However, few, if any, have focused on the far more difficult problem of optimizing recurrent neural networks (RNNs) aimed at processing temporal, sequential data such as time series, i.e., automated RNN design.

This study addresses the challenge of automated RNN design by developing a novel ANN topology optimizer based on concepts from artificial evolution and ant colony optimization (ACO). Specifically, we propose an algorithm called Ant-based Neural Topology Search (ANTS), which automatically constructs and optimizes the topology of RNNs, with a focus on time series data prediction. We further experiment with variations of our ANTS method in the following ways:

- In order to encourage the discovery of more sparsely-connected neural topologies, we investigate different schemes for dynamically modifying the pheromone traces deposited by ant agents that compose the swarm. Specifically, we introduce functions for introducing regularization into the overall optimization, slowly clearing out densely-connected synaptic areas by depriving poorly performing weights/edges of pheromone accumulation.
- We incorporate and analyze various weight initialization schemes and find that a strategy incorporating communal intelligence where best found weights are shared by the colony is highly effective.
- Inspired by the role-specialization that ants operate under within the context of real-world ant colonies, we extend ANTS to utilize different specialized ant agents to modularize the underlying synaptic connectivity construction process, which we find greatly improves solutions found by our metaheuristic.

Experimentally, we validate our proposed nature-inspired metaheuristic on an open-access real-world time series data set collected form a coal-fired power plant. A rigorous ablation study of the ANTS algorithm is conducted by analyzing the candidate network topologies it finds. A total over 1600 experiments with varying heuristics and hyperparameters were performed, which entailed training 32,000,000 different RNNs. Our results indicate that ANTS is able to build well performing, arbitrary RNN structures with connections that span both structure and time using both simple and complex memory cells. More importantly, ANTS is shown to significantly outperform the well-known neuro-evolutionary algorithm, NEAT [2], as well as the state-of-the-art evolutionary optimizer, EXAMM [3], which held the prior best results on this data set. Our ANTS source code is open source and freely available on our GitHub repository[1].

2   Related Work

With respect to neuroevolution of recurrent network topologies, a great deal of work already exists, ranging from stochastic alteration of the topology as in dropout [4] to something more sophisticated like that in the original NEAT [2] and its more modern incarnate HyperNEAT [5]. Other proposed approaches include EPNet [6], EANT [7], GeNet [8], CoDeepNEAT [9], and EXACT [10]. EXACT was extended to evolve RNNs that used LSTM memory cells (named EXALT) and shown to perform quite well on time-series prediction problems [11]. Later, the algorithm, retitled EXAMM, was generalized to evolve networks consisting of a library of recurrent memory cells [3]. These previously proposed ideas center around the use of a genetic algorithm [12], where optimization is inspired by approaches that draw from the evolution of organisms, of either Darwinian and/or Lamarckian nature.

Nonetheless, very few studies in the body of work described above consider ant colony optimization (ACO) [13] as the central optimizer for network topology, and even fewer in general focus on exploring how to evolve complex temporal models like the RNN, with EXALT and EXAMM being exceptions. Of the few that have investigated ACO, most existing work has used it to strictly optimize feed forward networks and, even in that case, have dominantly focused on either initializing the weights of the connections [14], or on reducing the dimension of the input vector solution space [15]. One notable effort that has used ACO for RNN optimization in some form is [16], which used ACO to optimize smaller neural network structures based on Elman recurrent networks [17].

This paper contributes to the domain of nature-inspired neural network topology optimization by proposing a novel metaheuristic for evolving the full structure of an RNN as opposed to prior studies that have applied the technique as only a partial component of the optimization process [18] or in smaller Elman RNN topologies with limited recurrent connectivity [16]. Furthermore, our algorithm is capable of utilizing the same full suite of recurrent memory cells as the state-of-the-art evolutionary algorithm EXAMM (LSTM, GRU, MGU, UGRNN, and Δ-RNN cells). To the best of our knowledge, we are the first to propose an ACO-based approach to automate RNN design, offering a powerful procedure

---

[1] https://github.com/travisdesell/exact/tree/adding_ant_colony.

that combines concepts of both neuro-evolution and ant colony metaheuristic optimization.

3   Ant-based Neural Topology Search (ANTS)

ANTS handles the optimization of ANN structures using a multi-agent system, where each agent (an ant) treats the ANN as graph structure, considering neuronal processing elements (PEs) as the nodes and the synaptic weights that connect PEs as the edges. In order to design the operations that these agents perform as well as the manner in which they traverse the ANN graph, we may appeal to the metaphor of ants and the collective they holistically form, *i.e.*, the ant colony. As a result, the agents will function based on simplifications of myrmecological principles, such as the mechanics of ant-to-ant social interaction.

At a high level, in ANTS, the individual ant agents operate on a single massively connected "superstructure", which contains all possible ways that PEs may connect with each other both in terms of structure, *i.e.*, all possible feed forward pathways that start from the input/sensory PEs and end at the output/actuator PEs, and time, *i.e.*, all possible recurrent connections that span many multiple time delays[2]. In our implementation, ants choose to move over connections between nodes (or neurons), probabilistically and as a function of a simulated chemical known as the "pheromone", which is placed on connections by ants based on how well they have been utilized to generate candidate RNNs.

ANTS was developed as an asynchronous parallel system for use on high performance computing resources, which has a master process that maintains the colony information and worker processes to (locally) train the RNNs. This parallel implementation is asynchronous, the master process generates new RNNs as needed for worker processes (which operate on separate, dedicated CPU or GPU resources) and updates colony information and pheromones as trained RNN results are returned. This results in a naturally load balanced algorithm with high scalability. From the overall superstructure, which the ant agents exclusively operate on, RNN subnetworks are extracted (as dictated by the current pheromone trace network available at the current simulation time step, which yields a map of nodes and connecting synapses, both recurrent and feed forward, visited by the ant agents) and sent to worker processes. The worker processes train the extracted RNNs locally with only a few epochs of back-propagation through time (BPTT). After a particular worker is done locally training a RNN subnetwork, the candidate's weight values and cost (fitness) function (measure on a validation subset of data) are communicated back to the swarm and superstructure (housed in the master process), adjusting the pheromone trace network and affecting future ant agent traversal behavior.

---

[2] Note that this superstructure is more connected than a standard fully connected neural network – each layer is also fully connected to each other layer as well, allowing for forward and backward layer skipping connections, with additional recurrent connections between node pairs for each time skip allowed.

Within the framework of ANTS, we investigate variations of its various underlying mechanisms. These include the use of communal intelligence by sharing the best weights found among the colony, allowing ant agents to also select from multiple memory cell types as opposed to operating exclusively with simple neurons, introducing specialized ants that have different graph traversal strategies, and constraining ant movement and manipulating the pheromone evaporation function in order to encourage the discovery of sparse RNN topologies. One particularly crucial element in our ANTS procedure is the introduction of different ant agent types or species, which is inspired by how real ants specialize to act according to specific roles to serve the needs of the colony [19]. Specifically, we consider designing ant agents that serve specific roles in constructing parts of candidate RNN subnetworks – some ants exclusively traverse feed forward synaptic pathways while others only explore recurrent synaptic pathways.

3.1   Communal Weight Sharing

Randomly initializing edges and recurrent edges' weights each time a new RNN is generated requires local tuning (via BPTT) for many epochs for the RNN to reach suitable generalization error, as they do not make use of any information gained by prior trained RNN candidates. It has been shown that the reuse of prior trained weights (*i.e.*, epigenetic or Lamarckian weight initialization) can significantly speed up the neuro-evolution process and result in better performing, smaller ANNs in general [20]. To apply similar use of prior knowledge, ANTS utilizes a communal weight sharing strategy. Each edge in the ant swarm's connectivity super-structure also tracks a weight value in addition to its pheromone value. These weights are randomly initialized uniformly $U(-0.5, 0.5)$. Each time a generated RNN performs well, the weights of its best performance, as measured on a validation data subset, are used to update the shared weight values in the swarm's super-structure.

Formally, we define phi (Φ) as a function of the population's best and worse evaluated RNN fitness, where W_{colony_i} is the colony's edge weight, W_{RNN_i} is the corresponding neural network's edge weight, fit_{pop_best} is the population's best fitness, and fit_{pop_worst} is the population's worst fitness. Weight initialization then proceeds as follows:

$$x = \frac{fit_{new} - fit_{pop\_best}}{fit_{pop\_worst} - fit_{pop\_best}} \tag{1a}$$

$$\Phi(fit_{new}) = min\left(max\left((1-x), 0\right), 1\right) \tag{1b}$$

$$W_{colony_i} = \Phi W_{RNN_i} + (1 - \Phi) W_{colony_i}. \tag{1c}$$

With respect to the function Φ, we investigated two variations. The first variant, as shown in Eq. 1, used the fitness of the RNN used to update the weights to determine how much these new (locally found) weight values effect those of the colony. The second variant of Φ was set to a predetermined constant instead of being calculated or adjusted by fitness. This process essentially allows for a running average (either with a fixed update or dynamic update based on fitness) of the best weights found for each connection in the superstructure. When a new RNN is generated, it uses the current weight values in whatever edges that were extracted from the superstructure on the master process. This allows for the colony to share information about the best weights found for each connection, adapting them in a manner similar to a running average as new best candidate RNNs and weights are found.

3.2 Memory Cell Selection

For any particular node in the super-structure, ANTS also has the ability to utilize the pheromones present to select which memory cell type a particular node will be in the generated network. A node could chosen to be either an LSTM [21], a GRU [22], an MGU [23], a UGRNN [24], or a Δ-RNN cell [25]. We refer the reader to these works for the formulations of these memory cells. Pheromones are deposited and updated for each of these memory cell possibilities as described below.

3.3 Altering Graph Traversal with Ant Species

As mentioned above, we explored various strategies for guiding ant traversal over the connectivity superstructure. Inspired by role specialization in real colonies, we implemented ant agents that explored the connectivity graph in specific ways. First, we started with a generic ant agent, called the *standard ant*, which was allowed to traverse through the massively connected colony superstructure in an unbiased manner. This, in essence, recovers the standard simple ant agent in classic ACO, which has complete freedom to explore any piece of a given graph structure. However, it became quickly apparent that this type of ant would get "stuck" in the network, generating a significantly high number of recurrent connections before finally reaching an output node (explained in Fig. 1). This meant that the RNN candidates extracted for local fine-tuning were rather dense, and in turn, compute-heavy (featuring many extraneous parameters as is characteristic of over-parameterized models).

To prevent this problem, our first tactic was to alter the pheromone deposit function by adding extra pheromones to forward paths upon initialization as well as after every pheromone update. If the total number of pheromones on the forward edges out of a node was less than 75% of the total number of pheromones on the recurrent edges out of the node, the pheromones on each forward node were multiplied by the ratio of the total sum of outgoing recurrent edge pheromones over the total sum of the outgoing forward edge pheromones. This biasing method yielded better proportions of forward and backward paths.

Even with this forward path bias added to the pheromone deposit function, when using standard ants, we found that ANTS still tended to favor the generation of fairly dense networks. Altering the number of ant agents used to explore

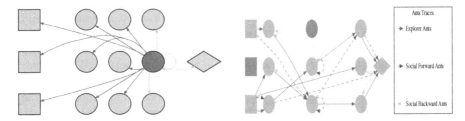

Fig. 1. Potential paths an ant can take from a given node (in orange) with the massively-connected superstructure. The number of recurrent paths (red) far outnumber the forward paths (green). This problem is exacerbated as the possible recurrent time scale increases, which results in multiple backward recurrent connections for each red connection, each going back a different number of time steps in the past. (Color figure online)

Fig. 2. In multi-role traversal, explorer ants (red) first select the forward paths in the network, creating a basic structure for the RNN. The social ant agents then select from the nodes chosen by the explorer ants with forward recurrent ants (blue) creating additional forward recurrent connections and backward recurrent ants (green), moving backwards from the output toward the input, creating backward recurrent connections between the same nodes. (Color figure online)

the structure as a means to control density of RNN candidates proved to help somewhat but was rather unwieldy and entailed far too much external human intervention. Instead, we developed an ant agent role specialization scheme that we found worked far better as an automatic control mechanism to control the network size and synaptic density.

The first agent role, the *explorer ant*, can only choose from forward connections in the connectivity superstructure. The connections selected by this specialized agent are utilized to generate the base neural structure upon which recurrent connections are then be added to. After the explorer ants have selected the possible nodes and forward connections, two additional specializations of what we call *social ants* are then used: *(i) forward recurrent ants* and, *(ii) backward recurrent ants*. Social ants are first restricted to only visiting nodes that have already been selected by the explorer ants. In the case of the forward recurrent ants, when a path is chosen, the ant specifically creates a recurrent connection that moves forward in the network along the same path, along with a selected time skip (determined by pheromones). Backward recurrent ants, on the other hand, move backwards through the network and, for each path between nodes they take, a backward recurrent connection is added, along with a selected time skip (also determined by pheromones). Figure 2 provides an example of possible pathways that these specialized agents can take in a colony superstructure.

In addition to the development of specialized ant agents as described above, we explored two modes for general ant movement; *(i)* ants were allowed to pick edges that could jump over layers in the colony (*i.e.*, the superstructure is massively connected, with a plethora of skip connections), or *(ii)* ants were only allowed to select edges between consecutive layers (*i.e.*, the superstructure is fully connected, with no skip connections). This was tested to see the impact that layer skipping would have on the sparsity and performance of generated RNNs. Jumping and non-jumping modes were tested for both the standard ants (with and without forward-path bias) and the specialized ant agent roles.

3.4   Updating Pheromone Values

Different strategies for pheromone placement were also examined. We define τ as the pheromone value, α as the pheromone decay parameter, W as the weights of the evaluated (candidate) RNN, and η as the candidate model's fitness. Specifically, we describe four different functional schemes used to model pheromone deposits.

The first strategy we implemented for ANTS is standard for classical ACO setups. This deposit scheme rewards well performing RNNs with a fixed (constant) pheromone deposit while penalized ill-performing RNN models by evaporating the pheromone trace by a constant evaporation value, C. Specifically, this approach is defined as:

$$\tau_{new} = \tau_{old} \pm C \tag{2}$$

The second strategy we implemented was one that used the fitness (value) as a parameter to guide pheromone deposit. This has been shown to improve ACO performance in prior studies [15]. This scheme is defined as follows:

$$\tau_{new} = (1 - \alpha) \cdot \tau_{old} + \alpha \frac{1}{\eta} \tag{3}$$

The third strategy was to use the values of the neural synaptic weights themselves to control/guide the deposit of pheromones. Specifically, we inserted a penalty on the weights, specifically an L1 penalty (assuming a Laplacian prior of the synaptic weight values), in order to encourage regularization that favored sparser connectivity structure. This form of weight decay is sometimes applied to ANNs when controlling for over-parameterization and sparse weight matrices (with many near hard-zero values) are highly desirable. L1 regularization was applied to the pheromone deposition calculation in the following manner:

$$\tau_{new} = (1 - \alpha) \cdot \tau_{old} + \alpha \left\{ \frac{1}{\eta + \frac{\gamma}{n} \|W\|} \right\} \tag{4}$$

The fourth and final strategy we employed was to insert an L2 penalty to regularize the RNN candidate weights. This assumes a Gaussian prior over the synaptic weight values and is sometimes referred to in ANN literature as "weight decay". We incorporate L2 regularization into pheromone deposition according to the following formula:

$$\tau_{new} = (1 - \alpha) \cdot \tau_{old} + \alpha \left\{ \frac{1}{\eta + \frac{\gamma}{2n} \|W\|_2} \right\} \tag{5}$$

We developed these L1 and L2 functional variations of pheromone deposit schemes in the hopes that they would ultimately encourage/reward the uncovery of sparse, compact RNN predictive models.

3.5   Pheromone Evaporation

Lastly, pheromone trace values (deposited on the superstructures synaptic edge pathways) were allowed to evaporate or "decay" after each generation of an RNN in order to reduce the amount of pheromones on synaptic edges that have not been recently beneficial and to encourage exploration [14,15,26]. Pheromone values are updated (or decayed) according to the following equation:

$$\tau_{updated} = (1 - \beta) \cdot \tau_{current} + \beta \cdot \tau_{original} \tag{6}$$

where $\tau_{updated}$ is the pheromone value after the update, $\tau_{current}$ is the current pheromone value, $\tau_{original}$ is the original baseline pheromone value, and β is the pheromone evaporation rate. This function evaporates the pheromone back towards the original baseline value.

4   Results

ANTS was compared to both NEAT and EXAMM, as well as traditional layered RNN architectures. All ANTS and EXAMM experiments generated 2000 total RNNs, training each for 10 epochs. NEAT, on the other hand, was allowed to generate $420,000$ RNNs. If we assume that a forward pass (forward propagation) and a backward pass (backprop calculation) are approximately the same computationally, this generously gave NEAT approximately 10 times the amount of compute time (as 2000 RNNs trained for 10 epochs would equivocate to $20,000$ forward and $20,000$ backward passes). The RNNs with non-evolvable (fixed) architectures were allowed to train for 70 epochs. Every experiment was repeated 10 times to compute means and standard deviations in order to ensure a proper statistical comparison.

ANTS used a colony superstructure with 12 input nodes, 3 hidden layers, each with 12 hidden nodes, and a single output node. Recurrent synapses could span 1, 2 or 3 steps in time. The resulting connectivity superstructure consisted of 49 nodes, 924 edges, and 3626 recurrent edges. While this may seem modest compared to modern convolutional architectures, which may consist of millions of connections, it is important to note that the RNNs generated from this superstructure are unrolled over 7200 time steps (according to the time series length of the training and testing data samples) when trained locally via backpropagation through time (BPTT). This means algorithms such as ANTS must handle (fully-unrolled) networks of up to $3,528,000$ nodes, $6,652,800$ edges, and $26,107,200$ recurrent edges with errors from the final output (predictor) potentially backpropagated over up to $28,000$ synaptic connections.

The dataset utilized in this study is an open access time series dataset taken from a coal fired powerplant. The data was introduced in previous neuroevolution studies for time series data prediction [11,27]. It consists of 12 possible parameters, recorded for 10 days with each parameter recorded at each minute. These 12 parameters were used to predict the flame intensity parameter (the response variable, in regression parlance). Results were generated by training

RNNs on 5 days worth of data taken from one of the coal burners from this data set. Fitness values (mean absolute error) were calculated on the other 5 days, which was data that was treated as a test set.

1,600 experiments were conducted in order to include all combinations of the ANTS options/variations (described below). Each experiment was repeated 10 times to obtain robust results. These ANTS experiments generated, trained, and evaluated 32 million RNNs. Experiments were scheduled on a high performance computing cluster with 64 Intel® Xeon® Gold 6150 CPUs, each with 36 cores and 375 GB RAM (total 2304 cores and 24 TB of RAM). Each experiment utilized 15 nodes. Overall, the experiments took approximately 30 days to complete.

4.1 Backpropagation Hyperparameters

All ANNs were trained with backprop and stochastic gradient descent (SGD) using the same hyperparameters. SGD was run with a learning rate $\eta = 0.001$ and used Nesterov momentum ($mu = 0.9$) to smooth out the local gradient descent. No dropout regularization was used since it has been shown in other work to reduce performance when training RNNs for time series prediction [18]. To prevent exploding gradients, gradients were re-scaled using gradient clipping (as prescribed by Pascanu *et al.* [28]) when the norm of the gradient was above a threshold of 1.0. To improve performance in the case of vanishing gradients, gradient boosting (the opposite of clipping) was used when the norm of the gradient was below a threshold of 0.05. The forget gate bias of the LSTM cells had 1.0 added to it as this has been shown to yield significant improvements in training time by Jozefowicz *et al.* [29]. Weights for RNN in all other cases were initialized as described in the section describing our communal weight sharing Sect. 3.1 scheme for ANTS and or by EXAMM's Lamarckian weight inheritance [3].

4.2 ANTS Options and Hyper-parameters

The influence/effect of individual ANTS hyper-parameters was carefully investigated in this study. A pheromone decay rate of $\alpha = 0.05$ and a pheromone evaporation rate of $\beta = 0.1$ were chosen as they were shown to be effective in preliminary tests and is within the recommended standard range [15]. The other ANTS parameters we considered were:

1. Number of ants : {20, 40, 80, 160}.
2. Regularization update parameter: {0.25, 0.65, 0.90}.
3. Initializing RNN using communally shared weights with constant Φ values of ({0.3, 0.6, 0.9}), using Φ as calculated by a function of fitness, and basic randomized weight initialization.

The application of the examined heuristics that appear in the figures and tables that follow are labeled as follows:

1. Function Φ: $\Phi()$
2. Constant Φ: $\Phi_{value\ of\ \Phi}$
3. L1 Pheromone regularization: $L1_{value\ of\ \gamma}$ (Eq. 4)
4. L2 Pheromone regularization: $L2_{value\ of\ \gamma}$ (Eq. 5)
5. Standard Ant Species: Without Bias (Std) and With Bias ($StdBias$)
6. Multi Species Ants:
   - Explorer Ants: Exp
   - Explorer Ants and Forward Social Ants: $ExpFwd$
   - Explorer Ants and Backward Social Ants: $ExpBwd$
   - Explorer Ants, Forward and Backward Social Ants: $ExpFwdBwd$
7. Layer Jumping: AJ
8. No Layer Jumping: OJ.

4.3 Performance of Individual Heuristics

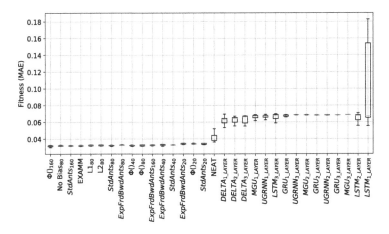

Fig. 3. Performance of NEAT, EXAMM, & individually applied ANTS heuristics against fixed memory cell RNNs.

Figure 3 presents the performance of ANTS when each heuristic is applied separately. Furthermore, it presents for comparison the performance of the state-of-the-art EXAMM, NEAT, and traditional fixed standard RNNs. While ANTS in this case (augmented only by individual heuristics) did not outperform EXAMM except for some outliers, both EXAMM and ANTS showed dramatically better performance than NEAT, even though NEAT was given a significant amount of extra compute time. ANTS, EXAMM and NEAT also significantly outperformed traditional RNNs. Some of the gain over NEAT is most likely due to the use of backpropagation by EXAMM and ANTS since NEAT uses fairly simple and non-gradient based recombination operations to adjust weights.

Table 1. Heuristic ranking statistics

	Top 10			Top 25			Top 100			Top 250		
	Mean	Median	Best	Mean	Median	Best	Mean	Median	Best	Mean	Median	Best
$\Phi()$	3(0)	4(0)	3(0)	9(0)	7(0)	9(0)	26(0)	23(0)	31(8)	58(0)	54(0)	49(8)
ConstΦ	7(0)	6(0)	7(0)	14(0)	14(0)	12(0)	60(0)	63(0)	54(8)	147(0)	149(0)	155(16)
NoΦ	0(0)	0(0)	0(0)	2(0)	4(0)	4(0)	14(0)	14(0)	15(0)	45(0)	47(0)	46(0)
L1	2(0)	4(0)	0(0)	9(0)	8(0)	3(3)	42(0)	34(0)	30(4)	96(0)	96(0)	91(4)
L2	5(0)	5(0)	6(0)	13(0)	12(0)	16(1)	40(0)	45(0)	38(3)	100(0)	98(0)	95(12)
StdAnts	0	0	0	1	0	0	3	0	0	20	19	0
StdBiasAnts	0	0	0	0	0	0	3	1	0	23	16	0
ExpAnts	0	0	10	0	0	25	1	0	100	10	6	250
ExpFrdAnts	6	7	0	14	15	0	45	49	0	98	103	0
ExpBkwAnts	0	0	0	0	0	0	0	0	0	0	0	0
ExpFrdBkwAnts	4	3	0	10	10	0	48	50	0	99	106	0
No Jump	0	0	5	0	0	13	0	0	52	0	0	128
Layer Jump	10	10	5	25	25	12	100	100	48	250	250	122
20 Ants	0	0	2	0	0	6	0	0	24	0	0	65
40 Ants	2	0	3	5	1	7	14	15	23	50	57	63
80 Ants	4	3	2	8	11	6	44	45	26	82	80	60
160 Ants	4	7	3	12	13	6	42	40	27	118	113	62

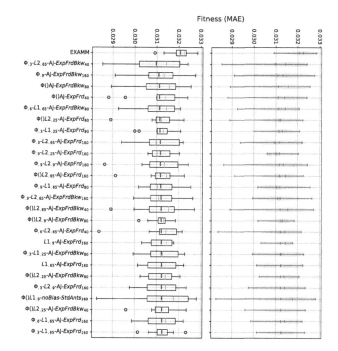

Fig. 4. Performance of EXAMM and the top 25 ANTS experiments

4.4 Performance of Combined Heuristics

The combined application of multiple different heuristics, as illustrated in Fig. 4, yielded ANTS results that outperformed *all baselines*, including the fixed RNNs, NEAT, *as well as* EXAMM. Table 1 provides statistics ranking each of the heuristics based on how many times the experiments that utilized them appeared in the top 10, 25, 100, and 250 best results as determined by the mean, median, and the best performance of the RNN generated in the experiment's 10 repeats. Values in parentheses are the number of times an experiment that only utilized that single heuristic appeared in that top ranking. The utilization of multiple heuristics dominated the top results, with individually-applied heuristics not appearing in the top 10, and only 4 times in the top 25 (only as best results).

Communal weight sharing proved to be very important, yielding strong performance, with all of the top 10 utilizing either functional or constant Φ parameters. Furthermore, it also occurred 2 (mean), 4 (median) and 4 (best) times in the top 10, and 14 (mean), 14 (median), and 15 (best) times in the top 25. Additionally, all of the best performing RNNs used layer-jumping ants, which tend favor more sparse connectivity patterns. Most of the best results used pheromone weight-regularization, with L2 regularization appearing at a nearly 50% rate in the top 10, 25 and 100 results. The regularization factor was also high, at 65% or 90%, for most of the 25 best experiments that used it.

All of the top 250 best results utilized the multiple ant species heuristic, which strongly supports the use of specialized ants. The number of ants varied between 20 and 160 for all the top 25 results in the mean and median case, with a larger number of ants tending to perform better. However the case of 20 ants did occasionally appear in the best cases, even sometimes in the top 10 and, furthermore, these networks tended to be rather sparse but very well performing. This may suggest that the experiments that utilized more ants had an easier time finding the most important structures, but also potentially had extraneous connections which were not needed. In contrast, the experiments with less ants had less of a chance of finding these important structures due to lower (overall) connectivity. This suggests that further optimizations could be designed to better guide ANTS towards the discovery of more efficient networks.

Perhaps one the most interesting items to observe is the performance distribution when multiple ant agent roles was used in ANTS. The entirety of the best found RNNs, up to the top 250 were from explorer ants only, so these generated RNNs only had recurrent connectivity in terms of whatever the various memory cells offered. However, for the mean and median performance of the experiments, nearly all the top 25, 100, and 250 consisted of explorer and forward recurrent roles or explorer, forward, and backward recurrent ant specializations – with only a very few of the only explorer ant only configurations showing up in the top 100 and 250. First, this suggests that backward recurrent connections (which are most commonly utilized in RNNs) were less effective than forward recurrent connections. Second, it also appears that adding these recurrent connections tended to make the RNNs perform significantly better on the average and median cases, while the RNNs which were generated with only explorer ants had the ability to occasionally find RNNs that generalized quite well. These results certainly suggest further study in order to better understand the effect of combining recurrent connections and memory cells. In addition, perhaps alternative strategies can be developed that retain the stability of adding recurrent connections while still efficiently finding well-generalizing RNNs.

5   Discussion

To the best of our knowledge, this work represents the first application of ant colony optimization (ACO) to the problem of neuro-evolution/neural architecture search for recurrent neural networks with varying recurrent time spans and more complex connectivity patterns, with the introduction of the novel Ant-based Neural Topology Search (ANTS) algorithm. ANTS generates candidate RNNs from a massively-connected superstructure (the colony/swarm), taking advantage of ACO for structural optimization and concepts from neuro-evolutionary/genetic approaches for maintaining populations of RNN candidates that are trained locally and asynchronously (making ANTS a memetic procedure as well). A hallmark of ANTS is its computational formalization of role specialization as done by real ant colonies – ant agents are prevented from getting stuck "wandering" around the superstructure through the use of different ant roles, which are constrained to only explore different components of the underlying complex graph space. We also utilize a noval communal intelligence strategy for sharing and updating the best found weights within the colony.

Our experimental results show that using ants with different roles generated RNNs that were not only sparse but performant – these candidates almost entirely outperformed the more standard ant traversal strategies even when standard ants were biased to select forward paths. Furthermore, communal weight sharing greatly improved the accuracy of the generated RNNs[3]. Additionally, allowing ants to jump (or skip) layers proved to not only boost performance but also to increase sparsity. Lastly, to our knowledge the introduction of L1 and L2 regularization into the ACO pheromone deposition process is quite novel if albeit a bit unconventional. Our results show by playing with the form of the pheromone adjustment function, we can increase the likelihood that sparser RNNs are found that also outperform schemes that do not incorporate regularization/constraints. The strategies we formalize in this work are generic and could be applied to any other ACO algorithm's pheromone update process.

The proposed ANTS metaheuristic not only provides advances and new concepts for the field of ant colony optimization research to further explore but also shows strong promise for its use as an alternative neuro-evolution algorithm for automated RNN architecture search. It significantly outperforms the well-known NEAT algorithm (even when NEAT is given an order of magnitude more computation), and, more importantly, ANTS outperforms the state-of-the-art EXAMM neuro-evolution algorithm on the studied time series problem.

---

[3] Corraborating prior studies that have also shown the benefits of similar initialization schemes [3, 20].

The work also opens up multiple avenues for future study and presents interesting questions. In particular, why were explorer ants able to find the best performing networks while performing quite poorly in the mean and median cases? Why did explorer ants combined with social recurrent ants perform extremely well in the mean and median cases but not in the best cases? Answering experimental questions such as these could lead to insights as to how recurrent connections that skip multiple steps of time interact with recurrent memory cells, potentially leading to the design of more expressive RNN structures that better capture longer-term dependencies in sequential data. Finally, future work should entail investigation of ANTS on other time series datasets as well as sequence modeling (and classification) problems more commonly explored in mainstream statistical learning research, such as language modeling [25,30].

Acknowledgements. This material is in part supported by the U.S. Department of Energy, Office of Science, Office of Advanced Combustion Systems under Award Number #FE0031547. We also thank Microbeam Technologies, Inc. for their help in collecting and preparing the coal-fired power plant dataset.

References

1. Yang, X.S.: Nature-Inspired Metaheuristic Algorithms. Luniver Press, Frome (2010)
2. Stanley, K.O., Miikkulainen, R.: Evolving neural networks through augmenting topologies. Evol. Comput. **10**(2), 99–127 (2002)
3. Ororbia, A., ElSaid, A., Desell, T.: Investigating recurrent neural network memory structures using neuro-evolution. In: Proceedings of the Genetic and Evolutionary Computation Conference, GECCO 2019, pp. 446–455. ACM, New York (2019). http://doi.acm.org/10.1145/3321707.3321795
4. Srivastava, N., Hinton, G., Krizhevsky, A., Sutskever, I., Salakhutdinov, R.: Dropout: a simple way to prevent neural networks from overfitting. J. Mach. Learn. Res. **15**(1), 1929–1958 (2014)
5. Stanley, K.O., D'Ambrosio, D.B., Gauci, J.: A hypercube-based encoding for evolving large-scale neural networks. Artif. Life **15**(2), 185–212 (2009)
6. Yao, X., Liu, Y.: A new evolutionary system for evolving artificial neural networks. IEEE Trans. Neural Netw. **8**(3), 694–713 (1997)
7. Kassahun, Y., Sommer, G.: Efficient reinforcement learning through evolutionary acquisition of neural topologies. In: ESANN, pp. 259–266. Citeseer (2005)
8. Xie, L., Yuille, A.: Genetic CNN. In: Proceedings of the IEEE International Conference on Computer Vision, pp. 1379–1388 (2017)
9. Miikkulainen, R., et al.: Evolving deep neural networks. In: Artificial Intelligence in the Age of Neural Networks and Brain Computing, pp. 293–312. Elsevier (2019)
10. Desell, T.: Large scale evolution of convolutional neural networks using volunteer computing. In: Proceedings of the Genetic and Evolutionary Computation Conference Companion, pp. 127–128. ACM (2017)
11. ElSaid, A.E.R., Benson, S., Patwardhan, S., Stadem, D., Desell, T.: Evolving recurrent neural networks for time series data prediction of coal plant parameters. In: Kaufmann, P., Castillo, P.A. (eds.) EvoApplications 2019. LNCS, vol. 11454, pp. 488–503. Springer, Cham (2019). https://doi.org/10.1007/978-3-030-16692-2_33

12. Holland, J.H., et al.: Adaptation in Natural and Artificial Systems: An Introductory Analysis with Applications to Biology, Control, and Artificial Intelligence. MIT Press, Cambridge (1992)

13. Dorigo, M.: Optimization, learning and natural algorithms. Ph.D. thesis, Politecnico di Milano (1992)

14. Mavrovouniotis, M., Yang, S.: Evolving neural networks using ant colony optimization with pheromone trail limits. In: 2013 13th UK Workshop on Computational Intelligence (UKCI), pp. 16–23. IEEE (2013)

15. Sivagaminathan, R.K., Ramakrishnan, S.: A hybrid approach for feature subset selection using neural networks and ant colony optimization. Expert Syst. Appl. **33**(1), 49–60 (2007)

16. Desell, T., Clachar, S., Higgins, J., Wild, B.: Evolving deep recurrent neural networks using ant colony optimization. In: Ochoa, G., Chicano, F. (eds.) EvoCOP 2015. LNCS, vol. 9026, pp. 86–98. Springer, Cham (2015). https://doi.org/10.1007/978-3-319-16468-7_8

17. Elman, J.L.: Finding structure in time. Cogn. Sci. **14**(2), 179–211 (1990)

18. ElSaid, A., El Jamiy, F., Higgins, J., Wild, B., Desell, T.: Optimizing long short-term memory recurrent neural networks using ant colony optimization to predict turbine engine vibration. Appl. Soft Comput. **73**, 969–991 (2018)

19. O'Donnell, S., Bulova, S., Barrett, M., von Beeren, C.: Brain investment under colony-level selection: soldier specialization in eciton army ants (formicidae: Dorylinae). BMC Zool. **3**(1), 3 (2018)

20. Desell, T.: Accelerating the evolution of convolutional neural networks with node-level mutations and epigenetic weight initialization. In: Proceedings of the Genetic and Evolutionary Computation Conference Companion, pp. 157–158. ACM (2018)

21. Hochreiter, S., Schmidhuber, J.: Long short-term memory. Neural Comput. **9**(8), 1735–1780 (1997)

22. Chung, J., Gulcehre, C., Cho, K., Bengio, Y.: Empirical evaluation of gated recurrent neural networks on sequence modeling. arXiv preprint arXiv:1412.3555 (2014)

23. Zhou, G.-B., Wu, J., Zhang, C.-L., Zhou, Z.-H.: Minimal gated unit for recurrent neural networks. Int. J. Autom. Comput. **13**(3), 226–234 (2016). https://doi.org/10.1007/s11633-016-1006-2

24. Collins, J., Sohl-Dickstein, J., Sussillo, D.: Capacity and trainability in recurrent neural networks. arXiv preprint arXiv:1611.09913 (2016)

25. Ororbia II, A.G., Mikolov, T., Reitter, D.: Learning simpler language models with the differential state framework. Neural Comput. **29**(12), 3327–3352 (2017)

26. Liu, Y.-P., Wu, M.-G., Qian, J.-X.: Evolving neural networks using the hybrid of ant colony optimization and BP algorithms. In: Wang, J., Yi, Z., Zurada, J.M., Lu, B.-L., Yin, H. (eds.) ISNN 2006. LNCS, vol. 3971, pp. 714–722. Springer, Heidelberg (2006). https://doi.org/10.1007/11759966_105

27. Ororbia, A., Elsaid, A.A., Desell, T.: Investigating recurrent neural network memory structures using neuro-evolution (2019)

28. Pascanu, R., Mikolov, T., Bengio, Y.: On the difficulty of training recurrent neural networks. In: International Conference on Machine Learning, pp. 1310–1318 (2013)

29. Jozefowicz, R., Zaremba, W., Sutskever, I.: An empirical exploration of recurrent network architectures. In: International Conference on Machine Learning, pp. 2342–2350 (2015)

30. Mikolov, T., Karafiát, M., Burget, L., Černocký, J., Khudanpur, S.: Recurrent neural network based language model. In: Eleventh Annual Conference of the International Speech Communication Association (2010)

Parallel and Distributed Systems

A MIMD Interpreter for Genetic Programming

Vinícius Veloso de Melo[1], Álvaro Luiz Fazenda[1],
Léo Françoso Dal Piccol Sotto[1], and Giovanni Iacca[2]([⊠])

[1] Federal University of São Paulo, São José dos Campos, São Paulo, Brazil
[2] Department of Information Engineering and Computer Science,
University of Trento, Via Sommarive 9, 38123 Povo, Italy
giovanni.iacca@unitn.it

Abstract. Most Genetic Programming implementations use an interpreter to execute an individual, in order to obtain its outcome. Usually, such interpreter is the main bottleneck of the algorithm, since a single individual may contain thousands of instructions that must be executed on a dataset made of a large number of samples. Although one can use SIMD (Single Instruction Multiple Data) intrinsics to execute a single instruction on a few samples at the same time, multiple passes on the dataset are necessary to calculate the result. To speed up the process, we propose using MIMD (Multiple Instruction Multiple Data) instruction sets. This way, in a single pass one can execute several instructions on the dataset. We employ AVX2 intrinsics to improve the performance even further, reaching a median peak of 7.5 billion genetic programming operations per second in a single CPU core.

Keywords: Genetic Programming · Interpreter · Vectorization · Multiple Instruction Multiple Data

1 Introduction

Genetic Programming (GP) [1] is an evolutionary algorithm that evolves computer programs to perform automatic programming. Standard GP represents individuals as s-expressions applying functions to variables, constants or other functions, which are recursively evaluated to obtain the individual's final value. This step is usually the bottleneck of the algorithm: for instance, when dealing with a classification or regression task, GP needs to employ an interpreter to calculate the outcome of each individual, for each sample in the dataset at hand.

Several researchers have investigated approaches to speed up the evaluation process, such as better individuals representation [2,3], compilation of individuals to machine-code [4,5], single-machine parallel (multi-core) evaluation [2], multi-machine distributed evaluation [6], or Single Instruction Multiple Data (SIMD) operations with hardware accelerators by means of FPGAs [7,8].

More recently, General Purpose Graphic Processing Units (GPGPUs) have also been proposed as a computing platform well-suited for parallel GP processes,

© Springer Nature Switzerland AG 2020
P. A. Castillo et al. (Eds.): EvoApplications 2020, LNCS 12104, pp. 645–658, 2020.
https://doi.org/10.1007/978-3-030-43722-0_41

with a seminal work in [3], and further extensions focused on sub-tree parallelization [9], two-dimensional stacks [10] and quantum-inspired linear GP [11]. Given
that GPUs have thousands of computing units, huge speedups can be achieved
since each unit executes the interpreter on a different block of data. However,
since GPUs are still considerably more expensive that CPUs (also due to the
recent high demand of GPUs from the crypto-currencies market, that led to a
further increase in the GPU prices), not everybody can have access to these
devices nowadays. Therefore, CPUs can be considered still the main GP computing platform, which justifies further investigations in the direction of exploiting various levels of parallelism on CPUs. For instance, previous literature has
proposed CPU-based approaches that try to exploit parallelism at instruction
level by means of SIMD instruction sets, such as Streaming SIMD Extensions
(SSE) instructions [2], or by converting individuals into SIMD assembly instructions [12]. This way, a single instruction such as an addition can be applied to
several data from an array at same time, resulting in large speedups.

Aiming at a further performance improvement in CPU-based GP, this paper
proposes the inclusion of MIMD (Multiple Instruction Multiple Data) instruction
sets in the GP interpreter. These MIMD operators are compiled to AVX2 (Intel
Advanced Vector Extensions version 2) intrinsics[1] and can perform up to four
float operations in parallel. It is important to note, though, that this approach
is not limited to CPUs: since we use an interpreter, any interpreted GP system
can benefit from our approach, even those based on FPGAs and GPUs.

The paper is organized as follows. Section 2 presents the related works.
Section 3 introduces our proposed approach. The experimental analysis is presented and discussed in Sect. 4. Conclusions are given in Sect. 5.

2   Related Work

Over the past few years, a number of approaches have been proposed to improve
the performance of GP, by implementing parallelism either at population level
(i.e., parallelizing the evaluations of multiple individuals), or at instruction level
(i.e., parallelizing the instructions within the evaluation of a single individual).

Most of the modern literature focuses on GPU-based implementations of GP.
In this regard, several works have recently achieved parallelism at population
level. For instance, Augusto and Barbosa [13] developed a GP system with the
OpenCL framework, instead of the regular CUDA programming language used in
most of the GPU-based GP literature [14–18], to parallelize multiple individual
evaluations. Although not as fast as CUDA, an interesting characteristic of such
framework is the automatic generation of machine-code for CPUs and GPUs
of any vendor that provide compatibility, whereas CUDA is only available on
Nvidia equipment. The authors tested their approach on different CPU and
GPU architectures, showing that, as expected, GPUs are several times faster
than CPUs.

---

[1] https://software.intel.com/en-us/node/523876.

In [19], Harding and Banzhaf have explored yet another alternative to OpenCL and CUDA, namely GPU.NET, a commercial closed-source tool for programming GPUs. They reported promising results, although hindered by the immature level of this technology, that still lacks proper debugging tools.

Staats et al. [20] introduced instead a Python framework named Karoo GP. In the paper, the authors replaced a previous scalar architecture (based on SymPy) with a vector architecture (based on TensorFlow), and tested both approaches on multiple CPU cores and GPUs achieving up to 15x speedup.

Earlier attempts were made to apply instead the parallelism at instruction level. Seminal works in this direction were proposed by Chitty [21], and Harding and Banzhaf [22], who first developed a GPU-based implementation of GP fitness functions. In both works, the authors followed a data parallel approach to achieve high speedups, but they used an individual-compiled approach rather than individual-interpreted.

Langdon and Banzhaf [3] have proposed another GPU implementation where they replaced the traditional prefix-based recursive interpreter by a Reverse Polish Notation (RPN) *postfix* stack-based interpreter. This was the first GP work using SIMD instructions in GPUs. The authors reported a 7x speedup of the GPU version over the CPU version.

Vasicek and Slany [12] proposed a method that is able to efficiently compile a Cartesian GP genotype to an efficient binary machine code, without the need to call the external C compiler. The generated machine code contains SSE/SSE2 SIMD instruction calls operating with 128-bit vectors which may process two to four floating point numbers at once, depending on their precision. However, in this method the translations are performed by the assembly code, thus being dependent on the specific compiler and hardware configurations.

Finally, Chitty [2] investigated the approach of Langdon and Banzhaf [3], but on CPUs. The author used a stack-based interpreter with several improvements such as SIMD instruction sets -including a Multiply-Add operator- and a multi-threaded blocking population parallel approach. In this case the execution time of GP was significantly reduced by better utilizing the cache memory and making efficiency savings. Thus the energy cost of executing GP was also significantly reduced. To the best of our knowledge, this work is the closest to the present paper: however, as it will become clear in the next section, here we introduce more operators, and we use *array* variables, with compiler flags set to obtain the automatic vectorization and generation of AVX2 codes, while in [2] this was manually implemented by means of custom operators based on SIMD calls.

3   Proposed approach

In the SIMD approach, a traditional GP interpreter executes only a single instruction at a time over the entire dataset. Thus, an individual with thousands of instructions performs thousands of loops through the data to calculate the result. In the best-case scenario, an individual should be compiled into a single large expression that passes a single time on the dataset. However, the compilation cost may be higher than running the interpreter. Here, we propose and evaluate a MIMD interpreter where the four arithmetic operations are fused to perform up to three instructions in a single loop.

By using MIMD operators, the interpreter should perform fewer memory accesses than the SIMD operators, due to a loop fusion over SIMD operators loops: this is because MIMD operators use a complex C++ arithmetic instruction in a single line instead of two or more single separated and dependent instructions, enclosed by separated loops.

The implementation used here uses the jump table idea (an array of information about the type of a node, including a function pointer, arity, name, and other characteristics) proposed in [23] where the authors state: *the primary benefit of such a jump table is that now we can select which function to execute with an array de-reference as opposed to a case statement. Although compilers will often compile a case statement into such a jump table, it will still do bounds checking on the index, and so will be slower than the hand coded jump table.* Thus, instead of checking conditions, the jump table allows for a highly efficient code that increments and de-references a pointer, references an array, and makes a function call.

In this paper, we are employing a *postfix* RPN GP interpreter with an explicit stack as proposed by Langdon and Banzhaf [3]. This modification allows the replacement of temporary arrays in the function operators, such as:

$$float* \; add(valarray \; a, \; valarray \; b) \; \{valarray \; tmp{=}a{+}b; \; return \; tmp;\}$$

by in-place operations on the stack like:

$$void \; add() \; \{stack[top\text{-}1]{+}{=}stack[top]; \; top{-};\}$$

where *stack* is a 2d-stack structure as used in [2], and *top* is the stack top. In the 2d-stack [2] the first dimension represents the maximal tree depth used, and the second dimension consists of the number of fitness cases. This structure allows better cache-hit rates.

The traditional and proposed operators are shown in Table 1. One may notice that there are only eight functions using four arguments, while the total would be $4^3 = 64$. However, allowing only eight functions of four arguments should be enough to evidence any difference in performance.

Let us assume that a, b, and c are actually positions on the stack. The equation $a{+}{=}b{+}c$ can be either written as $a \; b{+}c{+}$ with the traditional '+' operator or as $a \; b \; c \; A$ with the new operator. Similarly, $(a{+}b)*(c{-}d)$ can be either written as $a \; b{+}c \; d{-}*$ or $a \; b \; c \; d \; U$. Finally, one may sum these two expressions with the traditional operator: $(a{+}b{+}c){+}((a{+}b)*(c{-}d))$ as $a \; b \; c \; A \; a \; b \; c \; d \; U \; +$. One may obtain the same equation with the traditional operators using the following string: $a \; b{+}c{+}a \; b{+}c \; d{-}*{+}$. As one may observe, the MIMD operators result in a more compact expression, with 10 elements versus 13 in the previous simple example. This characteristic allows the creation of complex expressions with

Table 1. Traditional and proposed operators, where a, b, c, and d are arrays.

Opcode	#Args	String	Traditional operation	Proposed operation
A	3	a b + c +	a = a+b; a = a + c	a += b + c
B		a b + c −	a = a+b; a = a − c	a += b − c
C		a b + c *	a = a+b; a = a * c	a = (a+b)*c
D		a b + c /	a = a+b; a = a / c	a = (a+b)/c
E		a b − c +	a = a−b; a = a + c	a −= b + c
F		a b − c −	a = a−b; a = a − c	a −= b − c
G		a b − c *	a = a+b; a = a * c	a = (a−b)*c
H		a b − c /	a = a−b; a = a / c	a = (a−b)/c
I		a b * c +	a = a*b; a = a + c	a = (a*b) + c
J		a b * c −	a =a *b; a = a − c	a = (a*b) − c
K		a b * c *	a = a*b; a = a * c	a *= b*c
L		a b * c /	a =a *b; a = a / c	a = (a*b)/c
M		a b / c +	a = a/b; a = a + c	a = (a/b) + c
N		a b / c −	a = a/b; a = a − c	a = (a/b) − c
O		a b / c *	a = a/b; a = a * c	a = (a/b)*c
P		a b / c /	a = a/b; a = a / c	a = (a/b)/c
Q	4	a b + c d + +	a=a+b; c=c+d; a = a + c	a += b+c+d
R		a b + c d + −	a=a+b; c=c+d; a = a + c	a = (a+b)−(c+d)
S		a b + c d + *	a=a+b; c=c+d; a = a * c	a = (a+b)*(c+d)
T		a b + c d + /	a=a+b; c=c+d; a = a / c	a = (a+b)/(c+d)
U		a b + c d − *	a=a+b; c=c−d; a = a * c	a = (a+b)*(c−d)
V		a b + c d * −	a=a+b; c=c*d; a = a − c	a = (a+b)−(c*d)
W		a b + c d * /	a= a+b; c=c*d; a = a / c	a = (a+b)/(c*d)
X		a b + c d / −	a=a+b; c=c/d; a = a − c	a = (a+b)−(c/d)

shallower trees than those using only SIMD operators. Therefore, from an evaluation perspective, smaller stacks can be used, saving memory and processing time.

Although both the SIMD and MIMD versions use a stack to interpret the individuals present in the population, MIMD operations decrease the frequency of push and pop operations. MIMD operators also allow FMA (Fused Multiply-Add) instructions, otherwise impossible with SIMD. Instruction Level Parallelism (ILP) was found in the assembly code.

In the next section, we investigate the performance of an interpreter using the proposed MIMD operators. We will first investigate the performance of each of them to evaluate whether they are useful and what is the expected performance increase, and then analyze the overall performance of the MIMD interpreter.

4   Experimental analysis

In the experimentation, we evaluate the performance of the proposed operators on synthetic datasets, so we can control their dimensions. All datasets have ten variables, randomly sampled from as uniform distribution in the interval $[-1.0, 1.0]$. The number of cases is 100, 500, 1K, 5K, 10K, 50K, 100K, 500K, and 1M. This way, we investigate the performance on different data sizes on the CPU cache.

Regarding the interpreter, we test two versions. The first one is the SIMD interpreter, using only the four arithmetical operators with a protected division; thus, if the module of the denominator is less than $1e-8$, then the result is zero. The second version is our proposed MIMD interpreter with the operators presented in Sect. 3.

Since we are investigating the interpreter's performance, not the solution quality, our code only generates and evaluates a finite number of random individuals (there is no selection, crossover, and mutation) in a *single* generation. Individuals are generated in a ramped half-and-half approach, with depth 20 for SIMD and 4 for MIMD, to approximate the average number of instructions in the population, which will be used as an evaluation criterion. This difference in the depths is necessary because the operators in the SIMD interpreter execute a single instruction and require two arguments, while in the MIMD interpreter an operator can execute up to three instructions on four arguments.

Here, we investigated the performance with populations of 100, 500, 1K, 5K, and 10K individuals. In our experiment, we first generate the population and then investigate only the evaluation process to obtain the *GPops* per second [3] and the cache information.

We have implemented both interpreters in C++ and have compiled the source codes with Intel ICPC compiler using the following flags to enable auto-vectorization and AVX2 instructions:

$$-Ofast\ -std=c++11\ -funroll\text{-}loops\ -ffast\text{-}math$$
$$-march=native\ -mtune=native\ -xavx2\ -m64\ -fno\text{-}alias.$$

The *fno-alias* flag is necessary to inform the compiler that the vectors are independent from each other (there is no aliasing), allowing a better optimization. Also, because we are using a stack with indexes and a protect division operation, we must insert two *pragma* in each operator to *force* loop vectorization: *ivdep*, *vector always*, and *simd*. Also, memory alignment is forced with _mm_malloc function with 32 bytes, as recommended for AVX2 instructions. SIMD and MIMD operators use _restricted_ pointers to access the stack and data with __assume_aliased function on them. These procedures allow using our approach on the Intel C++ Compiler. Adaptations on these configurations are necessary to use other compilers, but performance may vary. In Fig. 1, the source-code function to perform OpCode I (Table 1) is shown, including the *pragmas* and specific data structure. As one can observe, the compiler identified the multiplication followed by the addition and employed the proper FMA Intel intrinsic[2]. Similarly the Fused Multiply Subtract operation was used for OpCode J (not shown).

The Intel compiler options joined with pragmas depicted above allows AVX2 code generation for an Intel CPU Haswell/Broadwell(R) processor line, as it

---

[2] https://software.intel.com/sites/landingpage/IntrinsicsGuide/#techs=FMA&expand=2549.

C++	Assembly
| ```
void eval_mult_plus()    {
  float * __restrict a = stack[top-2];
  float * __restrict b = stack[top-1];
  float * __restrict c = stack[top];
  __assume_aligned(a,32);
  __assume_aligned(b,32);
  __assume_aligned(c,32);

  #pragma ivdep
  #pragma vector always
  for (int i = 0; i < ncases; ++i)
    a[i] = (a[i]*b[i]) + c[i];

  top-=2;
  GPop+=2;
}
``` | ```
vmovups    (%r10,%rax,4), %ymm2
lea        (%r11,%rax,4), %r15
vmovups    32(%r10,%rax,4), %ymm3
vmovups    (%r9,%rax,4), %ymm0
vmovups    32(%r9,%rax,4), %ymm1
vfmadd213ps (%r15), %ymm0, %ymm2
vfmadd213ps 32(%r15), %ymm1, %ymm3
vmovups    %ymm2, (%r15)
vmovups    %ymm3, 32(%r15)
addq       $16, %rax
cmpq       %rbx, %rax
``` |

Fig. 1. Opcode I C++ source-code function (left) and assembly code fragment (right) showing the FMA operation (vfmadd213ps) employed by the compiler.

is possible to check in the assembly code generated by the same compiler, for both SIMD and MIND codes. The FMA (Fused Multiply-Add) instructions are also used for MIMD operators. Instruction Level Parallelism (ILP) was found in assembly code generated, including two FMA operations available for AVX registers in the supporting Intel CPU architecture.

The computational environment was an Intel(R) Xeon(R) CPU E5-2660 v4@2.40 GHz (CPU frequency scaling set for best performance in all computing cores), with CentOS Linux 3.10.0-327.el7.x86_64 and Intel Compiler icpc 17.0.4 20170411. We ran all the experiments using a single process (single-core), to execute 30 independent runs of each interpreter.

4.1   Evaluation

As explained above, both the SIMD and MIMD interpreters are compiled with the same optimization flags and use the same in-place two-argument operators and stack-based approaches. Therefore, in the experiments we evaluate only the improvement obtained by using the MIMD operators in the evaluation of individuals (ignoring the time to generate the strings).

Langdon and Banzhaf [3] defined Genetic Programming Operations per Second ($GPops/sec$), a metric for measuring the speed of a Genetic Programming implementation. $GPop$ is the number of instructions performed by an individual, including the number of variables, times the number of cases in the dataset. Thus, for an individual $ind=a \ b \ +$ and a dataset with 1K cases, $GPop = 3 * 1,000 = 3,000$.

Each operator proposed here is a single Genetic Programming operation. However, we must compare the number of instructions, as the MIMD interpreter may execute several of them at a time. According to Table 1, the operators with three arguments execute two instructions (for instance, $+, +$). Therefore, two $GPop$ are counted for these operators. Similarly, three instructions are counted for the operators with four arguments.

To compare the $GPops/sec$ of the two interpreters, we executed the Wilcoxon Rank-Sum Test assuming a significance level of $\alpha = 0.05$. Thus, if $p\text{-}value < \alpha$, then the difference between the performances is considered significant and the interpreter with the highest median is the winner.

4.2   Analysis of Each Operator

In this first analysis, we compare the performance of SIMD and MIMD operators according to the implementation shown in Table 1. We did 1 K independent runs of each operator for a dataset with 1M cases. For each run, we first copy data from temporary arrays to the required variables a, b, c, and d, and then execute the calculation. For the operations with only three arguments, we do not assign any value to d. This copy is to simulate pushing data onto the stack, in order to have a more realistic scenario. The average running times for each operator are shown in Table 2. As one may observe, for operators with three arguments, the speedup was approximately 17%, while for four arguments, the speedup was close to 25%. The average overall speedup was approximately 20%. This value is the expected speedup of the real-case scenario, as the tested equations combine two, three, and four argument operators.

As shown in Table 2, the speedup remains more or less the same inside the same class of operators (three argument and four argument operators). Thus, allowing only eight four argument operators should not introduce any bias towards a specific speedup value, while also providing a higher total speedup than that provided only by three argument operators.

Table 2. Running time of each operator.

Opcode	SIMD	MIMD	Speedup	Opcode	SIMD	MIMD	Speedup
A	138	118	1.169	M	137	117	1.171
B	138	118	1.169	N	137	117	1.171
C	138	120	1.150	O	137	117	1.171
D	144	122	1.180	P	138	119	1.160
E	138	118	1.169	Q	191	152	1.257
F	138	118	1.169	R	191	152	1.257
G	138	118	1.169	S	191	152	1.257
H	140	119	1.176	T	192	153	1.255
I	138	118	1.169	U	191	152	1.257
J	136	116	1.172	V	191	152	1.257
K	136	116	1.172	W	191	152	1.257
L	137	117	1.171	X	192	153	1.255
Average					155.75	129.417	1.198

4.3   Analysis of the Interpreter

In this section, we investigate whether the MIMD interpreter achieves the expected 20% speedup observed in the individual analysis of the previous section.

In Fig. 2, we present a plot of the overall results. The plot is a median of 30 independent runs for each configuration and shows how the number of $GPops/sec$ varies according to the number of evaluations allowed and the size of the dataset.

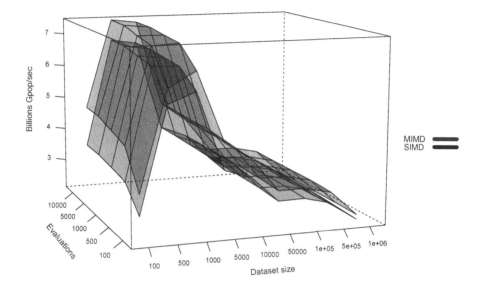

Fig. 2. Performance with respect to dataset size and number of evaluations.

First of all, the performance of the two interpreters show a similar pattern, which is an indirect indication that the MIMD operators are working properly.

As one can notice, the MIMD interpreter is able to outperform the SIMD interpreter in all configurations, executing more $GPops/sec$. A pattern that can be extracted from the plot is that the performance grows from 100 cases to 500 cases, stays stable for 1K cases and then starts dropping. The performance for 1M is lower than that with 100 cases. This is probably explained by the fact that larger datasets require more swap operations between memory and cache, decreasing the impact in performance from the MIMD operators.

The performance difference between the two interpreters is significant, but it also decreases as the dataset size increases. A possible explanation is again that, for larger datasets, the data swap between memory and cache is so frequent that the performance gain obtained with the MIMD operators is negligible. This is a crucial point, that suggests that further investigations are needed to find ways of reducing such swap and eventually increase the number of $GPops/sec$ even with larger datasets.

As for the number of evaluations, the results do not vary significantly when the population size increases. This behavior is expected as both interpreters are just evaluating more individuals on the same data.

The different *GPops/sec* can be better observed in Fig. 3, which shows Violin Plots comparing the distribution of performances of the SIMD and MIMD interpreters for the 30 runs, and the *p-value* of the Wilcoxon Rank-Sum Test, for each dataset size and number of evaluations allowed.

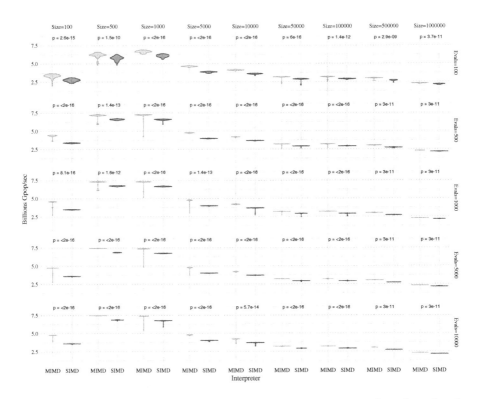

Fig. 3. Distributions of performances with respect to dataset size and number of evaluations.

As one can see, all the performance gains obtained by the proposed MIMD interpreter are statistically significant. The performance differences show the same pattern for all tested numbers of evaluations, as previously discussed when analyzing Fig. 2, with the MIMD interpreter processing consistently more instructions per second.

The speedups obtained by the MIMD interpreter are presented in Fig. 4 (top), where there is a line for each number of evaluations, depending to the dataset size. Again, there is no significant difference between the trends obtained with different numbers of evaluations, which was expected. However, differently from what happened to the number of $GPops/sec$, here the speedup is large on two dataset sizes (100 and 5K), but also decreases as the dataset size grows.

The unexpected behavior was observed for datasets of sizes 500 and 1K, that showed a substantial reduction in the speedup. In order to try to clarify this issue, we used PAPI(R) - Performance Application Programming Interface, an API which allows to access hardware counters to measure several aspects related to performance analysis, and obtain information about cache sizes and cache misses.

Figure 4 (bottom) shows the cache miss rate evaluated for three cache memory levels: L1, L2 and L3 over GPop ($L*_{misses}/GPop$) for a population of 100 individuals. For the CPU used in our tests, this cache memory levels has 448 KB, 3.5 MB, and 35 MB capacity, respectively. From the figure, it is possible to note three important facts: (a) L1 miss rate increases, starting at dataset size 500

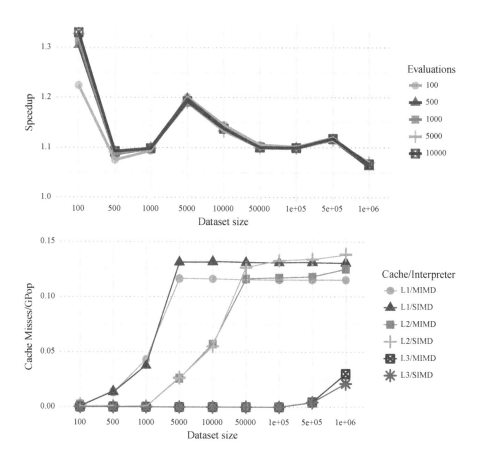

Fig. 4. Top: speedups (MIMD over SIMD) with respect to dataset size and number of evaluations (individuals tested). Bottom: cache misses of different cache levels and interpreters per GPop.

up to 5K, where it achieves a steady state; (b) L2 miss rate increases, starting at dataset size 5K up to 50K, then it plateaus until 500K, when it increases again; (c) L3 miss rate increases, starting at dataset size 1M.

The L1 miss rate increase at dataset size 500 causes no significant performance variation on *GPops/sec*. Until dataset size 5K, the *GPops/sec* rate continues to increase, due to an increase in the total number of operations. With a small number of GPop and, consequently, a small number of instructions issued, loop initialization, controlling instructions and array indexing influence the performance. However, as the array size increases, these controlling instructions become irrelevant.

The L1 and L2 miss rates that abruptly grow at dataset size 5 K significantly decreases the performance, as already seen in Figs. 2 and 3. The L2 miss rate continues to increase up to 50K. This L2 cache miss rate behavior decreases the *GPops/sec* rate quite in the same way (see Fig. 2). The L2 miss rate (as well as the performance in *GPops/sec*) reaches a stable state at 50K, up to 500K, but start to increase again at 1M, together with an L3 miss rate increase. This effect causes a further performance decrease.

Comparing the cache miss rate for SIMD and MIMD, it is possible to observe similar trends for both. However, the cache misses counts for L1 and L2 are greater in SIMD than MIMD: this is because SIMD uses more loops and load/store operations to deal with two or more single math instructions, as opposed to MIMD, where more math instructions are combined into a unique instruction.

5   Conclusions and Future Work

In this paper, we proposed a MIMD interpreter for GP, and evaluated its performance compared to that of a traditional SIMD interpreter. The proposed MIMD interpreter is based on a fusion of the four arithmetical functions into MIMD operators, which allow to execute up to three instructions in a single pass. Here, we tested only a few combinations of these functions, as the number of combinations increases exponentially with the number of functions. For instance, including *sin*, *cos*, *log*, etc. would create thousands of operators. Therefore, we recommend implementing the operators that provide the highest speedups.

Our experiments show that a median of 7.5 *GPops/sec* was achieved in a single CPU core running at 2.4 GHz. Further improvements might be obtained by extending the proposed implementation to use parallel programming on multicore CPUs and GPU co-processing. Algorithm and hardware acceleration could also be combined. In most of the times, algorithm speedup techniques always promote better results in parallel codes, however, a more detailed evaluation is required in order to check if the algorithm developed does not limit the concurrency, by requiring extra communication or synchronization.

We claim that swap operations between memory and cache are responsible for some of the observed effects, and show some supporting evidence in the cache miss rates. In future work, we could provide more metrics to justify that. We also want to investigate the impact of the proposed MIMD operators on actual

GP runs. In this case, there is the necessity of parsing the tree into the list of strings used by the interpreter, a step that is easily done by traversing the tree and identifying operators used in sequence in order to substitute them by one of the proposed operators. In this case, if more four argument operators were allowed, we should also have higher speedups, as the total speedup corresponds to an average between individual operators speedups.

Acknowledgements. This work was supported by Grant #2016/07095-5, São Paulo Research Foundation (FAPESP).

References

1. Koza, J.R.: Genetic programming as a means for programming computers by natural selection. Stat. Comput. **4**(2), 87–112 (1994)
2. Chitty, D.M.: Fast parallel genetic programming: multi-core CPU versus many-core GPU. Soft. Comput. **16**(10), 1795–1814 (2012)
3. Langdon, W.B., Banzhaf, W.: A SIMD interpreter for genetic programming on GPU graphics cards. In: O'Neill, M., et al. (eds.) EuroGP 2008. LNCS, vol. 4971, pp. 73–85. Springer, Heidelberg (2008). https://doi.org/10.1007/978-3-540-78671-9_7
4. Fukunaga, A., Stechert, A., Mutz, D.: A genome compiler for high performance genetic programming. In: Genetic Programming 1998: Proceedings of the Third Annual Conference, University of Wisconsin, Madison, Wisconsin, USA, pp. 86–94. Morgan Kaufmann (1998)
5. Nordin, P.: A compiling genetic programming system that directly manipulates the machine code. In: Advances in Genetic Programming, pp. 311–331. MIT Press, Cambridge (1994)
6. Fernández, F., Spezzano, G., Tomassini, M., Vanneschi, L.: 6. In: Parallel Genetic Programming, pp. 127–153. Wiley-Blackwell, Hoboken (2005)
7. Eklund, S.E.: Time series forecasting using massively parallel genetic programming. In: Proceedings International Parallel and Distributed Processing Symposium, pp. 1–5. IEEE, New York, April 2003
8. Heywood, M.I., Zincir-Heywood, A.N.: Register based genetic programming on FPGA computing platforms. In: Poli, R., Banzhaf, W., Langdon, W.B., Miller, J., Nordin, P., Fogarty, T.C. (eds.) EuroGP 2000. LNCS, vol. 1802, pp. 44–59. Springer, Heidelberg (2000). https://doi.org/10.1007/978-3-540-46239-2_4
9. Cano, A., Ventura, S.: GPU-parallel subtree interpreter for genetic programming. In: Proceedings of the 2014 Annual Conference on Genetic and Evolutionary Computation, GECCO 2014, pp. 887–894. ACM, New York (2014)
10. Chitty, D.M.: Faster GPU-based genetic programming using a two-dimensional stack. Soft. Comput. **21**(14), 3859–3878 (2016). https://doi.org/10.1007/s00500-016-2034-0
11. da Silva, C.P., Dias, D.M., Bentes, C., Pacheco, M.A.C., Cupertino, L.F.: Evolving GPU machine code. J. Mach. Learn. Res. **16**, 673–712 (2015)
12. Vašíček, Z., Slaný, K.: Efficient phenotype evaluation in cartesian genetic programming. In: Moraglio, A., Silva, S., Krawiec, K., Machado, P., Cotta, C. (eds.) EuroGP 2012. LNCS, vol. 7244, pp. 266–278. Springer, Heidelberg (2012). https://doi.org/10.1007/978-3-642-29139-5_23

13. Augusto, D.A., Barbosa, H.J.: Accelerated parallel genetic programming tree evaluation with OpenCL. J. Parallel Distrib. Comput. **73**(1), 86–100 (2013)
14. Harding, S.L., Banzhaf, W.: Distributed genetic programming on GPUs using CUDA. In: Workshop on Parallel Architectures and Bioinspired Algorithms, Raleigh, NC, USA, pp. 1–10. Universidad Complutense de Madrid, September 2009
15. Maitre, O., Lachiche, N., Collet, P.: Fast evaluation of GP trees on GPGPU by optimizing hardware scheduling. In: Esparcia-Alcázar, A.I., Ekárt, A., Silva, S., Dignum, S., Uyar, A.Ş. (eds.) EuroGP 2010. LNCS, vol. 6021, pp. 301–312. Springer, Heidelberg (2010). https://doi.org/10.1007/978-3-642-12148-7_26
16. Robilliard, D., Marion, V., Fonlupt, C.: High performance genetic programming on GPU. In: Proceedings of the 2009 Workshop on Bio-inspired Algorithms for Distributed Systems, BADS 2009, 85–94. ACM, New York (2009)
17. Robilliard, D., Marion-Poty, V., Fonlupt, C.: Population parallel GP on the G80 GPU. In: O'Neill, M., et al. (eds.) EuroGP 2008. LNCS, vol. 4971, pp. 98–109. Springer, Heidelberg (2008). https://doi.org/10.1007/978-3-540-78671-9_9
18. Robilliard, D., Marion-Poty, V., Fonlupt, C.: Genetic programming on graphics processing units. Genet. Program Evolvable Mach. **10**(4), 447 (2009)
19. Harding, S., Banzhaf, W.: Implementing cartesian genetic programming classifiers on graphics processing units using GPU.NET. In: Proceedings of the 13th Annual Conference Companion on Genetic and Evolutionary Computation, GECCO 2011, pp. 463–470. ACM, New York (2011)
20. Staats, K., Pantridge, E., Cavaglia, M., Milovanov, I., Aniyan, A.: TensorFlow enabled genetic programming. In: Proceedings of the Genetic and Evolutionary Computation Conference Companion, GECCO 2017, pp. 1872–1879. ACM, New York (2017)
21. Chitty, D.M.: A data parallel approach to genetic programming using programmable graphics hardware. In: Proceedings of the 9th Annual Conference on Genetic and Evolutionary Computation, GECCO 2007, pp. 1566–1573. ACM, New York (2007)
22. Harding, S., Banzhaf, W.: Fast genetic programming on GPUs. In: Ebner, M., O'Neill, M., Ekárt, A., Vanneschi, L., Esparcia-Alcázar, A.I. (eds.) EuroGP 2007. LNCS, vol. 4445, pp. 90–101. Springer, Heidelberg (2007). https://doi.org/10.1007/978-3-540-71605-1_9
23. Keith, M.J., Martin, M.C.: Genetic programming in C++: implementation issues. In: Advances in Genetic Programming, pp. 285–310. MIT Press, Cambridge (1994)

Security Risk Optimization
for Multi-cloud Applications

Rudolf Lovrenčić$^{(\boxtimes)}$, Domagoj Jakobović, Dejan Škvorc, and Stjepan Groš

Faculty of Electrical Engineering and Computing, University of Zagreb,
Unska 3, 10000 Zagreb, Croatia
rudolf.lovrencic@fer.hr

Abstract. Security proved to be a major concern when organizations outsource their data storage and processing. Encryption schemes do not provide solutions as they disable data processing in the cloud. Researchers have used constraint-based data fragmentation to increase security while maintaining availability. We build on this approach by applying fragmentation to the application logic in addition to the data in the database and propose a model for security risk assessment in a multi-cloud environment. By applying a multi-objective optimization algorithm to the proposed model, we determine pareto-optimal distributions of application and data fragments to the available cloud providers.

Keywords: Cloud computing · Multi-cloud applications · Risk assessment · Security optimization · Multi-objective optimization

1 Introduction

With the increased popularity of cloud computing in the past decade, it is no longer a question whether or not a company will embrace cloud computing. Rather, the question is when the technology will be implemented and which services should be migrated to the cloud. Remote access to a pool of computing resources reduces the up-front IT infrastructure costs and allows companies to meet fluctuating demands.

Current research indicates that the biggest challenges in cloud adoption are related to trust since companies may feel like they are losing control over their data [13]. Numerous data breaches and security vulnerabilities [8,12] prevent users from trusting *cloud service providers* (CSPs). Compliance with the industry specific regulations and even general information security regulations often

This research is co-sponsored by the European Union from the European Regional Development Fund through a research grant KK.01.2.1.01.0109 Cloud Computing Security During the Use of Mobile Applications. We acknowledge the support of the Ministry of Regional Development and European Union Funds of the Republic of Croatia as well as our research partners OROUNDO Mobile GmbH Austria and OROUNDO Mobile GmbH Subsidiary Croatia.

P. A. Castillo et al. (Eds.): EvoApplications 2020, LNCS 12104, pp. 659–669, 2020.
https://doi.org/10.1007/978-3-030-43722-0_42

make moving to the cloud difficult since regulations may differ from region to region. High flexibility of a cloud service makes exhaustive and continuous security revisions expensive or intractable [11].

Hybrid cloud environments enable users to combine their computing resources with the cloud to retain more control over their data. Confidential data can, for example, be stored or encrypted on premise before leaving the local environment. Such approach makes regulation compliance easier, but burdens the user with key management. Furthermore, encrypted data cannot be used by applications running in the cloud.

Recent trends show that the use of multiple cloud providers simultaneously is increasing to achieve higher service availability and damage reduction in the case of malicious insiders on a single CSP [1]. Such *multi-cloud* environments mitigate reliance on a single cloud provider.

The contribution of this paper is threefold. Firstly, we introduce a multi-cloud application model that assumes multiple application components and multiple data fragments. Secondly, we propose two risk metrics for assessing the risk of a given application deployment to the multi-cloud environment. Lastly, by using multi-objective optimization, we find a set of pareto solutions according to two proposed risk metrics.

1.1 Literature Review

Security is a major concern of the cloud platform and is one of the main research directions regarding the cloud computing [2]. Fragmentation has been recognized as a possible solution to improving data security while still enabling query evaluation at the provider side.

Using fragmentation as a method for increasing privacy in data storage has been explored [3]. Sensitive data relations can be broken to decrease information leakage in case of an attack. Confidentiality constraints have been introduced as a means for describing sensitive data relations. Algorithms for finding optimal fragmentation based on the constraints have also been proposed [3,4], but such algorithms do not touch on finding the optimal distribution of data fragments to the available servers.

Researches have used fragmentation and distribution between multiple cloud providers [10]. Similarly to earlier work [3], user defined constraints are taken into consideration during data fragmentation and distribution in the cloud. The paper shares motivation and assumptions with our work: cloud providers are non-colluding, usage of multiple CSPs enables better regulation compliance and minimal use of encryption maximizes data availability in the cloud. Work is focused on security in data storage and does not touch on data security during computations performed by the cloud applications.

Information entropy can be used to measure the sensitivity of connections between the data [9]. This can help in deduction of confidentiality constraints. Such approach requires the database to be filled with the actual or representative data which can be an issue when data distribution is not known in advance.

The rest of this paper is structured as follows. Section 2 presents a simple distributed database and distributed application model. Section 3 applies a risk assessment method for the distributed application deployed in a multi-cloud environment. Optimization algorithm and preliminary results of risk optimization are discussed in Sect. 4. Section 5 concludes the paper and explores possible future work.

2 Distributed Model

We assume that both, application logic and the data, are distributed. Since any cloud provider may be malicious, storage and computation are split and distributed among available CSPs. Optimal distribution of data fragments and application components ensures minimal information leak in case of an incident on a single CSP.

The application database is split into N_F data fragments and the application logic is split into N_C application components. *Data fragment F_i* is a portion of data that can be stored to any available CSP. Figure 1 illustrates vertical fragmentation on a simple table. The original table is split into two fragments: F_1 containing the name and the surname of a person and F_2 containing the payout amount for each person. Fragmentation aims to decouple the person and the payout amount. Malicious access to only one of the data fragments results in a significantly lower information leak than access to the both fragments. If F_2 is leaked, only payout amounts are known to the attacker. The names of involved persons are compromised if fragment F_1 has leaked. When such fragments are provided to the deployment optimization process for multi-cloud applications, it will attempt to deploy those fragments to different CSPs to maximize security.

F₁		F₂
NAME	SURNAME	PAYOUT
Cloe	Connolly	5000
Tom	Flynn	17500
Emma	Hills	12000

Fig. 1. Simple relational table split.

Similar to the data fragment, *application component C_j* is a segment of the application logic that can be deployed to and executed on any available CSP. Each component is able to perform three actions:

1. access data fragments (read or write),
2. receive data from other components,
3. send data to other components.

Result R_{ab} represents the data sent from source component C_a to the destination component C_b. Each result has exactly one source and exactly one destination application component.

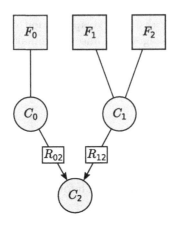

Fig. 2. Simple application model.

Figure 2 illustrates a simple application consisting of 3 components: C_0, C_1 and C_2. Components C_0 and C_1 access the data fragments and perform computations. Computation results R_{02} and R_{12} are sent to the component C_2.

Since the application components are treated as black boxes, no assumption can be made for their outputs. Consequently, results exchanged between the components must be treated as resources that carry information, likewise the data fragments. For example, component C_0 may simply forward input data to its output making the result R_{02} identical to F_0. Therefore, a *resource* ρ_k that the risk assessment process considers is either a data fragment F_i or result R_{ab} exchanged between the components.

3   Security Risk Assessment

Fragmentation can be used for increasing security in the data storage by breaking sensitive data relations to decrease information leak in the case of attack [3]. Security constraints are used for describing sensitive data relations.

User provides N_K security constraints for the multi-cloud application. Each constraint contains a subset of all resources. A *security constraint* $K_l = \{\rho_1, \ldots, \rho_n\}$ defines a property that sum of information of each resource ρ_k in the constraint is smaller than the information of all resources merged together. This concept is formalized in the expression 1 where $I(\rho_1, \ldots, \rho_n)$ is the amount of information leak when resources $\rho_1, \ldots, \rho_n$ leak together.

$$\sum_{k=1}^{n} I(\rho_k) < I(\rho_1, \ldots, \rho_n) \tag{1}$$

If all resources contained within a security constraint are present on a single CSP, the constraint is considered violated since more information will leak in case of an incident on that provider.

3.1   Resource Reach

A set of fragments and components where a resource ρ_k is available defines its *resource reach* $D(\rho_k)$. Therefore, the reach of a data fragment is a set that contains that data fragment and all components that access that data fragment. For example, resource reach of fragment F_1 shown in Fig. 2 is a set containing fragment F_1 and component C_1.

Results that components exchange are transferred from a single source component to a single destination component. Consequently, the reach of a component result is a set containing two elements: result source and result destination. Reach of the result R_{12} that can be seen in Fig. 2 is $D(R_{12}) = \{C_1, C_2\}$.

Resource reach enables efficient check if a constraint can be satisfied in the ideal case where unlimited amount of cloud providers is available. Constraint $K_l = \{\rho_1, \ldots, \rho_n\}$ can be satisfied in the ideal case if and only if:

$$D(\rho_1) \cap \ldots \cap D(\rho_n) = \emptyset \tag{2}$$

Evaluation of a distribution of fragments and components in the multi-cloud environment is also made simple with the use of resource reach. Violation of a security constraint $K_l = \{\rho_1, \ldots, \rho_n\}$ is checked in the following way:

1. The reach of each resource in the constraint is calculated: $D(\rho_i)$, $i = 1, \ldots, n$
2. *Cloud resource reach* $D_c(\rho_i)$ is calculated by substituting each fragment and component in $D(\rho_i)$ with a cloud provider where that fragment or component is deployed. $D_c(\rho_i)$ is therefore a set of CSPs where resource ρ_i is available.
3. Multi-cloud distribution satisfies constraint K_l if and only if:

$$D_c(\rho_1) \cap \ldots \cap D_c(\rho_n) = \emptyset \tag{3}$$

The procedure is repeated for each security constraint during the risk assessment of a particular deployment of fragments and components. Since the same resources are often part of multiple security constraints, computed cloud resource reach $D_c(\rho_i)$ may be cached to avoid duplicated calculations.

3.2   Risk Metrics

We define two metrics for assessing the security risk of a particular multi-cloud deployment:

1. violated security constraints,
2. individual security of resources.

The first metric penalizes when all resources within a security constraint are available on the same CSP. The second metric estimates security of resources individually and is responsible for pushing more important resources towards more trusted CSPs during deployment optimization. Given a set of available CSPs $P = \{\sigma_i, \ldots, \sigma_S\}$, trust estimate function $t \colon P \to \mathbb{R}^+$ must be provided by the user which assigns the trust estimate to each CSP. Higher trust estimate implies that the provider has a lower chance of leaking information. In addition to pushing resources to more trusted CSPs as much as possible, optimization process attempts to violate unsatisfiable constraints at the most trusted providers.

The risk for breaking security constraint K_l is calculated using the expression:

$$r_{1l} = \frac{p_l}{t(\sigma_l)}, \tag{4}$$

where $p_l \in \mathbb{R}^+$ is the penalty for breaking the constraint K_l and σ_l is the cloud provider where the constraint is violated. If multiple CSPs violate the security constraint, CSP with the lowest trust estimate is used.

Expression 5 computes individual risk of resource ρ_k with *value* $v_k \in \mathbb{R}^+$ assigned by the user.

$$r_{2k} = \sum_{\sigma \in D_c(\rho_k)} \frac{v_k}{t(\sigma)}, \tag{5}$$

More important resources should be assigned a higher value v_k. This enables critical resources to produce higher risks and have higher priorities in the optimization procedure.

4   Experimental Setup and Results

Metrics for assessing security provided in the previous section can be linearly combined. Total risk of a given deployment is then measured with a scalar. The issue with this approach is that the importance of each metric has to be expressed with a coefficient before optimization. Metrics can differ in scale rather greatly so choosing coefficients that yield good deployments may be difficult for non-trivial applications.

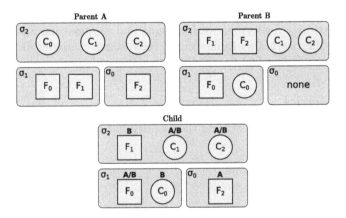

Fig. 3. Crossover example.

We use multi-objective optimization algorithm NSGA-III [5,6] to avoid attributing importance to optimization criteria before actual optimization.

Importance is attributed implicitly when one of the suggested deployments is chosen by the user. NSGA-III is a multi-objective evolutionary algorithm which aims to improve fit of a population of candidate solutions to a pareto front constrained by a set of objective functions. NSGA-II introduced elitism to the original NSGA algorithm. NSGA-III further improves the algorithm by using a method that increases solution diversity. This results in even distribution of solutions across the pareto front.

A solution is represented as a mapping of fragments and components to the cloud providers. In a scenario where three CSPs ($\sigma_0, \sigma_1, \sigma_2$) are available, three possible solutions for simple application (Fig. 2) are shown in Fig. 3 where crossover operation is visualized. In the solution that represents parent B, CSP σ_0 is unused, two data fragments and two application components are deployed to σ_2, and fragment F_0 and component C_0 are deployed to CSP σ_1. Genotype is implemented as a hash table that maps fragments and components to the CSPs.

Crossover operator uniformly selects a cloud provider for each component from one of the parents. Child solution illustrated in Fig. 3 is constructed by selecting CSPs for fragment F_1 and component C_0 from parent B. F_2 is deployed to the same CSP as in parent A, while CSPs for F_0, C_1 and C_2 could have been selected from either parent since they map them to same cloud providers.

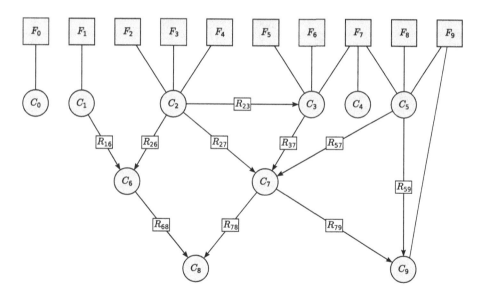

Fig. 4. Test application.

Two mutation operators are used with equal probability:

1. picks a random fragment or component and assigns it to a random cloud,
2. all fragments and components are assigned to random clouds (solution is reconstructed).

It has been found that the enterprise applications often consist of many distinct business logic and backend components [7]. Fortune 100 companies have applications with dozens, sometimes even reaching hundred components.

Our test application (Fig. 4) consists of 10 data fragments and 10 application components. We assume 7 available CSPs, σ_0 to σ_6, assigned with increasing trust values (σ_6 being the most credible). Such environment provides 7^{20} possible cloud deployments. The following set of security constraints is used: $\{F_0, R_{23}\}$, $\{F_2, F_6\}$, $\{F_3, F_4\}$, $\{F_3, F_6\}$, $\{F_3, R_{79}\}$, $\{F_7, R_{59}\}$, $\{F_9, R_{68}\}$, $\{R_{16}, R_{27}\}$, $\{R_{16}, R_{26}, R_{37}\}$, $\{R_{16}, R_{26}, R_{59}\}$. Penalization for breaking a security constraint is set to $p = 100$ for all security constraints.

Table 1 lists values of application resources. Results transferred between components have lower values than pure data fragments since we assume that output is arbitrary transformation of the input that is less useful to the attacker (e.g. aggregation).

Table 1. Values of test application resources.

Fragment	Value	Result	Value
F_0	100	R_{16}	35
F_1	200	R_{23}	55
F_2	300	R_{26}	15
F_3	400	R_{27}	65
F_4	500	R_{37}	35
F_5	600	R_{57}	85
F_6	700	R_{59}	95
F_7	800	R_{68}	45
F_8	900	R_{78}	25
F_9	1000	R_{79}	15

We use a population of 500 solutions and set maximum number of generations to 100 which results in 50000 evaluations of each objective function. Risks of solutions shown in Fig. 5 are achieved by the NSGA-III algorithm with 15% mutation rate. The algorithm consistently provides similar fronts. During our testing, random search never provided solutions below 2000 single resource risk. When presented with a pareto front, the user is able to make better decisions since valuing importance of each risk metric is made easier – trade-offs between possible solutions are visualized.

Table 2 lists solutions A and B marked in Fig. 5. Solution A violates three security constraints: $\{F_2, F_6\}$, $\{F_7, R_{59}\}$, $\{R_{16}, R_{27}\}$ on CSPs σ_5, σ_6 and σ_6 respectively. On the contrary, solution B violates only $\{F_2, F_6\}$ and $\{F_7, R_{59}\}$. Furthermore, both constraints are violated on the most trusted CSP σ_6 which results in significantly lower constraint risk. Solution A provides lower single resource risk as 15 resources are available on the single CSP while in B that is true for 11 resources. Solution A also makes five most valuable resources only available on the most trusted CSP σ_6 which contributes to lower single resource risk when compared to the solution A.

Deterministic strategies for finding optimal deployments can be successful when only database fragmentation is considered [10], but do not scale to applications with many logic components and data fragments. While solutions provided by heuristics might not be optimal, performance they offer opens up possibilities for real-time recalculation of security risk and redeployment of multi-cloud applications.

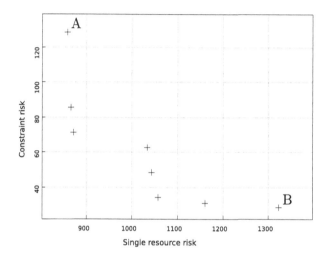

Fig. 5. Risks of deployments proposed by NSGA-III.

Table 2. Notable solutions from Fig. 5.

Solution A	
σ_4	F_0, C_8, C_6, C_0
σ_5	F_4, F_3, F_2, C_2
σ_6	$F_9, F_8, F_7, F_6, F_5, F_1, C_9, C_7, C_5, C_4, C_3, C_1$

Solution B	
σ_2	C_8, C_6
σ_3	F_0, C_0
σ_4	F_6, F_5, C_7, C_3
σ_5	F_1, C_9, C_1
σ_6	$F_9, F_8, F_7, F_4, F_3, F_2, C_5, C_4, C_2$

5   Conclusion and Future Work

In this paper, we introduced a model for assessing the risk of distributed application and distributed database deployed in a multi-cloud environment. Using the model, we performed multi-objective optimization which provided us with pareto set of deployments with regards to different security criteria. The approach is not exclusive to the multi-cloud setting. It can be applied wherever a multitude of deployment locations for application components and database fragments are available.

The proposed risk assessment model does not take time into consideration – it is completely static. Information about how often and which ratio of certain data flows through each application component would increase the level of detail that the model can describe. Verbosity of such model might become an issue, but supporting tools could be developed to assist with describing real world applications. For example, information entropy can be used to help the user determine security constraints [9].

While applying security risk optimization on existing distributed applications is possible, the best results are obtained when a multi-cloud application is constructed from the ground up with security in mind. Guidelines and patterns for such development should be established so that the right techniques (e.g. cryptographic protections) can be applied in the right situations.

Furthermore, supporting database mechanisms must be established to enable transparent usage of fragmented data while ensuring that constraints imposed on the data are valid (e.g. primary key).

References

1. AlZain, M.A., Pardede, E., Soh, B., Thom, J.: Cloud computing security: from single to multi-clouds (2012)
2. Buyya, R., et al.: A manifesto for future generation cloud computing: research directions for the next decade. ACM Comput. Surv. (CSUR) 51, 1–38 (2019)
3. Ciriani, V., di Vimercati, S.D.C., Foresti, S., Jajodia, S., Paraboschi, S., Samarati, P.: Combining fragmentation and encryption to protect privacy in data storage. ACM Trans. Inf. Syst. Secur. (TISSEC) 13, 1–33 (2010)
4. di Vimercati, S.D.C., Foresti, S., Jajodia, S., Livraga, G., Paraboschi, S., Samarati, P.: Fragmentation in presence of data dependencies. IEEE Trans. Dependable Secure Comput. 11, 510–523 (2014)
5. Deb, K., Jain, H.: An evolutionary many-objective optimization algorithm using reference-point-based nondominated sorting approach, part I: solving problems with box constraints. IEEE Trans. Evol. Comput. 18, 577–601 (2013)
6. Deb, K., Pratap, A., Agarwal, S., Meyarivan, T.: A fast and elitist multiobjective genetic algorithm: NSGA-II. IEEE Trans. Evol. Comput. 6, 182–197 (2002)
7. Hajjat, M., et al.: Cloudward bound: planning for beneficial migration of enterprise applications to the cloud. ACM SIGCOMM Comput. Commun. Rev. 40, 243–254 (2010)
8. Hashizume, K., Rosado, D.G., Fernández-Medina, E., Fernández, E.B.: An analysis of security issues for cloud computing. J. Internet Serv. Appl. 4, 5 (2013)

9. Hong, T., Mei, S., Wang, Z., Ren, J.: A novel vertical fragmentation method for privacy protection based on entropy minimization in a relational database. Symmetry **10**, 637 (2018)
10. Hudic, A., Islam, S., Kieseberg, P., Rennert, S., Weippl, E.: Data confidentiality using fragmentation in cloud computing. Int. J. Commun. Netw. Distrib. Syst. **1**, 1 (2012)
11. Kelbert, F., et al.: Securecloud: secure big data processing in untrusted clouds (2017)
12. Modi, C., Patel, D., Borisaniya, B., Patel, A., Rajarajan, M.: A survey on security issues and solutions at different layers of cloud computing. J. Supercomput. **63**, 561–592 (2013)
13. Subashini, S., Kavitha, V.: A survey on security issues in service delivery models of cloud computing. J. Netw. Comput. Appl. **34**, 1–11 (2011)

Using Evolutionary Algorithms for Server Hardening via the Moving Target Defense Technique

Ernesto Serrano Collado$^{(\boxtimes)}$, Pedro A. Castillo,
and Juan Julián Merelo Guervós

University of Granada, Granada, Spain
info@ernesto.es, {pacv,jmerelo}@ugr.es

Abstract. The *moving target defense* from cyberattacks consists in changing the profile or signature of certain services in an Internet node so that an attacker is not able to identify it uniquely, or find specific angles of attack for it. From an optimization point of view, generating profiles that change and, besides, optimize security is a combinatorial optimization problem where different service configurations are generated and evaluated, seeking the optimum according to a standard server vulnerability evaluation score. In this paper we will use an evolutionary algorithm to generate different server profiles that also minimize the risk of being attacked. Working on the well-known web server nginx, and using an industry-standard web configuration, we will prove that this evolutionary algorithm is able to generate a sufficient amount of different and secure profiles in time for them to be deployed in the server. The system has been released as free software, as is the best practice in security tools.

Keywords: Security · Cyberattacks · Performance evaluation

1 Introduction

Many different techniques are used to deflect cyberattacks, that is, attempts to gain access to certain assets through running code remotely; these techniques include hardening of services, as well as deception. *Moving target defense* [1, 2] includes both: the system must be hardened as a point of departure, but additionally it is going to be changing its attacker-facing profile and features to make its identification, and thus selection of an attack surface, more difficult [3]. This kind of defense was initially proposed by the Federal Networking and Information Technology Research and Development (NITRD) Program for the first time in 2009 [4], and since then it has spawned all kind of methodologies and software tools to carry it out in practice. The effectivity of this defense technique is variable and will depend on the kind of attack [5], but at any rate it is a valuable addition to the set of tools that are used against cyberattacks

© Springer Nature Switzerland AG 2020
P. A. Castillo et al. (Eds.): EvoApplications 2020, LNCS 12104, pp. 670–685, 2020.
https://doi.org/10.1007/978-3-030-43722-0_43

nowadays; besides, it can be applied to several different services, every one with a different mechanism [6], which makes it a versatile, active defense methodology, applicable at many levels and in many different ways.

This kind of protection against cybersecurity threats can be implemented by a proper software configuration without the need to invest in costly security solutions. In order to measure how optimal a configuration is, an objective score must be used to measure security or its inverse, vulnerabilities [7]: The 'Security Technical Implementation Guides' or STIGs are the configuration standards for DoD systems provided by the 'Defense Information Systems Agency' (DISA) since 1998. These guides give some recommendations to hardening the configuration of software systems based on known vulnerabilities and his impact is classified using the CVSS score.

The 'Common Vulnerability Scoring System' or CVSS [8] is an open standard to measure computer and network security vulnerabilities. Scores range from 0 to 10, with 10 being the most severe. In order to protect properly a system, we need to optimize this score so that it gets as close as possible to zero without compromising any kind of functionality; however, a 0 score is almost impossible, or at any rate impossible to measure automatically. Low scores are, thus, desirable as a point of departure for using additional measures such as the moving target defense.

Many vulnerabilities can be caused by misconfiguration or an inadequate combination of parameters. In addition, a given service can have practically infinite possible configurations, some being less functional and/or vulnerable than others.

Also, to create a good mechanism of protection against cyberattacks, the moving target defense fools the attacker with a continuous change in the configuration of a given service, so meanwhile an attacker is fingerprinting your service to discover vulnerabilities, the method or algorithm applying this kind of defense will have changed the configuration so the attacker cannot define an attack based on the known vulnerabilities. In practice, you need to create an additional policy to change configurations, for instance every time an attack is detected or periodically, at random moments within a defined schedule.

In practice, the moving target defense implies a method that is able to yield several low-vulnerability service configurations. In this paper we are going to focus on the creation of a search method that is able to find, in every application, several configurations with a low vulnerability score. Depending on the (external) policy, the chief security officer of a network can run (or establish a policy to run) the search algorithm once for every scheduled change period, and obtain several candidate configurations than can then be applied to the service to make it become the *moving* target, as was required.

In this paper we will use a genetic algorithm, which is a search heuristic that can discover new, secure and diverse configurations by modeling a given configuration as if they were chromosomes and the different individual configuration options as if they were genes in that chromosome [9]. The main idea of genetic algorithms is that by mutation, crossing and selection of these chromosomes we will eventually obtain better configurations. Since mutations are random, they are a source of the diversity we are interested in here.

We need, however, a way to score every individual chromosome/solution. While CVSS is an abstract way to score security, we first need to decide on a system for which security is going to be optimized and, second, on a tool that will be able to automatically compute CVSS or a vulnerability score related to it. For the former, we will use an open-source OWASP project called Juice-Shop [10,11] that consists in a vulnerable e-commerce platform written in Node.js, Express, and Angular. This is one of the most typical web application configurations, being more complex than a simple welcome webpage and more similar to a real environment; however, we will also include tests for this kind of simple configuration.

Once the system that is going to be tested is chosen, we need to quantify the security of a given configuration; for that purpose, we can use tools like OWASP ZAP [12]. OWASP ZAP is an open-source security analysis tool for web applications developed by OWASP, crawls and analyzes a specified site for security vulnerabilities, yielding a scalar value based on the number of vulnerabilities found in a site. This score is an alternative to CVSS and STIG, with the added advantage that it can be assessed automatically via that tool. There is no direct relationship between CVSS and ZAP score, although in general a low number in vulnerabilities will result in a low CVSS score.

Using these two test systems and the automatic ZAP tool as a fitness score, our moving target defense evolutionary algorithm will rely on the diversity of each generated configuration to improve the security of our system. This is based on the entropy of our random generated and mutated values but this random configuration can be wrong or vulnerable so we test that configuration and by the genetic algorithm evolve that configuration to get a good one. The same process is be applied to the resulting configurations to improve the security through generation, but as we more evolve the configuration we get a much more secure system but we lose diversity. We need to boost diversity while keeping security high, depending on our system.

Thus, the main objective of our paper will be to design a new system that is able to create a MTD in current industry-standard services. In order to do that we intend to use real systems, using real (or at least real benchmark) workloads, which are also deployed using best practices: Docker containers. Instead of ad-hoc scoring techniques for every parameters, we use also a standard tool for scoring the vulnerabilities of these techniques, from which standard score can be deduced. We will also work with a popular open source service, the nginx web server. Finally, as is a standard practice in the cybersecurity world, the whole system is released under a free software license.

The rest of the paper is organized as follows: next we present a brief state of the art in the subject of moving target defense. The methodology and results are presented in Sect. 3, followed by our conclusions.

2   State of the Art

The so-called moving target defense, or MTD, was proposed by the first time in 2009 [4] as part of an officially sponsored research program to improve the cyber-capabilities of American companies and organisms. The NITRD proposed different axes of research that included models of MTD mechanisms, assessing the problems and opportunities of randomization of service configuration and profiles, and creating automatic policies that are able to reduce or eliminate human intervention in the enforcement of this kind of defense. This MTD is targeted towards making what is called the attack surface [13], that is, the different mechanisms by which the attacker would be able to gain access, unpredictable [2], and thus either too expensive or too complex to pursue. An attacker, in this case, will probably try and pursue different targets, thus reducing security costs for the defender.

This program was pursued using different kind of techniques, of which a good survey is made in [6] and more recently in [14,15]. These techniques include bioinspired algorithms; which have been often used in the area of cybersecurity; for instance, even before proposing the moving target defense technique, evolutionary algorithms were applied to intrusion detection systems [16]. Some authors have proposed using evolutionary-based optimization techniques to improve detection of SQL injection attacks and anomalies within HTTP requests [17]; other authors [18] focus on detecting SQLIA (SQL Injection Attacks) and XSS (Cross Site Scripting) at the application layer by modeling HTTP requests with the use of regular expressions. In general, either by evolution of rules or programs or by finding the best solution in combinatorial optimization problems, such as the one we are dealing with in this paper. More recently, Buji et al. in [19] have applied evolutionary algorithms for a general enhancement of security in real systems.

Curiously enough, a bioinspired and ad hoc technique called *symbiotic embedded machines* (SEM) were proposed by Cui and Stolfo [20] as a methodology for *injecting* code into systems that would behave in a way that would be similar to a symbiotically-induced immune system. Besides that principled biological inspiration, SEMs used mutation as a mechanism for avoiding signature based detection methods and thus become a MTD system. Other early MTD solutions included the use of rotating virtual webservers [21], every one with a different attack surface, to avoid predictability and achieve a variable attack surface. However, while this was a practical and actionable defense, no specific technique was proposed to individually configure every virtual server, proposing instead manual configuration of web servers (such as nginx and Apache), combined with plug-ins[1]. A similar technique, taken to the cloud, was proposed by Peng et al. [22]. In this case, a specific mechanism that uses different cloud instances and mechanism for moving virtual machines between them is proposed; still,

---

[1] It should be noted that some of the proposed configurations, such as nginx + mod_rails, are simply impossible, since mod_rails is an Apache plugin, apart from being specifically designed for Ruby on Rails applications.

no specific mechanism was proposed to establish these configurations. Although most of the effort is devoted to creating a MTD for servers, it can also be applied to software defined networks (SDNs) [23].

After the early *bioinspired* approaches to MTD, explicit solutions using evolutionary algorithms were conceptually described for the first time by Crouse and Fulp in [24]. This was intended mainly as a proof of concept, and describes 80 parameters, of which just half are evolved. The GA minimizes the number of vulnerabilities, but the study also emphasizes the degree of diversity achieved by successive generations in the GA, which impact on the diversity needed by the MTD. Lucas et al. in [25] applied those theoretical concepts to a framework called EAMT, a Python-based system that uses evolutionary algorithms to create new configurations, which are then implemented in a virtual machine and scored using scanning tools such as Nessus. Later on, John et al. [9] make a more explicit and practical use of an evolutionary algorithm, describing a host-level defense system, that is, one that operates at the level of a single node in the network, not network-wide, and works on the configuration of the Apache server, evolving them and evaluating at the parameter level using the above mentioned CVSS score. These two systems highlighted the need for, first, a practical way of applying the MTD to an actual system, to the point of implementing it in a real virtual machine, and second, the problematic of scoring the generated configurations. In the next section we will explain our proposed solutions to these two problems.

MTD can also be applied at a network level. Makanju et al. applied evolutionary algorithms in software defined networks by Champagne et al. in [26]. In this case the SDN have to respect the service level agreements, and a fitness function that takes into account the adaptation of the SDN to the environment. This work was continued by others in [27], but in this case the EA dynamically placed the controller in a network.

Moving target defense has many applications in the field of cybersecurity. For example, in hardware systems, such as the Morpheus processor that is able to change its internal configuration every 50 ms to difficult attacks [28], a technique like this would have prevented the Spectre vulnerability suffered by Intel processors that exploited failures in the speculative execution feature.

3   Methodology, Experimental Setup and Results

Considering the huge amount of network services with its multiple configuration options, it has been decided to limit this project to alter and optimize the configuration of an HTTP server, specifically nginx. In recent years nginx has surpassed Apache as the most used HTTP server in the world [29]. This service was chosen over Apache, as was John et al. did in [9], since this web server is nowadays much more popular, and can act as static webserver as well as a reverse proxy for web services; both configurations will be used and tested.

The last stable version of nginx (1.17) has more than 700 configuration directives, which in general constitute the user-facing attack surface. These parameters, focusing on the ones that will be evolved, will be analyzed next. The next

Subsect. 3.2 will outline the setup actually used for running the experiments, and results will be presented last in Subsect. 3.3.

3.1   Description of the Attack Surface Parameters

There is a huge number parameters that could potentially be chosen for our experiments so to validate our hypothesis we choose a subset of 9 nginx directives (Table 1) and 6 HTTP headers (Table 2), all of them related to security hardening. The subset is extracted from the DISA STIG recommendations for hardening webservers based in the CVSS score. Most of this values are defined as Apache HTTP server configuration values but have a nginx equivalent directive.

Table 1. Selected nginx directives list.

STIG ID	Directive name	Possible values
V-13730	worker_connections	512–2048
V-13726	keepalive_timeout	10–120
V-13732	disable_symlinks	True/false
V-13735	autoindex	True/false
V-13724	send_timeout	True/false
V-13738	large_client_header_buffers	512–2048
V-13736	client_max_body_size	512–2048
V-6724	server_tokens	True/false
	gzip	True/false

These are the directives that have been used in this paper; their equivalent STIG ID is shown in Table 1.

- worker_connections: Maximum number of simultaneous connections that can be opened by an nginx process.
- keepalive_timeout: Timeout period during which a client connection will remain open on the server side.
- disable_symlinks: Determine if symbolic links can be used when opening files. When activated and some component of the path is a symbolic link the access to that file is denied.
- autoindex: When activated it shows the contents of the directories, otherwise it does not show anything.
- send_timeout: The waiting time to transmit a response to the client. The wait time is set only between two successive write operations, not for the transmission of the complete response.
- large_client_header_buffers: Maximum number and size of buffers used to read the headers of large requests.

– `client_max_body_size`: Maximum allowed size of the client request body, specified in the 'Content-Length' field of the request header.
– `server_tokens`: Enable or disable the broadcast of the nginx version on the error pages and in the 'Server' response header. It is recommended not giving too extensive information of software versions, but we can cheat the attacker telling wrong server version info.
– `gzip`: Enable or disable the compression of HTTP responses. This directive doesn't affect directly the security but adds entropy to the different generated configurations.

Table 2. Selected HTTP headers list.

Header name	Possible values
X-Frame-Options	SAMEORIGIN
	ALLOW-FROM
	DENY
X-Powered-By	PHP/5.3.3
	PHP/5.6.8
	PHP/7.2.1
	Django2.2
	nginx/1.16.0
X-Content-Type-Options	nosniff
Server	apache
	caddy
	nginx/1.16.0
X-XSS-Protection	0
	1
	1; mode=block
Content-Security-Policy	default-src 'self'
	default-src 'none'
	default-src 'host *.google.com'

The web servers also send a number of headers, which can be configured also. These are presented next, with possible values represented in Table 2.

– `X-Frame-Options`: The 'X-Frame-Options' header can be used to indicate whether a browser should be allowed to render an embedded page. Web pages can use it to prevent *clickjacking* attacks, making sure that their content is not embedded in other sites.
– `X-Powered-By`: The 'X-Powered-By' header is used to specify the software that generated the response. It is recommended not giving too extensive information in this header because can reveal details that can facilitate the task

of finding and exploiting security flaws. Doesn't affect directly to the security by itself but adds entropy to the generated configurations.

- X-Content-Type-Options: The HTTP response header 'X-Content-Type-Options' indicates that the *MIME* types announced in the 'Content-Type' header should not be changed to avoid 'MIME type sniffing' attacks.
- server: The 'Server' header contains information about the software used by the server. It is recommended not giving too extensive information of software versions, but we can cheat the attacker telling wrong server version info. Doesn't affect directly to the security but adds entropy to the generated configurations.
- X-XSS-Protection: The HTTP 'X-XSS-Protection' response header is a feature that stops pages from loading when they detect reflected cross-site scripting (XSS) attacks.
- Content-Security-Policy: The HTTP 'Content-Security-Policy' response header allows web site administrators to control resources the user agent is allowed to load for a given page.

3.2   Experimental Setup

To write the genetic algorithm we have chosen the Python programming language due to the availability of the OWASP ZAP API in that language. In addition, although this project does not require high performance, several publications indicate a very good performance of the Python language when working with genetic algorithms [30]. The implementation has been written for this project, and is a simple implementation of a canonical genetic algorithm; this has been released as free software together with the rest of the framework. The genetic algorithm works generating a population of n individuals. Each individual is a chromosome of 15 gens, each gen referring to the nginx directive or HTTP security headers shown in the previous subsection.

After generating the population we calculate the fitness of that population using OWASP ZAP, which gives a scalar value with the number of known vulnerabilities a configuration has. The OWASP ZAP Python API calling a container with the Docker version of OWASP ZAP; this simulates a real environment using the example.com domain and the generated configuration. This API will yield the mentioned scalar value depending on the number of known vulnerabilities found for that configuration.

Once every individual has been assigned a fitness, we sort the population list in reverse order to set the better ones at the end of the list and get the p (pressure) values that we will evolve using mutation and crossover. This will be repeated during 15 generations.

For evolving the configuration we have written two different crossover functions that use either one or two points. We will run the experiments for each function to find out which one gives better results [31].

Also, we are mutating the population with a chance of 0.4 using two different mutation methods. One changing random gen with a random correct value or increasing/decreasing random gen. After the mutation, we calculate the fitness of the new element, sort the population and run again the algorithm until no more generations left.

OWASP ZAP is a heavy-weight process taking a certain amount of time to analyze each web configuration so we ran the experiments in three AWS EC2 t3.medium instances all running Ubuntu 18.04 LTS with Docker installed, each instance has 2 vCPU and 4 GiB of RAM. Each instance runs a different set of experiments of 16, 32 and 64 population size. To orchestrate the instances we used a simple Ansible playbook.

For the 16 individuals population size the experiment took an average of 35 min, taking 80 min in the 32 individuals population size and 180 min for the 64 individuals population size. This times are the reason of running each population size in different EC2 instances. The running time of all instances was 266 h, equivalent to 11 days of total processing time, having a total cost of $11.07.

A set of experiments has been carried out with the static site and the juice shop. These have been the parameters that have been varied

- Mutation is either random or one. In the first case, the selected configuration variable is changed by another random value. In the second case, one is added or subtracted from its value.
- Crossover uses either one or two points.
- Population goes from 16 to 64 in the case of the static web site, it stops at 32 in the juice shop.
- The evolutionary algorithm is run for 15 generations.

In this case, it's difficult to know in advance what would be the correct configuration for the evolutionary algorithm, so all these options have been tested and evaluated to check its influence in the eventual result. Experiments have been repeated, for each configuration, 15 times.

For the two different payloads we use, we need to change one line in the genetic.py code. This code, as well as the final results of every experiment, are available from the GitHub repository https://github.com/geneura-papers/2020-evostar-variable-attack-surface and are in fact included in the same repository as this paper, and processed as part of the source of this paper.

These results will be analyzed next.

3.3   Experimental Results

Since the MTD is based on the frequent and unpredictable changing of configurations, one of the first thing we need to asses is how long it takes to generate a set of different nginx configurations with low vulnerability. This is represented in Fig. 1, which plots the duration of all experiments for the static web (Static) and the juice shop (Juice Shop). Every experiment takes a substantial part of a day; it goes from 1% to approximately 12%, that is, less than an hour and up to two hours in the case of the static web site. The time grows linearly with the population, which indicates that it is dominated by the scoring performed by ZAP, every one of which takes approximately half a second for the juice shop, a

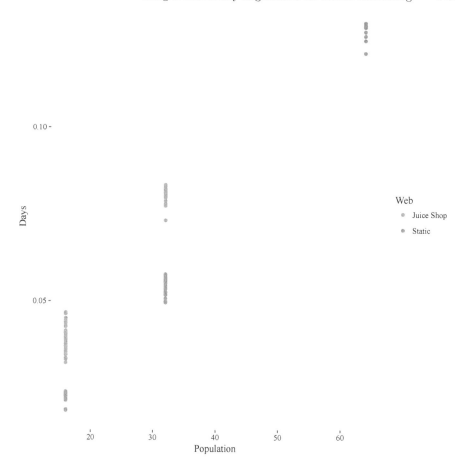

Fig. 1. Scatter plot representing the time, in days, it has taken for each experiment to be completed. Juice shop experiments were completed for populations = 16 and 32 individuals.

third of a second for the static web site. This time to generate a configuration constrains the frequency of change of configurations; on the other hand, every run generates several viable configurations.

This proves that our method, even using real-life scoring and deployment methods, is able to generate a good amount of configurations in a reasonable amount of time.

Of course, we need these configurations to have an acceptable degree of vulnerabilities. First it should be noted that acceptable ZAP scores go up to 15; more than that value will not be considered acceptable. These vulnerabilities captured by ZAP can be dealt with at a different level, but at any rate, it is always desirable to obtain as low a level of vulnerabilities as possible. We will analyze each of the two web payloads in turn, starting with the static web site, which is the simpler one.

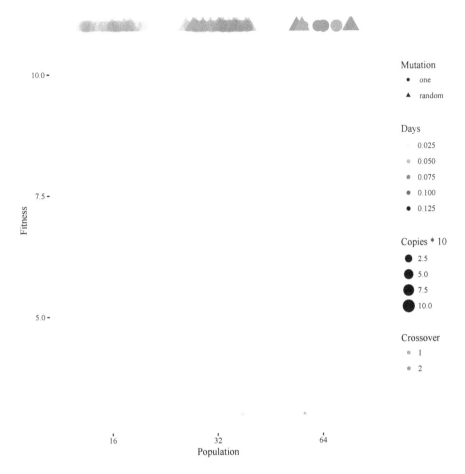

Fig. 2. Scatter plot for OWASP ZAP scores for every experiment using the static web site. A "Copies" value of 10 indicates that all individuals in the population have reached the highest score (proportion of the population equal to the highest fitness ==1). "Jitter" is used so that all data points can be visualized.

Figure 2 charts the results for the static website, representing the ZAP vulnerability score as y axis and the population as x axis. We need to assess the influence of this parameter in the final result; but at the same time we need to evaluate the importance of mutation operators that are being tested, as well as the relationship between the time employed and the results obtained.

This figure shows that most experiments result in a vulnerability score of 11, but in some exceptional cases a vulnerability score of 3 is reached. All these cases have used random mutation and a one-point crossover, so this might be a combination that, in a few cases, is able to obtain better results. The transparency of the points, which is related to time, only seems to depend on the population, that is, it is equivalent only to the number of evaluations. Better results, in fact, do not need more time.

It is also interesting to note the actual number of individuals found in every run, which is inversely proportional to the vulnerability levels that have been reached: while with ZAP = 11 all individuals in the population have the same value, if the level is equal to 3 a very small proportion of the population has the same value. This might indicate the need to run the evolutionary algorithm for more generations.

We will examine the next experiment, using the more complicated Juice Shop, to confirm or dismiss these results. These results are charted in Fig. 3.

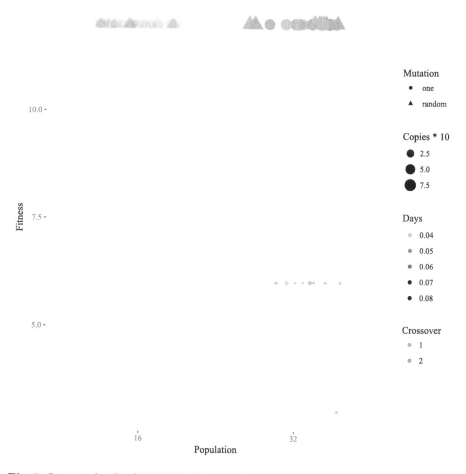

Fig. 3. Scatter plot for OWASP ZAP scores for every experiment with the Juice Shop site. "Copies" is the proportion of the population with the same ZAP score as the best; 10.0 indicates that the whole population has the same low vulnerability score (proportion equal to 1). Jittering is used to make the different results visible.

These results are substantially similar to the previous ones, but there are differences; for starters, the evaluation takes, as shown above, more time, so just the population levels of 16 and 32 could be tested. On the other hand, there are three level of vulnerabilities, with most experiments resulting in an acceptable (below 15), but the highest level of 11; a decreasing number of experiments reach 6 and very few ones get to ZAP = 3.

In the line of the previous results, the best results are obtained with 1-point crossover and random mutation, although for the medium level of vulnerability this is not so clear. Besides, when the additive mutation is used it results in more copies with the same vulnerability, or fitness.

In general, however, and in both cases, the evolutionary algorithm is able to find configurations with a low vulnerability level, but there seems to be a balance between obtaining many results and minimizing the vulnerability. However, in general, the objectives of this paper have been reached.

We will discuss these results next.

4   Conclusions and Discussion

After checking the results we can state that genetic algorithms can help us to improve the security of a system by generating many different low-vulnerability configurations for a real, and industry standard, server, thus being suitable to carry out the moving target defense along with passive or reactive policies of service configuration change. An evolutionary algorithm was successfully applied, allowing configurations to evolve diversely and securely, although there is a trade-off between them, with lower vulnerability configurations being generated in less quantity than others with a slightly higher vulnerability degree. However, low vulnerability configurations are consistently generated, which means that we could extract from a population different configurations with different degrees of vulnerability, contributing even more to the entropy of the system.

Some vulnerabilities can be caused by a bad configuration or by an unfortunate combination of configurations that it is difficult for an administrator to discover manually due to the large number of parameters and possible combinations. Thanks to a genetic algorithm it was possible to find more secure configurations. The configurations were represented as chromosomes and the algorithm took those chromosomes through a series of selection, crossing and mutation processes that resulted in even safer configurations than the previous generation. Using these evolved configurations we achieve the main objective of this paper, which is transforming our server into a moving target by changing the configuration with a reasonable periodicity (with a lower bound of approximately 4–5 h) using the configuration with the lowest (or second-lowest) generated by the algorithm.

These results open new and promising new lines of work. Focusing on the improvement of nginx, more directives as well as more security-related HTTP headers can be added. This will expand the search space of the evolutionary algorithm, and this can be a problem, which is why another possible future work would be to improve the genetic algorithm avoiding erroneous individuals in the initial population, generating in this way a safer population, and besides include some program of benchmark in our fitness function to know that besides safe, our configuration has a good performance.

However, one of the key issues is speed. The number of evaluations we are able to use in our evolutionary algorithm is relatively small for EA standards. We would need to speed up evaluation, and since it relies on an external tool, the only possible way is to use parallel evaluation by replicating the docker containers being tested and having ZAP score them at the same time. A small (4-fold, in the case of the cloud instance used in our problem) could be achieved this way. However, much better improvements could be achieved by using surrogate models [32]. This would mean training some machine learning model that is able to immediately issue a score for a certain configuration level. These surrogate models could be combined with real evaluations to give an accurate result, and be able to reach a good number of evaluations.

Finally, the algorithm itself can be improved, by testing different types of selection procedures, and tuning its greediness. This is something that can be done immediately, and will be one of our next steps.

Acknowledgements. This paper has been supported in part by projects DeepBio (TIN2017-85727-C4-2-P).

References

1. National cyber leap year summit 2009 co-chairs' report, networking and information technology research and development, September 2009
2. Jajodia, S., Ghosh, A.K., Swarup, V., Wang, C., Wang, X.S.: Moving Target Defense: Creating Asymmetric Uncertainty for Cyber Threats, vol. 54. Springer, Heidelberg (2011). https://doi.org/10.1007/978-1-4614-0977-9
3. Zhuang, R., DeLoach, S.A., Ou, X.: Towards a theory of moving target defense. In: Proceedings of the First ACM Workshop on Moving Target Defense, pp. 31–40. ACM (2014)
4. NITRD CSIA IWG Cybersecurity Game-Change Research and Development Recommendations, May 2009. https://bit.ly/2peOnfd
5. Evans, D., Nguyen-Tuong, A., Knight, J.: Effectiveness of moving target defenses. In: Jajodia, S., Ghosh, A., Swarup, V., Wang, C., Wang, X. (eds.) Moving Target Defense. Advances in Information Security, vol. 54, pp. 29–48. Springer, New York (2011). https://doi.org/10.1007/978-1-4614-0977-9_2
6. Cai, G.I., Wang, B.S., Hu, W., Wang, T.Z.: Moving target defense: state of the art and characteristics. Front. Inf. Technol. Electron. Eng. **17**(11), 1122–1153 (2016). https://doi.org/10.1631/FITEE.1601321
7. Yang, W.J., Cai, M.: A security configuration scoring system applying for configuration vulnerabilities. Comput. Mod. **8** (2012)
8. Common vulnerability scoring system version 3.1: Specification document. https://www.first.org/cvss/specification-document

9. John, D.J., Smith, R.W., Turkett, W.H., Cañas, D.A., Fulp, E.W.: Evolutionary based moving target cyber defense. In: Proceedings of the Companion Publication of the 2014 Annual Conference on Genetic and Evolutionary Computation, GECCO Comp 2014, Vancouver, BC, Canada, pp. 1261–1268. ACM (2014). https://doi.org/10.1145/2598394.2605437. http://doi.acm.org/10.1145/2598394.2605437

10. Luburić, N., Sladić, G., Milosavljević, B.: Utilizing a vulnerable software package to teach software security design analysis. In: 2019 42nd International Convention on Information and Communication Technology, Electronics and Microelectronics (MIPRO), pp. 1169–1174. IEEE (2019)

11. Kimminich, B.: OWASP juice shop project. Technical report, OWASP (2020). https://www2.owasp.org/www-project-juice-shop/

12. Bennetts, S.: OWASP Zed attack proxy. Presentation at AppSec USA (2013)

13. Manadhata, P.K., Wing, J.M.: A formal model for a system's attack surface. In: Jajodia, S., Ghosh, A., Swarup, V., Wang, C., Wang, X. (eds.) Moving Target Defense. Advances in Information Security, vol. 54, pp. 1–28. Springer, New York (2011). https://doi.org/10.1007/978-1-4614-0977-9_1

14. Lei, C., Zhang, H.Q., Tan, J.L., Zhang, Y.C., Liu, X.H.: Moving target defense techniques: a survey. Secur. Commun. Netw. **2018** (2018)

15. Ward, B.C., et al.: Survey of cyber moving targets, 2nd edn. Technical report, MIT Lincoln Laboratory Lexington United States (2018)

16. Wu, S.X., Banzhaf, W.: The use of computational intelligence in intrusion detection systems: a review. Appl. Soft Comput. **10**(1), 1–35 (2010). https://doi.org/10.1016/j.asoc.2009.06.019. http://www.sciencedirect.com/science/article/pii/S1568494609000908

17. Choraś, M., Kozik, R.: Chapter 8 - machine learning techniques for threat modeling and detection. In: Ficco, M., Palmieri, F. (eds.) Security and Resilience in Intelligent Data-Centric Systems and Communication Networks. Intelligent Data-Centric Systems, pp. 179–192. Academic Press (2018). https://doi.org/10.1016/B978-0-12-811373-8.00008-2. http://www.sciencedirect.com/science/article/pii/B9780128113738000082

18. Kozik, R., Choraś, M., Renk, R., Hołubowicz, W.: Modelling http requests with regular expressions for detection of cyber attacks targeted at web applications. In: de la Puerta, J., et al. (eds.) International Joint Conference SOCO'14-CISIS'14-ICEUTE'14. Advances in Intelligent Systems and Computing, pp. 527–535. Springer, Cham (2014). https://doi.org/10.1007/978-3-319-07995-0_52

19. Buji, A.B.M.: Genetic algorithm for tightening security. Technical report, Institutt for informatikk (2017). https://www.duo.uio.no/handle/10852/58270

20. Cui, A., Stolfo, S.J.: Symbiotes and defensive mutualism: moving target defense. In: Jajodia, S., Ghosh, A., Swarup, V., Wang, C., Wang, X. (eds.) Moving Target Defense. Advances in Information Security, vol. 54, pp. 99–108. Springer, New york (2011). https://doi.org/10.1007/978-1-4614-0977-9_5

21. Huang, Y., Ghosh, A.K.: Introducing diversity and uncertainty to create moving attack surfaces for web services. In: Jajodia, S., Ghosh, A., Swarup, V., Wang, C., Wang, X. (eds.) Moving Target Defense. Advances in Information Security, vol. 54, pp. 131–151. Springer, New York (2011). https://doi.org/10.1007/978-1-4614-0977-9_8

22. Peng, W., Li, F., Huang, C.T., Zou, X.: A moving-target defense strategy for cloud-based services with heterogeneous and dynamic attack surfaces. In: 2014 IEEE International Conference on Communications (ICC), pp. 804–809. IEEE (2014)

23. Al-Shaer, E.: Toward network configuration randomization for moving target defense. In: Jajodia, S., Ghosh, A., Swarup, V., Wang, C., Wang, X. (eds.) Moving Target Defense. Advances in Information Security, vol. 54, pp. 153–159. Springer, New York (2011). https://doi.org/10.1007/978-1-4614-0977-9_9

24. Crouse, M., Fulp, E.W.: A moving target environment for computer configurations using genetic algorithms. In: 2011 4th Symposium on Configuration Analytics and Automation (SAFECONFIG), pp. 1–7, October 2011. https://doi.org/10.1109/SafeConfig.2011.6111663

25. Lucas, B., Fulp, E.W., John, D.J., Cañas, D.: An initial framework for evolving computer configurations as a moving target defense. In: Proceedings of the 9th Annual Cyber and Information Security Research Conference, pp. 69–72. ACM (2014)

26. Makanju, A., Zincir-Heywood, A.N., Kiyomoto, S.: On evolutionary computation for moving target defense in software defined networks. In: Proceedings of the Genetic and Evolutionary Computation Conference Companion, GECCO 2017, pp. 287–288. ACM, New York (2017). https://doi.org/10.1145/3067695.3075604. http://doi.acm.org/10.1145/3067695.3075604

27. Champagne, S., Makanju, T., Yao, C., Zincir-Heywood, N., Heywood, M.: A genetic algorithm for dynamic controller placement in software defined networking. In: Proceedings of the Genetic and Evolutionary Computation Conference Companion, GECCO 2018, Kyoto, Japan, pp. 1632–1639. ACM (2018). https://doi.org/10.1145/3205651.3208244. http://doi.acm.org/10.1145/3205651.3208244

28. Gallagher, M., et al.: Morpheus: a vulnerability-tolerant secure architecture based on ensembles of moving target defenses with churn. In: Proceedings of the Twenty-Fourth International Conference on Architectural Support for Programming Languages and Operating Systems, ASPLOS 2019, Providence, RI, USA, pp. 469–484. ACM (2019). https://doi.org/10.1145/3297858.3304037. http://doi.acm.org/10.1145/3297858.3304037

29. w3techs: Usage survey of web servers broken down by ranking. https://w3techs.com/technologies/cross/web_server/ranking

30. Merelo-Guervós, J., et al.: A comparison of implementations of basic evolutionary algorithm operations in different languages. In: 2016 IEEE Congress on Evolutionary Computation (CEC), pp. 1602–1609, July 2016. https://doi.org/10.1109/CEC.2016.7743980

31. Dolin, B., Arenas, M.G., Merelo, J.J.: Opposites attract: complementary phenotype selection for crossover in genetic programming. In: Guervós, J.J.M., Adamidis, P., Beyer, H.-G., Schwefel, H.-P., Fernández-Villacañas, J.-L. (eds.) PPSN 2002. LNCS, vol. 2439, pp. 142–152. Springer, Heidelberg (2002). https://doi.org/10.1007/3-540-45712-7_14

32. Ong, Y.S., Nair, P.B., Keane, A.J.: Evolutionary optimization of computationally expensive problems via surrogate modeling. AIAA J. **41**(4), 687–696 (2003)

An Event-Based Architecture for Cross-Breed Multi-population Bio-inspired Optimization Algorithms

Erick Minguela[1], J. Mario García-Valdez[1(✉)],
and Juan Julián Merelo Guervós[2]

[1] Instituto Tecnológico de Tijuana, Tijuana, BC, Mexico
erick.vargas.minguela@gmail.com, mario@tectijuana.edu.mx
[2] Universidad de Granada, Granada, Spain
jmerelo@geneura.ugr.es

Abstract. Multi-population methods can combine multiple algorithms, with different parameters, interacting with each other at the same time. For instance, a genetic algorithm could find a promising global solution that is not optimal while another algorithm, more suitable for a local search, finds the global optimum. This approach has been followed extensively in recent years, with success. Moreover, there is a need for frameworks, architectures, and implementation models that can allow researchers the development of new parallel, asynchronous, heterogeneous, and parameter-free algorithms in a scalable way. In this work, we present an event-driven architecture, designed to distribute the processing of population-based algorithms asynchronously. The search algorithm uses a multi-population approach, creating multiple populations with different parameters of execution, allowing the implementation of multiple algorithms. In this work, we cross-breed Genetic Algorithms (GAs) and Particle Swarm Optimization (PSO). Experiments show that the framework allows the combined algorithms outperform, with a high probability, single-algorithm versions. The framework we provide also has few parameters to tune since single-algorithm parameters are selected randomly; in general, this will boost the diversity of every algorithm by itself.

Keywords: Multi-population · Asynchronous · Sub-population · Serverless · Distributed · Cross-breed multi-population

1 Introduction

In the past few decades, nature-inspired optimization algorithms have been applied to solve complex real-world problems [35]. Algorithms inspired by natural processes include evolutionary algorithms (EAs) [2] and swarm intelligence (SI) [14], among others. These population-based algorithms share the common characteristic of using an initial set of random candidate solutions that are later

© Springer Nature Switzerland AG 2020
P. A. Castillo et al. (Eds.): EvoApplications 2020, LNCS 12104, pp. 686–701, 2020.
https://doi.org/10.1007/978-3-030-43722-0_44

used to generate a new set of candidates, using a nature-inspired heuristic. Popular EAs are Genetic Algorithms (GAs), Genetic Programming (GP), grey wolf optimization (GWO) and Differential Evolution (DE), while examples of (SI) are particle swarm optimization (PSO) and ant colony algorithms (ACO).

As in nature, population-based algorithms are intrinsically parallel and asynchronous. Because of that, researchers have been proposing some form of parallelization since the earlier works [24] with the objective of increasing the speed of these algorithms. One of the first concepts proposed for parallelization was the island model, which lead to an increased performance [7,8] by dividing a large population into communicating subpopulations. Since then, the concept has been applied to other population-based algorithms and has been adapted by researchers to pursue other objectives besides the execution speed. Currently, researchers use the term multi-population based methods to describe those techniques using subpopulations as part of their strategy.

Multi-population based methods divide the original population into smaller subpopulations or islands, with every subpopulation carrying out the algorithm independently, with synchronous or asynchronous communication with the rest of the islands. This relative isolation helps in maintaining an overall diversity since each subpopulation will search in a particular area, at least between communications. The recombination mentioned above (mixing) or migration between subpopulations is needed to avoid a premature convergence of candidate solutions since smaller populations are known to perform better for a given problem than bigger populations. However, it gives them the added advantage of parallel operation. Additionally, and in some cases, multi-population algorithms scale better than expected due to the interaction between the algorithm and the parallelism of the operation [1].

However, in most cases, algorithms applied to each subpopulation are homogeneous, or at any rate, the same variant of the algorithm. As long as this parallel operation is not synchronous, other population-based algorithms, or, as a matter of fact, any algorithm, could be easily integrated. That is why several works based on multi-population are heterogeneous, integrating various optimization algorithms, and often performing better than single-population or homogeneous optimization algorithms [25,34].

Heterogeneous algorithms add another degree of freedom to the problem of finding the correct parameter settings for an algorithm; because some parameters affect the accuracy of the solution and the convergence speed of the algorithms as they tip the balance between exploration and exploitation of the search space. On the other hand, current studies show that by having a high number of subpopulations interacting in parallel, the effect of the individual parameters of each subpopulation is compensated by those selected in other subpopulations. In this work, we will use random settings within a specific range as results have shown this is a valid solution to this problem.

Some parameters, specially the population size, are kept fixed in order to control more easily the execution of the algorithm. For instance, by having the size of subpopulations fixed, it is easier to control the number of evaluations and the communication costs, when the algorithm is in operation.

A multi-population algorithm can benefit from having different algorithms and parameters in each subpopulation, interacting with each other at the same time, can benefit from the strengths of each. For instance, a genetic algorithm could find a promising global solution that is not optimal while another algorithm, more suitable for a local search, finds the global optimum. This approach has been followed extensively in recent years, with success. Moreover, there is a need for frameworks, architecture, and implementation models that can allow researchers the development of new parallel, asynchronous, heterogeneous, and parameter-free algorithms in a scalable way.

In this work, we present a new version of the event-driven architecture proposed in [9]; this is a so-called *serverless* architecture that asynchronously processes isolated and heterogeneous subpopulations. Each subpopulation is treated as an event, that is pushed asynchronously into a message queue. Events trigger stateless functions that receive the subpopulation and proceed to run an algorithm, using the parameters and population included in the message. After the specified number of iterations, each stateless function returns the evolved subpopulation by again pushing a message to another queue, used for receiving the resulting subpopulations. Subpopulations are received from the queue by a controller that is responsible for mixing the individuals from different subpopulations and producing new subpopulations. These new subpopulations are pushed again by the controller into the message queue, creating a loop. The cycle stops when the controller receives a subpopulation containing a candidate solution that satisfies a particular condition, or a maximum number of messages were received.

In this new version, we propose several improvements to the original. First, we propose alternative methods of migration between populations to compensate for differences in the execution time of the functions. The architecture includes external storage for the subpopulations it receives, instead of an in-process buffer, that was limited to a small number of sub-populations. Also, the migration or mixing process includes the capability of doing operations at the individual-level. We can see the proposal as a way of evolving and mixing a stream of populations that can very different as if their individuals belong to different species; the term we use to describe the solution is a cross-breed multi-population method.

To evaluate the capability of a cross-breed multi-population solution, we conducted several experiments using different benchmark functions, comparing the results of single versus cross-breed multi-population algorithms. For the experiments, we choose to compare the PSO and GA algorithms, as they are well understood, and there are several implementations in the literature. We implemented both algorithms as stateless functions, and more algorithms can be added in the same way.

The rest of the paper is organized as follows: the next section is devoted to analyzing the state of the art of multi-population, multi-paradigm, stateless evolutionary algorithms. The architecture proposed is presented in Sect. 3 and put to work in Sect. 4. Finally, we present our conclusions and future lines of work.

2   State of the Art

Multi-population based methods have been used extensively in recent years, with some journal papers dedicated exclusively to surveying the current state of the art [22]. Furthermore, Li et al. [18] described some of the challenges for multi-population methods in dynamic environments, e.g., how to dynamically adapt the number populations in response to the changes in the environment or how to determine the search area of each population. On the subject of heterogeneous populations, a recent survey on ensemble strategies Wu et al. [33] reports current advances on implementation techniques for multi-algorithm populations. They present several works on competitive and collaborative multi-populations as well as parametrization techniques. Multi-population techniques are heavily applied in dynamic optimization, from island-based parallel EAs [19], harmony search [32] and ACO [25]. There are also applications to combinatorial problems [28], and hybrid techniques using a combination of local and global operators [3].

Then there are also surveys dedicated to reporting current advances in the parallelization of particular population-based heuristics, from parallel PSO [17], using GPUs in particular [31], ACO [26] and distributed EAs [6]. The most common form of parallelization is to exploit the capabilities of multi-core CPUs and GPUs. Algorithms can run on a single workstation using a multi-core CPU, or a GPU with multiple processing elements or in multiple machines by using clusters, grids, or cloud services [17].

In this paper, we will focus on the use of cloud-based architectures that have been used extensively in the software industry, because of their high performance and lower overall cost. Recently, cloud providers such as Amazon Web Services (AWS), IBM Cloud, and Google Cloud, offers a new alternative to programming through interfaces called Serverless Computing [References]. These platforms consist of a simple mechanism where developers can upload the code into the service and execute it as many times as it is required, scaling and replicating automatically, allowing a parallel execution. This way, developers do not worry about servers, connections, and other configurations. In serverless, users pay only for what they use. In this case, the service provides the simple concurrent execution of stateless functions, and that is why it is called Function as a Service (FaaS) [4, 11]. When using a FaaS, the client pays for every single execution of the function. There is also the option to install some of these platforms locally; for instance, AWS (Amazon Web Services) lambda functions [4] or Apache Open Whisk [9]. The tendency in cloud-based architectures is to move from monolithic to serverless architectures, in this case we are using AWS lambda functions, as seen in Table 1.

Table 1. Software architecture generations.

Monolithic	Microservices	Serverless
Pay for each virtual machine and features	Pay for each microservice	Pay for each execution
Composed by virtual servers Client-server-database	Composed by virtual containers that execute small parts of a system	Composed by functions inside containers
OS installation required	OS only specified	OS not required

3   Proposed Architecture

Taking into account the requirements of the majority of multi-population methods and the advantages of cloud-native architectures, in this paper, we propose an architecture that allows the scalable processing of multi-populations. The approach follows the best-practices of cloud-based distributed processing and uses a queue as the communication channel between computing nodes. In our case, each population is pushed to a queue, to be consumed by stateless functions. Again, using a queue, populations are returned to a controller to be mixed with others. This architecture can accept the use of an indeterminate number of algorithms, allowing an easy cross-breed multi-population and continuous adaptability for different problems. The main components of the architecture and the flow chart are shown in Fig. 1.

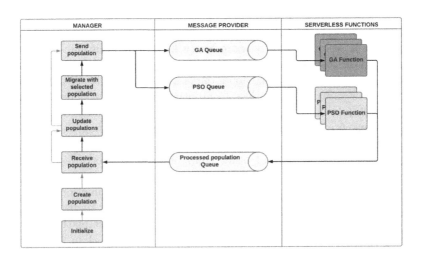

Fig. 1. General architecture flowchart.

The general architecture will be described next, and then we will focus on the most important components in the next subsections.

3.1   Architecture

There are three types of services in this model. First, there is a component responsible for the management of the algorithm in general, including starting and terminating the algorithm, and, additionally, the migration between subpopulations; this last particular task can be decoupled in other implementations. The second service is a message provider consisting of several scalable asynchronous queues. As a third component, we have a collection of serverless functions. We explain the data flow between these services in more detail next.

Manager. This component receives the configuration parameters of the experiment and initializes it; then it proceeds to create the number of subpopulations needed. Every time the manager creates a new population, it triggers an event that stores the new population into an external key-based data store implemented in MongoDB. This pool of populations will be used later for in the migration process. In previous works, this pool was kept in-memory and therefore was limited by its size. Also, the manager asynchronously pushes new populations into a message queue, which in turn triggers a serverless function, which will be described below. Because each sub-population requires the execution of a different algorithm in the cloud-service, there is a web socket assigned for each type of algorithm, push populations to their respective queue.

Once a population is processed by a stateless function, it is pushed to a queue containing the processed populations. The manager constantly pulls populations from this queue (Processed Populations queue). Each population it takes, it is mixed with one of the populations stored in the population pool, only when there is at least two populations in the pool. For this, the manager takes the best two populations from the pool and selects one randomly. Populations in the pool are sorted according to their best fitness. Populations are mixed by executing a crossing (migration) between them; we will explain this process below. As a result of the migration, we have now two new populations, which are resent back to their respective queues. This process is repeated until the number of assigned migrations for the multi-population [21,30] is completed. This whole process is performed asynchronously, avoiding the need to wait for the response of all serverless functions before operating any of the subpopulations [12,20].

Message Provider. Communication is a vital aspect of distributed systems and can be complicated to implement. Messaging systems have been used successfully in cloud computing environments because they are scalable and easier to use. When used as a service, they provide a secure, asynchronous, and highly scalable mean of inter-process communication. In this model, populations are messages. Messages are independent of the particular algorithm that is going to receive them. When implemented, there are no dependencies on time, implementation language, or operating system; systems can broadcast, publish, or subscribe to message channels, enabling many configurations. In this implementation, we use only three queues, one for each type of algorithm and one for populations returning to the manager.

Serverless Functions. Population-based optimization algorithms can be implemented as stateless functions in a serverless framework [29], receiving a configuration and a population as parameters, and returning the evolved population. The configuration parameter is needed because it contains all the information needed to execute the optimization algorithm and to report and identify the population when it is returned to the queue. The identifier is needed because many experiments with their corresponding multi-populations can be running at the same time.

This operation has to be executed in complete isolation, as a lambda function in the functional programming paradigm, so that they are compatible with a FaaS, where serverless functions can scale on-demand, and many copies of the same function could working at the same time. These functions are thus "pure" in the functional programming term: they have no side effects, which is why they are stateless: They receive a sub-population, and emit another one.

This is one of the main strong points of this kind of architecture. This lack of side effects allows easy, and automatic, scalability, with the only bottleneck being in the message queue itself.

3.2   Subpopulations

Each subpopulation is a structure with two main attributes:

– **Metadata:** This atribute includes all the data needed to configure and report the execution of the population. For instance, it has the algorithm, the parameters, objective function and the optimum value (when executing benchmarks). It also includes a trace of the execution, for instance, the number of evaluations per iteration, the best individuals, and their fitness value. It is necessary to explain that each population is independent, which means that even multiple benchmark functions could be optimized at the same time. The controller needs this data in order to migrate only populations working on the same problem.
– **Sub-population:** This is the actual collection of individuals in the population in their current state.

3.3   Migration

As we have mentioned earlier, an essential aspect of multi-population and crossbreeding methods is the communication between subpopulations after several iterations of isolated search. Individuals with some specifically chosen characteristics, such as a high fitness, maybe combined with a certain degree of similitude or difference to the host population, can be sent to other population so that they keep the whole set from premature convergence.

Our cross-breed architecture will use splitting point uniform crossover found in GA algorithms [15]. This method is applied in two levels; first, when selecting which individuals are going to migrate from one population to another, and later when single individuals are combined.

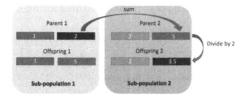

Fig. 2. Splitting point uniform process. The offspring in population two gets the result of summing the corresponding gene of the two ancestors and dividing it by two.

The method consists of randomly select which elements are going to participate in the migration. When selected individuals are going to be combined, the selected components, in this case, continuous values, are combined using the midpoint between the matching genes selected also at random [13, 16].

We exemplified this in Fig. 2, where we show two individuals that were randomly selected by the uniform mask as parents of two new individuals. Parents are shown on the top. First, the binary mask is applied. The uniform mask assigns a 0 or 1 bit randomly to each component of the vector. Those components having a 0 value are swapped with the other parent. For those with a 1 bit, the following operation is applied to replace the selected component in the child: each component is combined by adding both values and then dividing the result by two, as shown by the blue arrows. For example, for values 2 and 5, the new value would be 3.5, as we can see in Fig. 2. This kind of operator is more straightforward and less explorative than BLX-*alpha*, for instance [27]. In our case, the exploration part is left to the architecture itself.

4 Experiments and Results

In this section, we will first present the experiments that we have performed, including the selection of parameters, to then proceed to present and discuss the results in Subsect. 4.2.

4.1 Experiments

First, we will select those functions in which we are going to apply this framework. We will be working on continuous optimization since they are hard optimization problems and have also been chosen for benchmarks such as BBOB [10]; out of these functions, we have chosen Rastrigin, Sphere and Rosenbrock. They have a different degree of difficulty, can be scaled to different dimensions (as all the rest of the benchmark functions), and they can at least give us an idea of how single-breed (GA or PSO) algorithms perform compared to our cross-breed (GA+PSO) version.

We show the parameters used for these algorithms in Table 2. In every algorithm run, we will use as a stop criteria an error below 0.5E−8. The cross-breed algorithm itself used 10 sub-populations for each experiment and a maximum of

Table 2. Parameters used by the algorithms for all dimensions.

Parameter	Values for dimensions	
	2	10, 20, 40
GA generations	50	70
GA population size	100	200
GA mutation selection	Tournament3	
GA crossover selection	Tournament3	
GA crossover percentage	Random [10%, 80%]	
GA mutation percentage	Random [10%, 50%]	
GA crossover function	Splitting point uniform	
GA mutation Function	Gaussian	
PSO iterations	50	70
PSO vector size	100	200
PSO social factor	Random [0.5, 4.0]	
PSO individual factor	Random [0.5, 4.0]	
PSO inertia factor	Random [0.5, 4.0]	

4 migrations per subpopulation. Since this was intended mainly as a first approach to the performance of the cross-breed algorithm, we did not perform any optimization in the parameter space. Note that we use random parametrization for every population, except for the number of iterations before migration takes place and the population size (number of initial particles in the case of PSO). We kept this number fixed, and also did not vary it except for the smallest case (dimensions = 2). That was made mainly for the sake of a fair comparison between the two algorithms. However, in principle, and as a line of research that we could approach in the future, population size could be random or adaptive depending on the number of dimensions.

The maximum number of evaluations follows this equation:

$$Evaluations = 10^5 Dimensions \qquad (1)$$

This means that evaluations will scale from 200K for the 2 dimensions, un to 4 millions for 4 dimensions. This kind of parametrization is also usual in benchmarks, but of course we could use different parameters depending on the function and scaling in a different, and non-linear, way.

Every experiment was carried out 15 times, using a Dell Poweredge R730, with two Intel Xeon E5-2670v3 12-core processors, 128 GB of RAM and running Ubuntu Server 18.04 OS.

Results obtained in the experiments have been published with an open data license in URL hidden.

4.2   Results

Results are shown in Table 3, including averages (and standard deviation) and the best results for the 15 runs. The **Best** column show, among the 15 experiments, the best value reached. Except for two cases, the cross-breed algorithm is either the best or the same value as the best (in some cases where all algorithms reach the optimum, which is 0). There are two cases where the PSO algorithm reaches better values for the Sphere function, but in general, we can affirm that the cross-breed algorithm proposed here reaches either the best or a value that is very close to it.

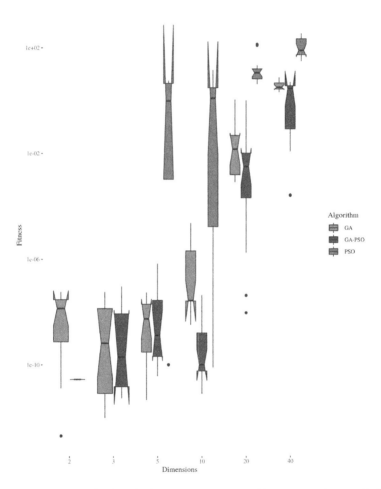

Fig. 3. Boxplots of results for the Rastrigin function. Please note the y axis is logarithmic.

Let us analyze the average behavior also via the boxplots shown in Figs. 3, 4 and 5. Averages for Rastrigin are either significantly better or similar to GAs;

Table 3. Experimental results. The **Best** column shows in *boldface* the best value among the three algorithms, or GA-PSO if it is the same value as the best.

Dimensions	Algorithm	Function	Average	SD	Best
2	Rastrigin	GA	1.65E−08	1.94E−08	0
2	Rastrigin	GA-PSO	0	0	**0**
2	Rastrigin	PSO	1.89E−12	7.31E−12	0
2	Rosenbrock	GA	1.24E−08	2.27E−08	1.62E−13
2	Rosenbrock	GA-PSO	6.91E−09	1.57E−08	**9.58E−14**
2	Rosenbrock	PSO	2.48E−06	9.59E−06	1.12E−12
2	Sphere	GA	4.37E−10	1.17E−09	4.53E−18
2	Sphere	GA-PSO	4.33E−14	1.37E−13	**0**
2	Sphere	PSO	7.80E−12	2.06E−11	0
3	Rastrigin	GA	1.21E−08	1.98E−08	9.98E−13
3	Rastrigin	GA-PSO	7.72E−09	2.40E−08	**0**
3	Rastrigin	PSO	0	0	0
3	Sphere	GA	4.20E−11	1.41E−10	1.74E−15
3	Sphere	GA-PSO	6.28E−10	2.39E−09	**0**
3	Sphere	PSO	3.30E−11	1.18E−10	0
5	Rastrigin	GA	1.27E−08	1.48E−08	4.68E−12
5	Rastrigin	GA-PSO	5.57E−08	1.71E−07	**0**
5	Rastrigin	PSO	6.54E−01	1.71E+00	0
5	Sphere	GA	5.89E−09	8.62E−09	4.41E−11
5	Sphere	GA-PSO	8.68E−09	1.74E−08	**0**
5	Sphere	PSO	1.48E−03	5.74E−03	0
10	Rastrigin	GA	2.38E−06	5.86E−06	3.22E−09
10	Rastrigin	GA-PSO	5.09E−09	1.15E−08	**8.01E−12**
10	Rastrigin	PSO	2.72E+00	3.87E+00	7.86E−11
10	Rosenbrock	GA	1.67E−04	2.88E−04	9.58E−07
10	Rosenbrock	GA-PSO	2.40E−04	4.63E−04	**3.62E−07**
10	Rosenbrock	PSO	4.43E+00	1.07E+01	4.17E−07
10	Sphere	GA	2.54E−08	2.13E−08	1.84E−09
10	Sphere	GA-PSO	1.30E−09	2.67E−09	**3.34E−11**
10	Sphere	PSO	3.08E−02	1.19E−01	4.50E−11
20	Rastrigin	GA	2.21E−01	4.30E−01	8.09E−04
20	Rastrigin	GA-PSO	7.38E−02	2.58E−01	**9.13E−09**
20	Rastrigin	PSO	2.55E+01	4.04E+01	3.99E+00
20	Rosenbrock	GA	1.10E−02	1.71E−02	3.48E−04
20	Rosenbrock	GA-PSO	5.61E−03	5.85E−03	**2.32E−05**
20	Rosenbrock	PSO	1.34E+01	3.68E+00	9.12E+00
20	Sphere	GA	9.23E−06	7.55E−06	1.85E−06
20	Sphere	GA-PSO	2.13E−08	2.95E−08	9.11E−11
20	Sphere	PSO	3.50E−07	9.46E−07	**7.04E−11**
40	Rastrigin	GA	3.56E+00	1.47E+00	1.95E+00
40	Rastrigin	GA-PSO	2.13E+00	1.83E+00	**2.46E−04**
40	Rastrigin	PSO	1.30E+02	1.12E+02	2.91E+01
40	Rosenbrock	GA	1.07E+02	1.66E+02	3.29E+01
40	Rosenbrock	GA-PSO	5.25E−01	4.71E−01	**1.85E−02**
40	Rosenbrock	PSO	3.68E−01	3.28E−01	3.27E−02
40	Sphere	GA	5.30E−03	1.85E−03	2.69E−03
40	Sphere	GA-PSO	1.41E−04	3.63E−04	2.00E−10
40	Sphere	PSO	2.07E−03	8.01E−03	**8.68E−11**

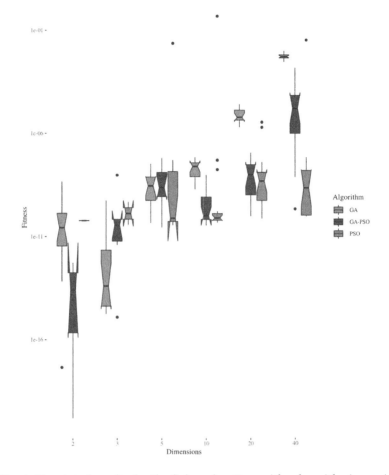

Fig. 4. Boxplot of results for the Sphere function, with a logarithmic y axis.

10 dimensions seem to be the case where the results for GA-PSO outperform the rest of the algorithms significantly; they are quite similar for more dimensions and slightly better, but similar for smaller dimensions.

GA-PSO does not show a significant advantage for the Sphere function, shown in Fig. 4, except for the smaller dimension; as the number of dimensions increases, so does the advantage of PSO. This is probably due to the big gap between the performance of the GA and the PSO algorithm. We will come back to this in the discussion.

Finally, averages for GA-PSO show little difference with the best average in the Rosenbrock function, as shown in Fig. 5. In the cases its average is not the lowest; the difference with the highest average is not significant.

These three functions show a different behavior; however, in most cases GA-PSO outperform the single-breed algorithms, and in some cases it shows an

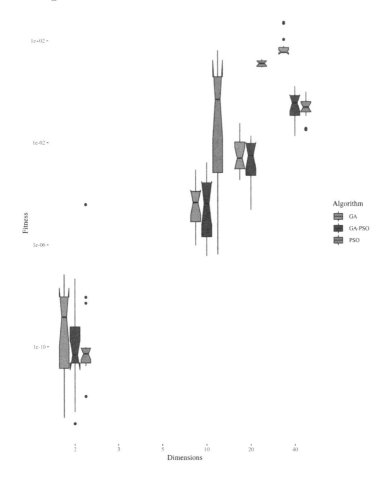

Fig. 5. Boxplot of results for the Rosenbrock function; y axis is logarithmic.

average behavior that is not significantly different from the best. We will discuss this findings in the next section.

5   Conclusions and Future Work

In this paper we have shown how a cross-breed algorithm, which uses GA and PSO; can be easily implemented using it. The cross-breeding actually occurs, allowing these combined algorithms outperform, with a high probability, single-algorithm versions. The framework we have provided also has few parameters to tune, since single-algorithm parameters are selected randomly; in general, this will boost diversity of every algorithm by itself.

Since we are using a serverless architecture, high-performance is achieved, each single experiment lasted between 30 to 40 s. And the whole set of experiments took about 3 h to complete. Scalability has as only ceiling the amount of individuals memory can hold, but its main advantage is that the architecture itself is able to accommodate as many sub-populations as we need. The limits is something that we will need to explore in the future.

The results obtained are probably due to the increased diversity cross-breed algorithm bring, boosting exploration without sacrificing exploitation; since results obtained by the two intervening algorithm are slightly different, the intermediate disturbance hypothesis, which has been used to explain results in PSO [5] as well as evolutionary algorithms [23], helps keep diversity high. However, in cases where the results for GA and PSO are quite dissimilar, as is the case for the Sphere function, the cross-breed algorithm might, in some very specific cases, obtain worse results than the cross-breed GA-PSO algorithm. However, the maintenance of diversity makes this difference relatively small, and the fact that it works better on the rest of the cases more than compensates.

To get a continuous improvement it is believed that it is required a sort of mutation applied to the sub-populations. This mutation would be a swapping type, taking the algorithm parameters from the best and the worst sub-populations, increasing the possibilities to get an optimal result, preventing get stuck into a local optimum. Of course, it is expected to use this architecture using more algorithms than GA and PSO.

Other futures avenues of research to explore would be to use other kind of algorithms, such as Estimation of Distribution Algorithms or Differential Evolution, brought into the mix. Scalability will also be something we will working on in the future, trying to find what are its limits and how they depend on the type of problem that is solved.

We also think about experiemtning other types of migration and comparing them.

Acknowledgements. This paper has been supported in part by projects DeepBio (TIN2017-85727-C4-2-P) and TecNM-5654.19-P.

References

1. Alba, E.: Parallel evolutionary algorithms can achieve super-linear performance. Inf. Process. Lett. **82**(1), 7–13 (2002). https://doi.org/10.1016/S0020-0190(01)00281-2
2. Back, T.: Evolutionary Algorithms in Theory and Practice: Evolution Strategies, Evolutionary Programming, Genetic Algorithms. Oxford University Press, Oxford (1996)
3. Bai, X., Yan, W., Ge, S.S., Cao, M.: An integrated multi-population genetic algorithm for multi-vehicle task assignment in a drift field. Inf. Sci. **453**, 227–238 (2018)
4. Baird, A., Huang, G., Munns, C., Weinstein, O.: Serverless reference architectures with AWS lambda, November 2016
5. Gao, H., Kwong, S., Yang, J., Cao, J.: Particle swarm optimization based on intermediate disturbance strategy algorithm and its application in multi-threshold image segmentation. Inf. Sci. **250**, 82–112 (2013)
6. Gong, Y.J., et al.: Distributed evolutionary algorithms and their models: a survey of the state-of-the-art. Appl. Soft Comput. **34**, 286–300 (2015)

7. Gorges-Schleuter, M.: Explicit parallelism of genetic algorithms through population structures. In: Schwefel, H.-P., Männer, R. (eds.) PPSN 1990. LNCS, vol. 496, pp. 150–159. Springer, Heidelberg (1991). https://doi.org/10.1007/BFb0029746

8. Grosso, P.: Computer simulations of genetic adaptation: parallel subcomponent interaction in multilocus model. Ph.D. Dissertation, University of Michigan (1985)

9. Merelo Guervós, J.J., García-Valdez, J.M.: Introducing an event-based architecture for concurrent and distributed evolutionary algorithms. In: Auger, A., Fonseca, C.M., Lourenço, N., Machado, P., Paquete, L., Whitley, D. (eds.) PPSN 2018. LNCS, vol. 11101, pp. 399–410. Springer, Cham (2018). https://doi.org/10.1007/978-3-319-99253-2_32

10. Hansen, N., Auger, A., Ros, R., Finck, S., Pošík, P.: Comparing results of 31 algorithms from the black-box optimization benchmarking BBOB-2009. In: Proceedings of the 12th Annual Conference Companion on Genetic and Evolutionary Computation, pp. 1689–1696. ACM (2010)

11. Hellerstein, J.M., et al.: Serverless computing: one step forward, two steps back. arXiv preprint arXiv:1812.03651 (2018)

12. Jimeno, H.M.A., Sánchez, M.J.L., Rico, R.H.: Multipopulation - based multi - level parallel enhanced Java algorithms. J. Supercomput. **75**, 1697–1716 (2019). https://doi.org/10.1007/s11227-019-02759-z. (0123456789)

13. Kaya, Y., Uyar, M., Tekin, R.: A novel crossover operator for genetic algorithms: ring crossover, May 2011, 2014

14. Kennedy, J.: Swarm intelligence. In: Zomaya, A.Y. (ed.) Handbook of Nature-Inspired and Innovative Computing, pp. 187–219. Springer, Boston (2006). https://doi.org/10.1007/0-387-27705-6_6

15. Kramer, O.: A Brief Introduction to Continuous Evolutionary Optimization, pp. 45–54. Springer, Heidelberg (2014). https://doi.org/10.1007/978-3-319-03422-5

16. Kramer, O.: Genetic Algorithm Essentials. Springer, Heidelberg (2017). https://doi.org/10.1007/978-3-319-52156-5

17. Lalwani, S., Sharma, H., Chandra, S., Kusum, S., Jagdish, D., Bansal, C.: Review - computer engineering and computer science a survey on parallel particle swarm optimization algorithms. Arab. J. Sci. Eng. (2019). https://doi.org/10.1007/s13369-018-03713-6

18. Li, C., Nguyen, T.T., Yang, M., Yang, S., Zeng, S.: Multi-population methods in unconstrained continuous dynamic environments: the challenges. Inf. Sci. **296**, 95–118 (2015)

19. Lissovoi, A., Witt, C.: A runtime analysis of parallel evolutionary algorithms in dynamic optimization. Algorithmica **78**(2), 641–659 (2017)

20. Løvbjerg, M., Rasmussen, T.K.: Hybrid particle swarm optimiser with breeding and subpopulations. In: Proceedings of 3rd Genetic Evolutionary Computation Conference, pp. 469–476 (2001)

21. Ma, H., Shen, S., Yu, M., Yang, Z., Fei, M., Zhou, H.: Multi-population techniques in nature inspired optimization algorithms: a comprehensive survey. Swarm Evol. Comput. **44**(July 2017), 365–387 (2019). https://doi.org/10.1016/j.swevo.2018.04.011

22. Ma, H., Shen, S., Yu, M., Yang, Z., Fei, M., Zhou, H.: Multi-population techniques in nature inspired optimization algorithms: a comprehensive survey. Swarm Evol. Comput. **44**, 365–387 (2019)

23. Merelo, J.J., et al.: Testing the intermediate disturbance hypothesis: effect of asynchronous population incorporation on multi-deme evolutionary algorithms. In: Rudolph, G., Jansen, T., Beume, N., Lucas, S., Poloni, C. (eds.) PPSN 2008. LNCS, vol. 5199, pp. 266–275. Springer, Heidelberg (2008). https://doi.org/10.1007/978-3-540-87700-4_27

24. Mühlenbein, H., Gorges-Schleuter, M., Krämer, O.: Evolution algorithms in combinatorial optimization. Parallel Comput. **7**(1), 65–85 (1988)

25. Nseef, S.K., Abdullah, S., Turky, A., Kendall, G.: An adaptive multi-population artificial bee colony algorithm for dynamic optimisation problems. Knowl.-Based Syst. **104**, 14–23 (2016)

26. Pedemonte, M., Nesmachnow, S., Cancela, H.: A survey on parallel ant colony optimization. Appl. Soft Comput. **11**(8), 5181–5197 (2011)

27. Picek, S., Jakobovic, D., Golub, M.: On the recombination operator in the real-coded genetic algorithms. In: 2013 IEEE Congress on Evolutionary Computation, pp. 3103–3110. IEEE (2013)

28. Pourvaziri, H., Naderi, B.: A hybrid multi-population genetic algorithm for the dynamic facility layout problem. Appl. Soft Comput. **24**, 457–469 (2014)

29. Roberts, M.: Serverless architectures, pp. 1–36 (2016)

30. Santander-Jiménez, S., Vega-Rodríguez, M.A.: Comparative analysis of intra-algorithm parallel multiobjective evolutionary algorithms: taxonomy implications on bioinformatics scenarios. IEEE Trans. Parallel Distrib. Syst. **30**(1), 63–78 (2018)

31. Tan, Y., Ding, K.: A survey on gpu-based implementation of swarm intelligence algorithms. IEEE Trans. Cybern. **46**(9), 2028–2041 (2015)

32. Turky, A.M., Abdullah, S.: A multi-population harmony search algorithm with external archive for dynamic optimization problems. Inf. Sci. **272**, 84–95 (2014)

33. Wu, G., Mallipeddi, R., Suganthan, P.N.: Ensemble strategies for population-based optimization algorithms-a survey. Swarm Evol. Comput. **44**, 695–711 (2019)

34. Wu, G., Mallipeddi, R., Suganthan, P.N., Wang, R., Chen, H.: Differential evolution with multi-population based ensemble of mutation strategies. Inf. Sci. **329**, 329–345 (2016)

35. Yang, X.S.: Nature-Inspired Optimization Algorithms. Elsevier, Amsterdam (2014)

Author Index